CW00740467

We Lead
Others Follow

First Canadian Division 1914–1918

We Lead
Others Follow

First Canadian Division 1914–1918

Kenneth Radley

Vanwell Publishing Limited

St. Catharines, Ontario

Vanwell Publishing acknowledges the financial support of the Government of Canada through the Book Publishing Industry Development Program for our publishing activities.

Design: Carol Matsuyama
Front cover design: Renee Giguére
Cover layout: Carol Matsuyama
Cover photograph: Canadians returning from the forward trenches, November 1916.
LAC PA 832.

Vanwell Publishing Limited
1 Northrup Crescent
P.O. Box 2131
St. Catharines, Ontario L2R 7S2
sales@vanwell.com
tel: 905-937-3100
fax: 905-937-1760

Printed in Canada

Library and Archives Canada Cataloguing in Publication
Radley, Kenneth, 1943–
We lead, others follow: First Canadian Division 1914–1918/Kenneth Radley.
Includes bibliographical references and index.
ISBN 1-55125-100-0
1. Canada. Canadian Army. Canadian Division, 1st—History. 2. World War, 1914–1918—
Regimental histories—Canada. I. Title.
D547.C2R32   2006   940.4'1271   C2005-907673-9

———————————

To the officers and men
of 1st Canadian Division, 1914–1918,
and especially to those
who marched up the line never to return.
All honour to them.

———————————

Our God and soldiers we adore
When at the brink of peril, not before.
The danger past; they're both alike requited,
Our God forgotten and our soldiers slighted.

—FRANCIS QUARLES, "EPIGRAM" 1630

Contents

CONVENTIONS

Decorations

Decorations have been omitted throughout in the interests of clarity since including them would have meant providing a chronology of award. The omission is not intended to offend, and with great respect, an apology is here tendered.

Capitalization

Levels of Command. "Army" has been capitalized throughout, and the context indicates whether the national Army or the formation is intended. Other levels of command are not capitalized unless a specific formation or unit is indicated.

Ranks. "General Officers" includes brigade commanders because in 1914–1918 they were Brigadier-Generals. After the war they were styled "Brigadiers" and were no longer General Officers. The term "Other Ranks" (ORs) refers to personnel other than commissioned officers.

Units and Formations

In 1914–1918 "unit" referred to all levels of command, even platoon. Today only organizations that have Commanding Officers are called units; companies and platoons are sub-units; organizations above battalion—brigade, division, corps and Army—are formations. These modern terms will be adhered to throughout. Examples of the style adopted for the levels of command are as follows: First Army, XVII Corps, 29th Division, 56th Brigade, 6th Battalion. To distinguish between Imperial (British) and Canadian formations, the former from division down will be identified as Imperial; thus, 29th (Imperial) Division, 56th (Imperial) Brigade. Imperial battalions are also identified as to regiment; for example, 6th Battalion, Seaforth Highlanders (Imperial). Canadian units and formations are identified simply as 1st Division, 1st Brigade, 1st Battalion.

ILLUSTRATIONS

MAPS

ACKNOWLEDGEMENTS

W riting history is not as solitary a pursuit as some might think. A combination and a result of collection, collation and interpretation of information and the injection of one's own ideas, the process is never a one-man show. Inevitably, the historian requires assistance.

Many people helped during the preparation of this book. Librarians and archivists in Ottawa and in Saskatchewan provided published and unpublished books, manuscripts, journal articles and documents. The staff of the National Defence Headquarters Library in Ottawa were particularly helpful, especially Heather Campbell, who patiently and promptly acted on what must have seemed to her endless requests for books and journals over a two-year period. These requests were so frequent she must surely at times have wished me (or herself) elsewhere. I am also grateful to Trina Gillis of the Saskatchewan Archives Board for making available the very useful unpublished memoirs of Brigadier-General George Tuxford. My sincere thanks also to Simon Robbins of the Imperial War Museum for directing me to several memoirs of Canadian soldiers who served during the Great War. These would not otherwise have come to my attention.

Doctors A. Douglas, N. Hillmer and J. Granatstein offered useful advice and constructive criticism on numerous points major and minor. Some of their comments ended up in the final version. I would also like to thank Doctors A. Bennett and D. McDowell for their encouragement and friendship during my stay at Carleton University, Ottawa. I especially wish to thank Doctor S.F. Wise, who supervised those sections of the book originally submitted as my doctoral dissertation.

I also wish to thank those individuals and organizations who generously gave permission for the use of previously published maps. Map 1, published in *Valour Remembered: Canada and the First World War* (Ottawa: Minister of Supply and Services, 1982), and Maps 4 to 9, originally published in Colonel G.W.L. Nicholson, *Official History of the Canadian Army in the First World War: Canadian Expeditionary Force, 1914–1919* (Ottawa: Queen's Printer, 1962), are used courtesy of the Canadian Forces. Maps 3, 10, 11, 13, 14 and 15, used courtesy of the Calgary Highlanders and the Calgary Highlanders Regimental Funds Foundation, were originally published in Daniel Dancocks, *Gallant Canadians: The Story of the Tenth Canadian Infantry Battalion, 1914–1919* (Calgary: The Calgary Highlanders Regimental Funds Foundation, 1990). Map 3, drawn by Major W.R. Bennett, was taken with the permission of The Royal Regiment of Canada Association from Major D.J. Goodspeed, *Battle Royal: A History of The Royal Regiment of Canada,*

1862–1962 (Toronto: The Royal Regiment of Canada Association, 1962).

Finally, I would like to thank my wife Lillian for her support and encouragement over the years. The fact that she has long been the world's best adjutant and quartermaster is a terrific bonus for this author.

PREFACE

*I was sorry to leave the First Division. There was always
something just a little special about the people who wore
the red patch.*

—COLONEL C.P. STACEY

Any man who ever wore one would agree with Stacey.[1] Who could argue with such an obvious truth? The genesis of this present study of 1st Division during the Great War of 1914–1918, *We Lead, Others Follow*, was the realization by the author, formerly an officer with The First Battalion, The Queen's Own Rifles of Canada (which in the 1960s wore the "Old Red Patch"[2] of 1st Division), that no account of this famous division and its splendid service in the Great War had ever been written.[3] In fact, until now, no studies of any Canadian divisions have existed!

Such a gaping hole in Canadian military history surprised several Commonwealth officers with whom the idea of writing a study of one Canadian division was discussed. One British officer was more shocked than surprised since he was aware that more than half of the 70 or so British divisions that served during the Great War had been the subject of some very fine divisional histories by such competent historians as Cyril Falls, who considered a division to be the real "unit" of the war.[4] Most of those who were party to the discussion assumed that Canadians had been as interested and as quick to tell the story of Canada's fighting divisions, and since we only had four divisions in the field, surely they were all "written-up" long ago. One individual, learning that this was not so, remarked upon what may be the inverse relationship, in that there was perhaps no particular interest in these histories because in an Army with so few divisions, historical interest inclined to the smaller family represented by a battalion. Moreover, our battalions are substance (albeit they are usually under strength), while our divisions just now are only potential.

In any event, while 2nd, 3rd and 4th Divisions have reason to complain about historical neglect, 1st Division has been particularly hard done by. Did anyone realize that Old Red Patch did not enjoy the advantages that later divisions did, such as less hurried mobilization, a longer period of training, signposts to mark the way ahead and the luxury of reflecting on the lessons learnt by a predecessor? Was it appreciated that 1st Division led the way? It stood up first at the front, it was the most experienced of our divisions, and many of its officers went on to senior command and staff appointments in it or other divisions. In fact, 1st Division was the first nonregular division to join the British Expeditionary Force (BEF), beating the first Imperial Territorial Division (the 46th) to France by two weeks and the first New

Army Division (the 9th Scottish) by three months.[5] This in itself reveals much about the national temper and the strong loyalty to the Empire at the time.

Although the historical slate marked "1st Division" has not been entirely blank these past 80 years and more, the story has not been easily retrievable. The Introduction that follows this Preface renders, *inter alia*, the historiography of the division. Let me just say here that there is something of 1st Division in each of the one-volume Canadian official histories, and data exists here and there in many, many books and articles, including those publications relating to other Canadian divisions. While these are not generally forthcoming about extraneous matters, they do contain the odd nugget on Old Red Patch. If nothing else, they reveal how other divisions benefited from 1st Division's blaze.

An adequate picture of 1st Division, or any aspect of its life in the Great War, can come only from thorough study of the primary sources, which is a customary (and mandatory) destination for those who try to write history. I cannot claim to have read *all* the documents pertaining to 1st Division, but over a 12-month period I did read the records pertaining to the division and its constituent formations and units, plus the records of its staff branches and a representative slice of the records of divisional artillery and engineers.

Despite this earnest study and despite being a long-serving and well-experienced officer, I, like every military historian, have had to struggle with the "empirical difficulty [of] describing the soldier's life. No one but he knows what it is."[6] In fact, more than that, only the soldier who has experienced combat *knows*. Very few in Canada today have ever had to say "Follow me, men," draw a very deep breath and snick the safety catch off. For real excitement, combat must surely take precedence over everything else in a man's life. It must be akin to being bitten by a rattlesnake. Only a man with experience can appreciate these sensations. Without direct knowledge of either, I am left to rely upon the historical record and upon the lessons of 35 years as a professional officer. If nothing else, they have been helpful in studying what is involved in planning for battle—today we call it "battle procedure"—and how difficult that is. These lessons also grant an appreciation of the basic nature of soldiers and, more importantly, the knowledge that this nature changes very little. Whiners, barrack-room lawyers, malingerers and all manner of villains, but also splendid, tough, forthright soldiers, marched with the XX Augusta, with Wellington in the Peninsula, and with 1st Division under Arthur Currie, and then Archibald Macdonell in Flanders and France. Army life can be very complicated, but at the same time it remains very basic. The simple experience and the exhilaration of marching with a battalion is at the heart of what it means to be a soldier. Indeed, there is a devil in the drum!

However, since peacetime soldiering is obviously not combat, it behooves us to contemplate two very pertinent sets of remarks, the first by an astute French officer:

> Anyone can discuss high strategy . . . the broad principles of war are simple and anyone can understand them . . . a lecturer is quite clear . . . when he says that to beat an army you turn a flank and break the centre if you want an Austerlitz, or envelop both flanks to obtain a Cannae; and if he concluded by saying that these results are nevertheless sometimes difficult to attain, everyone will agree and go home satisfied, their minds full of first principles . . .
>
> It is another matter to try to describe the details of a fight and to be capable of doing so a man must have been through it all himself. He must know what it means to lead a section through the mud and under shrapnel fire, and to be hung up in the enemy's wire. He must understand men, their arms, their methods; have seen them at work under all sorts of conditions and be capable of realising their feelings and their behaviour under fire. This is why it is difficult to find a man capable of writing a good detailed description of a fight. Obviously, too, an infantryman is not the best person to treat of cavalry and artillery fights, similarly airmen or artillerymen are apt to omit details of primary importance if called upon to write about the action of a small infantry unit.[7]

These remarks just cannot be dismissed. I do not see, for example, how an infantry officer could have written *The Guns of Normandy*. Nor do I see how a gunner could have written *Battalion*.[8] Imagine how strange ancient Rome would seem if, instead of reading the words of Roman historians, we had only reports by visiting barbarians. The second set of remarks, courtesy of Somerset Maugham, is no less apt:

> It is not necessary to eat a whole sheep in order to describe the taste of mutton, but it is advisable at least to have tasted a lamb chop.[9]

What a comfort it would be to think that rummaging through dusty archival boxes is at least a lamb chop, and perhaps it is, but this does not prepare one to command at any level, nor does it adequately prepare one to criticize those who have commanded. Nevertheless, it would be naive to ignore the ancient Norse wisdom that says "I know a thing that never dies, Judgement over the dead."[10] But no generation should pass judgement on another without being as aware as possible of the facts; nor should any generation contaminate the past with today's assumptions and values, encrusted as these often are with the giddy tenets of one "ism" or another. Each generation must accept the fact that people of the past had different values. As John Baynes so admirably says,

> it is essential to study the actions of those who lived in the past with a sympathetic mind. To jeer at those who have gone before us is a game fraught with pitfalls. After all, it will only be a fraction of time before we ourselves are the stuff of history. Most of us try to make a decent job of our lives, and though we make many mistakes, we feel entitled to a certain understanding of our difficulties and problems before judgement is passed on us. The least we can do is examine the actions of our forebears with generosity, and attempt to see clearly all the influences which affected them.[11]

Another significant difficulty is assessing just how complete or accurate your sources are. Consider, for example, war diaries. Research convinced me that battalion war diaries are often of questionable value. In 1914–1918 the CO was responsible to see "that the War Diary is written up to date, and initials entries to it daily . . . in order that it may later on form the basis for the historical records of the Battalion."[12] What he wanted entered was entered and what he did not, was not. As one CO said, "Of course, the story of a battle is never really as one writes it—one couldn't write it as it is!"[13] Often the quality of the diary worsened just as the situation it described did. Brigade diaries were marginally better, while divisional diaries were the best of the three levels despite being based on situation reports which, inevitably, were amended later. Of course, regimental officers usually question whether anyone at divisional headquarters knows what is going on in the forward trenches, and they have little patience with the rejoinder that only the division sees and understands the "big picture." Another question that comes to mind is the extent to which anyone had any training in writing war diaries. In addition, as a Royal Navy officer pointed out, the motive of a "Report of Proceedings" (the naval equivalent of war diaries) can be to "show the actions of the ship or squadron concerned in the best possible light."[14] For all these reasons, and although war diaries are a valuable source, I do not entirely share Charles Stacey's opinion that "if a division's log is available, you can write the history of that division with confidence."[15]

Take, for example, the diaries that may or may not have been maintained at the Second Battle of Ypres in April 1915. The evidence suggests 1st Division "probably" kept a war diary, but it was "replaced" by a narrative of events.[16] Denis Winter claims, but offers no evidence, that 3rd Brigade's war diary was burnt so as not to demolish its commander's reputation. The 3rd Brigade, he says, was not the only arsonist.[17] Apparently, 1st Brigade kept a "proper" diary, but any diary represents what the diarist, usually a tired and distracted man, *thought* was happening at the time, and it was written in an extreme hurry a few, several, or many days later. If written the same day, diary entries may reflect more excitement than fact. Often, even dates are wrong. Battalion diaries, too, were subject to "amplification."[18] The question is, in which do you place the greater confidence—unit diaries or diaries of their parent formations?[19] None of them being infallible, comparison is a must.

Sometimes even the formations involved in particular actions were wrongly identified. In September 1918, commenting on a magazine article that had credited 2nd and 3rd Divisions with the attack on 3 June 1916 at Mount Sorrel, Sir Arthur Currie informed the editor that the attacking division had been the 1st. Currie then forgave him: "I dare say, you are not to be blamed for making this mistake as no doubt the facts have been furnished you by the War Records people, who very seldom get things as they should do."[20]

A good example of how imaginative narratives about combat can be is Lord Moran's comparison of how a German raid was reported officially and how the press reported it, and then his account of what actually transpired. On 5 January 1917 First Army said the enemy had "attempted a raid" but was driven off, leaving several dead. The next day *The Times* described how the enemy raiders "succeeded in entering our trenches," but they were quickly driven out. Lord Moran then gave the facts of the matter:

> Readers of *The Times* would scarcely deduce from this that the Boche stayed forty minutes in our trenches extracting fifty-one prisoners . . . that a corporal and two men stuck to a machine gun otherwise there was little fight shown, and that subsequently the officer commanding this battalion was removed from his command.[21]

Overall, then, the sources present contradiction and dilemma. Unanimity is seldom found outside a cemetery! The military historian has always to contend with what General Sir Ian Hamilton saw as a very difficult aspect of military history: "On the actual day of battle naked truths may be picked up for the asking; by the following morning they have already begun to get into their uniforms."[22] We would do well to remember what Vladimir Nabokov suggests: "What you are told is really threefold: shaped by the teller, reshaped by the listener, concealed from both by the dead men of the tale."[23] Some of what I say in this start on the history of the Great War Canadian divisions may well be contentious, but then I have sought to speak directly as befits a soldier. I would also echo ye olde wisdom that the more you know, the more you know you don't know. Nevertheless, I believe this study of 1st Division will help "sift out the improbable from the impossible, the possible from the improbable, and the probable from the possible in order to obtain some foundation on which to build."[24]

Notes to Preface

1. C.P. Stacey, *A Date with History* (Ottawa: Deneau, 1983), p. 132.
2. Documents pertaining to the origin of division patches are in Library and Archives Canada (LAC), RG9IIIC3, Vol. 4006, Folder 2, File 4. On 24 August, 1916 the Canadian Corps authorized divisional identification insignia in the form of cloth patches, three inches wide by two inches high. The colour red was allocated to 1st Division. Document Q.29 directed that these be worn on the back below the collar, a deviation from the Imperial practise of wearing divisional patches on the upper sleeves of the tunic and the regimental sign on the back. An amendment permitted the patches to be worn in either place. All Canadian divisions chose the sleeves. Later, divisional patches were also painted on helmets, front and back. The system designed by corps HQ made it possible to see at a glance a man's division, brigade and battalion. Brigades were identified by a coloured "designation," the colour telling the brigade, and the shape of the designation identifying the battalion. The first brigade in each division wore green, the second red and the third blue. Shapes were as follows: the first battalion of each brigade wore a circle two inches in diameter above the divisional rectangle; the second battalion of each brigade a "hemisphere" (half-circle) two inches in diameter; the third battalion a triangle with a two inch base; and the fourth battalion a two inch square. Thus, the men of 1st Battalion, 1st Brigade, 1st Division, wore a green circle above the red divisional rectangle. The reasoning behind the shapes reveals a highly logical brain at work: a circle has one line, therefore first battalion; a semi-circle two lines; a triangle three lines and a square four lines. The terms "Red Patch" and "Old Red Patch" originated with Major-General Sir Archibald Macdonell, General Officer Commanding 1st Division from June 1917 to the Armistice. According to Colonel H.S. Cooper of the 3rd Battalion, the term came into use at Hill 70 (August 1917). When Currie asked how the attack was going Macdonell replied that Red Patch was on all its objectives. The term caught on like wildfire, said Cooper (RG 41, CBC interview). The historian of the 2nd Battalion thought the patches came to mean almost as much as regimental colours. Macdonell, he said, "established a proprietary claim to the sobriquet, 'The Old Red Patch' and applied it to the Division. In turn, the troops gave that name to Sir Archibald himself." (Colonel W.W. Murray, *The History of the 2nd Canadian Battalion [East Ontario Regiment] Canadian Expeditionary Force* [Ottawa: Mortimer Ltd., 1947], p. 145). A coloured chart of the entire Canadian patch system is in Colonel G.W.L. Nicholson's *Official History of the Canadian Army in the First World War: Canadian Expeditionary Force 1914–1919* (Ottawa: Queen's Printer, 1962).
3. The term "Great War" is appropriate for at least two reasons: first, in a good many ways the war was the most significant episode in our history; and, second, it was an unprecedented experience for most of our people.
4. Cyril Falls, *War Books: An Annotated Bibliography of Books About the Great War* (London: Greenhill Books, 1989), p. xiv. R.H.S. Spaight, *British Army Divisions in the Great War 1914–1918: A Checklist* (Richmond, Surrey: Robin Spaight, 5 Kelvin Court, 1978) lists all published British divisional histories, most of which are now being reprinted in the United Kingdom.
5. Spaight, *British Army Divisions in the Great War*, pp. 11, 30. 1st Division was the eleventh division of the BEF to reach the Western Front. The first ten were the regular Imperial divisions: 1st, 2nd, 3rd, 4th, 5th, 6th, 7th, 8th, 27th and 28th. One other

regular division, the 29th, formed in March 1915 and in April went to Gallipoli. The last regular division, the Guards Division, was not formed until August 1915.

6.   Colonel G.M.C. Sprung, *The Soldier in Our Time: An Essay* (Philadelphia: Dorrance and Company, 1960), p. 21.

7.   Colonel Grasset, "How to Write a Description of a Battle," translated by Brigadier-General W. Evans, *Journal of the Royal Artillery* 56 (January 1930): 91–92. Vital matters can escape the inexperienced very easily. Anyone who has instructed young officers in minor tactics and has started by simply letting them look at a platoon deployed tactically will recall their look of sudden comprehension of the command problem when they saw just how much space a platoon of 36 men occupied.

8.   George G. Blackburn, *The Guns of Normandy: A Soldier's Eye View, France 1944* (Toronto: McClelland & Stewart Inc., 1995). Blackburn served with 4th Field Regiment, Royal Canadian Artillery. Alastair Borthwick, *Battalion: A British Infantry Unit's Actions from El Alamein to the Elbe, 1942–1945* (London: Baton Wicks Publishing, 1994). Borthwick's unit was the 5th Battalion, Seaforth Highlanders.

9.   Quoted in Barrie Pitt, "Writers and the Great War," *Journal of the Royal United Services Institute* (August 1964): 247.

10.   Quoted from the *Havamal* in Roland Huntford, *The Last Place on Earth* (London: Pan Books Ltd., 1985), p. 392.

11.   John Baynes, *Morale, A Study of Men and Courage: The Second Scottish Rifles at the Battle of Neuve Chapelle 1915* (London: Cassell, 1967), pp. 13–14.

12.   *Notes for Commanding Officers* (Aldershot: Gale and Polden, 1918), p. 361; LAC, RG9IIID3, Vol. 4866, provides as good a definition of war diary as any: "A war diary is an account of the daily activities of a military unit or formation. The diary was to record all important orders, despatches, instructions, reports and telegrams issued and received, and decisions taken as well as the daily situation (i.e. movement of the unit), important administrative matters, changes in establishment or strength, meteorological notes and the description of field works constructed or quarters occupied. Appendices usually provide more detail than could be written in the diary itself and include orders, reports, telegrams, sketches, maps and tabular statements."

13.   David Fraser, ed., *In Good Company: The First World War Letters and Diaries of The Hon. William Fraser, Gordon Highlanders* (Salisbury, Wiltshire: Michael Russell, 1990), p. 321. A modern example of creative military writing was the daily situation report produced by the headquarters of the United Nations Forces in Cyprus: the report that went to New York and the report for local circulation were two very different documents. The first was invariably very much shorter!

14.   Admiral Sir Peter Gretton, quoted in Robert Rhodes James, "Britain: Soldiers and Biographers," *Journal of Contemporary History* 3 (1968): 93.

15.   Stacey, *A Date with History*, p. 230.

16.   Tim Travers, "Currie and 1st Canadian Division at Second Ypres, April 1915: Controversy, Criticism and Official History," *Canadian Military History* (Autumn 1996): 14. This article, together with Travers' "Allies in Conflict: The British and Canadian Official Historians and the Real Story of Second Ypres (1915)," *Journal of Contemporary History* 24 (1989), provides a fascinating account of the diaries controversy.

17.   Denis Winter, *Haig's Command: A Reassessment* (London: Viking, 1991), p. 307. In view of the unbalanced nature of this book one hesitates to even cite it. Before using it the reader would be wise to consume as much salt as possible!

18. LAC, RGIIID1, Vol 4691, Folder 50, File 1. This file contains an undated, unsigned three page document entitled "War Diary of 14th. Battalion." It compares the "Original War Diary for April, May and June 1915 . . . with the amplified copy of the same Diary for the same months." To give just one example, the seven lines of the original entry for April 22 grew to 18 lines in the "amplified" version.

19. Robert Rhodes James, "Thoughts on Writing Military History," *Journal of the Royal United Services Institute* (February 1966): 102–106, is very useful on the advantages and disadvantages of war diaries as sources.

20. LAC, MG30E100 (Currie Papers) Vol. 2, General Correspondence M–R, 20 September 1918, Currie to Brigadier-General J.G. Rose, Paymaster General, London.

21. Lord Moran, *The Anatomy of Courage* (London: Constable, 1945), pp. 72–73.

22. General Sir Ian Hamilton, *A Staff Officer's Scrapbook During the Russo-Japanese War* (London: Edward Arnold, 1906), p. v.

23. Vladimir Nabokov, *The Real Life of Sebastian Knight* (Norfolk, Conn.: New Directions, 1968), p. 52.

24. Major-General Sir Ernest [Ole Luk-Oie] Swinton, R.E., *The Green Curve and Other Stories* (London: William Blackwood & Sons, 1916), p. 45.

INTRODUCTION

*The Red Patch, well that was all the introduction that you
needed, if a chap had a Red Patch, he was a pal and you knew
he'd back you to the hilt.*

—LIEUTENANT-COLONEL H.S. COOPER
3RD BATTALION

Cooper's comment and Stacey's assessment in the preface share a
theme: Red Patch was a family. An infanteer comes to see his battalion as family and home, and should he, God forbid, be sent to another battalion, even of the same regiment, his new unit would be alien at first. He
may also extend feelings of kinship to his brigade, and his division may also
be a family, albeit a very large one. What is important is the sense of belonging, which is essential for success in war. The subject of this book is one particular military family, 1st Division, Canadian Expeditionary Force (CEF).
This division, the first ever put in the field by the Dominion of Canada, served
on the Western Front from 1915 to 1918, participating in the major battles of
Second Ypres, Festubert, Mount Sorrel, the Somme, Vimy, Hill 70, the Second
Battle of Passchendaele, Amiens, Drocourt-Queant and Canal du Nord.[1]

The preface mentions several reasons for the choice of topic. Perhaps the
key was 1st Division's reputation. On the one hand, the division had a history
of trouble and strife during its time in England in 1914–1915. On the other
hand, the Minister of Militia greeted the officers of the new 2nd Division
thus: "I understand, gentlemen, that you are going to live down the reputation of the 1st Division in England. Well, all I can say is that you'll have quite
a time to live up to their reputation in France."[2]

When "Wully" Robertson, one of the most remarkable British officers
ever, was Commandant of the Staff College, Camberley, he had insisted that
"Students should be quite clear as to what the problem was before they
began to think out the solution."[3] What, then, is the problem? From all the
evidence, documentary or otherwise, it seems that 1st Division had a good
reputation. It alone of the Canadian divisions was given and is still known
by a sobriquet, in this case "Old Red Patch." Such a distinction is ordinarily
evidence of enduring respect. Imperials seem to have admired the division.
One Guards private thought the British Expeditionary Force (BEF) had put
"splendid troops in the field, such as the first contingent of the Canadians."[4]
Regimental officers, too, and not just Canadian officers, appear to have
regarded it very highly; for example, Robert Graves wrote, "It was a matter
of pride to belong to one of the recognized top-notch divisions—the Second,
Seventh, Twenty-ninth, Guards, First Canadian."[5] Four reasons, at least,

make this assessment a tremendous compliment to Old Red Patch. First, the other divisions on the list were all Imperial. National pride being what it was, and Graves being a fighting man himself, he would not have extended membership in such an exclusive club out of generosity or mere courtesy. He *meant* what he said. Second, the tribute was unique because the 1st was the only non-regular division on his list. Third, it is unlikely that a junior officer would have been placed or qualified to make this comparison; his comment probably echoed the opinions of his superiors whose scope was sufficient to judge the merit of divisions. Finally, reflection on the list as a whole makes it clear that the 1st was in exceedingly fine company. The 29th, for example, won fame at Gallipoli and burnished its record on the Western Front. That splendid division suffered about 94,000 casualties, which "if not a record [was] among the highest totals in any division." Its share of Victoria Crosses (VC)—27—was a record.[6] The 2nd, 7th and Guards Divisions won 18, 14 and 16 VCs, respectively. The officers and men of 1st Division won Queen Victoria's Cross "For Valour" 24 times.[7]

Attempting the comparison implicit in Graves' remark would be impossible here since it would entail study, at the very least, of Graves' four divisions and all four Canadian divisions. Nor is there any way to do so objectively; for one thing the divisions that fought in Flanders and in France endured no common test.[8] In short, to assert that 1st Division was the best or one of the best or even a better division would be indefensible. Thus, this book will make no comparisons.

One other useful introductory point comes courtesy of Major W.K.M. Leader who stresses that if the *aim* or, in the earlier terminology, the *object* is "stated correctly to begin with, and is kept in mind all the time, one is probably more than halfway towards a solution of the problem."[9] The same applies to a book. Moreover, the reader is entitled to know exactly what the author is about and how he proposes to get there. The central idea of this book is that 1st Division became a good division. What made it a good one, that is to say what took it from raw militia to a good, professional fighting formation, was competent command and control, thorough staff work and sound training. This in itself is a sizeable and complex matter. To try to add the story of the ordinary soldier's life would far exceed the space available within a reasonably sized book. Consequently, a subsequent companion volume will focus on the ordinary soldier and the junior officer, the two being those most at risk in war.

A good division is an effective one. More precisely, it is a combat effective one. The simple test of effectiveness is victory or defeat. Effectiveness also means that a formation kills more than it loses. 1st Division was not a good division when it formed at Valcartier, or during its training on Salisbury

Plain; in fact, it was not even a division. It only started to become one in February 1915 when it reached the Western Front, where it also began the long, arduous passage to becoming a good division, a process that would continue during that year and the next. Before Vimy the 1st was learning to be a good division; afterward it was. What enabled it to become and remain good or effective were the three elements listed near the end of the last paragraph. No list will please every man—some will question the inclusion (or exclusion) of this or that, some might think the list too long, others might think it too short—but the three encompass and are at the centre of every operation. These professional matters are the meat and potatoes of military history. After the war Sir Arthur Currie recalled that if training was right, if leadership was what it should be and if preparations were complete, then Canadians could do anything. After Vimy and Passchendaele he thought fighting spirit explained success, but only when it was developed by training and by leadership.[10] Leadership was at the heart of the Canadian Expeditionary Force's (CEF's) experience.

Initially the list included two other elements. The first, the support provided by higher formation, is a central fact of the hierarchical structure of Army organization. Because it is inherent in command and control, staff work and training it would be illogical to list and treat this support separately. The story of 1st Division cannot be restricted entirely to it since by definition a division is subordinate to and dependent on higher formation, in this case the Canadian Corps. Just as a history of a rifle company cannot ignore its parent battalion, a history of 1st Division cannot ignore its parent corps. Being subordinate, the 1st operated on corps, Army and BEF policy, and its command and control, staff system and training exhibited conformity. This is not to say that 1st Division lacked freedom to experiment and innovate, but it practised such initiatives at its level of responsibility. Corps exercise of command included implementing on a corps basis those divisional ideas or combinations of ideas it deemed worthy. Corps, Army and BEF developments, decisions and support must be considered for these levels provided much of what the 1st needed to function and become and remain a good division; for example, heavy artillery was on corps, not divisional establishment, after the 1st arrived in Flanders in early 1915.

Technology, the other element on the initial list, will not be treated separately either since it, too, was intrinsic in command and control, staff work and training. It provided the tools with which to do the job and it drove doctrine. Leadership had to integrate technology, a process easier said than done. Technological and doctrinal innovation played a key role, but not a decisive one in the war as a whole because neither side had a technological monopoly or a better doctrine. Each side was professional enough to adjust to the other's innovations, meaning that a quick, clear-cut victory was impossible. Technology cannot always provide solutions because human factors get in the way. It is simplistic and misleading to say that the British were diverted away from basic tactical lessons in 1915 and 1916 because they emphasized "traditional military qualities such as discipline, courage, optimism and high morale."[11] God forbid our nation should ever have to depend on an Army that lacked these qualities! The lessons of experience could not be implemented without them. When it comes right down to it, then or now, a weapon or other technology is only as good as the man using it.

Early 1916, according to Hugh Urquhart, "marked the time of transition between a warfare in which individualism was afforded a certain amount of consideration, and one in which the machine and machine methods were gradually driving it to the wall." "Mechanical forces," he went on, were just gathering strength in late 1915 and early 1916, and it would be many months before they played a vital part. Nevertheless, the machine was encroaching on battalion life, reducing the "human touch and identity . . . imposing more onerous and exacting duties [and] making battalion organization complex."[12]

At least three fairly recent studies reflect upon this and other factors that drove doctrine and the conduct of operations. One study looks closely at the differing German and British "philosophies" of warfare. "Philosophy" is not a word that appeals much to the combat soldier since it smacks too much of the theoretical and the "schoolies" and as such it is distant from the practical exercise of command. "Concept of operations" is more meaningful and immediate. While the British concept clearly influenced every division's operations, divisions did not shape the concept, Major-Generals being somewhat down the chain of command and divisions being something less than *higher* formations. Divisions worked within a given concept, conducting operations as directed and supported by corps. Consequently, this book does not discuss the differing philosophies.[13]

Another study sees the central problem as the difficulty of integrating morale and human qualities (the "psychological battlefield") with weapons and firepower (the "technological battlefield") or, in other words, "the problem of relating tactics to firepower." In some aspects—machine-guns as an example—Tim Travers believes the integration had not been "thought through."[14] Machine-guns, in fact, provide the best example of how practical experience alters not only doctrine but organization. But it was not 1st Division that had not thought through. The decision to remove machine-guns from battalions, organize them into companies under brigade control and then further organize them into battalions and brigades had not been taken at divisional level. Divisions had to live with such decisions and learn from them, as will be related in later chapters. At the tactical level (divisions and down) battle as a matter of course was coal-face, hands-on work: the intimate use of the tools at hand, psychological and technological all at once. Within its level of responsibility, 1st Division had a solid record of integration.

Urquhart's remarks above did not mean that he thought the human factor in war no longer mattered. As an experienced combat officer—company commander, then brigade major and then battalion commander—he knew better. According to another study, while firepower remained lord of the battlefield in the end it was not because of weapons and machines, but because of the application of reason on "the still and mental parts."[15]

It must also be said that this book is not a history of the war, the BEF, the CEF, or 1st Division's entire career. Nor does it analyse the 1st as a social institution, this being of far less importance than the professional attributes that made the division a good one: command, control, staff work and training of and by the division. The focus here is the infantry. The artillery will receive its just due, as will the engineers, but much less attention is paid to functions such as transport, supply and medical support. The cavalry is not a part of this study, and tanks are discussed only briefly in reference to command and control and training.

A gunner might think the focus skewed since it has often been said that the Great War was an artillery war. It is true that artillery caused 59 percent of all casualties: "Artillery was the killer; artillery was the terrifier. Artillery followed the soldier to the rear, sought him out in his billet, found him on the march."[16] "Ubique" (everywhere) is a word on the artillery cap badge. And who can forget Private Jakes' lament in Frederic Manning's classic *The Middle Parts of Fortune* : "There's too much fucking artillery in this bloody war."[17] In contrast, Herbert Plumer, General Officer Commanding Second Army and an infantryman, when asked whose war it was, replied that it was an infantryman's war. It is hard to say how Currie, who had been gunner and infanteer, would have responded to such a question. He might well have done so in colourful fashion since he was known for profanity. He might have said it was an infantry war because 85 percent of Canadian casualties were sustained by the infantry. Of 1st Division's 24 VC winners, 23 were infantry. The twenty-fourth was Captain Francis Scrimger, Medical Officer (MO) of the 14th Battalion.[18] Of the four actions of war—move, fire, charge, hold— some artillery can move and all of it can fire, but it cannot charge or hold. Only the infantry does all four. Only the infantry gets to battlesight range where the issue is decided. Another officer, speaking of a later war, highlighted this timeless fact: "After all, command of a support arm such as artillery does not carry responsibility for many tactical decisions."[19]

After the analytical components had been settled, the results of research had to be organized to support the book's central contention. One option, a straight-line chronological narrative running from 1914 to 1918, in which the three components would be analysed together successively over the course of events, would have resulted in considerable repetition as developments in each were described. As the book progressed the central idea set out above would become less sharp. In addition, the three elements do not entirely suit a strictly chronological accounting. While training, for example, is the process of teaching men to lead other men in combat, it also teaches men how to train others for combat. Much of this occurs away from actual operations. On the other hand, to relate the story strictly topically would make the analysis of each stand out, but at the expense of the contextual narrative so essential in military history.

Reflection suggested a combination. The story will begin with a chronological account of command and control, staff work and training from Valcartier to Salisbury Plain and then to Flanders to that point at which Old Red Patch first took charge of a sector of the Front. This provides a start line for analysis. The book concludes with an accounting of how the division stood in mid-1918 in comparison to its state in April 1915. In between, one element at a time will be discussed, taking care to relate each to the record of selected battles or actions: Second Ypres and Festubert-Givenchy (1915); Mount Sorrel and the Somme (1916); Vimy, Hill 70 and Passchendaele (1917); and the first half of the "Hundred Days" of 1918.

Command and control precede staff in this book for the simple reason that command historically preceded the staff, which first came about in ancient times when warriors formed groups too large for a commander to control without having someone carry his orders and act as his eyes beyond the range of his voice. 1st Division trained to fight, of course. This being so, training might have come first, but as it is a command and staff responsibility—together they set policy, content and conduct—and because one of the objectives of operational analysis is to validate and improve training, or to reject it and indicate alternatives, it hardly seemed reasonable to examine training before appreciating the role of command and staff.

The objectives of *We Lead, Others Follow*, the first discrete study of 1st Division (or any aspect of its career), share two themes: fairness and balance. The first objective is to provide an appropriate perspective by setting the division within the context of the order of battle: it was one of four divisions in the Canadian Corps, which was one of 23 corps fielded by the Empire. The second is to ensure that the substantial British contribution to Canadian skill at arms is recognized. The third is to portray 1st Division and its performance accurately using Canadian military terminology, values and culture. The fourth objective is to focus attention on the general officers of the

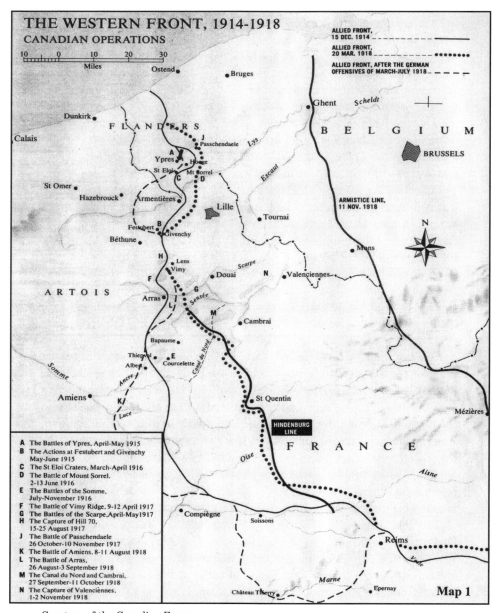

THE WESTERN FRONT, 1914-1918
CANADIAN OPERATIONS

ALLIED FRONT, 15 DEC. 1914
ALLIED FRONT, 20 MAR. 1918
ALLIED FRONT, AFTER THE GERMAN OFFENSIVES OF MARCH-JULY 1918

A The Battles of Ypres, April-May 1915
B The Actions at Festubert and Givenchy May-June 1915
C The St Eloi Craters, March-April 1916
D The Battle of Mount Sorrel. 2-13 June 1916
E The Battles of the Somme, July-November 1916
F The Battle of Vimy Ridge, 9-12 April 1917
G The Battles of the Scarpe, April-May 1917
H The Capture of Hill 70, 15-25 August 1917
J The Battle of Passchendaele 26 October-10 November 1917
K The Battle of Amiens, 8-11 August 1918
L The Battle of Arras, 26 August-3 September 1918
M The Canal du Nord and Cambrai, 27 September-11 October 1918
N The Capture of Valenciennes, 1-2 November 1918

Map 1

Courtesy of the Canadian Forces

division—not just the divisional commanders (Alderson, Currie and Macdonell) but also the brigade commanders whose enormous contributions have been largely forgotten.

One final introductory matter remains. The preface emphasizes that a study of 1st Division has been long overdue, and it mentions the literature that heretofore served as a "catch-as-catch-can" history. The historiography that follows is necessary for two reasons: first, the history of the quest and the evidence itself are inseparable, and second, the historiography is as important as the history.

The first attempt at an official history was Colonel A.F. Duguid's *Official History of the Canadian Forces in the Great War, 1914–1919,* General Series, Vol. I: *From the Outbreak of War to the Formation of the Canadian Corps, August 1914–September 1915.*[20] The title reveals the volume's inability to stand as a history of 1st Division which was not tested until April 1915. Because he was working on the basis that the volume was the first of eight, his text is burdened with "insignificant information,"[21] mostly about the days in Valcartier.

One of the earliest explanations as to why Duguid's volume did not appear until 1938 was provided by J.F.B. Livesay. In March 1933 Livesay asked Currie to write his war memoirs, not just because he wanted to see Currie's story in print, but also in frustration with Duguid: "I pretty much despair about the Official War History, what with the politicians. I doubt whether Col. Duguid is the man for the job. It seems to me he cannot see the wood for the trees."[22] A former Major of the 8th Battalion thought Duguid had another shortcoming: "He's one of those meticulous people who wouldn't write a line until he was certain in a hundred ways."[23] Three other possible reasons for the long delay have been offered. The British Official Historian, Brigadier-General Sir James Edmonds, claimed that "the Canadian strategy was not to publish . . . first, but to 'force' the Canadian narrative onto the British Official History." In a letter in 1926 Duguid offered a less Machiavellian explanation: Canadian concern that the British history be accurate had distracted those who were to write the Canadian history. He also told George F.G. Stanley that he felt unable to write the whole history until after the death of Sir Richard Turner, who nearly lost the battle of Second Ypres for the Allies.[24] In any case, the story simply never got told and Duguid's volume tracked a very cold trail.

Nor does the more recent official history provide comprehensive coverage. One can imagine the reaction of Colonel G.W.L. Nicholson, a professional and long-serving officer, to the order to write a one volume history of Canada's part in the Great War. He would not have been unfamiliar with being between Scylla and Charybdis, but trying to execute this historical "Mission

Impossible" must have made life very difficult. As he said, events were told "only in broad outline, for the limitations imposed by the covers of a single book have ruled out the inclusion of much detail . . . [and] individual treatment of the contribution made by many arms and services."[25] Coverage of 1st Division was necessarily abridged.

In contrast, Australia and Australian history have been much better served. Under C.E.W. Bean there appeared in Sydney between 1921 and 1942 the 12 volumes of *The Official History of Australia in the War.* Two volumes on Gallipoli and four on France celebrate the infantry story. Bean emphasized tactics and featured personal details because he was determined not only to write the history of the forces but to celebrate the deeds of front-line soldiers. Each Australian division is comprehensively examined.[26] Despite its enormous detail, which can deter the average reader, Bean's history is a great work, quite unlike anything else in modern military history.

It should not be supposed that the British official history can serve as an account of the Canadian Corps or of 1st Division. One reason for this is proportion: the Canadian Corps was just one of 23 corps in the five Western Front Armies of the BEF. At no time did it exceed 10 percent of British strength at its lowest in this theatre. The 14 volumes of Brigadier-General Sir James Edmond's *History of the Great War, Military Operations, France and Belgium,* published in London from 1925 to 1947, focus on the British Army and on British operations and generally they consider Dominion formations far less vigorously and thoroughly. This is not to say that Edmonds can be avoided; indeed, it is hard to see how anyone who seriously studies or writes about the war can do so without his work. Despite its faults the series is indispensable since so many of the documents on which it was based are no longer available.[27]

Nor do any of the relatively few non-official histories tell the story of 1st Division. While those by Desmond Morton and Jack Granatstein and by John Swettenham are genuine contributions to Canadian Corps history, they do not focus on 1st Division. The same is true of the accounts of Vimy by Pierre Berton, D.J. Goodspeed, Brereton Greenhous and Stephen J. Harris, Alexander McKee and Herbert Fairlie Wood; of the books on Second Ypres by Daniel G. Dancocks and J. McWilliams and R.J. Steel; and of Dancock's accounts of Passchendaele and the Hundred Days of 1918. There is nothing dramatically wrong with any of these accounts, although some of their conclusions are debatable. For one, Dancocks is too inclined to see Currie as a military genius at Second Ypres. All of these books attribute Canadian success almost entirely to good planning and good artillery, or to Currie after Vimy. All focus on *one* operation and one operation does not make a good division, or a good divisional history. As the old German military axiom has it, *Zweimal ist nicht einmal noch* (Twice does not mean once again).

Another category is personal memoirs. Few relate specifically to 1st Division. This group includes Harold Peat's *Private Peat* (1917) and Harold Baldwin's *"Holding the Line"* (1918). Both are highly entertaining (especially Peat), but they are also fanciful and somewhat in the line of recruiting tracts. While they are very good on soldier activities and philosophy, their reliability is often highly questionable and their focus is as narrow as the small slice of trench from which a private or a sergeant fights. Captain Frederic Curry's *From the St. Lawrence to the Yser* (1916) gives a wider perspective and is more useful, but it ends in 1915, as does Lieutenant-Colonel John Currie's *The Red Watch with the First Canadian Division in Flanders* (1916). Lieutenant James Pedley's *Only This: A War Retrospect* (1927) is more reflective and its frankness about the out-of-the-line pursuits of a junior officer and the characteristics and abilities of his superiors enhances its value; however, he did not join 4th Battalion until December 1917. Finally, O.C.S. Wallace's collection of the letters of Lieutenant C.A. Wells of the 8th Battalion is not particularly revealing, because of Wells' understandable reticence about describing combat to his parents. A sub-group of personal memories is oral history, published and unpublished. William Mathieson's *My Grandfather's War* (1981) and the 17 part CBC Radio program "Flanders' Fields" (1964) are typical. While these are often revealing they share an inherent weakness. The memories of old men, which are short and unreliable, sometimes defy reason, and the usual embellishments of the years, caused by confusion between memory and imagination, confirm my doubts about oral history.[28]

As for biographies of Canadian front-line commanders, only Julian Byng, Arthur Currie, George Pearkes and Andrew McNaughton have received serious scrutiny. No literary monuments exist for the other commanders of 1st Division, or for the commanders of other Canadian divisions, brigades and battalions. They remain the faceless ones, which, from a national point of view, is sad. Nor are there any accounts of 1st Division's three brigades in the Great War. Nor did every infantry battalion in the division become the subject of a full-length history—as did every infantry battalion of 1st Division in the Second World War.

Overall, Cyril Falls' comment that "the Great War has resulted in the spilling of floods of ink as well as of blood."[29] does not apply to Canada. Our flood has been rather shallow! Fortunately, amidst all this historiographic gloom there is some sunshine. Of 1st Division's 12 battalions, eight have been the subject of histories, some by men who actually served in them. These books vary considerably in style and quality, but all are useful; in fact, they are vital. One other battalion has a history in the form of the unpublished memoirs of its most famous and longest-serving commanding officer. For the three battalions that lack comprehensive histories, there exist some useful pamphlets and commemorative materials. These materials, archival records and the published literature suffice to enable a good picture of 1st Division.[30]

Clearly then, Canadian divisions are virgin ground for historians. Why this is so is less apparent. Ever since Agamemnon and the siege of Troy, generals have borne a disproportionate share of the shame and the glory of war. Marshal Joffre captured this professional hazard nicely when he commented, "I don't know who won the Battle of the Marne, but if it had been lost, I know who would have lost it."[31] The standard explanation for defeat is incompetence or unpardonable errors in judgement by the commander. This idea of individual fault is so appealingly simple that it is very easy to extend it to making Colonel Duguid, the CEF's erstwhile historian, solely responsible for the shortcomings of the Canadian Great War historical record.

Some might think that the accomplishments of our soldiers were forgotten only because of time, it now being more than 80 years since the Armistice. With almost all of the men of the Great War gone, that struggle could seem as remote as the Napoleonic Wars. Geography could be considered a factor, too, since most Canadians have not seen and never will see any of the Canadian monuments and cemeteries in Europe. But geography and time are excuses, not reasons, for forgetting. Neither geography nor time seems to have caused Australians to have national amnesia about their record during the Great War; anyone who has ever attended Anzac Day ceremonies, which are held every April 25 wherever there are Australians, knows that record and knows also that wonderful Australian pride.

Behind the Canadian amnesia is the fact that about one-third of the people of this country during the Great War were either indifferent or hostile to the war effort. Is this why the Hall of Fame on Parliament Hill, which was intended to house the statues of Canada's Victoria Cross winners,[32] never became a fact, and why there is no Vimy Day, no counterpart to Anzac Day? No one would deny a French Canadian contribution to the war. Most of the few who served at the front did so honourably and well, but they were numerically a very small presence in the Canadian Corps and in 1st Division. Only one of the Canadian Corps' 48 battalions was French Canadian. Only one of 1st Division's 48 rifle companies was French Canadian.[33] In each case the French Canadian contribution, two percent of the total, hardly reflects percentages of our national population. Had the French Canadian contribution been substantial imagine how much more could have been achieved for Canada. It was the English speaking population that largely bore the burden of the war and made the attendant sacrifice.

How little our people know of the endeavours and the valour of those who served at the front! This is entirely appalling when one considers the sacrifices of regimental officers such as Major F.A. Robertson, DSO, who lost an eye on the Somme but soldiered on until he lost a leg in August 1918.[34] As Lord Moran said,

> It is strange how some good fellows keep on their feet, drifting back when their wounds are healed . . . Something in their stock tethers them to the life . . . The value of these brave souls is beyond numbers, week by week they count for more. They are the backbone . . . Without them I cannot think how an improvised army could endure so much.[35]

The Canadian Corps was built and then held together on the long path from Second Ypres to Vimy and on to the Armistice by regimental officers such as Robertson. Vimy, now an enduring Canadian legend, marks for many people the passage of Canada, in 1917 only 50 years a Dominion, from colony to nation. Perhaps, then, Sir John Fortescue's remarks about his country also apply in considerable degree to Canada: "It is not too much, I think, to say that we owe our national existence to our regimental officers." Duguid thought Canadians had been robbed of "the preservation of the tradition of self-sacrifice, and . . . the precious heritage so dearly bought in battle overseas during the most momentous years in Canadian history."[36] W.B. Kerr saw the neglect of our war record as a "sad commentary upon our . . . lack of pride in our national achievements, and our failure to appreciate history as a road map through the treacherous and rugged terrain of . . . politics and war."[37] When we fail to treasure our history we should not expect the publications of others in the wider world to do so. How can we legitimately criticize Oxford University Press for publishing companion volumes of Australian and New Zealand military history, but not a companion to Canadian military history? If we do not care, why should others?

Every student on Canadian Army "Method of Instruction" courses was imprinted with a formula that neatly summed up the process: tell them what you are going to tell them, tell them and, finally, tell them what you told them. This applies equally well to the written word. Having done the first, I will start by telling of the birth and early infancy of 1st Division in Canada, England and Flanders.

Notes to Introduction

1. A record of 1st Division's battles and engagements is in Appendix II.
2. Hughes is quoted in Saskatchewan Provincial Archives, R.2.247, "The Great War as I Saw It," unpublished memoirs of Brigadier-General George Tuxford, p. 34.

3.   Brigadier the Rt. Hon. Sir John Smyth, *Leadership in Battle, 1914–1918: Commanders in Action* (London: David & Charles, 1975), p. 49. Robertson, the only man in the British Army who successively held every rank from Private to Field Marshal except WO1, became Commandant of the Staff College in 1910. He was Chief of Staff to Sir John French in 1915 and, finally, Chief of the Imperial General Staff. He retired in 1920. For a splendid appraisal of "Wully" see John Terraine, " 'Wully' Field Marshal Sir William Robertson, Bart, GCB, KCVO, DSO," in John Terraine, *1914–1918, Essays on Leadership and War* (Poole, Dorset: The Western Front Association, 1998), pp. 55–89.

4.   Stephen Graham, *A Private in the Guards* (London: Macmillan And Co., 1919), p. 16. Graham was a well-known author when he enlisted. *A Private in the Guards* was his twelfth book.

5.   Robert Graves, *Goodbye to All That* (London: Cassell, 1957), p. 161. Graves' book is possibly the best source in the English language for the individual and collective experience of trench warfare. He was a Captain in the Royal Welsh Fusiliers, a regiment whose many battalions gave splendid service. Modern historians share Graham's and Graves' opinions of 1st Division. To give just one example, Travers, "Allies in Conflict," p. 319, calls it one of the four or five outstanding divisions of the BEF.

6.   Captain Stair Gillon, *The Story of the 29th Division: A Record of Gallant Deeds* (London: Thomas Nelson & Sons Ltd., 1925), p. vii; J.G. Fuller, *Troop Morale and Popular Culture in the British and Dominion Armies, 1914–1918* (Oxford: Clarendon Press, 1990), p. 30, calls the 29th "the most famous division in the British Army." Robert Rhodes James, *Gallipoli* (London: B.T. Batsford Limited, 1965), pp. 243, 343, thought it "incomparable." Geoffrey Serle, *John Monash A Biography* (Melbourne: Melbourne University Press, 1982), p. 475, relates that Monash thought the 29th "magnificent."

7.   Arthur Bishop, *Our Bravest and Our Best: The Stories of Canada's Victoria Cross Winners* (Toronto: McGraw-Hill Ryerson, 1995). 1st Division's first Great War VC went to Lance-Corporal Fred Fisher (13th Battalion) on April 23, 1915 and the last to Sergeant William Merrifield (4th Battalion) on October 1, 1918. The 2nd, 3rd and 4th Canadian Divisions shared 33 VCs during the Great War. A list of 1st Division VCs is at Appendix IV. Canadians won 70 VCs during the Great War, out of a total of 633 VCs awarded. During the Second World War 182 were awarded (Smyth, *Leadership in Battle*, p. 11.)

8.   Peter Simkins, ed., "Co-Stars or Supporting Cast? British Divisions in the 'Hundred Days', 1918", in Paddy Griffith, ed., *British Fighting Methods in the Great War* (London: Frank Cass, 1996), pp. 53, 56–57, 68, suggests that 11 of the 50 Imperial divisions engaged in the Hundred Days, for example, had more "battle days" than the Canadian "divisional average" and that 4th Canadian was the most engaged Canadian division. He bases his survey on 1,187 operations, including 221 Dominion operations (100 Canadian). He defines operation as ranging from strong offensive patrols and battalion actions to full scale set-piece assaults by several divisions at a time, such as Amiens in August 1918.

9.   Major W.K.M. Leader, *An Elementary Study of Appreciations Orders and Messages* (London: Sifton, Praed & Co. Ltd., 1936), p. 4. Object and objective are often confused. The difference lies in terms of the proverbial chicken whose object (or aim) was to cross the road and whose objective was the other side. Without a clear aim there is no telling what can happen. E.S. Russenholt, *Six Thousand Canadian Men Being the*

History of the 44th Battalion Canadian Infantry, 1914–1919 (Winnipeg: The Forty-Fourth Battalion Association, 1932), p. 47, believed 10th Brigade's assault on Regina Trench in October 1916 failed because of obscure and ambiguous brigade orders that, contrary to recognized tactical principles, contained a series of alternative proposals instead of a single, definitive aim. 10th Brigade's GOC at the time was W.St.P. Hughes.

10. LAC, MG30E100 (*Currie Papers*), Vol. 1, General Correspondence (A-F), letter to Premier H.C. Brewster of B.C., 31 May 1917; Vol. 15, Folder 43, Currie to Charles Vining, 2 April 1927; RG9IIIC1, Vol. 3854, Folder 71, File 7, Currie, GOC Canadian Corps, to Second Army, 20 November 1917; 3rd Brigade War Diary, 9 May 1917. Currie's remarks largely echo the ideas expressed in what would have been one of the first military manuals he was exposed to, *Field Service Regulations, Part I: Operations* (London: HMSO, 1909; reprint, 1912). *FSR* said (p. 13) "Success in war depends more on moral than on physical qualities . . . but even high moral qualities may not prevail without careful preparation and skillful direction."

11. Tim Travers, "Learning and Decision-Making on the Western Front, 1915–1916: The British Example," *Canadian Journal of History* (April 1983): p. 92. All in all, this is not one of Travers' best, primarily because it is over-theoretical and ignores his own warning about "over-interpreting euphemistic language," which he says was revealing of an attitude that hindered learning lessons. It also condemns commanders for not knowing what they could not possibly have known. Hindsight is indeed the best commander!

12. Hugh M. Urquhart, *The History of the 16th Battalion (The Canadian Scottish Regiment) Canadian Expeditionary Force in the Great War 1914–1919* (Toronto: Macmillan, 1932), pp. 117–19.

13. Martin Samuels, *Command or Control? Command, Training and Tactics in the British and German Armies, 1888–1918* (London: Frank Cass, 1995), is the best source on the differing philosophies.

14. Tim Travers, *The Killing Ground: The British Army, The Western Front and the Emergence of Modern Warfare, 1900–1918* (London: Unwin & Hyman, 1987), pp. 62, 253.

15. Ulysses (William Shakespeare, *Troilus and Cressida*, Act 1, Scene 3) quoted in Shelford Bidwell and Dominick Graham, *Fire-Power: British Army Weapons and Theories of War, 1904–1945* (London: George Allen & Unwin, 1982), pp. 4, 38.

16. John Terraine, *The Smoke and the Fire: Myths and Anti-Myths of War, 1861–1945* (London: Sidgwick & Jackson, 1980), p. 132. Ronald Clifton, "What is an Artillery Brigade?" *Stand To!* 31 (Spring 1991): 34, estimates that 100 million 18-pounder shells and 25 million 4.5 inch howitzer shells were fired during the war. Over five million tons of ammunition were shipped to France during the war. Clifton, "What is a Heavy Battery?" *Stand To!* 35 (Summer 1992): 32, notes the presence of over 6,700 guns with the BEF in November 1918.

17. Frederic Manning, *The Middle Parts of Fortune* (London: Peter Davies, 1929), p. 222. Manning's book is probably the best English language war novel.

18. Anthony Eden, *Another World, 1897–1917* (London: Allen Lane, 1976), p. 124; A.M.J. Hyatt, *General Sir Arthur Currie: A Military Biography* (Toronto: University of Toronto Press, 1987), p. 22 and note 30; Lieutenant-Colonel C. Beresford Topp, *The 42nd Battalion, C.E.F. Royal Highlanders of Canada* (Montreal: Gazette Printing Co., Limited, 1931), p. 3.

19. Brigadier R.N.L. Hopkins quoted in D.M. Horner, *Crisis in Command: Australian*

Generalship and the Japanese Threat, 1941–1943 (Canberra: Australian National University Press, 1978), p. 229. This seems already to have been forgotten, it being one of those facts every generation must learn anew, viz, Jonathan Bailey, "British Artillery in the Great War," in Griffith, ed., *British Fighting Methods in the Great War*, note 3, p. 43. This article is pure "gunner." Only a gunner would call manoeuvre a preoccupation! Gunners are peculiar people. Infantry readers would contend that artillery supports rather than has or conducts operations. The artillery's mission is still to enable the infantry to close.

20. Published at Ottawa by The King's Printer in 1938.
21. A.M.J. Hyatt, "Official History in Canada," *Military Affairs* (Summer 1966): pp. 94–95.
22. LAC, MG 30E 100 (Currie Papers), Vol. 27, File 7, letter of March 28, 1933. In 1933 J.F.B. Livesay was the General Manager of the Canadian Press.
23. LAC, RG 41, Vol. 8, CBC interview with Major C. Smellie. Stacey, *A Date with History*, pp. 64–67, is very informative about Duguid the man and the historian. Duguid's superiors were no doubt frustrated about the lack of progress with the history, yet Duguid remained. Consequently, Generals MacBrien, Thacker and McNaughton, in their capacities as Chief of the General Staff, must share some of the blame for the fiasco of the Canadian official history of the Great War.
24. Travers, "Currie and 1st Canadian Division at Second Ypres," p. 14; "Allies in Conflict," pp. 310–11. Edmonds claimed that Duguid told him that the Canadian CGS (MacBrien) had instructed him to falsify the record of Second Ypres. What is also evident in both articles is Edmond's strong bias against Currie. LAC, RG 24, Vol. 1755, Duguid to Lieutenant-Colonel Gordon Hall, June 8, 1926; George F.G. Stanley, review of "Welcome to Flanders Fields: The First Canadian Battle of the Great War: Ypres 1915", by Daniel G. Dancocks, *Queen's Quarterly* 97 (Spring 1990): 187.
25. Nicholson, *Official History of the Canadian Army*, p. xii.
26. Falls, *War Books: An Annotated Bibliography*, p. 7, calls Bean's contribution, in which strong criticism abounds, "a serious and painstaking record."
27. The British official history is one of only 11 entries awarded three stars by Falls in his 315 page *War Books: An Annotated Bibliography*.
28. The CBC transcripts are in Library and Archives Canada (LAC), RG 41. The best survey of the earlier Great War literature is still W.B. Kerr, "Historical Literature on Canada's Participation in the Great War," *Canadian Historical Review* 14 (December 1933): 412–36. He is especially helpful for some of the more obscure soldier accounts and regimental histories. Kerr served with 4th Division. John Currie's battalion, the 15th, was known informally as the "Red Watch."
29. Falls, *War Books: An Annotated Bibliography*, p. xiii.
30. The 2nd, 3rd, 8th, 10th, 13th, 14th, 15th and 16th Battalions have full-length histories. The memoirs, "The Great War as I Saw It," were written by George Tuxford, first Commanding Officer, 5th Battalion. The 1st, 4th and 7th Battalions lack full-length chronicles.
31. Quoted in Trevor Royle, *A Dictionary of Military Quotations* (London: Routledge, 1990), p. 84.
32. Bishop, *Our Bravest and Our Best*, p. 64.
33. The expert in the matter of French-Canadian enlistment is Desmond Morton. See *When Your Number's Up: The Canadian Soldier in the First World War* (Toronto: Random House, 1993), pp. 61, 278; "The Limits of Loyalty: French-Canadian Officers and the First World War" in *Limits of Loyalty*, ed. Edgar Denton (Waterloo, Ontario:

Wilfred Laurier University Press, 1979), p. 82; and "The Short, Unhappy Life of the 41st Battalion, CEF," *Queen's Quarterly* 81 (Spring 1974): 75. Also very useful are C.P. Stacey, *Canada and the Age of Conflict: A History of Canadian External Policies*, Vol. 1 1867–1921 (Toronto: Macmillan, 1977), pp. 235, 237; and C.A. Sharpe, "Enlistment in the Canadian Expeditionary Force 1914–1918: A Regional Analysis," *Journal of Canadian Studies* (Winter 1984): p. 29. Desmond Morton and J.L. Granatstein, *Marching to Armageddon Canadians and the Great War, 1914–1919* (Toronto: Lester & Orpen Dennys, 1989), p. 33, note that Militia Department figures show 14,100 French-speaking soldiers in the CEF in mid-1917, of which "fewer than half" were recruited by Quebec battalions. *The Times History of the War*, Volume XVI (London: The Times, 1918), p. 254, reported in March 1918 that 16,000 French-Canadians were overseas. Morton's and Stacey's figures show that four percent of the 364,000 Canadians who went overseas were French speaking.

34. LAC, MG30E100 (Currie Papers), Vol. 43, Diary entry 26 August, 1918. The DSO (Distinguished Service Order) was awarded to officers for meritorious or distinguished service in the field, or before the enemy. Starting in January, 1917 award of the DSO was restricted to services in action.

35. Moran, *The Anatomy of Courage*, pp. 117–18.

36. Sir John Fortescue, *The Vicissitudes of Organised Power, The Romanes Lecture* (Oxford: Clarendon Press, 1929), p. 39. Fortescue became famous for his multi-volume history of the British Army. Colonel A. Fortescue Duguid, "Canadians in Battle, 1915–1918," *Canadian Defence Quarterly* 13 (October 1935): 27.

37. Kerr, "Historical Literature on Canada's Participation in the Great War," pp. 427–28.

CHAPTER ONE

"In the Beginning . . ."

The very lifeblood of our enterprise.
—HOTSPUR, *HENRY IV,* I, IV, 1, 28

Fielding a division was quite an undertaking for a young nation of less than eight million people who had little experience of war or the formation and workings of a large Army—or even of nationhood, since for the most part Canada ran to London time, not Ottawa time. Her most recent experiences of war were the South African War (1899–1902), the North West Rebellion (1885) and the 1884 expedition to rescue "Chinese Gordon" from the Mahdi at Khartoum. Canadians in that abortive mission totalled 386 men who served not as a formed unit but as individuals dispersed throughout the Imperial force. Canadians who served in the North West and in South Africa totalled about 8,000 in each case, and the highest level at which Canadian officers commanded was battalion.[1] By 1904 there was a Canadian Army in all but name, although it was not much of an Army.[2] Authorized 5,000 men that year, the Permanent Force stood at only 3,110 a decade later. Fortunately, some reserves existed: between 1904 and 1913 the number of men undergoing annual Non-Permanent Active Militia training rose from 36,000 to 55,000.[3] At 8:45 P.M. on Tuesday, August 4, 1914 when word came to Ottawa that the British ultimatum to Germany had expired, Canada (not quite a nation), with some forces (not quite an Army), was, with the rest of the Empire, at war. When the news reached Toronto large crowds sang "God Save the King." The chorus echoed almost everywhere across the Dominion.[4] Men rushed to the colours, worried that any delay might cost them the excitement of a war that would surely soon be over.

Being first in time and in title entails commitment, obligation and expectation that never goes away and never decreases. From the start much was expected of the 1st Division. As the war wore on, that expectation increased in view of the Division's seniority and growing reputation. At Vimy, after more than two years at war, the 1st stood right of the line, perhaps by chance or because some staff officer (or more likely, Arthur Currie himself), realizing that for the first time in our history four Canadian divisions would attack together, made strong representations to have the 1st in the place of honour. In any case, this was proper since the 1st Division had been first to fight at Second Ypres, where the 1st Field Battery of 1st Brigade, Canadian Field Artillery (CFA), had fired the first round for the Canadian Army.[5] With justification, Archibald Macdonell, the last GOC of the 1st in the Great War, could proclaim in the last summer of the war what those who wore the Red Patch had always done: "We lead, others follow."[6]

In 1914 all this was yet to come. At Valcartier the officers and men of 1st Division saw themselves as the standard setters. From 1st Division came the cadres of the others. Those who in time were scattered throughout the Canadian Corps in command and staff positions (where many became distinguished) did not forget that their experience, their opportunity and their pride had begun with Old Red Patch. They took with them the ethos of 1st Division.[7] Visible evidence of being first was the "special prerogative" (Currie's words) that in September 1914 authorized members of the original first contingent to wear coloured shoulder straps. Although the straps were a badge of pride, they never quite attained the status of the Old Red Patch. The man who wore both was good *and* lucky *and* one of the few. In December 1916 the "originals" of 3rd Battalion totalled only five officers and 68 Other Ranks (ORs). In 1917 Private Harold Peat of the 3rd, speaking of 1st Division as a whole said, "Today there are only a few hundred men entitled to wear [this] distinction."[8] By February 1918 just over 100 of the officers who came out in February 1915 were still with 1st Division.[9]

Another circumstance of 1914 that remained with the 1st throughout was its administrative and legal status. Upon mobilization the contingent was considered "Imperial [with] the status of British regular troops." Later (July 1916) the British Army Council decreed that CEF members were "attested to serve . . . as Imperial soldiers . . . fully subject to the Army Act," but in September it was realized that the CEF was

> not in fact "Imperial" [that is] raised by HM beyond the UK . . . to form part . . . of the regular forces [and] paid and maintained . . . by . . . UK. It was, *per contre* . . . raised by order of the King in one of his overseas Dominions, to form part . . . of the Armies of the British Empire . . . paid . . . and maintained . . . by the Parliament of Canada.[10]

Notwithstanding, the Army Act still applied and Canadian officers received Imperial Commissions (Temporary) so they could take rank with British Regulars.[11] This ensured parity between officers of equal rank regardless of service and experience, a fact that became important when Canadians were appointed to the staffs of Imperial formations.

Such matters were not on the immediate agenda in 1914. Nor, fortunately, did Dominion soldiers have to fight immediately. The first problem, mobilization, was exacerbated by an order to military district commanders from the Minister of Militia, Sam Hughes, to proceed on an entirely new basis: pay no attention to "memorandum C.1209, dated 1st October, 1911 [the mobilization plan] . . . This letter need not be acknowledged; its contents are not to be discussed; and nothing is required from you in the nature of a report."[12] This amazing letter, ignoring the wisdom that a fire is no place to organize a fire brigade, scrapped the mobilization plan and took Headquarters and the Militia Council out of the picture. It also meant that professional soldiers and their staffs at divisional area and district headquarters were out, since Militia HQ could now deal directly with the 226 militia infantry units by lettergram. On 6 August Hughes ordered them to recruit, but did not specify to what strength. This "personal call to arms, like the fiery cross . . . in former days"[13] restricted the Militia units to dispatching drafts to an embarkation point. Two days later Hughes further upset calculations:

> Each infantry battalion was instructed to provide a contingent of the strength of a double company (two hundred and fifty) or a single company (one hundred and ten) . . . In other words, in the infantry . . . the whole system of territorial identity . . . was destroyed; the work of years in the building up of a regimental spirit and affiliation founded upon personal relations and comradeship was undone. . . . The situation which developed . . . is hard to describe . . . Commanding officers commenced to ask all sorts of questions as to the grouping of detachments, the command of . . . battalions, the composition of the headquarters, the uniform . . . and so forth . . . These perplexities led to a tangle of telegrams . . . at such crosspurposes that no review of them is possible. To add to the confusion, Militia Headquarters, or . . . the Minister, ignored the usual military channels.[14]

Had the original mobilization plan been adhered to, much of the confusion

> might have been avoided. But the Minister . . . after calling for volunteers . . . formed them into numbered battalions bearing no relation to the number allotted to the militia battalions then in existence. To accommodate the C.E.F. volunteers he constructed a mobilization camp at Valcartier, complete with four miles of rifle ranges, streets,

buildings, lighting, telephones, baths and sanitary conveniences. It was a magnificent achievement but wasteful and unnecessary.[15]

The commanding officers did an admirable job of sorting out the mess. They gathered their *ad hoc* battalions and entrained them for Valcartier, Quebec, where they would be organized, trained—although time for that was fleeting—and otherwise made ready for the Atlantic crossing. Thinking officers like Louis Lipsett had known well the flaws in the prewar militia: many units were well below strength and too many were nothing but social clubs. He and others like him could not immediately correct all the prewar shortcomings, but they worked hard at strengthening the ties of kinship, friendship and cap badge. It was said of Lipsett, who had been responsible for standardizing prewar militia training, that his personality, ability and sound knowledge made him a "power of efficiency [giving him] an influence such as had never been wielded by any other Western officer . . . Many Generals, Colonels and their officers . . . had reason to bless the soundness of his teaching."[16] But Lipsett was a Regular and the Minister did not like regulars. However, Hughes had the ability to astonish both Regular and Militia officers. His romantic sense of tactics would become evident at Valcartier where he would order one officer to "Form Square," a tactical formation hardly to be recommended in 1914.[17]

Had the traditional structure been retained instead of being replaced by Celtic caprice, units would have filled out to establishment in more orderly fashion. Officers like Lipsett would have known intuitively that Hughes' way would have an adverse impact. If Hughes had read Kipling, he had forgotten the admonition that "it takes a deal of time, money and blood to make a regiment."[18] Being a politician, not a soldier, Hughes did not know how fundamental the regimental system was to efficiency and high morale, nor did he appreciate the extent to which men identified with their regiment. Politicians did not have regimental marches, which explains why they were habitually out of step. How difficult it must have been to summon up enthusiasm for bodies known solely by numbers and lacking that great talisman called a regimental cap badge.[19] Nor did he understand that while a battalion or a division can be created at the stroke of a pen, this does not give either life:

> The larger a unit the longer it will take to weld itself into a unity, and evolve a proper pride in itself. *Esprit de corps* for want of a better word. The division that has had no previous existence in peace cannot get an issue of this essential self-esteem with its other mobilization stores. Six months or a year of active service must pass before it understands its meaning; for units and brigades have first

to learn to row in the same boat before the divisional consciousness will grow.[20]

Starting from scratch would not have been necessary had the original mobilization plan been retained. The enormous individual effort taken by COs and officers to build units from the companies of various regiments distracted from the real business of learning how to soldier and how to command. Hughes' nameless orphan battalions were an abomination in the eyes of almost everyone. Every CO in 1st Division had to struggle daily to create and maintain *esprit de corps* from nothing. A first step to improve matters added regimental titles to the unit numbers; for example, 8th Battalion appended "90th Rifles;" 13th Battalion, "Royal Highlanders of Canada;" and 16th Battalion "The Canadian Scottish."[21] Another initiative, distinctive cap and collar badges and shoulder titles, took longer to appear since they had to be designed, approved and manufactured. By mid-1916 every infantry battalion had such accoutrements. The importance of badges is evident in the following order that became standard practise in 1st Division: "As soon as drafts reach the depot they will be supplied with regimental badges, shoulder titles, collar numerals and Divisional patches without any delay. Commandant[s] will seek to build up a Battalion and Brigade spirit by this and other means."[22]

As frustrating as all this was, within Hughes' scheme lurked a greater demon. Mobilization, Hughes' style, put everything in the shop window, so to speak. His decision to continue creating new battalions, instead of having the battalions tied to the regional centres in Canada that could keep them up to strength, resulted by October 1915 in 90 infantry battalions when only 65 were actually required. By December 1916 over 200 battalions had gone to Britain, where many were broken up and the men sent to reserve battalions for training.[23] A scramble ensued to find places for unemployed officers—the 4th Battalion, for example, ended up with two lieutenant-colonels, an anomaly of mobilization—but after Ypres the practise ceased. While brigadiers probably found it useful to have lieutenant-colonels in waiting, in the units it no doubt irritated majors whose stay in that rank would be lengthened because of the presence of another lieutenant-colonel, often one who had no previous connection with the unit. It was not only unfair but just plain awkward.[24]

For the men of the dispersed battalions and for their officers the break-up was painful. Many were convinced that "Hughes' recruiting system was not only a confidence trick, betraying promises made to prospective colonels and their men, but also it threatened the efficiency and morale of the CEF."[25] While subalterns were always in demand due to heavy casualties, the disbanded battalions created a large surplus of captains and above, which grew alarmingly until mid-1917 when individuals were given the choice of either reverting to lieutenant and going to France with other units or returning to Canada. Morale and recruiting suffered.

Not until March 1917 did a sound system of infantry reinforcement exist. Before that time combat units often suffered from want of men. After Second Ypres 1st Division, having taken heavy casualties, had to be made up to strength, as far as that was possible, by the Canadian Cavalry Brigade, which had been asked to volunteer for infantry duty despite having had "no infantry training, absolutely none at all." Going into the trenches as infantry without any indoctrination in trench warfare created considerable anxiety.[26] The problem in June 1915 was described thus:

> The 1st Canadian Division was reduced in strength and exhausted just as the British formations were, and its troubles further increased by the lack of an assured supply of reinforcements . . . [T]he promiscuous grouping of contingents at mobilization made it extremely difficult to deal with the question . . . To make good the losses . . . the only drafts on hand in England were the base companies of the units already arrived, totalling one to two thousand. To meet the need Canadian Headquarters had to break up completely organized battalions . . . The drafts [so] obtained . . . were distributed broadcast amongst the units of the 1st . . . irrespective of previous affiliations, by men drawn from anywhere between the Atlantic and the Pacific. These sources . . . exhausted no further reinforcements were available . . . Because of this . . . the . . . 16th, after the battle of Festubert, [was] not replenished until nearly the end of July. The Battalion was down to less than half establishment . . . In the ranks one man was doing the duty of two, and they were men tired in body and mind.[27]

It is not difficult to see how this could cause many needless casualties. At one point in 1916 only 1,000 reinforcements were available out of 25,000 men undergoing training in England.[28] The system, made worse by the low standard of training, came to be seen as a farce. Corrective measures began in December 1916 when all Canadian infantry in Britain were organized into six reserve brigades, consisting of 26 reserve battalions. Early in 1917 the infantry was put into 12 territorial regiments, each of which had reserve battalion(s) and frontline battalions, the idea being to ensure that recruits from one province would go, as much as possible, to units from that same province.[29]

Neither Lieutenant-Colonel John Creelman, Commanding Officer of 2nd Field Artillery Brigade, nor Captain H.S. Cooper of the 3rd Battalion (a self-styled "militia johnny" who finished the war as a Colonel) had anything good to say of Hughes. Creelman called him the "mad Mullah of Canada," while Cooper said, "It took the greatest genius of all times to make the muck-up that he made of the mobilization of the First Canadian Division." Captain D.H.C. Mason, 3rd Battalion, described confusion at Valcartier as so total that it would not have surprised anyone if Hughes had been assassinated.[30] One private summarized matters thus: "The word 'confusion' has become synonymous with 'Canadian Contingent' and just recently I have heard it referred to as the 'Comedian Contingent' (not bad that, as anyone knows who has had the misfortune to serve in it)."[31]

Hughes mostly ignored the artillery, which did things very differently thanks to Edward "Dinky" Morrison, Director of Artillery since 1913. He had won the DSO for a conspicuous act of gallantry and leadership in South Africa, but in 1914 he was of even more service to his beloved guns and to the Army as a whole. His initial contribution was intelligent, calm and systematic mobilization:

> General Morrison was responsible for the fact that the Divisional Artillery consisted practically of complete units selected from the existing Militia batteries, under their own officers, instead of, as the Minister at first proposed, new batteries being organized from material drawn from every part of the Dominion. This regard for homogeneity undoubtedly had much to do with the marked efficiency of the artillery arm.[32]

Much of the Canadian-made equipment adversely affected 1st Division, albeit only briefly. With three exceptions, most of the shortcomings were remedied before it reached the Front. The first shortcoming, the American Colt machine-gun, quickly gave way to the superior British Vickers and no harm was done. The other exceptions were the soldier's best friends: his rifle and his shovel. In both cases Hughes insisted on the issue and retention of poor equipment. The MacAdam shovel, a combination entrenching tool and shield, was his "special interest": it had been patented by his female secretary. Despite being too heavy to carry and to dig with (thanks to its useless shield), 25,000 went to England. After failing user trials in France, all were disposed of as salvage, no particular harm having been done other than wasting shipping space and people's time.[33] The troops received good British entrenching tools in lieu.

A far more serious shortcoming was the Ross rifle, which did great damage for a considerable time. It was a sorry political tale, one the infanteer paid for in blood. Its most "passionate proponent" and its "most ferocious defender" was Hughes.[34] The truism, efficiency in the use of the weapon is what gives the soldier confidence, was so as long as that weapon was the Lee-Enfield, but it could not apply to the infamous Ross rifle. No matter how carefully the rifle was treated it would not fight for the Canadian soldier, except as a sniping rifle where dead accuracy mattered more than sturdiness, size and rapid fire capability. The Ross jammed at awkward moments—an inconvenient flaw since most moments in combat are awkward ones. By May 1915 the Ross was so despised that COs had to report on its lack of suitability. 2nd Brigade responded as follows: 10th Battalion, "quite unreliable"; 8th Battalion, "entirely unsatisfactory"; 7th Battalion, "jammed frequently"; and 5th Battalion (Tuxford, an officer who spoke his mind straight-out, no prevarication), "The men . . . have lost confidence in [it] . . . I strongly object to taking my men into action with the Ross."[35] 1st and 3rd Brigades were of similar mind. At a subsequent divisional conference Tuxford expressed the consensus, which condemned the Ross: "The rifle was a long one and unwieldy. It was not properly balanced. The small of the stock was often crossgrained in the wood, in which case it was easily broken. The rear sights were fragile and easily damaged and above all . . . the rifle jammed."[36] In the absence of any immediate decision, and lending legitimacy to what was already happening, COs told their men to scrounge Lee-Enfields. Imperials, when being relieved by Canadians, learned to mind their rifles carefully lest they be relieved of these, too. One Canadian ditty went like this:

> Roamin' through the tranchees, Ross Rifle by my side,
> Roamin' through the tranchees, couldn't fire it if I tried,
> Oh, I've put 'em to the test, the Lee-Enfield I like best,
> When I go a-roamin' through the tranchees.[37]

After Festubert, Victor Odlum, CO of the 7th Battalion, reported that his unit had not a Ross left, everyone having acquired a Lee-Enfield. Soon thereafter (June), a more official issue of the superb British rifle commenced:

> We . . . were warned to be ready for a carrying party, the whole brigade, and we carried in Lee-Enfield rifles to the infantry . . . And I had three . . . I got into the line and it was a Scottish battalion. And I saw this kiltie . . . so I said to him "Hey, Jock, you want a Lee-Enfield rifle?", and he looked down . . . grabbed it . . . picked up his own rifle . . . and slung it out to No Man's Land, and I was supposed to take back 3 Ross Rifles.[38]

Perhaps C.E. Montague sums up the disenchantment with the Ross best of all:

> Yet hardly had its use, in wrath, begun when there broke upon the untutored Canadian foot-soldier a revelation withheld from the Hugheses of this world. He perceived that the enemy, in his perversity, did not intend to stand up on a skyline a thousand yards off to

be shot with all the refinements of science; pointblank was going to be the only range, except for a few specialists; rapidity of fire would matter more than precision; and all the super-subtle appliances tending to triumphs at Bisley would here be no better than aids to the picking of mud from trench walls as the slung rifle joggled against them . . . The Canadians got, in the end, a rifle not too great and good for business.[39]

The wisdom of the change and the quality of the British rifle came home dramatically to Private Don Fraser who in November 1915 recovered from No Man's Land a Lee-Enfield that had been beside its dead owner for 10 months and "notwithstanding . . . in less than a half an hour's cleaning still fired a shot through it. It was an astonishing exhibition of the serviceability of the little British rifle."[40] The soldier knew that if he pulled his Lee-Enfield through (cleaned it), then it would pull him through.

The men of the 1st Division shared some characteristics that would influence its career. They, and all Canadians, were British subjects, an Imperial people, sharing an enormous pride in the Empire which covered a quarter of the world and included a quarter of its population. They subscribed to the sentiment on a popular patriotic postcard, which proclaimed "WHAT WE HAVE WE'LL HOLD." Most 1st Division soldiers, missionaries of this pride, were British born and almost entirely English-speaking. Of its 48 rifle companies only Number 4 Company, 14th Battalion was French-speaking. In 1914 and 1915 even many Canadian born soldiers thought themselves British. Private Vick Lewis of the 4th Battalion recalled, "We weren't considering ourselves too much as Canadians, we were considering ourselves as British." D.H.C. Mason, 3rd Battalion, thought the men all felt part of the British Army. Lieutenant John Cartwright, also 3rd Battalion, described how "enthusiastic" Canadians were about being part of an Empire Army.[41] Identification with the BEF was common throughout 1st Division and this featured constantly in letters home during the first two years of the war. In 1915 Corporal William Neale of Medicine Hat advised his mother to write to him at "D Company 10th Battalion 2nd Brigade 1st Canadian Division British Expeditionary Force." In September 1916 Lieutenant Clifford Wells headed his letters "8th Battalion, Canadians, BEF." One historian suggests that Dominion soldiers "were content, even proud, to be called British until about the middle of the First World War when their own prowess . . . at a time when the troops from the British Isles were inevitably decreasing in quality, gave them a growing sense of separate nationality."[42] Even so, in 1918 at least one battalion was still BEF, *vide,* Christmas card, "8th Canadian Battalion (90th Rifles), B.E.F., France"[43]

When Robert Labatt, CO of the 4th Battalion, was declared unfit for service, Lieutenant-Colonel Arthur Birchall, Imperial Royal Fusiliers, took command.[44] No one saw anything odd in that. Private E.W. Russell, who left England for Canada in 1913 and joined the 5th Battalion in 1914, recalled that the CO, the Second in Command (2IC), the OC and his platoon commander were all English. It is unclear to what period of the war Russell refers, but this does not matter since all the COs of the 5th, successively George Tuxford, Hugh Dyer and Lorne Tudor, were British born; so too was its Adjutant, Edward Hilliam. Sergeant Harold Baldwin remembered the battalion being mostly "Britishers."[45] In the 7th Battalion the CO, Lieutenant-Colonel W.F.T. (William) Hart-McHarg, and the Adjutant, Captain Stanley Gardner, were British born.[46] The CO of the 8th Battalion, Louis Lipsett, was a professional British officer. As for the 10th Battalion, its first CO, John Rattray, and about three-quarters of its men were British born.[47] Of the 13th Battalion's original 1,017 men, 65–75 percent were British born. According to Lieutenant Ian Sinclair "With us being a kilted regiment . . . all the Scots tried to get to either the 48th [15th Battalion] or the Black Watch[13th Battalion]." Another subaltern recalled that 75 percent of his company were Scottish born.[48] Lieutenant Paul Villiers, 15th Battalion, said the unit was "81% the sons of Scotch farmers."[49] Finally, in 1914 nearly half the officers and 80 percent of the men of the 16th Battalion were British born. Of 268 officers who served in the 16th during the war half were British born, as were 3,300 out of 5,223 ORs.[50]

Of 1st Division as a whole, T.S. Morrissey of the 13th Battalion said it was "well over half English, Scots or Irish." Ian Sinclair thought that "a very high proportion of all the Canadian battalions [were British]. Some . . . were almost entirely . . . Old Country born." In fact, of the 36,267 members of the first contingent, 63 percent originated from the British Isles or elsewhere in the Empire.[51]

Many of these men were former British Regulars:

> Next to the colonel, the most important figure in many new CEF battalions was an elderly British veteran who acted as regimental sergeant-major. He and the sergeants, chosen from those with any prior military experience, indoctrinated raw Canadians in their new way of life. British soldiers were the backbone of many CEF units, passing on the customs and language of Indian cantonments of a decade earlier.[52]

They also passed on their professional skills. "No group was more influential than the 18,959 ex-British regulars, barely 3.1 percent of the total [of the CEF] but conspicuous in almost every unit history and memoir."[53]

Even more important was the veteran element in 1st Division. Private E. Seaman, 3rd Battalion, recalled the "large proportion . . . who had served in . . . India or South Africa, various other parts of the Empire." Private Vick Lewis of the 4th said that "at least 40 percent were South African veterans."[54] The officer who would become the division's first GOC, E.A.H. Alderson, had been a Brigadier-General in South Africa, where he had gained the respect of Canadians such that it was said the men "would follow him anywhere."[55] Lieutenant-Colonels Julian Byng (later GOC the Canadian Corps), Hubert Gough (later GOC Fifth Army and a man under whom Currie refused to serve a second time), and Herbert Plumer (later GOC Second Army and a man Canadians were delighted to serve under) all soldiered in South Africa. There Plumer had praised Canadian gunners for their "endurance, skill and tenacity." The Canadians, for their part, had regarded him "with the greatest confidence."[56] Also in South Africa as Chief of Staff to Major-General John French was Colonel Douglas Haig, with whom Arthur Currie, who had not served in South Africa, was to have a good and comfortable relationship.

A significant number of Canadians who served in South Africa attained considerable importance in 1st Division or elsewhere in the CEF:

> Of the 106 generals in Canadian forces during the Great War, at least thirty-four were Boer War veterans. Seventeen . . . served in France, among them R.E.W. Turner, A.C. Macdonell, R.G.E.[sic] Burstall, V.W. Odlum, E.W.B. Morrison, A.H. Macdonell, R.G.E. Leckie, V.A.S. Williams, W.A. Griesbach, A.H. King, and H.B.D. Ketchen . . . others such as Lieutenant-Colonels William Hart McHarg, J.E. Leckie, H.A.C. Machin, A.T. Ogilvie, and R.H. Ryan also played a prominent part in that larger conflict.[57]

Three of these officers penned memoirs of their service against the Boers. Captain William Hart-McHarg's observations were prescient of what was to come. He was blunt about the shortcomings he had seen: unsatisfactory equipment such as webbing, water bottles and blankets; "barrack-square" oriented training; a "drill-book" approach to tactical manoeuvre; and "bad management" and "supercilious indifference" by some officers to the needs of their men. Nor did he spare the Laurier-mould politicians, who he condemned as irresolute procrastinators. After Paardeburg he voiced a military lesson and a truth that many others did not: "The thought uppermost in my mind was what a power the modern rifle is in the hands of a man who knows how to use it, acting on the defensive."[58]

Given the substantial number of former soldiers in its ranks 1st Division could claim to have the experience level of a Territorial division. This leavening gave it an advantage over many New Army divisions; for example, Ivor Maxse's 18th Division contained "few old soldiers, or Boer War veterans."[59] Regular Imperial divisions also had the benefit of the experience of Boer War veterans. The 7th and 29th Divisions enjoyed another advantage in that most of their units were regular battalions brought home from stations overseas. As such, they had a higher strength establishment in 1914 than did the home-based units and unlike 1st Division they had no need of a large scale injection of reservists who would need time to renew their skills and knowledge.[60] A large influx of former soldiers was never all roses. Men who were years away from the colours could be difficult to absorb, many being "old Soldiers"—which brings its own set of problems. W.N. Nicholson describes one advantage a regular division had from the outset:

> We served with the Guards in the XIVth Corps and nothing impressed me more . . . than the unconcern with which their staff treated details. Whereas every particular had to be most carefully considered by us, and every unit fed with a spoon, my opposite number in the Guards passed on the barest orders, knowing they would be adequately dealt with by the many trained Regular officers and NCOs of all his units.[61]

This happy state, in which orders could be shorter and less detailed, was not at first enjoyed by 1st Division. It was like the New Army Imperial divisions, which

> did not start from scratch; but from rock bottom. Their organization and administration did not mean a skilled workman applying oil as necessary to a machine in full running order; the machine had never been put together, every spring and pinion had to be tested and adjusted. The machine revolved; but with an inordinate quantity of grit in its innards. The skilled workman, who incidentally was none too skilled, since he had never had practise, spent the greater portion of his time on the sawdust and shingle.[62]

Over time 1st Division became far less British and the number of Boer War veterans decreased. By Hooge (June 1916) the division had lost almost its entire original strength. On the long road from Second Ypres to Mons Old Red Patch left many of its best by the wayside. Each of its infantry battalions lost the whole of its number at least once. Such a toll meant that from 1916 on, the men of 1st Division were overwhelmingly Canadian born. No precise figures are possible, but by the time victory came 1st Division casualties totalled nearly 52,000 killed or wounded (once, twice, three or more times), plus prisoners.[63]

This chapter has set 1st Division within the military context of 1914 and has described the circumstances of its raising and their impact on its career. Some circumstances were unique to 1st Division. At the start, its Boer War veterans and its former soldiers, who were mostly British, were a strong presence that helped the 1st learn the fundamentals and come together as a division. The other divisions, by the time they were raised, drew many of their veterans, who were more and more Canadian as time wore on, from 1st Division. The other divisions did not experience such a hurried and confused beginning; they learnt from 1st Division. Had Macdonell been with the 1st in 1914 and remarked "We lead, others follow" then, as he did in 1918, the comment would have been just as true.[64]

This chapter has also highlighted some of the terminology in use in the Army in 1914. Understanding the language of Army life is very helpful, for without this, one can miss all sorts of important nuances. One has also to learn a unique culture, a significant part of which is organization. Organization may be mundane, but it cannot be ignored, for it is central to the waging of war and the first step to understanding command and control, the staff system and training. The next chapter concerns the organization of 1st Division as it was in the beginning.

Notes to Chapter One

1. Desmond Morton, *Canada and War: A Military and Political History* (Toronto: Buttersworth, 1981), pp. 25, 31, 41.
2. Desmond Morton, *Ministers and Generals: Politics and the Canadian Militia, 1868–1904* (Toronto: University of Toronto Press, 1970), p. 200.
3. Nicholson, *Official History of the Canadian Army,* pp. 6–7. The Permanent Force consisted of one infantry regiment and one artillery regiment, two cavalry regiments and the cadets of the Royal Military College, Kingston.
4. Major D.J. Goodspeed, *Battle Royal: A History of the Royal Regiment of Canada, 1862–1962* (Toronto: The Royal Regiment of Canada Association, 1962), p. 71. The habit of showing 8:45 P.M. as 2045 hours was resisted because it was not until October 6, 1918 that the Army implemented the "new 24-hour system of reckoning time." (LAC, 2nd Brigade War Diary)
5. Daniel G. Dancocks, *Welcome to Flanders Fields: The First Canadian Battle of the Great War: Ypres, 1915* (Toronto: McClelland & Stewart, 1988), p. 123.
6. LAC, MG30E318 (3rd Battalion), Vol. 24, Folder 188, 1 August 1918.
7. LAC, 1st Division Administrative and Quartermaster (A & Q) War Diary, 31 January 1916. In January 1916 only one staff officer and two staff clerks of the original staff were still with the 1st. 3rd Division, for example, was given the senior A & Q staff officer and five others. Military Advisory Board, *Canada in the Great World War: An Authentic Account of the Military History of Canada from the Earliest Days to the Close of the War of the Nations.* Vol. VI. *Special Services, Heroic Deeds, etc.* (Toronto: United Publishers of Canada Limited, 1921), pp. 315–19. From 1st Division came one corps

commander, seven division commanders and 11 brigade commanders. Currie was the Corps commander. The division commanders were R.E.W. Turner, H.E. Burstall, M.S. Mercer, L.J. Lipsett, D. Watson, F.O.W. Loomis and G.B. Hughes (5th Division). The brigade commanders were R. Rennie, D. Watson, G.E. McCuaig, A.H. Macdonell, H.M. Dyer, V.A.S. Williams, F.W. Hill, D.M. Ormond, E. Hilliam, R.J.F. Hayter and V.W. Odlum.

8. LAC, RG9IIIC3, Vol. 4006, Folder 2, File 4. Correspondence of mid-1917 lists the colours of the straps as follows: infantry, blue (except 8th Battalion which wore green because it was a Rifle Regiment); artillery, red; engineers, a small red oval with the letters C.E." in blue; signals, French grey; cavalry and veterinary corps, yellow; medical corps, maroon; and Army Service Corps, white with two blue pipings. Goodspeed, *Battle Royal*, p. 171, nominal roll; Harold R. Peat, *Private Peat* (Indianapolis: Bobbs-Merrill Company, 1917), p. 22.

9. Military Advisory Board, *Canada and the Great World War: An Authentic Account of the Military History of Canada from the Earliest Days to the Close of the War of the Nations*. Vol. V. *The Triumph of the Allies* (Toronto: United Publishers of Canada Limited, 1920), pp. 67–71. The names of 56 originals are in LAC, 1st Division A & Q War Diary, February, 1918.

10. LAC, RG9IIIC3, Vol. 4040, Book 5, War Office, 17 July 1916. *Instructions Governing Organization and Administration* (Ottawa: Government Printing Bureau, 1916), p. 8. In courts-martial proceedings Canadians were described as "soldiers of the regular forces."

11. Colonel A. Fortescue Duguid, *Official History of the Canadian Forces in the Great War, 1914–1919*, General Series Vol. I, *From the Outbreak of War to the Formation of the Canadian Corps August 1914–September 1915, Chronology, Appendices and Maps* (Ottawa: King's Printer, 1938), Appendices 44, 89. Canadians were commissioned as Lieutenants, not as Second Lieutenants, which was the Imperial practise (Alexander McClintock, *Best O' Luck* [Toronto: McClelland, Goodchild & Stewart, 1917], p. 28; O.C.S. Wallace, ed., *From Montreal to Vimy Ridge and Beyond: The Correspondence of Lieut. Clifford Almon Wells of the 8th Battalion, Canadians, B.E.F., November 1915–April, 1917* [Toronto: McClelland, Goodchild & Stewart, 1917], p. 64).

12. David W. Love, *"A Call to Arms": The Organization and Administration of Canada's Military in World War One* (Calgary: Bunker to Bunker Books, 1999), Chapter 8, pp. 55–86, provides a full account of the mobilization, recruiting and reinforcement of the CEF. The mobilization plan, C.1209, stipulated two mobilization scenarios, winter and summer, the main differences being the point of assembly and whether mobilization would encompass the entire Militia (units recruiting to full strength as part of a multi-divisional force), or just an overseas contingent of one infantry division, one cavalry brigade and artillery as appropriate. In either case, the Militia Council, the Minister of Militia and the Adjutant General were to direct mobilization, and commanders of divisional areas and districts were responsible for recruiting and equipping the required units from their areas and districts. The Permanent Force was to administer and train the men and to supply key personnel.

13. Dancocks, *Welcome to Flanders Fields*, p. 44.

14. Urquhart, *History of the 16th Battalion*, p. 6.

15. George F.G. Stanley, *Canada's Soldiers, 1604–1954: The Military History of an Unmilitary People* (Toronto: Macmillan, 1954), pp. 310–11. When 2nd Division formed its men were enrolled and remained in their military districts until just before embarkation, thus avoiding much of the confusion of the initial mobilization.

16. "Major-General Louis James Lipsett, C.B., C.M.G.," *Canadian Defence Quarterly* 6 (April 1929): 296–97. Three of Lipsett's students on the 1914 Militia staff course were Lieutenant-Colonels Arthur Currie and Bert Leckie and Major Garnett Hughes.

17. Dancocks, *Welcome to Flanders Fields,* p. 60.

18. Quoted in Kim Beattie, *48th Highlanders of Canada, 1891–1928* (Toronto: 48th Highlanders of Canada, 1932), p. 1.

19. The term "regiment" is often confusing to the non-military reader. In Commonwealth Armies an artillery or armoured regiment is the smallest self-supporting unit in these arms. During the Great War an artillery regiment was called a brigade. The infantry equivalent was called a battalion. An infantry regiment is usually made up of more than one battalion; The Queen's Own Rifles of Canada, for example, consisted until 1970 of 1st and 2nd Battalions (Regular) and 3rd Battalion (Militia). In Commonwealth armies an infantry regiment is not a tactical organization: the infantry fights not as regiments, but as battalions and brigades. During the Great War one of the infantry battalions of the Western Ontario Regiment served in the 1st Division, while another battalion of that regiment served with 2nd Division. 1st Brigade of 1st Division consisted of the 1st Battalion, Western Ontario Regiment; the 2nd Battalion, Eastern Ontario Regiment; the 3rd Battalion, Toronto Regiment; and the 4th Battalion, Central Ontario Regiment. Thus, the brigade consisted of one battalion from each of four different regiments.

    So strong is the regimental spirit that we identify certain individuals and functions in battalions as "regimental." The senior warrant officer in a battalion is the Regimental Sergeant-Major. "Regimental" means smart, soldierly, according to regulation. Men had regimental numbers, not battalion numbers. In a battalion Regimental Police sometimes assisted in maintaining discipline. The wounded man requiring evacuation began his journey to the rear at the Regimental Aid Post, which was a battalion organization. And finally, men who were employed on duties away from their unit were said to be "extra-regimentally" employed. The battalions of a regiment could be very different in character, but when all was said and done, they were still regimental.

20. Colonel W.N. Nicholson, *Behind the Lines: An Account of Administrative Staffwork in the British Army, 1914–1918* (London: Jonathan Cape, 1939), p. 154.

21. The 13th Battalion styled itself as it did because most of its men came from the prewar 5th Royal Highlanders of Canada. For the same reason the 8th Battalion incorporated the prewar designation "90th Rifles." "The Canadian Scottish" was probably inevitable since the 16th Battalion was formed of men from four Highland regiments, whose stations were Victoria, Vancouver, Winnipeg and Hamilton. When Currie spoke to the officers and men of 3rd Brigade on a parade on 9 May 1917, he addressed them not as the 13th, 14th, 15th and 16th Battalions but as the 48th Highlanders, the Royal Montreal Regiment, the Royal Highlanders of Canada and the Canadian Scottish (LAC, 3rd Brigade War Diary, May 1917). Having commanded a regiment before the war Currie knew the meaning of regimental spirit.

22. LAC, RG9IIIC3, Vol. 4031, Folder 26, File 7, 1st Brigade to units, 10 October 1917.

23. Morton, *When Your Number's Up,* p. 54.

24. During the war the terms "Commanding Officer" (CO) and "Officer Commanding" (OC) were generally used interchangeably, which was careless since this practise ignored certain critical legal distinctions about command. In an infantry battalion the senior officer on establishment, the lieutenant-colonel, was the CO. His appointment gave him powers of command, promotion and discipline that officers, even of equal

rank, who were not COs could not exercise. An OC on the other hand, commanded a sub-unit; he might be "OC A Company" or "OC 3 Platoon," but in either case, his powers were limited. The 8th Battalion (Lipsett) got it right: its first commandment was "The C.O. is thy Colonel, thou shalt have no other C.O. before him." (LAC, MG30E60 [Matthews Papers], Vol. 3, Folder 12, "The Ten Commandments")

25. Desmond Morton, *A Peculiar Kind of Politics: Canada's Overseas Ministry in the First World War* (Toronto: University of Toronto Press, 1982), p. xi. Morton provides the best account of the muddle created by Hughes and how it was cleaned up.

26. LAC, RG 41, CBC Radio Program *Flanders' Fields*, No. 6, "A World of Stealth," A.G. Jacobs and E.A. King, pp. 9–10.

27. Urquhart, *History of the 16th Battalion*, p. 88.

28. Sir Charles Lucas, gen. ed., *The Empire at War*, 5 vols. (Oxford: Oxford University Press, 1921–1926), Vol. 2, *Canada*, by F.H. Underhill, pp. 153–54.

29. Morton, *A Peculiar Kind of Politics*, p. xi; LAC, Canadian Corps A & Q War Diary and MG30E46 (Turner Papers), Vol. 8, Folder 48, show the line and reserve battalions in 1st Division in 1918 as follows:

Regiment	Line	Reserve
1st Quebec	13, 14	20, 23
1st Central Ontario	4	3
	3, 15	12
Eastern Ontario	2	6
Western Ontario	1	4
Manitoba	16	11
	8	18
Saskatchewan	5	15
Alberta	10	21
British Columbia	7	1

Before 1918 the linkages between line and reserve battalions were not fixed. Documents pertaining to reinforcements show that prior to 1918 reinforcements reached line battalions from several reserve battalions, sometimes from more than one simultaneously. *Ad hoc* arrangements fostered confusion, waste and duplication of effort. The linkages in LAC, MG30E100 (Currie Papers), Vol. 43, differ slightly.

30. LAC, MG30E8 (Creelman Papers), Diary, 19 November 1916: RG 41, CBC interviews, Colonels H.S. Cooper and D.H.C. Mason.

31. LAC, MG30E237 (Sinclair Papers), Diary, 9 February 1915.

32. "Editorial," *Canadian Defence Quarterly* 2 (July 1925): 321.

33. Nicholson, *Official History of the Canadian Army*, pp. 26–27; Morton, *When Your Number's Up*, p. 18.

34. Morton, *A Peculiar Kind of Politics*, p. 13; Fraser, *In Good Company*, p. 266. Fraser, CO of the XVIII Corps School (GOC Ivor Maxse) in January 1918, provides another excellent example of the pernicious influence of politicians on weapons, viz, a proposal in early 1918 to replace the Lewis gun with the Madsen, which front line troops considered as much inferior. Favourable consideration of the Madsen in the British House of Commons caused Fraser to comment (p. 265) that "the ignorance of politicians of the subjects they talk about is colossal." It could also be said that if a soldier must not be politically minded, then it is just as true that a politician must not be militarily minded.

35. LAC, RG9IIIC3, Vol. 4044, Folder 1, File 12, 7 May 1915.

36. Tuxford, "The Great War as I Saw It", pp. 3–4. Only one CO (unidentified) spoke in favour of the Ross.

37. G.R. Stevens, *A City Goes to War* (Brampton, Ont.: Charters Publishing Company Limited, 1964), p. 35.

38. RG41, CBC Radio Program, *Flanders Fields*, No. 7 "Apprentices at Arms," pp. 27–28, comments by Victor Odlum and Private A.G. Jacobs.

39. C.E. Montague, *Disenchantment* (London: Chatto and Windus, 1922), p. 41.

40. Major H.C. Singer, *History of the 31st Canadian Infantry Battalion C.E.F.* (Calgary: privately printed, [1939]), p. 46.

41. LAC, RG 41B, CBC interviews.

42. "Letters from France," *Stand To!* 31 (Spring 1991): 34, 36. Neale was killed at Givenchy in June 1915; Wallace, ed., *From Montreal to Vimy Ridge*, p. 190; Michael Glover, *A New Guide to the Battlefields of Northern France and the Low Countries* (London: Michael Joseph Limited, 1987), p. 9.

43. Card in the author's collection.

44. LAC, Service Records of Robert Hodgetts Labatt and Arthur Percival Birchall. Birchall was killed in action at Second Ypres.

45. Imperial War Museum 76/170/1, Private E.W. Russell, "A Private Soldier's View on the Great War, 1914–1918," p. 46. Russell's 49 page memoir is very informative on training and personalities. LAC, Service Records; Harold Baldwin, *"Holding the Line"* (Chicago: A.C. McClurg & Co., 1918), p. 4.

46. NAC, Service Records. Edward Hilliam went on to command 25th Battalion, then 10th Brigade and, finally, an Imperial brigade. William Hart-McHarg was killed in action at Second Ypres. Stanley Gardner commanded the 7th Battalion from July 1917 until his death from wounds in September 1918.

47. Daniel G. Dancocks, *Gallant Canadians The Story of the Tenth Canadian Infantry Battalion, 1914–1919* (Calgary: The Calgary Highlanders Regimental Funds Foundation, 1990), p. 6.

48. R.C. Fetherstonhaugh, *The 13th Battalion Royal Highlanders of Canada, 1914–1919* (Montreal: The 13th Battalion Royal Highlanders of Canada, 1925), p. 6; LAC RG 41, CBC interviews of Colonel Ian Sinclair and Lieutenant-Colonel T.S. Morrissey.

49. LAC, MG30E236 (Villiers Papers), Vol. 4, Diary. The figure "81" may seem too precise, but from his diaries it is clear that Villiers was a very precise man. By all accounts he became a very good BM.

50. Urquhart, *History of the 16th Battalion,* p. 415.

51. LAC, RG 41, CBC interviews; RG 9IIIC1, Vol. 3889, Folder 45, File 7, states that out of a total CEF enlistment of 590,572, British-born totalled 221,495 and a further 7,256 were native to various British colonies. Morton, *When Your Number's Up*, p. 278, gives the percentage of British-born in the CEF as 52 percent. The figure of 63 percent is in Duguid, *Chronology, Appendices and Maps*, p. 58.

52. Morton and Granatstein, *Marching to Armageddon*, pp. 50–51.

53. Morton, *When Your Number's Up*, p. 279.

54. LAC, RG 41, CBC interviews of Privates E. Seaman and Vick Lewis.

55. Carman Miller, *Painting the Map Red: Canada and the South African War, 1899–1902* (Montreal: McGill-Queen's University, 1993), p. 231.

56. Plumer retained the confidence of Canadians during the Great War. LAC, RG 41, Vol. 21, "Generals" folder. Brigadier-General J.A. Clark, GOC 7th Brigade, said of Gough

and Plumer: "But we were to be assigned to the command of General Gough at Passchendaele and he [Currie] strenuously objected, said he wouldn't serve under him with the result that we were transferred to the Second Army, General Plumer, who all soldiers loved. The Higher Command seniors loved him and his juniors loved him and his men loved him . . . he had a great white moustache and a kindly face and, even if you never had a word with him, you just instinctively looked at him and liked him and Currie both liked him and trusted him and we served there." Currie himself, in a letter to the manager of the Canadian Press in January 1933 (LAC, MG30E100 [Currie Papers] Vol. 27, File 7) characterized his relationship with Plumer thus: "I may say that my experiences with General Plumer were always of the happiest. He always had supreme confidence in the Canadian Corps." Cyril Falls, *The History of the 36th (Ulster) Division* (Belfast: M'Caw, Stevenson & Orr, Limited, 1922), p. 122, shows that all the BEF, not just the Canadians, preferred Plumer to Gough. One "distinguished" British officer (Falls does not name him) put the difference thus: "We felt that . . . Messines was won at Zero [hour], and that . . . Ypres was lost long before it." Although he does not say so directly, Falls puts the difference down to Plumer and Harington, Plumer's Major General General Staff (MGGS), as opposed to Gough and his MGGS, Malcolm. "The difficulties at Ypres were infinitely greater than at Messines; that everyone recognized. But in the former case they did not appear to be met with quite the precision, care, and forethought of the latter. The private soldier felt a difference. He may have been unfair in his estimate, but that estimate was none the less of importance. For what the private soldier felt had a marked effect upon what the private soldier, the only ultimate winner of battles, accomplished."

57. Miller, *Painting the Map Red*, p. 425. The Burstall mentioned is H.E., not R.G.E. Harry Burstall, a Permanent Force gunner, became GOC 2nd Division in 1916. Blunt and forthright, he was a master gunner and a good tactician. Richard Turner, who was to command 3rd Brigade and then 2nd Division in the Great War, was a Lieutenant in the Royal Canadian Dragoons when he won his VC during the Battle of Liliefontein on November 7 1900. General A.C. Macdonell went on to command 1st Division in the Great War. Most of the named officers commanded brigades or battalions in 1914–18.

58. W. Hart-McHarg, *From Quebec to Pretoria with the Royal Canadian Regiment* (Toronto: W. Briggs, 1902), pp. 46, 54, 60–61, 67–70, 132, 136, 158. Other books by Canadian South African War Veterans include E.W.B. Morrison, *With the Guns* (Hamilton: Spectator Printing Co., 1901), and W.A. Griesbach, *I Remember* (Toronto: The Ryerson Press, 1946).

59. Captain G.H.F. Nichols, *The 18th Division in the Great War* (London: William Blackwood and Sons, 1922), p. 5. This book is a gem, one of the best works of its kind.

60. C.T. Atkinson, *The Seventh Division 1914–1918* (London: John Murray, 1927), pp. 4–5, 108; Gillon, *The Story of the 29th Division*, pp. v–vi.

61. Nicholson, *Behind the Lines*, pp. 183–84.

62. *Ibid.*, pp. 195–96.

63. Casualty figures were compiled from battalion histories and from LAC, MG30E100 (Currie Papers), "Brief Review Operations Canadian Corps, 1915, 1916, 1917, 1918." If anything, the figures are probably low.

64. LAC, MG30E318 (3rd Battalion), Vol. 24, Folder 188, Macdonell to brigades, 1 August 1918.

CHAPTER TWO

Divisions: First the Fundamentals

Generally, management of the many is the same as management of the few. It is a matter of organization.
—SUN TZU

Old Red Patch became a division in name on 1 September 1914, but like "The Ship That Found Herself" (Kipling), it had to discover itself and come together to work in unison before it could be a division. This chapter has three objectives: to describe 1st Division's initial organization, to introduce some of the key players and to describe the Valcartier and Salisbury Plain experiences in terms of staff work, command and control and training. Only by knowing its initial organization and competence can one track its evolution and improvement. To know the division one must also know the commanders, the staff officers and the trainers, who, after all, made it a good formation. Knowledge of their background, experience and potential is essential.

In Chapter One the battalions of the new division mobilized. Now they have arrived and settled in at Valcartier and are on the parade ground for the first time as a division. Described below is what *should* have been there, not necessarily what *was* there.[1] No division has ever fielded its official establishment in every respect. Five years previously, in 1909, during a special Imperial Defence Conference in London, the nations of the Empire had settled on the same organizations, tactics and training in the expectation that standardization would permit easier integration during wartime. Nevertheless, discrepancies existed. How could it be otherwise, given the course of mobilization and the fact that only 80 Permanent Force instructors were on hand to train over 25,000 men? The only regular battalion in the pre-war Army, The Royal Canadian

Regiment (RCR), went not to Valcartier where its instructional skills would have been so useful but to Bermuda where it did guard duty until it finally went to France in November 1915.[2] 1st Division at Valcartier was truly a rough cut. Experience would result in numerous changes to its establishment.[3]

Before us, in patient obedience to the Army dictum "Hurry up and wait," are some 18,000 men massed in six blocks: the HQ, less the GOC who had not yet been appointed; three infantry brigades; the artillery in four brigades and one heavy battery; and a block of what the uncharitable might call the "odds and sods"—the supply train, engineers (who were known as "sappers"), signals, and field ambulances.[4]

Each infantry brigade consisted of four 1,000-man battalions. An old soldier's story says 1,001, the odd one being the bandmaster, or, as some say, the padre. What is strange to our eyes is that the battalions have eight rifle companies, each divided into four sections under sergeants. Two sections, known collectively as a "half-company," were supposedly the command of a subaltern. Such an organization would have hindered fighting efficiency; it is hard to even think of a "half-company" as a tactical organization since it lacks balance. Each battalion also had two Colt machine-guns, but no trench mortars since these did not exist in the divisions of the Empire in 1914.

As for the "long arm" (artillery), it differed from the artillery of Imperial Regular or Territorial divisions. A Regular Division had three field artillery brigades, each with three batteries of six 18-pounder guns, 54 in all; a field howitzer brigade with three batteries of six 4.5 inch howitzers each, or a total of 18 barrels; and a heavy battery of four 60-pounder guns—a total of 76 guns, four more than a German division.[5] A Territorial Division had only 68. Both types had four ammunition columns. A Regular Division included about 4,000 gunners. Pre-war Canadian militia batteries had conformed to the four-gun Territorial pattern, but on arrival at Valcartier they converted to six. On parade were the 1st Canadian Field Artillery (CFA) Brigade, Ottawa; 2nd CFA Brigade, Montreal; and 3rd CFA Brigade, Toronto. The heavy battery came from the Maritimes. Gunner strength was about 3,200 all told. Not until 1st Division arrived in Flanders would it be joined by a howitzer brigade, and then it was an Imperial brigade.

Once upon a time there were only three arms: horse, guns and foot. But then the sappers were added, and rather prominently, too. In 1914–1915 1st Division had two field companies, each of just over 200 men under a major. The field company was then the largest sapper unit. Experience would reveal the inadequacy of these numbers.[6] Pre-war manoeuvres, being compressed in time and concentrated on the fighting arms, had made sapper training hasty and superficial. Most sappers in 1914 had never seen defensive works of any extent, their experience being limited to siting individual trenches.[7] Here the sapper often committed that most heinous of sins: siting trenches while standing erect, rather than lying prone. A six-foot sapper standing erect had a picture of the ground very different from and superior to that of the infanteer, whose eyes, when he occupied the trench, were lower by six feet or more. If he had to fight from a trench sited by an erect man the infanteer frequently found that he had little or no field of fire or observation.

The division also had one signal company of 163 men from the Canadian Signals Service, then a separate branch of the engineers but not a separate corps. It maintained communications with flanking divisions and between divisional brigades and units. Communications included telephone, telegraph, visual signals and pigeons.[8] Medical services were provided by three field ambulances, each with about 250 all ranks under a lieutenant-colonel; each ambulance could handle 150 patients.[9]

Finally, we see the divisional train, an Army Service Corps unit of 428 men under a lieutenant-colonel. The central consideration in supply was that everything the soldier needed had to be put in his hand; he must not have to turn back to get what he needed to push on or to hold what he had taken. From static supply facilities known as "Base," supplies were sent forward to "Railhead." From there, corps supply columns took supplies to refilling points where divisional trains made up of 142 two-horse wagons and four motor vehicles assumed responsibility for carriage and distribution of mail and supplies. Trains took supplies forward to the artillery, divisional troops and divisional HQ and to the dumps or refilling points of the brigades. Brigades then took the loads forward to their HQs and units. Because ammunition expenditures were predicted and varied enormously, separate columns handled ammunition to avoid swamping the divisional train. Then, from brigade refilling points, ammunition was usually taken forward by "carrying parties from the battalions in the line or, where large quantities were required, by ordering battalions in support and reserve to furnish the . . . men."[10] Infantry officers worried about their men becoming exhausted by such labour; their business, above all, was fighting. Depleted, tired sub-units became less capable when they had to work and fight.

A division, 18,000 men or more and over 5,000 horses,[11] equated to a small city, one that was larger in 1914 than Charlottetown, now our smallest provincial capital. Supplying a division was a formidable task requiring 200 truck or waggon loads of supplies daily.[12] A division provided all the services of a city as well as moving itself lock, stock and barrel, including field ambulances, artillery, arms and ammunition, and taking along all the food required by men and horses, with extensive reserves of everything. On the move a division filled 20 miles of road. Moves were fairly frequent, sometimes with scant warning, and they had to be executed rapidly, often under very adverse conditions.

Making an effective team out of all these elements depended upon competent command and control, good staff work and thorough training. The first two also involve training, and all three are concerned with learning. A pertinent question to ask (and answer) is, what did Valcartier do for the division with regard to these aspects? The short answer is just the basics: drill, marching, physical training and range work.

As we watch the troops on parade, three characteristics would register in our eyes: dress, deportment and organization. Of the first there was little uniformity: as late as 27 September, only two days before it took ship, 10th Battalion still had many men in civilian clothes. Numerous items of equipment were also missing or in short supply. Outfitting became a "protracted affair," a process that together with organizational instability "played havoc." "Having arrived with no unit organization . . . training [was] further disrupted by repeated changes in the composition, location and command of the units." Chaos reigned supreme in some units; 2nd Battalion, for example, had five COs in one day; Sam Hughes fired 10th Battalion's first CO because he was a Liberal. Overall, Valcartier was "reminiscent of units without officers and . . . officers without units."[13]

Nor did the kit on issue contribute to building soldier confidence. Tunics and boots would be defeated by active service. The boots were particularly sorry: any moisture caused them to rot rapidly and their thin soles and overall light construction made them poor for marching. Greatcoats, too, were shoddy, their thin cloth no guard against rain or cold. The leather Oliver load-carrying harness, in service even before the Boer War, soon became very uncomfortable on long marches, and it could not carry as much ammunition as the British webbing; in short, it was unsuitable, as were the horse harnesses and the waggons, water carts, trucks, cars and ambulances. 1st Division was fortunate in having most of this rubbish quickly replaced by superior British-made equivalents, except for the boots; some men were still wearing the Canadian boots as late as June 1916.[14] A far more serious problem, the Ross rifle, was discussed in Chapter One.

As for deportment, the drill should have been satisfactory since it had occupied much of the training time. Each of the three Sundays that the troops spent in the camp were filled with an inspection by the Governor General. No doubt Fridays and Saturdays featured endless rehearsals. With only 80 instructors available much of the responsibility for training fell to units where the experience of former soldiers helped to achieve a "fair standard."[15] One subaltern recalled training as nothing but musketry and drill. His photograph shows him in service dress with double Sam Browne belt and side arms, revolver on the right and sword on the left. Another subaltern said, "Officer training in the morning . . . was sword drill . . . the motions of attack and defence with a sword . . . the only time we ever used a sword in the course of the war."[16] It is easy to sneer at this now until one remembers that between Valcartier and reality was an ocean across which no officers or non-commissioned officers (NCOs) had yet returned wise in what was valuable and what was not.

Training also included route-marching and musketry. The first is as old as war itself, and the second is a prerequisite of good fighting men. If nothing else, these were a useful start. Range firing being top priority, the extensive ranges were in constant use once they were ready in mid-August. By mid-September nearly all infanteers had fired the qualifying practise (50 rounds at distances up to 300 yards), and those who needed extra practise had repeated the course. Shooting in one battalion apparently showed such "marked improvement" that Sam Hughes, quite ignorant or forgetful of the British Regular's ability to get off 15 aimed rounds in 60 seconds (the famous "Mad Minute"), boasted that the men could "handle a rifle as no man had ever handled it before."[17]

Little, if anything, was learned of tactics; there were only two exercises and these involved just night outpost duties. Even if they had had the latest manual, *Infantry Training (4-Company Organization) 1914* (published on 10 August), and even if they had been in four companies instead of eight, the units were going to a war that was very different from the war envisaged in the manuals. No one anticipated trench warfare. Speaking for his pals, one NCO in 2nd Battalion said, "All expect two or three weeks in England, some time on lines of communication, and a winter of sieges of some fortress on the German frontier. Of course, it may be quite different, but that is the general guess."[18]

Despite only four weeks training, Hughes puffed that his "boys" were fully trained when they reached Britain, a claim that was nonsense, given the confused and haphazard mobilization and the equally disorganized training in a Quebec camp that was still in the throes of construction. The British realistically judged the new arrivals to be at the level of third-week recruits, which must have been disappointing to the War Office in view of the need to get divisions to France as quickly as possible. Had the training been anywhere near what Hughes claimed, the 1st would probably have crossed to France in late November or early December. M.C. McGowan, 1st Battalion, agreed with the British: "1st Division . . . weren't highly trained at all . . . training was practically nil." So did Hugh Urquhart: "There was no thorough course of training at Valcartier . . . [T]he short period of time spent there, twenty-five days in the case of the 16th Battalion, . . . did not permit of thoroughness."[19]

Much of what by definition is command and control did not come into play at Valcartier. At the end of the four weeks training, officers and NCOs knew what they were commanding, but they had yet to know their men and their men them. This applied to the relationship between commanders and staff officers. At unit level Adjutants were learning their new business from the ground up. One unidentified Adjutant, forced to type his own orders, reversed the carbons and thus the impressions on the copies. Unfazed, he annotated them: "To read these orders hold them up to the looking glass."[20] A bigger challenge, such as producing a new plan for moving overseas (necessitated by the decision to send 31,000 instead of 25,000 men), was beyond the officers at Valcartier. An ad hoc organization under Lieutenant-Colonel William Price got the contingent embarked and away, "not a single package" having been left behind.[21]

It cannot be said for certain what attitudes towards command were held by Lieutenant-General E.A.H. Alderson of the British Army when he became GOC 1st Division after its arrival in Britain in October 1914. The commander was the mainspring; upon his personality and leadership all depended. Only he could instill the spirit that made a division effective. Alderson, aged 55, may not have been strikingly charismatic but he was sound. He got the green Canadian division ready to soldier; that is to say, he got it ready to learn to soldier. As an experienced Regular he had a set of previously tested ideas with which to start. Although the concept "train two up and think two down" did not originate with him, it is reasonable to suggest that even early in the war he had this in mind. In practise this meant that soldiers and officers were trained to command two levels up; the OC of a platoon, for example, had to be made fit to command a battalion, for that need could arise.[22]

As for thinking "two down," Alderson must surely have thought how he would carry out brigade tasks and, were he a brigadier-general, what tasks he would assign his battalions. Such foresight would have helped his untested subordinates to plan the execution of his orders. Quite possibly this had been his practise while commanding a division in India before the war. It is unlikely that his three new brigadiers realized that obeying an order also required concentrated thought on the level from which it was issued. In theory, they should also have been thinking about division, but lacking the knowledge initially to do so, they focussed entirely on the duties of their own rank. Each commander in 1st Division struggled to grasp the intricacies of the tricky art of command. None had experience of war at brigade or even battalion level; two of the three had no experience of war at any level. For the Brigadiers— Malcolm Mercer, 1st Brigade; Arthur Currie, 2nd Brigade; and Richard Turner, 3rd Brigade—the pressing problem was to learn *how* to command their brigade.[23] How far does peacetime training fit a man to command in war? No one can say how he will react until he has actually experienced war. Who would do well was unpredictable: "The emergence of a commander on earth," said Sir Ian Hamilton, "is as great a mystery as that of the emergence of the queen-bee into the air."[24]

The artillery, at least, was under a Regular, Lieutenant-Colonel Harry Burstall. One of only two Canadian divisional commanders who were Staff College graduates, he would prove a highly competent GOC of 2nd Division.[25] As a subaltern he had served in the South African War, as had Edward "Dinky" Morrison, to whom Burstall owed his appointment as divisional artillery commander. Morrison, an editor of the *Ottawa Citizen* in civilian life, had been a militiaman for many years. His initial and crucial contribution to the war effort—efficient mobilization of the artillery—was described in Chapter One.

Morrison's second contribution and his sterling character are evident in the way Burstall obtained the senior gunner appointment. When in 1914 Morrison was offered that post he deferred to Burstall because he thought the long-serving Regular better fitted for it and he was happy to accept command of an artillery brigade under Burstall. Dinky Morrison may have been small in physical stature but he was big in heart and in mind. His generosity, integrity and strong sense of duty impressed everyone. J.B.S. MacPherson, a gunner himself, said of Morrison, "He fought for his men and he saw to it that his men fought for him."[26] Noted as a strict disciplinarian, Morrison also had the ability to get the best out of his staff and his command. His fearless nature and his determination to wreak maximum execution with the ammunition that was expended meant that usually he spent more time with his batteries than with his staff. His personal motto was "Kill Boche" and he worked hard to reduce "every artillery problem to this simple solution."[27] Morrison subsequently became artillery commander of 1st and then 2nd Division, later replacing Burstall as senior gunner of the Canadian Corps in December 1916.[28]

Herbert Thacker, an Indian born Permanent Force officer, was initially a senior gunner with 1st Division. When 2nd Division formed in May 1914 he was appointed artillery commander of that Division, but in September he and Morrison switched, Thacker going to the well-established 1st Division and Morrison going to the newly organized 2nd—"a very different matter from taking over a formation already functioning . . . The efficiency of the 2nd . . . Divisional Artillery was the best possible evidence of the abilities of the man who commanded it."[29] All in all, the gunners were to be well served by their senior officers during and after the war. Morrison and Burstall, in particular, built well-deserved reputations.

In England a process of standardization of Canadian batteries, which would take more than a year to complete, began with a reversion to four-gun batteries in order to conform to the organization of Imperial Territorial divisions. This one-third reduction in field guns would be compensated, to some extent, by the eventual introduction of trench mortars. The second major change was the removal of the heavy battery (60-pounders). Thus on arrival in France 1st Division had three field artillery brigades (each made up of four batteries of four guns each) and an Imperial howitzer brigade of two batteries, giving a gun strength of forty-eight 18-pounders and eight 4.5 inch howitzers.

Infanteers, too, coped with constant change that put them in "the throes of a great bustle, learning . . . new weapons . . . new tactics and . . . many adjustments of organization."[30] They were soon involved in the controversy about the number of companies that should populate a battalion. Ivor Maxse thought the Army was

> hampered and thrown back by an eight company system, which destroys the initiative of subordinates without increasing the legitimate control of superior commanders . . . The eight company battalion was very convenient when we fought in lines of two or more closed ranks, and the commanding officer and captains could be heard by every man in those ranks. But, it is unsuitable to the wide and deep formations which modern weapons compel a battalion to assume in an attack, and it is positively detrimental to cooperative fire tactics, which are based on the initiative of individuals in the firing line backed by the supporting fire of their comrades behind.[31]

His unvoiced question was, "What can the average man handle?" He believed that four companies better defined the chain of command and were the optimum in the sense of span of control. The demise of the half-company structure was most notable in that it gave subalterns a definite command: a platoon.[32] To those who thought the change would allow junior officers too much initiative, Major-General Thompson Capper, soon to be GOC 7th (Imperial) Division, retorted that seniors must be sufficiently far forward to control subordinates and, in any case, initiative was to be encouraged, not stifled.[33]

David Watson, CO 2nd Battalion, recalled the incredible organizational dance in England. On 1 November the division, conforming to British practise, went to four companies, back to eight three weeks later, to four again in December and within days back to eight before settling at four for good in January 1915. Such aggravating indecision did little to foster good staff and line relationships. Some battalions, perhaps with pretensions of grandeur, copied the Guards' fashion of designating companies numerically (1, 2, 3 and 4) while others were content to letter them A, B, C, and D. Each company of 250 men under a major or a captain was divided into four 50 man platoons each under a subaltern. Each platoon consisted of four 12 man sections under sergeants.[34]

One other innovation, which marked the start of a series of major organizational changes, was the introduction of two additional machine-guns in February 1915, making a total of four per battalion.[35] Of the more important changes in the BEF that year, mention must be made of the first issue of Lewis guns, "one per infantry battalion in six selected divisions . . . on the 14th July."[36] Their impact upon tactics, command and control, and training will be discussed in subsequent chapters.

Most COs, not surprisingly, were Militia officers. No disparagement is intended. Napoleon quipped that there are two occupations where an amateur is often better than a professional, one being prostitution and the other war.[37] The 1st Battalion, largely from Windsor, London and other western Ontario centres, commenced its service under Frederick William Hill, a former mayor of Niagara Falls. He went on to command the 9th Brigade from February 1916 to the Armistice. The 2nd Battalion, mostly men from eastern Ontario, had as CO David Watson, formerly of the 8th Royal Rifles and by profession a newspaperman. He may have been an "old Hughes crony," but at Second Ypres he would lead his battalion with "considerable distinction," and "his lean, seamed face, with its twisted, sardonic smile under its jaunty field cap, [was] seen at every crisis point."[38] Shortly afterward he took over 5th Brigade and later 4th Division.

The other two battalions in Malcolm Mercer's 1st Brigade were the 3rd, hailing entirely from Toronto and the 4th, a "Central Ontario" unit raised in Barrie, Brampton, Hamilton and Niagara Falls. The CO of the 3rd, Robert Rennie, a 52-year-old businessman, had commanded The 2nd Queen's Own before the war. Private E. Seaman recalled Rennie's disgust on being told that some of the men were "cooty" ridden (verminous): "I will not take one lousy man to France. So clean yourselves up." But the news was out; the 3rd ever after was the "Dirty Third." Rennie became GOC 4th Brigade in November 1915, a command he held until the Armistice.[39] The 4th Battalion would have four COs in less than a year. Robert Labatt, who took the battalion to England, went on sick leave in January 1915. His replacement, Arthur Birchall, would be killed at Second Ypres where the 4th lost half its strength. Despite his brief tenure he made a strong impression, as did his Adjutant, Captain Webber of The RCR. Private Guy Mills remembered "the complete contrast between this very severe, straight, reserved CO and the fun-loving and sporting adjutant . . . Remarkably enough they . . . fit . . . like two fingers in a glove." Webber, too, was killed at Second Ypres.[40] Labatt then resumed command, but within a month again was evacuated sick, never to return. His successor, Malcolm Colquhon, was CO from June 1915 to June 1916.

Arthur Currie's 2nd Brigade included one battalion from each Western province. The 7th Battalion, entirely from Vancouver Island, the Lower Mainland and the Kootenays, was under William Hart-McHarg, who had little chance to prove himself because he was killed at Second Ypres in 1915. His 2IC and successor, Victor Odlum, in a letter to his dead CO's mother said "It almost broke my heart to lose him. We have got along so well together, and he was such a splendid type . . . His loss almost totally unnerved me." [41] Odlum subsequently assumed command of 11th Brigade in mid-1916. Saskatchewan contributed the 5th Battalion, a unit raised from various cavalry regiments by George Tuxford, a hard-driving rancher from Moose Jaw and former CO of the 27th Light Horse. It was the only infantry battalion whose reveille and other bugle calls were sounded in cavalry fashion. Some of the men were still wearing cavalry breeches when the 5th first went into the line. Sergeant Harold Baldwin recalled how its title, "5th Western Cavalry," was

> a big joke to our comrades of the Second Infantry Brigade, and indeed to the whole division, and we were . . . "The Disappointed Fifth," "The Wooden Horse Marines," "The Fifth Mounted Foot," Etc. . . . Judge of our astonishment when we had taken our places in the trench and . . . a hail came from the German trenches . . . "Hello, you Fifth, what have you done with your horses?" And in the morning . . . on the German parapet . . . was a little wooden horse—a child's toy . . . Two or three of the boys opened up on the dummy horse and knocked it down . . . a moment or two later . . . the dummy reappeared, swathed in bandages . . . Fritz displayed a rare sense of humour in this instance and we enjoyed the joke immensely.[42]

As shrewd as he was colourful, Tuxford knew his unit's unique features would strengthen spirit and cohesion. "Tuxford's Dandies" achieved a sterling reputation. Currie said the 5th "never lost an inch of ground to the enemy, nor ever failed to take its objective."[43] His Medical Officer, G.M. Davis, who left the 5th in July 1915 for similar duties with the Cavalry Brigade, described his new CO as not "such a fusser" as Tuxford. Sergeant, later Captain, F.C. Bagshaw thought Tuxford "selfish, bull-dozing, grabbing but he was . . . courageous . . . lots of guts." Later as a brigadier (3rd Brigade) Tuxford was disliked by his peers because of his habit of grabbing undue credit for himself.[44]

The 10th Battalion, an amalgamation of the 103rd Calgary Rifles and the 106th Winnipeg Light Infantry, represented Alberta and Manitoba. Its commander, Lieutenant-Colonel John Rattray, was summarily dismissed at Valcartier because of his politics, and was succeeded by Russell Boyle, a tough Boer War veteran and one of only four COs in 1914 who were graduates of the Militia Staff Course. He would be killed at Second Ypres, after which the 10th carried on under temporary commanders until June when Rattray resumed command. Rattray remained with the battalion until September 1916 when he took command of a training brigade.

Manitoba also contributed its very own battalion, the 8th Battalion (90th Rifles), known as the "Little Black Devils" because of its cap badge, a black metal devil above the regimental motto stemming from Riel Rebellion days— *Hosti Acie Nominati* (Named by the Enemy in Battle).[45] The 8th would gain a fine reputation largely due to its first CO, Louis Lipsett. Even those who considered him a hard taskmaster soon recognized him as a born leader who was fearless and determined to set the example and look after his men. Renowned for his relentless search for new and better ways to kill Germans, Lipsett was also approachable and possessed a fine sense of the human touch, qualities that gave him the ability to inspire men. Major Lester Stephens summed him up thus: " Lipsett was a good soldier, you know." J. Pritchard, 8th Battalion, called him a "wonderful soldier and a wonderful man." While he brooked no nonsense, he was not without humour. Major Paul Villiers, Brigade Major 3rd Brigade, recalled a dinner where Lipsett's guests included Brigadier-General J. Seely (GOC Canadian Cavalry Brigade), Lieutenant-Colonel Winston Churchill (CO 6th Battalion Royal Scots Fusiliers) and one Private "Foghorn" MacDonald, an extremely "foul-mouthed man" there for one purpose, "to horrify Winston and Seely."[46] Lipsett had lasting impact on those who followed him in command. Thomas "Tommy" Raddall, for example, a subaltern under Lipsett, was a much admired officer and a strict disciplinarian. Known as a "hell-fire colonel," Raddall's death at Amiens in August 1918 would cause great sadness amongst superiors and subordinates alike.[47]

3rd Brigade, usually called the Highland Brigade, included men from British Columbia, Manitoba and all points east. It is ironic that its GOC, Richard Turner, who needed strong COs, had a mixed bag in the sense of competence, while Currie, much his superior as a brigade and then a division commander, who needed the support of strong COs far less, enjoyed sound performance from his four.

The 15th Battalion, mostly men of Toronto's 48th Highlanders, had as CO John Currie, a 46-year-old Member of Parliament and a close friend of Sam Hughes. Ian Sinclair categorized Currie as "very much more of a politician than an officer . . . one of the type of civilian-soldier . . . worshipped by the poorer element among the ranks but service under whom, for an officer, is sheer misery." [48] At Second Ypres he followed a "curious" itinerary away from his unit during the battle. At one point he appeared in Ypres, supposedly to gather and take stragglers forward, which was a rather strange set of priorities for a CO. Later he parked himself in Arthur Currie's 2nd Brigade Report Centre where he had to be "man-handled out" (reason not given) by a staff officer. Finally, his inexplicable journey to Boulogne resulted in an order from Turner to rejoin his unit at once or be arrested. Daniel Dancocks thought John Currie may have been suffering from shell shock. Colonel John Creelman, 2nd CFA, had another explanation: "Currie was . . . drunk at Ypres, while half his battalion was being killed and the other half being taken prisoners. I know this because he was in my dugout on April 24th where he had no business to be . . . this skunk is passing as a hero."[49]

The 14th Battalion, from Montreal, was the non-Highland battalion in Turner's 3rd Brigade. Frank Meighen, a milling company executive, took the battalion to France and it was under his command until his promotion in June 1915, two months after Second Ypres. He was replaced by Lieutenant-Colonel W.W. Burland, who had been 2IC. He commanded until October 1915 when F.W. Fisher took over.[50] Thus, the 14th had three COs in 11 months. Only 4th Battalion matched that, and then only because one of its COs was killed at Second Ypres.

Turner's other Montreal unit was the 13th Battalion. Its first CO, 44-year-old Frederick Loomis of Sherbrooke, was not immediately or universally popular (COs never are). At Valcartier one subaltern thought, "Loomis lost his head as usual and mucked things up completely. The Colonel was *quite* excelling himself in giving wrong orders and generally messing things up, and the general opinion . . . is that the sooner we get rid of him the better." Loomis proved his critics wrong, going on to replace Lipsett first as GOC 2nd Brigade in July 1916 and then as commander of 3rd Division from September 1918 on. Currie, commenting on Loomis as a brigadier said, "Brigadiers like him do not grow on gooseberry bushes [and] I would not lose him for the world."[51]

Finally, from Victoria, Vancouver, Winnipeg and Hamilton men of the Gordons, the Seaforths, the Camerons and the Argylls, respectively, came together as the 16th Battalion under Robert Leckie, a 34-year-old mining engineer and South African War veteran. He faced the formidable task of forging a unit out of the forced marriage of four Highland regiments. Some thought he could have been more forceful in this process, but his training skills and perseverance built a battalion that could fight like hell. In August 1915 he replaced Turner as GOC 3rd Brigade, an appointment he held until being seriously wounded in February 1916. His brother John then assumed command of the 16th, the only case of brother succeeding brother in the CEF. John Leckie had been in South Africa twice and had a DSO to show for it.

"Stocky and powerfully built, well-read, breezy, with twinkling little eyes, ruddy complexion, and possessing a keen sense of humour . . . it was impossible to spend any time . . . with him without finding oneself entertained and interested." Ready for any adventure, "he passed along most beaten paths . . . and ventured on others of which the majority . . . knew nothing outside of story books." Having commanded the 16th Battalion from August 1915 to November 1916 and then a reserve brigade, Leckie would volunteer in 1918 to lead the Canadian contingent serving in North Russia (Murmansk).[52]

The battalions generally all had fine men as 2ICs. When Tuxford left the 5th on promotion, Major Hugh Dyer took over, and when he left, also on promotion to command a brigade (7th), his 2IC, Major Lorne Tudor, became CO. Sergeant Harold Baldwin said of "Dad" Dyer at Second Ypres: "At about three in the afternoon we saw a figure approaching . . . we knew it to be our dear old major . . . He was well over sixty [he was actually 54], but a hero's heart belonged to him . . . the sheer, dogged spirit of that old warrior." Sergeant A.W. Griffith remembered him as a "very kindly man," one so solicitous of the men's welfare that he mused about getting "a firm like Eaton's to ration us in the trenches."[53] Within the units were other majors and junior officers who would rise to command battalions and beyond. Lieutenant Albert Sparling of the 10th Battalion, for example, became CO of the 4th Battalion. Captain Edward Hilliam, Adjutant of the 5th Battalion and eventually a brigadier, was remembered as "a soldier from his feet up."[54] Many, many men of that first contingent, on being commissioned in the Canadian or Imperial forces, took command of units and distinguished themselves; for example, the last wartime CO of the 14th Battalion, Dick Worrall, began the war as an NCO and finished it as a Lieutenant-Colonel with the DSO and the MC.[55]

Training in England on the Salisbury Plain in Wiltshire, where 1st Division spent the first winter of the war, was only marginally better than it had been in Valcartier. Few thought it strenuous or thorough. Several of the problems that had plagued training at Valcartier—shortage of equipment and instructors—persisted and new ones arose, such as days on end of torrential rain which converted training ground into bog. W. L. Gibson, 4th Battalion noted: "October 1914. Moved camp on several occasions on account of mud. Very little training. December. Little training, too much mud. January 1915. Not much training, too much mud."[56] Hugh Urquhart recalled the 16th Battalion losing two of its four days on the rifle ranges because of heavy snow and dense mist. With so many units sharing the ranges, time-tables had to be strictly followed: bad luck but no re-scheduling. In theory, each infanteer fired 155 rounds while on Salisbury Plain and constantly practised magazine loading and rapid firing with drill rounds, but this and the 50 live rounds each man had supposedly fired at Valcartier were hardly likely to enable the men to attain the Regular's pre-war ability to stagger the enemy with 15 rounds rapid.[57]

In December a particularly severe storm wrecked some of the camps, forcing resident units to pack up and move. This, and the pressing need for repairs elsewhere, resulted in many men being put to construction work. For more than two weeks in early January the 16th Battalion went completely over to navvying: "We are now common labourers . . . doing all sorts of work; loading junk for the building of new huts . . . digging trenches and laying pipes for water." Captain Frank Morison claimed that this involved every man with skills such as carpentry. As a result, the 1st was dubbed "The Constructive Division." He suggested that "notwithstanding its lack of military training" the division was surely the most physically fit ever to leave the British Isles. COs became very unhappy with the situation. By the end of the third week in January R.L. Boyle, CO of the 10th Battalion, was angrily clamouring for the return of the 234 men he had lost to labour tasks.[58]

2nd Division's experience is in sharp contrast. "During the first month in camp [June 1915] the weather was generally warm and fine, and as a result rapid progress was made in the routine of training. Company and battalion drill and manoeuvres, trench digging and similar work occupied most of the time." Other 2nd Division men noted how thorough the training was in Britain: "We had to work, and real hard, too."[59]

January 1915 brought better weather and, as noted above, a permanent four-company battalion. The instability before the new year had had serious impact; officers had been moved from pillar to post, causing much confusion in instruction, repetition and duplication of effort and neglect of some training.[60] Lack of knowledge about conditions in France also inhibited training. It was not enough that training prepare men for battle; the training had to fit the sort of battle they were expected to fight. Some thought the training in open warfare "quite useless [considering] the strongly entrenched positions the Germans had taken up." The real requirement was to master trench warfare, whose "exact principles had not been developed."[61] Anthony Eden, an Imperial subaltern, agreed:

> We seemed to concentrate too much on open warfare, the importance of which was continually being emphasized from above, whereas all we learnt from returned wounded and others showed that trench warfare was there to stay for quite a while . . . We did spend a short spell, it may have been as much as forty-eight hours, in practise trenches . . . But . . . the outcome . . . was confusion rather than instruction. I consoled myself . . . that once in real trenches overseas, we would . . . be free to sort things out for ourselves.[62]

An air of unreality surrounded the whole effort. Stories filtering through from the Front related some techniques of trench warfare, but these were not much practised since no one had any experience of them. They also contradicted the training manuals. Ian Hay thought the war "terribly hard on the textbooks," meaning the *Field Service Regulations, (FSR)* and *Infantry Training (4-Company Organization), 1914.* His claim that these manuals recommended forward slope over reverse slope positions erred, but it does indicate the potential (and actual) confusion.[63] "Rumours of a return to medieval warfare" circulated, while other stories suggested the power of artillery and machine-guns.[64]

In late January battalions began exercising together, but much of this was "rendered useless . . . by the mishaps . . . which generally upset amateur tactical schemes." Divisional exercises were even worse:

> The complete Division, all arms, was assembled with the intention, as far as it was possible for battalions to judge . . . of moving across the Plain in line of battalions (massed) and then wheeling to either right or left . . . [T]he first part of the scheme went . . . without incident; but when the wheel commenced both flanks turned inwards— nutcracker shape—and order was lost beyond redemption . . . [W]hen it became evident that the mass was in hopeless confusion the flanking units . . . were ordered to march back to camp independently.

Overall, "training, to which much hard work should . . . have been given, was never completed in satisfactory fashion." Only 40 of 16th Battalion's 130 days in Britain were available for training.[65] 15th Battalion spent the first two months on construction work. Even in January, when the training picked up, "too many fatigues" continued. Weather and construction labour "seriously hampered" 14th Battalion's training in December and January and 13th Battalion's, too, although the 13th spent less time at labour, having resumed training on 10 January.[66] 1st and 2nd Brigades experienced much the same.

This profile of 1st Division near the end of its time in Britain shows that it was by no means well-trained. How could it be, in view of its brief sojourn there and the appalling weather that had so hindered training? Even the soldier's vital skill, musketry, had suffered. As for commanders, they had not yet held in their hands the lives of their men and the fate of their division. Nor had staff officers had much impact. Their time had been spent learning all they could to prepare for the actualities of executing their commander's will at the Front. Commanders and staff officers had little more to go on than *FSR* and *Infantry Training*. The former manual, being concerned with leading troops, made no mention of training at all, while the latter was concerned with open, not trench warfare. Neither manual said much about command or staff work at division and brigade. An arduous education process lay ahead, the learning curve lifting sharply upward from a rock-bottom starting point:

> But apart from office procedure a working knowledge of war cannot be acquired by sitting in somebody's else's pocket; however well stuffed with knowledge that pocket may be. Bitter lessons that have been learnt by bitter experience, often entailing much loss of life, cannot be passed on. They will never be apprehended until they have been branded red hot on the inner consciousness. [67]

Clearly, 1st Division had a far piece to go before it would be capable, let alone good.

Flanders would be a start.

Notes to Chapter Two

1. No attempt has been made to document individual facts or groups of facts in the description of divisional organization. Doing so would have resulted in a copious and mind-boggling array of notes. The picture that is presented is a compilation and comparison of appropriate British and Canadian data. The reader especially interested in order of battle should consult *Stand To!*, the journal of the Western Front Association, for details of British organizations. The articles by Ronald Clifton and Colonel Terry Cave are most useful. Most helpful for Canadian organizations were Military Advisory Board, *Special Services, Heroic Deeds*, etc. and Love, "*A Call to Arms*." The latter is definitive and indispensable. At this point the reader, if he has not already done so, should refer to Order of Battle, Appendix III.

2. Duguid, *Chronology, Appendices and Maps*, appendix 133; Library and Archives Canada (LAC), RGIIIC3, Vol. 4054, Folder 26, File 1, Operation Order, 18 November 1915; Morton, *When Your Number's Up*, p. 145.

3. LAC, MG30E100 (Currie Papers), Vol. 43, "Canadian War Establishments." This 22 page document lists personnel changes to establishment of arms and services subunits, formations and HQ from corps down to field bakery. It also lists corps schools, railway and forestry troops and non-CEF organizations but not "amendments to transport" and to superseded establishments since these could not be accurately cited. The document's importance lies in its revelation of the enormous effort required to build a corps from scratch and the difficulty of incorporating changes. It is not dated, but it refers to other documents of various dates in June 1918. As it speaks of documents "now in use," it must have been produced before the Armistice.

4. Dancocks, *Gallant Canadians*, p. 7. At Valcartier a fourth infantry brigade existed. Its role was to serve as a reinforcement depot. It disappeared from divisional establishment in October 1914. Consequently, neither it nor its battalions are further discussed here. Arthur Banks, *A Military Atlas of the First World War*, 2nd ed. (London: Leo Cooper, 1989) profiles various national divisional organizations. Of the major combatants only

the Russian division was larger in manpower. The typical German division, at 17,000 men, had 72 guns. Artillery "brigade" requires explanation lest this cause the reader unused to Army organizational peculiarities to think this breed of brigade equal in size to an infantry brigade; in fact, an artillery brigade, being the command of a lieutenant-colonel, equated to an infantry battalion or a cavalry regiment, not an infantry or cavalry brigade.

5.   Major-General A.G.L. McNaughton, "The Development of Artillery in the Great War," *Canadian Defence Quarterly* (January 1929): pp. 60–63. By 1918 the Canadian Corps had over 750 guns and howitzers. The 18-pounder, which in 1914 could reach out 6,500 yards, had by 1918 achieved 9,500 yards. The corresponding figures for the 60-pounder were 10,000 and 15,000. The 4.5-inch howitzer range remained about the same (6,500 yards). German artillery throughout the war outranged ours, gun for gun, by about 30 percent. A British decision after the Boer War had sacrificed range for mobility in the mistaken belief that mobility was more important. What had been overlooked was the fact that fire could be massed without moving the guns. Lt.-Col. C.N.F. Broad, "The Development of Artillery Tactics, 1914–1918," *Journal of the Royal Artillery* 39 (October 1922): 66–67, says that the introduction of the German 5.9-inch howitzer as a horse-drawn field piece in 1914 was a very nasty surprise since it outranged everything we had except the 60-pounder.

6.   *FSR*, pp. 18–19. Engineering tasks included preparing defences, erecting wire obstacles, maintaining tracks and roads, providing water, manning light railways, tunnelling and mining and laying telephone cable. *FSR* stipulated that the infantry was responsible for constructing its own defensive works, but engineers were to assist and undertake any "special engineering" work. *Infantry Training (4-Company Organization) 1914* (London: HMSO, 1914), p. 111. The infantry saw its part as understanding the use of the various tools and the elementary principles of field fortification.

7.   Colonel R.N. Harvey, "The Effect of the War on Field Engineering," *Journal of the Royal United Services Institute* (May, 1922): pp. 194–96.

8.   Ronald Clifton, "What Is a Signal Company?" *Stand To!* 36 (Winter 1992): 6–8; LAC, MG30E100 (Currie Papers), Vol. 43, "Canadian Signal Service." Divisional signal company strength in 1918 was 415 in Imperial divisions and 301 in Canadian divisions.

9.   Military Advisory Board, *Special Services, Heroic Deeds*, pp. 104, 367–68.

10.   Major F.R. Phelan, "Army Supplies in the Forward Area and the Tumpline System," *Canadian Defence Quarterly* 6 (October 1928): 20. Ronald Clifton, "What Is a Divisional Train?", *Stand To!* 33 (Winter 1991): 26, states that the ASC in the BEF grew from 374 officers and 5,252 ORs in 1914 to 11,564 officers and 314,824 ORs in November 1918. John F. Meek, *Over the Top! The Canadian Infantry in the First World War* (Orangeville, Ont.: n.p., 1971), p. 16, notes that 14,030 men served in the Canadian Service Corps.

11.   The division's Veterinary Section (one officer and 25 ORs) did for horses what the field ambulance did for men. The importance of horses cannot be overstated. While motor vehicles gained in importance, horses provided much of the Army's ability to manoeuvre and supply itself. Healthy artillery horses were vital.

12.   Clifton, "What Is a Divisional Train?" p. 26. The daily ration in August 1914 included 1 lb 4 oz fresh or frozen meat or 1 lb preserved or salt meat, 1 lb 4 oz fresh bread or 1 lb biscuit or flour, 4 oz bacon, 2 oz dried vegetables, 3 oz cheese, tea, jam, sugar, salt, mustard, pepper, and lime juice, plus 1/2 gill rum and 2 oz tobacco per week. The daily ration was 19 lb oats and 15 lb hay for heavy draught horses and 12 lb hay for other

horses. Each man and beast carried one day's ration. The divisional train carried another day's ration for each man and horse and there was two days' iron ration per man and two days' reserve grain per horse in the parks on the Lines of Communication.

13. Dancocks, *Gallant Canadians*, pp. 6–7; Nicholson, *Official History of the Canadian Army*, p. 24; Murray, *History of the 2nd Canadian Battalion*, p. 2.

14. LAC, 15th Battalion War Diary, June 1916. The MO reported over 200 men suffering from severe problems "produced by bad boots and recent wet weather." Subsequent contingents were still suffering Canadian-made boots as late as May 1918. The best source for correspondence about equipment shortcomings is Duguid, *Chronology, Appendices and Maps*, pp. 145–60. For data on the continuing problem see LAC, RG9IIIC3, Vol. 4006, Folder 3, File 4, Vol. 4069, Folder 10, File 6, and MG30E432 (Sinclair Papers).

15. Goodspeed, *Battle Royal*, p. 75.

16. Frederic C. Curry, *From the St. Lawrence to the Yser with the First Canadian Brigade* (London: Smith, Elder & Co., 1916), frontispiece, pp. 33–34; Ian Sinclair, CBC Radio Program, *Flanders' Fields*, No. 2, "Canada Answers the Call."

17. Quoted in Nicholson, *Official History of the Canadian Army*, p. 24.

18. R.C. Fetherstonhaugh, *The Royal Montreal Regiment, 14th Battalion, C.E.F., 1914–1925* (Montreal: The Gazette Printing Co. Limited, 1927), p. 11.

19. LAC, RG 41, CBC interview; Urquhart, *History of the 16th Battalion*, p. 17.

20. Urquhart, *History of the 16th Battalion*, p. 18.

21. Nicholson, *Official History of the Canadian Army*, pp. 29–30. Loading on a trial and error basis resulted in units embarking on one ship, their equipment and horses on another (or several), and considerable wasted space on some ships, while others were crammed tight with men and equipment. Much of the confusion was caused by Sam Hughes. Having rejected on 21 September the loading plan prepared by the Director of Supplies and Transport (Ottawa) Hughes put Price in the position of having to produce a new plan "without reference to Headquarters or to previous schedule" and without an adequate staff. It is much to Price's credit that he got the contingent on its way as soon as he did.

22. Baynes, *Morale, A Study of Men and Courage*, pp. 73, 80–81. The CO of the 2nd Scottish Rifles at Neuve Chapelle on 13 March 1915 was Second Lieutenant W.F. Somervail. After a difficult night march he got his tired battalion into attack position on time, thus passing one of the main tests of the infantry officer. Four of the ten original war-time GOCs of the regular Imperial divisions that existed in August 1914 had been killed in action by the end of 1915. While the impact of such a loss of experience was very significant, the effects of the high casualty rates amongst majors and captains, who were potential battalion and brigade commanders, were incalculable.

23. All three commanded militia regiments before the war. Only Turner had combat experience, albeit as a subaltern. His VC must have counted greatly for his credibility. Alderson, commissioned in 1878, had served in the Boer War (1881), in the Egyptian War (1882) and in South Africa (1900–1902) where he commanded a mounted infantry brigade. He wrote two books on the profession: *Pink and Scarlet, or Hunting as a School for Soldiering* (London: Hodder, 1913) and *Lessons from 100 Notes Made in Peace and War* (Aldershot: Gale and Polden, 1908).

24. General Sir Ian Hamilton, *The Commander* (London: Hollis and Carter, 1957), p. 2.

25. Of the eight Canadians (Arthur Currie, Archibald Macdonell, Richard Turner, Harry Burstall, Malcolm Mercer, Frederick Loomis, David Watson and Louis Lipsett [I have

made him a Canadian]) who commanded divisions at the Front, only three are in *The Canadian Encyclopedia* (Second Edition). Macdonell gets 21 lines, Turner 22, and Currie 37. Ian and Sylvia Tyson, on the other hand, get 61 lines! One wonders about the editor's values.

26. Military Advisory Board, *Special Services, Heroic Deeds*, p. 24.

27. "Editorial," *Canadian Defence Quarterly* 2 (July 1925): 322. McNaughton's opinion of Morrison was that he was a good commander who provided his subordinates with full and firm support. (See John Swettenham, *McNaughton, Volume I, 1887–1939* [Toronto: The Ryerson Press, 1968], p. 132)

28. The terms "artillery commander" and "senior gunner" do not really convey the place of senior gunners at division or corps. How and why their roles changed is a very important and somewhat complicated aspect of command and control. For this reason more accurate terminology and an explanation have been left to Chapter Three.

29. Swettenham, *McNaughton*, p. 48.

30. Urquhart, *History of the 16th Battalion*, p. 101.

31. Brigadier-General F. I. Maxse, "Battalion Organisation," *Journal of the Royal United Services Institute* (January, 1912): p. 55. The only vestige today of the eight-company battalion is evident in the eight Guards companies seen yearly on the Queen's Birthday Parade. The article is still worth reading for the observations on training and on the difficulties inherent in the transition from peace to war.

32. Ibid., p. 54. Murray, *History of the 2nd Canadian Battalion*, p. 7, says that at Valcartier " platoon" was not in the Canadian military vocabulary. This was probably because Valcartier had no copies of *Infantry Training (4-Company Organization), 1914*, it having been published only on August 10. On its authority, battalions in England had gone to the platoon organization. This was introduced to Canadians upon arrival there. Curiously, Currie said in early 1917 that "before the war we endeavoured to make the platoon a self-reliant and self-sufficient unit of battle." (LAC, RG9IIIC3, Vol. 4053, Folder 29, File 16, report by Currie, 23 January 1917). Perhaps his memory played him tricks, or the word "before" may have crept inadvertently into his report.

33. Keith R. Simpson, "Capper and the Offensive Spirit," *Journal of the Royal United Services Institute* (June 1973): p. 55. Capper was killed at Loos (September 1915).

34. LAC, MG30E69 (Watson Papers), Diary; Murray, *History of the 2nd Canadian Battalion*, p. 7. LAC, 1st Division General Staff War Diary. After July 1916 company commanders were majors.

35. Alan Clark, *The Donkeys* (London: Hutchinson, 1961), p. 163, claims that Haig told the War Council in April 1915 that the machine-gun was an overrated weapon and two per battalion would do. This is very strange, indeed, since battalions had had four since February. It is even stranger to think that Haig, then commanding First Army in France, would have "minuted" anything to the War Council. If such a document exists, Clark should have cited it so that others could read it. The entire book gives a distorted view of British generalship in 1915.

36. Brigadier-General Sir James E. Edmonds, *Military Operations France and Belgium, 1915: Battles of Aubers Ridge, Festubert and Loos* (London: Macmillan, 1928), p. 89.

37. John Lukacs, *The Hitler of History* (New York: Knopf, 1997), p. 135.

38. Morton and Granatstein, *Marching to Armageddon*, p. 107; Morton, *A Peculiar Kind of Politics*, p. 41; H.F. Wood, *Vimy* (Toronto: Macmillan, 1967), p. 67.

39. LAC, RG 41, Private E. Seaman, 3rd Battalion; Peat, *Private Peat*, p. 28.

40. LAC, RG 41, Guy Mills, 4th Battalion; Brigadier-General A.C. Critchley, *Critch! The*

Memoirs of Brigadier-General A.C. Critchley (London: Hutchinson, 1961), p. 54; Dancocks, *Welcome to Flanders Fields*, p. 215; Peat, *Private Peat*, pp. 164–65.

41. LAC, MG30E300 (Odlum Papers), Vol. 16, Odlum to Mrs. Hart-McHarg, 26 April, 1915. Hart-McHarg's *From Quebec to Pretoria with the Royal Canadian Regiment* is in the bibliography under "McHarg, W. Hart." Only in his book and in Military Advisory Board, *Special Services, Heroic Deeds*, p. 322, is he shown thus. Everywhere else he is Hart-McHarg.

42. Private E.W. Russell, "A Private Soldier's Views on the Great War 1914–1918," Imperial War Museum, 76/170/1, p. 17; Baldwin, "*Holding the Line,*" pp. 118–19, 140.

43. LAC, MG30E100 (Currie Papers), Vol. 52, diary, 2 September 1918.

44. LAC, RG41, Captain F.C. Bagshaw, 5th Battalion; Daniel G. Dancocks, *Spearhead to Victory: Canada and the Great War* (Edmonton: Hurtig, 1987), p. 105.

45. Bruce Tascona and Eric Wells, *Little Black Devils: A History of the Royal Winnipeg Rifles* (Winnipeg: Frye Publishing, 1983), p. 67.

46. LAC, RG41, Lester Stevens, J. Pritchard and A.H. Fisher; MG30E236 (Villiers Papers), diary, Vol. 1, entry for October 1915. Martin Gilbert, *The Challenge of War: Winston S. Churchill, 1914–1916* (London: William Heinemann Ltd., 1971; reprint, London: Mandarin, 1990), p. 637, notes that Lipsett and Churchill had been at Sandhurst together. Churchill considered Lipsett's Canadians "wonderful fellows: like leopards."

47. Tascona and Wells, *Little Black Devils*, p. 112; CBC interview, H. Mowat.

48. LAC, MG30E432 (Sinclair Papers), Vol. 1, Folder 1-1, Biographical notes, p. 5.

49. Dancocks, *Welcome to Flanders Fields*, p. 248; LAC, MG 30E8 (Creelman Papers). On return to Canada after Second Ypres Currie was promoted. This was not the madness it seems: colonel was not a command rank, it being too senior for battalion and too junior for brigade. Currie was promoted out of a command in order to be put where he could pose no danger to troops!

50. Fetherstonhaugh, *The Royal Montreal Regiment*, pp. 62, 72. Dancocks, *Welcome to Flanders Fields*, p. 221, says that at Second Ypres Frank Meighen had been in charge of "miscellaneous troops" in the GHQ line while Burland commanded the two forward companies of the 14th. After leaving the battalion Meighen served in Canada and England. In 1918 he reverted to Lieutenant-Colonel in order to command the 87th Battalion (Canadian Grenadier Guards), 11th Brigade, 4th Division.

51. Imperial War Museum, P 443, diary, Stanley Brittain, 17 September 1914; LAC, MG30E46, Turner Papers, Vol. 8, File 51, Currie to Turner, 5 December 1917.

52. Urquhart, *History of the 16th Battalion*, p. 97; Nicholson, *Official History of the Canadian Army*, p. 512; LAC, Service Record; MG30E83 (J.E. Leckie Papers), Vol. 1.

53. Baldwin, "*Holding the Line,*" p. 170; LAC, Service Record; MG30E442 (Griffith Papers), pp. 13–14; RG 41, CBC interview of F.C. Bagshaw; Tuxford, "The Great War As I Saw It," p. 68.

54. Baldwin, "*Holding the Line*" pp. 170–71.

55. Fetherstonhaugh, *The Royal Montreal Regiment*, p. 317.

56. Capt. W.L. Gibson, ed., *Records of the Fourth Canadian Infantry Battalion in the Great War, 1914–1918* (Toronto: MacLean Publishing Company Limited, 1924), p. 13.

57. Urquhart, *History of the 16th Battalion*, p. 30.

58. *Ibid.*, pp. 32, 34. Lt.-Col. Frank Morison, "The 16th and 10th Canadians at St. Julien," *Hamilton Association Journal and Proceedings*, 1920, pp. 133–34; Dancocks, *Gallant Canadians*, p. 13. The total number of men in 1st Division who were labouring instead

of training cannot be stated with any certainty, but the numbers were significant and so was the adverse impact on training.

59. Singer, *History of the 31st Canadian Infantry Battalion*, p. 22; Lieut. R. Lewis, *Over the Top with the 25th* (Halifax: H.H. Marshall, Limited, 1918), p. 7.

60. Urquhart, *History of the 16th Battalion*, p. 32; Goodspeed, *Battle Royal*, p. 82.

61. Curry, *From the St. Lawrence to the Yser*, p. 49.

62. Eden, *Another World*, p. 71.

63. Ian Hay [Major-General John Hay Beith], *The First Hundred Thousand, Being the Unofficial Chronicle of a Unit of "K(I)"* (Toronto: William Briggs, 1916), pp. 95–96; *Infantry Training (4-Company Organization), 1914*, p. 150; *FSR*, p. 146. While reverse slope positions shortened the defender's field of fire, they prevented the enemy knowing the exact nature of the defence and enabled greater freedom of movement for defenders. Artillery compensated for the shorter fields of fire.

64. Major Bryan Cooper, *The Tenth (Irish) Division in Gallipoli* (London: Herbert Jenkins Limited, 1918), p. 19.

65. Urquhart, *History of the 16th Battalion*, p. 30.

66. Beattie, *48th Highlanders of Canada*, pp. 28, 32; Fetherstonhaugh, *The 13th Battalion*, p. 25; Fetherstonhaugh, *The Royal Montreal Regiment*, p. 21.

67. Nicholson, *Behind the Lines*, p. 64.

CHAPTER THREE

At My Command (1)

If officers desire to have control over their commands, they must remain habitually with them, industriously attend to their instruction and comfort, and in battle lead them well.

—STONEWALL JACKSON, NOVEMBER 1861

The contribution of command and control to the reputation of Old Red Patch as an effective formation is the subject of this chapter and the next. From the very top, in this case the BEF, right down to the infantry section, the smallest fighting organization, a commander's chief responsibility was "fighting his command." At every level he had to plan how to employ his resources to achieve the assigned mission, and he had then to see that his plan was implemented. He had to ensure that his men could fight and had the will to do so, he had to establish and maintain operational routines, and he had to integrate new organizations, technology, specialists, tactics and command structure.

Dictionary and thesaurus treat the nouns "command" and "control" synonymously, but this ignores certain military realities. For instance, command is a legal distinction unique to the Armed Forces. In 1914–1918 the law was the *Army Act* as enforced by *King's Regulations* and the *Manual of Military Law*. As Stonewall Jackson pointed out (above), while control is part of command there is a difference, a difference Major-General Chris Vokes also voiced: "Command is often not *what* you do but the *way* you do it." Vokes thought that E.L.M. Burns, under whom he served in Italy, missed the essential division between command and control: "All he had to do was tell me what he wanted done. But not how to do it."[1] No two officers will or can have the same style of command. It is an unwise superior who tries to force a subordinate to conform to his idea of "how." Grouping, which is the attachment or detachment of formations and units to or from a formation issuing an operation order, also reveals the difference between command and control. At Mount Sorrel in June 1916, First Army gave the Canadian Corps additional resources: 8th (Imperial) Brigade *under control,* and some artillery *under command.* The crucial difference was this: the Imperial brigade remained under command of First Army, meaning that Canadian control of this brigade was limited in some respects, while the additional artillery, having come under command of the Canadian Corps, could be deployed as the Corps commander wished and its fire was *guaranteed* to the Corps.[2] Control, one of the tools of command, executes what is ordered. Like command, it depends upon timely information, efficient organization and good battle procedure—that whole process during which a commander prepares and gives orders and his troops deploy.

Readers unfamiliar with command and control probably find it easier to contemplate the higher levels of command and the strategy or operations that are their responsibility.[3] Army and corps can be dealt with in broad-brush fashion. How exactly they fit together and do their work need not be gone into at great length and the story will still remain intelligible. Higher-formation commanders think necessarily in terms of numbers, not of men. Tactics, on the other hand, reduces the horizon to the men who populate the smaller commands and those who lead them: division (although it, too, can be somewhat remote), brigade, battalion, company, platoon and section. The lower levels were made up of close-knit teams, the best featuring a high standard of individual weapons skills and physical toughness, sufficient trained specialists (such as signallers and Lewis gunners), officers and NCOs qualified to lead their commands, and well executed battle procedure. At unit and sub-unit levels tactics had to be decided upon in the direct application of men and weapons *to* the ground and *on* the ground. The basic building blocks, upon which all else rested, were the section and the platoon. This is why they were (and are) so important.

When reflecting on the lower levels of command, the reader must keep two matters foremost in mind: numbers and the space they occupy. The smaller the organization the more of it was in contact. A section of 12 men was *all* in contact; everything, so to speak, was in the shop window. The Sergeant's concern was only a few yards of trench: his sphere of interest and control was minute, his tools with which to influence the action were limited and his initiative (what little was expected of him) was restricted to immediate vicinity and circumstance. Above the section level, officers commanded. A platoon, with four times the manpower, occupied more frontage. Its OC, a subaltern, could field a reserve of one or more sections, a capability that made the platoon effective tactically. He had more scope and more was expected of his initiative, so much so that his command came to be seen as perhaps *the* most important one. It is ironic that the most junior, and usually the youngest, officer should have had that responsibility added to the awesome burden of being in charge of other men's lives—but then platoon commanding was a young man's game.

At company level (four times the manpower of a platoon) and at battalion level (four times again) responsibility widened and more weapons had to be managed, but, again, commanders had limited scope for planning.[4] COs, however, being responsible for intimate execution of plans, had considerable discretion in modifying details. Once a CO was given a task, how he carried it out was his business. He expected to command without interference, except for the inspection necessary to judge progress and for the direction and even disciplinary action that came his way if he faltered. Stepping up one notch to the first formation, the brigade level, its GOC, a brigadier-general, kept some of his infantry out of the line, retaining perhaps one battalion in support and another in reserve.

Another step up was division, a self-contained formation that moved as a single body with its own artillery, engineers, transport, medical and other support. It was the first level at which all-arms coordination took place and where sizable reserves were committed. It was also the key point for the transmission of intelligence upward. Its responsibility was much larger than a brigade's. When massing a division for attack, deciding on a narrow or wide front was a lesson of experience. The defence, too, featured more or less concentration, the problem and the lesson being when to thin out or thicken up. Saying that a division was defending an area was customary and true in the sense of mission, but the reality, Canadian or otherwise, was very different:

> All three brigades were in the line, side by side, each with two battalions 'up,' one in close support, and one back in reserve doing what was ironically calling 'resting'; . . . six battalions out of the 13 [including the divisional pioneer battalion] in the division held the line. Each of these front-line battalions would normally have two . . . companies 'up' and two held back in support positions . . . [T]he six front-line battalions at quiet times held the whole divisional front with about thirty-six platoon posts, and since a platoon could rarely put more than thirty men on duty, we may conclude that the divisional front was held by about 1,000 out of its, say, 10,000 infantrymen.[5]

This reality also applied in the attack where strength was deliberately reduced by the left-out-of-battle (LOB) policy implemented after the Somme.[6]

A division was not independent; it set doctrine to a limited extent and relied upon corps for support (heavy artillery, for example). Corps was the lowest level that planned and fought the longer battles. "Even at Division," said Captain J.R. Cartwright, "there weren't a great many major decisions to be made . . . they were all made higher up at Corps and even at GHQ [BEF General Headquarters]." An engineer officer from 1916–1918, E.L.M. Burns, wrote that narrow fronts left division commanders with little "scope for the exercise of tactical genius . . . The orders came down from above and they framed the action . . . pretty tightly; their execution was more . . . staff work than . . . initiative by the commanders.[7] This is too strongly worded since GOsC, who were responsible for the detailed tactical plan, usually exercised considerable discretion in formations, organization, and jumping-off lines. In 1st Division, for example, leading waves were moved forward into No Man's Land at Mount Sorrel just before attacking on 13 June 1916, thus sparing the men some of the German artillery fire.[8]

1st Division and the Canadian Corps existed in three dimensions of command. First, Imperial command: The 1st was a division of the BEF, and the Corps was, in the original terminology, an "army corps" of the BEF.[9] Second, the Corps was a national Army that remained together for virtually all of the war. Finally, command was tactical. A brigade could be shifted from one division to another as necessary, or battalions could be moved between brigades. Creating composite brigades was entirely possible, too; at Mount Sorrel two such brigades went temporarily from 1st to 3rd Division.[10] From time to time, Imperial divisions came under Canadian command, as did five in 1918, for example.

What was required of command is best summarized in the code "You were only their fathers; I was their Officer."[11] Officers served at the sovereign's pleasure. They were *commissioned*, not *enlisted*. Each new officer, now His Majesty's "Trusty and well beloved," received that splendid document called the King's Commission, "the greatest honour that can be conferred upon any man." So important was the officer that he was not given a service number.[12] His commission bound him to his duty; it was an ethos to live by. Soldiers selected for commissioning from the ranks were officially discharged from the Army and then commissioned. Unlike enlistment, a commission could be resigned. This may seem minutia, quaint, even frivolous, but the distinction was useful and practical. In mid-1917 GOC 1st Brigade reminded COs that officers were appointed, commissioned, transferred, seconded, or dismissed the service, but they were never enlisted or discharged; "the use of these two terms, improperly, indicate to me that some officers have not a proper appreciation of the terms and conditions of their service."[13] One of the benefits was that the incompetent or otherwise unsatisfactory officer and the Army had a quick way out of a bad contract without resort to a destructive and embarrassing trial which, while it removed the individual, also sullied the service. In 1914–1918 the universal fact was that

> the value of officers can never be rated too highly. From top to bottom they are the leaders on whom victory depends. The value of a formation, no matter what its size, depends on the character and personality of its commander, whether he be a colonel or a lieutenant. A company can be what its commander makes it; the men will catch his fire and enthusiasm.[14]

Ecclesiastes 1:18 states a cruel irony applicable to good officers, men and formations: "He that increaseth knowledge increaseth sorrow." As GOC 1st Division (A.C. Macdonell) said, "Increasing fame brings increasing responsibilities. More and more is naturally expected."[15] In the infantry, where the quality of the officer "was the most vital factor," rapid turnover meant constant loss of wisdom and experience. Also, shortages of officers "became more and more acute [and] the quality worsened."[16] Attrition is about numbers but also about the impact of the strain of responsibility. Arthur Currie understood the terrible ebbing away of a man's strength:

> Every day the pressing need for suitable and honourable employment for war torn Commanding Officers from the front becomes more apparent. This is a fact which must . . . be dealt with. Certain Commanding Officers, who have rendered most excellent and gallant service, will in a short time become so war worn as to become inefficient. If such is the case it would be unjust and cruel to adversely report upon these Officers. The necessity for providing for them where their war wisdom can be taken full advantage of exists.[17]

The personality of a CO had marked impact upon the discipline, efficiency and happiness of his unit. While the last could not be his primary concern, the good CO realized its importance in achieving and maintaining the first two. Command had to be exercised in a relaxed manner, for only a happy unit could be successful, and in a happy unit juniors did not fear their seniors, but the relaxed manner had of necessity to be accompanied by the strictest attention to detail if things were to be kept up to the mark. The unit with a personable and competent CO did its job happily and well, while the unit with a competent but miserable CO was an efficient, but unhappy one, in all likelihood. The unit suffering under the mediocre or just plain bad CO, who lacked the personality to help carry command off and perhaps was also labouring under the severe disadvantage of having replaced a good CO and not being able to fill his boots, was doubly cursed in that it was inefficient *and* unhappy. Good company commanders and a good 2IC could compensate somewhat for the last type of CO especially, but the strain on the unit told.

Wherever there was a good CO, there was a good battalion. 2nd Battalion under David Watson became known as a well-disciplined and aggressive unit that dominated No Man's Land. 16th Battalion was considered easygoing, which is not to say that it was ineffective for it was also a hard-fighting unit, but its administration and march and trench discipline were somewhat casual. Some thought its first CO, Robert Leckie, "before all else, a first-class soldier"; some did not.[18] 8th Battalion's very fine reputation began with its first CO, Louis Lipsett. Of the nine infantry COs who survived Second Ypres he was the outstanding one, a leader of high ability in the judgement of his peers.[19] He went on to shine as a brigadier and then as GOC 3rd Division until his transfer to 4th (Imperial) Division in September 1918 and his death in action a month later. Lipsett was "sniped" while forward on reconnaissance. As well as being informed by subordinates, he had always preferred to look for himself when he commanded 2nd Brigade and then 3rd Division. Private Will Bird remembered a night in February 1917 when as a sentry he saw someone coming up the trench—an officer, because the man carried no rifle. "He stayed and stayed," said Bird, and the conversation ranged from life back in Alberta to how Bird liked the infantry. Eventually it came out that the visitor was Lipsett, which Bird was disinclined to believe until he was made a present of a postcard-sized snapshot. Bird, who was no great respecter of officers, was mightily impressed with Lipsett. He still had the snapshot in 1930 when his war memoirs were published.[20] Lipsett became perhaps the best division commander in the Canadian Corps. He came to think of himself as a Canadian, so much so that he planned to settle in western Canada after the war.[21]Despite Lipsett's strongly expressed desire to remain with 3rd Division, Currie either did not protest or did not protest loudly enough to reverse Haig's decision to move Lipsett, possibly because Currie wanted all four division commanders to be Canadian.[22]

Conversely, 14th Battalion had severe disciplinary problems and failed to establish a good reputation under F.W. Fisher, who on Currie's recommendation was replaced by R.P. Clark, a Major from the 2nd Battalion, in March 1916. Neither Currie nor Tuxford, Fisher's brigade commander, suffered incompetence well or for long. Part of Fisher's discipline problem was bilingualism, an "uncommonly awkward" creature in an infantry battalion. Before Clark took command Tuxford reorganized the battalion by redistributing the French Canadians of Number 4 Company throughout the unit. Paul Villiers, at the time Staff Captain of 3rd Brigade and later its Brigade Major, believed that Fisher's departure became inevitable after two cases of desertion to the enemy in December 1915. In the first case (23 December) one man in an outpost murdered his companion and went over to the enemy. The second case, which occurred on Christmas Day, was of a "French-Canadian Sergeant [who] suddenly . . . disappeared over the parapet and made for the German trenches. No one fired on him as he went over." Such disturbing incidents caused anxiety amongst units that had the 14th as a neighbour in the line. The CO of the 15th Battalion (W.B. Marshall), for example, complained directly to Currie in early March 1916 when two platoons of Number 4 Company left their trenches without orders, retiring some distance behind the line, thereby leaving a gap on the flank of the 15th. Villiers also noted that under Clark, and later Gault McCombe, the 14th became an efficient unit.[23] A unit's style and aggressiveness also matched those of its CO. His impact just cannot be overemphasized, as this extract from one of Currie's letters shows:

> Yesterday . . . the enemy launched a counter-attack which was met and defeated by a bayonet charge, leaving one hundred prisoners in our hands. The Battalion which did this was to go over the top this morning. During last night it was again counter-attacked and its line forced back, but the Colonel . . . led his men in a counter-attack, got back to the line from which he jumped off this morning, and in the operation captured another hundred prisoners. At zero hour . . . he was on the tape and went across according to plan. You cannot get anything which exemplifies the fighting qualities of a Battalion more than this.[24]

The best account of how COs change a battalion was written by Lieutenant James Pedley, MC, who joined the 4th Battalion in December 1917:

> My first impression of Harry Lafayette Nelles was not altogether favourable. He was too well-dressed, too smooth, and . . . even a newcomer could see that the accord which should exist between a commander and his officers was lacking. As a matter of fact, Colonel Nelles was having a hard time those days. He had pushed himself, so the word went, into prominence through his concentration on the display side of soldiering, had become a sort of 'Brasso King' in the commands which he had heretofore held, and it was his ability to keep the soldiers outwardly clean under adverse conditions which had resulted in his obtaining the coveted promotion to battalion commander over the heads of many officers in the division senior to himself. Only about 22 years of age, some said, at the time of his advancement he was the most junior major of the division, but I think that cannot have been the case . . . I seem to remember . . . that Nelles was the man [who] built the comfortable mess . . . at Chateau de la Haie; and I can well believe it. He liked a bit of swank. He had not been in the line since early in the war . . . and he

followed Lieut.-Col. A.T. Thomson, D.S.O., M.C., a man of totally different type, who had been the idol of the battalion, adored alike by officers and men, and whose death in the line had plunged the unit in grief. A battalion of infantry is a chameleon, ceaselessly changing its colour to suit the changing complexion of its commanding officers. The Fourth . . . followed the rule. It had started out under Birchall by earning the sobriquet 'The Mad Fourth', a catch which stuck right to the end . . . But the madness . . . appears to have been an intermittent fever. Birchall engendered it, Colquhoun advertised it, Rae damped down the fire. For with the coming of Rae we first discern another element . . . cold discipline. One gathers that when the prim little colonel was finally promoted to the staff he left behind him a well chastened set of madmen. He was a while steady Rae, even a brilliant Rae, but a Rae that gave out little or no heat. Thomson succeeded; things began immediately to warm up. In the summer and fall of 1917 . . . Thomson led a mob of enthusiasts. more it was the 'Mad Fourth' in all verity . . . The morale of the battalion reached its crest. Its fighting ability was prodigious. But this result had been achieved only at the expense of the sartorial perfection which had been the keynote of the Rae regime. Birchall, I fear, would have turned over in his grave at the sight of the battalion in those Passchendaele days. Under Thomson's command the Fourth had achieved a tradition of raggedness and dirt, superimposed upon its ancient reputation for hard fighting. Then Thomson fell, caught by a sniper's bullet . . . Nelles' job was to smarten up the unit without sacrifice of the esprit de corps, hardwon by dint of battles. He must burnish the sword, yet not impair its strength. It would be no mean feat, and for some time . . . his success hung in the balance. It was not long after my arrival that the story came back to us how Colonel Nelles had said at a party . . . that he was as popular as a skunk at a garden party. And indeed it was so. Colonel Nelles never became the popular idol that Thomson had been; but as the months went by and he showed that in addition to his bent for smartness he had tactical ability far beyond the average, a sense of justice, and (more important still) his full share of personal bravery, a better feeling grew. At the end there were few grumblers and a great share of the credit for the success of the Fourth . . . must be laid at the feet of Colonel Nelles. He had the excellent qualities of youth as well as youth's defects. His energy and enthusiasm, while often the cause of needless work for his officers and men, had this redeeming feature that he made few blunders of note and probably saved us from

more useless tasks than he imposed. I always found him fair . . . and
. . . reasonable in his judgements.[25]

Good judgement stems from experience, routine or otherwise, just as doctrine does. Hope is about the only thing that springs into being fully mature.
Judgement and doctrine are easy to criticize when one has the advantage of
hindsight; it is easy to forget that "the historian's omniscience about the battlefield is not only unreal but privileged."[26] Often the armchair
Generalfeldmarschell who criticize commanders and campaigns lack not
only the experience but the technical literacy to do so. Theory, right from the
start, is the "very opposite of practise, and not infrequently the laughing
stock of men whose military competence is beyond dispute."[27] In any case,
the theorist can comfortably pronounce for he will not have to meet the test.

Canadian commanders in the Great War had a less secure future. They
had immediately to command and could not rely on doctrine to create and
develop their method of command. Each commander suffered from inexperience and lack of military education, insufficient trained staff officers to assist
them, and the difficulty, beyond these basics, of understanding new technology and getting it into the hands of soldiers trained in its use. Each had to
assemble the practical experience that cumulatively made up his skills and
came to characterize his style of command. Men without experience are usually conservative, a charge laid against the commanders of 1914–1917, who
were often pilloried for their methods as a whole. Some of the condemnation
was entirely justified, but some was also quite unfair considering that the
commanders' much improved *educated* performance in 1918 was scarcely
mentioned. Commanders who survived into 1918 were quite changed from
earlier in the war. It is unhistorical to condemn the commanders of 1914–1917
for not displaying the wisdom of 1918.[28]

Doctrine strongly influenced training and organization. The definitive
statement on pre-war doctrine, "The British Army and Modern Conceptions
of War," appeared in the *Journal of the Royal United Services Institute* in
1911. Its anonymous author concluded that doctrine, or rather the lack of it,
had been a significant factor in several setbacks of the South African War.[29]
The cynical and age-old view that "tactics is the opinion of the senior officer
present" could hardly fill the void. Doctrine, more precisely, is a "philosophy
of combat," or better, the "tactical principles on which to base both training
and the conduct of war."[30] Doctrine can also be strategic, but it is the tactical that concerned 1st Division.

Was not *Field Service Regulations (FSR)* British Empire doctrine in 1914?
In the absence of anything else it was but it hardly sufficed, being just regulation or, as the 1911 article said, "regulations and instructions." As its

author suggested, the General Staff had provided a method of action but had failed to give the Army a doctrine. A doctrine was a "clear conception of the main principles of war," while a method of action was "application of those principles."[31] 1st Division's concern was really method.

It would have been convenient if innovations in technology could have been in step with innovations in tactics, but they seldom are. Between concept and effective use lies a wide gap. Usually, urgency and expediency force the incorporation of new technology within old doctrine. From the beginning war was hard on the manuals: "above all, we . . . learned to revise some of our most cherished theories."[32] Integration was fundamental, for as *FSR* stressed, "The full power of an army can be exerted only when all its parts act in close combination, and this is not possible unless all members of each arm understand the characteristics of the other arms."[33] Many months passed before this was even close to true of the BEF, the Canadian Corps, or 1st Division, specifically in relation to the attack, a phase of war far more difficult than the defence. "Combination" is a key word for no single innovation in itself proved a war-winner. Each innovation had to get in step with the infanteer, who in the end would close with the enemy and decide the issue. Within 1st Division, Lewis guns, for example, were well integrated, but mortars were less so because of technological limitations. The literature, especially soldier memoirs and diaries, shows this. To say that "*most* officers . . . did not know how to integrate technology and human factors such as morale, discipline, courage, etc.," is a blanket statement that should not apply to Regimental officers nor, in fact, to officers up to divisional level.[34]

A complicating factor in achieving integration was the absence in 1914 of the schools—infantry, artillery, engineers and services—to develop and integrate corps doctrines. Nor did infantry-artillery cooperation strike much of a chord. Establishing a doctrine for the new style warfare had commanders groping in their past experience and in the manuals, where they found "nothing to fit the novel situation." This left them to rely on old methods. Inevitably, "casualties . . . became the only guides to tactical improvement!"[35] It should not be supposed that a new or improved doctrine emerged from one battle. "The human imagination," said Captain G.C. Wynne, "is so unreliable that actual experience is needed before changes can be made to an established doctrine."[36] Misinterpretation was common because the ground rules kept shifting. Also, once the Army was engaged, it became much harder to appreciate the lessons of experience and there was less time to do so.

Upon arrival in Flanders in February 1915, all ranks began learning the lessons of war, starting with a fundamental of trench warfare: "The gradual establishment of a systematic and orderly trench routine was a process of great educational value."[37] The initial tour in the trenches marked the beginning of the habit and the standard procedures that were necessary for the day-to-day routine and the rapid acquisition of the soldier's art. They would ensure that nothing was overlooked and would provide a well-understood plan for dealing with any enemy initiatives, such as raids. One precaution, "Stand To," dictated that one hour before daylight and one hour before dusk every man was in his fighting position. These wearying watches went unremarked by those who calculated the sacrifices of war. Once reduced to standard drills, routine matters required no orders, and reinvention of the wheel was avoided. Thus began standing orders for battle, or standard operating procedures, in the form of "Trench Orders."[38] Education included approved methods of annoying and upsetting the enemy. Experience also awakened the strongest of all fellowships, that of the warrior. The Corps commander and the C-in-C expressed satisfaction with 1st Division's first tour in the line. The bill for tuition and for the first stirrings of doctrinal revision came to 278 casualties.[39]

At Second Ypres on Thursday, 22 April 1915 Canadians were aggressive, even rash, when they attacked Kitchener's Wood near St. Julien in what became the Ypres Salient. Just after 10:30 P.M. GOC 3rd Brigade, Richard Turner, VC, ordered the 10th and 16th Battalions to counter-attack at 11:30. It was 11:30, however, before the two units, together about 1,500 strong, got into position. Consequently, the assault was ordered for 11:45. "Formed up in the moonlight," said the keeper of the 16th Battalion's War Diary, "10th Batt. in front on two company width, double rank, thus forming 2 lines 30 yards apart." 10th Battalion formed up in similar fashion.[40] At 11:48 the battalions advanced, the three-minute delay being immaterial since artillery support was virtually nil. Two hundred yards or so from the enemy the 10th encountered a hedge reinforced with barbed wire, through which both battalions quickly scrambled and then reformed. But the noise of their passage had alerted the enemy. The mad charge that ensued got the two units into the woods and through to the other side, but severe casualties and the inability to get reinforcements forward resulted in their withdrawal before noon.[41] At Ypres Canadians displayed discipline and high morale, but they were too raw to be called skilled. Their doctrine was more incidental than conscious.

Canadians had not been engaged in March at Neuve Chapelle, an attack featuring such innovations as detailed maps produced from aerial photography ("wonderful maps," said Haig); a heavy concentration of artillery fire on a narrow front (one gun for every six yards of enemy trench); and highly redundant communications (telephone lines laid triplicated and crossed over in an interlocking grid).[42] Nor did 1st Division participate in the attack at Aubers Ridge, an attack that proved a great disappointment for the BEF. It failed to achieve even the partial success of Neuve Chapelle, in part because its planning and execution was not an improvement over that of Neuve Chapelle, especially in regard to fire support. The principle that the width of the attack should be proportional to the artillery available to support it was not applied as it should have been. This was particularly significant at Aubers Ridge where the enemy defended a system of three trench lines instead of the single major trench they had occupied at Neuve Chapelle. Mass versus dispersion was a dilemma: attack on a broad front, meaning that artillery support would be spread thinner, or attack on a narrow front, which thickened fire support for the assault, but allowed the enemy to concentrate and subject the attacker to flanking attacks and intense fire. In fact, Aubers Ridge was regressive in the way it separated firepower and assault power, thereby turning the BEF away from the integration of infantry and support weapons, which was so necessary to provide even a chance of breakthrough, as opposed to break-in.

Initially, tactical innovation also lagged since General Headquarters did not analyse and disseminate lessons in an organized way for the benefit of the entire BEF. Still, GHQ was involved far more than has been acknowledged. As early as February 1915 headquarters began issuing guidance pertaining to lessons.[43] Significant aspects of BEF, French and enemy doctrine, training and equipment were also being published in the Central Distribution Section and Stationary Services (CDS/SS) series.[44] The search for lessons became constant and insistent, the BEF being just as diligent as the enemy in this search. After every battle or action commanders expected to be asked, "To what do you attribute the success (or failure)?" and "What lessons can be drawn?" Their answers received close attention as part of the quest for a clear and consistent vision of what to do and what not to do. This process of validating or rejecting previous practise became a major aspect of the exercise of command. Even a representative sample of Canadian questions and answers, and of the minutes of conferences held to discuss lessons, with the emphasis on 1st Division responses, fills hundreds of pages.[45]

Learning lessons was not an ever-upward curve of comprehension. Despite recognizing the primary lesson of Neuve Chapelle—the German line could be broken given enough artillery support—Sir Henry Rawlinson's attack on Aubers Ridge in May 1915 lacked a sufficiency, thus indicating that command "was not a consistent process of learning . . . [L]essons already mastered might then go disregarded and have to be learned all over again."[46] In the Canadian Corps formation commanders and senior staff officers displayed no reluctance to directly criticize. After the Canadian counterattack on 13 June 1916 at Mount Sorrel, Corps praised the divisions for their conduct of the operation but also reminded them of the tactics suggested earlier: "Although the counter-stroke . . . was [a] success, an immediate assault

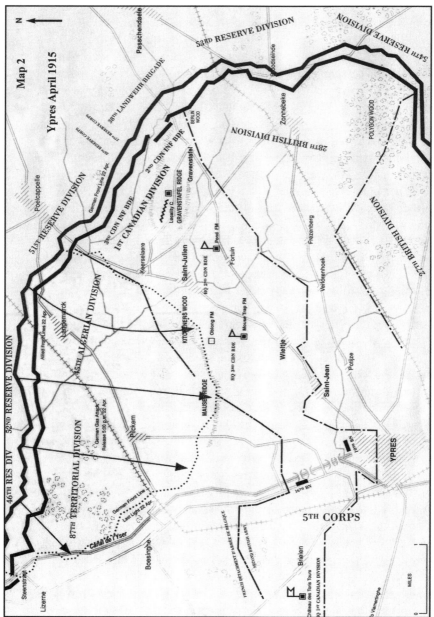

Courtesy of The Calgary Highlanders and The Calgary Highlander Regimental Funds Foundation (map prepared by 2Lt I.R. Spratley)

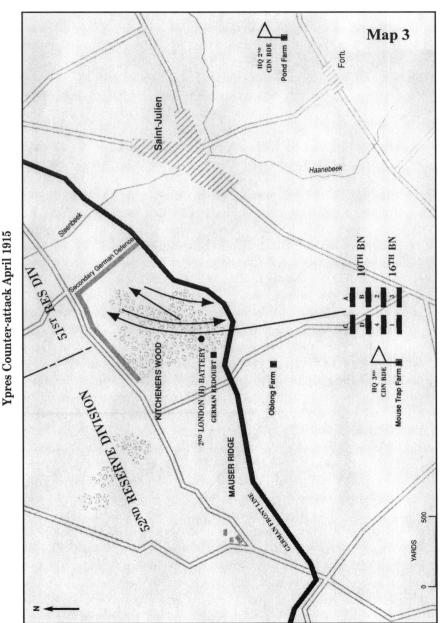

Map 3

Ypres Counter-attack April 1915

Courtesy of The Calgary Highlanders and The Calgary Highlander Regimental Funds Foundation (map prepared by 2Lt I.R. Spratley)

on . . . 2nd June from an unopposed locality would have prevented the enemy's consolidation and therefore have been less costly."[47] When things went wrong, the repercussions extended down through battalion and company to platoon commanders who had to explain what had gone amiss. The lower the level of inquiry, the more detailed the inquiry became. An enemy attack on 26 April 1916 on 1st Brigade near Hill 60, for example, led Corps to ask more than 20 specific questions, mostly about counterattacks and enemy wire cutting, all "with a view to obtaining lessons."[48] Questions might be simple or very complex, often with a hint of dissatisfaction; if enemy raiders entered a brigade's trenches, for example, there would be a question about the extent to which "X" Battalion had been patrolling. If the raiders got away with prisoners, the questions became accusatory, so much so that it was easy to visualize fingers being pointed.

Considerable information about lessons also circulated extra-officially. A sheaf of documents from 1st Australia New Zealand Army Corps (ANZAC) to "my dear Radcliffe" in August is a good example of the value of the network. From his counterpart, C.B.B. White, Brigadier-General Radcliffe received "some useful notes by one of our best brigade commanders . . . his orders for certain operations . . . some training orders by the same brigade . . . [and] a sample of divisional orders, which . . . are the best available, although they go into a great amount of detail."[49] Radcliffe, always looking to improve operational efficiency, passed most of the package down to divisions.

Divisions were intimately involved in lesson gathering and analysis; in fact, they were the node of the system. The covering memoranda and lengthy manuscript annotations show how carefully HQ 1st Division studied lesson documents before sending them to brigades, whose commanders, in turn, added comments useful to the battalions. Comments often reflect not only the official position on tactics but the originator's personal philosophy; in April 1917 William Griesbach's "Notes for the Guidance of Battalion Officers" said exactly how he wanted reports rendered.[50] Lessons of the Somme, for example, were quickly and widely circulated, even though the information had "not in all cases been thoroughly sifted, so that some of the points raised are open to discussion." Many interim reports are surprisingly thorough, indicative of close observation, careful investigation and attention to detail. One especially good report draws conclusions on the effectiveness of weapons (Stokes mortars and grenades), clearing captured trenches, assault formations, carrying parties and passage of information, closing with what were the most important lessons: infantry must keep close to the creeping barrage, being initially not more than 100 yards behind and closing to 50 yards once they saw the fire was accurate; consolidation required fresh troops, meaning that commanders had to keep a reserve in hand; and limited objectives should be set.[51]

Preliminary reports were usually followed by thorough analyses. The danger that such documents taken into trenches could be lost and operations compromised was often accepted because it was more important that the lessons reach units quickly.

Appreciations dealing with projected operations and "principles and methods to be followed to inflict maximum casualties" took longer to prepare. An appreciation was simply an orderly sequence of reasoning that led logically to the best solution to a problem. They appeared with increasing frequency from 1916 on. In January Louis Lipsett, then GOC 2nd Brigade, in a particularly finely crafted appreciation (there are many by him in archival files) warned of the necessity for "drastic changes": "During 1916 we may base our hopes of success on: (i) A more intense and heavier artillery bombardment. (ii) Larger numbers of infantry, arriving without check when required. (iii) More perfect Staff arrangements." The enemy's counter—greater depth of defence, more machine-guns (concealed and strongly protected) and large quantities of hidden wire—had serious implications for consolidation. The nub of the tactical problem, in the absence of reliable communications, was how to quickly get fresh troops, and then their supplies, to the right place. Ever the realist, he thought it "over sanguine to expect that Staff work will run without mistakes under such conditions." Lipsett's recipe for success included limited objectives and movement in short bounds; continuous artillery support directed from forward and hardened observation posts (OPs); flanking attacks whenever possible; consolidation on either side of captured trenches but never in them; intense bombardment (not long bombardment, which simply warned the enemy); reserves at all levels; training, briefing and rehearsals before all attacks; and evening or night advances to lessen effects of enemy fire. He thought the best time to attack was four hours after dawn at the earliest and the later the better—two or three hours daylight in which to consolidate being adequate—considering that troops could work all night without being subject to observed fire. This was possible because *effective* fire then was *observed* fire. Many of his ideas featured in future operations.[52]

Other longer term assessments of operations included the compilations stressing the reasons for success or failure and the annual "Lessons Learned During the Year's Fighting." The 1917 Canadian edition of the latter is very impressive, with detailed answers to questions on organization, equipment, weapons, tactics, support by other arms, communications, transport and training. Its value lies not just in its content but in its revelation of the process and progress of learning throughout 1917.[53] Such assessments also highlight an inevitable aspect of the education of commanders: "Special value is to be gained by studying causes of failure." Inevitably, "we learn wisdom from failure much more than from success. We often discover what will do by finding out what will not do; and probably he who never made a mistake never made a discovery."[54]

Discoveries and mistakes also featured in modifying battalion organization, which challenged commanders throughout as much as the learning and passing on of lessons did. In February 1918 a lecturer at the Senior Officers' School, Aldershot, listed several reasons for difficulties in battalion organization: heavy casualties, insufficient replacements, the need for constant training, inexperience, and "extraction of men for outside work—Trench Mortars, Tunnelling Companies, etc., etc."[55] For battalion commanders and officers the loss of knowledge and skills and the reduction of fighting strength meant constant reorganization, as well as increased training to compensate for the loss of leaders; in addition, more training meant more trainers, thus further reducing unit strength.

The real point made by the lecturer concerned the integration of new weapons, part of a larger problem that worried commanders for most of the war-specialization. The very word conjured up narrowing of focus and detraction from team effort, especially that of the platoon, the basic organization of the Army. As early as July 1915, GOC 3rd Brigade (Turner) thought specialization excessive but its evils, which adversely affected organization, training and tactics, remained generally unrecognized for a time.[56] Backing the wrong horse, when it came to integrating technology, could have very serious consequences; the Ross rifle was the classic case. An example of the right horse is the mortar. For once, the soldier could not voice the old complaint that the weapon in his hands was the product of the lowest bid.[57]

Good examples of structural integration were artillery and engineer commands, which had so much to do with 1st Division's skill at arms and its achievements. Initially, some senior officers of these arms at Army, corps and division headquarters occupied a rather nebulous category. The senior divisional artillery officer (a brigadier-general), for example, seldom commanded or controlled but merely advised, despite his title of "Commander Royal Artillery" (CRA). This situation lasted until mid-1917 when he became GOC in the same sense as infantry brigadiers, with a staff and the authority to issue orders. Experience had shown the necessity

> for coordination and control in the artillery beyond that of Division, and that the position of the artillery advisors . . . was unsatisfactory and responsible for . . . friction and discord. An energetic performance of their duties infringed on the prerogatives of subordinate commanders and staffs, whilst a more retiring attitude resulted in their advice being either not sought for or ignored when tendered.[58]

The change, which enabled all guns within range to engage, was an improvement at least as important as the introduction of the tank, especially since the artillery's mission was to clear the way for the infantry.

The claim that German artillery was "fully integrated" as early as 1 March 1917, is invalid. For the Riga offensive in September 1917 "the necessity for a higher centralisation of [artillery] command was realised . . . As no artillery commander existed at Army H.Q. one had to be extemporised."[59] This innovation did not reach the Western Front until early 1918. Only then could German artillery be said to be fully integrated. Before that time, while it retained its technological superiority,

> one of the greatest advantages we had . . . was in organization . . . enemy artillery was invariably fought on a divisional front; as a consequence they experienced great difficulty in bringing to bear . . . an adequate volume of fire. So, too, [their] artillery intelligence was collected and coordinated on a divisional front and they experienced difficulty in passing this information quickly to adjoining formations . . . We, on the other hand, fought as a corps with the result that the whole force of our artillery was immediately available . . . and the whole of our intelligence system was centred on those [with] the means to take immediate and effective action.[60]

The Commander Royal Engineers (CRE) also began as a mere advisor. In theory, COs of field companies (in 1915 one per infantry brigade) reported directly to him, while they were responsible for the work done in their brigade areas. CRE was responsible for work in line with the divisional plan, a task of great difficulty since brigadiers differed about what to do and how: "One . . . holds a section for eight days and commences work which he considers necessary, then he is relieved by another . . . who holds different opinions, the result being new work is commenced and the previous tour's work is left incomplete and of little or no value.[61] Occasionally, CRE convinced the GOC that he should intervene. One brigade was admonished: "The GOC does not approve of dividing up small parties of sappers . . . If you have any special work . . . CRE will be instructed to . . . carry it out." It became policy that "Brigadiers or officers ordering RE [Royal Engineers] . . . will, where possible, give the order in writing and must be prepared to show that the situation was urgent enough for the issue of these orders."[62] Putting the Commander Royal Engineers on the same basis as the Commander Royal Artillery resolved many ambiguities.

Integration of Vickers machine-guns, Lewis guns and mortars was still a work in progress at the end of the war. From 1915 on the roles of the first two increasingly diverged.[63] The Lewis gun, said H.S. Horne, GOC First

Army, was the "battalion Machine-gun, and accompanies the Infantry"; but not the Vickers, because its role was different.[64] The Lewis gun, according to GOC 1st Brigade (Griesbach), was "not in the same class [being] only a fore-runner of the automatic rifle with which all ranks will one day be armed." [65] These opinions failed to still the clamour of the infantry for machine-guns.

The first issue of Vickers machine-guns (two and then four), to battalions seemed to confirm infantry ownership but by June 1915, machine-gun "experts" had sold their case that the Vickers was a new "fourth arm" requiring special tactics, training and organization that only those experts could provide. While it is cynical, perhaps, to say it, the usual motive for want-ing control of any weapon is control of the men who are to use it. Increased establishment means a larger promotion pyramid. This aspect would not have escaped the attention of infantry battalions, who are, by nature, suspicious. The selling point in the "expert" argument was that although machine-guns under the direct command of COs could act in close cooperation with units, close cooperation of machine-guns within the brigade was not usually possi-ble. Consequently, infantry units lost their Vickers to the new Machine-Gun Corps, which formed cavalry machine-gun squadrons, motor machine-gun batteries and infantry brigade machine-gun companies (16 Vickers each). All Canadian infantry brigades had a machine-gun company by February 1916.[66]

While the Vickers had shortcomings—its weight significantly reduced its mobility (this was obviously less critical in defence than in offence), and for most of the war "no proper appliances for night-firing" existed—technical deficiencies were not the primary reason for the separation of the Vickers from the infantry. In view of the scarcity of machine-guns in 1915, most brigade commanders concurred with the decision because they believed it would ensure the close cooperation of machine-guns on a brigade basis and enable the centralized control that would allow them to use the few available weapons to the best advantage. The shift of the weapons from infantry battalions to brigade machine-gun companies (these eventually were reorganized into machine-gun battalions) seemed to be the only option that would enable coordinated interlocking machine-gun defence. Moreover, as concentrations of enemy artillery fire grew more intense and protracted, it became clear that whole sections of trench and their garrisons could be blown out by such fire. Numbers of machine-guns grouped behind the for-ward trenches were a ready means to maintain brigade positions in the event of break-ins wrought by enemy artillery. Machine-gun companies, in short, could provide defence in depth at a low cost in manpower; in rough terms the fire of one machine-gun crewed by 10 men equalled the fire of 100 riflemen.[67]

At the time the advantages of brigading machine-guns seemed to out-weigh the disadvantages. Once brigaded, machine-guns could be fought on a brigade basis under the brigade machine-gun officer (BMGO), whose other major responsibility was to ensure machine-gunners were properly relieved and rested. This latter task was made easier because the new organization permitted the creation of a reserve. Prior to this, an infantry battalion going into rest usually left its machine-guns behind to support the incoming battalion; consequently, machine-gunners became exhausted, training suffered, and the battalions had constantly to learn new personalities and new ways. These problems had bedevilled the artillery until the formation of reserves in the form of the Army Field Artillery Brigades. On the other hand, the inadequate establishment of a machine-gun company meant that it could not supply, transport or feed itself, or even provide itself with sufficient ammunition, and consequently it relied upon infantry battalions for such support. A CO ordered to give his Vickers to somebody else, and then to fetch and carry to keep that somebody going, fell into a dark, even ugly, frame of mind.

To what extent the real impact of the decision to separate machine-guns from the infantry was realized at the time it was taken cannot be stated with certainty. What had occurred was the separation of firepower and assault power, which was a rejection of the idea that the infantry should have the weapons at hand to provide effective, immediate direct fire support, thereby giving it the means to overcome the enemy by its own integral resources. In short, firepower was not to be "a scalpel in the hands of the infantry." [68] It is not unreasonable to suggest that the separation was inhibiting and contradictory in the development of the all-arms concept of operations.

It may be that the real motive behind the organization of the machine-gun companies was not so much efficiency or improvement but mere economy. At the start of a war the country and the Army often find the cupboard bare due to the shortsightedness of politicians. As a result many men die, while the Army has no choice but to resort to what is most expedient. Had there been at the start a stock of machine-guns sufficient to give, say, 16, to each infantry battalion, then the question is, Would the infantry battalions— the heart of the fighting Army—have been stripped of theirs in order to form brigade machine-gun companies? Probably not.

The separation left each battalion with four Lewis guns (eight by the end of 1915), a weapon not universally welcome at first. While it is highly unlikely that the British Official Historian ever lugged one or fired one in anger, his assessment of it as "a cumbrous, heavy and not too reliable automatic rifle"[69] was shared by many who crewed it or had to depend upon its fire. One Lewis gun officer complained about its magazines being heavy and hard to refill. Another called it "a very shoddy affair after the Vickers."[70] But once the necessity for thorough cleaning was realized, and men became attuned to and trained on it, and effective fire and movement tactics had been worked out, its merits were recognized. By the end of 1916 each infantry platoon had one Lewis gun, and two by May 1918. All told, by mid-1918 1st Division had over 400 Lewis guns.

By April 1918 each Canadian division also had 96 Vickers, making a total of over 500 automatic weapons per division.[71] 1st Division had arrived in France in 1915 with four! By early 1916 divisions had 64 Vickers: 16 in each brigade machine-gun company and 16 in the divisional machine-gun company that joined the division in early 1917.[72] The addition of the last led "almost inevitably to the next step . . . a machine-gun battalion, a separate divisional unit independent of brigade authority."[73] Horne's recommendation, which had much to do with the decision to adopt a battalion structure, was supported, he said, "by a large proportion of the Divisional and Infantry Brigade Commanders." He believed the new machine-gun battalions enabled not only a more even distribution of tasks and fairer promotions but better control over training and discipline of machine-gunners. Training particularly concerned him. In his opinion infantry brigadiers and COs should understand the tactics of machine-guns but did not. Consequently, "the more the necessity for experts," in this case the divisional machine-gun officer (DMGO), who would ensure uniform training and best use of machine-guns.[74] Horne seems to have ignored one thing: if brigadiers had retained tactical control of their machine-guns they in their own interest would soon have attained greater proficiency in machine-gun use and they would have seen that their COs did, too.

In 1st Division Griesbach (1st Brigade) and Tuxford (3rd Brigade) favoured a machine-gun battalion.[75] Those opposed (including infantry COs) thought centralization would make the Vickers progressively more remote from the infantry, in much the same way that artillery had become more centralized and remote during the nineteenth century. As men were posted in from training centres in England the gulf between machine-gunners and infantry battalions widened. The new gunners knew nothing of the brigade to which they were attached and the brigades knew fewer and fewer of the machine-gunners, who came to be almost as remote as artillery gunners and sappers. Loss of understanding and knowledge often made cooperation much less than what the new organization was supposed to provide; it also led to a souring of relations.

Machine-gun company organization also posed serious dilemmas for the BMGO and later the DMGO. The June 1917 offensive at Ypres typified their difficulties. The elements of the brigade machine-gun companies ordered to accompany the assault came under the command of brigade commanders. The remainder of the brigade machine-gun companies and the divisional company were under the DMGO initially but later some sections came under direct brigade command. The DMGO had thus to command substantial elements and move others without the help of sufficient staff. The unfortunate brigade machine-gun company commanders had to serve two masters: "God and Mammon, the brigade and the DMGO; and there was grave danger of his holding to one and despising the other."[76] A system in which the officer responsible for discipline and training had no authority was a poor one. The desire to marry these was a contributing factor in the formation of machine-gun battalions.

Another factor, and one that drove a deep wedge between infanteers and machine-gunners, was the concept of using predicted indirect barrage fire against enemy rear areas. This could only be effective if groups of weapons were devoted to the task. A single Vickers' beaten zone (the area within which 75 percent of its fire will fall at a given range) was at 1,000 yards about 300 yards long by five yards wide. As the range increased to 2,000 yards, the zone shortened and widened, being 70 or so yards long and about seven yards wide. At longer ranges the trajectory also became much steeper, making the fire more effective against troops in shell-hole defences.[77] Consequently, machine-gun experts desired massed indirect machine-gun fire.

Indirect fire's earliest and most influential exponents were George Lindsay and Raymond Brutinel. Lindsay first articulated the idea of "long-range searching fire." He originally called it "long-range annoyance fire," but ceased using that term probably because it seemed to hint that the fire was of nuisance value only. By August 1915 he was recommending the idea of indirect, overhead predicted and plunging fire. Brutinel, however, was the "true father of the machine gun barrage."[78] When it came to the planning and conduct of attacks, the question was, "what could the machine-gun companies (and battalions) do?" The answer was, support attacks by providing indirect, overhead fire, thereby thickening the artillery barrage—and even replacing it should the infantry get beyond the range of artillery, which could not move forward as quickly as machine-guns. Brutinel planned and executed the first such barrages in September 1915, another in early 1916 and yet another at Courcelette in September 1916. Thereafter such barrages routinely featured in Canadian attacks and the idea was taken up by many Imperial formations.

One major problem with the concept of indirect fire was the lack of adequate communications. Machine-gunners were often unaware of immediate situations confronting the troops they were supporting and could only fire according to pre-arranged timetables, or in response to a visual SOS. This inflexibility inhibited support. The more serious problem, however, was the difficulty, and usually the impossibility, of observing indirect fire. As one Canadian machine-gunner said, "Indirect fire is not very satisfactory—you cannot see your target and, of course, do not know what damage, if any, is done."[79] Given the state of target acquisition at the time, luck played a major part in indirect fire, and in view of communication shortcomings, not much could be done to provide timely damage assessments. Many infantry officers considered indirect barrage fire a distraction from more immediately useful direct fire support. Indirect fire did fray enemy nerves and morale and produced some casualties but as one machine-gun officer concluded, "The general result must be regarded as probably considerable but certainly incalcuable."[80] In short, machine-guns would have been better used directly, a conclusion with which few would disagree today.

The separation of infantry and machine-guns also created personnel problems. Many Regimental officers saw postings to machine-guns as career inhibiting.[81] Other Ranks were as reluctant. The CO of 4th Battalion, for example, found that "good men were disinclined to transfer . . . as they thought they lost their chances of promotion."[82] COs could usually see the need for good men to be sent to the machine-gun companies but company and platoon commanders often succumbed to the temptation to send their worst.[83] Even the best of intentions lost something in the translation: Currie ordered Macdonell to provide 50 of the "best and brainiest men" to the Machine Gun Corps, Macdonell told Griesbach to send 50 of the "best"; his BM simply told battalions to select "50 men."[84]

Despite all this, in time machine-gunners built a strong company spirit and a feeling of superiority took hold, sometimes excessively so, as the following report from the CO of 2nd Battalion shows:

> An urgent letter was received from brigade attaching extracts from a letter received from the OC 3rd Brigade Machine-Gun Company. These extracts are detrimental to the soldierly qualities of the 2nd Canadian Battalion and are attached. This officer is being asked if he has any further observations to make. His reply will also be attached.[85]

This was indicative of a situation in which machine-guns inevitably

> like so many other self-proclaimed elites, tried to portray itself as an ardently innovative and professional body at the same time as it had to fight a continuous—and losing—battle against infantry regiments who wanted to draft their worst, rather than their best, men into it. In practise, it was not quite as elite as it liked to make out, yet [it] always clung stubbornly to an elusive sense of its own importance.[86]

Martin Samuels rightly believes that the creation of the Machine-Gun Corps may have improved technical efficiency but the separation of machine-guns from the infantry was too high a price to pay. Captain J.C. Dunn spoke for many when he called division of the command of infantry weapons an "insane act." It was not reversed until after the war, "although *from August 1918 onwards a Machine-Gun Section was attached to each infantry battalion and acted under the orders of its O.C.*"[87] Loomis of 2nd Brigade, the only Brigadier in 1st Division opposed to machine-gun battalions, could take some credit for this:

> The Machine Gun is an Infantry weapon, and its employment in warfare cannot be separated from the Infantry with success.
>
> Machine Guns cannot be handled in the fight by a formation higher than the Battalion, successfully.
>
> Barrage fire is not the normal function of the Machine Gun in warfare but it is, however, a very valuable tactical use for the weapon in actions for a limited objective or position warfare.
>
> Barrage fire is therefore secondary and the true function of the Machine Gun should not be misunderstood because we are and have been employed in position and trench warfare.
>
> Every Machine Gunner should be an Infantryman. A Rifleman first and a Machine Gunner second: he should be a part of the organization of the Battalion. If the Machine Guns were . . . it would be quite easy to assemble them under Brigade for barrage fire or to group them under Division or under Corps for the same purpose.
>
> The present Machine Guns should be divided among the Battalions. Each Battalion should have a Machine Gun Officer and a Machine Gun Section. Any other system, such as Machine Gun Companies, with Brigade or Machine Gun Battalions with Division or Corps, give rise to so many difficulties of transport, supply, administration, tactical control and communications that the force would not be effective in a fight and will, in fact, become an obstacle and may be the cause of failure.
>
> I consider that no Machine Gun Officer is needed at Brigade, Division or Corps. The regular Staff should be able to handle the Machine Guns, both in training and tactically, if sound principles are not departed from in organization. Staffs are now so overloaded with specialists, personnel, fancy formations and paraphernalia that the Army could not move or fight for twenty five miles. [88]

Loomis's ideas have been quoted in their entirety because they offer timeless truths whose wisdom was not generally seen by others until the last summer of the war.

Another close support weapon, the trench mortar, began to come onstream in 1916. By May each Canadian brigade had one battery (eight light Stokes three-inch mortars).[89] These light mortars and the artillery's medium and heavy mortars were referred to as "unwelcome" for three reasons: they were inaccurate, often falling in friendly trenches where they killed just as surely as enemy fire; they had an irritating habit of going into action at the same time as tired men were trying to recoup the sleep lost the night before on some working party or other; and they drew retaliatory fire.[90] The enemy was of similar mind: *Leutnant* Ernst Junger complained bitterly that mortars, having fired and annoyed the enemy, skedaddled, leaving the infantry to "meet the bill as usual." [91] Everyone soon realized, however, that mortars excelled at producing casualties. Loomis emphasized this: "Experience . . . confirms . . . that the brigade batteries should be doubled in strength . . . No troops can come through a proper trench mortar barrage and no trenches under continuous bombardment by them can long remain tenable."[92] Experience also revealed the shortcomings of insufficient battery strength. With only 4 officers and 46 other ranks a battery required outside assistance for transport, digging parties, and ammunition carriers. Open warfare, which demanded continuous rapid movement, marginalized the fighting value of the light battery.[93] The obvious solution, to increase battery strength, was impossible. GOC 1st Division (Macdonell) supported Griesbach's proposal to give each battalion two Stokes mortars on establishment. Loomis wanted to do with trench mortars exactly what he had proposed to do with the brigade machine-gun companies: "That two Stokes guns and one quarter of the personnel be transferred to each infantry battalion in the brigade, becoming an integral part of the Battalion."[94] If anyone had grasped the necessity for an infantry battalion to be a balanced, all-arms team capable of providing its own close support, Loomis and Griesbach had. Their ideas about mortars and machine-guns strike a modern chord.

Individual weapons such as hand and rifle grenades had also to be integrated, a task not as straightforward as it sounds. The battalion in 1914, whose sole weapons specialists were the crews of the Vickers, gradually became a very complex entity with a wide range of weapons and specialists. By early 1916 all was not well in the sense of organization. Some of the more difficult questions were: What is the place of the specialist? What should be the division of responsibility between company and specialist officers? What should the battalion HQ look like? What blend of weapons will make the battalion most effective tactically? Perhaps the central question was, how can unit interior economy (which had been disturbed by detachments and specialists) be re-established? The answers to these questions had to restore "drive" to units and maximize the "manoeuvring and attacking power of the platoon and company."[95]

Detachments, whether specialists or "employed men," reduced fighting strength. The former included Lewis gunners, bombers (battalion and company), signallers, runners, snipers, scouts and instructors. Employed men, defined as men "on duties other than the above" and ammunition carriers, either lived with and were rationed by their battalions or they were detached away but remained on battalion strength, which meant they could not be replaced by reinforcements; this regulation satisfied accountants but not battalions, for it meant that holes could not be filled.[96] Detachments eventually reduced "the platoon to a mere skeleton . . . 15 or 20 riflemen . . . without the weapons . . . to develop its full power. In these circumstances . . . the Platoon organization has become practically a dead letter."[97]

The best account of the injury that specialization inflicted upon the company and the platoon as fighting entities comes courtesy of the historian of the 16th Battalion, who saw the issue as being how to accommodate the "stormy petrels [whose] selection . . . for special duty brought strife, and [whose] entrance into the battalion interior economy caused more trouble." These petrels, "the cause of most, if not all, of the trouble which centred around the specialists," were the bombers who ended the long-standing principle that all infanteers carry the same weapon. Bombers even wore a special badge to set them apart. On return from training they exercised "lordship" over the companies. OCs were deemed to know nothing of bombing tactics and were not to "tamper" with bombs in any way, or assign bombers other duties.[98] This left the battalion bombing officer, a subaltern, in charge, much to the displeasure of OCs, who quite rightly demanded, "Who fights the company front anyway?" The bombing officer, "hitherto a despised underling, popularly (but maliciously) reputed to have been appointed . . . through inability to handle a platoon," had become a star, the confidant of COs, BMs and GOsC.[99] As more and more men became trained bombers, "The rifle was neglected, the infantry was almost reduced to the power of a strong right arm."[100] Soon the bomb had ascended to a factitious position entirely out of proportion to its real value. One report told of a soldier who followed a solitary German for half a mile at a distance of 300 yards trying to get close enough to bomb him, ignoring completely his rifle which could have done the job nicely! 2nd Brigade, in its final report on the Somme, mentioned this exact sort of amnesia, remarking that bombs had often been used when the rifle would have done better. [101]

One Imperial subaltern—he could just as easily have been Canadian since the loss of detailed or detached men sapped Canadian fighting strength just as surely as it did British—eloquently described the impact of specialization at platoon level:

I once had a lovely platoon, sir,
The finest platoon ever seen,
They could drill 'neath the sun, or the moon, sir,
They were fit, and their rifles were clean.

They could march, and they knew how to shoot, sir,
And to bayonet sacks upon sticks, sir,
Equipped from the cap to the boot, sir,
—Their number was fifty-and-six.

They were infantry right to the core, sir,
They trusted in bullets and steel
To finish the terrible war, sir,
—It bucked them all up a good deal.

But as soon as we landed in France, sir,
Such terrible changes began
That hardly a man had a chance, sir,
Of being an Infantry man.

For some for the transport have left, sir,
And one cuts up beef for the Staff,
And others, of whom I'm bereft, sir,
Mend trousers that suffer from "STRAFE".

There are some who are Sanit'ry men, sir,
—(We tread upon dubious paths)—
And some became sappers, and then, sir,
They lived among boilers and baths.

The M.G.C. pinched a few more, sir,
—And blood-thirsty beggars they be—
They're especially out for the gore, sir,
Of Huns that are carrying tea.

One's running a photograph show, sir,
Another is making a map,
There are servants and grooms, one or two, sir,
They all leave a bit of a gap.

There are some who are officers now, sir,
While others wield clippers and shave,
There are bandsmen all under a vow, sir,
To hearten the steps of the brave.

> *The few that remain use the bomb, sir,*
> *Proficient in anarchist lore,*
> *They handle H.E. with aplomb, sir,*
> *I look on with obvious awe.*
>
> *If my men are all details am I, sir,*
> *A detail myself! and if so,*
> *Am I O.C. Platoon still, and why, sir,*
> *Is what I should just like to know.*[102]

Men employed away or at battalion HQ often added up to about 200 men, one-fifth of battalion establishment. Since units were never up to strength, the actual reduction always exceeded one-fifth. In February 1917 GHQ estimated a loss in fighting power of about 3,500 men per division across the BEF. As Radcliffe said, "the calls [for] men for every sort of extra regimental employment . . . are the bug-bear of a Battalion Commander."[103] Commanding a battalion got harder every day. GHQ first sought to reduce the loss. "By a careful application of the regulations under which reinforcements may be demanded . . . by pooling, and by rigorous combing-out, it should be possible to reduce this number so that it does not exceed an average of 150 men per battalion." This initiative restored over 1,800 fighting men to each division. Then to maximize the number of fighters, as opposed to administrators, GHQ limited the strength of unit and sub-unit HQs, and set guidelines for company and platoon strength, specifying for the latter a minimum of 28 and a maximum of 44. Then the specialists, "the intruders, who used to dictate to company men . . . were shorn of their privileges by absorption into the companies." Their privileges had incensed company men to the point where the very word "specialist" raised hackles. First Army ordered it eliminated because the proficient rifleman was equally a specialist, and Lewis gunnery, bombing and rifle bombing were, like musketry and bayonet fighting, "Skill at Arms" rather than specialist training.[104] What GHQ was after was an all-arms fighting platoon, the specialists restored to their platoons and companies, the rifle and bayonet as the most important weapons, and every soldier available to work and carry regardless of his weapon.[105]

An even more complex challenge was achieving the best combination of the four platoon elements (and weapons): riflemen (Lee-Enfield rifle), rifle grenadiers (rifle grenades), bombers (hand grenades) and Lewis gunners (one Lewis gun, later two). The whole process was one of experimentation. When remodelling began in late 1916 and early 1917 Canadian Corps HQ offered as a guide a platoon of one officer and 48 ORs in four sections: two 13-man mixed rifle and rifle grenade sections, one 12-man Lewis gun section and a 9-man bomb (hand grenade) section; plus platoon HQ consisting of only the platoon commander and the platoon sergeant. This is odd because Corps, while extolling the supreme importance of the platoon commander, had not provided him with a headquarters that could sustain him in command. At this time the all-arms concept could not extend to sections because a platoon had only one Lewis gun. Also, the combination of riflemen and rifle grenadiers caused a mixture of weapons that were not complementary.[106] Another oddity about the model is the separation of *hand* grenades (bombs) and *rifle* grenades, despite several editions of "Notes on the Somme Fighting" that recommended "every bombing squad must be furnished with a proportion of Mills Rifle Grenades and Rifle Smoke bombs [for] keeping enemy bombers at a distance and blinding machine-guns or Strong Points."[107]

Canadian divisions enjoyed considerable discretion in platoon organization, the only limitations being that establishments be uniform in each division, efforts to train platoon commanders be redoubled and every rifleman be trained as a bomber, rifle grenadier or Lewis gunner. 1st Division made the Corps guide an order: "This is the organization GOC 1st Division wishes tested and put into operation at once." It also moved the rifle grenadiers to the bombing section, giving the platoon a Lewis gun section, two rifle sections and a grenade (hand and rifle) section, for a total of one officer and 40 ORs. Two men were added to Platoon HQ, thereby making it a sustainable entity. A week later, incorporating brigade suggestions, 1st Division increased platoon strength to 43 ORs. On 10 January Corps authorized all four divisional platoon establishments.[108] Thus, the Canadian Corps had created an all-arms platoon that made integrated tactics possible for the first time. The BGGS (Radcliffe) later wrote that the new platoon "was adopted early in the winter [of 1916/1917] . . . some six weeks before the G.H.Q. instructions on the subject were issued. The actual details . . . consequently varied from those laid down by G.H.Q. but the guiding principles were the same."[109]

In February 1st Division conformed to the organization in *SS 144 The Normal Formation for the Attack*, with standard nine-man sections and specialization by section: No. 1 Section, bombers; No. 2 Section, riflemen; No. 3 Section, rifle grenadiers; and No. 4 Section, Lewis gunners. Platoon HQ included the OC, the platoon Sergeant, a batman and a runner. Platoon strength of one officer and 39 ORs increased on 23 February by the addition of one man to each of Sections Nos. 1, 2 and 3, giving the platoon a strength of 42 ORs. Thus, the platoon comprised

Platoon HQ—OC, platoon Sergeant, batman, runner
No. 1 Section (Grenade)—NCO, eight bombers, one sniper
No. 2 Section (Rifle)—NCO, nine riflemen
No. 3 Section (Rifle Grenadier)—NCO, eight grenadiers, one rifleman
No. 4 Section (Lewis gun)—NCO, five gunners, three riflemen

Lt Gen Sir E.A.H. Alderson, first
GOC 1st Division, awards the
Distinguished Conduct Medal to
Lance Corporal Frank Cox, 10th
Battalion, for his part in a raid on
4/5 February 1916.
(LAC PA-005592)

Lt Gen Sir Arthur Currie, second
GOC of 1st Division and later GOC
Canadian Corps. June 1917.
(LAC PA-001370)

GOC Canadian Corps and Senior Staff Officers. l–r: Brig Gen J.G. Farmar, DA & QMG; Brig Gen P.P. deB. Radcliffe, BGGS; Lt Gen Sir J.H.G. Byng, GOC. May 1917. (LAC PA-001259)

Visit of His Majesty King George V to Canadian Corps, August 1916. From the right: Lt Col J.H. MacBrien; Lt Col R.J.F. Hayter, BM 1st Brigade; Brig Gen J.H. Elmsley, GOC 8th Brigade; Brig Gen F.W. Hill, formerly CO 1st Battalion; Lt Col G.S. Kearsley, GSO1 1st Division; Lt Col G.R.Frith, AA & QMG 1st Division; Lt Col N.W. Webber, GSO1 2nd Division; Colonel P.E. Thacker, CRA 1st Division; Brig Gen H.D.B. Ketchen, GOC 6th Brigade; Brig Gen R. Rennie, GOC 4th Brigade and formerly CO 3rd Battalion; Lt Sir B.S. Brooke; Colonel G.L. Foster; Brig Gen P.P. deB. Radcliffe, BGGS; Brig Gen A.C. Currie; Brig Gen W.D. Lindsay, Chief Engineer,Canadian Corps; Brig Gen J.G. Farmar, DA & QMG; HM The King; Lt Gen J.H.G. Byng, GOC Canadian Corps; Brig Gen H.E. Burstall, CRA Canadian Corps; Lt Col A.E.G. Mackenzie, CO 26th Battalion. (LAC PA-000582)

Maj Gen Sir Archibald Macdonell,
GOC 1st Division, June 1917 to
Armistice.
(W.J. Topley/LAC PA-042974)

Maj Gen Sir Archibald Macdonell and Staff, 1st Division, April 1918. Front row, l–r: Lt
E.D.P. Hardy; Hon Lt Col F.G. Scott, Senior Divisional Padre; Capt. W.W. Mitchell; Lt
J.M. Macdonell; Capt. E.G. Palmer; Maj F.R. Phelan; Maj C.G. Saunders. Centre row, l–r:
Maj W.D. Wedd, GSO2; Lt Col J.L.R. Parsons, GSO1; Brig Gen H.C. Thacker, CRA; Maj
Gen Macdonell; Lt Col J. Sutherland Brown, AA & QMG; Col R.P. Wright; Lt Col H.H.
Matthews, GSO2. Back row, l–r: Capt J.D. Paterson; Maj J.C. de Bolinhard; Capt J.A.G.
White; Lt P. Gilou; Lt Col H.F.H. Hertzberg; Maj C.H. Vandersluys; Maj P. Hennessey;
Maj B.W. Brown; Maj G.K. Killam; Maj O.H. Mabee; Col G.P. Templeton; Capt T.H.
Plumer. (LAC PA-002620)

Brig Gen F.O.W. Loomis, GOC 2nd Brigade (centre front) and Staff, Passchendaele, November 1917. Note the regimental badges on some helmets. (LAC PA-002179)

Brig Gen G.B. Hughes, Lt Gen Sir R.E.W. Turner and Maj P.F. Villiers (right). (LAC C 002072092, in Villiers Papers, MG 30E 236, vol. 4)

Brig Gen George Tuxford (centre front) and Staff, 3rd Brigade, December 1918.
(LAC PA-003790)

Lt Gen Sir R.E.W. Turner,
GOC 3rd Brigade until
August 1915.
(LAC PA-006315)

Brig Gen W.A. Griesbach, GOC 1st Brigade, February 1917 to February 1919.
(LAC PA-007298)

Brig Gen F.O.W. Loomis (left) and Brig Gen George Tuxford, commanders 3rd Brigade,
March 1916 to March 1918 and March 1918 to Armistice. (LAC PA-007580)

GOC and Staff, 2nd Brigade, June 1916. Front row, l–r: Capt W.H. Collum; Capt P. MacKenzie. Centre, l–r: Maj J.M. Prower, BM September 1915 to August 1916 and CO 8th Battalion September 1916 to April 1918; Brig Gen L.J. Lipsett, Maj B.M. Humble, Acting CO 7th Battalion in June, 1916. Back row, l–r: Capt H.W. Harbord; Lt H.E. Knobel; Capt G. Norton; Maj T.H. Raddall, CO 8th Battalion April to August 1918, KIA. (LAC PA-000048)

GOC 1st Brigade and Staff, July 1916. To the right of Brig Gen G.B. Hughes (centre front) is his BM, Maj H.F. McDonald, who was wounded September 1916 and replaced temporarily by Maj P.F. Villiers. (LAC PA-000352)

GOC and Staff, 2nd Brigade, April 1918. Seated, l–r: Maj R.H. Winslow; Capt H.D. Ives;
Capt R.J. Paget. Centre, l–r: Lt S.C. Graham, Maj J.P. MacKenzie, BM; Brig Gen F.O.W.
Loomis; Capt E.H.L. Johnson, Capt E.L. Brown. Back row, l–r: Lt H.W. Dawson; Capt
Grant; Lt M. de Bishop. (LAC PA-002636)

Battalion Commanders, 3rd Brigade, December 1918. l–r: Lt Col D. Worrall, 14th
Battalion; Lt Col C.E.Bent, 15th Battalion; Lt Col C.W. Peck, 16th Battalion; Lt Col K.M.
Perry, 13th Battalion. Worrall is the only non-Highlander. (LAC PA-003788)

These changes reflect increased emphasis on the rifle grenade, the platoon "howitzer."[110] So popular did it become that the expenditure of bombs rose dramatically. One officer in 5th Battalion fired 258 in one night in early 1916.[111]

What is obvious about this new "Battle Platoon" is its elasticity: "The various sections can be formed up to suit the task they have to undertake."[112] Second, the platoon now had the capacity for mutual support. Third, standardized battle platoons greatly simplified training in the field and at the schools and lessened the time required to adjust to operations and commanders. The most striking point is that the platoon had only *one* rifle section, a situation that surely marks the apogee of specialization. This worried many Regimental officers, one of whom commented with words that usually describe the path of a disease: "By this time specialization had run its course through our armies."[113]

After Vimy, First Army sought opinions on the worth of the new platoon. The four battalions of 1st Brigade applied the following adjectives to it: satisfactory, effective, very satisfactory, excellent. 4th Battalion also noted how the new ability of platoon commanders to resolve difficulties by themselves enhanced their self-confidence. The other two brigades were equally keen on the new platoon. 14th Battalion called it a "thoroughly well balanced fighting body," while the 8th thought it had given platoon commanders a much greater sense of responsibility and offered more tactical flexibility. 5th Battalion suggested strengthening the Lewis gun section so more ammunition could be carried.[114] Currie was

> perfectly convinced that our success was greater and . . . more easy of accomplishment by the adoption of that organization. Every advantage claimed for it was fully proven by results. It developed in . . . Platoon Commanders initiative, resourcefulness, and a more intimate knowledge of the power of the weapons . . . It gave the men greater confidence in their ability to overcome any resistance . . . while the cooperation of these arms was more thoroughly understood and practised than would otherwise have been the case.

Later, more experience having accrued, he called the new platoon

> a great success . . . all four sections of the platoon, the Lewis gunner, the Riflemen, the Bomber and the Rifle Grenadier were used to their fullest extent in close cooperation with each other and with neighbouring platoons. This organization had enforced a higher training of the Platoon Commander and had demonstrated to him his responsibilities and the capabilities of the various arms with which his men are now equipped.[115]

As for the weapons themselves, the wheel had come full circle. Pre-war and early war handiness and reliance on the rifle—the Regular in 1914 could get off 15 *aimed* rounds a minute—had been lost. Territorials, men of the New Army and men of the Dominions had not that skill at arms and could not achieve it in trench warfare. Thus, the rifle had given way to the cult of the bomb. In the hard light of experience, though, the rifle began to re-assert itself. First Army told its Corps in May 1917 that "trench warfare has undoubtedly had the effect of lessening the confidence of the British soldier in his rifle and no effort should be spared in the endeavour to approach the very high standard of the original Expeditionary Force."[116] The place of the rifle had become clear:

> *Alf is old as a soldier goes,*
> *With hair that is rapidly turning grey;*
> *Ever since Mons he has strafed our foes*
> *In his own cool, calm, methodical way.*
> *He learned to shoot on a Surrey range,*
> *His aim is steady and quick and true.*
> *'Bombs,' says Alf, 'are good for a change,*
> *But it's the rifle will pull you through.'*[117]

During the war the infantry had evolved through four stages: *just* infantry, the rise of specialists, the decline of specialists, and INFANTRY writ large. According to Liddell Hart, "the key to the problem was simply the old master key adapted to the new lock," or, as the Chief of the Imperial General Staff (CIGS) said in 1927, "You will remember what happened in the late war; we jumped to one conclusion after another and in the end . . . came back to what . . . had been taught at the beginning—the use of the rifle." [118]

In the autumn of 1917 divisions were asked again if the platoon was satisfactory and, if not, what alterations were required. 1st Division, showing that the problem of detachments discussed above had not been solved, complained that it was difficult to field a platoon 30 strong: with casualties, strength fell to 20 or even 15, at which point the new organization became unworkable. The 1st offered no solution (divisions did not control unit establishments) but suggested that the grenade section be replaced by another rifle section, giving the platoon two rifle sections, a rifle grenade section and a Lewis gun section. As a basic principle 1st Division argued that every man must be a rifleman first, and a Lewis gunner, rifle grenadier or bomber second. In open and semi-open operations, where rifle and bayonet would dominate, Griesbach of 1st Brigade saw no need for separate rifle grenadier and bomber sections. He was not alone in this. The CO of 4th Battalion, A.J. Thomson, wondered whether an entirely new style of platoon would be required for open warfare. The former GOC 2nd Brigade (Lipsett) thought that because the platoon had frequently to be divided for manoeuvre, each of its sections should be self-contained. Flexibility would be greatly improved if the platoon were reduced to three sections: two 14-man mixed sections (riflemen, rifle grenadiers, bombers) and one 8-man Lewis gun section. "The object," he said, "is a uniform method of arming all Infantry other than Lewis guns . . . as soon as the . . . soldier can be trained in all branches of Infantry work."[119] As always, Lipsett was forward-thinking.

These reports had hardly gone forward when some Imperial divisions went to a three-section platoon: one Lewis gun section and two equally sized sections composed of riflemen, rifle grenadiers and bombers. The Canadian Corps complied but not for long. By May 1918 the Corps, left untouched by the great German spring offensive, was about to return to a four-section platoon. 1st Division sought the opinions of brigadiers who in turn asked the COs what they thought it should look like.[120] The consensus (two rifle sections and two Lewis gun sections) was implemented and retained until the Armistice. Canadian battalions also adhered to the four-platoon company. George Tuxford, GOC 3rd Brigade, when asked by one of his COs in October to permit reorganization on a three-platoon basis, emphasized the numerous substantial tactical reasons against such an idea: "I would like to point out the idea of 'four' . . . four platoons, four companies, four battalions and the principles governing firing line, support and reserve . . . relief and relations with neighbouring formations."[121] And so the 4-4-4 Canadian battalion finished out the war. Had sufficient Lewis guns been available earlier many officers might have proposed a platoon of three (or perhaps four) sections, each containing a manoeuvre element of men trained to rifle and bayonet, and rifle and hand grenade, and a fire element called the Lewis gun group; in short, they might well have arrived at the modern all-arms platoon consisting of three equally sized all-arms sections.

This chapter has highlighted the most significant command and control challenges facing 1st Division commanders which were precursors to and concomitant with their basic responsibility of conducting operations. The commanders proved their ability to learn and teach the hard lessons of war; they integrated machine-guns, mortars and other weapons as effectively as possible given the direction from above and the technological limitations; and they solved the dilemmas posed by specialization, in the end making the platoon a balanced all-arms fighting organization. Their endeavours in these areas established and maintained the foundation of 1st Division's capacity for combat and its reputation for effectiveness. The next chapter examines the proof of the pudding: their conduct of operations.

Notes to Chapter Three

1. Major-General Chris Vokes, *Vokes My Story* (Ottawa: Gallery Books, 1985), pp. 184, 186. Vokes was GOC 1st Division in Italy in 1943.

2. LAC, Canadian Corps General Staff War Diary, June 1916, Appendix II. The term "grouping" does not appear to have been used during the Great War. It is not in either edition of *Notes for Commanding Officers*, or in *FSR*. What appears instead in most orders is a list of attachments and detachments in the "Intention" section, usually under the heading "Preliminary Moves."

3. The military art applies to three levels: strategic, concerning national and theatre-level groupings of operational formations; operational, involving the Army and corps levels of command; and tactical, entailing combat at division and below. Strategic relates to campaigns, operational to the conduct of operations within a campaign, and tactical to the conduct of combat action within an operation.

4. LAC, RG9IIIC1, Vol. 3843, Folder 44, File 1. On the Somme in 1916 a company frontage, typically, was 150 yards. A battalion occupied 300 or so yards.

5. Charles Carrington, *Soldier from the Wars Returning* (London: Hutchinson, 1965), pp. 87–88.

6. LAC, RG9IIIC1, Vol. 3861, Folder 90, File 3. In the event of decimation LOB (left-out-of-battle) personnel could reform the unit. In September 1916, LOB policy said that not more than 20 officers per battalion would accompany the attack and 15 percent of Senior NCOs and specialists would be LOB. A year later (RG9IIIC3, Vol. 4061, Folder 8, File 2) the policy was that not more than 21 officers would take part in an attack, including either the CO or the 2IC, and either the OC or 2IC of each company, but not more than two OCs in all. Also, 108 ORs were LOB per battalion. LOB policy is detailed in *SS 135 Instructions for the Training of Divisions for Offensive Action* (London: HMSO, December 1916 and February 1918), p. 58. The contemporary term for LOB was the "nucleus."

7. LAC, RG41B, CBC interview. Cartwright served as Aide-de-Camp to three GOsC. Lt.-Gen. E.L.M. Burns, *General Mud Memoirs of Two World Wars* (Toronto: Clarke, Irwin and Company Limited, 1970), p. 75.

8. Reginald H. Roy, ed., *The Journal of Private Fraser, 1914–1918, Canadian Expeditionary Force* (Victoria: Sono Nis Press, 1985), p. 160.

9. For senior commanders in 1st Division and the Canadian Corps see Appendix V. LAC, MG30E100 (Currie Papers), Vol. 37, File 166, "Organization of the Canadian Corps in the Field," 15 June 1918, p. 3. For matters of operations and discipline the Canadian forces in the field were under the Commander-in-Chief. For matters of organization and administration the Canadian Government retained responsibility, but because such matters frequently bear on operations and discipline (and vice versa) these were coordinated by Canadian authorities and GHQ.

10. LAC, RG9IIID3, Vol. 4813, Corps General Staff War Diary, June 1916; Colonel Terry Cave, "The Canadian Corps Order of Battle," *Stand To!* 24 (Winter 1988): pp. 11–12. No permanent changes of battalions within 1st and 2nd Divisions were made, but 3rd and 4th Divisions experienced such changes.

11. Major-General A.C. Duff, *Sword and Pen: Some Problems of a Battledress Army* (Aldershot: Gale and Polden Limited, 1950), p. 9. Duff was paraphrasing two lines from "In Memoriam" by E.A. MacIntosh, *Up the Line to Death: The War Poets, 1914–1918*, edited by Brian Gardner (London: Methuen, 1976), p. 95).

12. "An Officer's Code," *Canadian Defence Quarterly* 3 (July 1926): 479. With the exception of the word "Temporary" in the upper right corner and the designation of the component of the forces into which the officer was commissioned, the wording of the King's Commission, 1914–1918, is identical to today's Queen's Commission. For an example of a Temporary Commission see Malcolm Brown, *Tommy Goes to War* (London: J.M. Dent & Sons Ltd., 1978), p. 20. When Clifford Wells was commissioned as a lieutenant in June 1916, he told his parents in a letter that "As an officer, I have now no Regimental Number." (Wallace, ed., *From Montreal to Vimy Ridge and Beyond*, p. 71). He did have a new metal officer's identity disc, having turned in his fibreboard one. Decades passed before Canadian officers were given numbers. The post-Second World War individual number for an officer commenced with a "Z" (indicating officer), then a letter designating his province and finally a few or several numbers. Numbers assigned today make no distinction between officers and men.

13. LAC, RG9IIIC3, Vol. 4024, Folder 3, File 4, Griesbach to COs, 24 July 1917.

14. Nicholson, *Behind the Lines*, p. 48.

15. LAC, RG9IIIC3, Vol. 4077, Folder 3, File 13, 14 September 1918.

16. Nicholson, *Behind the Lines*, p. 223. This comment applies to any Army. Using the figures in Appendix C, Tables 1 and 3, in Nicholson, *Official History of the Canadian Army*, pp. 546–48, roughly one in every eight CEF officers died due to enemy action. For ORs the ratio is 1 in 13. As was pointed out in the Introduction to this present book, roughly 85 out of every 100 casualties were infantry.

17. LAC, MG30E100 (Currie Papers), Vol. 2, General Correspondence (S–Z), letter of 8 March 1918.

18. Urquhart, *History of the 16th Battalion*, pp. 96–97; LAC, MG30E100 (Currie Papers), Vol. 15, Folder 43. Currie, who was not impressed with the leadership of either Leckie brother, thought Urquhart's portrayal of them overly generous.

19. Tuxford, "The Great War as I Saw It," p. 64. The other COs in 2nd Brigade agreed that if Currie became a casualty, Lipsett should command, even though he was not the senior CO.

20. Will R. Bird, *Ghosts Have Warm Hands* (Nepean, Ontario: CEF Books, 1997), pp. 14–15.

21. "Major-General Louis James Lipsett, CB, CMG," p. 299.

22. LAC, RG 41, Vol. 8, CBC interview with Major C. Smellie, 8th Battalion. Smellie thought that Lipsett departed for another reason. Smellie claimed to have been told by Victor Odlum (2IC and then CO of the 7th Battalion) that Lipsett was "a little put-out and a little jealous" when Currie got the Corps. Lipsett had apparently said to Odlum that he was more experienced, and had it been a "straight forward thing," he would have gotten the Corps. According to Smellie's account, Odlum told Lipsett "You know perfectly well that you couldn't . . . For obvious reasons, the Corps commander . . . had to be a Canadian and nothing else could have been done." Smellie's personal opinion and that "of the troops that I knew" was that Lipsett should have gotten the Corps because while Currie "had the ability to keep good men around him . . . I don't think he had anything to write home about." Mutual jealousy may well have played a part in Lipsett's departure. Certainly, Lipsett had all the qualities that would have made him a fine Corps commander, but we can only speculate about how he would have done. The fact that he was given a Regular division indicates that Haig thought highly of him.

23. Military Advisory Board, *Canada in the Great World War: An Authentic Account of the Military History of Canada from the Earliest Days to the Close of the War of the*

Nations, Vol. III, *Guarding the Channel Ports* (Toronto: United Publishers of Canada Limited, 1919). Pages 91–92 discuss the dangers attending bilingualism in an infantry battalion. LAC, RG 24, Vol. 1828, GAQ 7–21, contains Currie's recommendation and Marshall's report. According to his Service Record (LAC) Fisher was "permitted to resign" from the Army in February 1917. Tuxford, "The Great War as I Saw It," p. 153; LAC, MG30E236 (Villiers Papers), Vol. 4, Folder 7, Vol 1, pp. 58–59, Diary of Major P.F. Villiers; RG9IIIC3, Vol. 4008, Folder 6, File 8, Record of Courts Martial in 1st Division. In the year from July 1915 to July 1916, the 14th Battalion had the highest rate of desertion and the highest rate of self-inflicted wounds in the division. The latter offence infuriated senior commanders who saw a high rate as a sure sign of poor morale, bad leadership and something very wrong in a unit. As good an officer as Clark was, it took him months to get the 14th on track.

24. LAC, MG 30E100 (Currie Papers), Vol. 2, General Correspondence (M–R), Currie to Dudley Oliver, Manager, Bank of Montreal, London, 2 September 1918. The battalion was the 5th, Lieutenant-Colonel Lorn Tudor, DSO (Currie Papers, vol. 43, Diary entry, 2 September). Tudor was awarded the DSO for "conspicuous gallantry and ability to command." The full citation is in David K. Riddle and Donald G. Mitchell, eds., *The Distinguished Service Order to the Canadian Expeditionary Force and Canadians in the Royal Naval Air Service, the Royal Flying Corps and Royal Air Force, 1915–1920* (Winnipeg: Kirkby-Marlton Press, 1991), p. 105. Tudor's first DSO had been awarded in 1917. LAC, MG30E75 (Urquhart Papers), Vol. 3, Folder 6. This action must finally have made it obvious that Tudor was burnt out. He had been with the 5th from the start, moving up from platoon commander to CO and never missing a fight. On 18 October Currie told General Turner that Tudor was coming to England for rest and that he had been failing in health for over a year.

25. James H. Pedley, *Only This: A War Retrospect* (Ottawa: Graphic Publishers, 1927), pp. 38–41. Nelles, DSO and Bar, MC, was 27, not 22 (Service Record, LAC). He led the 4th until the end of the war. Arthur Birchall, a British officer, was CO from February to April 1915 when he was killed in action. His replacement, Malcolm Colquhoun, was CO until June 1916. William Rae, DSO, replaced him and on leaving the 4th in June 1917 went to Corps HQ as a staff officer. Alex Thomson, his successor, was killed in action in November 1917. Gibson, *Records of the Fourth Canadian Infantry Battalion,* contains a photo of each CO. 4th Battalion is one of the four battalions of 1st Division lacking a full battalion history.

26. Bidwell and Graham, *Fire-Power,* p. 64.

27. Carl von Clausewitz, *On War,* ed. and trans. by Michael Howard and Peter Paret (Princeton, N.J.: Princeton University Press, 1976), p. 169.

28. Traver's *The Killing Ground* is not true to its title in that 1918 is virtually ignored. Military education is a subject often misinterpreted. Several reviewers, for example, have missed the point that "Educated" in John Terraine's *Douglas Haig: The Educated Soldier* (London: Hutchinson and Co. Ltd., 1963; reprint, London, Leo Cooper, 1990), refers to education in its special military sense and also to the fact that Haig, like any other soldier, became educated in war and by war. For these reviews see the *Journal of the Royal United Services Institute* (August 1963); *History Today,* September 1963; and the *New Statesman,* 26 April 1963. The last is rife with factual error and epitomizes the old wisdom that a little knowledge is a dangerous thing!

29. The article was in the September issue, p. 1184.

30. Samuels, *Command or Control?,* pp. 5, 22; Bidwell and Graham, *Fire-Power,* p. 2.

Rank has much to do with a man's perspective on doctrine: Generals offer battle and officers conduct operations in which combat results; the soldier is the one who fights.

31. "The British Army and Modern Conceptions of War," p. 1203. Its author seemed not to realize that unlike the French and the Germans, who knew precisely their enemy, the requirement of the British to be prepared to fight anywhere in the world hindered doctrinal definition and development.

32. Hay, *The First Hundred Thousand*, p. 96.

33. *FSR*, p. 14. In the original text the first half of the quoted sentence was in bold type.

34. Travers, "Learning and Decision-Making on the Western Front," p. 91. Author's italics. Generalization is difficult because everything differed from unit to unit.

35. Captain B.H.L. Hart, "The Soldier's Pillar of Fire by Night: The Need for a Framework of Tactics," *Journal of the Royal United Services Institute* (November 1921): p. 621.

36. Captain G.C. Wynne, *If Germany Attacks: The Battle in Depth in the West* (London: Faber and Faber Ltd., 1940), p. 5.

37. Atkinson, *The Seventh Division*, pp. 131–32.

38. *Canadian Corps Trench Orders* (London: HMSO, October 1915); *Canadian Corps Trench Orders* (Army Printing and Stationary Services, July 1916); *Canadian Corps Standing Trench Orders* (Army Printing and Stationary Services, July 1917). The 1915 and 1916 editions have 12 pages each, while the 1917 edition has double that, reflecting greater sophistication and concerns. All three editions contain guidance on duties, sentries, care and use of weapons, sanitation, communications, work parties, arrangements in case of attack, rations and cooking, rum issues, reliefs and foot care. The 1917 edition also includes a section on patrols.

39. Dancocks, *Welcome to Flanders Fields*, p. 139.

40. LAC, MG30E46 (Turner Papers), Vol 1, File 4, Diary of Operations; 10th and 16th Battalion War Diaries, April 1915.

41. Ibid; Dancocks, *Gallant Canadians*, pp. 29–34. 10th Battalion came out with only five officers and 188 ORs, the 16th with five and 263. Foch called the attack "the finest act in the war."

42. Robin Prior and Trevor Wilson, *Command on the Western Front: The Military Career of Sir Henry Rawlinson, 1914–18* (Oxford: Blackwell, 1992), pp. 24, 33–34.

43. LAC, RG9IIIC3, Vol. 4004, Folder 3, File 3.

44. Brigadier-General J.E. Edmonds and Captain G.C. Wynne, *Military Operations, France and Belgium, 1915: Winter 1914–15, Battle of Neuve Chapelle, Battle of Ypres* (London: Macmillan, 1927), p. vii, say that instructional pamphlets did not appear in any number until after Loos in September 1915, experience being insufficient before then to compile pamphlets of much value. A full list of the Central Distribution Section (CDS) and Stationary Services (SS) series is in Peter T. Scott, "The CDS/SS Series of Manuals and Instructions: A Numerical Checklist," *The Great War, 1914–1918*, 1. Of the 14 listed in *Notes for Commanding Officers* (1918), pp. 32–34, most were used in this book and are in the bibliography. Of the 550 or so published by the end of 1917, 450 concern tactics, lessons and training; the rest relate to administration. It is easy now to criticize these publications as plodding or inadequate, but those who had to use them were no doubt more appreciative of their guidance than historians of today might realize. A useful summary of the formation, growth and work of the Army Printing and Stationary Services is on pp. 200–204 in *Statistics of the Military Effort of the British Empire During the Great War, 1914–1920* (London: War Office, March 1922).

45. Entire archival volumes consist of minutes of corps and division conferences; for example, RG9IIIC3, Vol. 4007, and RG9IIIC1, Vol. 3827, contain minutes of conferences chaired by commanders and senior corps and division staff officers
46. Prior and Wilson, *Command on the Western Front*, p. 88.
47. LAC, RG9IIIC1, Vol. 3859, Folder 85, File 4, 27 July 1916.
48. LAC, RG9IIIC1, Vol. 3859, Folder 85, File 3, memo, 2 May 1916.
49. LAC, RG9IIIC1, Vol. 3842, Folder 43, File 9. These documents helped in the exchange of sectors between 1st ANZAC and the Canadian Corps in August 1916. The quid pro quo was copies of all Canadian maps and schemes, which C.B.B. White praised for their comprehensiveness. Comparison of the exchanged documents shows the high degree of standardization of staff work in the BEF. White, the extremely capable Australian who had planned the evacuation of Gallipoli (the plan was a model of precise and clear thinking, which in execution got the Allies out without loss), became Major-General Sir C.B.B. White. Radcliffe at the time was the senior operational staff officer, the Brigadier-General General Staff, at Canadian Corps HQ.
50. LAC, RG9IIIC3, Vol. 4033, Folder 4, File 5, 4 April 1917. As GOC of 1st Brigade, Griesbach issued a long series of instructions in his "Book of Wisdom." These very valuable how-tos and how-not-tos reveal Griesbach's attention to detail and his solid training skills. William ("Billy") Antrobus Griesbach, 36 years old at the start of the war, initially went overseas with the cavalry but returned to Edmonton before Christmas 1914 to command the 49th Battalion, then forming in that city. In February 1917, having shown himself to be a fine battalion commander, he was promoted to command 1st Brigade.
51. LAC, RG9IIIC1, Vol. 3843, Folder 44, File 1, II (Imperial) Corps, 17 August 1916.
52. LAC, RG9IIIC3, Vol. 4053, Folder 24, File 16, "The Offensive," 20 January 1916.
53 LAC, RG9IIIC1, Vol. 3859, Folder 85, File 8, Canadian Corps to Second Army, 20 November 1917; File 2, "Canadian Corps G.116/3-23 and Divisional Replies." The table of contents of divisional responses fills three foolscap pages listing 57 topics which range alphabetically from "Administration of Platoons" to "Working Parties." The entire response, set out in point form, fills 39 foolscap pages, of which 1st Division contributed 12.
54. LAC, RG9IIIC3, Vol. 4026, Folder 11, File 3, Corps to divisions, 3 November 1916; Brigadier-General J.J. Collyer, *The Campaign in German South West Africa, 1914–1915* (Pretoria: Government Printer, 1937), preface.
55. *Notes for Commanding Officers* (1918), p. 334.
56. LAC, 1st Division General Staff War Diary, July 1915, Appendix 9; Urquhart, *History of the 16th Battalion*, p. 189.
57. Peter T. Scott, "Mr. Stokes and His Educated Drainpipe," *The Great War, 1914–1918* 2 (May 1990): 80–95, provides an excellent account of getting the Stokes three-inch trench mortar into the hands of the troops. Although the mortar was first test-fired on 30 January 1915, it was the end of the year before the first 200 were issued to training centres and March 1916, before it entered front line service. Scott briefly describes the competition, the West Spring Gun, in "Trench Weaponry: 3 The West Spring Gun," *Stand To!* 5 (Summer 1982): 16. With its 24 springs at full tension, the West had a maximum range of 240 yards, less than one-third of the eventual range of the Stokes; its bomb weight was much less than the 11-pound bomb fired by the Stokes. Nor could the West match the high rate of fire of the Stokes. In one case in September 1916, a battery of eight Stokes mortars put 750 bombs on target in 15 minutes, a rate

exceeding six a minute per tube. For comparative purposes, in 1917 the 18-pounder field gun was set an "intense" rate of four rounds per gun per minute (LAC, RG9IIIC1, Vol. 3843, Folder 46, File 5, Artillery Instruction No. 3, First Army, 22 March 1917).

58. Lt.-Col. A.F. Brooke, "The Evolution of Artillery in the Great War: IV, The Evolution of Artillery Organisation and Command," *Journal of the Royal Artillery* 52 (1925–26): 377–79. The senior gunner at Corps underwent the same metamorphosis, becoming General Officer Commanding Royal Artillery (in October 1915), as did the senior gunner at Army. Heavy artillery also came under a GOC.

59. Timothy L. Lupfer, *The Dynamics of Doctrine: The Changes in German Tactical Doctrine During the First World War*. Leavenworth Papers, no. 4 (Fort Leavenworth, Kansas: Combat Studies Institute, 1981), pp. 13, 19–20. Lupfer studiously avoids giving the British credit for anything while consistently making the Germans paragons of military virtues. He includes only doctrinal improvements in German artillery. Brooke, "The Evolution of Artillery in the Great War, IV," pp. 385–86.

60. McNaughton, "The Development of Artillery in the Great War," p. 164.

61. Colonel H.F.H. Hertzberg, "The Reorganization of the Engineering Troops of a Canadian Division, Great War, 1914–1918," *Canadian Defence Quarterly* 1 (July 1924): 41.

62. LAC, RG9IIIC3, Vol. 4051, Folder 19, File 11, 1st Division to 2nd Brigade, 4 April 1917; RG9IIIC1, Vol. 3843, Folder 44, File 1, II (Imperial) Corps, 17 August 1916.

63. Paddy Griffith, "The Lewis Gun Made Easy: The Development of Automatic Rifles in the Great War," *The Great War, 1914–1918*, 3 (September 1991): 108–15. This article, which was the basis of Chapter 7 of Griffith's *Battle Tactics of the Western Front: The British Army's Art of Attack, 1916–18* (New Haven, Conn.: Yale University Press, 1994), is a fine piece on the Lewis gun, machine-guns, and the organizational and doctrinal controversies thereto. The Lewis gun, calibre .303, was an air-cooled, bipod-mounted, shoulder-controlled weapon with an effective range of less than 500 yards. The gunner could empty its 47-round magazine in five or six seconds but continuous fire played hell with accuracy and brought on stoppages—to which the temperamental Lewis gun was prone anyway (the manual lists 28 types of stoppage). Short bursts of four or five rounds, on the other hand, were the good gunner's method since this produced aimed, controlled effective fire. The Vickers .303 calibre machine-gun, in use in both world wars and into the 1960s, was a "Medium Machine-Gun." This tripod mounted, water-cooled, belt-fed weapon had an accurate range of 600 yards and an effective range of 1,100 yards but it could reach out as far as 4,000 yards. While it was capable of continuous fire (a belt of 250 rounds per minute was considered rapid fire), it was most effective and economical when fired in bursts of 10–20 rounds. Its tripod, weight 44 pounds, featured mechanisms that could set the Vickers on fixed lines, a significant advantage over shoulder-controlled automatic weapons. It could, for example, traverse the enemy's parapet with deadly accuracy, despite smoke or darkness, and it could lay down long range indirect fire in precise patterns, although the efficacy of the fire was debatable. The gun itself weighed 33 pounds, plus 10 pounds of water, for a total of about 87 pounds. At 28 pounds the Lewis gun was lighter but its full magazine at 4.5 pounds was almost two pounds heavier than the equivalent number of rounds in a Vickers belt.

64. LAC, RG9IIIC1, Vol. 3852, Folder 65, File 12. Horne to GHQ 2 November 1917. Horne was a gunner, which tended to influence his concept of machine-gun doctrine.

65. Ibid., Griesbach to 1st Division, 27 October 1917; RG9IIIC3, Vol. 4024, Folder 3, File 4, Griesbach to battalions 24 July 1917. He was close to the mark, although it would

be a semi-automatic rather than an automatic rifle that would enter general service in the Canadian Army after the Korean War, which marked the last hostile use of the Lee-Enfield by Canadian soldiers. Griffith, "The Lewis Gun Made Easy," p. 108, notes that the British Army led the way in the deployment of automatic rifles (in 1914 terms the Lewis gun). This was an extremely important "first." The Germans, lacking any equivalent until the end of 1916, used captured re-chambered Lewis guns. The BEF maintained separate machine-gun and Lewis gun schools throughout the war, the former opening in December 1914 and the first of the latter in June 1915. A description of the first months of operation of these schools is in Tony Ashworth, *Trench Warfare, 1914–1918: The Live and Let Live System* (New York: Holmes and Meier Publishers, Inc., 1980), pp. 60–61.

66. Brig-Gen. Sir James E. Edmonds, *Military Operations, France and Belgium, 1916: Sir Douglas Haig's Command to the 1st July: Battle of the Somme* (London: Macmillan, 1932), p. 64; *1915, Battles of Aubers Ridge, Festubert and Loos*, p. 299; Cave, "The Canadian Corps Order of Battle," pp. 9–10. LAC, 1st Division A & Q War Diary, entry for 10 December 1915 indicates that 3rd Brigade was the first Canadian brigade to have a machine-gun company. Its establishment was eight officers and 139 ORs. These companies, commanded by captains or majors, were some of the smallest independent commands in the Army.

67. Major R.M. Wright, "Machine-Gun Tactics and Organization," *Army Quarterly* (January 1921): p. 295, stresses that a suitable luminous aiming-mark was not on general issue until after the Armistice. Wright, an officer in the Guards Machine-Gun Regiment, was a well-experienced machine-gun officer. His article reflects his own opinions and his experience in only one division but, as he quite rightly points out (p. 290), "There is no reason to suppose that [other machine-gunners'] experiences were widely different." Bill Rawling, *Surviving Trench Warfare: Technology and the Canadian Corps* (Toronto: University of Toronto Press, 1992), p. 178, puts the separation of the Vickers down to the lack of mobility. Wright, Paddy Griffith, ed., *British Fighting Methods in the Great War* (London: Frank Cass, 1996), pp. 8–9, and Samuels, *Command or Control?*, pp. 115–16, make an irrefutable case for tactics as the root cause of the organizational shift. The latter three sources also provide a comprehensive analysis of the advantages and disadvantages of the separation of machine-guns from the infantry, something Rawling could not do in his brief account (two paragraphs, pp. 178–79), which relates primarily to the training of machine-gunners and the organization of machine-gun battalions.

68. Samuels, *Command or Control?*, p. 86.

69. Brig-Gen. Sir James E. Edmonds, *Military Operations, France and Belgium, 1918 March–April: Continuation of the German Offensives* (London: Macmillan, 1937), p. 471.

70. Carrington, *Soldier from the Wars Returning*, p. 177; Charles Edmonds [Carrington], *A Subaltern's War* (London: Peter Davies Limited, 1929), p. 38; Captain F.C. Hitchcock, *Stand To: A Diary of the Trenches, 1915–1918* (Norwich, Norfolk: Gliddon Books, 1988), p. 133.

71. Nicholson, *Official History of the Canadian Army*, p. 383. Imperial divisions had 64 Vickers and 336 Lewis guns (Major A.F. Becke, *History of the Great War, Order of Battle of Divisions*, Part 1: *The Regular British Divisions* [London: HMSO, 1935], p. 127). German divisions, depending on infantry company configuration, had either 252 or 360 automatic weapons. In either configuration they had more machine-guns but

fewer automatic rifles (Lewis gun equivalents). See *SS 356 Handbook of the German Army in War. April 1918.* (London: HMSO, 1918), pp. 54–61. What should also be factored in is a very effective weapon we did not have in mid-1918 and the Germans did: the MP 18 Bergmann submachine-gun. Brigadier-General Victor Odlum is pictured examining one in August 1918 in Mike Chappell, *The Canadian Army at War*, Osprey Men-at-Arms Series, no. 164 (London: Osprey Publishing, 1985), p. 18.

72. The fourth company was authorized in January 1917 (LAC, RG9IIIC3, Vol. 4056, Folder 32, File 10).

73. Wright, "Machine-Gun Tactics and Organization," p. 310.

74. LAC, RG9IIIC1, Vol. 3852, Folder 65, File 12, letter to GHQ, 2 November 1917.

75. LAC, RG9IIIC1, Vol. 3852, Folder 65, File 12, Horne to GHQ, 2 November 1917. How the Corps as a whole answered is significant because the results contradict Horne's statement that most favoured a battalion organization. Presumably the results in I (Imperial) Corps, which with the Canadian Corps made up First Army at the time of the survey, allowed him to make this claim. The only Canadian divisional commander opposed to the idea was Watson of 4th Division. Only four of the 12 Canadian infantry brigadiers favoured a machine-gun battalion organization. 2nd and 4th Division brigadiers opposed it. 1st and 3rd Division brigadiers were, in both divisions, two to one in favour.

76. Wright, "Machine-Gun Tactics and Organization," p. 307.

77. Ibid., p. 306.

78. Griffith, *Battle Tactics of the Western Front*, pp. 123–24.

79. Roy, *Journal of Private Fraser*, p. 251.

80. Wright, "Machine-Gun Tactics and Organization," p. 294.

81. Fraser, *In Good Company*, pp. 71–72. On being told that he was going to a machine-gun company Fraser complained to his diary that such an appointment was a dead end for anyone who wanted to get on. To his relief, he went instead as a brigade Staff Captain.

82. LAC, RG9IIIC1, Vol. 3864, Folder 99, File 4, private letter from Lieutenant-Colonel William Rae to BGGS (Radcliffe), 16 December 1916.

83. Wright, "Machine-Gun Tactics and Organization," p. 292.

84. LAC, RG9IIIC3, Vol. 4025, Folder 6, File 3, April 1918.

85. LAC, RG9IIIC3, Vol. 4014, Folder 26, File 1, 2nd Battalion report on Hill 70, 24 August 1917. There is every indication here of a very angry CO.

86. Griffith, "The Lewis Gun Made Easy," p. 109.

87. Samuels, *Command or Control?*, p. 115; Captain J.C. Dunn, *The War the Infantry Knew, 1914–1919* (London: Jane's Publishing Company Limited, 1987), p. 183. Author's italics.

88. LAC, RG9IIIC1, Vol. 3852, Folder 65, File 12, Loomis to 1st Division, 2 November 1917.

89. Major N. Hudson, "Trench Mortars in the Great War," *Journal of the Royal Artillery* 47 (April 1920): 17, 19–21. Hudson described mortar characteristics as cheapness (of mortar and ammunition), great destructive power, simplicity of use and training, and lightness and high trajectory. Regarding employment, he categorized them as follows: heavy mortar—an immobile weapon whose primary object was demolition; medium mortar—unsuitable to accompany the infantry in the assault, its primary object being destruction of wire and trenches; and the light mortar—relatively mobile with a high rate of fire and suitable to accompany the infantry, its primary function being to kill men. His categorization has to do considerably with weapon and projectile weights:

9.45 inch heavy mortar, 3,500 lb and 152 lb; 2-inch medium, 500 lb and 52 lb; 6-inch medium, 375 lb and 48 lb; and Stokes 3-inch light, 100 lb and 11 lb. The ranges in yards of each type were: heavy (9.45 inch), 1,140, rising to 2,300 by 1917; medium (2-inch), 540, medium (6-inch), 1,800; and Stokes, 430, rising to 800 in 1917.

90. Major D.J. Corrigall, *The History of the Twentieth Canadian Battalion (Central Ontario Regiment), Canadian Expeditionary Force in the Great War, 1914–1918* (Toronto: Stone & Cox Limited, 1935), p. 97; Bernard Adams, *Nothing of Importance: A Record of Eight Months at the Front with a Welsh Battalion*, October 1915 to June 1916 (Uckfield, East Sussex: The Naval and Military Press, n.d.), p. 183. Adams sarcastically defined the types of trench mortar officers as those who could never be found but who left an NCO with instructions not to fire without his orders; those who could not fire without brigade orders; those afraid to give their positions away; those out of ammunition; and those who fired just when a working party was in the forward trenches. The title of this book is unfortunate, since it does contain a good deal of importance to study of the Western Front.

91. Ernst Junger, *The Storm of Steel* (London: Chatto and Windus, 1929; reprint, London: Constable, 1994), pp. 40, 44. This book celebrates the *Fronterlebnis*, the front experience of the combat soldier. Junger served four years on the Western Front. Amongst his many decorations was Germany's highest award, the *Pour le Mérite* (the equivalent of the Victoria Cross), which he won as an infantry company commander. Junger was wounded 14 times, the last injury suffered in August 1918. He also served in the German Army in the Second World War. Born 29 March 1895, he died on 17 February 1998, aged 102! A recent biography is Thomas Nevin's *Ernst Junger and Germany into the Abyss, 1914–1945*.

92. LAC, War Diary, 2nd Brigade, entries for 5 December 1917 and 31 January 1918.

93. LAC, RG9IIIC3, Vol. 4052, Folder 22, File 8 and Vol. 4053, Folder 24, File 16. Scott, "Mr. Stokes and His Educated Drainpipe," p. 95, describes an experimental model that is thought to have seen very limited service near the end of the war. Known as the "GHQ Equipment," it dispensed with bipod and had a much smaller baseplate, two features that improved mobility. It looked very much like the 60-mm mortar in use after the Korean War. It would have been fired in much the same way: over "open sights," so to speak, with the holder, his hands grasping a bracket mounted on the tube, setting the angle of fire, and hence the range, by extending or drawing back his arms.

94. LAC, MG30E15 (Greisbach Papers), Vol. 3, File 16A, November 1917; RG9IIIC3, Vol. 4028, Folder 17, File 20, report of 4th Battalion, November 1917; Vol. 4053, Folder 24, File 16, Macdonell to Canadian Corps 26 May 1918; Loomis to Macdonell 21 May.

95. LAC, RG9IIIC1, Vol. 3864, Folder 99, File 3, BGGS to divisions, 27 December 1916 and 10 January 1917. *Notes for Commanding Officers* (1918 edition), p. 345, defined interior economy as the system by which the duties of all ranks were coordinated so as to maintain the efficiency and well-being of the unit.

96. LAC, RG9IIIC1, Vol. 3864, Folder 99, File 3, 27 December 1916; First Army to Canadian Corps, 9 December 1916. The regulations are in RG9IIIC3, Vol. 4058, Folder 36, File 2.

97. Ibid., BGGS to divisions, 27 December 1916. In Imperial battalions detachments created an administrative and housekeeping headache by not being under any organizational umbrella: an HQ Company was not authorized because detached men had to remain on strength of their parent sub-unit (LAC, RG9IIIC1, Vol. 3864, Folder 99, File 3). Many Canadian infantry COs, usually on their own hook, formed such a

company under the Adjutant for purposes of discipline and for "the improvement of the interior economy" (LAC, RG9IIIC3, Vol. 4062, Folder 12, File 1, 5th Battalion order, 3 October 1916).

98. Urquhart, *History of the 16th Battalion*, pp. 101, 104–105; LAC, RG9IIIC1, Vol. 3859, Folder 85, File 4. In October 1915 the BGGS, then Tim Harington, emphasized, as part of a "lessons learned" synopsis, that as many men as possible had to be trained in bombs because all platoons had to be prepared to carry out bombing attacks. One of the photographs in *We Lead, Others Follow* shows General Alderson decorating Lance-Corporal Cox, a bomber in 10th Battalion.

99. Urquhart, *History of the 16th Battalion*, pp. 105, 118.

100. Ibid., p. 105; Hay, *The First Hundred Thousand*, p. 232.

101. Bernard McEvoy and Capt. A.H. Finlay, MC, *History of the 72nd Canadian Infantry Battalion Seaforth Highlanders of Canada* (Vancouver: Cowan & Brookhouse, 1920), p. 74. Currie, summarizing the lessons of the Somme up to mid-August, 1916, referred to the same sort of bomb-happy tactics in 1st Division (LAC, RG9IIIC3, Vol. 4051, Folder 19, File 8, Currie to 2nd Brigade, 15 August). 2nd Brigade's report is also in this file.

102. Lieutenant Cyril Winterbotham, "O.C. Platoon Enquiries," in Lyn Macdonald, ed., *Anthem for Doomed Youth* (London: The Folio Society, 2000), pp. 37–38. Winterbotham was killed in action on the Somme in 1916.

103. LAC, RG9IIIC1, Vol. 3846, Folder 51, File 7, p. 7 of Radcliffe's lecture ("Vimy Ridge Operations") to the Senior Officers' School.

104. Urquhart, *History of the 16th Battalion*, p. 105; *SS 143 The Training and Employment of Platoons* (France: Army P and S Service, February 1918), p. 3, refers not to specialists but to men "trained . . . in special duties." LAC, RG9IIIC3, Vol. 4031, Folder 26, File 7, 17 June 1917.

105. LAC, RG9IIIC1, Vol. 3864, Folder 99, File 3.

106. LAC, RG9IIIC1, Vol. 3864, Folder 99, File 3, Corps to divisions, 27 December 1916.

107. LAC, RG9IIIC1, Vol. 3843, Folder 44, File 1, 15 August 1916; RG9IIIC3, Vol. 4028, Folder 17, File 20, 1st Division to brigades, 23 August 1916.

108. LAC, RG9IIIC3, Vol. 4063, Folder 13, File 1, 2nd Brigade to battalions, 29 December 1916; 2nd Brigade War Diary, January 1917; RG9IIIC1, Vol. 3864, Folder 99, File 3, Corps guideline, 10 January 1917. The other divisions were closer to the Corps guideline, platoon strengths being 48 ORs in 2nd Division and 49 in 3rd and 4th Divisions.

109. LAC, RG9IIIC1, Vol. 3486, Folder 51, File 7, p. 6, "Vimy Ridge Operations."

110. *SS 143 Instructions for the Training of Platoons for Offensive Action* (1917) provided tactical guidance. Every OR, except the number one on the Lewis gun, was a rifleman and a bomber. Those in No. 2 Section had to be trained on either the Lewis gun or the rifle grenade. Every man in the rifle grenade section carried "at least" six bombs, the section total of 56 or more bombs being only slightly smaller than the number of hand grenades in the grenade section.

111. LAC, 5th Battalion War Diary, 16 March 1916; Rawling, *Surviving Trench Warfare*, p. 51. What caused this considerable expenditure is not revealed.

112. This, said Russenholt, *Six Thousand Canadian Men*, p. 80, is what the new platoon was styled. LAC, RG9IIIC3, Vol. 4031, Folder 26, File 8, 1st Division to brigades, 23 February 1917.

113. Lt.-Col. Cuthbert Headlam, *History of the Guards Division in the Great War 1915–1918*. Volume I (London: John Murray, 1924), p. 119.

114. LAC, RG9IIIC1, Vol. 3864, Folder 99, File 3, First Army, 4 May 1917; Vol. 3846, Folder 51, Files 1–7; War Diaries, 2nd Brigade and 5th and 14th Battalions, April 1917.

115. LAC, RG9IIIC3, Vol. 4028, Folder 17, File 20. GOC 2nd Division (Burstall) agreed. Lipsett (3rd Division) did not think that Vimy had been a thorough test of the platoon. Watson of 4th Division believed the new platoon was an "undoubted" success, being the ideal, self-contained sub-unit. However, he pointed out that the ideal demanded a far higher standard of training of platoon commanders.

116. LAC, RG9IIIC3, Vol. 4053, Folder 24, File 16, First Army to I, II, XI, XIII and Canadian Corps, 9 May 1917; Vol. 4031, Folder 26, File 7, First Army to Canadian Corps, 11 July 1917.

117. Dunn, *The War the Infantry Knew*, p. 355.

118. Hart, "The Soldier's Pillar of Fire by Night," p. 621; Lord Milne quoted in Travers, *The Killing Ground*, p. xix.

119. The Corps' request and the divisional responses are in LAC, RG9IIIC1, Vol. 3859, Folder 85, File 2; MG30E15 (Griesbach Papers), Vol. 3, File 16A. Thomson's letter, dated 17 September 1917, is in RG9IIIC3, Vol. 4024, Folder 3, File 2.

120. LAC, RG9IIIC3, Vol. 4025, Folder 6, File 3.

121. LAC, RG9IIIC3, Vol. 4043, Folder 1, File 17; Vol. 4044, Folder 3, File 15, Tuxford to battalions, 8 October 1918.

CHAPTER FOUR

At My Command (2)

*For I am a man under authority, having soldiers under me; and
I say to this man, Go, and he goeth; and to another, Come, and
he cometh; and to my servant, Do this and he doeth it.*

—MATTHEW 8:9

The preceding chapter examined several matters that commanders had to
resolve if 1st Division were to grow professionally and become more effective
in unleashing the hurricanes of compressed violence known as combat.
Solutions came only when the commanders, like the division, had grown in
competence. Over time, they learned not only what to do but the best way to
do it. This chapter examines the conduct of operations, a commander's primary responsibility, including the controls inherent in battle procedure
(a vital part of how a division fought). It also illustrates the evolution of command competence from raw to good to professional between Second Ypres
and Passchendaele.

In February 1915 E.A.H. Alderson, the only General Officer in the division
with experience of war as a General Officer, took the division to Flanders
where it went into the line under instruction, its brigades being paired with
Imperial brigades. In April the division assumed responsibility for a sector of
the line near Ypres where it faced its first real test. To cover his front of
4,500 yards Alderson deployed 2nd Brigade (Currie) right and 3rd Brigade
(Turner) left, each with two battalions forward, one in support and one in
division reserve. 1st Brigade (Mercer) was in Corps reserve about two miles
west of Ypres.

Raw commanders and raw divisions seldom perform brilliantly on first
acquaintance with war. Too much is unknown or unappreciated for that to
occur. Given this, it hardly seems productive to dwell at length on the mistakes

made at Second Ypres. Command and control, certainly, were not what they should have been but it is hard to see how this could have been otherwise. The same applies to staff work, which will be examined in later chapters. What is notable is that the Battle of Second Ypres was the first active field command for all of Alderson's subordinates, and it marked the first ever attack by a Canadian formation when on the night of 22/23 April Turner attacked Kitchener's Wood with two battalions.

Second Ypres is the starting point in the refinement of Canadian command and control and the part they were to play in the transformation of 1st Division into a good division. One crucial aspect of command is confidence. When Geddes' Detachment (a composite brigade of four Imperial battalions) came under command on 23 April it deployed to fill the gap that had opened on the Canadian left flank. Alderson had a difficult choice: keep the detachment under Geddes, who was a professional officer but without a proper staff, or assign its battalions to one (or more) of his brigadiers, whom he did not know all that well and who were inexperienced but at least they had staffs, albeit neophytes. Alderson went with Geddes, who, as it turned out, had a difficult time executing the mission assigned to his *ad hoc* brigade.[1]

Communications, or rather their inadequacy at Second Ypres (and throughout the war) also hindered command. Broken field telephone lines and tardy and inaccurate reports played a significant role in the battle. One source of confusion was HQ locations: Turner's brigade HQ was too far forward, while Alderson's divisional HQ was too far back for it to influence events in timely fashion. Orders proved so slow in arriving that when they did many were irrelevant; on one, Turner sarcastically wrote "An example of the value of information received from the rear."[2] Communications forward were hardly better: at one point the St. Julien garrison under Lieutenant-Colonel Loomis was ordered to counterattack, but, fortunately, the order was cancelled before he could start with the 15 men he had available.[3] Loomis also continued to command 13th Battalion, most of which was forward, the split responsibility being unenviable and, in the circumstances, impossible. Infantry-artillery liaison was nil, which hardly mattered since most guns were out of range. Division and Corps, too, remained ignorant for some hours of Turner's order to withdraw to the GHQ Line, a decision which nearly lost the battle.[4] In the end, though, despite shortcomings in command and control at division and 3rd Brigade HQ, the line held, thanks mainly to the steadiness of Regimental officers and men, Canadian and British, and the efforts of Currie and COs like Lipsett and Tuxford. Perhaps the salient fact about command and control at Second Ypres, and the most encouraging one, was that battalion command in general was far better than anyone might reasonably have expected.

Within a month 1st Division was engaged at Festubert, followed four weeks later by the action at Givenchy. At Festubert 3rd Brigade again opened the Canadian part of the operation. At 5:25 P.M. on 18 May 1915 the 3rd, with an Imperial brigade on its left, attacked positions south of the wood known thereafter as Canadian Orchard. For the first time barbed wire was a factor to contend with; indeed, this new man-made obstacle complicated operations severely then and afterward. It also produced casualties, as indicated in this realistic estimate by a fictional French general: "Say, five per cent killed by their own barrage . . . Ten per cent loss in crossing no-man's-land, and twenty per cent more in getting through the wire."[5] The last figure may seem high but wire slowed an attack and caused troops to bunch up, thereby presenting lucrative targets for the defender.

Infantry Training (4-Company Organization), 1914, made no mention of wire. Artillery then had two tasks: kill men and wreck field defences. Shrapnel was most effective at the first, high explosive (HE) at the last—but not field gun HE shells, which were too light to have much effect against trenches. The Empire's field gun, the 18-pounder (range 6,500 yards in 1914), was designed to fire shrapnel against infantry in the open. Until early 1915 it fired only shrapnel and pyrotechnic star shell. The German equivalent, the "77," fired shrapnel or HE out to 7,000 yards, a clear superiority in ammunition and range but one significantly reduced by faulty doctrine that had the gunners burst their shrapnel 30 feet up, too high for optimum man-killing.[6] Neither shrapnel nor HE were particularly effective at cutting wire. Most men thought shrapnel better since it cut the wire clear of the pickets that secured it and left it in small pieces, unlike HE, which left the wire broken but still an entanglement.[7] Fuses in HE shells in 1915/1916 were such that the shells buried themselves before detonating, resulting in much of the explosive force going straight up instead of against the wire. Also, the craters caused by HE severely impeded the attacker. For these reasons, and because HE was in short supply until 1917, production having been concentrated on the simpler shrapnel shell, wire cutting was left mostly to field guns firing shrapnel, which had to burst three or four feet above the wire in order to cut it. The inherent shortcomings of shrapnel, which lost effectiveness at longer ranges, meant heavier expenditure of ammunition (and longer preparatory firing), and it demanded extreme accuracy and very careful observation of the results. At longer ranges accurately assessing the adequacy of the cutting became harder.

Wire-cutting was perhaps the least of Turner's worries at Festubert where his brigade attack quickly collapsed due to intense artillery and machine-gun fire. A contributory factor was inadequate time for battle procedure. Army had set Zero for 4:30 P.M. but orders were not issued until 1:55

and when they reached Turner the time was nearing Zero, which then had to be postponed.[8] All some units got by way of orders was attack immediately: "there was no time to be lost." Some companies were uncertain that they had even reached their assembly areas since no guides met them. One OC did not know whence he was to attack, or what he was to attack. With no time for reconnaissance of the ground and with maps a jumble of letters and numbers representing points on the ground and printed upside down with north at the bottom of the sheets, Turner's brigade attacked. "Forehand decisions . . . little more than guesses; the only course . . . to go ahead and make the best of the situation." Direction-keeping proved impossible and units were soon mixed and bunched up, a situation conducive to nothing but increased casualties.[9]

That night (18 May) Alderson took under command the Imperial 51st (Highland) Division and the guns of 2nd and 7th (Imperial) Divisions. Without a proper staff to run this *ad hoc* corps, command and control and fire planning suffered from the start. As it was, "liaison . . . between infantry and artillery [was] still in the experimental stage."[10] The CRA, then mere advisor, not commander, and without an adequate staff, found himself responsible for coordinating the fire of four divisions, something in the order, by establishment, of 190 field guns and 30 howitzers. Not all were present: the artillery suffered from shortages of guns and ammunition and "showed plainly that they did not have full limbers."[11] Counter-battery capability at the time was more hope than reality.

On 20 May Alderson attacked, 2nd Brigade to take a point identified as K.5 and 3rd Brigade to seize M.10 just north of K.5. A house near a wood, M.10 was a recognizable feature, but K.5 was not and Currie could not identify it. Despite this, and the heavy fire that made his assembly trenches a shambles, Alderson refused Currie's request for a postponement. Once again, assault battalions became entangled, evidence of less than definitive orders regarding control (boundaries, for example), although it must be said that the ground was very difficult. Fire support was inadequate. Neither brigade accomplished much. 2nd Brigade's second attempt the next evening achieved a small lodgement but heavy fire snuffed it out soon after daylight.[12] Another attack on 24 May, this time with adequate artillery and after careful reconnaissance and thorough preparation, took K.5, the only tangible gain of Festubert, which overall cost nearly 2,500 casualties. It all came down to superior enemy artillery and, for 1st Division, sheer frustration.

Givenchy in mid-June was on a much smaller scale, the assault being just one battalion (the 1st) from Mercer's 1st Brigade. The smaller scale and the more than ample time for battle procedure enabled assault units to be as ready as they could possibly be.[13] Attaining the objective, two strong points some 150 yards apart, would secure 7th (Imperial) Division's flank for its attack. The plan was imaginative. Artillery support was crucial since an attack on such a narrow front would receive enfilade fire. The fire plan called for intense fire to destroy the wire and for the placement, the night before Zero, of three 18-pounders in the Canadian trenches, two of them 75 yards distant from the southern objective and the third some 300 yards from the northern objective. At Zero minus 15 minutes these guns would engage the strong points over open sights.[14] At Zero minus two, sappers would explode a giant mine near the southern objective. Once the infantry, bombing their way from south to north, took the two points, work parties from another battalion would connect them to the Canadian trenches. Bomb depots were established well forward.

But the best of plans seldom survive first contact. Givenchy epitomized the wire problem: long grass prevented the actual wire damage from being ascertained; pickets and strands of wire were damaged but not the coils, since shrapnel could not cut them and HE only tossed them about; wire often "appeared" to be cut but was not; and the cutting was only "fair" (or less). Because artillery and infantry reports on cutting differed, mutual confidence suffered. The CRA insisted that in future the infantry had to say, before the assault, whether or not the wire had been satisfactorily cut. Mercer reported another problem inherent in wire cutting: while the wire was being cut, the protracted fire told the enemy where the attack would come and he then saturated the area with fire.[15] The next day (16 June) Rowland Fielding summed up the Canadian experience at Givenchy:

> I am told that the Canadians . . . captured three lines of trenches without casualties. Yet this morning, there are left only a Maj and 60 men, the rest . . . knocked out during the night by bombs and shell-fire. Apparently, more than one thing went wrong. The troops on the left . . . seem to have been hung up and there was also a hitch about the mine [which] unexpectedly blew back through the gallery leading to it, at the mouth of which were congregated the bombers as well as their reserve of bombs. All were destroyed . . . when the enemy counter-attacked; bombing along the captured trenches, there was no one to meet them except for riflemen, who were rapidly reduced to a negligible quantity . . . the few survivors . . . were compelled to fall back.[16]

Also, heavy enemy fire prevented connecting the captured trenches to the Canadian line, forcing reinforcements to cross open ground. Few reached the beleaguered 1st Battalion, which soon had to withdraw. Givenchy, all told, cost 1st Division 600 casualties.[17]

The imperfect infantry-artillery coordination shows in 1st Division's

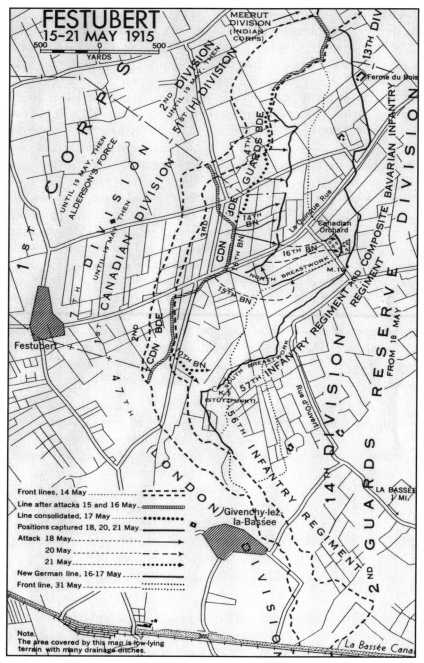

Courtesy of the Canadian Forces (reproduced by Army Survey Establishment.
Compiled and drawn by Historical Section G. S.)

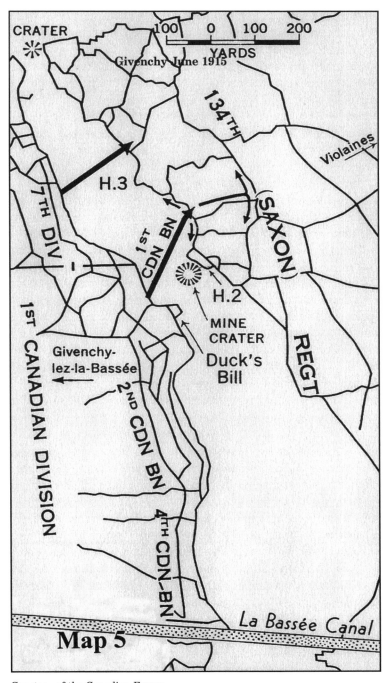

CRATER

100   0 \ 100   200
YARDS

Givenchy June 1915

134TH

Violaines →

H.3

7TH DIV

1ST CDN BN

SAXON

H.2

MINE
CRATER
Duck's
Bill

REGT

1ST CANADIAN DIVISION

Givenchy-
lez-la-Bassée

2ND CDN BN

4TH CDN BN

La Bassée Canal

Map 5

Courtesy of the Canadian Forces

report: "A distinct pause . . . when, at 6 P.M., the artillery lifted from the front-line trenches. This was sufficient to give the enemy warning . . . and to enable him to reman . . . the trenches." Currie's complaint that "every time we have been in trenches lately we have suffered more or less from fire of our own guns," incensed Burstall, who called this "absurd and improbable." The argument showed the frustration and the terrible stresses of trench warfare. When the 18-pounder inserted opposite the northern strongpoint failed to wreck it, gunner credibility took another jolt but their reputation was restored somewhat when the two southern guns reduced the southern strongpoint to rubble.[18]

Much of this was negative but then Festubert and Givenchy were early days on the long, hard road to effectiveness. Afterward, during the quiet months of the last half of 1915, 1st Division (and the Canadian Corps whose HQ opened on 13 September) analysed past events and identified the lessons. In October C.H. (Tim) Harington, the BGGS, summarized the key lesson: "the Commander . . . coordinating the attack [must] take measures to secure the ground he has won . . . reorganize his troops and husband his resources for a fresh effort." In the event that the enemy endangered the gains, the commander had to counterattack at once, or, in the worst case, recognize when the opportunity for that had passed, at which point it was better to take the time to prepare a deliberate counterattack . In sum, "Use your initiative." Choosing hurricane or protracted bombardment presented another tough decision, as did whether or not to widen the bombardment (ammunition permitting) so as not to reveal the main axis of the attack. Harington also stressed reconnaissance of routes forward, ground and positions.[19]

In part, these ideas echoed those of the Corps commander, E.A.H. Alderson, GOC 1st Division from October 1914 until he assumed command of the Canadian Corps. He had been "the ideal choice for the chore of whipping the [first] Canadian contingent into a coherent and effective fighting force" capable of withstanding the German onslaught at Second Ypres in April 1915.[20] During the summer of 1915 he continued to improve 1st Division's capabilities, so much so that he handed over in September a division well organized, equipped and trained, one secure in its operational routines and one made experienced and better by the challenges of Festubert and Givenchy.

Alderson's choice to replace him was 40-year-old Arthur Currie, in Alderson's view far and away the best of the Canadian brigadiers. Currie would command 1st Division for 22 months, almost half of its war service. "Dogged, dependable, thorough and increasingly knowledgeable" and "unquestionably the ablest senior officer the Canadian Corps had produced," he would make 1st Division, in Sir Henry Horne's words, "the pride and wonder of the British Army."[21] Currie, while he was not a soldier's soldier, being unable to inspire troops, had been the "sole bright spot" at Second Ypres where he had revealed himself as a natural leader; one aspect of this was evident in some remarks by Alderson's GSO1 (General Staff Officer 1st Grade) about Currie's calmness and determination.[22] Second Ypres established Currie's reputation. While he had little opportunity there and later at Festubert and Givenchy to display his talents as a planner of offensives, it was clear that he had tactical ability beyond his peers in 1st Division. During his time as GOC 2nd Brigade he trained his brigade well, including his COs who, in accordance with Currie's command style, had the freedom to train their units so long as the training matched Currie's philosophy of training hard and earnestly. His promotion to command of 1st Division was clear recognition of his ability.

On becoming GOC he stressed the lessons of the spring and summer of 1915. His GSO1, Harvey Kearsley, put on paper what they considered the greatest obstacles to offensive success: wire, concealed machine-gun emplacements, and strong points. "Notes on Recent Operations," which followed, addressed control measures before and during an attack, including the preferred assault formations—three or more waves, each one divided into lines. Its other major topic detailed traffic control, which was vital: "No trouble that is spent on the . . . problem will be wasted."[23]

Commanders had also to keep their men in the trenches. This was not new; 300 or so years before 1915 references to this responsibility were not uncommon. Thomas Hobbes, for example, thought, "He that enrolleth himself a soldier . . . is obliged not only to go into battle but also not to run from it without his captain's leave."[24] Hobbes, other political philosophers, and soldiers of his time and afterward, including the great Confederate General, Robert E. Lee, knew that no amount of training and discipline would bring every soldier to his duty every time. Thus, in 1862 the Confederate Provost implemented a system featuring straggler lines, posts and patrols to prevent men leaving the battle line.[25] Lee knew that the only way to prevent desertion was to "visit the offence . . . with the sternest punishment, and leave the offender without hope of escape by making the penalty [death] inevitable."[26] Unfortunately, inconsistent enforcement prevented achieving the end that made "the avenue to the rear . . . absolutely closed up in the mind." These sentiments were shared by many Great War officers, including Louis Lipsett, CO 8th Battalion: "No man is allowed to leave the trenches under any circumstances without a pass signed by an officer.[27]

Obviously, Canadian straggling and desertion were more threat than serious harm but they had to be watched since discipline had not entirely closed that avenue to the rear. Some sources say that a system to prevent men leaving the trenches was implemented after the Somme when severe casualties (the

3rd Brigade alone lost 3,000 men) caused a noticeable fall in morale and a corresponding increase in disciplinary problems. In fact, the *Field Service Pocket Book* (1914) tasked military police with the return of stragglers to their units. As early as January 1916 such a system existed in the BEF. In February 1st Division ordered daily battle straggler reports to be sent to the assistant provost marshal.[28]

Final preparations for the Somme the night before the offensive included the deployment of "Battle Stops" (sometimes called "Battle Straggler Posts") a mile or so behind the front. Military police, detailed men, divisional mounted troops and elements of the divisional cyclist company deployed in three lines behind the front, each line consisting of several stops and a straggler collecting station. Flying patrols moved between the stops and visited places where stragglers were most likely to congregate, such as exits from communication trenches where posts had not been sited. The patrols were to stop all men who were moving to the rear without written authority to do so or men who were not moving as part of a formed body; identify them, noting particularly those who were unarmed (casting away arms was an offence warranting the death penalty); gather the unwounded and arm them, if required, with weapons taken from wounded men; and then, if necessary, escort them forward to their units. Those enforcing the system had sweeping powers, including the authority to shoot anyone making to the rear and refusing to halt when challenged. War ate away at enthusiasm and self-discipline even in the best divisions. Firm discipline and punishment did more to sustain 1st Division (and the Canadian Corps) than our permissive and self-indulgent society likes to accept or know.[29]

During the first quarter of 1916, 1st Division digested the lessons of 1915 and began to master trench discipline, for which a better term might be "battle discipline." That hard work was paying off is evident in the division's reaction to enemy raids on 24 April (2nd Brigade), 26 April (1st Brigade), and on 5 and 7 May (2nd and 3rd Brigades). Despite severe damage to the trenches, and in some sectors their virtual obliteration, in only one instance (26 April) did the enemy make a lodgement, and this he held less than an hour. Lipsett, always quick to suggest refinements, thought casualties would have been fewer had some units conducted a more "elastic" defence, with fewer men manning the parapets and more reliance on concealed wire, enfilade machine-gun fire and ready counterattack forces. 1st Division's conduct delighted the Corps commander. GOC Second Army was "extremely pleased."[30]

In May Alderson handed the Canadian Corps over to Lieutenant-General Julian Byng and returned to Britain as Inspector General of Canadian Forces there. He was not to hold a field command again. Alderson has been assessed as a "better than average soldier" and a "good commander who had earned the respect . . . of those under him."[31] Conversely, he has also been categorized as a "mediocre combat commander," primarily because he lost control of the situation at Second Ypres (April 1915), where he was GOC 1st Division, and because of St. Eloi (April 1916) where 2nd Division in its first fight had not shown well, so much so that immediately thereafter, inquiries commenced "to determine the responsibility for the St. Eloi fiasco." In both battles he had not been well served by subordinate formation commanders, nor had he acted as expeditiously and forcefully as the situations required. His greatest contribution during the 18 months he commanded Canadians was in getting 1st Division and then the Canadian Corps ready for operations. "To him must go no small part of the credit for building the staunch Canadian force that within a year was to win its spurs as a corps on Vimy Ridge."[32]

Byng came to the Canadian Corps with solid credentials. Commissioned in 1883, he had served in the Sudan War (1884) and in the South African War. A cavalryman, he took command of a cavalry division in 1914 and then the Cavalry Corps in France; thereafter he was GOC IX Corps in the Dardanelles, and then GOC XVII Corps from February 1916. His manner on arrival probably puzzled many Canadians until they realized that behind his outward casualness was a mind that framed and asked the most penetrating questions, leaving everyone in no doubt about what he expected. His lack of pretension and his willingness to be frequently well forward, where he could see for himself, endeared him to all ranks; his energy and desire to make the Corps the best it could be through good discipline and relentless training won their respect. Training, in particular, became a key factor in Corps performance, as did thorough planning and staff work, a characteristic that epitomized Canadian operations from 1916 on.

Just three days after joining the Corps Byng had to contend with a strong German attack launched against 3rd Division at Mount Sorrel commencing in the early hours of 1 June. The tight situation might not have developed or might have been immediately recoverable had not the enemy barrage crippled the defence by killing GOC 3rd Division (Mercer) and wounding GOC 8th Brigade (Williams), who was then captured. For a time it was known only that the two were missing. When the senior brigadier in the division, the CRA, E.S. Hoare Nairne, was ordered to take command it took him some time to reach the divisional HQ; it took even longer for the senior battalion commander in Williams' brigade to take over. In the interim, the GSO1, Lieutenant-Colonel Ross Hayter, took the necessary action to maintain the line. Byng soon realized that the brigades of 3rd Division had been hammered to the point where they were in no condition to restore the front. Consequently, he ordered 1st Division to provide two brigades to Hoare Nairne for a counterattack on 3 June. The regrouping and other battle procedure took time. The counterattack ordered for 2:00 A.M. by Hoare Nairne proved impossible because some battalions could not get forward on time and those that did, having marched all night, were exhausted. At 1:59 GOC 2nd Brigade (Lipsett) reported that he would first have to fight to secure his assembly trenches, a situation hardly conducive to a good start or to confidence. So hurried was the battle procedure that 13th Battalion received perhaps the shortest verbal orders on record: "Mount Sorrel is your objective. Go to it." Following several postponements of Zero, which did nothing to reduce confusion (order, counter-order, disorder), four separate attacks, each in battalion strength, were launched in broad daylight between 7:00 and 8:35 A.M. All failed. The enemy had had too much time to consolidate.[33] Currie summed it up: "The difficulties were extremely great, the 3rd Brigade had to march from seven to nine miles, pass through most terrific barrages, form up and attack over ground which they had never seen . . . while no one knew just exactly where either our troops or hostile troops were." Captain Walter Crichley, 10th Battalion, thought the whole attack "a pretty bad show." Private Fraser, 31st Battalion, said it "should never have been delivered."[34]

Command, as always, entailed assessment of subordinates, some of whom did not measure up. Currie wrote Victor Odlum, then recovering in hospital, that Major Bernard Humble, who commanded the 7th Battalion during the assault, "will [hardly] do to succeed you," an assessment probably based on what he perceived as lack of a grip. Told to report to the CO of the 10th Battalion (J.G. Rattray), who was to lead a combined attack, Humble apparently made only one attempt to contact the 10th by runner and this not until 2:30 A.M. At 5:00 A.M. a captain from the 7th finally established contact. Judging by his report, Humble seems to have contented himself with passing messages between the brigade, 10th Battalion and the four companies of the 7th that, under two captains, participated in the counterattack. He simply did not take hold.[35]

A subsequent counterattack on 13 June, the first Canadian planned deliberate attack of the war, proved very different. Figuratively and factually the two counterattacks, on 13 and 3 June, were like night and day. Zero on 13 June was 1:30 A.M. under the cover of night, unlike the daylight and "hopeless" Zero on 3 June. That attack's sole gain was start positions for the subsequent attack, later described as an "unqualified success" thanks to good artillery support and thorough preparation.[36] For the night attack tight control measures included the establishment of brigade and division "Advanced Report Centres" and parties of runners to relay messages (which greatly improved passage of information and communications generally), and navigation aids, such as railway flares set out to delineate boundaries and coloured flares to indicate progress.[37]

Three battalions made the actual assault. Lieutenant-Colonel W.D. Allan displayed his great tactical sense: it being a night attack, he decided there would be no firing, just bayonets, which added to the surprise; prior to Zero he moved part of his 3rd Battalion into No Man's Land; and on consolidation he ignored the captured enemy trench, instead digging a new line some 100 yards distant. The two latter decisions helped the unit avoid some enemy artillery fire. Allan's "quiet but forceful personality" contributed to his reputation as a "remarkable" man. One of his officers said of him: "What Billy Allan thinks to himself today, the whole battalion is thinking tomorrow." That is quite an accolade. 3rd Battalion spent 5 to 9 June in the line, during which time it identified the whole of the enemy outpost line and the sub-unit commanders had ample time to view the ground. On 9 June the 3rd went into rest, not returning to the line until Sunday, 11 June, when it had time for further reconnaissance prior to issue of battalion orders. During its reconnaissance 16th Battalion found a disused trench, which became its assembly trench and was free of fire for most of the time. Overall, time sufficed for careful battle procedure in every unit. It was very smooth.[38]

Mount Sorrel brought home several lessons. One lesson reiterated the value of well-briefed guides, another the merit of holding the front lightly with reserves close by in deep dugouts. 3rd Division stressed the "importance of good wire," a tacit admission that its failure to maintain its wire properly had made it easier for the enemy to penetrate the division's trenches. On 13 June none of the assault units reported any particular difficulty with enemy wire. One lesson of Givenchy was overlooked at Mount Sorrel: enemy artillery had continued its nasty habit of burying or destroying stocks of bombs and ammunition. Both 1st and 3rd Divisions recommended that in future these be held in deep dugouts, or, if these were not available, in smaller, more widely separated dumps.[39]

Summing up, while the enemy made some initial gains, all were given up by 14 June. He lost nearly 6,000 men during the period 2–14 June. The Canadian Corps suffered almost 8,500 casualties, 4,396 of these from 1st Division. Officer casualties were especially high. Paul Villiers, at the time a junior staff officer at divisional HQ, reported that in his old battalion (16th) of three NCOs who were commissioned the day before the attack, two came out each in command of a company and the third was 2IC of another.[40] The Germans later blamed their failure to hold the ground on superior enemy artillery. The British official history offered a simpler explanation: "the better soldiers won."[41]

With the crisis past, Byng looked for ways to worry the enemy. The German lines in the ruined village of Hooge, some 2,500 yards north of Mount Sorrel, and a small lodgement halfway between the two became the

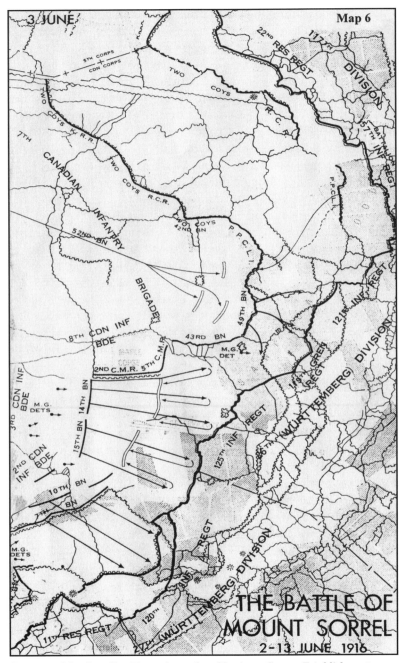

Courtesy of the Canadian Forces (reproduced by Army Survey Establishment.
Compiled and drawn by Historical Section G. S.)

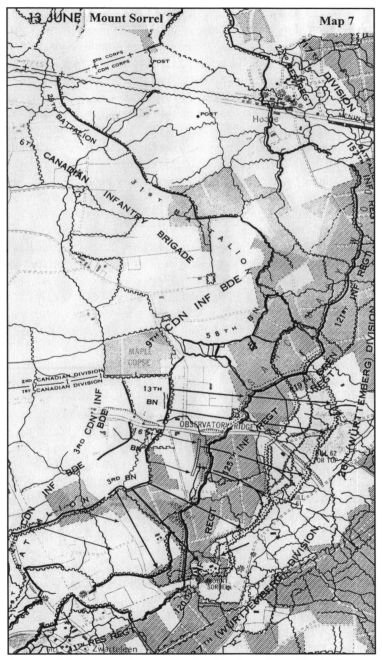

Courtesy of the Canadian Forces (reproduced by Army Survey Establishment.
Compiled and drawn by Historical Section G. S.)

objectives of an attack by Garnet Hughes' fresh 1st Brigade on 8/9 July. Explaining the failure to take these, he and the CO of the assault battalion (the 4th) blamed "non-destruction" of the wire. 2nd Brigade, ordered to attack a week earlier, saw the operation postponed for 24 hours and then cancelled because of wire. Postponement was ordered because of dust, which had prevented accurate artillery fire and observation of its efficiency in cutting the German wire. The next day the dust had cleared and the 18-pounders renewed their cutting efforts, this time satisfactorily. But the attack was cancelled once more because the CO of the assault battalion convinced his brigadier (Frederick Loomis) that the fire over two days had twice warned the enemy, making chances of success very poor. Here, and later at the Somme, "the type of shell was in many instances unsuitable . . . those who were there will recollect their disheartening task of endeavouring to cut wire with field gun shrapnel."[42]

Relative quiet marked the rest of the summer in the Ypres salient, the highlight being 7th Battalion's defeat of an attempt to recapture the Bluff, a strongpoint on the north bank of the Ypres-Comines Canal southeast of Ypres. Lieutenant-Colonel S.D. Gardner, who had been CO for only five days, responded energetically, preventing the enemy achieving anything whatsoever. Byng and the Army commander echoed Currie's comment: "The more I think of your handling of the situation . . . the better pleased I am."[43]

A tactical error by an officer of 16th Battalion in the line in the Hill 60 sector in July 1916 was less pleasing, causing strong "disapproval of the Higher Command for the loss of a prisoner."[44] When the officer, a captain commanding the listening posts of the right company of the 16th, withdrew his men into a sap where they could avoid the worst of the mortar fire, they lost their ability to warn of a raid, this being exactly what the enemy had counted on. The OC the listening posts of the left company of the flanking battalion, the 13th, also withdrew some of his men. Although he left some sentries in place, they were not so located to warn of a threat. The raiders entered the Canadian trenches at the inter-battalion boundary, no men of the 16th Battalion being in position to prevent them, and the 13th Battalion being ignorant of the intrusion until it was attacked from the open flank. The total bill for the neglect came to one officer and 10 ORs killed, 29 ORs wounded and one missing. Furious, Currie wrote the brigade commander:

> In withdrawing all his posts [the Captain] showed a lack of tactical knowledge which one does not expect in one of his rank. Had he paid sufficient attention to the lessons of Trench Warfare or had these lessons been sufficiently impressed on him . . . he would have expected a raid or at least made arrangements to deal with a raid . . .

The whole affair is a serious reflection on the training and discipline of this Battalion; it shows an indifference to the teaching of the War and a lack of appreciation of the responsibilities of officers, which I will not tolerate.

When Tuxford responded that he had personally "explained a good many things" to the COs and 2ICs of both battalions Currie, unappeased, ordered all concerned to be at his HQ two days hence. No doubt, strong language ensued. Currie, and Tuxford, too, may well have reminded these Regimental officers of the wisdom that says, "Do your duty and you have nothing to fear; just be damned sure you know what your duty is."[45] While the affair greatly annoyed him, Currie knew mistakes were inevitable. Officers and men had come a very long way but they required further training and experience. The word got around. Brigadiers emphasized being prepared; Hughes, for example, warned that officers and NCOs must "take hold," and all ranks had to know what to do in emergencies. He also ordered additional patrols: "Do not permit a single German to get in front of his parapet."[46]

By 4 September 1916 the Canadian Corps had relieved 1st ANZAC on the Somme (Pozieres). 1st Division held the whole of the new front (3,000 yards), leaving 2nd and 3rd Divisions in reserve to prepare for the attack that the C-in-C intended to launch in mid-September. On the left, 3rd Brigade worked hard repairing very battered trenches and beating off counterattacks. 1st Brigade had a quieter time, except for 2nd Battalion, which, as ordered, attacked an enemy salient on 9 September, the aim being to pinch it off as a pre-cursor to the coming offensive. The salient, about 500 yards long, was 150 to 200 yards away, a distance that was reduced by half once a jumping-off trench had been dug 50 to 75 yards in advance of 2nd Battalion's lines. At Zero, 4:45 P.M., intense artillery fire opened on the enemy and the assault commenced, fire lifting at Zero plus three just as the infantry reached the enemy line. Within twenty minutes 2nd Battalion reported success, due to the short, intense bombardment (surprise), the arrival on the objective of the infantry at almost the second that the fire ceased (more surprise and perfect timing), and, above all, good planning and battle procedure. The excellence of this operation can be surmised from the fact that Currie chose to keep copies of Lieutenant-Colonel A.E. Swift's splendid Operation Order and other relevant orders and reports in his papers. It is no exaggeration to say, as an early account did, that the attack featured "a precision that left nothing to be desired."[47] Swift's intelligence officer (IO) hit the mark when he wrote at the time:

A minor operation demands as much careful thought and studious enquiry as any large one. There are still the hundred and one things to be considered. Information must be exact; communication is vitally important; the consolidating wave must know where and how it is to work; the wounded must be tended; prisoners are expected and guards have to be detailed; and everyone must know just exactly what the operation is, why it is done and when it takes place. The responsibility lies ultimately with the CO and his operation order must meet every contingency. Undoubtedly the whole reason for the latest trench-snatching operation being termed "brilliant" lies in the completeness of the preparation.[48]

This well planned and equally well executed operation shows how far 1st Division had come in 18 months. Any of its 12 battalions would probably have done as well.[49]

1st Division played no part in the Battle of Flers-Courcelette until 18 September, three days after it began. That morning it deployed on 2nd Division's left flank, ready to do its part in executing the Army plan which called for two corps, II (Imperial) on the left and Canadian on the right, to capture the ridge running northeast of Courcelette to the Schwaben Redoubt north of Thiepval, thereby ending enemy observation of our rear areas and affording us the advantage of overlooking his. Each corps had half the 6,000 yard frontage. Zero was set for 12:35 P.M., Tuesday, 26 September. The Corps' Operation Order, issued more than 48 hours before Zero, is notable in two aspects: first, for its emphasis on control, specifically an exchange of liaison officers (LOs) between 1st and 2nd Divisions and between the 1st Division and the 11th (Imperial) Division of II Corps; and, second, its direction that 1st Division echelon one battalion behind its left assault battalion to fill any gap that might develop between the 1st and the 11th. This proved not only prudent but prescient.[50] Initially, the 1st had three objectives: the Zollern Graben, Hessian and Regina Trenches, the last including Kenora Trench, a spur that ran eastward from Regina and was covered by Sudbury Trench some 500 yards to the south. Subsequently, its final objective became a line running along Kenora, then across an open area to Hessian and along it to the Corps left boundary. The amendment to the Operation Order left Regina Trench, on the reverse slope of the ridge northwest of Courcelette, until later, intelligence (especially about wire) being sketchy.

Currie opted to attack with Tuxford on the right and Loomis on the left, each assaulting with two reinforced battalions (one additional company each). Because of the change in objectives, the GSO1 (Kearsley), issued two Operation Orders, one on 22 and the second on 24 September, plus, a day later a two-page "Reference"; the latter's conditional language ("if," "should," "if practicable"), usually frowned upon in operational writing, in this case revealed Byng's aggressiveness and his willingness to let Currie decide if 1st Division could or should push on to take Regina Trench. To this end, Byng gave Currie 4th Brigade from 2nd Division under command, thereby providing a ready exploitation force.[51] Operation Orders reflect 1st Division's customarily thorough battle procedure. On receipt of the first order Loomis (2nd Brigade) issued a preliminary Operation Order, which laid on rehearsals and brought together all detailed men in one area, assigning them duties such as battle stop, stretcher bearer, and carrier for bombs and ammunition. 3rd Brigade (Tuxford) decided not to hold rehearsals but otherwise its battle procedure was as thorough, and more so when it came to such control measures as liaison.[52]

At Zero the brigades got off to a good start. 2nd Brigade attacked in four waves, each battalion accompanied by two brigade machine-guns and Stokes mortars.[53] Artillery fire was "extremely effective," more so than the enemy's which did not disrupt operations unduly despite catching the last assault wave before it was clear of Canadian trenches.[54] Before 1:00 P.M. the 2nd had taken its first objective, Zollern Graben Trench, despite heavy enfilade fire from the left flank where 11th (Imperial) Division was supposed to be but was not. After reorganizing, the 2nd moved on, quickly securing Hessian Trench.

By 3:30, seeing no sign of the 11th and fearing a counterattack, John Prower, the CO of 8th Battalion, the left assault unit, ordered the extra company he had been given to barricade the left flank. Immediately Loomis knew of the problem, he ordered 7th Battalion forward to dig and occupy a new trench running north-south between Hessian and Zollern Graben Trenches. He also requested and received pioneers from 3rd Division to help build the new flank. 7th Battalion ended up doing most of the work because the 150 pioneers who arrived and were ordered to the new trench "refused to trust the guide and returned . . . at 12 midnight numbering 30 All Ranks and in a demoralised condition." 1st Division pioneers, on the other hand, "worked faithfully and secured excellent results."[55] Firm contact with the 11th was not established until the next day.[56]

3rd Brigade was also well away at Zero, helped by "beautiful" fire support. Its last assault wave, like the 2nd Brigade's, suffered from artillery fire before it vacated the jumping-off trench. Rather than deploy machine-guns and mortars with the assault waves Tuxford used the former in the indirect role and kept the latter at his HQ; he saw no use for them owing to the difficulty of transporting ammunition. He thought the machine-gun fire had "great moral effect," but did not elaborate. At least two COs were less complimentary: 4th and 5th Battalions complained that in opening before Zero, the machine-gunners spoiled any chance of surprise and the flash of their fire drew artillery fire. Clearly, fire support coordination was flawed. In a technical sense, the machine-gunners were at fault but responsibility lay with the brigadiers. Two hours after Zero, 14th and 15th Battalions, despite heavy casualties, held Kenora Trench and the open space between it and Hessian Trench. Here the spade, the soldier's second best friend, came into furious play. By late afternoon a new trench dominated the open space. Kenora could not be held, however. An attempt to re-take it failed, the 14th by this time reduced to some 75 men.[57]

Shortly after the relief of 1st Division on 28 September, Loomis complained that 11th (Imperial) Division's failure "in maintaining touch with us [and] capturing the strong positions which over-looked and commanded our area prevented us from giving very much attention to Regina Trench."[58] This was true but continued enemy occupation of Kenora Trench also had much to do with it. 3rd Division and the 11th took all of Hessian Trench by 30 September but the attack on Regina Trench, the next Canadian objective, by 2nd and 3rd Divisions on Sunday, 1 October, fared poorly. By the end of the day the assault troops (now fewer) were back in their start trenches.[59]

On return to the line on the night of 4/5 October 1st Division took over the right of the Corps line, 3rd Brigade on the left and 1st Brigade on the right. While the infantry connected advanced positions with new trenches and dug jumping-off trenches for the next assault set for 4:50 A.M. on Sunday, 8 October, the gunners struck at the enemy trenches and his wire, cutting it in many places; but each night the gaps were filled with concertina wire. 1st Division's objective, a two-mile stretch of Regina Trench, included the formidable "Quadrilateral," so named because of the double rows of east-west trenches meeting double rows of north-south trenches.

1st Division's assault brigades attacked on 8 October with two battalions each. The events of that day, which became known as the Regina Trench Disaster, strongly influenced Currie's ideas on command and control.[60] Uncut wire prevented 13th Battalion from getting into Regina Trench, and only a hundred or so men of the 16th did. The most junior subaltern in 4th Battalion, W.H. Joliffe, described the men becoming "sitting ducks" as they bunched up to try to get through the wire. Congestion increased when the 4th crowded into the enemy trenches that were held by the 3rd Battalion, which had not encountered wire.[61] The enemy responded with intense artillery fire and an endless rain of bombs which separated the two battalions and then rolled them up. Lacking any bombs with which to retaliate— the supply had been exhausted and more had not come forward—and with no ammunition left for its sole remaining Lewis gun, 3rd Battalion fought hand-to-hand, the struggle so severe that one officer was forced to shoot a number of men who "could not be induced to counterattack." Both units had to withdraw. Losses equated to the virtual destruction of three battalions.

Joliffe had become senior subaltern of the 4th Battalion.[62]

1st Brigade's ordeal continued afterward. The Army commander demanded from Corps "a full report upon the attack [including] . . . reasons for failure" and answers to many other questions such as:

1. The jumping-off place. Did the Infantry start from trenches or did they line up in the open? Was the jumping-off place satisfactory as to siting, and what was the average distance from the objective?

2. The artillery barrage. What was the rate of advance and was the infantry able to keep close up to it?

3. Was the wire satisfactorily cut? What reports had been received from the infantry on this point prior to the attack?

4. Was liaison between infantry and artillery satisfactory?

5. What were the reasons for the retirement of the 1st Bde . . . Has this Brigade made proper preparations for the supply of bombs etc? When the counterattack was delivered, was artillery support properly forthcoming?

6. Was the communication between 1st Brigade Headquarters and the Battalion Headquarters satisfactory?

7. What lateral communications was there with the left of the III Corps?

8. What orders were issued by the Brigade Commander, and why was it that no counterattack was ordered and organised? [63]

Currie's report filled seven pages. His answers to the first four paragraphs were: the jumping-off place was satisfactory; the rate of advance was such that the infantry kept up to the barrage; the wire was not satisfactorily cut, and reports on it prior to the attack were inaccurate; and infantry-artillery liaison was not what it should have been. As for paragraph 5, he said that 1st Brigade did not retire but was forced back by artillery, weight of numbers and lack of bombs. Currie held off commenting on "proper preparations" until the conclusion of his report. Liaison (paragraphs 6 and 7) was satisfactory. Finally, 4th Battalion counterattacked but Corps countermanded Currie's order for 1st Brigade to counterattack.

There were, in fact, *three* investigations: General H.P. Gough's demand, a 1st Division Court of Enquiry, and Currie's personal investigation.[64] Gough was more interested in reasons for failure than in culpability; he sought lessons that could teach the entire Army. The Court of Enquiry, established "to investigate the circumstances under which the 1st Canadian Infantry Brigade

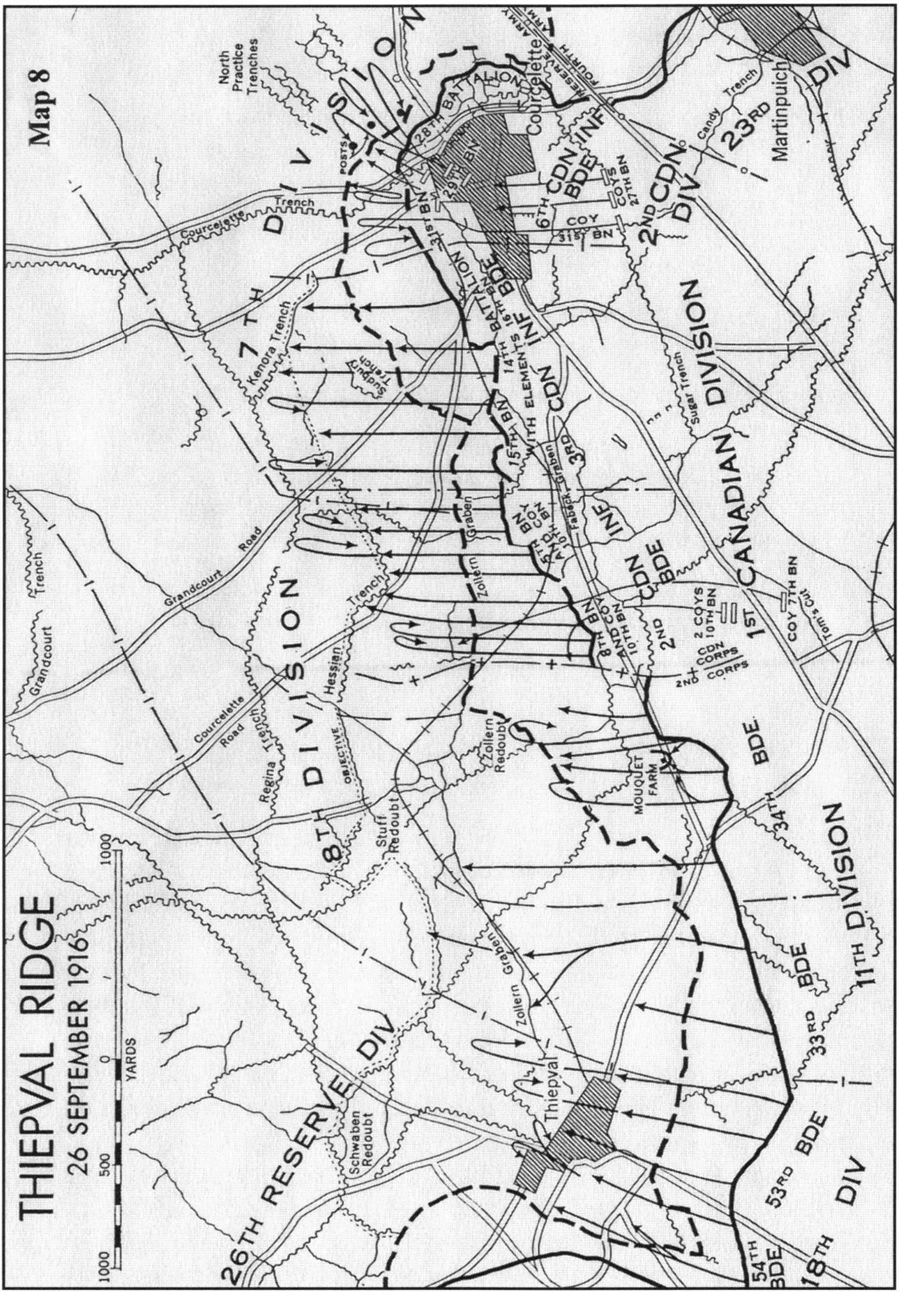

Map 8

THIEPVAL RIDGE
26 SEPTEMBER 1916

Courtesy of the Canadian Forces

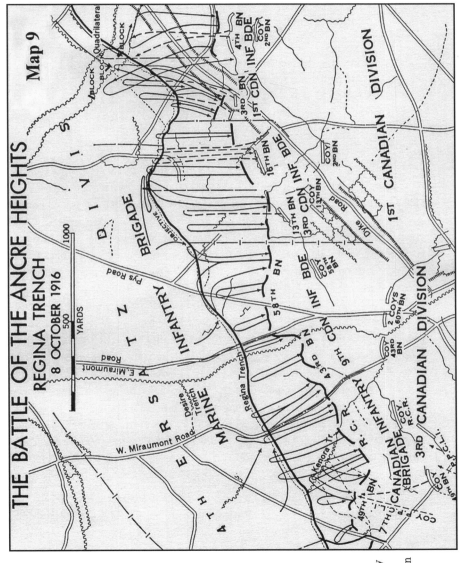

THE BATTLE OF THE ANCRE HEIGHTS
REGINA TRENCH
8 OCTOBER 1916

Map 9

YARDS

500   1000

Courtesy
of the
Canadian
Forces

retired from certain captured positions," had to consider the matter of blame. Was there a command problem in Hughes' 1st Brigade (paragraphs 5, 6 and 8)? Its President, GOC 3rd Brigade (Tuxford), required answers to 21 questions posed by HQ 1st Division regarding attack strength, number of officers involved, casualties, dispositions, enemy reaction, consolidation, number of bombs carried per man, and bomb resupply, and several questions whose tenor is obvious, relating specifically to retirement:

14. What were the reasons for the retirement?
15. Was the order given to retire? If so by whom?
16. Were any steps taken to stop the retirement?
17. Did any of our men surrender? If so how many and where?
18. How many men of each unit got back to our original Line?
19. To what extent did the units suffer during retirement?
22. In your opinion was retirement justifiable?[65]

Gough left Currie (and Byng) to search for every possible tactical lesson. Despite his bad reputation in certain aspects, Gough was a good enough Army commander to let subordinates do their duty. In taking the unusual step of conducting a personal investigation, Currie showed his determination to find out what had gone wrong and why. He was the responsible officer; it was his division that had failed. "Retire," like "Withdraw," conjures up shortcomings that cry out for explanation.

Hughes' part in the attack had been limited because he had not returned from leave until 6 October when he attended the final pre-attack conference held by Lieutenant-Colonel A. E. Swift. As acting GOC in Hughes' absence, Swift had planned the assault.[66] Currie learned that while the 4th had rehearsed the attack for two days, its men had not been properly briefed. He did not comment on the Operation Order issued by the 4th but he criticized 3rd Battalion for its unclear orders and lack of rehearsals. He personally spoke to NCOs from both units who did not know what or where the objective was or with whom they were to join up—strong evidence of inadequate supervision by the acting GOC and the BM (who had been less than a month in that appointment).[67] The Court of Enquiry made only one finding:

This Court finds that there was no general retirement in this action but that the 3rd and 4th Battalions were pushed back, fighting, after a very severe bombardment, by sheer weight of numbers. Our lack of bombs, which it appears could not be got up in sufficient numbers, contributing to this effect.[68]

In the concluding paragraphs of his report Currie blamed uncut wire, not poor orders, for the failure. Also, after bombing their way into Regina Trench, assault troops had insufficient bombs left to hold the gains and had no option but to "get out." Carrying parties taking bombs forward during the day suffered 60% casualties. Had the attack started in the afternoon, Currie thought, the ground could have been held until dark when more bombs could have been delivered forward.[69] The artillery's failure to destroy the wire received far less attention in the after-action reports. For the assault divisional howitzers were allowed only 1,000 rounds each for all tasks, and Corps heavy and medium howitzers had only one heavy or two medium rounds per yard of trench. Spread over the divisional frontages, each about one mile wide, the allocation was parsimonious. After 8 October no limit applied: "each section of trench must be completely obliterated."[70]

Currie listed one other lesson ("The getting of the trench does not mean the getting of the objective.") and one requirement ("The development of qualities of leadership and resolution in officers").[71] His report could not possibly have satisfied. No more could be usefully said or done but to make the changes that would prevent such things in the future. The shortcomings were corrected. 1st Division learned.

One of the great dilemmas of command was whether to attack on a broad front, which thinned artillery support, or to attack on a narrow front, which thickened fire support but allowed the defender to deliver flanking attacks and intense fire. On the Somme Haig tried both options. He set unattainable objectives; the concept and the plan were flawed; and he persisted when he ought not to have.[72] But those who condemn everything about it forget how severely the enemy suffered. German regimental histories commonly refer to "the Hell on the Somme." One general staff officer called it "the muddy grave of the German Field Army." General Ludendorff said "the German Army . . . was utterly worn out." Field Marshal von Hindenburg warned that a second Somme battle had to be avoided.[73]

Many lessons were drawn from the Somme even before it ended. Despite the fact that a manual issued during the course of a great battle could hardly be definitive, *SS 119 Preliminary Notes on the Tactical Lessons of the Recent Operations* was issued in July and again in September 1916. Its main lessons included a renewed reliance on the rifle and bayonet, rather than on the bomb; the identification of the platoon as the "ultimate unit"; and the division of the assault force into four functional groupings. The latter comprised fighting platoons whose task was to press forward; moppers-up, who were to secure the ground won, destroy strongpoints and eradicate any enemy coming up from the deep dugouts; support platoons that formed an immediate ready reserve; and carrying platoons whose men bore the necessities to sustain the assault and the consolidation. During an advance the support and carrying platoons moved in column, commonly referred to as "worms," while the fighting platoons and moppers-up advanced in line. The pattern was lines for fighting and worms for movement.[74] Worms could move faster than waves, which meant they could quickly follow and remain close to the waves, thereby being readily available to support the leading troops. *SS 119* was considerably more sophisticated than earlier *SS* manuals.

Throughout the autumn operational staff officers laboured at preparing a definitive manual, *SS 135 Instructions for the Training of Divisions for Offensive Action*. When issued in December it included seven pages on infantry-artillery coordination, stressing, *inter alia*, the necessity for the infantry to hug the barrage and to cross No Man's Land as quickly as possible.[75] The most notable aspect of *SS 135* is its emphasis on battle procedure; the whole of the introduction and Appendix A relate to preparation and training, including reconnaissance, fire planning, and command and control. It enjoins the divisional commander, immediately he has done his reconnaissance and formed his plan, to issue a "Warning Order" and any necessary preliminary instructions, thereby providing maximum time for subordinates' battle procedure before issue of the executive Operation Order. 1st Division (and the Canadian Corps) also benefitted from Currie's three day visit to the French Army at Verdun. His 16 page report, which was widely distributed within the BEF, includes what the French had learned about command and control at Verdun and Currie's distillation of his own experience as GOC.[76]

On 3 November the BGGS (Radcliffe) sought the opinions of formation and unit commanders "as to the lessons to be derived . . . in order that valuable experiences . . . may be turned to the best account in future operations." The very great distance 1st Division had come professionally is shown in the comprehensive asking and answering of sophisticated tactical questions. The responses of the division, its brigades and eight of its 12 battalions (Tuxford, GOC 3rd Brigade, chose not to forward battalion replies but to collate them into one brigade report) exceed 100 pages.[77] One of the highlights concerned artillery, the essential points being the necessity for the closest possible coordination with the infantry; precise control and direction; and the principle of fire *and* movement, not fire *then* movement: "Formerly when we wanted to take an enemy position we first endeavoured to destroy it by heavy artillery fire, and the cessation of that fire was the signal for the Infantry to advance . . . Now, the beginning of the artillery fire marks the beginning of the Infantry advance." The infantry had to tuck right up to that fire, arriving at the enemy line virtually with the last fall of shot and giving the enemy no time to re-man his parapet. Infantry normally kept about 100 yards behind the falling shells but could get closer if the guns were firing from behind them since the blast was thrown forward. Another highlight was command, the responses echoing *SS 135*: maximize time for battle procedure. Warning orders had become routine.[78]

The responses also stressed control measures, dividing them into two categories: organization before and organization during the attack. The first included measures designed to get the assault troops to their assault positions on time and in good order. Regimental Police enforced march discipline, manned traffic control centres and sign-posted assembly and communications trenches "In" and "Out," thereby keeping traffic flowing and troops on track. When necessary jumping-off lines were also marked. Command posts that were sufficiently hardened to withstand shells were prepared for division and brigade and often even for battalion HQs by sappers and pioneers.

John Prower, who had been CO 8th Battalion for about three months and before that BM 2nd Brigade (September 1915 to August 1916), submitted the best battalion report on lessons. Its thoroughness and its solid ideas, some of which were unique, made it very well received. One idea recommended that a "feel" wire strung along the overland routes used for bringing reinforcements forward would help prevent troops becoming lost during darkness. Another point said the siting of artillery Observation Posts (OPs) should not be left to inexperienced subalterns. In many cases OPs were being sited a thousand or more yards behind the front line despite the availability of better sites immediately behind or even in the front line. Poor choice of OPs meant gunner officers could not always even see SOS signals, let alone respond to them. Tuxford of 3rd Brigade knew personally of requests for SOS fire that had gone unanswered for too long or had not been answered at all. He, Prower and the CO of 5th Battalion all pointed out that artillery OPs required their own telephone lines, otherwise they tied up command nets. Loomis of 2nd Brigade thought forward observation officers (FOOs) were inexperienced in observing and correcting fire, which was no doubt true but he seemed to have forgotten that the only way to get experience was to direct fire.[79] Clearly, infantry-artillery coordination was not yet what it should be. Overall, said Prower, "I cannot say how strongly I feel about the importance of Preliminary Work." COs would hold up their end but division had to become more involved. It was no good CRE or CRA ordering this or that if he then did not see the job done.

Control measures during the attack were equally vital. Using flares and having machine-guns fire on fixed lines helped with the problem of keeping direction at night. Contact with flanking formations, higher HQ and the artillery, as well as communication between base and front, had to be improved. LOs depended on these communications; when they were inadequate, it was futile "to expect liaison between Infantry and Artillery" forward of brigade HQ. Prower's closing thought probably caught the attention of all: "The Divisional Commander, the CRA and the CRE hold the success or failure of the operation in their hands and very often they do not realise it." At the time CRA and CRE were still advisors and would not function as commanders for a few more months.

For a CO, once the attack began, the most frustrating thing was the inability to influence the situation until it had cleared up sufficiently to enable him to judge where to use his reserve. Prower thought that a CO participating in a brigade or division attack should not hold a reserve, because that would tie him too long to his HQ and thereby prevent early reconnaissance of any gains. His suggestion that the reserve be provided by brigade was not a good one: in view of communication inadequacies the brigadier would not know when to send the reserve forward; because of distance the reserve could well arrive too late; and in moving forward it could well be savaged by enemy fire before it could do any good.[80] CO 5th Battalion spoke for all when he commented, "A patchy situation is extremely difficult."[81] In fact, battalion command became "patchy" immediately after Zero: Dan Ormond, CO 10th Battalion, said that for 20 minutes or more after Zero a CO had to depend on subordinates. This made the platoon commander and his training very important.[82] For a CO, the location of his HQ became a "Catch 22": he had to be forward but he had also to maintain communications with brigade Battle HQ (Tactical HQ, or Tac HQ, as we know it today). Command was best exercised from a known HQ location but a feel for the battle and first-hand information could only be obtained by going forward. No really satisfactory answer obtained.

One aspect of control and communications and of all-arms cooperation that received increasing emphasis in the last half of 1916 was ground-air liaison by aircraft contact patrols; they were tasked to keep HQs informed of progress during attacks, to report on enemy opposition and to pass messages between troops, HQs and the artillery. The initial difficulty in establishing the contact system was one of recognition: how was the sender of a message to know that the recipient was friend and not foe (the recipient had the same problem); and how was each to know that the other had understood the message? These problems were soon more or less resolved, and while improvements were clearly necessary, British, Australian and Canadian reports during and after the Somme reveal a general recognition of the airplane's tactical value, especially, as Currie said, in reporting the location of attacking infantry.[83]

Brigade reports in August 1916 and Currie's response show that while "flares in bunches of threes [were] easily distinguished," certain problems had appeared. First, to thwart enemy imitation, the colour of the flares had to be changed frequently. Second, flares had to be carried by many men, not just a few. If only leaders—who were most likely to become casualties—carried flares, the flares would be destroyed or lost. But this was not what lay behind the Corps' complaints to divisions in November that the infantry "frequently" failed to show flares when called for by contact aircraft.[84] Garnet Hughes, then GOC 1st Brigade, reported that while all ranks "thoroughly appreciated" contact patrols, a large number of flares had to be carried to ensure that leading troops retained flares in the attack. Battalion reports from all three brigades indicate that sufficient flares were not getting forward. Currie then ordered that every man carry a flare, these "so fixed that [the men] cannot easily throw them away." Tuxford and Currie knew of the "general feeling" that using flares gave away positions. Reluctance to use flares could only be overcome by training and discipline but this was easier said than done, even in well-disciplined battalions like the 10th, whose CO stated in one report, "All orders shown to me set out that flares must be shown when required." Beside this statement was a handwritten comment, quite probably in the brigade commander's hand: "Yes—but it was not done—Discipline!!"[85]

Despite the shortcomings of flares and ground signal panels (it was not yet clear which was the most effective), the contact patrols proved a useful communications and control measure that helped dissipate some of the customary fog of war. "More careful training of individuals" and "frequent drills with aeroplanes" would further enhance infantry-air cooperation.[86]

On being relieved by Watson's 4th Division on 10 October, 1st Division, together with the 2nd and 3rd, left the Somme for a quiet sector between Arras and Lens, near Vimy. The 4th, which remained behind with II (Imperial) Corps, would greatly distinguish itself in the last Canadian operation on the Somme, the capture of Regina Trench. 1st Division (and the Canadian Corps) stayed some months in the Vimy area. A captured enemy document best sums up the achievements of 1916. Lesson One of "Lessons Learnt from the Battle of the Somme," issued by 53rd Reserve (Saxon) Division, said: "The Infantry attacks with great energy, usually full of confidence in the enormous mass of artillery engaged. The ground captured is stubbornly defended . . . Hitherto, in all the engagements, our infantry has been fully conscious of its own superiority over that of the enemy."[87] Our commanders, whose troops had been long in defence, worried that their men were less alert and the Germans were getting off lightly. J. Byng, Lieutenant-General, Commanding Canadian Corps, wondered if everything possible was being done to damage enemy personnel, material and morale. In view of "future eventualities" (Vimy), he urged the divisions to wear out the enemy, disturb his rest, destroy his shelter and dislocate his traffic. He left unsaid the fact that the perpetrator soon suffers similar perturbation.[88] But the gingering up put the edge back on, as did the preparations for the Vimy Ridge attack. These had started even before Christmas. One enormous benefit was the new "106" instantaneous fuse, which detonated a shell on contact, thereby making HE (high explosive) much more effective against wire. Now firing HE fitted with the new fuse, howitzers could also effectively engage enemy wire on reverse slopes. For Vimy, 88 percent of the artillery allocated by First Army (558 18-pounders, 186 4.5 inch howitzers and 120 medium trench mortars) would target enemy wire; even this was no guarantee since artillery could not always be counted upon to cut adequate gaps in wire more than 2,000 yards distant.[89]

The artillery appreciation for Vimy is particularly interesting for its revelation of the thorough competence of the "long arm." From Zero minus 20 days to Zero, heavy and medium howitzers alone expended 16,000 rounds on wire destruction and 91,000 on trench destruction. 1st Division's share of field, medium and heavy artillery drenched its 2,000-yard front with a total of 9,937 rounds every day. Afterward, every brigade and battalion report said of enemy wire: "No obstacle." Control measures included incredibly redundant liaison and communications, resulting in excellent fire support. Only the heavy artillery received adverse comment: 1st Brigade (Griesbach) found it difficult to control because of too few FOOs. Two of his COs reported "considerable difficulty . . . from shorts." This did not occur in the other two brigades; perhaps Griesbach did not get his fair share of FOOs. Tuxford of 3rd Brigade called fire support "magnificent."[90]

In a command and control sense thorough study of the Vimy records shows just how carefully the Canadian Corps and 1st Division incorporated the lessons of 1916, including those relating to ground-air cooperation. In addition to the routine means of contacting aircraft—lamps, horns and flares—each brigade agreed with its supporting squadron on a location at which men would be stationed to retrieve messages from the aircraft. 1st Division ordered that every rifleman carry two flares and that these would only be fired from the bottom of trenches in hopes of reducing the enemy's ability to locate Canadian positions.[91] Because "the necessity for close liaison with the R.F.C. [Royal Flying Corps] [was] now fully appreciated," artillery brigade commanders were urged to have as many battery commanders as possible visit their supporting squadron to get to know the pilots and observers and to become fully conversant with the methods and difficulties of artillery-aircraft communications. Artillery instructions detailed the main difficulty in artillery-aircraft liaison:

> Experience has shown that it is useless for a pilot to send down corrections unless he knows what battery to send them to, as otherwise batteries accept corrections which are not applicable to themselves, with disastrous results. Further, it is necessary that no other batteries should be shooting in the immediate vicinity, say 200 to 300

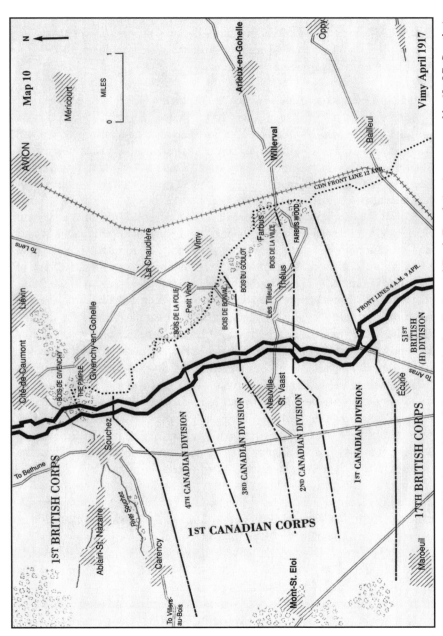

Courtesy of the Calgary Highlanders and The Calgary Highlanders Regimental Funds Foundation (map prepared by 2Lt I.R. Spratley)

yards of the target on which the pilot is working, as it is usually quite impossible for him to pick out his own shells from a large number falling in a limited area, and false corrections are the result. [This] points to the necessity for a definite programme of tasks [and] the necessity for a carefully worked out time-table for all targets requiring aeroplane registration.

The instructions also specified the requirements for preparing, coordinating and executing these timetables. Also included was explicit direction on air photography, which was essential before and after bombardments.[92] Even a cursory read of these instructions confirms the conclusion that "already by 1917 the BEF's effective air-artillery combination of photography and firepower meant that no German . . . anywhere on the battlefield could consider himself safe."[93]

The divisional report on operations from 9 April to 5 May noted how valuable the RFC had been in registration for artillery and in photo reconnaissance but it made no other mention of aircraft. From the infantry point of view, aircraft, including contact patrols, had not been much in evidence. None of the brigades and only one of the 12 battalions remarked on it, and the latter merely said, "The machine allotted . . . was not seen." Behind this absence of activity was, as Corps HQ said, weather "very unfavourable for flying." References to rain or snow and poor visibility feature in most reports.[94] Nor do reports on Arleux and Fresnoy, which followed the Vimy Ridge success, contain much on air activity. They do reflect the continuing reluctance of the infantry to use flares despite Currie's warning that those who did not show them were "liable to be fired on by our own artillery." Brigadiers passed this on to units, adding that flares were especially important when final objectives were reached.[95] Canadian Corps' reports on Vimy and its aftermath praised the RFC for its assistance despite "deplorable" losses, which occurred because of "machines in every way inferior to those of the Germans."[96]

Another innovation at Vimy was the widespread issue of maps down to senior NCO level, including 1:10,000 and 1:20,000 visibility and topographical maps. Officers also received "Special" maps, 1:5,000 scale—12 per CO, 12 per company commander and 8 per platoon commander. One side of the special map had a message form on which the user was to number and note the time and place of writing. The reverse had a map of the German trenches upon which the user was to mark his position.[97]

None of the brigade or battalion commanders complained about communications at Vimy; the usual comment was "Good throughout." Deeply buried cable, redundant lines down to brigade HQs and artillery batteries and the use of all means of communication, voice and visual, ensured satisfaction. 1st

Division had also ordered the connection of brigade report centres to the division centre and had established battalion report centres under battalion IOs, who collected and communicated all messages from observers and companies to the CO, brigades and flanking units.[98]

Clearly, control measures featured prominently in orders. Of the 24 points that the GSO1 (Kearsley) raised with 1st Brigade, half dealt with control: the brigade order required clarification of the movement times of HQs (and their locations); lateral liaison laterally, Battle Stops; and consolidation. From the other two brigades he sought clarification in only a few minor matters. Traffic control facilities and procedures were very thorough, including the opening of traffic control posts, a Battle HQ for each brigade, and one battalion HQ in the tunnels and galleries. Above ground, Regimental Police closely regulated traffic and carefully signed routes to make traffic patterns clear to all. Luminous stakes showed each assault unit the way into communications trenches where guides met and took them on to their assembly trenches. Each brigade assigned 44 men to Battle Stops to prevent straggling. All ranks were warned not to fall out to attend to wounded men. Other means of maintaining control included painting stripes on haversacks so that waves could be easily distinguished and proper distance maintained. This did not please third wave battalions; their assigned colour was yellow.[99]

When it went in at 5:30 A.M. on 9 April the assault was virtually textbook perfect. 4th Battalion suffered only four casualties between its jumping-off trench and the first objective. Ready but untouched meals on the tables in the dugouts testified to how hurriedly the enemy had departed. 3rd Brigade noted that 120 rounds per man had been more than ample, "considering the little use to which the rifle was put." As Tuxford said, "The extraordinary success that the operation met with, running as it did absolutely according to timetable, emphasized the value of the training received; the artillery preparation and cooperation, and the individual confidence of every man." 1st Division attributed success to a good plan, excellent artillery support, good intelligence, sound leadership, confidence and discipline.[100] Vimy was the epitome of good battle procedure. Luck was a lady, as well, for the enemy, quite contrary to his doctrine, held his counterattack divisions too far back for them to be able to intervene—"one of the dramatic tactical failures of the war," said one historian.[101] Given time to consolidate, the Canadians made their new ridge positions unbreakable.

In June the most important changes in the Canadian Corps involved command. Arthur Currie replaced Sir Julian Byng who left to assume command of Third Army. Neither promotion came as a surprise. 1st Division's new GOC, Archibald Macdonell, who came from 7th Brigade, was largely unknown in 1st Division but would very quickly make it his.

Field Marshal Haig thought that one of Byng's greatest contributions to the Corps was his elimination of most of the "jealousy and friction" that had existed between the Canadian divisions in 1915 and the first half of 1916. As Haig also pointed out, Byng's dissatisfaction with Canadian training in Britain had initiated a process of change that wrought significant improvement.[102] As a field commander, Byng had guided the Corps through Mount Sorrel, the first attack he had conducted, and through the dark days of the Somme, where he had not been comfortable with the rigidity of Army plans for the attacks. One of the first to grasp the significance of the lessons of the Somme, he ordered divisions to conduct a detailed analysis to determine the reasons for the lack of success, particularly failure of the artillery to cut the wire, the inability to identify objectives, the poor training of reinforcements, and the inappropriateness of assault formations, thus initiating a process of doctrinal review that was to become a permanent feature of Corps operations. Organizational adjustments were not ignored either. Here, in the words of one Canadian brigadier, Byng "revolutionized a lot of our organization and made it much more sensible." Byng participated—indeed, decisively so—in the evolution of the battle platoon in the Canadian Corps and in the departure from rigid linear formations in favour of the new tactic of section "rushes," a development that greatly enhanced combat effectiveness.[103] He also had the gift of being able to inspire men. His integrity and moral courage were apparent in his refusal of the elder Hughes' demand that his son, Garnet, be given command of 3rd Division after Major-General M.S. Mercer was killed in action. Byng was well known for his strong support of subordinates, right or wrong. All of these qualities made him not only respected but liked, and the Corps was sorry to see him leave.

Arthur Currie brought to his new appointment the traits that had served 1st Division so very well. Currie had gone from militia Colonel to Lieutenant-General in 33 months, showing better and better as each month passed and as his responsibilities broadened. After assuming command of 1st Division in September 1915, he had taken full advantage of the several relatively quiet months of late 1915 and early 1916 to learn the business of a division commander. He learned it so well that in Byng's mind no other officer would do to take over the Canadian Corps.

At first sight Currie did not look the part. He had, unfortunately, a physique that recommended itself to caricaturists and critics alike. He was over six feet tall and weighed well over 200 pounds, and his huge, pear-shaped torso was divided by a Sam Browne belt, which rode up above the large bottom of the pear, looking almost like a brassiere. Private Frank Baxter recalled hearing one soldier ask another, in reference to Currie's bulk, "Who'd want to be three-to-a-loaf with that bugger?" Lieutenant

James Pedley thought Currie's nickname, "Guts and Gaiters," appropriate. Pedley, one week with his unit (4th Battalion), confused his Brigadier, William Griesbach ("soldierly of face and bearing") with the Corps commander, Arthur Currie ("coarse and obese"). "Instinct," said Pedley, prompted him to salute Griesbach first, a discourtesy for which he was severely rebuked. Pedley thought Currie lacked the "winning personality that makes a man beloved as well as great." It is unfortunate that junior officers and ORs were not more aware of Currie's concern for them. He did not like to see them "mucked about," a good example being his reaction to the decision by the teetotaller COs of the 7th and 10th Battalions (Victor Odlum and J.G. Rattray) to deny the men their rum ration: "Currie raised hell, asking them whose rum they thought it was."[104]

Often commanders at every level become "Dad" or "Daddy." General Sir Herbert Plumer, GOC Second Army, was exactly that. So obvious was his concern for the lives of his men that they, in turn, greatly admired him. A soldier querying an Australian battalion, "Where are you off to, Aussie?" received the telling reply, "We don't know but thank God we're going to Daddy Plumer's Army.[105] Currie was never "Daddy," unlike his successor, A.C. Macdonell.

Currie may not have been an inspirational leader but he was a strong one and a firm disciplinarian. He knew good men when he saw them, and he knew how to get the best out of them. Those nearest him came to admire him greatly. Even Pedley agreed that Currie was "great."[106] At Mount Sorrel (June 1916) his initiative in sending forward elements of the 10th Battalion saved the immediate situation by sealing off the German penetration. He then rapidly formed the two composite brigades that under 3rd Division successfully counterattacked. After the Regina Trench "disaster" (October 1916) Currie vigorously pursued its lessons. His analysis, which spared neither himself nor his subordinate commanders, aimed at identifying the reasons for failure and ensuring they were not repeated. The search for lessons became a prime characteristic of Currie the division commander and Currie the Corps commander.

A 53-year-old professional officer when he became GOC Old Red Patch in July 1917, Macdonell also believed strongly in lessons and in the incessant teaching of them—convictions absorbed during his days as a mounted policeman and as a Permanent Force cavalry officer in South Africa and in Canada. In May 1915 he took his regiment, Lord Strathcona's Horse, to France and on promotion in December he assumed command of 7th Brigade. Opinions on him were divided. While this is true in regard to all officers, Macdonell had very mixed reviews, indeed. Although he was "Daddy" to some, others called him "Batty Mac." Lieutenant Pedley described one exhortation (Macdonell was famous for these):

>"Who are you?" Macdonell would shout.
>"The Red Patch" came our answering yell.
>"Are you with me?" from the platform.
>"Yes!" from the crowd.
>If we didn't yell loud enough the first time, the performance was
>repeated until we did. You could stand even that kind of thing from
>Batty Mac, who had been eighteen years a subaltern.[107]

Major H.S. Cooper of 3rd Battalion thought Macdonell "a wonderful chap, marvelous."[108] Brigadier-General J.E.B. Seely, who commanded the Canadian Cavalry Brigade, considered Macdonell "one of the most remarkable men alive." He especially recalled Macdonell's "various mottoes" and his character:

>To grouse was a crime; nobody groused. Shell-shock was a delusion:
>all through the war nobody had shell-shock. To surrender
>unwounded was disgraceful: nobody surrendered unwounded.
>Altogether he was the embodiment of a fine military tradition,
>owing little to precedent, everything to character.[109]

Private E.W. Russell of 5th Battalion credited Macdonell with "the reputation of giving every thought for the welfare of the men." Private William Woods of 1st Battalion disagreed. He believed that while Macdonell cared about Old Red Patch, he "did not give a damn" about the men who wore it. Woods considered Macdonell a "Yes Man" who should never have been given 1st Division. In his opinion William Griesbach had a better claim, being a far better officer. Macdonell (and Currie), he said, did not know enough "to come in out of the rain.[110] A private soldier's perspective cannot be strategic, of course, especially when written late in life. The "unconventional" Macdonell, exhibited a "vivid behaviour . . . and terse exposition [that made him] a personality about whom the rear rank wove many far-fetched stories."[111] Tough and colourful, with the ability to zero in on faults in tactics or whatever caught his eye Batty Mac became a good brigadier, so good that Currie chose him, from amongst some very good brigadiers, to command 1st Division. Currie would not be disappointed.[112]

After Vimy and the follow-on operations (Arleux and Fresnoy) the Corps went over briefly to the defensive. The subsequent assault on Hill 70, on the outskirts of Lens, on 15 August made a good start for Currie as GOC. It also showed that the Corps could move swiftly from one phase of war to another. Unlike Vimy, where faulty German deployment had made consolidation easy, retaining the gains at Hill 70 would be the hard part of the operation. Anticipating this, he ordered special attention to consolidation: systematic and complete mopping-up; special measures for dealing with machine-gun emplacements and dugouts located between trench lines; and rapid defensive preparation, including wire "in view of the heavy counterattacks to be expected." The Corps, as it happened, defeated no fewer than 21 counterattacks launched over three days.[113]

Once again, time for battle procedure was ample. Upon being told on 7 July to capture Lens, Currie pointed out that high ground on both sides dominated Lens. Better, he said, to seize Hill 70, a position so vital to the enemy that he would try to recover it and would expend much blood in the attempt. By 10 July, with Army convinced that Hill 70 should be the objective, staff planning intensified. On 16 July the assault divisions, the 1st and the 2nd, went into the line, the 1st on the left. From north to south the assault brigades were the 3rd and the 2nd.[114] Just as at Vimy, artillery support was lavish; each division attacked behind a barrage from 125 guns. Heavy artillery pulverized strongpoints and trenches, while counter-battery assets struck at enemy gun lines. Mortars thickened the fire, supplemented by massed machine-guns firing in the indirect role. These machine-guns came under control of the formation whose area they covered but brigades could not move them or alter their fire.[115] The RFC attacked, destroyed enemy observation balloons, and engaged rear area targets such as the most likely concentration areas and heavy artillery gun positions. Contact patrols flew at several specific times. Macdonell, in his first order as GOC 1st Division, warned that if the infantry expected support, it must contact the aircraft but that only forward troops should use flares.[116]

Battle procedure for Hill 70 is laid out nicely in 1st Division's report. Upon receipt of its orders, the division directed brigades to organize their trenches for the attack in accordance with *SS 135*: prepare assembly, jumping-off and communications trenches, with the required signing; establish Battle Stops (each brigade worked on the basis of 10 posts, four men at each, and two Collecting Stations); and assign Trench Police for traffic control. Just as at Vimy, advanced Report Centres opened. Other preparations included construction of HQ bunkers, selection of areas for dumps, and organization of brigade carrying parties; in 3rd Brigade, as an experiment, a pack mule company was devoted entirely to moving ammunition forward.[117]

Zero came at 4:25 A.M. on Wednesday, 15 August, just as dawn broke. By 6:00 A.M., some 90 minutes later, both divisions were consolidating on the final objectives. The infantry and the 150 or so Vickers that had accompanied them made ready to meet the first of the counterattacks that began after 7:00 A.M. Artillery and the Vickers smashed the attacks, a pattern that persisted until the enemy finally gave it up early on18 August. 1st Division casualties from 15 to 21 August totalled 3,000. Currie estimated 20,000 enemy casualties:

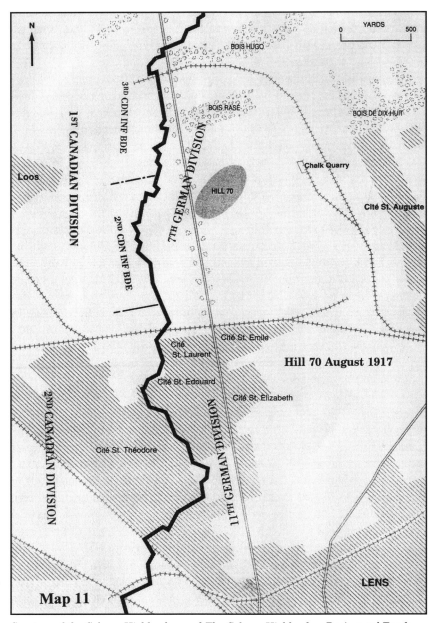

Map 11

Hill 70 August 1917

Courtesy of the Calgary Highlanders and The Calgary Highlanders Regimental Funds Foundation (map prepared by 2Lt I.R. Spratley)

"Our guns, machine-guns and infantry never had such targets, FOOs could not get guns for all their targets . . . It was a great and wonderful victory. G.H.Q. regard it as one of the finest performances of the war.[118]

Aircraft contact patrols did not feature largely at Hill 70. Macdonell's comment that 16 Squadron's patrols rendered "valuable assistance" seems pro forma considering that the division "Narrative of Events" for 15 August (a very detailed 14-page log with 196 entries) mentions only one contact report, and the logs for 16 to 18 August (a total of 18 pages with over 200 entries) contain none. 2nd Brigade's only reference to contact said that aircraft did not "O.K." or drop any messages. Tuxford (3rd Brigade) remarked that enemy aircraft often had the air to themselves. One of his COs, G.E. McCuaig of 13th Battalion, complained that "our aeroplanes did not show up." Lieutenant-Colonel Bent of the 15th Battalion said that his unit saw no aircraft at all. None of the other battalions in the two assault brigades mentioned contact aircraft in their reports. Two battalions (5th and 10th) described extremely active enemy aircraft flying at low altitudes, firing machine-guns, spotting positions, and registering artillery, this in a short time bringing very heavy fire.[119]

Overall, Hill 70 confirmed the lessons of Vimy: prepare thoroughly and in detail, train hard, and build in redundant control and communications. Consolidation was another key factor. Had the attack not been so well planned and supported, which enabled rapid consolidation, determined counterattacks might have allowed the enemy to restore his lines. As it was, the two Canadian divisions broke up five German divisions in three days. This in itself is a good definition of effectiveness.

After a breather, the Corps returned in October to Second Army (Plumer) in the Ypres Salient. On 18 October it relieved the Australians northeast of Ypres, an area of some familiarity, 1st Division having held part of the ground in 1915. For Passchendaele the C-in-C intended an initial three-phase operation, each phase separated by three or more days, to secure the village of Passchendaele. Next, the high ground east and north of the village would be secured. The whole operation was aimed at acquiring full observation over enemy positions to the northeast. Opposed were three regiments deployed in two zones: an outpost zone some 500 to 1,000 yards deep, featuring large numbers of hardened concrete machine-gun emplacements (named "Pillboxes" because of their profile) that were impervious to field artillery; and behind this the main line, backed up by counterattack forces in dugouts. Canadian Corps objectives in Phases One and Two (26 and 30 October) were assigned to 3rd and 4th Divisions. Once again, the plan included massive, closely coordinated fire support. After considerable difficulty in locating and redeploying the available artillery, the GOCRA (Morrison) had in hand 210 18-pounders,

190 howitzers and 26 heavy guns to shoot the two divisions on to their objectives.[120] In the event, Phase One attained footholds on higher and drier ground; from these good positions Phase Two achieved gains of up to 1,000 yards on a 2,800-yard front, an excellent basis for subsequent phases.

In preparation for Phase Three, during the early morning of 5 November 1st and 2nd Divisions completed their relief of the 3rd and 4th Divisions. By 4 A.M. the next day the troops were in their jumping-off trenches, 1st Division on the left. Currie had planned a two stage attack, Stage One (6 November) to seize the village and, four days later, Stage Two to secure the crest of the ridge. Griesbach, whose 1st Brigade would execute the first stage, ordered a two battalion assault. Once his leading wave held the first objective, about 1,300 yards distant, the second and third waves would leapfrog to take the second and final objective. Leapfrogging was necessary because of the enemy deployment. Snuffing out the pillboxes would take time, which meant delay and the loss of the barrage cover that would continue toward the next objective. Consequently, Griesbach rejected the "Straight-Through" system where the leading waves went directly to the most distant objective. While a leapfrog necessitated a passing through by waves—always an awkward time—it offered the advantage that each wave had only one objective to worry about. Because of the nature of the defence—no well-defined trench system but rather pillboxes and strongpoints—systematic mopping-up and maintenance of contact with the flanks were vital. As for command, he ordered that every man in every section be "told off in order of seniority so as to replace any section commander who may become a casualty, so that at no time will a section be without a definite leader."[121] Communications did not pose the usual problem, because it took only three hours to secure the village.

Afterward, when asked what had ensured success, Griesbach answered that it was good battle procedure and command and control. Early information, which permitted thorough study, greatly helped, too. Once in the line, a steady stream of brigade officers had started to reconnoitre. In fact, the time available had been such that COs became thoroughly familiar with preliminary plans and the ground, and Griesbach had time to consult them prior to issuing his confirmatory orders the day before Zero. The troops, too, had a full day to adjust to the ground. His other principle—"success lies always in snuggling up close to Brother Boche"—obtained; it was always better, he said, to form-up as closely as possible to the enemy, then get to "personal contact," taking advantage of enemy "disinclination . . . to fight at close quarters with the bayonet with our people." Griesbach also made special mention of the very difficult terrain:

> There was very little suitable ground upon which troops could be assembled, and the enemy's new plan of giving up his out-post line

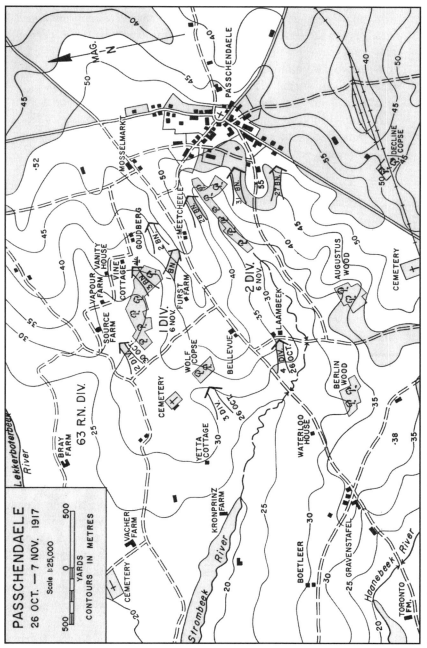

and walking his barrage backwards shortly after Zero, complicated this difficulty . . . the forming up . . . was almost in mass. This was a highly dangerous and hazardous method but the only method which presented itself. The situation was dealt with by two expedients: (i) A very short preliminary bombardment of the enemy's front line system (two minutes) (ii) A swift thrust on the part of leading troops and a hasty and close following up on the part of rear troops, who throughout . . . managed to keep just in front of the retiring barrage. I am bound to say that this Brigade . . . was favoured with exceptionally good luck. Had the enemy brought his barrage down on our massed troops it would have been a very serious matter.[122]

Luck is always a factor, of course but Griesbach's orders and his report show that he left little to chance. 1st Brigade was thoroughly prepared and the plan was as good as ever man could make it. Casualties did not exceed a thousand.[123]

2nd Brigade's turn came on 10 November. Loomis' two-battalion assault secured the whole of the brigade's objective by noon, just six hours after Zero. No infantry counterattack ensued, reaction instead being a fierce and protracted artillery barrage that shook the 2nd Brigade but could not eject it from its newly won positions. Loomis' explanation of success almost echoes Griesbach's. Casualties were nearly 1,300.[124]

1st Division suffered just over 3,000 casualties from 1 to 15 November. Macdonell offered several "salient" points for the success. Each brigade had studied its own problem, worked out the best plan and allowed everybody plenty of time to study it. Early deployment had given brigades time in daylight to become familiar with the ground. Also, every soldier knew his place in the chain of command: "nothing could produce lack of control." Numerous brigade coordinating conferences had resolved every detail. The excellent fire plan had also played a key part in the success. Barrage lifts of 100 yards instead of 50 yards and a move forward rate of 100 yards per eight minutes enabled advancing "in the old Infantry way by rushes . . . thereby saving many lives." Aircraft patrols, just as at Hill 70, were not prominent, 21 Squadron RFC flying only one patrol on 6 November and then, due to very poor weather, none until 10 November when three were flown. These patrols produced no information of value. None of the battalions in the two assault brigades (1st and 2nd) reported any contact patrols; 5th Battalion reported one unusual air event on 10 November: "One aeroplane with our markings flew along our front very low, dropping lights and using a hooter. The numerous German aeroplanes made no attempt to engage it and finally it disappeared . . . escorted by two German planes. Evidently this was a ruse . . . to get our dispositions."[125] Macdonell concluded his report thus: The men were fit, they were not overloaded, they were confident in their officers and in themselves and though they expected a hard fight they were, in their words, "Good for it."[126]

When asked to what he attributed the success, Currie offered several ideas that applied throughout and others that although they applied only to the operations of 3rd and 4th Divisions, were important since their experience helped 1st and 2nd Divisions: fighting spirit, adequate preparation, construction of plank roads and tramlines, and thorough reconnaissance carried out in close cooperation with the artillery. Currie did not mention aerial photography but it was the most useful RFC contribution at Passchendaele. Despite very bad weather aircraft photographed the area twice weekly, this being "all the more essential since the landscape kept being changed . . . under the battering of artillery and rain.[127] 1st Division's plan and orders for the November attacks had also stressed mopping-up because of the severe difficulties and many casualties caused on 26 October when some pillboxes escaped ruin, leaving the occupants free to savage assault waves from flank and rear. Also on that occasion, in the first two attacks the initial barrage at eight minutes had been too long, and heavy casualties were incurred from the counter-barrage during the wait. For the November attacks the initial barrage lasted only two minutes.[128]

Thus, for Canadians, ended the Third Battle of Ypres, or Passchendaele as it is better known. The whole operation is still controversial. Here we must leave it as Nicholson did: "Passchendaele carried the process [of destruction of the German Army] a long step forward."[129] Currie's methods made the Canadian Corps one of the "centres of tactical excellence [that] gradually accumulated." It came to be recognized as a formation that could be relied upon for any task, including the really tough ones, like Passchendaele, which fell to "brilliant organization and method."[130]

The question is, did commanders in 1st Division learn? The answer is yes. They showed readiness to adapt, ability to innovate, and consistent improvement in many aspects of their conduct of operations. The research undertaken for this book has not unearthed any claim by Currie or his successor as GOC 1st Division, Macdonell, about Canadian tactics being unique, or that Canadians waged war in some fashion distinct from any of the good Imperial corps or divisions. Possibly the most definitive statement Currie made about Canadian doctrine is in his *Interim Report* for 1918: "The laying down of a definite . . . tactical doctrine was necessary by reason of the different organization, the greater strength, and the particular methods which characterised the Canadian Corps."[131]

Macdonell's approach to command resembled Currie's, although he was perhaps more methodical and not as imaginative. Both were thorough planners, both encouraged initiative—indeed, they demanded it of subordinates—and both expected a great deal of their officers, staff and line. Batty Mac was a stern disciplinarian, perhaps more so than Currie. He dealt severely with the perpetrators of transgressions that he believed to be injurious to the division's reputation but in cases where he thought the transgression to be honest error he could be less severe. He invariably exhibited strong loyalty and support of subordinates. Macdonell also took enormous pride in Old Red Patch (he originated the sobriquet), a pride that swelled as he watched his division perform so well at Hill 70 and at Passchendaele. He had become a very good division commander. During the summer campaign of 1918 his performance was particularly impressive.

Currie provided sound guidance both for the Corps and for 1st Division when he commanded it, as did Macdonell, his tactical ideas mirroring Currie's. Change could be thoroughly discussed and easily implemented since Currie, unlike his Imperial counterparts, always dealt with four knowns: four divisions that remained under his command virtually throughout and four division commanders who were permanent fixtures. Happy is the Corps commander whose divisions have few changes of command for they will develop qualities upon which he can calculate and rely. But doctrine always "depends on the situation," meaning that the doctrine and the method applied to one scenario will not necessarily fit another. A good principle or doctrine is like a good coat: it will bear brushing. Canadian divisions knew that.

What had begun in 1915 was professionalization. The unprecedented numbers of men to be organized and fought, numbers with which no man had any experience, dictated that the BEF acquire regulation, codification and certification. By 1916 these elements were building a professional Army. While close coordination of all arms and services won battles, it was the infantry that decided the issue. Success stemmed from the fighting spirit and the skillful and determined use of weapons in conjunction with ground and manoeuvre, by the individual soldier, unit and commander. Leadership had to put all together. It took time for commanders at all levels to learn their jobs from A to Z and for corporate knowledge to accrue. Once it was there, the Officer Corps, despite heavy losses, had a benchmark and the capability of exercising continued sound direction, both in planning and in execution. In the aggregate, command and control in 1st Division at every level became and remained competent, making the division effective.

Notes to Chapter Four

1. Nicholson, *Official History of the Canadian Army*, p. 67.
2. Goodspeed, *Battle Royal*, p. 103. A good deal has been written, much of it uninformed condemnation, about Great War Generals commanding from the rear. What must be realized is that at the time command could only be effectively exercised from locations where up and down information converged. Technology (communications) was key. The trick was to site a HQ neither too far forward, nor too far rearward.
3. J.L. McWilliams and J.R. Steel, *Gas! The Battle for Ypres, 1915* (St. Catharines: Vanwell Publishing, 1985), p. 115.
4. Nicholson, *Official History of the Canadian Army*, pp. 75–76.
5. Humphrey Cobb, *Paths of Glory* (New York: Avon Books, 1973), p. 82. Cobb, an American, served with the 14th Battalion from 5 October 1917 to the Armistice. His service record is in LAC, RG 150 (1992–93/166, Box 1821).
6. LAC, RG9IIIC1, Vol. 3859, Folder 86, File 9, Canadian Corps report, 20 October; Lt.-Col. A.F. Brooke, "The Evolution of Artillery in the Great War. III," *Journal of the Royal Artillery* 51 (April 1924): 266, said the artillery's role was to affect enemy ability to fire "so as to afford the infantry the opportunity to assault." Bailey, "British Artillery in the Great War," pp. 23, 25, 27, 31, 35, 37, summarizes artillery doctrine by period thus: 1914—to assist the infantry to establish fire superiority (today we would say to win the fire fight) and to neutralize, not destroy the enemy; 1915—the perception grows that destruction, not neutralization, was the task; 1916—mass destruction; 1917—the zenith of destruction; 1917/1918—a shift back to neutralization; and 1917/1918—neutralize or destroy as appropriate. Shrapnel was named after Lieutenant-General Sir Henry Shrapnel (1761–1842) who invented a hollow shell filled with musket balls and a bursting charge with a timed fuse.
7. Brigadier R.J. Lewendon, "The Cutting of Barbed Wire Entanglements by Artillery Fire in World War One," *Journal of the Royal Artillery* 112 (September 1985): 115; Edmonds and Wynne, *Battle of Neuve Chapelle: Battles of Ypres*, pp. 78, 91.
8. At that time two scenarios drove Zero. If the enemy barrage was not likely to be heavy, the first scenario considered Zero to be "the moment at which our barrage lifts from the enemy front trench, the Infantry timing their advance so as to be close under our barrage before it lifts." The alternative scenario, which was to apply when the enemy was expected to put down a heavy barrage very quickly, set Zero as the moment our barrage began. This was the signal for the infantry to leave their trenches. Either option had potential for things going astray. Lieutenant-Colonel C.N.F. Broad said Zero was the hour at which the barrage opened ("The Development of Artillery Tactics, 1914–1918," p. 80). One GOC warned that Zero was only an approximation. "Watch the barrage" was his rule. See Gillon, *The Story of the 29th Division*, p. 101. Today Zero, now known as "H-Hour," is the time at which the infantry crosses the start line. All timings are reckoned from that.
9. Urquhart, *History of the 16th Battalion*, pp. 74–76; Fetherstonhaugh, *The Royal Montreal Regiment*, p. 55. Assembly trenches were where the assault force assembled, what today we call the forming-up place. At its forward edge was the jumping-off trench, which was just what it says it was: the place from whence the attack started, in today's terms the start line. It was important that it was parallel to the enemy line so that assault waves jumped off square to their objective. As the CO of 10th Battalion pointed out, it was not always possible to show all ranks their objective; if the jumping-off

trench was parallel then they could be told, if nothing else, to go straight ahead. (LAC, RG9IIIC3, Vol. 4026, Folder 11, File 3, 3 November 1916). When it was not parallel scouts determined the line with a compass and marked it with white cloth tape pegged down with iron stakes.

10. Lucas, gen. ed., F.H. Underhill, *The Empire at War: Canada*, p. 103.

11. Beattie, *48th Highlanders of Canada*, p. 86.

12. LAC, 1st Division General Staff War Diary, Narrative of Events, May 1915.

13. Nicholson, *Official History of the Canadian Army*, p. 105.

14. Military Advisory Board, *Guarding the Channel Ports*, pp. 187–89. Using the guns in the direct fire role was the idea of the CRA, Brigadier-General Burstall.

15. LAC, RG9IIID3, Vol. 4824, 1st Division General Staff War Diary, June 1915, Appendices 7, 11, 14, 15 and 1st Brigade report, Appendix 17. Throughout the war, long grass and weeds that concealed or partially covered wire made damage assessments problematical, even with air photographs. Often wire could not even be identified.

16. Rowland Feilding, *War Letters to a Wife: France and Flanders, 1915–1919* (London: The Medici Company, 1929), p. 22.

17. Prior and Wilson, *Command on the Western Front*, p. 98.

18. LAC, RG9IIIC3, Vol. 4011, Folder 15, File 9, 1st Division report, 20 June 1915; Vol. 4824, 1st Division General Staff War Diary, June 1915, Appendices 19–20; RG9IIIC3, Vol. 4011, Folder 15, File 9, 1st Division report. See also note 8 above for the ambiguity about Zero at the time.

19. LAC, RG9IIIC3, Vol. 4053, Folder 24, File 16, 7 October 1915, Harington to divisions. This was followed (3 November) by "Notes in Connection with Offensive Operations," the main point of which was reinforcing and supplying assault troops, i.e. consolidation (RG9IIIC1, Vol. 3859, Folder 85, File 4; Vol. 3842, Folder 42, File 2A).

20. Dancocks, *Welcome to Flanders Fields*, p. 84. For Alderson's pre-war career see Chapter Two of this present study.

21. R. Craig Brown and Desmond Morton, "The Embarrassing Apotheosis of a 'Great Canadian': Sir Arthur Currie's Personal Crisis in 1917," *Canadian Historical Review* 60 (January, 1979): 43–44; Hugh M. Urquhart, *Arthur Currie: The Biography of a Great Canadian* (Toronto: Macmillan, 1950), p. 156. Horne, GOC First Army, made the comment on 3 May 1917, just after Vimy.

22. Dancocks, *Welcome to Flanders Fields*, p. 336. GSO1 was the title of the senior operational staff officer at division HQ. Such terms and the staff system as a whole will be detailed in subsequent chapters.

23. LAC, RG9IIIC3, Vol. 4044, Folder 3, File 5, 29 October 1915. The purpose of traffic control was to keep traffic moving, especially priority traffic such as ammunition vehicles. Controls included signing, traffic control posts, allocation of routes to specific purposes and such restrictions as imposing one-way traffic flows and closing routes for specific periods. The staff planned traffic control, while an Assistant Provost Marshal in each division enforced it.

24. Hobbes is quoted in Robert D. Heinl, *Dictionary of Military and Naval Quotations* (Annapolis, Md.: U.S. Naval Institute, 1966), p. 91.

25. Kenneth Radley, *Rebel Watchdog: The Confederate States Army Provost Guard* (Baton Rouge, La.: Louisiana State University Press, 1989), pp. 126–27.

26. Quoted in A.L. Long, *Memoirs of Robert E. Lee* (New York: J.M. Stoddart & Company, 1887), p. 630.

27. Graham, *A Private in the Guards*, p. 2; LAC, MG30E60 (Matthews Papers), Vol. 3, Folder 12, Trench Orders, May 1916.

28. Christopher Pugsley, *On the Fringe of Hell: New Zealanders and Military Discipline in the First World War* (Auckland: Hodder & Stoughton, 1991), p. 123, and Brereton Greenhous and Stephen J. Harris, *Canada and the Battle of Vimy Ridge, 9–12 April 1917* (Ottawa: Canada Communication Group, 1992), p. 43, say the system began during the Somme. *Field Service Pocket Book* (London: General Staff, War Office, 1914), p. 225; Edmonds, *Haig's Command to the 1st July: Battle of the Somme*, p. 313; LAC, RG9IIID3, Vol. 4839, 1st Division A & Q War Diary, 31 January and February 1916, Appendix 2.

29. LAC, RG9IIID3, Vol. 4839, 1st Division A & Q War Diary, 31 January and February 1916, Appendix 2.

30. LAC, RG9IIIC1, Vol. 3859, Folder 85, File 3; RG9IIIC3, Vol. 4011, Folder 15, File 11, Lipsett to 1st Division, 9 May 1916, reports of 1st Division, April and May 1916; RG9IIIC1, Vol. 3842, Folder 42, File 8, Second Army to Canadian Corps, 2 May. A commander defending a position must decide, with due regard for the ground and his resources, whether to conduct an oyster or a peach defence. The former entails a hard crust, with most of the defenders on the outer shell. They can hold the attacker for a long time but should he break through, then the soft interior is in grave danger. The peach, conversely, has a thin outer edge, designed to delay and weaken the attacker, and a central reserve capable of counterattacking and crushing an enemy that breaks in. Knowing which to choose is another of those so difficult command decisions.

31. Major D.J. Goodspeed, *The Road Past Vimy: The Canadian Corps 1914–1918* (Toronto: Macmillan, 1969), p. 40; Wood, *Vimy*, p. 53.

32. Dancocks, *Welcome to Flanders Fields*, p. 84; Nicholson, *Official History of the Canadian Army*, pp. 145,147.

33. LAC, 1st Division General Staff War Diary, June 1916, Appendix 30; Fetherstonhaugh, *The Royal Montreal Regiment*, p. 86; Beattie, *48th Highlanders of Canada*, p. 131. At the outbreak of war the Adjutant-General, Colonel V.A.S. Williams, took command of Camp Valcartier. In late 1915 he assumed command of 8th Brigade.

34. LAC, MG30E300 (Odlum Papers), Vol. 15, Correspondence book, February–December 1916, Currie to Odlum, 8 June; Dancocks, *Gallant Canadians*, p. 78; Roy, *Journal of Private Fraser*, p. 147. The divisional report on operations for the period 2–13 June (LAC, RG9IIIC1, Vol. 3842, Folder 43, File 1A) makes only two references to aerial reconnaissance, one noting a report on enemy artillery on 3 June and the other stressing that bad weather prevented reconnaissance, thereby making heavy artillery registration impossible (Nicholson, *Official History of the Canadian Army*, p. 152). In contrast, given favourable weather, aerial photography could be "exceptionally good," as it was during the Bluff operation in March 1916 (LAC, RG9IIIC3, Vol. 4074, Folder 2, File 4).

35. LAC, MG30E300 (Odlum Papers), Currie to Odlum 8 June; 10th and 7th Battalion War Diaries, June 1916.

36. Beattie, *48th Highlanders of Canada*, p. 137; Edmonds, *Haig's Command to the 1st July: Battle of the Somme*, p. 241.

37. LAC, RG9IIIC3, Vol. 4050, Folder 19, File 4, report of 3rd Battalion; 8th Battalion War Diary, June 1916, Appendix 5; 2nd and 3rd Brigade War Diaries, June 1916.

38. Goodspeed, *Battle Royal*, pp. 130, 141–42; Urquhart, *History of the 16th Battalion*, p. 142.

39. Goodspeed, *Battle Royal*, p. 144; LAC, RG9IIIC1, Vol. 3842, Folder 43, File 1A, 3rd Division report, 30 June 1916.

40. Canadian casualty estimates range from a low of 8,000 (Nicholson, *Official History of the Canadian Army*, p. 154) to 9,000 (Goodspeed, *Battle Royal*, p. 150). LAC, RG9IIIC1, Vol. 3842, Folder 43, File 1A, 1st Division report, p. 7. Officer casualties were highest in 3rd Brigade (LAC, 16th Battalion War Diary, June 1916).

41. Edmonds, *Haig's Command to the 1st July: Battle of the Somme*, p. 245.

42. LAC, RG9IIID3, Vol. 4813, Corps General Staff War Diary, 9 July 1916; 2nd Brigade War Diary, July 1916, Appendices A and B; 1st Brigade War Diary, July 1916, Appendix B; McNaughton, "The Development of Artillery in the Great War," p. 163.

43. LAC, RG9IIIC3, Vol. 4065, Folder 2, File 14, Currie to Gardner, 29 July 1916; Canadian Corps Special Order. 2nd Brigade's re-publication of the Corps order was signed by Major Bernard Humble, Staff Captain, and Gardner's predecessor in command.

44. Urquhart, *History of the 16th Battalion*, p. 151.

45. LAC, RG9IIIC1, Vol. 3842, Folder 43, File 6, Currie to 3rd Brigade and to Canadian Corps, 19 July 1916; 3rd Brigade War Diary, July 1916. The CO of the 16th Battalion at the time was Lieutenant-Colonel J.E. Leckie. See Chapter Three, note 18.

46. LAC, RG9IIIC3, Vol. 4074, Folder 2, File 6, 26 October 1916.

47. LAC, MG30E100 (Currie Papers), Vol. 35, File 176; Lucas, gen. ed., Underhill, *The Empire at War: Canada*, p. 133.

48. LAC, 2nd Battalion War Diary, September 1916, report by Lieutenant W.W. Murray. Total casualties were 71 killed and 199 wounded.

49. LAC, MG30E300 (Odlum Papers). This includes the 14th Battalion, which had been a troublesome unit at first but then improved immensely under Lieutenant-Colonel R.P. Clark. In a letter of 8 June to Victor Odlum, Currie remarked how very well it had done.

50. LAC, RG9IIIC1, Vol. 3842, Folder 43, File 12.

51. Ibid.

52. LAC, RG9IIIC3, Vol. 4051, Folder 19, File 6, 2nd Brigade report; 3rd Brigade War Diary, September 1916.

53. LAC, RG9IIIC3, Vol. 4051, Folder 19, File 6, 2nd Brigade report; Vol. 4053, Folder 24, Files 20 and 22, 5th and 8th Battalion reports; Vol. 4065, Folder 2, File 12, 7th Battalion report; Vol. 4072, Folder 8, File 10, 10th Battalion report. None of 2nd Brigade's reports comment on the usefulness of the attached machine-guns and mortars.

54. LAC, 2nd Brigade War Diary, entry for 26 September; Captain Wilfrid Miles, *Military Operations: France and Belgium, 1916: 2nd July 1916 to the End of the Battles of the Somme* (London: Macmillan, 1938), p. 398.

55. LAC, RG9IIIC3, Vol. 4052, Folder 19, File 6, reports of 2nd Brigade and 8th Battalion.

56. Ibid., report of 8th Battalion; Vol. 4065, Folder 2, File 12, 7th Battalion report, 30 September; Miles, *2nd July 1916 to the End of the Battles of the Somme*, pp. 399–407. 11th Division found itself soon after Zero in the midst of several strongpoints from which heavy fire emanated. Within minutes its assault brigade was too mangled to be effective and the attack stalled.

57. LAC, RG9IIIC3, Vol. 4053, Folder 19, File 6, 2nd Brigade report; Folder 24, File 20, 5th Battalion report; 3rd Brigade War Diary, September 1916, Appendix 50; 14th Battalion War Diary, September, Appendix 2. Tuxford may have thought the sound of the machine-gun indirect fire to be a morale raiser.

58. LAC, RG9IIIC3, Vol. 4051, Folder 19, File 6, 2nd Brigade report.

59. Lucas, gen. ed., Underhill, *The Empire at War: Canada*, p. 144. 5th Brigade went in with 1,717 men and came out with 773. Overall, casualties were about half of the five assault battalions.

60. Fetherstonhaugh, *The 13th Battalion*, p. 142. Nicholson, *Official History of the Canadian Army*, p. 186, called it a "fiasco."

61. LAC, RG9IIIC3, Vol. 4080, Folder 4, File 2, Statements of Lieutenant-Colonel C.W. Peck, CO 16th Battalion, Lieutenant E.B. Hart and Sergeant F.M. Watts; RG 41, Vol. 7, interview with Lieutenant W.H. Joliffe; 3rd Battalion War Diary, 8 October 1916.

62. LAC, 1st Division War Diary, Appendix 16, October 1916. 3rd Battalion, which went in with 14 officers and 481 ORs, came out with 1 and 85, while the 4th lost 510 out of 600 all ranks. Overall, casualties exceeded 1,300. LAC, RG 41, Vol. 7, interview with Lieutenant Joliffe. An officer issues orders to bring his men to the place where they can kill the enemy. In so doing he is also ordering the death of some of his own men. Most men prefer to postpone the time of their passing for as long as possible, an aim that may cause them to feel that avoiding combat is the wisest course. For the individual this may well be so but leaders cannot permit that. In this case, the avoidance occurred in such circumstances that the officer was forced to the most Draconian action, something that he would not have wished to do.

63. LAC, RG9IIIC3, Vol. 4026, Folder 11, File 3, General H.P. Gough to Canadian Corps, 10 October.

64. LAC, MG30E100 (Currie Papers), Vol. 35, File 176. Currie's written summation of his personal investigation, which he sent to Corps, is dated 16 October. To this report he attached the findings of the Court of Enquiry.

65. LAC, RG9IIIC3, Vol. 4026, Folder 11, File 3. The other members of the court were Lieutenant-Colonel C.E. Bent, CO 15th Battalion, and Major L.F. Page, 5th Battalion.

66. LAC, RG9IIIC3, Vol. 4026, Folder 11, File 3, Hughes' report, 11 October.

67. LAC, MG30E100 (Currie Papers), Vol. 35, File 176. Swift was appointed GOC a training brigade in England on 3 November and then went on promotion to 14th Brigade, which was disbanded in early 1918. He did not return to active command. The BM, Major W.A. Adams, took up a staff appointment in England in February 1917.

68. LAC, RG9IIIC3, Vol. 4026, Folder 11, File 3.

69. LAC, 13th Battalion War Diary, 8 October 1916; RG9IIIC3, Vol. 4026, Folder 11, File 3, 1st Division report, 12 October. Currie noted that poor weather meant aerial photographs of the enemy wire were not available.

70. LAC, GOCRA War Diary, October 1916, Appendix A, Artillery Instructions.

71. LAC, RG9IIIC3, Vol. 4011, Folder 17, File 1, Corps to 1st Division, 3 November, and 1st Division to Corps 25 November; Vol. 4026, Folder 11, File 3. Currie emphasized that a "fairly large" proportion of the assault force consisted of officers and men who had never been in a trench before and he did not have the "old" officers to supervise them. Furthermore, many of the newcomers had never thrown a bomb.

72. Edmonds, *Haig's Command to the 1st July: Battle of the Somme*, p. 288. Before the battle began, Sir Henry Rawlinson assumed that nothing could survive a week long rain of fire by 1,500 guns—some 1,550,000 rounds—and the troops would be able to simply walk over and take possession. This proved optimistic. His GOCRA, Major-General J.F.M. Birch, did not dispute Rawlinson's assertion; to some extent Rawlinson may have been repeating his senior gunner's opinion. GOC and GOCRA were in agreement on a flawed premise.

73. Ibid.,pp. 288, 494; Miles, *2nd July 1916 to the End of the Battles of the Somme*, p. 555.

74. *SS 119 Preliminary Notes on the Tactical Lessons of the Recent Operations* (Army P & S Services, July 1916).

75. *SS 135*, pp. 12–13, 17, 52. The Currie Papers (LAC, MG30E100, Vol. 49) contain a draft entitled "Instructions for the Training of Divisions Withdrawn from the Frontline."

76. LAC, RG9IIIC3, Vol. 4053, Folder 24, File 16.

77. LAC, RG9IIIC3, Vol. 4011, Folder 17, File 1.

78. *SS 135*, pp. 14–15; LAC, RG9IIIC3, Vol. 4023, Folder 1, File 10.

79. LAC, RG9IIIC3, Vol. 4011, Folder 17, File 1, Tuxford to division 21 November and CO 5th Battalion (Dyer) to 2nd Brigade 20 November; Loomis to division 21 November.

80. Ibid., Prower to 2nd Brigade 19 November.

81. Ibid., Dyer to 2nd Brigade, 20 November.

82. LAC; RG9IIIC3, Vol. 4051, Folder 19, File 8, Ormond to 2nd Brigade, 15 November.

83. LAC, RG9IIIC1, Vol. 3859, Folder 86, File 6, "Notes on the Somme Battle." This British report, which covers operations to the end of August, collates and comments upon the ground-air experience of four Imperial divisions. GHQ released the report to all Armies of the BEF. Australian reports on airplane contact patrols were also on general distribution (Vol. 3842, Folder 43, File 9, report of 4th Australian Brigade, 16 August 1916), as were reports by Canadian divisions (Vol. 3843, Folder 44, File 1, report of 4th Division, 15 August). Currie's report as GOC 1st Division is in RG9IIIC3, Vol. 4028, Folder 1, File 10, 15 August. The contact system as set out in *SS 135* (Appendix B) published in December 1916, provided for the exchange of signals between aircraft and battalion and brigade HQs, between aircraft and artillery, and between aircraft and attacking infantry; the latter exchange took place at pre-arranged times and/or places, or "on call" as necessary. Detailed contact procedures, based on the experience of the Somme, included how and when to sound klaxon horns as signals, and the use of flares, signalling lamps, ground signal panels and wireless; the last was only used for sending target information to the artillery since otherwise the nets would become jammed and fire support would not be possible or prompt.

84. LAC, RG9IIIC3, Vol. 4023, Folder 1, File 10; Vol. 4026, Folder 11, File 3, Corps report dated 3 November; RG9IIIC1, Vol. 3842, Folder 43, File 9, Australian report.

85. LAC, RG9IIIC3, Vol. 4026, Folder 11, File 3, 1st Brigade report, 20 November; Vol. 4011, Folder 17, File 1, 1st Division order, 25 November; War Diaries of 3rd Brigade, 5th and 10th Battalions, November 1916.

86. LAC, RG9IIIC3, Vol. 4051, Folder 19, File 8, 2nd Brigade to 1st Division, 21 November; 5th Battalion War Diary, November 1916.

87. LAC, RG9IIIC1, Vol. 3843, Folder 44, File 5, translation published by 1st Printing Company, RE, November 1916.

88. LAC, RG9IIIC3, Vol. 4046, Folder 4, File 2, Canadian Corps to 1st Division, 14 March; 1st Division to brigades, 17 March.

89. LAC, RG9IIIC1, Vol. 3844, Folder 48, File 2, First Army to Canadian Corps, 4 January 1917; Lewendon, "The Cutting of Barbed Wire Entanglements by Artillery Fire in World War One," p. 115; Brooke, "The Evolution of Artillery in the Great War, III.," pp. 43, 46; Captain Cyril Falls, *Military Operations France and Belgium, 1917: The German Retreat to the Hindenburg Line and the Battles of Arras* (London: Macmillan, 1940), p. 239.

90. Artillery appreciations and allocations are in LAC, RG 24, Vol. 1828, GAQ 7–16 and RG9IIIC1, Vol. 3843, Folder 46, File 4. Some idea of the strain on the gunners is evi-

dent in the fact that one 9.2 inch howitzer battery (150 men) took in 150 tons of ammunition in one night, this between two days of hard firing. Brigade and battalion reports are in Vol. 3846, Folder 51, Files 1 and 4. The gunners' exhaustion is not difficult to imagine.

91. LAC, RG9IIIC1, Vol. 3844, Folder 48, File 4, "Instructions for Offensive Operations, March 1917;" RG9IIIC3, Vol. 4026, Folder 10, File 9, 1st Brigade "Instructions for the Offensive;" Vol. 4061, Folder 7, File 1, 2nd Brigade Operation Order 185, 6 April, and "Instructions No. 3," 26 March; RG9IIIC1, Vol. 3846, Folder 51, File 3, 7th Battalion Operation Order 49, 7 April.

92. LAC, RG9IIIC1, Vol. 3843, Folder 46, File 6, "Artillery Instructions for the Capture of the Vimy Ridge," 28 March 1917.

93. Griffith, *Battle Tactics of the Western Front*, p. 157.

94. LAC, RG9IIIC3, Vol. 4026, Folder 11, File 5, 1st Division report dated June 1917; RG9IIIC1, Vol. 3846, Folder 51, Files 1, 3–5, reports of Corps HQ, brigades and battalions.

95. LAC RG9IIIC1, Vol. 3846, Folder 51, Files 1, 2 and 4; Vol. 3847, Folder 54, File 6, 1st Division Operation Order 164, 1 May; 14th Battalion Operation Order 81 (War Diary, May 1917).

96. LAC, RG9IIIC1, Vol. 3846, Folder 51, Files 5 and 7.

97. LAC, RG9IIIC1, Vol. 3844, Folder 48, File 4. Special maps were also referred to as Message Maps.

98. Ibid., Corps Scheme of Operations, 5 March 1917; Vol. 3845, Folder 49, File 4, 1st Division orders, 22 March; File 5, 3rd Brigade amended Operation Order, 31 March. Power buzzers were also used at Vimy but infrequently thereafter, mainly because the equipment was heavy. Power buzzers had a range of about 2,000 yards. Instead of a continuous line the system used a base line some 200 yards long for transmission and an induction amplifier at the receiver end.

99. LAC, RG9IIIC1, Vol. 3845, Folder 49, Files 4 and 5, Operation Orders; Vol. 3844, Folder 48, File 3, Canadian Corps Conference Minutes, 30 March; Vol. 3846, Folder 51, File 2, 2nd Brigade report, 2 May; Fetherstonhaugh, *The 13th Battalion*, p. 168. A 3rd Battalion Operation Order dated 5 April (Appendix 1, April 1917 War Diary) refers to another control measure, namely "Battle Flags": "The Division flag is dark blue and yellow and will be carried . . . two per platoon and will be used to indicate to the Artillery the line gained by the leading Infantry . . . flags carried by the 2nd Canadian Division . . . is a yellow flag, with a black maple leaf centre . . . battalions will carry a light flag with the base bright red and the superstructure bright green. These superstructures will be cut to represent the markings of the Battalion. These will be carried on the flanks of Battalions . . . four per Battalion, carried by Battalion Scouts." This is the only reference to such flags in the operational documents pertaining to Vimy. If these flags were actually carried 3rd Battalion made no reference to them, or their practicality and effectiveness in its post-Vimy report. No references to such flags were seen in the study of other Canadian operations. The whole idea seems so impractical that it is unlikely to have got beyond the experimental stage.

100. LAC, RG9IIIC1, Vol. 3846, Folder 51, Files 2, 4 and 5. Total brigade casualties were: 1st Brigade, 583; 2nd Brigade, 1109; 3rd Brigade, 1041.

101. Wynne, *If Germany Attacks*, p. 180.

102. Jeffrey Williams, *Byng of Vimy General and Governor General* (London: Leo Cooper, 1983), p. 130. Haig made the comments to the King in a letter dated 28 July 1916.

Haig had probably been informed of the mutually insulting remarks made about divisional capabilities that had passed between 1st and 3rd Divisions earlier that month. (LAC, RG9IIIC3, Vol. 4024, Folder 4, File 9).

103. LAC, RG 41, CBC interview, Brigadier-General Alexander Ross (GOC 6th Brigade).

104. LAC, MG30E417 (Baxter Papers), p. 10; Pedley, *Only This: A War Retrospect*, p. 57; LAC, RG 41, CBC interview of Sergeant F.C. Bagshaw, later Captain and Adjutant 5th Battalion. Rattray left the 10th in September 1916, and served in a number of appointments in Britain thereafter. Odlum left the 7th in July 1916 on promotion to command 11th Brigade; his new command got its rum ration.

105. Geoffrey Powell, *Plumer, the Soldier's General* (London: Leo Cooper, 1990), p. 151.

106. Pedley, *Only This: A War Retrospect*, p. 57.

107. Ibid., p. 176.

108. LAC, RG 41, CBC interview.

109. Major-General the Rt. Hon. J.E.B. Seely, *Adventure* (London: William Heinemann Ltd., 1930), pp. 218–19.

110. LAC, MG30E220 (Papers of Pte. E.W. Russell, 5th Battalion), "A Private Soldier's Views on the Great War 1914–1918," p. 18; MG 31 G29–31, File 8, Private William Woods, commenting in 1994 on Desmond Morton's *When Your Number's Up*. By all accounts Griesbach, ever the disciplinarian, was highly respected by the men.

111. Stevens, *A City Goes to War*, p. 91.

112. The unpublished biography of A.C. Macdonell by J.A. Kennedy-Carefoot (LAC, MG30E20, Vol 1) is uninformative on Macdonell as GOC 1st Division. His time as GOC receives only 25 pages and these, like the whole of the work, are almost entirely anecdotal and hagiographic.

113. LAC, RG9IIIC3, Vol. 4061, Folder 7, File 4, 27 July; Brigadier-General Sir James E. Edmonds, *Military Operations, France and Belgium, 1917* Volume II, *7th June–10th November, Messines and Third Ypres* (Passchendaele) (London: Macmillan, 1948), pp. 223–25, 228. The initial counterattack was mounted by one regiment from 7th Division and another from 11th Reserve Division. Subsequently two regiments of 4th Guards Division, one regiment of 185th Division, elements of 1st Guards Reserve Division, and a storm-troop regiment mounted counterattacks.

114. LAC, RG9IIIC3, Vol. 4014, Folder 25, File 1, Canadian Corps Scheme of Operations, 26 July; Vol. 4027, Folder 12, File 1, 1st Division Instructions, 22 July.

115. LAC, RG9IIIC3, Vol. 4014, Folder 25, File 1. Ammunition was plentiful, the machine-guns having 20,000 rounds per gun, and field artillery alone expended 150,000 rounds from 14–18 August.

116. LAC, RG9IIIC3, Vol. 4014, Folder 25, File 1, Corps "Scheme of Operations—Capture of Hill 70," 26 July; Folder 26, File 3, 14th Battalion Operation Order 151; RG9IIIC1, Vol. 3850, Folder 62, File 1, 1st Division "Instructions for the Offensive Hill 70—July 1917."

117. LAC RG9IIIC1, Vol. 3850, Folder 62, File 1, 1st Division "Instructions for the Offensive Hill 70—July 1917." 1st Division Operation Order and 3rd Brigade Instructions, 22 July; 10th Battalion War Diary, August 1917, Appendix 18.

118. LAC, MG30E100 (Currie Papers), Vol. 42, Diary; RG9IIIC3, Vol. 4014, Folder 25, File 2, 1st Division report. Almost 1,400 Germans were captured.

119. LAC, RG9IIIC3, Vol. 4014, Folder 25, Files 2–3 and Folder 26, File 3; Vol. 4052, Folder 21, File 1; Vol. 4077, Folder 3, File 10. The division logs contain six reports by 43 Squadron whose task was aerial reconnaissance. Macdonell expressed his appreciation for the reports and squadron efforts in engaging enemy movement with machine-guns.

120. Nicholson, *Official History of the Canadian Army*, p. 318.
121. LAC, RG9IIIC3, Vol. 4031, Folder 26, File 7. By mid-1917 platoon commanders routinely checked that all ranks knew the seniority in the platoon and that they were practised in assuming command: "Platoon Commanders will prove section commanders, seconds-in-command of sections, next senior soldiers and so on, frequently." One of the last actions done before an operation commenced was to "prove": as a formal drill, each man on command, in order of seniority, raised his right forearm parallel to the ground, thus signalling to his OC that he knew his place in the chain of command. MG30E15 (Griesbach Papers), Vol. 2, Folder 13, 1st Brigade report, 15 November; RG9IIIC3, Vol. 4015, Folder 29, File 1, 1st Brigade plan, 1 November.
122. LAC, RG9IIIC3, Vol. 4028, Folder 17, File 20, 1st Brigade report, 16 November. The two assault battalions formed up in an area only 350 by 200 yards.
123. LAC, MG30E15 (Griesbach Papers), Vol. 2, Folder 13.
124. LAC, RG9IIIC3, Vol. 4052, Folder 21, File 3, 2nd Brigade report.
125. 1st Division's report on Passchendaele operations from 4 to 12 November is in LAC, RG9IIIC1, Vol. 3853, Folder 68, File 3. 1st and 2nd Brigade reports are in MG30E15 (Griesbach Papers), Vol. 2, Folder 13 and RG9IIIC3, Vol. 4052, Folder 21, File 3 respectively. For battalion reports see Vol. 4052, Folder 21, File 2. Reports of the battalions of 1st Brigade are in Vol. 4033, Folder 3, File 3 (1st Battalion); Vol. 4044, Folder 3, File 1 (4th Battalion); and November 1917 War Diaries (2nd and 3rd Battalions). Most battalions reported that their flares were too wet to fire.
126. LAC, RG9IIIC1, Vol. 3859, Folder 85, File 8, 1st Division report, 22 November 1917.
127. Griffith, *Battle Tactics of the Western Front*, p. 156.
128. LAC, RG9IIIC1, Vol. 3859, Folder 85, File 8, 1st Division report, 22 November 1917, and Corps report, 20 November; MG30E15 (Griesbach Papers), Vol. 2, File 13, 1st Brigade report.
129. Nicholson, *Official History of the Canadian Army*, p. 330.
130. Paddy Griffith, "The Extent of Tactical Reform in the British Army," in Griffith, ed., *British Fighting Methods in the Great War*, p. 2; Terraine, *Douglas Haig: The Educated Soldier*, p. 345.
131. Lt.-Gen. Sir A.W. Currie, *Canadian Corps Operations During the Year 1918: Interim Report* (Ottawa: Department of Militia and Defence, 1919), p. 24.

CHAPTER FIVE

A Staff to Serve the Line (1)

*Staff officers cannot be improvised; nor can they learn
their duties, like the rank and file, in a few weeks or
months; for their duties are as varied as they are important.*
—FIELD MARSHAL LORD ROBERTS, 1902

Operational success depended to a very considerable extent on the competence of Staff Officers in particular and the efficiency of the staff system as a whole. This chapter and the next examine staff work as one of the three elements that contributed to the evolution of 1st Division from a raw division to good division. The staff system in which the division operated and the division's role will be described, including characteristics, organization, responsibilities and functions and working methods. Where the staff was obtained, and the preferred Staff Officer profile will be featured, along with the relationships between staff and command; between staff, Regimental officers and men; and between the Canadian and Imperial levels of command and staff.

Several characteristics of the system require emphasis as they provide the context for assessment. The first is quality, the subject of the next chapter. For now suffice it to say that everything revolved around quality; it was the whole point of the system. Staff work, the systematic management of paperwork, was what turned ideas into reality. The test of staff work was to get the right troops to the right place at the right time with all that was required to achieve their mission. This fundamental truth applied to every level at which the staff existed.

Second, the BEF had *one* staff system, not one per division nor one per corps—although Army commanders exercised considerable discretion because of Haig's style of command. Canadian Corps staff responded in much the same way as any other corps of the BEF would. Similarly, Corps knew that in executing orders 1st Division would adhere to the system. The GOC the 1st expected the same from his brigadiers, who, in turn, expected battalions to conform. Despite some variations—Canadian divisions had extra Staff Officers and individual commanders had particular preferences when it came to staff work—all levels adhered to BEF practises. It could be no other way. 1st Division lacked the wherewithal, even if it had been so inclined, to stand alone.[1]

Third, while strong-minded Staff Officers had particular ideas about how things should be done, the system was *their* system. A divisional Staff Officer who routinely practised the experimental, habitually reporting in unwanted or unexpected ways, risked being at odds with his superiors in the staff chain and with his GOC, who would have heard very quickly about errant staff from the Corps commander. At brigade, the wise senior Staff Officer avoided causing the divisional staff any concern, extra work, or annoyance. At all levels the primary Staff Officer took care in his relationship with the next lower level of commander because he was at least one rank inferior. The rank difference made it easy for lower commanders to use the higher staff to convey their ideas upward, including criticism, without suffering any loss of face or dignity in the eyes of the higher commander. Personalities could detract from this, but generally the system worked well. Clearly, Staff Officers had to be carefully chosen. When the whole object was maximum universality and standardization, a *prima donna*, no matter how brilliant, could upset the whole cast.

Finally, adherence had more to do with individual background than with simple obedience. Imperial officers filled most senior staff appointments at Corps for the entire war and at 1st Division until December 1917. At HQ 1st Division the incumbents were all Staff College graduates; their staff methods came from the same manuals and the same experience; they worked first for a British GOC (Alderson) and then for two Canadian GOCs (Currie and Macdonell) who, having been raised in the system would have seen little reason or need to change it; and they reported to British Staff Officers, much like themselves and whom they most likely knew, at Corps. Some of their Canadian colleagues were graduates of the militia staff courses, which adhered to the Camberley pattern, or of the wartime staff courses that taught, not surprisingly, the system. For all these reasons, 1st Division responded in accordance with the BEF system. It must also be said that 1st Division's initial experience of war differed very little, if at all, from that of any non-Regular Imperial division (one could almost say "any other" so strong was the presence of the British-born in 1st Division). Its attitudes towards command and staff would not have been markedly different.

The obvious question is, who were the staff? John Masters' account of the staff branches, which he aimed at readers with little military knowledge, is a useful start:

> Broadly speaking, all the problems that an army faces come under three headings. Two of these headings would still apply if it were not an army but a collection of civilians, as say, a city or a province. Those two are—the problem of people and the problem of things . . . The third sort of problem [has] to do with fighting.[2]

The Adjutant-General's Branch, or A Branch, looked after "people" or, specifically, their personal administration, which included pay, promotion, records, discipline, confinement, law, personnel appointments, medical matters, burying casualties, discharges and interior economy, or "housekeeping" as soldiers say. The Quartermaster General Branch, Q Branch, handled "things" which included supply, ordnance, equipment, weapons and materials, mail, transportation and veterinary services. The A and Q branches, and the services that performed such functions, had to establish an interior economy and come together quickly in order to support 1st Division even before it set foot in France.

A definition of "services" is owing. An Army consists of arms and services. The first kills the enemy. At the beginning of the war the arms were infantry, artillery and cavalry. Engineers, or "sappers" as they were known, were also considered an arm because although their usual purpose was not to kill the enemy, they were as far forward as the other arms and often became involved in combat. Eventually, these four arms were joined by a new arm, armoured troops, who fought in landships called tanks. The arms were supplied with all that they needed to fight by the services, which then included supply, transport, ordnance, medical, military staff clerks, veterinary, legal, pay, burial services and military police.

"Fighting," the business of the General Staff (GS), or G Branch, included plans, operations, policy, operational movement, communications, training and intelligence. The proposing and planning of operations by G Branch gave the lead to which the A and Q Branches had to respond. To ensure primacy, G Branch had responsibility at each formation for staff coordination. The GOC commanded and issued his orders through G Branch. Below Army, A and Q Branches worked as one, meaning that the senior G Branch officer had only one opposite number, the senior AQ officer. In early 1916 Canadian Corps HQ summed up the system this way: "GS Branch. . .settles policy and deals with. . .operations, war efficiency and training. The A & Q Branch deal with the provision of personnel and material respectively."[3] As for the working relationship, John Masters sums it up best:

Obviously, the G.S. branch is the most important, and also must be the prime mover, since it is no use . . . Q people sending rations to Rome if the G.S. are attacking Paris. But the other branches are far more than deferential housekeepers. The G.S. can plan the most gorgeous battle that ever was, but it will result in an even more gorgeous snafu unless they have made certain that Q can bring up the required ammunition, and that A can fit their columns into the available road space. The three branches must always work in close cooperation, and always as a part of their commander's will, not as a separate entity.[4]

In short, G's concern was what was desirable, and A and Q advised what was feasible. When a sufficiency existed, work commenced on making the desirable happen.

The definitive study of the Great War staff summarized Staff Officer personalities thus: "All the dull dogs gravitated to 'A.' 'Q' always produced light-hearted men; while 'G', perhaps of necessity, were at all times obsessed by the war."[5] One officer's recollection about G being the domain of professional Staff College-trained officers pertained to 1st Division where three of the four senior G officers during the war were p.s.c. (passed staff college).[6]

At Corps, senior G was the Brigadier-General General Staff (BGGS), whose subordinates included the GSO1, a key appointment since this officer (a Lieutenant-Colonel) was responsible for operations; two or three General Staff Officers 2nd Grade (GSO2s); three or four General Staff Officers 3rd Grade (GSO3s); and an additional GSO2 tasked specifically with intelligence duties. When in February 1917 GHQ promulgated staff responsibilities for training, a GS01 (Training) was appointed at Army and a GS02 (Training) at Corps.[7] On the AQ side, the senior officer, a brigadier-general, was the Deputy Adjutant and Quartermaster General (DA & QMG) under whom laboured a Lieutenant-Colonel Q, a Major A and a Major whose chief headache was movements.[8]

A happy circumstance about being on staff of a Canadian division arose from the most significant difference between Canadian and Imperial corps. While Canadian divisions fought under other corps, their return to the Canadian Corps was a given. Imperial divisions, conversely, moved from corps to corps since fresh troops often had to go to an active sector, while exhausted troops went to a quiet sector to rest and refit. Frequent changes forced Imperial formations to adapt constantly to other personalities and ideas:

> There were not many popular corps staff in the eyes of their divisions
> . . . One of the chief reasons for the divisional dislike of all corps was
> the latter's lack of uniformity; not only had each its own system of
> 'returns' but their whole method of staff work was diversified . . . If

corps had kept their own divisions far greater uniformity would have been gained, a corps spirit would have been fostered and the fighting value of the formation increased. The Australians and the Canadians owed something of their success to their brigading. While the XIVth Corps were lucky in always having the Guards.[9]

The British Official Historian thought cooperation was better between the divisions of a homogeneous corps such as the Canadian or Australian corps, whose divisions nearly always remained with their corps, any attachments elsewhere being infrequent and brief. Thus, Dominion divisions came to know and respect their corps commanders and staff. Conversely, Imperial corps were foster parents, assuming from time to time any number and succession of charges. Imperial divisions frequently did not stay in one corps long enough to even know the staff.[10] On the other hand, because an Imperial corps tended to remain for a long period in any particular sector, its staff became so familiar with the corps area, front and rear, that more assistance could be provided to newly joined divisions than if the corps area frequently changed. As a rule, corps moves were infrequent and when they did occur they were more a side-step than a move to an entirely new sector. An Imperial corps HQ had little experience of life on the road.

The divisional staff organization replicated that of corps HQ, but at reduced rank level. Senior G, the GSO1 (a Lieutenant-Colonel), was the kingpin, being responsible for planning and execution of operations, orders, training and intelligence. Were he GSO1 of an Imperial division he would be assisted by a GSO2 (major) and a GSO3(captain). In Canadian divisions the GSO1 had two of each grade, a luxury that

> came about in the early days . . . when nearly all staff appointments were held by British officers. But Canadian officers in the same grades were put alongside them to learn the business . . . When the British staff officers departed, the double establishment was left, and was filled with Canadian officers who had acquired the necessary experience. This arrangement contributed to the efficiency of Canadian staff work. While one experienced and fully-trained staff officer could handle these jobs, when they had to be done by officers whose military training for the most part had begun in 1914, the extra man was useful.[11]

Each GSO1 had his own ideas about the precise responsibilities of subordinates and each exercised his discretion in assigning duties. The "curious dislike" of delegating responsibilities exhibited by Imperial GSO1s[12] did not feature in 1st Division where GSO1s, cognizant of their responsibility for training, displayed no reluctance whatever in delegating and working subordinates hard. Lieutenant-Colonel John Parsons, for example, made his senior GSO2, Lieutenant-Colonel Harold Matthews, responsible for office routine and training. His junior GSO2, Major Basil Wedd, looked after liaison between infantry and artillery, trench mortars and machine guns, coordination of communications, codes and anti-gas precautions. The senior GSO3, also a Major, sorted out intelligence. The junior GSO3, a captain, minded the War Diary, the Summary of Operations, work reports, condition of defences and dispositions and moves. All G officers and attached officers and staff learners had to "keep in touch with the general situation . . . and make frequent visits to Brigades, Battalions and Batteries."[13]

Major Paul Villiers, GSO3 from January to October, 1916 (the GSO1 was Harvey Kearsley), recalled his duties as writing the War Diary; being in general charge of all codes, ciphers, correspondence and reports; and constantly collecting information:

> The first essential . . . is for each commander to know exactly where all his units are and to know how they are situated, i.e. what they require in the way of reinforcements, ammunition, bombs, water, rations, R.E. Stores, etc. It is the business of every Staff to obtain this information at all costs and to keep all the units of the formation acquainted with the position of the units on its flanks. Thus, the Brigade Staff must verify the positions of all battalions of their own Brigade and of the flank . . . Brigades . . . and they must ensure that each Battalion knows where its neighbouring Battalion is. Similarly, the Division Staff must . . . keep themselves informed as to the actual line reached by their Brigades, and to keep the latter posted as to the positions of Brigades on their flanks.[14]

Liason officers were another valuable source of information. During the Somme, 1st Division instituted a very effective system. Each level of command from company to brigade assigned one LO to the next higher HQ. During the day he remained with his unit, going each night to the HQ to which he was accredited, there passing on information before returning to his unit the next morning.[15]

The senior AQ officer, the Assistant Adjutant and Quartermaster General (AA & QMG), was equal in rank but not in status to the GSO1. His three subordinates handled Q, A and movement. In July 1918 of the 28 Staff Officers in HQ 1st Division, only the AA & QMG (a Canadian) was p.s.c. In September 1916 two were p.s.c. (both British), and in December 1917 the A & QMG (Canadian) and the GS01 (British) were staff trained.[16]

At brigade the Brigade Major (BM) was kingpin. His province was operations, training and intelligence. Then, as now, he filled a key position, one of the most demanding in the Army and, for him personally, a make or break appointment. Currie considered it to be one of the most important of all: "Unless it is filled by a trained staff officer, loss of efficiency will occur, and too great additional responsibility [will be] thrown upon the Brigadier." From the start Currie had been fortunate in his BM, Hubert Kemmis-Betty, p.s.c. At the end of 1915 Currie flatly stated that no Imperial serving as a BM in 1st Division could be replaced by a Canadian without "great loss" of efficiency. No junior Canadian would be appointed or recommended for BM unless he was a trained Staff Officer: "Sentiment must not sway our better judgement." Most GOsC refused to accept less than the most experienced officers as BMs: correspondence on Captain Talbot Papineau, for example, shows that while he was thought an "entirely satisfactory" GSO3 by Byng and Currie, neither would recommend him "for the next step, namely Brigade Major in the field" until he had additional experience.[17] One former BM depicted the appointment thus:

> The BM is chief of staff, and coordinates the work of the whole . . . "AQ" as well as "G". He sets the tone and rules the roost. If all goes well, he gets the credit; if things go ill, he deserves the blame . . . But . . . it is by the "AQ" staff work that brigade tends to be judged. The closest harmony and cooperation is needed . . . friction or isolationism is fatal. The BM must be *primus inter pares*; but he must not boast of it.[18]

One British BM, later a prime minister, was Anthony Eden. "To be a brigade major," he said, " was a job I had always coveted . . . The brigade and its staff seemed of exactly the right size and scope for individual efforts to be rewarding, while the contacts with units were close enough to have a human interest . . . The work was strenuous." Captain Bernard Montgomery, a BM for almost two years, echoed Eden: "There is no doubt that a Brigade-Major's job is the most interesting of all Staff jobs. But it is hard work."[19]

Major Paul Villiers, who in August 1916 had been eight months a GSO3 at 1st Division, agreed. Brigade major had been his ambition because it was "by far the best" job open to a young Staff Officer. When at the end of that month Major Harold McDonald, BM 1st Brigade, suffered severe wounds, Villiers, aged 32, became acting BM: "My joy may be imagined when I was told that if I did this work to the general's satisfaction I should probably keep the appointment." However, his new GOC, Garnet Hughes, gave him a rough welcome and a worse ride:

> The general loathed everything and everybody English with a

mania that was really a disease. When I arrived . . . he said that he only wanted a Canadian and not any Goddamned Englishman! . . . he absolutely refused to help me become *au fait* with the situation . . . I had 10 very hectic days of perpetual abuse. At the end of 10 days a new Bgde Maj was appointed and the Brigadier sent for me and asked me if I would like to stay . . . Because if so he would go and see the Div Commander and try and get me appointed. I told him quite plainly that no consideration on earth would make me accept the appointment. Further I reported the whole matter to Gen. Currie G.O.C. of the Div . . . I got a very nice letter from the Brigadier apologising. We became good friends after.[20]

What is significant here is neither Hughes' irascibility, nor the window that Villiers affords into personalities, but rather that Hughes was soldier enough to recognize Villiers' competence despite his inexperience. From his own time as a BM at Second Ypres, Hughes knew that to a very considerable extent the fortunes of a brigadier depended upon his BM. A comfortable, mutually respectful and supportive relationship spelled prosperity. Indeed, such a situation was essential.

Villiers discovered that others had it even worse. A GSO3 from 1st Division, on visiting a forward brigade in early October, found the BM walking about in the open during a heavy enemy barrage. Asked why he was not under cover in the brigade HQ bunker, the BM replied that the Brigadier was there![21]

In that same month Villiers became a permanent BM, replacing Major M.O. Clarke, BM 3rd Brigade, who went to Second Army as a GSO2. Villiers had made a reputation for himself as GSO3, not just because of good staff work but also because at Mount Sorrel (June), having requested and been allowed to join his old battalion, (the 16th) for the attack, he had gone forward "most gallantly."[22] In giving Villiers the news, Harvey Kearsley, the GSO1, warned that the GOC, George Tuxford, had complained about the appointment. Villiers recalled his introduction to Tuxford as rather unpromising:

> *Gen*: Well, Villiers, you know that you are to come to me as Brigade Major?
>
> *Maj*: Yes, Sir.
>
> *Gen*: Well, I didn't ask for you and I don't want you. But as the GOC says that you have got to be tried I propose to start you fair and square. I wanted a Staff College officer . . . Can you write orders?
>
> *Maj*: Yes, Sir.

> *Gen*: Can you read orders?
>
> *Maj*: Yes, Sir.
>
> *Gen*: Can you read your own writing?
>
> *Maj*: Yes, Sir.
>
> *Gen*: Have you confidence in yourself?
>
> *Maj*: Yes, Sir.
>
> *Gen*: Right, now these are my ideas. I am a farmer out West, and as such employ a lot of machinery. When I engage a mechanic I hand him over the machine and he runs it. If it wants oiling and it begins to squeak I get another mechanic. So now you know how we stand.

Despite this "precarious" beginning Tuxford proved absolutely fair, so much so that Villiers served him for 14 months with "genuine pleasure," calling his time as Tuxford's BM "the most delightful and enjoyable period of the war."[23]

On arrival Villiers astutely realized that "if a Brigade Major can only put himself in real touch with the COs . . . half his difficulties are smoothed away." His daily routine put him in the trenches with battalion COs from 6:30 to 11:00 A.M., at which time he returned to Brigade HQ, dealt with the mail, conferred with the GOC, and visited the reserve battalion, or the Divisional School where brigade soldiers were on course, after which more correspondence faced him on every conceivable subject from "Gum boots" to "Lessons Learnt." During moves he made it his habit to march for a time with each battalion and talk to each CO.[24] It was a full day and then some, but he had an advantage over Major Anthony Eden. In Imperial brigades the BM's only assistant was a Staff Captain who worried himself (and the BM) with numerous (and onerous) AQ matters. Villiers had one Captain to handle AQ and another (the junior) to look after intelligence, leaving him free to focus on operations.

Colonel W.N. Nicholson thought the standard of BMs had deteriorated because of high casualties and insufficient replacements. Another reason for the deterioration was the preference of young officers for A & Q, where their "previous business training stands them in good stead, as they have to deal with concrete facts." Certainly it became harder to find suitable BMs and GSO2s. If it took 12 to 18 months for an officer to progress from Staff Captain A or Q to the more senior divisional A & Q appointments, then the production of GSO1s and BMs took even longer.[25] While training time and experience inevitably decreased, 1st Division did not seem to suffer any significant decline in BM quality. None of its brigades had more than seven BMs during the war. Some BMs may have moved on faster than was preferable, but their next appointments indicate that they were highly thought of, most going on to battalion command or more senior staff appointments.

One officer, successively a BM, a GSO2 at division and finally a GSO2 at Corps, compared the staffs thus:

> The staff of a higher formation closely resembles a rugger fifteen, in which a multitude of individuals must be welded into a team. The brigade staff is [where] individual merit counts proportionately more and team work slightly less . . . corps headquarters is a symphony orchestra, while brigade headquarters is a string quartet. In the big orchestra, minor individual shortcomings may be concealed in the crash of the music; but teamwork and loyalty . . . are . . . paramount.

Of his time at division he said, "Its charm lies in the daily comradeship on equal terms of many officers of different arms of the service. Properly led, a divisional staff is a proud and lively association . . . in the fullest sense a community."[26] An excellent example, perhaps the best, of the experienced and practical Staff Officer at work, and how such an officer absorbed the lesson that he was the servant of the infantry, is the 1st Division Staff Officer who in June 1917 told 2nd Brigade that Army was

> enquiring into the loss of a certain amount of Iron Rations—Beef and Biscuits. We must show a certain amount destroyed by shell fire, between the 9th and 21st April 1917. Could you please give me a certified statement showing the amounts destroyed by shell fire . . . I understand you had between 2,000 and 3,000 Rations destroyed in this way. If you are not quite clear in this matter call me up on the phone.[27]

Units had no Staff Officers as such, no red tabs (gorget patches), no large HQ, just the adjutant (a captain or even a lieutenant) who in 1914–1918 functioned as G, A, disciplinarian and general factotum. The CO, concerned with commanding his battalion, relied upon him to organize the daily routine, run an office, cope with correspondence, write orders, answer queries from brigade, anticipate company needs, stave off troubles and ensure proper deportment of ORs and junior officers. As the chief executive officer the adjutant acted in the CO's name and authority, becoming well known throughout the battalion. A good adjutant became more influential than anyone, except the CO. He could even carry an indifferent CO for some time—weeks, perhaps a few months—but if he was not a good adjutant he could quickly ruin morale no matter how good the CO was. A quick mind helped because some COs cared little about administration, as the acting adjutant of 5th Battalion discovered:

> You know, Tuxford didn't know enough about the economy of running a battalion . . . he wouldn't allow me to leave him, you see he

had lost his adjutant . . . He wouldn't let me go to make out returns. I knew that returns should have been made . . . giving the list of casualties . . . He wondered why the hell we weren't getting any reinforcements. Col. Lemier from the staff . . . came . . . to talk to Tuxford [who] was complaining that he hadn't got reinforcements. He said, "I suppose you sent in your B213." He said, "Oh, yes." [Later] Tuxford said "What's a B213?" I said I had never sent them in because he wouldn't give me time to make them out.[28]

It must have seemed to adjutants that the only burden they were spared was Q (stores and supply), which fell to the unit quartermaster. 8th Battalion's third commandment testifies to the importance of the adjutant: "Thou shalt not take the name of the Adjutant in vain, for the C.O. will not hold him guiltless that taketh his name in vain."[29]

The best way to learn how to be a Staff Officer was to attend Staff College. A decade before the war few officers considered the course of much value, but by 1910 or so the letters p.s.c. were considered magic. Graduates could see that the course had given them greater clarity of mind, better speaking and writing skills and the ability to function better as a member of a team. By 1913 one student, having completed the first year at Camberley, realized that it had made him a better officer and that there was more to soldiering than he had imagined. Also, he had seen the benefit of learning the work of other branches and he had gained many good friends—no small thing for him or the Army. In 1914 the Canadian stock of Camberley graduates was nine, plus three still in training![30] Canada's traditional military shortcoming, staff training (or rather the lack of it) stemmed mostly from an inability to find suitable candidates. None of the 12 graduates were available or immediately fit for senior staff positions in 1st Division; even Camberley graduates were considered only ready for junior appointments. As for graduates of pre-war militia staff courses, even the duties of junior staff positions exceeded the capabilities of most.[31] In 1914 the only other trained Staff Officers available in Canada were eight British or Indian Army officers holding temporary Canadian Militia commissions and seven British Staff Officers attached to various Militia District HQ. Some rejoined their units in the British or Indian Armies, and some, like Lieutenant-Colonel Louis Lipsett, took command of Canadian units. The other way to learn field staff work was to actually do it, but in pre-war Canada no permanent formations existed and the only experience anyone had came during short field exercises when temporary and understrength formations were created.

Consequently, most Canadians, command and staff, commenced their war without the confidence of other Canadians or of their Imperial superiors, peers and subordinates. Credibility came slowly for inexperienced, largely untrained and unknown officers. When Julian Byng, for example, became GOC in May 1916 he knew only the BGGS, C.H. (Tim) Harington. Even the division commanders were strangers to him.[32] While command inexperience raised concern in 1914, an infusion of British officers as commanders was neither necessary nor acceptable. The GOC, however, had to be British since no Canadians then had experience of command above battalion. Going from battalion to division would have been a far stretch for anyone, no matter how competent.

Initially, 1st Division (and later the Canadian Corps) staffed itself with "temps," just as Territorial and New Army divisions did. The newcomers had very little to go on, the "Staff Manual" (*FSR*) having only one and a quarter pages on staff duties in brigades and nothing on staff duties at division or corps. As a whole, *FSR* was so general, without concrete examples of staff work, that one Australian, voicing what was no doubt the consensus, thought it "as much use . . . as the cuneiform inscriptions on a Babylonian brick."[33] This situation had a pronounced impact. While Nicholson described the regular Staff Officer as a "sheet anchor," he did not hesitate to express his preference for the first class temp over the mediocre regular, which was as it should be. But he was no less forthright in emphasizing reservist shortcomings. A gifted reservist could match his Regular colleague in performing a specific task in light of existing conditions, but when these conditions changed the Regular could rely upon his training and experience, while the reservist had always to begin again.[34] Amateurism has very clear limitations. Whatever one chooses to think about Staff Officers, one of the "cankers of a calm world and a long peace"[35] was the desperate shortage in 1914 of trained ones.

To become truly competent a Staff Officer also required command experience as a Regimental officer. War meant that Staff Officers were trained not in the classroom, but on the battlefield. In this hard school, militia staff qualifications were not held in much regard. One graduate who did not shine as a BM, but became a brigade commander in the division and, finally, GOC of a division, albeit one that did not get into action, was Garnet Hughes, son of Sam Hughes. Richard Turner, GOC 3rd Brigade at Second Ypres, was "poorly served by his staff, especially the brigade-major, Garnet Hughes."[36] His shortcomings as a BM largely explain Currie's belief that Hughes was incompetent.

The work that Staff Officers did and how they did it is encompassed in that discipline known as Staff Duties (SD). It provides the nuts and bolts of a Staff Officer's technique. This technique, which takes considerable time to acquire and master, employs a particular methodology, language and procedures for written and other staff work. SD differ from Army to Army, but generally includes dissemination of information and instructions (communications, conferences, visits and liaison); organization of offices and HQs (physical layout and procedures); and preparation of written correspondence (letters, messages, appreciations, instructions, orders, standard operating procedures, movement orders and tables, staff tables and minutes of conferences).

Conferences were an important part of the system. In a corps as close-knit as the Canadian Corps, the BGGS became closely involved in the training and guidance of divisional GSO1s and his ideas, methods and personality strongly influenced BMs and even division and brigade commanders. Visits between HQs were routine and Staff Officers conferred as often as, if not more frequently than, commanders did, which was useful since staff matters that were ironed out in advance or after such visits facilitated and expedited operational decisions. The BGGS, for example, attended the weekly conference of his staff superior (the Major-General General Staff [MGGS]) at the HQ of the Army to which the Canadian Corps was subordinate. On return to his own HQ he apprised his GOC of what had transpired and he conferred with divisional GSO1s, who then returned to their HQs to brief the BMs. A & Q staff were similarly engaged. Staff Officers at all levels also routinely attended their commander's conferences; in fact, they organized them. As well, a GOC who was attending higher formation conferences usually took his senior G officer along. Any Staff Officer visiting a subordinate HQ, formation or unit had always to take immediate action on return to his own HQ on any matters raised during his visit and then advise what he had done, or what he contemplated doing. The wise Staff Officer never made promises that could not be kept.

To execute his responsibilities the Staff Officer practised military writing, a universal system of formats, language and procedures that stressed great attention to detail and absolute thoroughness as much as was humanly possible. Deployment, control and administration of a division and due regard for men's lives left no place for broad-brush canvas art or carelessness with facts and figures. Staff Duties aimed at universality and standardization. Formation commanders, of course, amplified staff school training by specifying their preferred style in SD. When Tuxford of 3rd Brigade, for example, instituted a standard orders format for brigade relief in the line, 1st Division liked it so much that it was entered into general use throughout the division.[37] Griesbach, GOC 1st Brigade, demanded standardized battalion reports because the format facilitated preparation of brigade reports and helped make them comprehensive. He also urged COs to maintain a "Narrative Book" showing times and incidents and anything that influenced their minds. Within Old Red Patch, the aim of standardized operation orders was to ensure that officers "writing orders under difficulties will instinctively conform to the form, and the recipients . . . will know where to look for [that] which affects them."[38]

Other benefits accrued. First, universal techniques helped to improve coordination between HQs and formations, especially when everyone was labouring under the severe strain and pressure of time imposed by operations. Second, when all HQs worked in similar fashion, everyone could adjust more readily to rapidly changing situations. Third, knowing the standardized format and procedures made it less likely that a harried Staff Officer would omit a crucial fact or paragraph. Fourth, a standard style or method of expression stressing clarity, accuracy, brevity, relevance and logic assisted clear presentation: no verbosity, no ambiguity such as orders to the Light Brigade to "charge the guns." Staff Duties strove to ensure identical sequence, layout, phraseology and general principles at whatever level the order originated. All of this in 1914 had yet to be learned. There was a long way to go at that time because *FSR* thought it "neither necessary nor desirable that definite rules should be laid down as to the form in which operation orders should be drafted."[39]

Finally, good or bad SD was a matter of perception and reputation. The operation order that was correct in every aspect—format, content, tone, and minor SD such as abbreviations—inspired confidence and respect, and indicated that the issuing officer and his HQ were up to the mark. The final test of staff work was this: were you the commander would you sign that which had been prepared? Would you stake your reputation on it being right? If your answer was "no," then the document had to be reworked. An infanteer's task was butcher's work, with little finesse about it, but the orders that got him to his place of work demanded enormous care. That was the whole point of SD.

Being a Staff Officer involved more than masterful SD, though. No officer was intuitively a Staff Officer, let alone a good one, nor could a competent Staff Officer be extemporized, not even junior ones. No amount of training could help the officer who could not get on with others. While training and experience helped, this could not do much for an individual who was severely handicapped by want of energy, moral courage, determination, character, intelligence and common sense (the two are complementary but different), imagination, a reasonable manner (it was an art to get his way without quarrels and bickering), and the ability to delegate, to name just a few. Good Staff Officers were not ready stock in quartermaster stores, nor was knowledge.

In late 1916 it was a simple matter for Field Marshal Douglas Haig to say to General Sir Henry Horne, GOC First Army, "Horne, take Vimy Ridge." His whole order is barely two pages long. Horne, turning to the GOC the Canadian Corps (one of three corps in First Army), ordered, "Byng, take Vimy Ridge." Horne's plan fills less than two pages. His operation order is even shorter.[40] At the bottom of the chain of command it was even simpler:

the OC of a platoon or a company in the first wave blew his whistle, shouted "Charge" and led his men over the top. There was no need to commit this operation order to paper. Complications lurked in the large gap between Army and platoon: move masses of men forward, group and prepare the artillery and engineers to support the infantry assault, and provide them a myriad of supplies and other support.

A division had become a very complicated machine by 1915, driven by the chain of command. Command had to overcome friction (opposition) from the enemy, from allies, from nature, from superiors who had strong ideas, from subordinates who might have had other ideas, and even from staff. Field Marshal Slim, speaking to a Staff College in 1952, offered the timeless advice that in the end the commander must "drive through . . . against *every* kind of opposition." His modus operandi was "No details, no paper and no regrets": that is, leave platoon commanders to do platoon commander's work, reduce paper work to the absolute minimum; and do your best and even when you get it wrong you must not have regrets.[41] In 1914–1915 Canadian brigadiers lacked the extra-regimental experience and training that would have provided such insight. They became rather more involved in platoon commander's work than anyone anticipated, and initially they struggled with and contributed to a torrent of paper. Those who were good and lucky and had good Staff Officers were blessed. Very few of the latter were about. In any case, how was the inexperienced commander to control his staff and understand their limitations? Each new brigadier was still trying to comprehend his brigade (only one of them had been infantry for any appreciable time). Almost every problem was new and approached only from the perspective of narrow experience. Such commanders could easily be misled and were hard to serve, even (or perhaps especially so) if their BM was staff trained.

While the staff was a method of control in itself, and Staff Officers facilitated command, they had "no executive authority of command but merely act[ed] for the O.C. and [were] the servants of all in their respective duties."[42] As a rule, Staff Officers did not demand what their superior had not demanded, for to be caught out at this by subordinate commanders could wreck Staff Officers' effectiveness and prospects. Maintaining good relations with superior and subordinate headquarters and with Regimental officers and troops was imperative. This was not always easy. Under certain circumstances, say, the temporary absence or the loss of their commander, Staff Officers might be in charge, as Lieutenant-Colonel Hubert Kemmis-Betty, BM 2nd Brigade, was at Second Ypres in April 1915. Second Ypres also provides an example of a Staff Officer being given sweeping powers. When General Plumer, then GOC V Corps, learned that 2nd and 3rd Canadian Brigades had lost contact, meaning that a gap had opened in the line, he ordered GOC 1st Division

(Alderson) to close it. This prompted a surprised and mortified Alderson, who had not been made aware of the gap or of Turner's order to 3rd Brigade to withdraw, to order his GSO2, Lieutenant-Colonel G.C.W. Gordon-Hall, forward with powers to take whatever action he deemed necessary, including the authority to fire commanders. Plumer also told Gordon-Hall that if necessary he should appoint another officer to command. Once forward, Gordon-Hall reviewed the situation, formed a plan to close the gap and issued orders to Garnet Hughes, Arthur Currie, M.S. Mercer and Bush (GOC 150th Imperial Brigade). (Turner was en route to Alderson's HQ.) Gordon-Hall was a good judge of ability: in Britain he had said that Currie would be a "great asset," which he certainly was at Second Ypres. After the battle, Gordon-Hall was adamant that Turner, in refusing to commit his reserve, had wrought "disastrous consequences."[43] Another example of a Staff Officer filling in was Ross Hayter, GSO1 of 3rd Division, who for a time assumed command at Mount Sorrel in June 1916.[44]

Staff work made the wheels of the machine go round with staff providing the "lubrication" to the chain of command.[45] Knowing when, where and how to apply it had to be learnt. Mistakes were easily made. Overcoming the friction mentioned above was very difficult and usually thankless. After the war one former Staff Officer provided a very useful analogy. He saw the staff as a trouser button, saying

> there are few to praise it while it goes on with its work, and very few to abstain from cursing when it comes off. When a Staff's work is done well the front line only feels as if Nature were marching . . . along some beneficent course . . . But when someone slips up, and half a brigade is left to itself . . . the piercing eye of the front line perceives . . . how pitifully ill the Brass Hats deserve of their country. If you are an infantryman the Brass Hats above you are, in your sight, a kind of *ex officio* children of perdition.[46]

The match of commander and senior Staff Officer was critical. The ideal was that they be different: if one was a generalist then the other should be a man of detail; if one was reserved then the other should be outgoing. Replacing either had to be carefully done since this meant significant change in mood and approach within the formation. At its simplest, the staff was the instrument through which a commander exercised command. It existed to provide him the relevant facts he needed to form his ideas and decisions, to ensure he was aware of any possible consequences of his decisions, to convert his decisions into orders and to convey them to those who had to act upon them. Staff Officers had also to ensure that formations and units were made ready by being brought up to strength and by training and rehearsing for operations, both in routine procedures and in new or amended doctrine. However, no matter how precise an order and how good routines and processes were, prompt or complete execution was never guaranteed. This does not mean that 1st Division staff were more or less careless than any other division; it just means that routines did not always receive the attention they deserved, and individuals erred. For example, a Guards officer taking over from Canadians at Hooge in June 1916 complained of inheriting a mess:

> Mined trenches, confluent craters, bodies and bits of bodies . . . a stink of death and corruption . . . The Canadians fought extremely well and are brave and enterprising, but they are deficient in system and routine. No troops can be first-rate unless they are punished for small faults and get their meals with regularity. The Canadians are frequently famished and never rebuked, whereas the Brigade of Guards are gorged and damned the whole time.[47]

This had little, if anything, to do with Imperials looking down on Dominion troops, nor did it reflect permanent bad habit by 1st Division. What it reflected was consciousness of superiority (the mark of the very best) and the inevitable charge by an incoming division that everything had been "lamentably neglected by the outgoing troops." Such conceit was not restricted to Imperials. A battalion of the 1st Division, relieving a Canadian battalion of another division, just as loudly complained of the "horrible condition [of the trenches]; no work had ever been done . . . food and ammunition lying about all over . . . It was ever the same." By early 1917 one battalion historian could say of 1st Brigade units that given "their outstanding qualities on active operations . . . it can be readily understood why the battalions . . . possessed no particular genius for self-abasement."[48] The same was true of 3rd Brigade. In August, just before Hill 70, A.C. Macdonell, who had taken command of 1st Division in June, overheard Cy Peck, the CO of 16th Battalion, assuring his men that "the Brigade Commander, the Divisional Commander, the Corps Commander knows, and God knows you are the best of men—none ever better."[49]

Tim Harington, in August 1916 BGGS Canadian Corps, provided GSO1s with "Diary of Orders, etc, Concerning the NAB Trench" an amusing but instructive example of friction hard at work inhibiting work, and "how *not* to do a job of work." He also expressed his confidence (and an unvoiced warning) "that the Army will have no cause to make a similar complaint against the Canadian Corps."

> July 19th. 'A' Corps ordered to dig . . . to connect with left of 'Nth' Division tonight. Approximate distance to be dug; shortest line 350

yards, longest 450 yards. Orders acknowledged. No mention made of any intention to vary them.

July 20th. Information received . . . that trench had been started from quite the wrong place . . . explanation called for from 'A' Corps.

July 22nd. 'A' Corps confirm and furnish explanation. Danger and difficulty of carrying out orders represented.

July 23rd. Memo to 'A' Corps impressing necessity of orders being obeyed or explanation furnished. Also stating decision re trench will be made after further consideration.

July 24th. Acknowledgement of above . . . by 'A' Corps and report of its substance having been passed on.

July 25th. Proposals of GOC 'Nth' Division for modified work approved in consequence of strong representations made by 'A' Corps as to difficulty of, and heavy casualties likely to be incurred in, carrying out orders originally issued.

Aug 3rd. Progress report showing some 200 yards of communication trench dug . . . Proposals made for further work, including one for the identical trench for which orders were first issued.

Aug 4th. Proposal approved by Army Commander and necessity pointed out of great care being exercised before any operation is pronounced impossible or even difficult and dangerous.

Aug 9th. Further progress report called for.

Aug 11th. Progress report submitted showing of original trench ordered:—a) 200 yards of trench giving sufficient cover by day but still requiring a good deal of work to make it really satisfactory. b) 110 yards partly dug. c) One strong post commenced. d) Estimated that another four nights work will be necessary before it is possible to move across by day.

Therefore, 27 days after the original order was given it is anticipated that communication on the line originally ordered . . . will be established . . . though there still remains a good deal to be done. [50]

Another example of friction marked 3rd Brigade's trials and tribulations when the brigade was going into reserve that same month. "Pleasant anticipations" also brought numerous problems; none of the promised transport appeared; searching for the billets that had been assigned to the 3rd, advance parties coped with cold, pouring rain, and billets that three times running were full of other troops. "No excuse would be accepted . . . for failure to provide proper quarters. They [would be] a target of all complaints just and unjust." ANZAC, 3rd Brigade's neighbour in reserve saved the day, generously readjusting its accommodation so that upon arrival the 3rd had reasonable quarters. [51]

If these few examples seem to encompass too long a period (June–August 1916) they are intended simply to represent staff mistakes made during that time. Their importance lies in the fact that such how-not-tos continued for two years after the outbreak of war, which in itself indicates the elusive nature of efficiency and the difficulty of overcoming friction. They also suggest supervisory shortcomings, as does the digging of two sets of HQ bunkers for 3rd Brigade above the Douve River six months earlier—an irritating waste of time and effort, resulting from the absence of a "well-defined brigade policy of work and staff supervision to ensure that it was carried out [without which] each unit will run its own course, and sometimes did." Such incidents brought a sharper focus: "Staff Officers must be given definite jobs to supervise . . . One officer cannot control traffic, carrying parties and working parties."[52] Divisional staff had also to be involved intimately in supervision; such a commitment was not always the case, as John Prower, CO 8th Battalion (and formerly BM 2nd Brigade), complained:

> As a rule a large portion of the work preparatory to an attack had to be done by a brigade which was not going to make the attack itself. Therefore the Schedule of Preparatory Work must be drawn up by the Divisional Staffs and throughout must be under *Divisional Supervision*. The C.R.E. himself must superintend the laying out of Jumping Off, Assembly and Communication trenches; a Divisional Staff Officer must locate positions for Dumps, must see the Dumps are properly formed and filled. Many times the men of Brigades who had to make an assault were overworked immediately beforehand because important preparatory work was left undone by disinterested Brigade Staffs.[53]

The lesson was this: a soldier would stand for considerable "mucking about," but he would not fight the better for it. An exhausted, hungry soldier did not train well; he adapted poorly and suffered a loss of confidence. "Tommy is best when Tommy has dined," said one soldier poet.[54] The better commanders—Plumer, Byng, Lipsett, Currie, to name just a few—emphasized that the staff existed to assist the fighting troops and the services. Plumer, for one, repeatedly told his staff, "Gentlemen, remember that [you] are the servants of the infantry." Harington, who by August 1916 was Plumer's MGGS, warned, "If there is anybody on the staff who throws sand on the . . . machine he must go."[55] The forgetful were not long with Plumer's staff, nor were those who bragged (like the fly on the truck axle), "Just look at all the dust we are making!"

Operations meant movement of troops, equipment and supplies, control of which involved numbing staff work. If there has ever been a Staff College graduate who could avoid shuddering in horror when reflecting on exercises that demanded the production of written movement orders, then we have a prodigy. Actually producing such orders surely caused the same shudder or worse. In 1916 it took a 20-page order just to move one division, which occupied 15 or so miles of road space, or if moving by rail required 38 trains of 50 cars each, each car having eight horses or 40 men.[56] Movement orders, while critical, were tedious and prone to going wrong:

> A single brigade on the move with its transport occupied at least three miles of road. With the tail of the column an hour's march behind the vanguard and the obligatory ten minutes' rest in every hour, it took two hours and a half, marching easy, to cover that distance. If one such procession met another at a crossroads proceeding in the opposite direction, the subsequent contretemps could hold up ten thousand men in a chain reaction that stretched for miles and hours behind and could throw out the carefully planned arrangements.[57]

One staff function that really did not come into its own until 1915 was intelligence. 1st Division had a major role in bringing this about. As the first Canadian division to need intelligence it had to establish an intelligence staff and system. Before looking at the division's initiatives, one must summarize the place of pre-war intelligence as exercised by the Corps of Guides (established 1903). Currie's characterization of the Corps' pre-war role as "chiefly directed to reconnaissance and scout duties" indicates its limited usefulness when it came to intelligence—which is not the same as reconnaissance.[58] Intelligence is a product, while reconnaissance is a means of collection. Also, reconnaissance collects information, not intelligence. Information only becomes intelligence after analysis has put it in a form upon which commanders can base decisions.

While the value of intelligence had been realized to some extent before the war, it took the experience of the trenches to reveal how central it had become in the conduct of war. Intelligence had to be hand and glove with operations; it existed to support operations and therefore it could not be an end in itself. In late 1914, when it was seen that reconnaissance units would be of very little use, Guides officers were assigned to new staff appointments dedicated to intelligence: 1st Division gained a GSO3 (Int), and the three brigades each got a Staff Captain (Int) in October 1914.[59] Commencing in 1915 infantry battalions appointed an intelligence officer. Too much should not be read into this; at that time intelligence organizations were "more or less" and "no fixed unit personnel establishment was ever slavishly followed."[60] Intelligence staff at 1st Division eventually included a GSO2 (Int) and one Order of Battle analyst primarily responsible for preliminary interrogation of prisoners and examination of documents. GSO2 (Int) oversaw intelligence policy and duties, and liaison between the infantry and supporting arms down to battalion level, through the Staff Captain (Int) of each brigade. Duties of the GSO3 included artillery liaison, targets and shoots, control of observation post equipment and coordination, and organization of brigade and battalion intelligence.[61]

Early in the war divisions had no sophisticated means of collecting intelligence, air photography being in its infancy and artillery techniques such as flash-spotting and sound-ranging not yet in vogue. Topographical intelligence became very important because of the highly inaccurate state of maps.[62] Troops in contact—the infantry—were the main source of tactical intelligence, and what they provided came mostly from snipers and patrols. Even with the advent of new technology, patrols remained a primary source. Patrolling, which was an art requiring good navigational and leadership skills, was a highly dangerous and tricky affair for the junior officers who led patrols night after night. During one patrol in May 1917 Lieutenant Charles Powers, the IO of the 14th Battalion, and one of his Corporals had a lighter moment, although they did not then recognize it as such. Crawling towards a crater, thought to be disused, they suddenly heard a voice say in perfect English, "Hello, there. Come and have some breakfast." Quickly looking up, they saw a German watching them from the crater, not 10 feet away. They declined by quickly heading for home.[63] Considerable information also came from raids, which grew in importance, frequency and size. Commanders constantly emphasized their value, seeing them as a stiffener of morale.

The CEF adhered to the philosophy common to most European armies in 1914, including the German and British Armies, that intelligence was a normal staff function of G Branch. A British officer, for example, could well have gone during the course of his career from operations (O sub-branch) to intelligence sub-branch, or from operations to movements or vice versa, and back again at various formation levels. Many Canadian officers, amongst them Lieutenant-Colonel H.H. Matthews, DSO, preferred this system because they thought a specialist corps was "a danger which was to be carefully avoided" and they believed that G Staff Officers had to be capable of operational and intelligence duties since these did not fundamentally differ.[64]

But operational duties and intelligence duties did differ. While intelligence was seen as a G staff function, it proved as susceptible to specialization as the infantry battalion had. Intelligence Staff Officers wore the green cap band and gorgets prescribed for miscellaneous appointments, rather than the scarlet of G Staff. Miscellaneous appointments also included recruiting staff, musketry instructors and catering and gymnastics instructors, none of whom were *habitués* of front-line trenches. This explains why many infantry officers referred commonly to intelligence staff as "scrimshankers," despite the fact that green-tabbed subalterns were usually to the fore looking for early indications of a possible attack or of changes in enemy dispositions and order-of-battle. This was just one part of the uphill battle facing intelligence personnel.

Getting intelligence up and running proved far easier than convincing commanders and other Staff Officers that it was good only to the extent to which it was used. Establishing the credibility of the product, let alone its accuracy, was even more difficult, since intelligence and intelligence officers lacked a track record. Currie noted after Vimy that while the staff throughout the Corps appreciated the value of intelligence, Regimental officers, including COs, required "greater stimulation of interest."[65] He did not elaborate. Perhaps he was getting at the cool reception that frequently greeted intelligence Staff Officers sent down to brigades and battalions for information. Another complication for 1st Division intelligence staff lay in the very nature of their function: intelligence production was a relatively slow business. Delay meant some degree of separation from reality. In 1st Division, intelligence began to circulate in the daily "Intelligence Summary" published from March 1915 onward. Currie said the 1st Division was "about" the first in the BEF to produce "regular, daily" Intelligence Summaries.[66] Whether the summaries originated at division, corps or Army, readers dubbed them the "Daily Lies" or "Comic Cuts"—if they were even read. Considerable truth abided in the complaint that they were nothing but extracts from the *Daily Mail* of two days past.[67] Humour at the expense of the staff was not peculiar to the British. Credibility had to be earned by every individual employed in intelligence duties in every division.

Another characteristic of intelligence, one shared with every "watchkeeping" activity, was the period of silence that ruled between the vastly shorter periods of excitement. When others at HQ 1st Division saw "not much happening," they no doubt asked, "Why do you need all those people?" At such times the intelligence specialist was seen as someone who could and should be doing something useful, such as filling in as a Duty Officer, arranging this or that, or assisting here, there and everywhere. One Staff Captain (Int), charged with designing his brigade's 1915 Christmas card, was flattered to think that someone actually thought he could do something, a compliment that seldom came his way. Perhaps he had been guilty of what many saw as the major sin of the practitioners of intelligence: prevarication. Intelligence, Canadian or otherwise, could (and can) only assess capabilities, not intentions. While the following example is exaggerated, it does show the impact of the limitation:

> The enemy might attack, or he might elect to remain on the defensive, or he might do both, either tomorrow morning at 5:30, 12 noon or at any hour of the day or night within the next two years. If there was an attack, it might confidently be expected from the North or from the South, while there was undoubtedly signs of a very good possibility of a drive from the East . . . while it is impossible at the present time to arrive at any conclusion with any degree of inexactitude, I must say that . . . the general opinions . . . seem to indicate that . . . broadly speaking. . . .[68]

It also hints that intelligence assessments could be wrong. Error happens in any staff function, but when it concerns intelligence eyebrows and tempers rise because commanders and operations staffs hate unpleasant enemy surprises. Indications of impending enemy operations can be misinterpreted or entirely missed. At Second Ypres 16th Battalion advised brigade of strange pipes projecting above the German parapet, but at brigade and then at division, intelligence formed "no ideas . . . of their purpose" despite French reports of a prisoner who had talked about an "asphyxiating gas" attack. When a second prisoner stated that there were no gas bottles in the area, the first prisoner's statement was considered too improbable to believe. Neither report was collated with other indications of possible offensive action, such as forward movement of troops, including artillery, and captured maps showing new deployments and positions well forward. While it would have been very difficult to determine exactly when the enemy would attack, increased patrolling might have provided more clues. In the event, the enemy achieved tactical surprise, French intelligence having failed to convince French commanders of the real and immediate threat. Canadian intelligence, doing real intelligence work for the first time, was just as unsuccessful.[69] Thereafter, the 1st Division as a formation was not again surprised as a result of intelligence failure. Localized attacks could not always be foreseen, however, and small scale enemy operations would continue to achieve some successes, just as Canadian operations did.

Canadian military intelligence was really advanced by officers of the calibre of Lieutenant-Colonel Charles Mitchell. In 1914 as a Major he had been appointed the first GSO3 (Int) of 1st Division. His imagination and determination created an intelligence *system* that began to enjoy an enviable reputation under his successor, John Parsons (GSO1 of 1st Division from December

1917). Together, they established for the Canadian Corps what today would be called the intelligence process: effective collection, collation, analysis and dissemination. *The Times History of the War* went so far as to say that other Armies largely copied the system that began in 1st Division.[70]

At each brigade HQ, Staff Captain (Int) was responsible for liaison with supporting arms, for establishing brigade observation posts and for coordinating the siting and activities of all posts within the brigade area; for intelligence training; and for commanding the brigade intelligence section that included eight observers (two being fluent in German), two draughtsmen and a clerk. The exact nature of the first task, so critical as it applied to artillery, bears reiteration since it contains the meat of a lesson learned the hard way. Staff Captain (Int) was directly responsible to his GOC for ensuring that

> destructive and retaliatory shoots [were] being carried out against known targets, giving L.O.'s definite coordinates and all information available. L.O's will inform their H.Q. of the requests of the Brigade, it being left to the Artillery to arrange the method by which the tasks are carried out. *The Infantry will say whether or not the task has been satisfactorily carried out.*

This could only be done by observation from the forward trenches. At Mount Sorrel (June 1916) Captain J.P. MacKenzie (Staff Captain [Int] and later BM of 2nd Brigade), watching wire-cutting by artillery in preparation for a counterattack, reported the work proceeding satisfactorily at 3:15 P.M. Other circumstances caused postponement of the attack (for nine days as it turned out) which meant more wire-cutting and more observing, since in the interim the enemy could be relied upon to mend and thicken his wire.[71] Artillery intelligence became especially valuable. Using the then new techniques of sound-ranging and flash-spotting, observers could plot the location and type of enemy fire units; when correlated against known enemy weapons characteristics, doctrine and tactical organization, this footprint enabled the piecing together of a comprehensive enemy order of battle, a vital ingredient in the planning and execution of operations. Such analysis also had the immediate purpose of providing targets. The artillery preferred that trained artillery officers perform the artillery intelligence function, but the work was closely coordinated and the information was routinely shared with intelligence staffs.

One aspect of Canadian intelligence organization seems to have been neglected. By 1915, although there existed a system designed to ensure an orderly progression of G Staff Officers consistent with their training and experience, no such system for those in intelligence appointments appears to have been formally instituted until mid-1918 when "qualifying appointments" were set.[72] No written prerequisites for "lower" appointments appear to be extant. Perhaps they were thought redundant since some prior experience in intelligence at brigade or battalion clearly stood a GSO2 or a GSO3 at division HQ in good stead. An inexperienced officer thrust into a divisional intelligence appointment could hardly have done the HQ or himself much good.

How well a Staff Officer worked bore a direct relationship to what sort of career he had had. Peacetime principles had discouraged or even forbidden Imperial officers from being employed continuously on the staff, or specializing in one staff branch, be it G, Q or A. The British official history is very informative on the enormous difficulty come 1914 of obtaining sufficient competent Staff Officers and ensuring a balance of experience. In the pre-war Canadian military situation this had not been of particular concern, but once in the field 1st Division experienced the same difficulties:

> To fill the ever-increasing number of staff appointments good regimental officers, to the detriment of their units, were taken; the system of "learners" was introduced, and . . . short Staff College courses were held. During the war the staff officer produced was not, however, an all-round man, but trained only in one particular branch, or merely in one side of it. Even the few commanders and staff officers who were fully trained had no experience of a force of more than a division, and . . . they had to deal with improvised bodies of intelligent amateurs . . . Orders had to contain more details, and subordinates required more nursing and supervision.[73]

The BGGS, who worried that the staff branches would become "watertight" compartments, recommended as much interchange as possible between them. His suggestion that when an officer was absent, an officer from another branch could fill in (or even short exchanges of four to six weeks might be arranged) was usually not taken up since most commanders preferred experience over experimentation in operations.[74] In reality, the shortage of trained officers meant that divisions often relied on Staff Officers who were learning their duties during operations. Sometimes "over-anxious staff officers nursed . . . commanders too much, thereby curbing and discouraging initiative; on the other hand, proper staff guidance and help were not always forthcoming when most needed." [75]

Few commanders willingly released good Staff Officers to other duties and, in any case, the supply of such officers trailed far behind demand. Accordingly, once on the staff, officers tended to remain there. As well, an officer who had started, say, in G Branch usually stayed there because he was less likely to make the serious mistakes that he might make in unfamiliar

waters. Moreover, to move him created the problem of who would train
him and when. The disadvantage of continued specialization—the loss of
opportunity to gain a broader outlook and experience of staff work—was
considered easier to bear, even though commanders then had to watch that
officers serving continuously in one Branch worked not just as members of a
branch team, but also of the staff team.

A balanced profile in which an officer returned periodically to regimental
duty, thus remaining conversant with unit life, was the best insurance that
he would be unlikely to commit the folly of imposing academic staff solutions
on units. The preferred profile featured increasingly senior appointments
across the various levels of formations. Ross Hayter followed a path about
as well-rounded as one could get:

October 1914—September 1915	BM, 1st Brigade
September 1915—January 1916	GSO2, 1st Division
January 1916—August 1917	GSO1, 3rd Division
August 1917—December 1917	GSO1, 1st Division
December 1917—October 1918	GOC, 10th Brigade
October 1918—Armistice	BGGS, Canadian Corps

It is as if all along he were being groomed for finer things. In view of his
competence this is quite likely the case.[76] Captain William Herridge also had
a solid profile, going from Staff Captain 2nd Brigade to GSO3 4th Division, to
BM 2nd Brigade. Harold McDonald followed a similar pattern. Paul Villiers
went from Staff Captain to BM to GSO3, all in 1st Division, and for a time
thought he might go to GHQ as a GSO2. In the event, though, he went to 29th
(Imperial) Division, which he described as "very remarkable . . . commanded
by a very remarkable General . . . The immortal 29th of Gallipoli fame."[77] In
due course Villiers would have been appointed GSO1 of a division.

In December 1916 the selection and training of Canadian Staff Officers
became a matter for the War Office and for what Haig called the "Canadian
authorities." In February 1917 his military secretary asked First Army to
ascertain if the Canadian Corps would accept a proposal for the attachment
of Canadians, say, three or four officers from each division, as staff learners
to British formations for three-month periods after which they would return
to their units. When the Canadian Corps passed this on, 1st and 3rd Divisions
promptly responded with lists of nominations. Major-General David Watson
(4th Division) opposed the idea, preferring the system in the Corps of attaching officers for instruction at all formation HQs. Major-General H.E. Burstall
of 2nd Division agreed, adding his concern that officers who took the attachments might not return to the Canadian Corps. He was open, however, to submitting names of Canadian officers for Imperial staff appointments, as

opposed to attachments. Byng subsequently told First Army that once Imperial officers holding staff appointments in the Canadian Corps had been replaced by Canadians he would pursue the proposal of having Canadian officer attachments to Imperial formations.

The internal system that Watson preferred featured one supernumerary officer attached to each brigade HQ staff for 30 days. Those recommended for further training went on to division, corps or Army for 10 days as understudies at either G Branch or A and Q Branches, or they worked "on [their] own account as opportunity occurs," or they even filled in for a junior Staff Officer. Starting in early 1917, an officer who sought appointment to one of these Staff Learner positions had to be nominated by his CO and then approved by brigade, division and, in some cases, even by the corps commander. Progress reports, including recommendations for additional training or employment, were mandatory. In May, in keeping with Byng's priorities, senior Canadians were attached as understudies to Imperial Staff Officers within the Canadian Corps, the idea being to enable Canadians to qualify to fill such appointments permanently. Lieutenant-Colonel William Rae, CO 4th Battalion, became supernumerary GSO2 at Corps HQ, and Lieutenant-Colonel John Parsons, GSO2 (Int) at Corps HQ, shadowed the GSO1 of 1st Division.

Byng, taking up the offer by First Army, recommended the attachment of six officers as learners to Imperial divisions.[78] By mid-1917 several Imperial divisional HQs had become accustomed to Canadians on staff, an arrangement clearly in the British interest but also a generous one since a Canadian in a GSO2 slot deprived an Imperial officer of such an appointment for a time. Haig wanted more Canadians with Imperial formations "even at the expense of exchanging an officer of somewhat less experience and training for an Imperial officer."[79] He also proposed to offer Canadians who had been evacuated, sick or wounded, attachments or even appointments if they had served on the staff in France, once they were fit and provided they were recommended. Staff Officers, he thought, should be interchangeable in order to guarantee uniformity of doctrine, training and organization and to enhance understanding and sympathy. Consequently, he urged cross-postings of Dominion and Imperial officers.[80] Haig knew that officers so employed would be effective, not just because they were carefully selected, having exhibited the best qualities of the Staff Officer, but because they shared a common Army culture. The most important fact about the staff system, which benefitted every division in the BEF, was that Staff Officers approached and did their work in similar fashion.

This chapter has set 1st Division firmly in the context of the BEF staff system, whose central characteristics came to be universality and standardization. In so doing, it has identified who the staff were, where they came from, what they did and their working practises, the whole of this a necessary precursor to the question of quality: viz, staff work's part in the transformation of the 1st into a good and effective division.

Notes to Chapter Five

1. For senior Staff Officers in 1st Division and Canadian Corps HQ see Appendix VI. Urquhart, *Arthur Currie*, p. 118. Currie, as GOC 1st Division, refused to replace British officers with Canadians: the case was not "Canadian or otherwise [but] the best man for the job."

2. John Masters, *The Road Past Mandalay* (New York: Harper & Brothers, 1961), p. 81. A complete breakdown of staff organization and functions is in *Field Service Pocket Book*, pp. 25–29. See also Love, "*A Call to Arms*," pp. 107–109.

3. LAC, RG9IIIC1, Vol. 3827, File 5, "Staff Work in Armies," 13 January 1916.

4. Masters, *The Road Past Mandalay*, pp. 81–82.

5. Nicholson, *Behind the Lines*, p. 298.

6. Carrington, *Soldier from the Wars Returning*, p. 105.

7. LAC, RG9IIIC1, Vol. 3843, Folder 44, File 1, GHQ, 14 February 1917; *SS 152 Instructions for the Training of the British Armies in France* (London: HMSO, June 1917), p. 4 and Appendix XIV "General Staff Officers (Training)."

8. LAC, MG30E117 (Parsons Papers), Vol. 1, "Composition of Headquarters, British Armies in France," p. 54. One of the striking things about the officers at Canadian Corps HQ in July 1918 is that only three of the 41 listed were p.s.c. Two were British, the BGGS and the DA & QMG. The Canadian was the Lieutenant-Colonel Q. Lists of December 1917 and September, 1916 show respectively three (two British and one Canadian) and seven p.s.c (four British and three Canadian).

9. Nicholson, *Behind the Lines*, p. 193.

10. Brig.-Gen. Sir James E. Edmonds and Lieut.-Col. R. Maxwell-Hyslop, *Military Operations France and Belgium, 1918* Volume V: *26th September–11th November, The Advance to Victory* (London: Macmillan, 1947), p. 179.

11. Burns, *General Mud*, p. 76.

12. Nicholson, *Behind the Lines*, p. 185.

13. LAC, MG30E117 (Parsons Papers), "Composition of Headquarters, British Armies in France," p. 110. Parsons was appointed in December 1917 serving until January 1919.

14. LAC, MG30E236 (Villiers Papers); MG30E60 (Matthews Papers), Vol. 7, Folder 25. Kearsley set out these requirements in mid-1916.

15. LAC, RG9IIIC3, Vol. 4028, Folder 17, File 20, Kearsley to brigades, 23 August 1916; Vol. 4056, Folder 32, File 10, 1 October 1916.

16. LAC, MG30E46 (Turner Papers), Vol. 3, Folder 17, pp. 152, 106. The July 1918 figures show that one in each of 2nd and 4th Divisions and two in 3rd Division were p.s.c.

17. LAC, MG30E75 (Urquhart Papers), Vol. 2, File 3, Currie to GOC Canadian Corps, 11 December 1915; MG30E46 (Turner Papers), Vol. 11, Folder 79 and Vol. 3, Folder 17, pp. 44, 50. The normal progression was GSO3, then BM, then GSO2. While A Branch was responsible for postings and appointments, including those to and about the staff, commanders had considerable (often the final) say in such matters. GOsC routinely requested and got particular officers on their staff, which made sense since knowledge of each other's character and methods was an advantage to all. They did not always

get their choice, of course. In September 1916, December 1917 and July 1918 none of the BMs in 1st Division were p.s.c. All, however, had been on the staff, either as Staff Captains, GSO3s or both.

18. Major R.G. Jessel, *G, A and Q: An Introduction to the Staff* (Aldershot: Gale and Polden Ltd., 1947), p. 18.

19. Eden, *Another World*, p. 149; Nigel Hamilton, *Monty: The Making of a General, 1887–1942* (London: Hamish Hamilton, 1981), p. 123.

20. LAC, MG30E236 (Villiers Papers), Vol. 4, Folder 7, Diary, Vol. 2, pp. 19–20. Villiers was British born. He joined the 16th Battalion on 22 September 1914. See photo.

21. Ibid., p. 23. Villiers does not identify the BM or the brigade. The 1st and the 3rd were the forward brigades at the time. If it was Hughes' 1st Brigade, which is most likely, the brigade had just suffered heavy casualties and been forced to withdraw from those sections of Regina Trench that it had captured. An investigation was ordered into the withdrawal. These events no doubt heightened Hughes' customary irascibility and occupied his mind to the exclusion of much else. Hughes may have been giving his newly appointed BM, Major W.A. Adams, the same sort of treatment he had just given Villiers, his BM of 10 days duration. While George Tuxford, GOC 3rd Brigade, could be very cranky, his BM, Major M.O. Clarke, had been BM for some time and must have had a good relationship with Tuxford or else he would not have stayed long with 3rd Brigade.

22. LAC, 16th Battalion War Diary, June 1916, Appendix 2.

23. LAC, MG30E236 (Villiers Papers), Vol. 4, Folder 7, Diary, Vol. 2, pp. 22–23. Tuxford's remarks are an excellent summation of the BM's place in the scheme of things.

24. Ibid., pp. 24, 28–29. The time taken was well spent. Villiers, by appointment Brigade Major, by rank Major, had to get on well with battalion COs, Lieutenant-Colonels.

25. Nicholson, *Behind the Lines*, p.185; LAC, RG9IIIC1, Vol. 3870, Folder 112, File 2, First Army to Canadian Corps, 1 August 1917. First Army recommended that Staff Captains understudy BMs, but the usual Canadian practise was to select BMs from Staff Captains only when GSO3s were not available.

26. Jessel, *G, A and Q*, pp. 23–25.

27. LAC, RG9IIIC3, Vol. 4057, Folder 34, File 4, letter of 5 June 1917. On 6 June Captain W.D. Herridge, Staff Captain, 2nd Brigade, replied that 2,500 rations had been destroyed. His answer reveals a good sense of balance. He later become a BM.

28. LAC, RG 41, Vol. 8, Tape 2, p. 9, Sergeant (later Captain) F.C. Bagshaw; Meek, *Over the Top!*, p. 183. For his pains an adjutant received an extra 50 cents a day. The adjutant's duties are detailed in *Notes for Commanding Officers* (1918), pp. 356–58. D.S.V. Fosten and R.J. Marrion, *The British Army 1914–18* (London: Osprey Publishing, 1978), p. 30. Before 1916 regulations prescribed coloured cap bands and red and gold collar gorget patches for generals (Staff Officers in the rank of brigadier-general and above also had a thin line of red cord extending from the button at the top of the patch to the bottom), colonels and majors on the staff, the colours depending on the wearer's appointment. From 1916 on, junior Staff Officers at formation also wore these accoutrements. G Staff before and after 1916 wore scarlet, while Staff Officers of the services wore blue gorgets and cap bands. "Miscellaneous" appointments, which included intelligence Staff Officers, wore green. After the war only full Colonels and above wore gorget patches. During the war Staff Officers and commanders also wore armbands, the colour(s) revealing the level they served at: red for division, red-white-red for Corps, red-black-red for Army and red-blue for GHQ. Many photographs of

Currie show him wearing the Corps armband (see Hyatt, *General Sir Arthur Currie*).
29. LAC, MG30E60 (Matthews Papers), Vol. 3, Folder 12, "The Ten Commandments."
30. Colonel R. Meinertzhagen, *Army Diary, 1899–1926* (Edinburgh: Oliver and Boyd, 1960), pp. 57–58. Daniel G. Dancocks, *Legacy of Valour: The Canadians at Passchendaele* (Edmonton: Hurtig, 1986), p. 115, says there were only seven graduates. John A. English, *The Canadian Army and the Normandy Campaign: A Study of Failure in High Command* (Westport, Conn.: Praeger, 1991), p. 92, notes that there were 12 graduates and three still training in 1914. Captain M.V. Bezeau, "The Role and Organization of Canadian Military Staffs, 1904–1945," Master's Thesis, Royal Military College, Kingston, 1978, p. 45, figures there were 10 Canadian Camberley graduates. LAC Militia Reports, 1906–1914, is most accurate on this score: 12 graduates (nine before 1914 and three on training at the outbreak of war). Brian Bond, *British Military Policy Between the Two World Wars* (Oxford: Clarendon Press, 1980), p. 2, says the British Army in 1914 had only 447 p.s.c. officers.
31. Bezeau, "The Role and Organization of Canadian Military Staffs, 1904–1945," p. 41. The pre-war Permanent Force establishment, a mere 3,110, partially explains the problem of coming up with candidates. Canadian officers (Permanent Force only) had begun attending Camberley in 1903. Sometimes even the most careful choices did not pan out. Two candidates had failed the entrance examinations for the 1906–1907 course and all Canadian candidates had severe initial difficulties with the course. See also English, *The Canadian Army*, p. 92.
32. Williams, *Byng of Vimy*, p. 117.
33. Quoted in Edmonds, *Aubers Ridge, Festubert, and Loos*, p. viii.
34. Nicholson, *Behind the Lines*, p. 183.
35. W.J. Craig, *The Complete Works of William Shakespeare* (London: Magpie Books, 1993), p. 430 (*Henry IV*, part I, act 4, scene 2, 32–33).
36. Dancocks, *Welcome to Flanders Fields*, pp. 335, 337.
37. LAC, RG9IIIC3, Vol. 4077, Folder 3, File 11.
38. LAC, MG30E15 (Griesbach Papers), Vol. 3, Files 16A and 16B, RG9IIIC3, Vol. 4027, Folder 12, File 5 and Vol. 4028, Folder 17, File 20. Griesbach to battalions, 3 and 29 April 1917. His orders format (Information, Intention, Instructions) conforms to *Notes for Commanding Officers* (Aldershot: Gale and Polden, 1917), pp. 121–25.
39. *FSR*, p. 27. Experience soon confirmed the value of standard formats. See also Hay's comment near the end of Chapter Two herein.
40. Brigadier-General Sir James E. Edmonds, *Military Operations, France and Belgium, 1917: The German Retreat to the Hindenburg Line and the Battles of Arras: Appendices* (London: Macmillan, 1940), pp. 10–12, GHQ, 2 January 1917; pp. 23–25, Plan of Operations, First Army, 31 January; pp. 92–93, First Army Order, 26 March.
41. Field-Marshal Sir William Slim, "Higher Command in War," *Military Review* (May 1990): pp. 12–13.
42. LAC, RG9IIIC3, Vol. 4056, Folder 32, File 10, 1 October 1914.
43. Dancocks, *Welcome to Flanders Fields*, pp. 107, 266, 277; McWilliams and Steel, *Gas! 1915*, pp.145–48, 157.
44. LAC, RG9IIIC1, Vol. 3842, Folder 43, File 1A. At 10:15 a.m. on 1 June in the absence of the GOC 3rd Division (Mercer), who was forward on reconnaissance, Hayter ordered the reserve brigade to prepare to move. With the whereabouts of Mercer and one of the forward brigade commanders unknown, and the other in no position to get to HQ, Hayter was essentially in command until late afternoon when E.S. Hoare

Nairne assumed command. His report commended Hayter for his thorough knowledge and quick appreciation of the situation. Hoare Nairne also wrote of the excellent work of Major G.R. Stevens, BM 8th Brigade, "on whom the chief burden" fell after his GOC was wounded and captured.

45. Masters, *The Road Past Mandalay*, p. 81.
46. Montague, *Disenchantment*, pp. 35–36. Before (and after) the war Montague was a leader writer for the Guardian. Age 47 in 1914, he dyed his grey hair and lied about his age in order to serve. During the war he was a Staff Captain at GHQ. He also spent some time with III (Imperial) Corps during the Amiens battle. After the war he became a well-known novelist.
47. Headlam, *History of the Guards Division*, p. 124.
48. Inglis Sheldon-Williams and Ralf Frederic Lardy Sheldon-Williams, *The Canadian Front in France and Flanders* (London: A & C Black Ltd., 1920), p. 9; Herbert Rae, *Maple Leaves in Flanders Fields* (Toronto: William Briggs, 1916), pp. 107–108; Murray, *History of the 2nd Canadian Battalion*, p. 185.
49. Urquhart, *History of the 16th Battalion*, p. 198. Macdonell later recalled that he had gone to the battalion to tell Peck that certain matters in the unit could be done more efficiently, but having heard Peck's remarks he thought criticism out of place and did not see what more could be said by way of praise.
50. LAC, RG9IIIC1, Vol. 3842, Folder 43, File 8, Harington to Kearsley, Webber and Hayter (GSO1s 1st, 2nd and 3rd Divisions respectively), 11 August 1916.
51. Urquhart, *History of the 16th Battalion*, pp. 158–59.
52. Ibid., pp. 113–14; LAC, RG9IIIC3, Vol. 4074, Folder 2, File 4, 1 March 1916.
53. LAC, RG9IIIC3, Vol. 4051, Folder 19, File 8, Prower to GOC 2nd Brigade 19 November 1916. Prower was BM 2nd Brigade from September 1915 to August 1916.
54. A.P. Herbert, "The Cookers," in Macdonald, ed., *Anthem for Doomed Youth*, p. 149. Herbert, an officer of the Royal Naval Division, also wrote *The Secret Battle*, long considered a classic novel about how a man can reach breaking point.
55. Plumer is quoted in Eden, *Another World*, p. 137; LAC, RG9IIIC1, Vol. 4056, Folder 32, File 10. Harington is quoted in *Notes for Commanding Officers* (1918), p. 393.
56. LAC, MG30E54 (Major Frederick Phelan, 1st Division HQ, Papers), Folder 3. A division took seven hours to pass a given point. A brigade took about two hours to pass a given point.
57. Lyn Macdonald, *Somme* (London: Michael Joseph 1981), pp. 26–27.
58. Quoted in Maj. J.F. Hahn, *The Intelligence Service Within the Canadian Corps* (Toronto: Macmillan, 1930), p. xiii.
59. Major S.R. Elliot, *Scarlet to Green: A History of Intelligence in the Canadian Army, 1903–1963* (Toronto: Canadian Intelligence and Security Association, 1981), p. 25.
60. Ibid.; Hahn, *The Intelligence Service Within the Canadian Corps*, p. 60.
61. LAC, RG9IIIC1, Vol. 3872, Folder 117, File 3. In March 1918 GHQ authorized one intelligence company per Army. It was to have a section at Army HQ and corps sections corresponding to the number of corps in the particular Army. Corps HQ intelligence staff also had responsibility for security and counterintelligence within corps areas.
62. Inaccurate maps, poorly printed with south at the top of the sheets and coordinate numbers reversed, remained a problem throughout 1915 as Elliot, *Scarlet to Green*, pp. 27–28, indicates. Aerial photography made for better maps. Aircraft were also exploited for other purposes, such as artillery intelligence.
63. LAC, RG9IIIC1, Vol. 3845, Folder 50, File 4. Powers had earlier been awarded the

MC. He finished the war as a Major.

64. Elliot, *Scarlet to Green*, p. 61. Matthews had been CO of the 8th Battalion. His staff experience included stints as GSO3 (Int) and later GSO2 at 1st Division. The present author, having served for 34 years as an infantry and intelligence officer, supports Matthews' view. Its advantages far outweigh the disadvantages. LAC, MG30E318 (3rd Battalion), Vol. 23, File 173, 14 April 1923. Matthews' appointment as Assistant Director of Military Intelligence in 1924 delighted D.H.C. Mason: "I was so glad to hear . . . you were in charge of intelligence because it is something one frequently searches for at Ottawa and does not always find."

65. Maj.-Gen. Sir Ernest Swinton, "Intelligence and Spies," *Twenty Years After*, Supplementary Volume, Part 15, Chapter XXXII, p. 513. The *Concise Oxford Dictionary* defines the verb "scrimshank" as "to shirk duty." Battalion IOs did not usually suffer insult. They did not wear gorgets and they remained on strength and with their units. LAC, RG9IIIC3, Vol. 4061, Folder 7, File 1.

66. Hahn, *The Intelligence Service*, p. xvi; Elliot, *Scarlet to Green*, p. 26. Atkinson, *The Seventh Division*, p. 129, states, "Infantry activity was as before much restricted, though on February 19th [1915] the Intelligence Summary notes that there had evidently been a change in the regiment facing the 21st Brigade." Review of the divisional histories of the other regular Imperial divisions (only these reached the Western Front before 1st Division) reveals no mention of Intelligence Summaries. 7th (Imperial) Division seems to have a case that it was the first division to produce them. Perhaps the significant words are "regular, daily" and "about." The general format of Intelligence Summaries was: Operations (Own Troops and Enemy), Enemy Artillery Activity, Identification of Enemy Troops and Prisoners, and a weather forecast. A typical summary was two or three pages long.

67. Murray, *History of the 2nd Canadian Battalion*, p. 235; Lieutenant-Colonel The Hon Ralph G.A. Hamilton, *The War Diary of the Master of Belhaven* (London: John Murray, 1924; reprint, Barnsley, South Yorkshire: Wharncliffe Publishing Limited, 1990), p. 171.

68. Captain W.P. Lipscomb, *Staff Tales* (London: Constable & Company Ltd., 1920), pp. 27–28.

69. Urquhart, *History of the 16th Battalion*, p. 55; Elliot, *Scarlet to Green*, p. 27.

70. Elliot, *Scarlet to Green*, p. 36. Mitchell's competence is evident in the fact that following his stint as GSO2 (Int) at Canadian Corps (September 1915–October 1916) he became head of the Intelligence Branch at Second Army, and when the GOC (Plumer) went to Italy after Caporetto, Mitchell, at Plumer's insistence, went, too. Plumer was an excellent judge of men. *The Times History of the War*, Vol. XVI, p. 258.

71. LAC, RG9IIIC3, Vol. 4063, Folder 13, File 1. 1st Division detailed specific duties of battalion and brigade intelligence and provided guidance for the siting and operation of observation posts and snipers. The italics have been added to the last sentence of the quoted material since it enunciates a fundamental change in doctrine due to the repeated failure of artillery to cut enemy wire before an attack. The observation duties are related in 2nd Brigade War Diary, July 1916.

72. LAC, RG9IIIC3, Vol. 4063, Folder 13, File 1, Third Army to constituent corps 13 July 1918 established a hierarchy of senior intelligence appointments (Higher Appointments) and what experience an officer required (Qualifying Appointment) for advancement. For example, an officer hoping to be appointed First IO at an Army HQ had to have served as First IO at a Corps HQ.

Higher Appointment	Qualifying Appointment
First IO, Army HQ	First IO, Corps HQ
First or Second IO, Corps HQ	Divisional IO and either Second at Corps or Third at Army
Air Photographic Officer	Staff Captain (Int)

73. Edmonds and Maxwell-Hyslop, *The Advance to Victory*, pp. 592–93.

74. LAC, RG9IIIC3, Vol. 4032, Folder 28, File 1, Canadian Corps, "Notes on Training," 27 November 1917.

75. Miles, *2nd July 1916 to the End of the Battles of the Somme*, p. 570.

76. The fact that Hayter did not command a battalion prior to taking command of 10th Brigade did not hurt him or his brigade. Both enjoyed a fine reputation. While a man can become commander without ever having been on the staff, experience as a Staff Officer will help him know what it is reasonable to expect a staff to be able to do; it will enable him to judge his staff's efficiency and it will help him identify and correct shortcomings.

77. LAC, MG30E236 (Villiers Papers), Vol. 4, Folder 7, Vol. 3 of Diary. Urquhart, *History of the 16th Battalion*, page 473, lists all of Villiers' staff appointments.

78. LAC, RG9IIIC1, Vol. 3870, Folder 112, File 2. According to a letter of 17 June 1917 from Haig to the Army Council, "Canadian authorities" had inquired about the possibility of attaching more Canadian officers to Imperial formations. The "authorities" were presumably HQ Overseas Military Forces of Canada.

79. Ibid.; Vol. 3827, Folder 6, File 6, Conference of Army Commanders, 20 March 1917.

80. LAC, MG30E100 (Currie Papers), Vol. 2, General Correspondence (G–L), Haig to Secretary of War, 17 June 1917 (copy to Currie). As of June there were 18 Imperial Staff Officers in the Canadian Corps (12 General Staff, one A and Q and five BMs). Two Canadians were in staff appointments with Imperial formations, and three were under instruction. 39 learners were in place within the Canadian Corps. One Canadian had completed the Cambridge Staff Course (not specified whether junior or senior), and 10 Canadians had completed the GHQ Staff Courses (two senior and eight junior).

CHAPTER SIX

A Staff to Serve the Line (2)

I passed out of the Staff College . . . I believe I got a good
report, but do not know as nobody ever told me if I had
done well or badly: which seemed curious.

—MONTGOMERY OF ALAMEIN

Chapter Five concerned the staff system as a whole and 1st Division's place in it in particular. Montgomery's comment hints at the subject of this chapter: a report card or assessment of the quality of 1st Division's staff work, just as promised in the second paragraph of the last chapter. That paragraph also specified the test of staff work as getting the right troops to the right place on time with everything required to achieve the mission. To pass that test, which is also a purpose, staff work required certain attributes: accuracy, relevance, logic, brevity and clarity. This chapter analyses 1st Division's staff work in the field in light of these attributes and assesses it as one of the three elements by which the division became a good or effective formation.

Montgomery went on to become a famous commander, his reputation based partly on the talents of his chief Staff Officer, Freddie de Guingand. Another very successful partnership featured Sir Herbert Plumer, GOC Second Army, and his MGGS, C.H. (Tim) Harington, formerly BGGS of the Canadian Corps. Most Staff Officers, however, remain largely unknown, either because of a less spectacular partnership or because the partnership did not exist at a decisive level. Mediocrity described some Staff Officers.

Others became infamous for laziness, incompetence, or just plain non-effectiveness, giving the lie to their cap badge with its crown-and-lion emblem that historically represented the hallmark of quality.[1]

The description of a few basic circumstances about staff performance is necessary. First, in terms of a division, no level of the staff stands alone: staff quality is a cumulative assessment of division, brigade and battalion. The competent BM, for example, was a joy not only to his GOC but to battalions and to the divisional staff, especially the GSO1, his immediate superior in the staff chain. The impact of his competence extended also to Corps since its GOC and its BGGS had to think "two-down," meaning that high quality brigade staff work was vital. A divisional GSO1 who was tolerant of ineptitude or habitual carelessness by a BM would certainly have felt the ire of the BGGS and his own GOC, who would have heard about it on the command net (from the corps commander) and on the staff net (from the BGGS). Regimental officers were quick to judge the staff harshly. One 18-year-old platoon commander initially saw the staff as the personification of "Best men forward into danger, and less good men backwards into safety, the eliminating rule of war . . . at work." With some experience, and despite his youth, came wisdom: "Best men forwards and less-good men backwards is so natural a process that it requires much resolution on the part of the High Command to reverse the flow and keep an adequate number of good men for the essential work that must be done in the rear."[2] GOsC had also to ensure that Staff Officers not be "pushed on" without sufficient experience to perform capably in a higher appointment.[3]

Second, because of erroneous estimates or the enemy, plans had always to be revised, which is why

> Hard work and often over-work were commonplace at G.H.Q. and at formation and unit headquarters right up to the front line . . . at G.H.Q. there were "few, if any, officers who do not do a fourteen-hour day" . . . I have seen a Staff officer faint at table from sheer pressure of work, and dozens of men, come fresh from regimental work, wilt away under the fierce pressure of work at G.H.Q. . . . John Terraine has pointed out: "It can hardly be doubted that errors and breakdowns in staff work were far more likely to be due to fatigue through overwork than to the blithe incompetence for which the staffs were universally blamed."[4]

Finally, in 1914 the reputation of the staff as a whole was neither good nor enviable. The staff of every division, including 1st Division, had to work hard to reverse this. Inexperience and the varied and difficult demands suddenly facing newly appointed Staff Officers made the early going very difficult. The music-hall patter of Boer War days, which had asked, "If bread is the staff of life, what is the life of the staff?" and had answered, "One long loaf,"[5] became popular again and remained so well into the war. Sometimes the popular view, which saw a Staff Officer as a failed Regimental officer, became very pointed. In the spring of 1915 Arthur Currie, then GOC 2nd Brigade, approved the use of sawed-off shotguns but Sir John French, then C-in-C of the BEF, prohibited them because lead pellets contravened the Geneva Convention. 2nd Brigade retained them for sporting purposes "until the red band around the cap of a well- known staff officer, observing from a trench in the support area, was mistaken for a cock pheasant, whereupon the guns were withdrawn."[6]

One of the best of the "Old Bill" cartoons portrayed Tommy's rancour toward Staff Officers who, it was thought, seldom appeared up front. Spotting several red-tabbed officers in a forward trench, Old Bill comments ruefully to his mate, "There's evidently goin' to be an offensive around 'ere, Bert." Another cartoon illustrated the Regimental officer's disgust with incessant staff requests for "returns" (reports) and staff failure to recognize how these consumed the time and energy of combat officers. Here we see a haggard officer under heavy artillery fire, field telephone in hand, listening to some Staff Officer say, "Please let us know, as soon as possible, the number of tins of raspberry jam issued to you last Friday."[7] The cartoon is not exaggerated. 14th Battalion experienced such comic opera at Mount Sorrel in 1916: on 3 June, the day its counterattack failed, there arrived a runner breathless and nervous from having come forward through heavy artillery fire. His message asked how many men had subscribed to the War Loan![8]

Sometimes staff insensitivity drew absolute fury. During the heavy fighting near Hill 60 in the Ypres Salient in June 1916 2nd Battalion came under command of 3rd Brigade (Tuxford). Sent forward to relieve the 14th and 15th Battalions, Lieutenant-Colonel A.E. Swift and his men found themselves with both flanks in the air, no trenches to speak of, just shell holes and shallow ditches, and the situation altogether grim. Nevertheless, he consolidated the position, so much so that 1st Division praised 2nd Battalion for its thorough patrolling, which had precisely located the German line, as later proved by aerial photography. On June 5 Currie personally congratulated Swift. Later that day Swift received the following from the BM of 3rd Brigade:

> The GOC directs that you and your staff and senior officers commanding officers [sic] must make greater endeavours to get round the positions occupied by your companies . . . The reports as to the positions of your four companies were by no means accurate . . . Another Staff Officer of the 3rd Canadian Infantry Brigade . . . reports that the Company Commanders were not taking sufficient steps to move round and see their men and the positions . . . You will please render as usual the three situation reports which are required from Battalions when in the front line. You will also take

further steps to reconnoitre the ground between the front line
which was dug last night and suitable positions in rear.[9]

This missive, so wrong in tone and its timing hardly propitious, considering the severe fighting the 2nd Battalion had just experienced, contained an
error that any self-respecting brigade staff should have caught: "senior officers commanding officers,"which presumably should have read "senior
officers commanding companies." 2nd Battalion's historian later excused the
"incoherencies . . . on the ground that the staff were operating under great
nervous strain."[10] In soldier parlance, 3rd Brigade staff had the "wind up."
Still, prudence dictated that the wise soldier "honour the army Staff, that
thy days may be long in the corps Reserve, to which they may possibly send
thee."[11] The fact that the staff could determine a man's fate no doubt ran-
kled, too.

Such incidents say a great deal about the line-staff relationship in the
first half of the war. Clearly, the perfect Staff Officer did not exist, not even
in 1st Division, although the division was blessed with good senior staff from
the start, many being p.s.c. and experienced in the wider scope of the British
Army. While staff work generally and continually improved, errors continued. In January 1916 the BGGS (Harington) and GOC 2nd Brigade (Louis
Lipsett) concluded that mistakes were unavoidable in the conduct of ever
more complicated operations. This had not changed by 1917. Even after an
operation as fine as Vimy, close study of its lessons obliged First Army to reit-
erate several shortcomings because "the mistakes referred to are apt to recur
whenever offensive operations are undertaken."[12]

Staff Officers, whether p.s.c., Militia Staff, or wartime trained, played central roles in every operation, including relief in the line, a basic operation
that was a constant task for every division and one that had to be conducted
in pretty much the same fashion time and again from start to finish. Basic
or not, a relief demanded the close attention of staff and command.[13]
Operation Order No. 1, issued over the signature of Colonel C.F. Romer,
GSO1, on 27 February 1915 is significant not because of its subject but
because it marked the start of 1st Division's operational life, its genesis in
the sense of "First Book."The Order detailed how the 1st would relieve 7th
(Imperial) Division, making Canadians responsible for the first time for a
sector of the Western Front. This relief went well; the 7th made no complaint, or at least recorded none, which we might take as an indication that
the Operation Order featured good SD. So it should have, too, since Romer
was an experienced and competent Imperial officer.[14]

A divisional relief was relatively straight forward, which was reflected in
the brevity and simplicity of the order; however, it was not as easy as it

sounds since the relief was normally a night operation during which much could go wrong, especially when it involved green troops. It is a fact, too, that man is not usually at his best in the dark. An enemy attack during a relief was as dangerous as an attack delivered astride a unit or formation boundary. In both instances, responsibilities, unless they were absolutely clear, could become divided or uncertain down at the level where they had to be carried out. In the case of a relief, the euphoria caused by packing up to get out of the line could distract the departing unit and the arriving unit often lacked easy familiarity with the trenches. Delay also worried commanders since it usually caused congestion in the trenches, which made for good targets. Other hazards existed. If a CO, for example, had to relieve a Bantam battalion one of his first thoughts might be to curse his luck, for he and his men would be fortunate to find trenches that reached up to their waists and therefore plenty of digging loomed. More often, his anxiety centred around the condition of his new trenches: how good were they, how good was the information he was getting about the enemy opposite and how much work would have to be done to put the line in good shape? These things were not often a serious matter during an internal 1st Division relief but they no doubt surfaced to some degree when 1st Division units or brigades relieved elements of other divisions.

A brigade usually had two battalions in the line, a third "in support," the distance from the line dependant upon the ground and the situation, and the fourth battalion "in reserve," perhaps two or three miles back (or it might be tucked up closer if the situation demanded). A battalion in reserve usually meant that it was still under direct enemy observation, which inhibited training and rest. Periodically the battalions changed places, every few days or so depending on what was going on in the brigade sector. A battalion could also go into divisional reserve, where it was no longer under enemy observation but still might be shelled, or it could go well back, into Corps reserve, where it would be in safety. Very infrequently a battalion might spend a few days in Army reserve, or it might go into GHQ reserve—a paradise so far removed from the trenches that it was another world. Relief at brigade level worked in similar fashion but rotation was less frequent. Once or twice a year the entire division would be withdrawn for rest and training in Army reserve.

To ensure reliefs went smoothly a whole discipline was established which included a system of battle procedure for reconnaissance, giving of orders, and movement of troops in and out of positions. Relief started with a unit being warned by brigade that it would relieve the Xth Battalion in the front line, say, the following night. The CO then warned his companies, the unit QM, the MO and the TO (transport officer) and ordered company parades at dusk on the night of the relief so the men could be inspected to ensure they had the necessary kit, rations and ammunition for going into the line. When all was correct, the troops moved off at a time that would get them to the trenches at the precise time specified by brigade. Earlier an advance or reconnaissance party consisting of company 2ICs and three or four NCOs per company would have gone to the trenches to take over trench stores and to "recce" the positions. When the company main bodies arrived after dark, they were guided into the line; at the same time, incoming and outgoing commanders at all levels discussed the positions, enemy dispositions, wire, patrols and any peculiarities of the sector. Meanwhile, patrols had gone out to guard against surprise, and listening posts and other positions were handed over. As each platoon did so, this was reported to company HQs, which in turn reported "Complete" to battalion HQ where the incoming CO then signed for the trenches. The relief was officially over. The incoming unit now had full responsibility.

One Imperial officer, in a very detailed account of what this routine meant in the life of an infantry subaltern, recalled that in 1916 he spent 65 days in front-line trenches and 36 more in close support, "that is, 101 days which may be described as under fire." In addition, he was 120 days in reserve positions and 73 days out in rest. The remaining 72 days were spent at schools, in hospital, on leave, at base depot and travelling. During its 16 tours in the trenches, varying from one to thirteen days, his battalion was in action four times, in attacks or raids. "This must," he said, "be a typical experience shared by many hundreds of thousands of infantrymen who spent a year continuously at the front."[15] He was right: the time passed pretty much the same in 1st Division. A table prepared by the BM of 3rd Brigade, Major Paul Villiers, for the year 27 October 1916 to 26 October 1917 shows that the battalions of 3rd Brigade averaged 85 days in the trenches, 128 days in close support and 152 days in division or corps reserve, which included rest.[16] Hugh Urquhart, whose history of the 16th Battalion must surely be one of the most thorough battalion histories ever written, tells us where the 16th spent every day of its war, that is, all 1,363 days from 17 February 1915 to 11 November 1918: 347 days in trenches, 295 days in brigade support or reserve, 598 days in division or corps reserve, 104 days in Army reserve, and 19 days in GHQ reserve.[17]

A classic relief, and a very complicated one, occurred in April 1916 when the Canadian Corps relieved V Corps in the St. Eloi-Hooge sector, the first ever complete relief of one corps by another. The staff work to complete it (relief and movement orders, road allocations, and timetables for changes of command during the relief) makes up a solid one inch thick file. The conduct of this relief pleased Alderson. It reflected great credit, he said, on divisional and brigade staffs, comments echoed by GOC 1st Division (Currie) who thought it went "wonderfully well, although it was a move involving many and varied complications."[18] Sound planning, good SD and good discipline had done the trick. This corps relief is significant for two reasons. First, it shows how far Canadian staff work had come and how dramatically Canadian skills and confidence had grown in a relatively short time. It had only been about a year since Operation Order No. 1. Second, before this relief Imperial practise had been to relieve at division or lower but the arrival of the Canadian Corps (which was also a National Army whose government wanted it put into and taken out of the line as a whole) meant conducting corps reliefs.[19]

Second Ypres, 1st Division's initial battle, was not routine at all, being instead a rude and bloody awakening. Had he been asked, Garnet Hughes might have admitted that his pre-war Militia Staff Course scarcely prepared him to perform at the level of the other two BMs in 1st Division: Major Ross Hayter, 1st Brigade (Mercer), and Lieutenant-Colonel Hubert Kemmis-Betty, 2nd Brigade (Currie). Both were regulars and p.s.c. As circumstance would have it, Hughes found himself further burdened with 2nd and 10th Battalions (from 1st and 2nd Brigades respectively), which came under command of 3rd Brigade, adding to his control and coordination problems at a HQ too close to the firing line. Who had sited it so precariously cannot be said for sure but as BM Hughes would certainly have had a say. In any case, the order from his GOC (Turner) for an immediate counterattack by two battalions allowed no time for reconnaissance and little for planning. The Operation Order, signed by Hughes and issued at 10:47 P.M. on 22 April, included Zero (11:30), the location of the jumping-off line, the mission, the assault formation and an order to the guns to shell the far side of the objective, the woods later known as Kitchener's Wood.[20]

Daniel Dancocks thought Hughes should have been "more helpful" but did not say how. Turner's senior Staff Captain (Harold McDonald) put the two battalions into assault position, Hughes not arriving until afterward. Perhaps this curious delegation of such a vital task was what Dancocks meant. What Hughes could have done after the issue of the attack order is unclear; how "helpful" he was before Turner's decision is equally uncertain. Perhaps on his own, or at the urging of the two COs, he tried to influence Turner to allow more time for battle procedure but given the inexperience of all involved, that is unlikely.[21] Kemmis-Betty and his p.s.c., on the other hand, stood Currie in good stead; indeed, his confidence in his BM was such that he left him in charge of the HQ while he commenced a perilous search for the reinforcements he had been promised.[22]

Once 1st Division became engaged, little time was available to issue formal orders. Much of the written staff work came afterward in the form of lengthy brigade and battalion reports that featured long, unnumbered paragraphs, making easy reference difficult. Nor are they standardized in format, which must have been a nuisance to Staff Officers at division and corps. Notwithstanding, the reports even in minor SD are surprisingly good. 8th Battalion's reports stand out for their quality but then their author was Louis Lipsett, the only Regular Army (Imperial) CO in the 1st Division. He describes events as a professional soldier would: left, centre and right; front to rear; and he uses group headings throughout to indicate different subjects and paragraph headings where he thought them helpful.[23]

Grouping expediency, while necessary, also had a negative impact upon staff work at Festubert in May, it still being the case that unexpected change could affect the quality of staff work. Following the abortive attack by 3rd Brigade (Turner) on 18 May—enemy artillery stopped it cold almost as soon as it began—Alderson took under command 51st Highland (Imperial) Division plus the divisional artillery of the 2nd and 7th (Imperial) Divisions. The Army Commander (Haig) made the Indian Corps responsible for administration in Alderson's new and temporary corps, an awkward arrangement that lasted only four days. Lacking a HQ and a staff to run a corps, Alderson had to appoint his GSO1 (Romer) BGGS, meaning that staff work at HQ 1st Division suffered because it then had only one other qualified G Staff Officer and his only experience was a brief stint as GSO2. This partially explains the events of the next two days: brigade attacks without adequate fire support; ammunition shortages (the ad-hockery in making another corps responsible for administration, of which dumps were a part, stood condemned); little or no reconnaissance (one OC in one of the assault battalions found himself not knowing where the jumping-off line or the objective were, or how to get there); two attacks within a short period by 2nd Brigade, which lost its edge after suffering severely during the first attack; and for the attack on 20 May, less than five hours warning.[24] Most of what went wrong had more to do with command than with staff but the latter's reputation at the time made it a convenient villain and an explanation for heavy casualties. Overall, Festubert was "frustrating" and even a "fiasco," the whole at a cost of nearly 2,500 casualties in exchange for a gain of 600 yards on a one mile front. One participant remembered "getting out alive [as] one of the few pleasant recollections of Festubert."[25] Its only value, perhaps, lay in tempering the steel that 1st Division had displayed at Second Ypres.

Givenchy, which followed Festubert by a month, was classed as an action, not a battle, because it was on a smaller scale, involving just sub-units of two battalions of 1st Brigade. It differed also in that the brigade had two whole weeks to prepare, as opposed to the few hours at Festubert. Consequently, battle procedure (including staff work) stood as "a model for successful major engagements fought later."[26] The preliminary instructions (including warning orders) and Operation Orders issued for Givenchy are thorough and clear, so much so that one could consider them finely crafted. Given the time available, both sets of battalion orders (1st and 3rd) epitomize good SD: they are clear, concise and relevant. By contrast, at Festubert nothing much was clear; for example, no one from GOC 2nd Brigade down had known exactly where "K5" (their objective) was, or what its capture entailed. While the orders' format was not standardized at Festubert or Givenchy, Operation Orders generally adhered to *FSR* and contained "Information" (on enemy and one's own troops), "Intention" (mission), "Instructions" (timings, locations and other matters necessary to execute the order), and "Reports" (the HQ location). At this time administration, supply and communications also came under Instructions.[27] Despite the fine staff work Givenchy went awry soon after it began, mostly because of the failure of certain command and control measures, such as ensuring a sufficient and ready supply of bombs (hand grenades). Givenchy cost 1st Division 600 men.

1st Division's next major encounter as a division, the defensive operations and subsequent counterattacks at Mount Sorrel in June 1916, severely tested staff and commanders. Timing was crucial, and the events of that month repeatedly hammered home this point. Perhaps the biggest lesson concerned counterattack, the best time to do so being when the enemy had "expended his reserves in storming the entrenchments" and before he had consolidated—in short, immediately, despite, as *FSR* pointed out, "less time for preparation." The well-planned defence includes planned and rehearsed counterattacks but neither 3rd Division nor Corps had done their homework here. At 8:45 P.M. Corps HQ ordered 3rd Division to counterattack at 2:00 the next morning using 2nd and 3rd Brigades of 1st Division. At 9:20 P.M. Lipsett (2nd Brigade) asked 1st Division when he could expect orders. Two hours later HQ 1st Division received them, and time being short, Currie read 3rd Division's orders to Lipsett over the telephone. This began a race against time for some of the assault troops who had 11 miles to march. Despite the warning order issued before noon by 1st Division's GSO1, Harvey Kearsley, to 1st and 3rd Brigades to be prepared to move at short notice, and his follow-up order that had some units moving by 8:00 P.M., 3rd Brigade did not reach its assault position until 15 minutes before Zero. Further delays stalled matters until daylight when, nothing going right, the rockets that fired to signal the attack exceeded the specified number (six) and did not match the agreed pattern, raising doubts about whether or not they were the word to go.[28] The uncoordinated attacks that resulted from the confusion all failed.

Preparations for a deliberate counterattack began almost immediately.

Scheduled first for 6 June and then 7 June but time being inadequate, the counterattack was reset for 13 June. The BGGS (Harington) had been ordered to report to Second Army as MGGS on 7 June but Plumer left him with the Canadian Corps, saying, "You had better look sharp and get Mount Sorrel back, or I shan't have you at all."[29] Everyone, it seems, looked sharp. The heavy losses taken by 2nd and 3rd Brigades in the counterattack on 3 June had necessitated the rapid formation of two composite brigades, a regrouping that was accomplished expeditiously. 3rd Division's brigades were still in no condition to participate. Louis Lipsett, GOC of one of the composite brigades, had two of his own battalions (the 7th and 8th)) and two from 1st Brigade (the 1st and the 3rd), while George Tuxford, commanding the other composite brigade, had his 13th and 16th Battalions and the 2nd and 4th from 1st Brigade. Having been together in the division for over a year these units were not strangers to one another but the shuffle broke up familiar habits, forcing everyone to spend more time and effort ensuring that all were on net.

The minutes of a conference involving the BGGS, the GOsC 1st and 3rd Divisions and the GSO1s of all three Canadian divisions became one of the first entries in 1st Division's General Staff Log for Mount Sorrel. For the period 8 to 14 June the log runs to 15 pages. The conference resolved many matters and permitted the two composite brigades to commence preparing their Operation Orders even before the corps order was issued on 11 June. Both brigades issued their orders that same day. Lipsett's BM (Major John Prower) stuck to the standard format (Information, Intention, Instructions, Reports), all in three pages and absolutely clear. His definitive mission statement is irreproachable: it features the prescribed imperative "will," it is singular (there are no subordinate clauses joined by "and") and it is one clear, direct sentence without expressions such as "in order to" or "with a view to." Tuxford's order written by BM Major M.O. Clarke lacks a precise mission statement, although it is easily deduced from the second paragraph. Rather than detailing one brigade and then the other, the order skips back and forth; however, it is clear by the end of the first page who is to do what. The differences lie in the fact that Prower and Lipsett had been together since September 1915 while Tuxford and Clarke had been a team for less than three months.

The orders also reflect the differences in the two GOsC: Lipsett, the well-trained and precise infantry professional with a keen eye for SD; and Tuxford, a thrusting former militia cavalryman with less concern for operational writing of any kind. Both sets of orders met the test of staff duties. As for battalion orders, not surprisingly those for the 7th and 8th Battalions are in the Lipsett mould. 3rd Battalion's orders, which Lipsett criticized for a lack of definitiveness (one example being an imprecise line of advance, particularly for a night operation) were subsequently amended. He had no complaint with 1st Battalion's order. Tuxford's own battalions (13th and 16th) produced adequate orders, they having the advantage of knowing what he wanted. 4th Battalion's order, had it been issued as written, would have left recipients still searching at the bottom of the first page for the unit's mission. This order was not critical, however, since the 4th, like the 2nd, was in support, Tuxford having decided to attack with the 13th and 16th.[30] Overall, battalion orders showed better than those at Festubert but then they benefitted from the extensive time available for their preparation. Even so, imprecision in the vital Intention and Instructions sections remained the major weakness.

Tuxford thought his staff did well: "All worked energetically and hard. Major Clarke (BM), Capt. Urquhart, Capt. Cotton, made repeated trips to the front line . . . gaining valuable information." Lipsett was equally pleased with his staff.[31] Artillery Staff Officers were stretched because the temporary grouping of Corps heavy artillery and divisional artillery working out of 1st Division HQ, added to their burdens but they still produced excellent fire plans. As always, the inability to maintain communications with assault battalions hindered commanders and staff, as Lipsett indicated when he began a report with "The conditions . . . are something as follows." and this despite having "just been down and reconnoitred the position myself."[32] Better weather, accurate and heavy artillery support, and superior staff work made "the first Canadian deliberately planned attack in any force . . . an unqualified success." The Army commander (Plumer) later told GHQ that the Canadian divisions had suffered severely and had fought well.[33]

The Canadian Corps remained in the Ypres Salient through July and August, departing at the end of the latter for the Somme where it relieved 1st Anzac Corps in the Pozieres area. 2nd and 3rd Divisions commenced preparations for an offensive scheduled for 15 September, while 1st Division held the Canadian Corps' front. The attack, when it came, resulted in some gains but the main objective, the high ground northeast of Courcelette, remained in enemy hands.

Old Red Patch now had its turn, first becoming actively involved in preliminary operations on 18 September as a precursor to the Battle of Thiepval. 2nd and 3rd Brigades were tasked to take Thiepval village, Zero being set for 26 September. Kearsley, the GSO1, continued to demonstrate his professional acumen and leadership, especially in the quality of his staff work. His preliminary and executive Operation Orders (and an amendment made necessary by changes beyond his control) reflect a precise and ordered mind and a thorough grasp of the situation. Brigade orders, on the other hand, exhibit the same faults they had earlier. The BM of 3rd Brigade, Major M.O. Clarke, did not provide clear mission statements in either of the brigade's two orders and it is easy to get buried in the wealth of detail caused by his format: his decision to detail orders by phase (there were five phases) rather than by battalion results in considerable repetition. Battalion orders are generally satisfactory, surprisingly so for it must have taken adjutants considerable time to get the picture from Clarke's orders. 2nd Brigade's orders are not as good as earlier but the brigade's new BM, Captain W.H.S. Alston, had only arrived in late August and was now issuing his first order in that role. While his orders are lengthy (seven and eight pages), they are clearer than 3rd Brigade's. Alston plainly stated the mission in his second paragraph. Much to his credit (and as a junior officer) he had produced the better orders. Battalion orders reflect this.[34] Overall, brigade staff work had improved only marginally since Mount Sorrel, while battalion orders were considerably better.

Regina Trench operations commenced on 1 October, 2nd Division carrying the flag. A week later (on 8 October) 1st and 3rd Divisions had their turn, each attacking with two brigades, in 1st Division's case the 1st (Griesbach) and the 3rd (Tuxford). Kearsley maintained his customary high standard with three finely crafted Operation Orders between 5 and 8 October. The staff package for 1st Brigade, consisting of Operation Orders of the brigade and the two assault battalions, is impressive; each order, in identical format, consists of three pages, the first paragraph of each stating the Intention in one clear sentence. Overall, 1st Brigade's staff work is of high quality, a tribute to the new BM, Major W.A. Adams, who had joined the brigade in September. Unfortunately, the operation itself went very wrong, so much so that it was tagged the "Regina Trench Disaster" (see Chapter Four). Those who had been most actively involved in the planning did not remain long with the brigade: the acting GOC, Lieutenant-Colonel Swift, left 1st Brigade for England within a month, and Adams lingered until early 1917 when he, too, took up an appointment in England. 3rd Brigade again exhibits better battalion orders than brigade orders but the latter have improved over those of September. As a whole, division staff work is not dramatically better, but consistent and encouraging improvement is evident.[35]

Had it been left to its own devices at Second Ypres, Festubert, Mount Sorrel and the Somme, 1st Division would have been running with *one* qualified Staff Officer: Lieutenant-Colonel A.H. Macdonell, p.s.c.; he was undoubtedly a fine officer and one of the few Canadians with p.s.c. but he had not been a BM, a GSO2, or even a GSO3. It would have been asking a great deal to have made him GSO1. Fortunately, some very fine Imperial officers were at hand, thereby giving him and other Canadians time and opportunity to learn. He began as a GSO2 in 1st Division in February 1915.[36]

Amateur night at the General Staff had not been an appealing prospect for the professionals, who saw France as "no place for amateur soldiers."[37] There was no option, and obviously Staff Officers required formal training. Dominion officers attended not only their own but Imperial schools as well, starting with the GHQ staff courses in 1915 and then the staff courses that began at Cambridge in the autumn of 1917. Senior staff courses, which trained officers for the higher staff appointments (GSO1 and its equivalent in A & Q), accepted candidates who had been or were GSO2 or its equivalent in A & Q and "exceptionally promising" BMs who were not p.s.c. Junior staff courses trained officers for lower appointments such as GSO2, its equivalent, and BM. Candidates included BMs, GSOs3, staff captains and "specially selected" Regimental officers, including staff learners. Both courses lasted six weeks, which is very short but the concentrated and demanding syllabi related directly to operational requirements. A prerequisite for either course was staff experience at the front.[38]

With the influx of so many amateurs, many of whom were new officers as well as Staff Officers, it could "no longer be assumed that measures which would as a matter of course have been taken in the earlier stages of the war . . . [would] now always be carried out efficiently."[39] This anxiety about the competence of subordinates revealed itself in an increase in the length of orders at every level, this indicating over-supervision, which can be almost as damaging as under-supervision. For example, VIII Corps' "Scheme for the Offensive" for the Somme filled 69 close-typed foolscap pages. One officer wondered if "anyone ever lived long enough to read it through."[40] Too much paper had been seen as a significant problem long before the Somme but how to reduce the deluge evaded everyone. One British company commander—he could just as easily have been Canadian, or German, for that matter—recalled becoming "literally dazed" by the increasing volume of paper, which flowed downward to him (orders and instructions) and upward from him (reports and returns).[41] As early as October 1915 one acting BM said:

> the great thing out here is to have as little paper as possible and to cut down what you send on to battalions to a minimum. Also to be able to write orders shortly and clearly . . . I found this Brigade had brought out reams of useless paper. Which I had to go through and tear up, which I did ruthlessly.

Seven months later little had changed: "Far too much writing goes on in this sedentary war."[42] On the other hand, the BM of 3rd Brigade (Clarke), reporting on lessons learnt at "The Bluff" in March 1916, believed it "impossible to have too much detail. Everything, however insignificant, must be provided for . . . Orders should be full." Some truth resided in this but there had to be a limit. Currie, listing the lessons of Mount Sorrel in June 1916, put in first place "the education Battalions require in writing Operation Orders."[43]

Lecturing to students at the Senior Officers' School, Aldershot, in February 1917, Tim Harington, MGGS Second Army, warned of "far too much writing . . . a perfectly ridiculous" amount. "The next time this enormous army moves, it will move quickly . . . Almost a different brain is required . . . for this moving warfare. No time for drafting and submitting orders to a Senior Staff Officer."[44] Others, too, preached an end to "ponderous" staff work featuring "a good deal of working out of 'Appreciations,' and deliberate writing and issuing of orders."[45] This was easier said than done, for offensives became increasingly complicated in view of an ever more sophisticated enemy defensive doctrine. For Vimy, which has been described so often as the classic example of the set-piece deliberate attack against a well-established enemy, the G or "Part I (Tactical)" staff packages for Corps, 1st Division, its brigades and its battalions stack up six inches high. "Part II (Administrative)" doubles the pile. The main impression one gets is of absolute staff thoroughness at all levels.[46]

Staff work was simplified somewhat by staging the issue of instructions according to their content and the time remaining until the operation. Due to its great detail and the need for extensive coordination, the fire plan, including heavy artillery and counter-battery tasks, was issued separately from the Operation Order on 16 March. The fire plan is splendidly written. Morrison had a total of 863 guns, field and heavy, under his control, including the 144 guns and 48 howitzers of the four Canadian divisions, the 54 guns and 18 howitzers of the Army Field Artillery Brigade, and over 100 mortars. "Precisely at 5:30 A.M.," says the Corps report, "the intense artillery bombardment opened with sudden fury and the advance of the infantry began." Given the types and numbers of guns involved and the intense rate of fire for each, expressed in number of rounds per gun per minute, the initial minute alone would have featured about 2,500 rounds.[47] Such a weight of lead for that minute and all the other minutes in the fire plan registered heavily upon "the woeful waiting ones."[48]

It would be impossible to argue against the conclusion that the resounding success at Vimy was due largely to superb fire support. Good staff work and increased tactical skill also "greatly contributed": "The whole Canadian contingent, unsurpassed in potential quality, had made rapid progress in efficiency during the winter months."[49] In view of the unprecedented thoroughness and excellence of all the preparations it is tempting to say that the attack would have succeeded even if the German defence had not exhibited two fatal flaws—counterattack divisions were held too far back to be able to influence the situation (they were 12 to 24 hours' march away), and contrary to Ludendorff's orders, the Germans reverted to holding the forward area in the rigid style of the Somme, or *Halten, was zu halten ist* (Hold onto whatever can be held).

Staff preparations in 1st Division began in earnest with the receipt on 23 December of a warning order that demanded division "outline schemes" (preliminary plans) not later than 4 January. This warning order contained the essence of First Army's preliminary plan: a four-division attack in four phases, the aim being to capture Vimy Ridge and Thelus in order to deprive the enemy of observation of the area southwest of the ridge. Subsequently, Corps demanded "complete schemes" as soon as possible.[50] 1st Division would have the farthest to go, just over two miles to its fourth and final objective. Its initial frontage, 1,900 yards, narrowed to about 750 yards from the second objective onward. The 1st would attack with two brigades forward until they reached that point, whereupon 1st Brigade would assume the lead.

On 5 March the Corps' "Scheme of Operations," signed by the Acting GOC (Currie), went to First Army for approval. Three days later Horne responded with a dozen comments, directing that the scheme be "resubmitted after consideration . . . on the return of Lt. General Sir Julian Byng." Two weeks later, with the suggested amendments, it was issued to divisions and on 25 March, having received the brigade plans, 1st Division passed them on to Corps HQ.[51]

Meanwhile, 1st Division's "Instructions for Offensive Operations," signed off by the GSO1 (Kearsley) on 22 March, had been forwarded. It totalled 23 pages, not counting the table of contents, fire plan, appendices and maps, which doubled the instructions. An earlier issued 45-page "Preliminary Instructions and Orders" helped keep the final to only 23 pages. In this, 1st Division had followed the Corps lead: issue a preliminary to get preparations underway and allow maximum time to complete them, and then issue a final instruction as Zero gets closer and most, if not all, preparations have been confirmed and finalized. The first section of the Instructions of 22 March covers deployment, objectives and boundaries and in three full pages details exactly how to achieve consolidation on the final objectives. This section, the meat of the order, is a gem; read in conjunction with the map it is crystal clear, the epitome of good operational writing and indicative of why Kearsley enjoyed such a good reputation. Another section, equally good, covers all means of communications front, rear and lateral, including pigeons, power buzzers, field phones, runners, visual signals and wireless (assault brigades to division). The underlying principle is redundancy. This emphasis on consolidation and communication comes from recognition that these were the most problematic parts of offensives. Friday 30 March featured a conference to tie up loose ends and allow Byng to stress directly to division commanders such final preparations as precautions against straggling and timings for artillery observers to move forward.[52]

Brigade plans, which averaged 14 pages, were returned to brigades with Currie's and Kearsley's comments, which numbered 24 for 1st Brigade, 21 for 3rd Brigade and a mere 5 for 2nd Brigade. Most of the criticisms of Griesbach's plan concern sins of omission. The brigade seemed not to have understood that an entire engineer field company would be under command to assist in consolidation. Nor did its plan specify the location of brigade HQ and it made no mention of flanking brigades or how to maintain contact with them. It was not entirely clear how the third phase of the brigade attack tied in to the fire plan, how long troops would pause on the second objective, how enemy dugouts and strong points would be dealt with and how units would consolidate. 3rd Brigade's plan did not mention flanking formations and units, either. Most of division's criticisms of its plan related to administration, particularly medical arrangements and ammunition resupply. 2nd Brigade, too, made no mention of flanking forces, nor was it obvious which assault wave would pass through the first objective to seize the second. The other comments were minor. As amended, final "Instructions for the Offensive" were: 1st Brigade, 21 pages; 2nd Brigade, 40 pages; and 3rd Brigade, 29 pages.[53] Overall, brigade plans reflect a high standard of SD in 1st Division, and 2nd Brigade's plan comes off as best.

Brigade Operation Orders produced from the brigade plans were equally good. Canadian brigades seemed to have heeded the call of brevity, the average orders being a very reasonable five pages. By this time, minor SD had also vastly improved, all paragraphs being numbered and extensive use being made of paragraph headings. 1st Brigade's order starts with one-sentence statements of the corps and division missions and then gets right into 1st Brigade's role. The fourth paragraph states the mission explicitly, and the execution section is completely clear. Afterward, the BM, Major Hugh Urquhart, could say with pride that brigade paperwork was first class. Of the operation as a whole, 1st Brigade complained only of a shortage of stretchers. 3rd Battalion reported that it had executed the Operation Order "to the letter."[54] Captain William Alston, the BM of 2nd Brigade at Vimy, was one of only two Captains who served as BMs in that brigade. The reason that the brigade plan drew only five comments from division is simple: the plan is just plain well done. Everything Alston did for Vimy was quality: the plan, the work program prior to the attack, the preliminary instruction, the movement order and the Operation Order. Afterward, his GOC singled him out for his "work and self-sacrifice throughout." He must have been a very impressive junior officer. 2nd Brigade's only complaint was the scarcity of stretchers, which Alston put down to its Field Ambulance's extreme reluctance to part with them.[55] 3rd Brigade's staff work for Vimy is at least as good, thanks to its BM, Major Paul Villiers. He, too, remarked later about the shortage of stretchers, thereby making the complaint unanimous in 1st Division.

The obvious care taken in writing, reviewing and amending brigade Operation Orders seems to have been echoed in battalion Operation Orders. Having more than adequate time to prepare them helped, too. Battalion orders in the division averaged five pages. Most battalions issued a separate administrative order, and some also distributed preliminary instructions, which outlined all the preparations required for the move forward to assembly areas. Thus the Operation Orders were kept short.[56]

The length of formation orders still worried some. Hugh Urquhart, BM 1st Brigade, thought "control or staff oversight went to the extremes of paternal government."[57] There is some truth in this. The volume was increased by the type of operation—a deliberate attack—which gave the whole team the luxury of a very long time in the huddle. Given the several pre-attack conferences, the pile of paper should have been thinner. Still, the dramatic improvement in the writing of Operation Orders since the Somme is evident. Tuxford concluded his report by saying:

> The key note of the success may be said to be the coordination of the preparatory work. The instructions received from the Division were so clear that it very largely facilitated the Brigade Instructions to units and theirs to Companies, etc. The exchange of ideas and opinions, the dissemination of views . . . and the progress of work were all contributing factors.[58]

Brigade reports testify to the soundness of the planning. The move forward to assembly areas during the night before the attack at Vimy had gone splendidly, with no confusion or delay. All units reached their positions in good time, some as much as five hours before Zero, thereby avoiding any uncertainty due to unfamiliarity with the jumping-off trenches. 13th Battalion was as pleased as any battalion could be at Vimy for it enjoyed not only the customary rum ration—"VC Mixture"—but also hot soup.[59] Griesbach (1st Brigade) said the entire operation had gone in accordance with the Operation Order, all tasks being performed on time. All ranks knew exactly where they were at all times during the attack, thanks to the rehearsals over taped ground and the excellent maps and air photos. 3rd Brigade (Tuxford) operations also went "without a hitch . . . and well on time." 2nd Brigade (Loomis) said much the same.[60] Currie attributed rapid success to confidence and discipline, sound leadership, artillery support, good intelligence (he thought the deductions of his GSO2[Int], Major W.R. Bertram, "uncannily accurate"), and a good plan:

> I have no suggestions to make as to how it could have been improved except in minor details. I wish to place on record my appreciation of the splendid work of Lt. Col. R.H. KEARSLEY, D.S.O., 5th Dragoon Guards, the G.S.O. 1 of the Division, who, owing to the staff being shorthanded, was called upon to work practically day and night from the beginning of March to May 5th, when the Division was relieved, and of Lt. Col. J. Sutherland BROWN, D.S.O., Royal Canadian Regiment, the A.A. and Q.M.G. of the Division, who made such excellent administrative arrangements.[61]

A serious shortcoming in command and staff work before Vimy had been tardy issue of orders. 1st Division reminded the brigades of this less than 48 hours before Zero (9 April): staffs at every level "must realize the difficulties of getting these orders to front line troops." One of the main factors in success, according to the BGGS (Radcliffe), was that "plans matured in time to complete all preparations, owing to early decision on the part of higher command (Divl. Objectives allotted Jan. 31st 1917)."[62] Such a luxury of time would not always be the case, which is why First Army warned:

> There is always the difficulty that if definite orders are issued too soon they have to be cancelled or much amended before the operation takes place and this cancelling of orders at the last minute is often a greater evil than their late issue. At the same time, it must be the endeavour . . . to assist the troops by every means . . . by warning orders . . . and by making every effort to get orders down to units at the very earliest possible moment. A great deal of time is often wasted . . . not only in drafting orders . . . but also in getting the order out . . . it should be realised that every minute saved in higher formations may mean the receipt of orders two or three hours earlier by the troops who have actually to carry them out on the ground.[63]

Vimy demonstrated that Canadian potential had become reality. The planning and execution of the two-division attack (1st and 2nd) on Hill 70 on 15 August reiterated and reinforced this reality. "Impeccable" is a word entirely appropriate to the whole Hill 70 operation. Currie's first Corps Scheme of Operations (he had become GOC in June) totals eight clear and succinct pages, not counting the fire plan that as usual was issued separately. Knowing that without the hill the Germans could not overlook Lens, meaning that they would make the most vigorous efforts to get it back if they lost it, he stressed consolidation and breaking up the inevitable counterattacks. The 48 Vickers machine-guns attached to the assault brigades (2nd and 3rd) were to move in close support as rapidly as possible, selecting good fire positions on the final objectives and making these into strongpoints with the help of sappers who accompanied the infantry. Once wired in and strengthened, these strongpoints would stop the enemy and channel him into killing grounds. An attachment to the Scheme of Operations set out in three pages the "Action of Massed Machine Guns," for in addition to those with the infantry, a further 160 would provide supporting fire and barrages day and night.

The fire plan also played a key role in consolidation by concentrating on likely enemy assembly areas and on approaches to the hill, these targets having been pre-selected during careful study of the ground.[64] Fire also struck hard at enemy wire, so much so that it presented no obstacle. 2nd Brigade's GOC (Loomis), personally inspecting the German line while consolidation was still underway, reported that it had been made a shambles by heavy artillery, an assessment seconded by Tuxford of 3rd Brigade.[65] In addition, counter-battery fire had eliminated more than a third of the enemy gun batteries and many of his mortars.

In format, the Instructions for the Offensive signed by Kearsley follow those he wrote for Vimy. Section I outlines the general plan, the division's task, the attack method and consolidation, which is stressed, just as at Vimy, this time being accompanied by maps portraying deployment for consolidation. Another section details the operation and control of the 72 Vickers machine-guns allocated to 1st Division, in addition to its own 48. Brigade plans went to division for approval. Turn-around was short; 2nd Brigade's plan, submitted on 21 July, came back so quickly that the 2nd issued its Operation Order on 24 July. 3rd Brigade's plan came out as quickly. 1st Brigade, being in support, did not become as involved. For Hill 70, 2nd Brigade had a new BM, Major John MacKenzie, posted in from 8th Battalion. He combined operations and administration in one Operation Order, the first part detailing operations. Within that, he presented the Instructions in seven sections (operations, locations, communications, artillery, machine-guns, LOB (Left Out of Battle) and equipment), each starting on a new page regardless of the length of the preceding section. The second part (administration) was organized in similar fashion. The result is a longer order (35 pages) but it is well spaced and highlighted by both marginal and paragraph headings. A useful innovation was an Index of Maps which made the document very easy to use. 3rd Brigade's plan and Operation Order drawn up by Villiers continues the very high standard he had set at Vimy. Both brigade orders also paid close attention to consolidation, including the organization of large carrying parties, in order to avoid a repeat of Regina Trench where inability to get sufficient bombs forward had been the main cause for withdrawal from the enemy trenches. If graphic evidence of good planning and thorough reconnaissance is sought, 3rd Brigade orders are the place to look; they even include useful diagrams of strongpoints that would block enemy approaches.[66]

For Hill 70, Captain J. Miller, Adjutant of the 10th Battalion (2nd Brigade), wrote a splendid Operation Order, perhaps the finest battalion order seen in the preparation of this book. So pleased was GOC 2nd Brigade (Loomis) that he commended Miller in his brigade report. Miller's order is not quite three foolscap pages long. Having stated the Corps mission and general plan (one sentence each) and the division and the brigade general plans (two sentences each), he presented the battalion's general plan, its mission and the company boundaries (one sentence each). Then in 20 brief subparagraphs he detailed the battalion plan and artillery support. This succinct order was a far cry from the earlier battalion Operation Orders that had repeated irrelevant sections of formation orders. Miller's CO, Dan Ormond, insisted on adherence to 1st Division's guidance on preparing Operation Orders: "only such information should be put in . . . as directly concerns the particular formation or unit to whom the order is issued."[67] 16th Battalion's order is another example of an order that concentrated on what the battalion had to do and how, with sufficient information (and no more) on where it fit into the larger operation. The longest battalion Operation Order in the two brigades was only six pages, with most at four pages. Overall, Hill 70 reveals a very great improvement in battalion SD. At this time the Senior Officers' School at Aldershot somewhat unrealistically stressed that a battalion Operation Order should not exceed two pages. It is hard to see two pages catering for anything more than very simple situations.

In the event, by 4:45 A.M. (20 minutes after Zero), 1st Division had secured its objectives, and within an hour all final objectives, less some small bits in 2nd Brigade's area, were being consolidated. Just after 7:00 A.M. German counterattacks commenced, first locally and then in strength. Every one of their 21 counterattacks (Currie's count) were broken up by artillery, mortars and machine-guns.[68] GOC 2nd Brigade (Loomis), responding to a Corps Intelligence Summary on 17 August that touted the barrage as "very successful" (which it was overall), reported that it had not been effective on the reverse slope of Hill 70 and that along his second objective fire had burst "about 100 feet too high," meaning that it had had no effect on the enemy's capability to produce fire. This explained why 2nd Brigade had been the longest in achieving the final objective and why it suffered the highest number of casualties (1,651) in the assault force. Perhaps more howitzers and mortars should have been allotted to reverse slope targets. While his comments did not feature in Section 18, Lessons to be Learned, of 1st Division's report (Loomis had not intended they should; he kept the matter low key by addressing them to "1st Div G" and not GOC), it can be assumed that they were closely studied by the artillery, especially the comment about excessive burst height.[69]

Nevertheless, Hill 70 typified sound tactics and superb planning. Neither brigadier complained about staff arrangements, and the stretcher problem at Vimy had not reappeared. Loomis reported that everything had "worked well under a most severe test."[70] The obvious professional progress and the results delighted Currie (and the C-in-C):

> The Chief was immensely pleased and always regarded Hill 70 as one of the finest minor operations of the war—a fact which Andy McNaughton tells me the German files confirm. When the Committee on battle honours met after the war they first determined not to include Hill 70. I wrote to the Chief and personally appeared before the Committee for the express purpose of insisting that a battle honour be given for that engagement. I daresay it is the only honour which the Canadians share with no one.[71]

1st Division's Operation Order for the defence of Hill 70 and Lens east of Loos is particularly interesting because it shows how smoothly the 1st could revert to the defence, having previously demonstrated that a transition to offence went just as smoothly. It also reflects the very high standard of staff work achieved by mid-1917. Founded on a fine appreciation by Archibald Macdonell, who had assumed command of Old Red Patch on 9 June, the Operation Order has in fact the best written and the most comprehensive of any of the divisional defensive schemes examined. Currie's Instructions for Defence (a model of superior SD, particularly in the defensive concept, principles and organization that Currie wanted implemented) ordered every level of command to defend in depth, to designate a counterattack force and to make a detailed reconnaissance of the routes and ground that such a force would have to use (the lesson of Mount Sorrel had been learned). Having identified and described the area, including the most likely enemy approach and the ground "to be defended at all costs" (in today's terminology the "vital ground," that real estate without which a defensive position cannot be maintained), Macdonell set out 1st Division on the ground, two brigades up and one in reserve. One cannot help but be impressed with the artillery "retaliation" policy, which said simply, "Fire on Request." That is "gunpower" of substance.[72]

In the autumn of 1917 Haig gave the Corps a very tough mission: seize the last German-held high ground around Ypres. The operation was multiphased, the first and second phases (26 and 30 October) involving two divisions, which were relieved preparatory to the next phases (6 and 10 November). Consequently, a series of Instructions, together with several Operation Orders had to be issued.[73] Because 1st Division did not participate until 6 November, its staff had three full weeks to prepare. By mid-October detailed maps and Intelligence Summaries had been issued. Even before the issue of Corps Instructions on 23 October the 1st was well into its battle procedure, a situation that allowed it to issue Operation Orders before the end of October. Its objective was the high ground north of the village of Passchendaele, while the 2nd Division on its right would secure the village. On 24 October the GSO1 (Ross Hayter) issued Instructions on training relevant to the coming attack, despite not knowing the start line or the enemy situation, these being dependent upon the progress made by 3rd and 4th Divisions in the initial phases.[74]

Following the attacks on 26 and 30 October, 1st and 2nd Divisions prepared to relieve the 3rd and 4th Divisions, the relief, in 1st Division's case, coming on 3 November. On 2 November Hayter sent the division plan, which committed 1st Brigade (Griesbach) to the attack on 6 November, to Corps for approval. 3rd Brigade was in divisional reserve and the 2nd went into Corps reserve. Good staff work being concurrent, Griesbach had given division his two-page brigade outline plan on 1 November: a two-battalion assault in two phases. That same day he issued his Instructions for the Offensive, a precise and succinct eight pages, followed on 4 November by the Operation Order, an equally precise five pages. Fifteen pages for the whole package (sixteen counting a one-page addendum signed by the BM) is indicative of his focus and insistence on standardized SD.[75] The package is easy to read and admirable for its economy; for example, his two-page outline plan is incorporated as the first half of the execution section of his Instructions for the Offensive. Griesbach may have been more involved in their production than normally since his BM (Hugh Urquhart) had left shortly before to take command of a battalion and he was probably unsure of his acting BM. Griesbach's operational writing is the epitome of clarity, with no verbiage and no ambiguity, virtually every sentence being a direct statement, and most featuring the word "will." In this regard, the order is much like the many memoranda in his "Book of Wisdom," which he issued for the tactical guidance of COs. The one word that sums up his operational writing is "effective."

The orders (three pages each) of the two assault battalions (1st and 2nd), issued on 5 November, adhere to what was being taught in the COs' courses at Aldershot, especially in regard to keeping the objective clear.[76] Meanwhile, 2nd Brigade continued preparations for its attack on 10 November. At a conference of COs on 5 November the GOC (Loomis) briefed his plan: a two battalion attack by 7th and 8th Battalions. These verbal orders were followed by a confirmatory Operation Order two days later.[77]

The whole of the documentation for Passchendaele says much about the quality of the staff work in 1st Division. First, the staff principle of concurrent activity is evident, instructions and orders being issued successively in short order thanks to sound battle procedure, including timely warning orders, and full use of conferences, thereby resolving many matters without recourse to lengthy orders. Second, all formation instructions and orders are brief, the first in only one case exceeding 14 pages and the second never longer than seven. Battalion orders do not exceed five pages and are usually three, primarily because, as was the rule in 1st Division since Vimy, they adhered to what that level of command had to know. Third, the staff work reflects improved and more sophisticated battle procedure, specifically in control, as discussed in an earlier chapter. Fourth, because multiphase operations generate many "ifs," flexibility becomes a virtue and a necessity. When 3rd Division did not quite get all of its objectives on 30 October, 1st Division had to make several amendments to its plans several times, with no discernible adverse impact. Throughout, staff and commanders adapted rapidly to change and in fact demonstrated great ability to anticipate. Finally, Canadian appreciations displayed a keen eye for the implications of ground, which posed special problems because of so many "large tracts of mud and water." The "guiding feature" was "the impassable condition of some of the ground to be traversed."[78]

Despite being the most trying Canadian experience of the war (October–November saw almost 16,000 casualties), Passchendaele was also "a triumph of organized effort carried out almost exactly to timetable." Official historians, Canadian and British, agree: the former noted the "ample evidence of . . . the efficiency of his [Currie's] well organized staff in the smoothness and despatch [of] preparations for the Canadian assault"; while the British historian thought the operation reflected "the high standard of staff work and training [and] as at Vimy Ridge and on Hill 70 [Canadian] tenacity and endurance."[79] These remarks were particularly noteworthy given that the operations were conducted under circumstances very different from those at Vimy and at Hill 70: "No previous training . . . over taped trenches was possible. Plans and dispositions were made at comparatively short notice and with more or less indefinite information as to the exact position and condition of the 'jumping off' Line and the disposition and strength of the enemy."[80] On the other hand, as Griesbach pointed out, while the jump off was hazardous and the going extremely bad, the plan was "more or less stereotyped." Loomis added that there had been more than ample time for reconnaissance; even NCOs had a chance to look over the ground from jumping-off positions. Still, he made special mention of his BM, Major John MacKenzie, whose "concise orders and attention to detail contributed to a large extent to success," and of W.D. Herridge, Staff Captain A, for his plan for evacuating the wounded, a major problem due to ground conditions.[81] In short, first class staff work marked Passchendaele.

The "Hundred Days" campaign of 1918 would see the Canadian divisions advancing as the spearpoint of the blow to end the war. Amiens and Canal du Nord in particular show not only how fine 1st Division's staff work had become but also the very high quality of its command and control and training. For this reason 1918 has been left to a later chapter for showing how this all came together.

A significant part of the story of the admirable staff work in Canadian formations concerned the British professionals who joined Corps HQ. They held the two most senior staff appointments throughout the war. One hesitates to use that much debased word "outstanding," but the incumbents were exactly that.

Four British officers served as BGGS. Tim Harington, appointed when the Corps formed in September 1915, remained until August 1916 when on promotion he became MGGS, Second Army. He was considered "one of the best"[82] by Lieutenant-Colonel T.S. Morrissey, a Canadian who served as a BM and then as a GSO2. Known for his sharp sense of humour and his charm, Harington perfectly complemented Byng and then Plumer, all three being plain, honest soldiers. Plumer was the best, the most personable, and the most trusted of the Army commanders. Harington, his "legendary" MGGS, shared his penchant for hard work. British, Canadian and Australian combat soldiers considered Second Army the best commanded and administered Army in the BEF. The men knew that attacks would be thoroughly planned and well supported, time in the line would be fairly shared, they would be well supplied and housed when relieved, and any moves they made would be well organized and swift.[83] Plumer and Harington saw to this by frequent contact with their subordinates, by ensuring that liaison officers spent two of every seven nights in front line trenches and by having groups of COs as weekend guests at training sessions at Army HQ. Byng, not surprisingly, copied some of these practises during his time as GOC the Canadian Corps, and Currie insisted on them. Second Army became the Army under which every division wanted to serve. Philip Gibbs, the war correspondent, summing up Plumer, Harington and Second Army, said:

> The staff work . . . was as good in detail as any machinery of war may be, and the tactical direction . . . was not slip-shod or haphazard, as so many others but prepared with minute attention to detail . . . Harington . . . was highly wrought . . . but he was never flurried,

never irritable, never depressed or elated by false pessimism or false optimism. . . . There was a thoroughness of method, a minute attention to detail, a care for the comfort and spirit of the men . . . which did at least inspire the troops with the belief that whatever they did . . . [they] would be supported.[84]

Harington's replacement, P.P. deB. (Percy) Radcliffe, was widely regarded as an "outstanding planner" and "the ablest tactician" in the Army. He came to the Canadian Corps from II (Imperial) Corps where he had been BGGS; previously he was a GSO1 at Third Army and before that AA & QMG of 8th (Imperial) Division. That he was highly thought of is evident in his appointment in April 1918 as Director of Military Operations at the War Office.[85] His fine common sense shines through in his reaction to a Q staff proposal that extra pay might offer some recognition of the infanteer's hard lot. While sympathetic, Radcliffe wisely observed, "I do not think the payment of working parties in the front line feasible. If you pay men extra to dig a trench, how much will you pay them to take one?"[86] His replacement, and the third British BGGS, N. W. "Ox" Webber, was another "fine type of Imperial officer."[87] Currie especially appreciated Radcliffe's and Webber's services, so much so that he specifically thanked them in his interim report on operations during 1918.[88] In October 1918 the equally capable R.J.T. (Ross) Hayter, whose career has been summarized in Chapter Five, replaced Webber. Hayter had made a reputation in 1st Division for his quick appreciations of fast-moving situations and for sound judgement.[89]

The corresponding A and Q Branch appointment, the DA & QMG, was held by T.B. Wood until June 1916 and then by George Farmar until the Armistice. Known as "Jolly"[90] because of his ready wit, charm and ability to get along with virtually everyone, Farmar had friends everywhere. This very gifted officer displayed "outstanding talent and energy." Herbert Fairlie Wood said, "His experience, understanding and patience not only created a climate of cooperation but taught Canadian staff officers how best their duties could be carried out. The hostility with which the fighting soldier regarded the staff . . . was never a serious factor in the Canadian Corps after the Somme." Captain F.R. Phelan called Farmar the most efficient officer he had ever met.[91]

Within the four Canadian divisions the number of British senior Staff Officers varied. 1st Division had British GSO1s until John Parsons replaced Hayter as GSO1 in December 1917. The GSO1s before Hayter—Harvey Kearsley and C.F. Romer—also received appointments as BGGS, Kearsley at VI (Imperial) and Romer at III (Imperial) Corps. Kearsley, in particular, was a fine officer. Paul Villiers remembered him as "the embodiment of all that a staff officer should be . . . his courtesy, tact and geniality won him all hearts . . . I was extremely fortunate to start my career on the staff under him."[92] On the A and Q side, British officers held the appointment of AA & QMG of 1st Division until March 1917 when Lieutenant-Colonel J.S. Brown was appointed. As for the BMs of 1st Division, Canadians replaced British officers at the following times: 1st Brigade, September 1916; 2nd Brigade, August 1916; and 3rd Brigade, January 1918. In 2nd Division the GSO1 was British until November 1917 when Lieutenant-Colonel D.E. MacIntyre became the first Canadian GSO1. 3rd Division had a British GSO1 throughout the war, while 4th Division had Lieutenant-Colonel W.E. Ironside until January 1918. He later became Chief of the Imperial General Staff (CIGS), as did two other officers who served with Canadian formations. With one exception, all who served as AA & QMG in 2nd, 3rd and 4th Divisions were Canadian.[93]

In summary, in 1915 about a third of the Staff Officers were British but by the end of the war only the BGGS and DA & QMG at Corps and the GSO1 at 3rd Division were British.[94] These British officers, the "cream of the British Army," according to Brigadier-General Victor Odlum, made an enormous contribution to Canadian fortunes. Currie called them "expert students of the art of war . . . the best trained soldiers" he had ever met, which is why he insisted on retaining Webber and Farmar at Corps HQ. The three men remained lifelong friends. Andrew McNaughton, who would assume Currie's mantle during the Second World War, said of his Great War British brothers-in-arms: "We had . . . the pick of the British Army. They were absolutely superb . . . they taught us much. We had . . . staff officers . . . the like of which no other corps had . . . We owe them an immense debt of gratitude."[95]

Lieutenant-General E.L.M. Burns goes so far as to compare (twice) the relationship between the Canadian commander and the British Staff Officer to the "Prussian system, under which a senior but somewhat obsolescent general would nominally command . . . but the real control would reside in a younger member of the Great General Staff." This is much overdrawn, as Burns realized, since later in his book he torpedoed the thought by stressing that all Canadian divisional commanders had proven themselves in command of brigades and that some had also been fine battalion COs.[96] Currie simply would not have been so dominated by any Staff Officer, no matter how brilliant. The same is true of his successor as GOC 1st Division, A.C. Macdonell. During a career as gunner officer, then infantry officer, then Northwest Mounted policeman, then cavalry officer and finally as GOC a brigade and then a division, Macdonell impressed his forceful personality whatever the circumstances.

There is no doubt that in 1st Division from Second Ypres through to

January 1918 its British GSO1s—Cecil Romer, Harvey Kearsley and Ross Hayter—and from the autumn of 1914 to March 1917 its British AA & QMGs—T.B. Wood and Gilbert Frith—ensured superb staff work, while simultaneously training (never an easy task under the pressure of active operations) their Canadian understudies to the point where they could take over without in any way degrading 1st Division's effectiveness as a fighting formation. Teaching, which involves criticism, sometimes very sharp criticism, and retaining rapport can be tricky. That these British officers could impart hard lessons and maintain amicable relations with their Canadian superiors and subordinates is a striking tribute to their tact and professionalism. Indeed, most British officers who served with the Canadian Corps came to be regarded as Canadians and expressed their delight with that status. Colonel A.F. Duguid said that their "knowledge and experience freely applied were largely responsible for the technical excellence of its (the Canadian Corps) organization, administration and training and for the efficiency of its staff in the field."[97]

The excellence of 1st Division's staff work cannot be disputed. Romer got the division off to a good start. Kearsley built on this, setting a very high standard and demanding a good deal from his staff at division and from the BMs. Hayter and Parsons maintained that standard, their bywords being precision and thoroughness. Their work and staff work as a whole in the division had a central role in making it a good, reliable and effective formation.

Every Staff Officer, British and Canadian, in 1st Division (and in the Canadian Corps) knew full well Macdonell's and Currie's predilection for thorough training. Both men stressed officer training at every level, including holding many tactical exercises and meetings of COs at division and corps HQs to discuss tactical problems set by their GOC. The training of platoon commanders particularly interested Macdonell who saw their performance as the key to success.

Professionalization came with training, which included, not formally but from necessity, the ability to endure privation and fire, whether just the usual "hate" or the hurricane harbinger of assault. Gunfire at Mount Sorrel, for example, obliterated defences and defenders, removing half the COs of the 8th Brigade, its GOC, and the GOC 3rd Division. One battalion, under intense fire for over five hours, was left with one officer and 23 ORs out of the 22 and 680, respectively, with which it began the day.[98] Such losses marked the death of a unit, meaning that a new one had to rise in its place and be trained and led.

When Corps HQ asked about the lessons of the Somme 1st Division commanders could readily articulate them because of their experience, the greatest teacher of all. They had learned what to do and how best to do it.

This they had achieved gradually, sometimes dramatically and sometimes imperceptibly but always they had improved. Over many months they had witnessed how their staffs gained in confidence and competence and they felt justifiable pride in their own professional growth, which had been instrumental in bringing their commands to professional standard. They and their staffs had also learned by mid-1916 that training had to be a primary concern. In response to the query about the lessons of the Somme, Loomis of 2nd Brigade concluded: "The answer to every one of the questions . . . is TRAINING, a training that will not only result in securing discipline and higher technical knowledge but will also secure greater resourcefulness in officers, NCOs and men."[99] The infanteer, in Lord Tennyson's words, had always to be

Ready, be ready to meet the storm
Rifleman, rifleman, rifleman form![100]

Notes to Chapter Six

1. Fosten and Marrion, *The British Army, 1914–18*, p. 30. General officers, staff or line, wore a crossed sabre and baton within a laurel wreath surmounted by the Royal Crest (crowned lion on crown). Colonels wore only the Royal Crest.
2. Carrington, *Soldier from the Wars Returning*, pp. 39, 74.
3. For an example (Captain Talbot Papineau) see Chapter Five.
4. Nicholson, *Behind the Lines*, pp. xi–xii (Introduction by Peter T. Scott).
5. Ibid., p. vii.
6. LAC, RG 24, Vol. 1847, GAQ 11–71D.
7. Tonie and Valmai Holt, eds., *The Best of Fragments from France by Capt. Bruce Bairnsfather* (Cheltenham, Gloucestershire: Phin Publishing Limited, 1978), pp. 19, 97. The answer was probably "None," the general complaint being that the only jam the front line ever saw was a mixture of plum and apple, which was not a favourite. Somehow, as Army Service Corps moved the jam forward, the good kinds disappeared.
8. Fetherstonhaugh, *The Royal Montreal Regiment*, p. 89. The problem persisted. *Notes for Commanding Officers* (1918), p. 273, advised COs to ask brigade to hold "matters not of immediate importance" in abeyance until the unit was relieved. Such matters that did reach the unit should be held by the adjutant until the unit went into billets when it could then be actioned. This advice might seem superfluous since, surely, any good adjutant would have done exactly this but, keeping in mind the always heavy officer casualties and the ever younger and less experienced adjutants, the advice was necessary.
9. LAC, RG9IIID3, Vol. 4875, 3rd Brigade War Diary, Appendix 24 to June 1916.
10. Murray, *History of the 2nd Canadian Battalion*, pp. 95–97.
11. LAC, MG30E60 (Matthews Papers), Vol. 3, Folder 12, "The Ten Commandments." Going into Corps Reserve took a man well out of the line of fire.
12. LAC, RG9IIIC1, Vol. 3859, Folder 85, File 4, Lipsett, "The Offensive," 20 January, and Harington, 24 January; RG9IIIC3, Vol. 4053, Folder 24, File 16, First Army to Corps

9 May 1917. The lessons included the absolute necessity of early issue of orders. Tardiness was not a new problem by any means.

13. *FSR*, Section 12, stipulated that all operations required orders, verbal or written. If the former, confirmatory written orders had to be issued.

14. Romer replaced Colonel E.S. Heard on 24 February (Duguid, *Chronology, Appendices and Maps*, Appendix 842, p. 428). Before relieving the 7th (Imperial) Division the Canadian brigades were attached to Imperial divisions for instruction in trench warfare. Romer seems to have had a mixed reputation after he left 1st Division. GOC VI Corps (Aylmer Haldane) commented in 1916 that "in the 3rd Corps, Pulteney and his BGGS Romer never go to the trenches, so get little first hand information." (Travers, *The Killing Ground*, p. 109.) A partial explanation for this may be that Corps HQ was too far back, as was HQ 1st Division at Second Ypres. Romer, in each case, would have had considerable, if not decisive, say in their locations.

15. Edmonds [Carrington], *A Subaltern's War*, pp. 120–21.

16. LAC, MG30E236 (Villiers Papers), Vol. 4, Folder 7, Vol. 38 of diary, 18 November 1917. 1st Division General Staff War Diary for 1918 shows that for the first seven months of 1918 the division was 80 days in the trenches, 60 in reserve and about 70 out of the line.

17. Urquhart, *History of the 16th Battalion*, p. 416. This is also the best of the battalion histories. It is exceeded in its detail and in overall quality only by Rudyard Kipling's masterpiece, his astonishingly detailed two volume history of the Irish Guards.

18. LAC, RG9IIIC1, Vol. 3839, Folder 36, File 1.

19. Edmonds, *Haig's Command to the 1st July: Battle of the Somme*, p. 186; Nicholson, *Official History of the Canadian Army*, p. 140. Australians preferred going in and out as a corps, too.

20. LAC, 7th Battalion War Diary, April 1915, Appendix D.

21. LAC, MG30E46 (Turner Papers), Vol. 1, File 4, Diary of Operations, 3rd Brigade; RG9IIIC3, Vol. 4925, 16th Battalion War Diary, April 1915; Vol. 4870, 10th Battalion War Diary, April 1915; Dancocks, *Gallant Canadians*, pp. 29–34; *Welcome to Flanders Fields*, pp. 176, 187.

22. McWilliams and Steel, *Gas!, 1915*, pp.128–31. Currie left his HQ "shortly after noon." Soon afterward Kemmis-Betty was forced to move the HQ, the change in location leaving Currie for a time not knowing where to rejoin. At 1:45 Kemmis-Betty reported Currie missing and Lipsett (CO 8th Battalion) assumed command. McWilliams and Steel say that Currie's absence caused "some alarm," but from their account 2nd Brigade HQ seems to have continued to function effectively. With Lipsett in charge it would. Currie took an enormous risk in leaving his HQ and his command, it almost invariably being best that a commander remain where the bulk of his command is but the situation being so desperate and the need for reinforcement so urgent, he decided to act as he did, rather than send an officer of lesser rank. Currie knew that his rank could be a convincing argument should he find reinforcements and order them forward.

23. Minor SD in *FSR* included such things as using block capitals for places and names; how to write distances and directions; and a warning that "anything of an indefinite or conditional nature such as 'dawn,' 'dusk,' 'if possible,' 'if practicable,' 'should,' 'may,' is to be avoided." This sound advice, and most of the minor SD conventions in *FSR*, modernized, are in today's Canadian staff manual. Minor conventions are not unimportant, for they assist in standardization and they remind that "if you cannot get the little things right, you will not get the big things right." *Infantry Platoon*

    Commander's Aide Memoire (Camp Borden, Ontario: The Royal Canadian School of Infantry, 1959).

24. Urquhart, *History of the 16th Battalion*, p. 76.

25. Nicholson, *Official History of the Canadian Army*, p. 103; Dancocks, *Gallant Canadians*, p. 47; Lucas, gen. ed., Underhill, *The Empire at War: Canada*, p. 106.

26. Nicholson, *Official History of the Canadian Army*, p. 105.

27. *FSR*, Section 12. Modern Operation Orders have five sections, the headings being more precise and indicative of content: Situation, Mission, Execution, Administration and Logistics and Command and Signals.

28. LAC, 1st Division General Staff War Diary, June 1916, Narrative of Operations; Canadian Corps General Staff War Diary, Operation Order No. 17, 2 June; Edmonds, *Haig's Command to the 1st July: Battle of the Somme*, p. 236.

29. Edmonds, *Haig's Command to the 1st July: Battle of the Somme*, p. 238.

30. LAC, 1st Division General Staff War Diary contains all staff activities and battle procedure for the attack. 2nd and 3rd Brigade War Diaries, June 1916.

31. 3rd Brigade War Diary, June 1916, Reports on Operations.

32. LAC, RG9IIIC3, Vol. 4011, Folder 16, File 1.

33. Edmonds, *Haig's Command to the 1st July: Battle of the Somme*, p. 241; LAC, RG9IIIC1, Vol. 3842, Folder 43, File 1A, report and Plumer to GHQ.

34. LAC, RG9IIIC1, Vol. 3842, Folder 43, File 12, 1st Division orders; 3rd Brigade War Diary, September 1916; RG9IIIC3, Vol. 4051, Folder 19, File 6, 2nd Brigade orders.

35. LAC, RG9IIIC3, Vol. 4054, Folder 26, File 1, 1st Division Operation Order; MG30E100 (Currie Papers), Vol. 35, File 176, 1st Brigade orders and reports; 3rd Brigade War Diary, Appendices, October 1916.

36. Lieutenant-Colonel A.H. Macdonell is easily confused with his cousin, A.C. Macdonell, who commanded 7th Brigade (3rd Division) and then 1st Division, replacing Currie. The former Macdonell went on to command 5th Brigade in 2nd Division.

37. Simon Robbins, "The Right Way to Play the Game: The Ethos of the British High Command in the First World War," *Imperial War Museum Review* 6 (1991): 42.

38. LAC, RG9IIIC3, Vol. 4058, Folder 37, File 5, First Army, 7 September 1917.

39. LAC, RG9IIIC1, Vol. 3859, Folder 85, File 4, "Memorandum on the Lessons to be Drawn from Recent Offensive Operations," 5 October 1915.

40. Major A.F. Becke, "The Coming of the Creeping Barrage," *Journal of the Royal Artillery* 58 (January 1932): 32.

41. Major A.G. Wade, quoted in "The Staff The Myth? The Reality?" *Stand To!* 15 (Winter 1985): 50. He recalled that during his first 24 hours in command in the line he received: notes on trench warfare and on taking over trenches, battalion instructions on taking over trenches, a list of returns he had to render, rules for transport and sanitation, instructions for defence, orders on mining operations, notes on the use of flares, a brigade instruction on enemy snipers, a corps letter on dress, instructions on village fighting and withdrawal of work parties, additional notes on sniping, an intelligence summary, how to report wounded, divisional and brigade standing orders, "Notes from the Front" and "Things to be Remembered by Every Officer on Field Service."

42. Fraser, *In Good Company*, pp. 69, 85.

43. LAC, RG9IIIC3, Vol. 4074, Folder 2, File 4. Only 1st Brigade was involved in the defensive action at "The Bluff," a raised feature on the Ypres-Comines Canal. Currie's comment is in 1st Division General Staff War Diary, Appendix 8, July 1916.

44. Major-General C.H. Harington, "The Relations of the Staff to Commanding Officers, and Vice Versa, That of Commanding Officers to the Staff," *Notes for Commanding Officers* (1918), pp. 388, 391–92.

45. Military Advisory Board, *Guarding the Channel Ports*, p. 86.

46. First Army and Canadian Corps papers are at LAC, RG9IIIC1, Vols. 3844–3846. 1st Division and brigade papers are in RG9IIIC3, Vols. 4026, 4051, 4061 and 4077.

47. LAC, RG9IIIC1, Vol. 3843, Folder 46, File 5. First Army issued the order on rates of fire on 22 March. The artillery fire plan is in RG9IIIC3, Vol. 4011, Folder 18, File 2. The Canadian Corps report on Vimy is in RG9IIIC1, Vol. 3846, Folder 51, File 5.

48. Kim Beattie, "The Song of Death" in *"And You!"* (Toronto: Macmillan, 1929), p. 5.

49. Falls, *The German Retreat to the Hindenburg Line*, pp. 239, 303.

50. LAC, RG9IIIC1, Vol. 3844, Folder 48, File 2, First Army plan; RG9IIIC3, Vol. 4011, Folder 18, File 2, Corps preliminary plan and artillery plan.

51. LAC RG9IIIC3, Vol. 4011, Folder 18, File 2, corps preliminary plan and artillery plan; RG9IIIC1, Vol. 3844, Folder 48, File 2, First Army plan; First Army to Canadian Corps and Corps to divisions 20 March. Four of the 12 comments concerned the fire plan, which is not surprising since the GOC (Horne) was a gunner. None of the comments criticized the concept or main features of the Corps' plan.

52. LAC, RG9IIIC1, Vol. 3845, Folder 49, Files 4 and 5; Vol. 3844, Folder 48, File 3, Notes on Conference.

53. LAC, RG9IIIC1, Vol. 3845, Folder 49, File 4, brigade plans and Currie's remarks. Griesbach assumed command of 1st Brigade in mid-February. Vimy would be his first battle as GOC. His BM, Major Hugh Urquhart, also joined the brigade in February.

54. LAC, RG9IIIC1, Vol. 3846, Folder 15, Files 1 and 5, brigade and battalion reports, 19 and 17 April respectively.

55. LAC, RG9IIIC1, Vol. 3846, Folder 15, File 2, report of 2 May.

56. LAC, RG9IIIC1, Vol. 3846, Folder 51, Files 1–5.

57. Urquhart, *History of the 16th Battalion*, p. 189.

58. LAC, RG9IIIC1, Vol. 3846, Folder 15, File 4, report of 27 April.

59. Fetherstonhaugh, *The 13th Battalion*, pp. 169–70; Richard Holmes, *Firing Line* (Harmondsworth, Middlesex: Penguin Books, 1987), p. 249. Australian practise was to issue rum after an attack. Canadian practise was to issue rum before an attack. This is why rum was dubbed "VC Mixture." A healthy tot, or two if a second could be had, made a man bolder.

60. LAC, RG9IIIC1, Vol. 3846, Folder 1, File 1 and 2, 1st and 2nd Brigade reports; Folder 51, File 4, 3rd Brigade report.

61. LAC, RG9IIIC3, Vol. 4061, Folder 7, File 1, 1st Division report.

62. LAC, RG9IIIC3, Vol. 4028, Folder 17, File 20, 1st Division report, 7 April 1917; RG9IIIC1, Vol. 3846, Folder 51, File 7.

63. LAC, RG9IIIC3, Vol. 4053, Folder 24, File 16, First Army, 9 May 1917.

64. LAC, RG9IIIC3, Vol. 4014, Folder 25, File 1, Corps Scheme of Operations, 26 July 1917.

65. LAC, 2nd and 3rd Brigade War Diaries, August 1917; RG9IIIC3, Vol. 4014, Folder 26, File 2, brigade reports.

66. LAC, RG9IIIC3, Vol. 4027, Folder 12, File 1, 1st Division Operation Order; RG9IIIC1, Vol. 3850, Folder 62, File 1, Instructions for the Offensive; RG9IIIC3, Vol. 4014, Folder 26, File 2, 2nd Brigade Outline Plan; File 3, 3rd Brigade orders.

67. LAC, 10th Battalion War Diary, Appendix 19, August 1917; *Notes for Commanding Officers* (1917), pp. 122–23, are an example of an attack Operation Order.

68. Nicholson, *Official History of the Canadian Army*, p. 292.

69. Lucas, gen. ed., Underhill, *The Empire at War: Canada*, p.189; LAC, RG9IIIC3, Vol. 4014, Folder 25, File 2; Vol. 4052, Folder 21, File 1. The primary difference between a gun and a howitzer is described by Hugh Urquhart, *History of the 16th Battalion*, p. 117: "A gun gives scant warning but can be avoided by getting behind some impenetrable object. You hear the report of a howitzer and when you have presently forgotten about it something drops from the sky with a sickening thud, as the novelists say." In short, gun fire comes at you; howitzer fire rushes down on top of you.

70. LAC, RG9IIIC3, Vol. 4014, Folder 25, File 2, and Folder 26, File 2, 1st Division and 2nd Brigade reports respectively.

71. LAC, MG30E100 (Currie Papers), Vol. 13, File 39, General Correspondence (Q–Ri), Currie to Colonel J.L. Ralston (Minister of National Defence), 9 February 1928. The whole of Currie's letter is a fine testimonial to Haig, whom he obviously admired greatly.

72. LAC, RG9IIID3, Vol. 4839, 1st Division A & Q War Diary, entry for 1 July 1917; Vol. 4007, Folder 4, File 17 and Folder 5, File 8, Corps Instructions for Defence and 1st Division Scheme of Defence.

73. LAC, RG9IIIC1, Vol. 3853, Folder 69, File 2, Corps Instructions for the Offensive, Passchendaele No. 1–5.

74. LAC, RG9IIIC3, Vol. 4015, Folder 28, File 3, Hayter to brigades. Hayter had replaced Kearsley in August when Kearsley became BGGS VI (Imperial) Corps.

75. Ibid., 1st Division to Corps, 2 November; Folder 29, File 1, 1st Brigade to battalions (4 November).

76. LAC, War Diaries 1st Battalion (Appendix 3, November 1917) and 2nd Battalion (Appendix 11/3, November 1917); *Notes for Commanding Officers* (1917), p. 117.

77. LAC, RG9IIIC3, Vol. 4052, Folder 21, File 3, Minutes of Conference, 5 November; Vol. 4061, Folder 8, File 2, 2nd Brigade to battalions 7 November. Loomis' order was 20 pages long. The figure is offered for the record only, and no criticism is intended; the difference was simply one of style. Staff work in 2nd Brigade was competent beyond any doubt, Loomis maintaining the high standard set by Lipsett.

78. LAC, RG9IIIC1, Vol. 3853, Folder 68, File 3, 1st Division report. Artillery staffs had abundant headaches reorganizing the guns, which had been dispersed anywhere a fire position could be found, even as single guns, meaning that control and the ability to register properly had been lost. No one was even sure how many guns were available. All of this was put right by Morrison.

79. Lucas, gen. ed., Underhill, *The Empire at War: Canada*, p.193; Nicholson, *Official History of the Canadian Army*, pp. 314, 327; Edmonds, *7th June–10th November Messines and Third Ypres* (Passchendaele), p. 359.

80. LAC, RG9IIIC1, Vol. 3853, Folder 68, File 3, 1st Division Report, "Lessons and Deductions."

81. LAC, MG30E15 (Griesbach Papers), Vol. 2, Folder 13, 1st Brigade report 15 November 1917; RG9IIIC3, Vol. 4052, Folder 21, Files 2 and 3, 2nd Brigade and 8th Battalion reports; 2nd Brigade War Diary, November 1917.

82. Morton and Granatstein, *Marching to Armageddon*, p. 109; LAC, RG 41, CBC interview with Lieutenant-Colonel Morrissey, 13th Battalion. Harington came from a Territorial division where he had been GSO1. Powell, *Plumer, the Soldier's General*, p. 153, notes that Harington went from Major to Major-General in 14 months. Like the CIGS, Field-Marshal Robertson, Harington reached high rank without ever

commanding more than a company or squadron. His autobiography, *Tim Harington Looks Back* (London: John Murray, 1940), unfortunately is not revealing at all of his time with the Canadian Corps.

83. Russenholt, *Six Thousand Canadian Men*, p. 129.

84. Philip Gibbs, *Realities of War* (London: Heinemann, 1920), pp. 47–49, 389–90. A prolific author, Gibbs wrote 16 novels and 40 non-fiction books, four relating to the Great War.

85. Wood, *Vimy*, p. 58; Peter T. Scott, ed. "With France The 'W.F.' Plan and the Genesis of the Western Front: A Previously Unpublished Account by General Sir Percy Radcliffe, KCB, KCMG, CB, DSO," *Stand To!* 10 (Spring 1984): 11. Meinertzhagen, *Army Diary, 1899–1926*, p. 241, who worked for Radcliffe at the War Office, described him as a first-class soldier, very easy to work with, and with a personal charm that few men have.

86. LAC, RG9IIIC1, Vol. 3839, Folder 34, File 1, BGGS to Q, 12 March 1917.

87. Military Advisory Board, *The Triumph of the Allies*, p. 131; Currie, *Interim Report*, p. 85. Webber had previously been GSO1 of 2nd Division and he was a dedicated officer. He typifies the good meaning of the old adage "like father, like son." His father, Lieutenant Henry Webber, 7th Battalion, South Lancashire Regiment, was 68 when he was killed in action at the Somme on 19 July 1916. He is thought to be the oldest British soldier killed by enemy action whilst on active service in the Great War. His story is told by Julian Sykes, "Lt. Henry Webber," *Gun Fire* No. 7: pp. 162–67. For N.W. Webber, see *Who Was Who, 1941–1950 A Companion to Who's Who Containing the Biographies of Those Who Died During the Decade 1941–1950* (London: Adam & Charles Black, 1952), p. 1215.

88. Currie, *Interim Report*, pp. 6, 85.

89. LAC, RG9IIIC1, Vol. 3842, Folder 43, File 1A, 30 June 1916, 3rd Division to Corps.

90. LAC, RG9IIIC1, Vol. 3842, Folder 43, File 9, 1st ANZAC to Canadian Corps, 23 August 1916.

91. J.F.B. Livesay, *Canada's Hundred Days: With the Canadian Corps from Amiens to Mons, Aug. 8–Nov. 11, 1918* (Toronto: Thomas Allen, 1919), p. 39; Wood, *Vimy*, pp. 58–59.

92. LAC, MG30E236 (Villiers Papers), Diary, January 1916.

93. Cave, "The Canadian Corps Order of Battle," pp. 6–12.

94. LAC, RG9IIIC1, Vol. 3827, Folder 6, File 6. In March 1917 Byng stated that he could staff the Canadian Corps with Canadians "except for a few Imperial officers who could not at present be replaced."

95. Kenneth Charles Eyre, "Staff and Command in the Canadian Corps: The Canadian Militia, 1896–1914, as a Source of Senior Officers," Master's Thesis, Duke University, 1967, p. 135; LAC, MG30E100 (Currie Papers), Vol. 12, File 36, letter 9 December 1925 to John Nelson; Swettenham, *McNaughton*, p. 67. McNaughton, who became the Great War counter-battery expert, readily acknowledged the contributions of British officers to this speciality (pp. 68–71).

96. Burns, *General Mud*, p. 142.

97. Duguid, *From the Outbreak of War*, p. 53.

98. Lucas, gen. ed., Underhill, *The Empire at War: Canada*, p. 124.

99. LAC, RG9IIIC3, Vol. 4026, Folder 11, File 3, Corps to divisions; Vol. 4051, Folder 19, File 8, Loomis to division.

100. Alfred, Lord Tennyson, "Rifleman Form," quoted in Royle, *A Dictionary of Military Quotations*, p.168.

CHAPTER SEVEN

Training: Policy and System

Blessed be the Lord my strength, which teacheth my hands to war and my fingers to fight.

—PSALM 144

The great virtue of training is that it provides the individual and collective self-confidence that makes a division or an Army effective. An Army is not an Army all at once. "I have not got an Army in France really," said Haig in March 1916, "but a collection of divisions untrained for the field. The actual fighting army will be evolved from them."[1] This evolution required system, selection of training content, and when it came to the conduct of training, the staff and facilities. This chapter examines the system, including training philosophy, policy and components. The next chapter looks at the content, standard and conduct of training. The two chapters track the soldier along the path from Base Depot, Corps Reinforcement Wing, division, brigade (or Brigade School or Depot) to unit—in short, from rear to "up forward."

The training story necessarily goes beyond 1st Division. Just as the division's SD and staff system existed within a larger system of the BEF, so too did its training. Manuals were mostly Imperial, the system ran according to higher direction and policy, and officers and men studied or served on staff at Canadian and Imperial schools and depots. All training was based on the *Field Service Regulations (FSR)* and *Infantry Training (4-Company Organization), 1914.*[2] Nevertheless, training was flexible enough to meet Canadian capabilities, wishes and requirements.

In late 1914 the training problem involved taking the British Army from 10 to over 70 divisions with only sufficient trained officers and NCOs for 10. This expansion was nightmarish: one new battalion found itself with a CO aged 63, one regular subaltern having a broken leg, and a nearly deaf quartermaster who had been recalled from the retirement he had been in since 1907.[3] Canadians had a similar but much smaller training problem: training from a standing start sufficient officers and NCOs to fight 1st Division and then a corps of four divisions. The training of Dominion divisions was also an Imperial training problem since they were part of the BEF.

One of the main responsibilities of commanders was training; indeed, a strong case can be made for calling it their chief responsibility. Of the 20 chapters in each edition of *Notes for Commanding Officers*, a manual issued to new and potential battalion commanders attending the special course for COs at the Senior Officers' School, Aldershot, 17 concerned training.[4] It is strange, then, that the subject has been so neglected. One of the better bibliographies of the war devotes only one page (of 332 pages) to it. All 20 entries on that page are for training manuals, and there is not one assessment amongst them.[5] Ivor Maxse, whose philosophy was "training is everything," would find this absurd. It would surprise the Viscount Byng, who was adamant that "training in peace-time is the most important part of soldiering. In war-time it is second only to operations, and operations can only be as good as the training is efficient." Arthur Currie, too, would raise an eyebrow for he considered "confidence . . . born of good training" to be the key to success. William Allan, the greatly admired CO of the 3rd Battalion, would be aghast because he believed fighting ability came from "training-discipline-morale." Training first![6] Currie, no doubt, had officers like Allan in mind when he said a decade after the war, "Over there, if the training was right, the discipline was right, the leadership what it should be, and the preparation complete, there was nothing which Canadians could not do."[7]

Three reasons for the neglect are that the subject of training, like the training itself, is difficult and complex and the urgency of training never seems to survive the end of hostilities. Training in 1914 aimed to make "the infantry soldier mentally and physically a better man than his adversary."[8] What a man thought he was and what the Army wanted him to be were very different. Experienced soldiers passed on the wisdom that said, "Don't die for your country; make the other fellow die for his." At its most basic, the aim was to provide the man with the skill to kill. This seems very simple but training was never that. Maxse, as Inspector-General of Training, stressed that it had to deal with methods ("how to") rather than principles ("what to").[9] The truth of this was in the equation DRILL + WILL + SKILL = KILL, *as it applied to the training of the individual soldier.* Clearly, method mattered in firing a mortar or a Lewis gun but the tactical employment of these weapons had more to do with principles than method. While method usually sufficed for individuals, leaders had to lead and teach from first principles. Another awkward aspect of training was the many categories of trainees: recruits, NCOs (junior and senior), specialists of every description from cooks to snipers, and officers in a wide range of education running from a 10 day familiarization with mortars to the staff and COs' courses. In addition, training, whether individual or collective, had to be conducted in a wide variety of locales: informally in the field with units (what we now call "On the Job Training"), at brigade, division, corps and Army schools or reinforcement camps, and at bases in the rear and in the home country.

Basic training gave the recruit the skills he needed to survive.[10] It also instilled group values of spirit, pride, loyalty to comrades, cohesion and obedience (which is a particular virtue in combat) and the security of learned routine and behaviour. These were critical because a division, unlike a sports team, could not pick its own men but had to take in the good, the bad and the indifferent. In his very perceptive article on writers and the war, Barrie Pitt stresses the strengths built into men by training, and he cautions against accepting the bleak assessment of training, especially drill, as tedious. Whatever its shortcomings, no one has come up with a better way to instil that sense of obedience without which the soldier will not long survive. "Drill is not the end of training but it is unquestionably the first of it."[11] This is not to say that training had no faults, for it most certainly did. One shortcoming was the tendency to concentrate on drill to an extent altogether out of proportion to its importance, especially in the case of officers, whose courses "should be devoted primarily to teaching . . . work in the field."[12] A GHQ document from late in the war sums up another longstanding problem: how repetitive training irked "the *Trained Soldier* [for whom] the old system was absolutely wrong . . . We have got to evolve a system . . . suitable for the trained soldier, something simple and interesting; above all we have got to treat him as a human being and not as a machine." This was not a new thought. Early in 1915 one British brigade commander had stressed that the idea of turning a man into a machine was "abortive" because success depended upon the individual action of the infantry soldier.[13]

Most officers in 1914 had had little formal training. Young Canadians, suddenly officers commanding men, faced a harder task than Regular Army subalterns, who went to regiments of trained and disciplined soldiers and strong traditions, where their authority was unchallenged and they had the help of experienced NCOs and the advice and intervention of senior officers if necessary. Canadians were less fortunate. Behind them were usually an equally inexperienced OC and NCOs who had been chosen by caprice or trial and error. Some officers had experience, for example, Lieutenant-Colonel Louis Lipsett, p.s.c., a 40-year-old Imperial Regular who led the 8th Battalion. Two years later he commanded 3rd Division. But even Lipsett could not bridge that wide gulf all at once; he had to train himself to train and command his unit, then his brigade and then his division. He made mistakes. While it is better to learn from the mistakes of others, few men habitually do that, and commanders, like divisions, are not suddenly struck brilliant. As one subaltern said, "Generals are accused of lack of imagination . . . by men who have never commanded a platoon on a field day."[14] Indeed, how a good leader emerges is, as Ian Hamilton said, one of life's great mysteries.[15]

Before the war the main or perhaps the sole aim of training was the inculcation of discipline but in the field the emphasis shifted. By all accounts a strict disciplinarian, Lipsett was also an excellent trainer, but he and Canadian officers as a whole could not guarantee that pre-war and early war training were up to date. Front and rear areas were two different worlds, which partially explains the persistent shortcomings in training. Training establishments never quite caught up to reality. *FSR* and *Infantry Training (4-Company Organization), 1914*, sought to prepare troops for open warfare but, instead, the troops got trench warfare; by the time they had become experienced in such operations the requirement had spun the other way. Absence of systematic dissemination of the lessons of the front also explains why training initially trailed reality. Early attempts to institute a systemized exchange of information between those responsible for training at home, those responsible for training at the front and those doing the fighting foundered because of brief and infrequent liaison. In October 1915 one subaltern described visitors as

> Cook's tourists . . . Officers sent over from the Canadian Training Base for short periods of one or two weeks to receive practical instruction in trench warfare . . . They brought . . . some wondrous ideas about the proper methods of doing things, gathered from some official publications known as 'Notes From The Front' and were greatly surprised to find we were not in touch with this 'Trade' journal . . . These little handbooks were written by wise men wearing red tabs and living miles away from the Front, where the continuity of their thoughts is only interrupted by the tea hour, and not by the 'Jack Johnson' shells.[16]

That same month a subaltern visiting 5th Battalion from a training battalion in Britain complained about being allowed to stay only "two weeks in the trenches to get first hand information for training purposes."[17] Even in early 1917 training officers visiting from Britain had little time to see and learn. One Major from the 35th Reserve Battalion, visiting 1st Brigade in February to get "direct information of requirements and suggestions," stayed only six days.[18] From mid-1917 on liaison improved greatly. When he was OC 1st Division Reinforcement Wing, H.S. Cooper (3rd Battalion) recalled going "up the line" frequently:

> You had to keep yourself abreast, because tactics changed up there very quickly, one battle to another and you wanted to be up to date . . . to see and ask questions [for] the good of your training, you see, the good of your outfit . . . You've got to give the chaps that you're training an odds on chance for their life to do something.[19]

Visitors went in the opposite direction, too. One early visitor, Brigadier-General W.B. Lindsay, Chief Engineer of the Canadian Corps, travelled to Crowborough in January 1917 to inspect the Canadian Engineer Training Depot because of numerous complaints about the low standard of skills and knowledge of the engineer replacements arriving in the divisions. Lindsay discovered an incredible state of affairs:

(1) the Depot had forgotten that its sole purpose was training of reinforcements to keep engineer units in France supplied with qualified officers and ORs;

(2) the Depot, because it was under command of the garrison commander, had been used as a reservoir of personnel to do other tasks, this being fatal to . . . (1);

(3) despite a 10 fold growth in students Depot establishment had not increased;

(4) an alarming shortage of senior and experienced officers had left inexperienced subalterns in command of battalion sized units. Moreover, the few junior officers available spent most of their time on administrative duties;

(5) accommodation was unsatisfactory in every respect; billets, messing and even sanitation;

(6) engineering material for training were inadequate;

(7) instruction was not on the best lines in that it was out of date and discipline was neglected. Officer instructors had been too long away from the Front. Hours of instruction, 20 to 22 hours a week, were inadequate and this limited time was being consumed by pay parades, rifle inspections and other distracting administrative matters. In addition, the demand for men for fatigues, garrison duties and construction engineer services were breaking up courses.

(8) senior officers did no instruction, only administrative duties, which were heavy; and

(9) the lack of a definite syllabus and constant interruptions had prevented progressive training.

Given the absence of the basic conditions for good training it is no wonder that of its 203 officers and 2,280 ORs, only 26 and 77 respectively were classed as fully trained. These numbers provided abundant proof of the depot's failure to achieve its mission. The only "fix" was

(1) complete reorganization, which was essential;

(2) making the CO at Crowborough responsible for discipline only; for all else sappers would be under the Depot;

(3) relief of unqualified engineer officers and their replacement by experienced officers from the Front;

(4) increase in the establishment of the Depot;

(5) revision of course syllabus including 35 hours of progressive training per week;

(6) provision of adequate training materials; and

(7) senior officer involvement in training.

As the first step, an experienced and competent officer from the front took over as commandant. The numerous changes he made are beyond the scope of this book. Suffice it to say that he put things right, and sapper training dramatically improved, so much so that divisions made no further serious complaint.[20]

Another visitor in January 1917 was newly promoted George Tuxford, who arrived to take command of 14th Training Brigade until such time as a brigade became available at the front. Determined that the 14th benefit from his experience, he "started a series of trenches . . . such . . . as at the Front, not of the type . . . on the training grounds . . . and the Brigade practised . . . night reliefs and taking over the trench line. Recognizing the importance [of] bombs . . . I organized a Brigade Bombing School."[21]

William Griesbach, GOC 1st Brigade, arrived in July 1917 for a three-day senior officers' course at the Machine-Gun School at Grantham. He had much to say about machine-gun doctrine but, more importantly, he thought the school "absolutely first class . . . a most valuable institution very efficiently conducted," and the instructors appeared "anxious to maintain close touch with the progress of machine-gun work at the Front . . . [They] were careful to teach nothing which cannot be carried out at the Front so far as I could see." In October he returned to England, this time to inspect the reserve battalions (3rd, 4th, 6th and 12th) that reinforced 1st Brigade. Their weapons training impressed him, especially in the 4th, where it was "quite as good" as anywhere in France; but field engineering training left "much to be desired . . . [being] for the most part unreal and not up to date." "Sound principles" in placement of wire were not known or practised; in most cases the wire was erected too close to the parapet and failed to take advantage of the ground to achieve concealment. In one case, consolidation of a mine crater was "quite contrary to our experience . . . and [was] not only useless but dangerous." He urged that reports on front-line experience and enemy field engineering methods be issued to line and reserve battalions simultaneously.[22] He also learned that reserve battalions preferred that all instructors have front-line experience. Those without it found it hard to deal with other ranks who were undergoing refresher training after recovering from wounds. Regarding exchange postings he thought:

> While great strides have been made in this matter there is still room for much improvement. There should be less rigidity and more fluidity in the interchange . . . between Battalions at the front, Base Depots and Reserve Battalions and more careful selection of officers exchanged . . . A steady movement of officers backwards and forwards should be going on all the time.

On the whole, "The good work, . . . the system of training, . . . and the willingness and eagerness . . . to render the greatest possible service to front line people," impressed him.[23] Such favourable comment marked quite a change from the previous summer and autumn when the BGGS, Percy Radcliffe, remarked in exasperation how essential it was that "every man should throw a live bomb before going into action." At that time Tuxford had complained about "a number of the new drafts recently received [being] unaccustomed to the use of the . . . Mills bomb." Currie, too, was aware that many of the new men had never thrown a bomb.[24]

Another means to improve training involved visits to the front by the COs of reserve battalions and exchange visits between commandants of training centres on the continent and those of various training centres in England, including the Officers' School at Bexhill.[25] Although difficult to arrange, the visits resulted in significant improvement during the last year or so of the war. The requirement for close liaison between front and home came to feature strongly in training considerations.

One of the most pertinent questions about the training problem is the old Army one: "Who's in charge here?" *Infantry Training (4-Company*

Organization), 1914 made commanders responsible for training.[26] In early 1916 Haig reiterated training policy: "The division must be regarded as the unit of training and instruction."[27] General Officers Commanding were responsible for training along the lines of the manuals and the instructions that amplified them.[28] This was repeated in *SS 152 Instructions for the Training of the British Armies in France*, published in June 1917:

> Commanders of formations are responsible for the efficiency of the units under their immediate command. Commanding Officers are responsible for the training of all Officers, N.C.Os and men in their units. Various special Instructors are trained at Schools in order to assist Commanding Officers . . . Reinforcements . . . are trained at Training camps or with their units. Commanders should train the troops they lead into action. This is a principle which must never be departed from and nothing . . . is to be held to relieve Commanders of their initial responsibility. [29]

Thus, divisions generally trained without much interference from corps. Consequently, schools proliferated, and training manuals and instructions were not commonly interpreted, a situation exacerbated by shortages of equipment and instructors.

Infantry Training made no mention of a CO's responsibility to train subordinates in the art of teaching. During 1915 COs struggled to train young officers, including teaching them how to train others but in the aftermath of Second Ypres, Festubert and Givenchy, it became clear that the COs could not cope with these duties. As the CO of the 3rd Battalion pointed out, "there [had] . . . been a reduction in the number of experienced officers and men, and consequently . . . efficiency . . . [was] more than ever dependent upon the unremitting personal efforts of the O.C.'s." He asked company commanders to focus specifically on ensuring that platoon commanders understood their duties.[30] Recognizing that COs required help, Alderson supposed that divisional schools might be established to assist them. The requirement was just as obvious in Imperial divisions, "hence the growth of Army, Corps and Divisional Schools" in the BEF. Later, Macdonell considered that training was every leader's business: "teaching [new men] . . . the war wisdom learnt on many a hard fought field by their predecessors is a constant problem, and I wish all Officers and N.C.O's to get their backs into it." To provide more concrete and dedicated help he suggested adding supervision of training to the duties of battalion 2ICs, a task quite new to them. Specifically, he recommended that they visit brigade schools periodically to check on the training of battalion ORs.[31]

That the conduct of training remained a problem throughout is evident in the following diary entries by an officer on the staff of the XVIII (Imperial) Corps school:

> 17th February 1918. It is almost extraordinary how few officers do understand how to train, or to organise for training . . . To hear fellows talk one would think that every battalion in France was splendidly trained.

> 18th February 1918. We talked about their battalions and the things that came out were positively astounding . . . The battalions are not organised, and they CAN'T train. The state of affairs is incredible.

> 22nd February 1918. I tried an experiment . . . got all the Officers to air their grievances . . . Some quite interesting facts came to light . . . illustrating the extraordinary lack of organisation and method in some battalions.[32]

These comments are surprising since the GOC was Maxse, an officer considered by many to be one of the best trainers in the BEF. If his corps had such problems, it would be naive to think that Canadian battalions did not suffer, to some degree, from similar ills. Heavy casualties and the demands of a seemingly endless war impacted adversely on the training of every battalion, Canadian and Imperial. Hence the exhortations made by Macdonell, and the many others made by battalion and brigade commanders. Much of the litany of complaint about inadequate training arose from GHQ's failure to lead. In 1917 R.J. Kentish pointed out that "what has been done in the training line in France is due more to individual efforts of Army, Corps, Division and Brigade commands than to any clear direction from higher command (G.H.Q.)."[33] Not until the appointment of Maxse as Inspector-General Training for the BEF in May 1918 was a focus for training provided at the very top. Brigadier-General A. Solly-Flood had been appointed Coordinator of Tactical Training of Senior Officers in October 1916, a post soon expanded into a Directorate of Training with the intention of exercising that function in the BEF as a whole; but he and his directorate lacked the clout to have much impact.[34] Even the creation of Army schools resulted from the initiative of GOC Third Army (Sir C.C. Monro) rather than from GHQ. It has been said with some justification that GHQ largely ignored the schools and that formation commanders "learnt tactics from each other in a casual *ad hoc* manner, through personal contacts rather than through any system of conferences and meetings."[35] The extent to which that applied depended on the corps, however. Despite GHQ's isolation, a training system existed in the BEF and certainly in the Canadian Corps.

Because Imperial corps schools lacked the authority to enforce their instructions or methods, uniformity of training (and doctrine) was well-nigh impossible. In addition, most Imperial corps commanders had neither the time nor the inclination to ascertain the standard of training of a particular division, or to correct any defects, since the division would soon move on to another corps. The Canadian Corps, with its permanent slate of divisions, was spared this. In those corps where the commander expressed no strong interest, the uniformity of training suffered to some extent.[36] Byng's and Currie's abiding interest in training encouraged and, when necessary, bucked up training standards, providing an enviable coherence and commonality in the Canadian Corps. Their interest extended to the training of reserve battalions in England. Both editions of *Training in Canadian Reserve Battalions* (January and October 1917) emphasize the pressing need for a uniform training standard. One particular group of records in the National Archives (now Library and Archives Canada) contains a great many files pertaining to Canadian Corps, 1st Division and brigade conferences, as well as conferences and meetings chaired by senior staff officers; they were all called to discuss every conceivable aspect of operations, including training, which received considerable attention. Much of the correspondence originates with the particular Army in which the Canadian Corps served at the time.[37] This lends credence to Kentish's remarks, above, concerning the impact of the Army level of command on training, in the absence of central GHQ direction.

For most soldiers, relevant training began in France where they spent long hours digging trenches and practising attacking and defending them.[38] During the brigade attachments to Imperial divisions for a week in the line in February 1915, Private H. Campbell realized, "You learned more in 24 hours . . . than what you had learned with all your training . . . previously." While the tutorial was helpful and necessary, the raw Canadians really came to grips with war once they were on their own. Private G.W. Twigg, 4th Battalion, called Second Ypres "a glorious day for the Canadians [who] had practically no training." His CO, Lieutenant-Colonel A.B. Birchall, had warned the unit in England "You are going to require all your abilities and all your fitness to beat these Germans." But it took time to learn the discipline of battle. "We attacked . . . and we were an undisciplined mob. Our men weren't trained to keep their proper distance in extended order, and the leaders weren't trained, and the result was that our casualties were very heavy."[39]

At its simplest, training functioned in four sets: "home" (the British Isles), "base" (in various guises), schools (from GHQ down to brigade) and unit (where training was usually synonymous with operations: "Perhaps the best way to break into the game is to go through a 'show' the first thing and learn the worst there is to experience"[40]).

Strictly speaking, home should include Canada but it does not for three reasons. First, the training men received in Canada turned dull and green, like their brass, during the voyage across the Atlantic. Second, in Canada, a galaxy away from the war, no training immediacy existed, unlike in "Blighty" where all infantry recruits did their 14 weeks' basic training, often under the guidance of experienced instructors. Once 1st Division had left for Flanders, training in Britain concentrated on reinforcements. Even if shortcomings had not existed or had been corrected immediately, units would not have been entirely happy with the product, the universal judgement always being that reinforcements lacked discipline and training.

Currie, an artillery CO before 1914, became incensed at the low standard of gunner reinforcements. In a letter of December 1915 to Major-General J.W. Carson, Hughes' representative in Britain, he passed on the complaints of senior artillery commanders about the "most unfavourable" standard, the men "appearing to have had no training to speak of and [knowing] nothing of the elementary duties of gunners." Many of the newcomers had revealed that their training time on the 18-pounder totalled one afternoon. Others said they had seen one three times in their entire training. Said Currie:

> Now Carson, you and I know that this is . . . d—d rotten, and the men responsible . . . should be told so . . . We have to fight these men and the least the chaps who have the soft jobs at Shorncliffe can do is train them . . . Unless they are prepared to do this, they should be kicked out of the Canadian Service. They are as much slackers as the man who doesn't join at all. In fact some are worse because they spoil good men. This brings me to another question . . . The troops in England should be trained by men who have had experience here . . . We are entitled to the very best service from those on the other side, and that, I know you will see that we get, in so far as it lies in your power.[41]

Many gunners, Canadian and Imperial, did not then have a reputation for accuracy. That some of this resulted from inadequate technology or organization did not interest the infantry who were frequently subjected to friendly fire. Within a year, however, the picture was quite different:

> I was up in another artillery observation post the other day. The officer was showing me two points on the enemy's parapet between which he had to fire. He was describing them to me, and suddenly said, 'Half a minute,' gave an order down the speaking tube, and in fifteen seconds a round hit the parapet fairly. 'That is the right point,' he remarked, gave another order, another round fired. 'That is the left point,' said he. It was just as if he had reached out a gigantic arm

to touch the points he wished to show me on the enemy's parapet nearly a mile away.[42]

Of course, gunner training was technical and easier to teach and learn than infantry tactics.

In May 1915 Major Percy Guthrie, acting CO of the 10th Battalion after the death of Lieutenant-Colonel Boyle at Second Ypres, complained that of a draft of 250 men "very few . . . had even fired a shot, and none had fired their musketry course before being sent out."[43] This almost unimaginable neglect would have angered every officer and NCO in the 10th, or in any other infantry battalion. In July J.G. Rattray, the new CO, complained to the CO of the reserve battalion serving as his reinforcement unit that, at the very least, men should know how to entrench and be competent with their rifles, plus have a working knowledge of bombs and machine-guns, and they must expect strict discipline on arrival in the field.[44] Complaints about infantry training continued into and during 1916. In December, 3rd Brigade drafts did not appear "to have had much training and this will have to commence from the beginning." 2nd Brigade spoke "of the futility of attempting advanced work [with drafts] until the elemental rules of discipline and training have been most thoroughly mastered."[45] Canadian brigadiers would have agreed entirely with Imperial comments about some of the infantry they were receiving:

> reinforcements were sent to France and Flanders with inadequate initial training; that Officers and NCOs never received the sort of systematic training for their responsibilities which . . . should be essential prerequisites for promotion; and that battalions . . . were given insufficient time and resources for training between battles or spells in the line . . . tactical doctrine and knowledge of how to train men intelligently were deplorably ignored [and] . . . training at every level would have drastically reduced the casualty lists . . . a great deal of that loss [due] to inexperienced leadership and faulty basic training.[46]

One estimate says that of 50,000 Canadians who reached France between April 1915 and October 1916, almost half were only partially trained.[47] A primary reason for this was *Army Council Instruction No. 1968*. This appendix to *Training in Canadian Reserve Battalions* detailed the 14-week training syllabus for infantry recruits but not the standard they had to achieve. With this lack of certification recruits, ready or not, were sent off to France. The unready recruits made COs very unhappy. One Imperial spoke for any CO receiving such men when he said, "I still have my old grouse against the training at home. It's absolutely rotten. We have to train our men as we get them."[48]

A revised edition, issued in October, made the path ahead clear: "The only reason for the existence of any large reserves of Canadian troops in England is the necessity of supplying trained reinforcements to the field. Efficiency in training is the primary duty of every officer, non-commissioned officer and man in . . . Reserve units in the British Isles." Second, in stressing the responsibility of COs for training, it implied that the January edition had neglected the requirement for uniformity of battalion instruction. Third, in response to the many complaints about the low standard it directed that the fitness of recruits to proceed to the front would no longer be decided by length of training but by the new *Army Council Instruction No. 1230*, which required the recruit to pass tests in drill, musketry, bombs, bayonet fighting, gas measures, rifle bomb or Lewis gun, and rapid wiring, and to be issued a certificate showing that he had passed.[49] Finally, training of infantry drafts had also to meet the requirements of *SS 143 Instructions for the Training of Platoons for Offensive Action, 1917*, a publication written specifically for the new platoon, which held "all the weapons with which the Infantry are now armed."[50] The new platoon and the changing thinking about the efficacy of the various weapons had necessitated the revised edition of *Training in Canadian Reserve Battalions*, including some amendments to the recruit syllabus, the most important being a decrease in bomb training (from 15 to 12 hours) and the addition of 24 hours of rifle bombing or Lewis gun training (half the recruits were trained as Lewis gunners and the other half as rifle bombers). Musketry training remained at 153 hours.[51] Clearly, training now reflected the reality of the front.

The generally unsatisfactory standard before the issue of *Army Council Instruction No. 1230* bothered field commanders but they were deeply worried about the shortage of infantry reinforcements, an even more debilitating problem that had originated with Hughes' mobilization scheme. While the reinforcement system wasted resources, such as facilities and instructors, many of the officers and NCOs sent from the field as instructors were exhausted, some had just recovered from wounds (or were convalescent), and their instructional skills were often marginal due to lack of training or interest. Recruits trained by instructors without combat experience, on the other hand, suffered from the instructor's inability to impart relevant training.

In February 1916, Alderson won his case that it would be better to send semi-trained men to France to complete their training. By mid-1916 several "Base Training Centres" had opened: Le Havre for infantry and artillery; Rouen for infantry, cavalry and engineers; and Calais and Etaples for infantry. The centres had three objectives after testing the drafts: further train those not up to standard; bring training into line with the latest lessons from the front; and train men who might remain there for some time. Drafts could still be sent direct to divisions but this was unusual. Each centre had a "Bull Ring," the one at Etaples being the most famous, or more accurately, infamous. The ring, said Robert Graves, was designed "to inculcate the offensive spirit," but not a questioning spirit if a sign at the Etaples railway station is to be believed. The sign, prominently located to catch the eye of each new arrival, conveyed an easily understood message:

> *A Wise Old Owl Lived in An Oak,*
> *The More He saw The Less He Spoke*
> *The Less he spoke The More he Heard,*
> *Soldiers Should Imitate That Old Bird.*[52]

Lieutenant James Pedley of the 4th Battalion described a bull ring as

> a huge circular training area where troops could be finally tested in large batches for the line. A squad would cut in at some point in the circle in the morning and by the time each soldier had gone through the various diversions of the area he was to have his equipment fully and finally tested, and . . . his memory refreshed on all the points of his previous training. Musketry, bayonet work, drill, gas, bombing—there was originally a section for each branch.[53]

Etaples, which included No. 1 Canadian Infantry Base Depot (Colonel F.A. Reid), aimed at testing 2,000–3,000 men within three days. On day one, a newly arrived draft was kitted out, medically examined and checked for documentation. In the afternoon the tests began. Immediately a draft passed, it was reported available for the front. Until called for, it continued training in the above essentials and was lectured on trench warfare, discipline, weapons, interior economy and many other topics. Drafts that did poorly could be retained for additional training. A good draft could expect to be in and out within five days of arrival. Imperials ran the training but Reid administered the Canadians. In response to some complaints about training standards, he wrote to the COs in June 1917, inviting their criticism and suggestions on training. He also sent GOC 1st Division a copy of the syllabus.[54]

In September 1916 Corps HQ announced its intention to cease testing at base depots and instead send drafts directly to "Reinforcement Camps (Corps or Divisional)," this being possible because every man in the next infantry draft would come with a certificate showing his qualifications and proving that he had successfully completed the syllabus in Britain. The BGGS, seeking proof that training had improved, ordered and received divisional assessments of the standard of this draft. 2nd Division (Turner) found its draft satisfactory and better than previous ones, comments echoed by 4th Division (Watson) although he thought musketry required improvement. Currie (1st Division) found the draft generally "satisfactory," except for musketry. 13th Battalion thought the draft's musketry needed considerable attention, failures in elementary handling reaching as high as 50 percent, and the 20th and 23rd Reserve Battalions, which provided reinforcements to the 13th, no doubt heard about this. On the other hand, some receiving units expressed their satisfaction with the reinforcements: "New drafts . . . reflected the thoroughness of the training . . . now being given in the reinforcing battalions in England."[55] Overall, the drafts appeared "considerably improved" over earlier ones. Based on these assessments, Corps terminated the base depot test period.[56]

Subsequently, GHQ directed that with the exception of anti-gas training, base depots would no longer train infantry reinforcements, who would instead go directly to corps reinforcement camps to complete their training under Army arrangements. *SS 152 Instructions for the Training of the British Armies in France* had mentioned in general terms the functions of these camps, and GHQ amplified these terms on 25 September: each corps camp would have a small permanent staff (initially 16 all ranks) and a wing for each division in the corps. Each divisional wing would have a permanent staff of four and an instructional staff (from divisions) that was proportionate to the number of reinforcements (up to a maximum of 30 instructors) "when and as required" (that is, temporary attachments). Some instructors could be LOB officers and men. Training would be continuous, reinforcements being put in squads on arrival according to the qualifications on their individual certificates and then being trained as appropriate. Tests on training were considered unnecessary.[57] On taking over as OC 1st Division Reinforcement Wing, Major H.S. Cooper (3rd Battalion) found 30 instructors to be insufficient for his 2,440 students. Currie then authorized Cooper to retain 500 men until he could pick out 250 suitable instructors. Currie "wanted them trained . . . He was down . . . often enough to see that training went on."[58]

The Canadian Corps had, in fact, begun organizing a corps reinforcement camp early in September. As a first step, it abolished divisional entrenching battalions, transferring their personnel to the Canadian Corps Reinforcement Camp (CCRC), whose first CO, Lieutenant-Colonel W.J.H. Holmes, had commanded the Canadian Entrenching Group.[59] The CCRC held 100 reinforcements per infantry and pioneer battalion and 10 percent for other arms. Each of its four divisional wings, which included one training company per brigade, and the arms and services sections were responsible for the training of their reinforcements. The organization and functions of the CCRC remained pretty much the same until mid-1918 when GHQ, responding to the continuing dissatisfaction with reinforcement training standards, re-introduced an abbreviated version of the old qualification certificate and tests, similar to those formerly conducted by Base Depots, on musketry, rifle bombing, grenades, Lewis gun and rapid wiring.[60]

The third component of the training system in France was the schools that sprang up everywhere: "In this war we were all at school.[61] One of the first to open, the Machine-Gun School (22 November 1914), was graduating nearly 300 men a month by May 1915, rising to 500 in June, which also saw the establishment of the Lewis Gun School. The Officer Cadet School (estab-lished December 1914) was graduating 200 officers a month by May. By the end of 1915 schools open in France included:

> *G.H.Q.*: Lewis Gun and Light Trench Mortar, Machine Gun, Wireless, Cadet, and Royal Engineers; and a Staff College Course each winter. *Army*: Artillery, Infantry, Signal, Scouting, Observation and Sniping, Mine, Trench Mortar, Anti-Gas. *Corps*: Infantry, Bombing and Trench Mortar, Lewis Gun, Anti-Gas. *Cavalry Corps*: Equitation, Signals. *Miscellaneous*: Ammunition School of Instruction, Anti-Aircraft, Bridging, Cookery, Intelligence, Labour Corps Officers, Machine-Gun Corps, Light Railway (Forward), Mechanical Transport, Officers commanding Field and Army troops R.E., Young Officers, R.A.M.C., Tank Tactics, Transportation Units, Chaplains.[62]

Bernard Adams, a Welsh Lieutenant who attended a month-long young officers' course at Third Army in December 1915, gives the best account of the training at young officers' schools. He describes the general run of training at such schools; why they were necessary; their content, conduct and value; the composition of the student body and instructional staff; and the rest and leisure activities experienced during the month he was away from his unit. Adams also readily admits he knew next to nothing about organization, artillery, bombs and warfare in general, which is not surprising, because he had only arrived at his unit on 9 October. At the school he enjoyed the com-pany of more than 100 junior officers eager to learn about their new profes-sion. All the instructors were well experienced in warfare; rather than an academic program of theory and opinion, they presented fact derived from experience. Adams was especially impressed by the commandant's advice on achieving good morale and avoiding bad. Other lectures and discussions included artillery, engineer and flying corps roles and capabilities, sniping, patrolling, discipline, and the lessons, good and bad, learned from the recent Battle of Loos. The students also worked diligently on attack and defence schemes, map reading and trench routines. "In short," said Adams, "there was very little we did not do at the School." Free time was occupied with weekly concerts and trips to Amiens for sightseeing and socializing. Christmas dinner was enjoyed at a hotel in the city. When he returned to his unit in early January Adams felt "so much better equipped to command his men."[63]

Eventually, schools existed for every conceivable group and speciality. General Headquarters, Armies and Corps ran permanent schools with an approved establishment for the purpose of training "Instructors." Lower formations, strictly speaking, did not have schools; rather; divisions and brigades conducted temporary "classes of instruction" to train "Personnel and Instructors as may be necessary."[64] Considerable informal on-job training, or classes as time and circumstance permitted, continued in the trenches to correct error or to incorporate new ideas, but most training was conducted as formal courses behind the line. Classes of instruction, or schools (the usual term), offered little by way of frills or comfort, except that they were out of the direct line of fire, or any fire at all, and students could learn what they needed to survive. Edmund Blunden thought the real reason for the "number-less schools" in the BEF at this time (autumn 1917) was as much the desire to give officers and men a rest as to instruct them. Many student recollections share this theme. One Canadian called the schools "the temporary homes of promising N.C.O.'s, 'officers aspirant,' and officers needing a 'refresher.'" Another said they were a "welcome diversion" from the trenches. Charles Carrington wrote:

> Sergeants and 'young officers' (how I disliked that patronizing phrase!) were much exposed to educational treatment and if they had the greatest share of danger in the line they enjoyed the perquisite—now and then—of being 'sent on a course.' At least it would be safe and comfortable, at best it might be a mere holiday— a 'binge'.[65]

At first, like in so many other things, Imperials played a leading role. "It was about this time [July 1915] that the professional instructors of the 'Old Contemptibles' were replaced by Canadians and the division [1st] was able to do its own training." While "the men of the Maple Leaf took a pride in their schools," trainees were "recruits to all intents and purposes, and a stiff kindergarten curriculum" faced them. Instructors were notoriously difficult to please, dissatisfied with anything done on first attempt, which meant the constant shrieking of "As you were!" and having the recruits do it again and again. "I suppose it was good for our souls . . . but better the Somme and Passchendaele rolled into one putrid horror than an unlimited course of 'school.'" Personal likes aside, the schools made a vital contribution, their value being beyond dispute:

Very good institutions in every way. They kept the whole army *au fait* with the latest improvements, and improved the *entente* between the different branches of the service and units. All these courses of instruction went on, no matter what battle was being fought. Men were taken out in the middle of an action, and sent off in a Piccadilly bus to this or that house of knowledge.[66]

Canadian schools gradually became well known. The French thought highly of some. A delegation visiting a Canadian school at Bexhill went away greatly impressed with the use of live ammunition and bombs in training. The Commandant, Major A.C. Critchley, thought it absurd not to give men a better idea of what battle would be like, before they went across to France. He insisted on "pretty realistic" training, including lobbing hand grenades "with a very small detonating charge," to let trainees see what would happen.[67]

Specialists were a very large part of the actual and potential student population. Every new piece of kit from a weapon to pigeons for message carrying appeared to need a school. The plethora of specializations and the ever increasing numbers of specialists, which greatly enlarged the "school archipelago," had two very serious implications for battalion fighting strength.[68] Reflecting in mid-1916 upon the fact that when a specialty is created, it creates a specialist who must be trained, one commanding officer wondered at the "schools of all sorts [that] sprang up . . . and the demand for victims . . . so great . . . that the fact that there was a war on had apparently been overlooked."[69]

The second implication was the ever rising demand for instructors, who came mostly from line battalions. Units that were asked for men often did as they had done when they had to ante up for machine-gun companies and trench mortar batteries: they sent less than their best. Incompetents, malcontents and malingerers were foisted upon the schools, meaning a mixed standard of instruction; but fortunately, such miscreants were a very small minority amongst the generally enthusiastic and knowledgeable instructors in Canadian schools. By September 1917 the pressing need for instructors, "borrowed or secured, as best they can, from the fighting Battalions," caused Generals Currie and Turner to propose the formation of an Instructional Corps to provide the rear and the front with a pool of instructors. They would be allocated to reserve battalions as required, and would form instructional cadre for divisional or brigade schools in France, or assist in training battalions out of the line. It was estimated that the Canadian Corps School in France would require 48 officers and 100 sergeants, while the Canadian Training School in England could manage with 5 officers and 300 sergeants. Combat experience was to be a primary qualification for all instructors.[70]

However, their proposal ran into the old problem: an increased training establishment could only be provided by transfers from units and by training "specially selected" officers and NCOs. "Canadian War Establishments" (1918) makes only one reference to an instructor pool: "25 Instructors . . . to be *attached* to the Canadian Corps School and carried on the General List."[71] In short, no Instructional Corps was established.

Each command level had particular responsibilities for training. *SS 152 Instructions for the Training of the British Armies in France* was issued in June 1917. This extremely important manual codified the policy and system that was more or less already in practise. Although *SS 152* does not directly say so, its purposes, according to the documents leading up to its publication, were to standardize training and to prevent duplication of effort.[72] Several draft versions underwent earnest scrutiny. Canadian views, based on divisional comments, went to First Army on 26 February. In the interests of standardization Byng suggested that Army set the general lines for training and that the GS02 (Training) at corps should ensure corps schools adhered to them. Also, training had to be progressive: each class of school should offer a higher level of training than the school of the next lower formation. Thus, the Army school should train COs, company commanders, and instructors for schools of lower formations (bombing and other specializations). "The great want," he said, "was for trained company commanders." Army schools could best train them. Corps schools should train platoon commanders, adjutants, and drill and bayonet instructors, while division and brigade schools should look after musketry and specialist courses. David Watson, GOC 4th Division, thought training platoon commanders the most pressing need, while Currie of the 1st believed training platoon commanders how to train their platoons was more important.[73]

In March, First Army hosted several training conferences. One decision ruled out formal courses for adjutants because such training in reports and returns was better left to COs and to short attachments to brigade HQs. Participants thought officer training as a whole at Army schools too elementary and urged more tactical schemes on the ground and more teaching of lessons gleaned from recent fighting and minor operations. Also, officers should receive training at divisional schools before attending Army schools. The Army Commander (Horne) ordered instruction "taken up on progressive lines." Thereafter school lists were headed: "The aim of the various Schools . . . is to make the Teaching Progressive." The July list included the following GHQ schools: GHQ Staff Course, senior and junior (both six weeks long); small arms school, with machine-gun, Lewis gun and rifle branches; and schools or courses of bridging, communications, cavalry, engineers and transport. Army schools included central, trench mortar, musketry, artillery, scouting, signal, observation and sniping, anti-gas and cookery schools. The central school had five objectives:

(a) To train Company Commanders and Seconds in Command of Companies, and N.C.O.s of, and above the rank of sergeant, as subordinate commanders, and to fit them to become instructors.

(b) To hold periodical conferences of senior officers, to discuss questions of tactical and administrative interest.

(c) To conduct special experiments.

(d) To teach the tactical handling of machine and Lewis guns, light trench mortars, grenades and other appliances.

(e) To ensure uniformity of doctrine.[74]

Each command course included one officer and one NCO from each battalion in the Army and selected artillery and engineer officers, for a total of 150 officers and 150 NCOs or so. All candidates had to have previously attended a divisional or corps school. The third week featured a six-day "Senior Officers' Conference" attended by every infantry CO in the Army, plus selected artillery, engineer and staff officers. Schools would run even during operations, the students being mostly LOB officers and ORs.[75]

By June the schools and student bodies had been formalized into four categories: England, GHQ, Army and Corps. The schools in England trained staff officers (Cambridge), infantry officers selected to be COs (Aldershot) and artillery officers selected to be battery commanders. GHQ schools would train staff officers, engineer company commanders, officers and NCOs in the tactical handling of machine-guns and Lewis guns; they would also train musketry instructors. Army schools included signals and anti-gas schools and an infantry school to train company commanders and company sergeant majors. Commanding Officers' courses, a heavy and medium mortar school and a scouting, observation and sniping school were affiliated. An artillery school would train gunnery instructors. Corps schools included infantry and signal schools and an anti-gas school. The first, which would train platoon commanders and sergeants, had affiliated a bombing and light mortar school, a Lewis gun school and "(In the Schools of Overseas Forces) Senior Officers' and NCOs' Courses." This met Dominion wishes to control such training.[76]

Course loading documents show that in early 1918 schools in Britain offered two senior officers' courses (10 weeks in duration) on the basis of two or three vacancies per division, one senior and one junior staff officers' course (no allotment set). Various musketry schools offered three-week courses for instructors, two or three NCOs per division. GHQ offered numerous machine-gun and Lewis gun courses, which were heavily subscribed. Every other wireless and sapper course offered places for three students per division. Army schools offered courses in intelligence, method of instruction, musketry, mortars, artillery, signals and first aid. Most courses ran continuously. All schools and courses were open to every division in the BEF.[77]

These arrangements formalized what every corps in the BEF had been doing for two years or more. The Canadian Corps School that opened in 1915 soon gained several additions. The Officers' School, which had a permanent staff of 4 officers and 20 ORs (the staff was assigned in November 1916), ran a first course of 24 officers. Earlier, Second Army had authorized a Canadian Corps School of Instruction. In December this school, styled the Canadian Corps Training School, opened at Pernes, France. "A" Wing taught general duties to junior officers and NCOs, while "B" Wing conducted technical training of instructors in bombing, Lewis gun, Stokes mortar and sniping. Initial courses scheduled 60 officers and 120 NCOs ("A" Wing) and 18 officers and 162 ORs ("B" Wing). As it turned out, the first officer course had a total of 100, "some . . . straight from England and others who had been in the front line but whose training wanted brushing up." The school's first Commandant, Major A.C. Critchley, fresh from touring training centres in Britain where he had found the training "quite useless . . . the instructors . . . teaching tactics . . . long out of date," insisted on all instructors having front line experience.[78] Once in full operation the school had a stream of visitors, including the GOC and his staff. Currie noted in his diary in January 1917 that the school was running to full capacity.[79]

In Byng's view the Canadian Corps School had three purposes: to train instructors in weapons and trench warfare, to train junior officers and to bind the corps together. There had been some concern that interdivisional relations were not what they should have been, so much so that in July the BGGS (Harington) spoke to the Officers' School thus: "It is right and proper to believe, and to make your men believe, that there is no other battalion or division that can hold a candle to your own but it is unsoldier-like . . . to belittle or run down any other unit . . . it must be everyone's object to promote . . . good comradeship.[80]

Very soon after assuming command of the Corps in June 1917, Currie turned his attention to training. On 2 July, the day after the Dominion's 50th birthday, which was celebrated at 11:00 A.M. by all guns firing three rounds, he issued training orders to "prevent overlapping and the . . . waste of Instructors." The Corps School would continue to train platoon commanders and NCOs as drill and bayonet instructors. Divisional training centres (each centre organized in three battalions, one per brigade) would train NCOs and

Lewis gun, bombing and mortar instructors. All reinforcements would train at divisional training centres before joining their units. Mandatory subjects included drill, musketry, bayonet fighting, bombing, Lewis guns and all-arms cooperation within platoons. NCOs were trained in minor tactics, instruction of drill and bayonet fighting, and interior economy. The latter encompassed duties in trenches and billets, elementary military law, supply of rations and ammunition, keeping duty rosters and warning men for duty (because the Corps had the highest and worsening rate of absence in First Army).[81] Brigades and units would train specialists as required. Currie's strong proprietary interest in training is evident in his direction that henceforth Corps HQ would approve divisional plans for training their battalions. August 1917 saw the opening of a bombing and trench mortar school, a Lewis gun school and an infantry school (taking in the officers' school established in November 1916). In October a signals school joined. For the rest of the war courses ran continuously.[82]

As for divisional schools, the War Office had formally approved their establishment in October 1916. 1st Division opened its School of Instruction for junior infantry officers and selected NCOs on 19 November, and by the end of the month three courses were in progress. Subjects included tactics, map reading, musketry, field engineering, organization, military law and discipline and drill, plus lectures on various topics (for example, artillery support) by visiting officers. In fact, 1st Division had been running courses long before this formality. In April it had opened a divisional grenade and trench mortar school to which Stokes mortar batteries were attached for training.[83] Parent brigades had to supply additional instructors and staff because every infanteer had also to be trained in bombing and Lewis gunnery.[84]

The strong commitment to training is evident in the numbers of students. Figures for 1917 are most useful since during this year corps schools were fully running, with permanent facilities and staff and with policies and system mostly codified and uniform, even before *SS 152* came out in June. Canadian students at GHQ, Army, and Corps schools averaged 41 officers and 147 ORs per week. March–May was the low period (31 officers, 86 ORs), understandably since the Corps was heavily committed for much of the time (Vimy came in April). Late fall and early winter featured a significant increase in attendance per week (50 officers and 219 ORs). Not surprisingly, a disproportionate number of the students were officers; inevitably, as an officer became more senior, his school time increased. Overall, during 1917 1,255 officers and 4,434 ORs attended higher formation schools; in fact there were probably more, but figures for some weeks are not available and corps and division numbers differ.[85]

Figures for attendance at divisional training wings, including the brigade schools (often referred to as training depots), are not as complete. Records are annotated with "No Training-Moving" or "Special Training for Offensive Operations" opposite some weeks. Sometimes active operations closed one or all three brigade schools. Moving considerably inhibited training. From 18–25 July 1917, 1st Brigade did no training because of difficulty in finding a suitable school location. A week later it finally found a home but then had to repair it instead of train. 3rd Brigade's new school lacked accommodation, battle firing and rifle ranges, bombing facilities and trench systems. Travel to distant rifle ranges ate up training time. 2nd Brigade, however, found good facilities, allowing training to be in "full swing" almost immediately—including instruction on models of the German lines, which proved "very useful." After another divisional move in October the new locations had most of what was required, allowing all three brigade schools to resume training within a day or two.[86]

Brigade schools hosted impressive numbers of students:

1917	January–March 1918
1st Brigade,	**1st Brigade,**
231 officers, 8,684 ORs	147 officers, 2,558 ORs;
2nd Brigade,	**2nd Brigade,**
234 officers, 8,482 ORs	170 officers, 2,418 ORs;
3rd Brigade,	**3rd Brigade,**
317 officers, 9,839 ORs;	167 officers, 3,927 ORs
Total:	Total:
782 officers, 27,005 ORs.	484 officers, 8,903 ORs.

Numbers peak two or three weeks before the start of major operations and then taper off during and immediately after them. Passchendaele is a good example: during the week ending 10 October almost 2,500 students were at brigade schools, the figures then falling to less than half.

3rd Brigade topped the tally every week for the first three months of 1918 and for most of 1917, not because of any significant difference between the three brigades in number of days in reserve (at such times more men could attend training) or in number of casualties (the higher the casualties were the more reinforcements had to be trained) but most likely because of the priorities and preferences of the brigadiers.[87] Tuxford (3rd Brigade) and Griesbach (1st Brigade) stand out because of their demanding and hard-charging ways, traits they had exhibited in plenty as COs. Tuxford was especially rugged. It is not surprising to see in his training schedule for December 1916/January 1917 a reminder that "if battalions desire to work on Christmas Day instead of New Year's Day, care must be taken that the progressive programme . . . is strictly adhered to." They were exceeded in their devotion to training only by Macdonell, GOC 7th Brigade until June 1917 and then GOC 1st Division; throughout he was known as a relentless trainer. Hugh Dyer, who replaced Macdonell at 7th Brigade and had been Tuxford's 2IC earlier in the war, may have equalled Tuxford and Griesbach in their determination to make their commands the best they could be. Loomis (2nd Brigade) was perhaps the better all-rounder despite what may have been a lower enthusiasm for training. He took command of 3rd Division (*vice* Lipsett) in September 1918.[88]

Brigades, like divisions, conducted courses continuously long before brigade schools were authorized. In mid-1917 the GSO1 (Kearsley) warned brigades that the GOC intended to form brigade schools and that COs would have to rely on these "to turn out specialists to their satisfaction." As early as January 1917, brigade "Classes of Instruction" (*SS 152*'s phrase) had been doing just that. Each battalion had what was then called a "Battalion Training School" where reinforcements and returning casualties received refresher training under brigade supervision. What Kearsley wanted to know was

1. Shall a certain number of men from any number of platoons stay back when the Battalion is in the Line and in Support?

2. Shall untrained and partially trained men go straight to their platoon and complete platoons under their own N.C. O's and officer attend the School—thus keeping up the idea of the platoon being an independent Unit?

3. Length of Course?

4. The school should cease to exist as such when the Brigade is out of the Line, so that the whole Battalion can be under the Commanding Officer.[89]

The situation in No. 1 had been the norm for months, *SS 135* having set LOB policy. No. 2 was not put into effect; returning casualties would continue to receive refresher training on their way back to units. The length of the course depended on the particular weapon or skill. Although not a question, No. 4 was a direction that was not rigidly enforced since circumstances sometimes demanded that brigade schools remain open. Closing them offered two advantages: battalions retained a full slate of officers for training and the instructors were handy to give their parent units the maximum benefit of their expertise. Macdonell allowed his brigadiers to close brigade schools as they wished and to return the instructors to their battalions, but with one proviso: "keep . . . ten likely men per battalion in training for Lance

Corporals under . . . one good Instructor and one ditto Assistant Instructor." Divisional schools often closed for similar reasons.[90]

Reporting on his visit at this time to the brigade school, the BM of 3rd Brigade, Major Paul Villiers, noted the excellent work of its commandant, Major Dick Worrall, 14th Battalion, and his staff, and that the syllabi and administrative procedures formed a valuable resource "should the Brigade School system come into force." On the day of his visit 72 men graduated. Villiers laughed to hear that the men of this draft had been told in Britain that once at the front they would not have to shave or clean anything but they were "to be tough." Worrall was concerned about some shortages of training equipment because the "Brigade School [was] not a recognized unit."[91] Life became easier in July when brigade schools were approved. Thereafter all personnel in excess of battalion war establishment trained at the schools until required as reinforcements.[92] Over the summer the schools provided useful training on "miniature" trenches representing the German positions, on taped attack training grounds, again representing enemy positions, and on "Plasticine Relief Maps" of the enemy lines. Obtaining sufficient qualified instructors remained a serious problem, so much so that in October Tuxford directed COs to ask the COs of their reserve battalions in England to send 12 instructors in the next draft.[93] The shortage of instructors was never made good.

Another contentious aspect of training, depending on one's perspective, concerned the relationship between training and rest, a relationship that was always uneasy no matter what the colour of the uniform. Guidance on the training to do when units were at rest featured in the syllabus of the Canadian School for Infantry Officers at Bexhill and at the COs' Course at Aldershot where students were reminded that battalions should be trained "sensibly and in moderation," advice that was also passed on to platoon commanders at the Canadian Corps Officers' School in France. Reality was very different.[94] In February 1918 an Imperial officer, when told that his name had been put in for leave, wrote: "I am very doubtful about it as I fancy we shall be going to rest soon. Commanding officers are not supposed to take their leave whilst in rest, as 'rest' is always spelt 'intensive training.' What the men really want is to sit still and get themselves clean."[95] Across the line *Leutnant* Ernst Junger expressed a similar view in early July when he described duties as minimal, "not as it was in the early days, when the amount of training . . . during the days of rest almost passe[d] belief. Training ought to be like a prayer: short and earnest. Nothing is more mischievous than exaggeration."[96] One of the great irritations to a soldier, German, British or Canadian, was arms training despite his use of weapons every day in the line. For the enemy and for the BEF training filled the time of troops out of the line. Even the best troops were kept hard at it because commanders worried about them losing their edge. Commanders also took advantage of the natural relationship between training and discipline: as the one intensified, the other tightened. Training had always to prepare men to fill in for casualties.

Most commanders could not abide "idle hands." Tuxford, for example, said before Second Ypres: "It is a great mistake to imagine that troops when in reserve . . . indulge in pure relaxation. On the contrary, every effort is made to perfect the men's training . . . hard training. Route marching . . . bombing . . . practising the attack . . . all manner of schemes." Three summers later his brigade was training "hard and intensive . . . tactical schemes . . . embracing platoons, companies, battalions and brigades."[97] COs made training a priority. One hoped "for a proper rest soon—the battalion needs it badly—a chance to really train the men." One subaltern saw the Army's concept of rest as "stiff training all the morning and games in the afternoon." In mid-1917 Canadians "indulged in Corps Rest in . . . the centre of a tremendous training ground . . . There was much enforced idleness in the line but none at 'rest.'"[98] Only the most naive could miss the real purpose of going into rest. When the 5th Battalion went into reserve in August 1917 Private Russell remarked that "from the training it seemed something more arduous was soon to be undertaken." Typically, the men referred to "rest" as "being fatted for the slaughter."[99]

Hard, constant training was not just personal preference. It was GHQ and Army policy, Canadian Corps policy and 1st Division policy. When the all-arms platoon came into being only hard training could get it performing effectively. Every training syllabus of units in reserve emphasized platoon training. In May 1917 Macdonell directed that it be intensive but that the men should have two or three days' rest before it commenced. Griesbach ordered COs to remind company commanders that they had to ensure platoon commanders were attentive to their duties, including the planning and conduct of platoon training but they were not to do the work for platoon commanders, who had to be permitted to make and correct mistakes. On 10 May Byng advised First Army that "the training being carried out by 1st Canadian Division is entirely Platoon and Company training. Reinforcements are being brought in and allotted to their Platoons, which are then being trained as complete units." Clearly, the focus at the most senior levels when it came to training was on the platoon.[100]

In August another of Macdonell's typically direct, homely training directives concentrated on the platoon: "Training will be vigorously carried out, and as all work and no play makes Jack a dull boy, pains will be taken to have . . . games, competitions and recreations." Nothing must interfere with training, he said. Platoon commanders had to instruct their platoons themselves, mastering the material under supervision of company commanders out of hours. As only he could, Macdonell included a decisive maxim: "Officers and N.C.O's must be kept up to a high standard and made to pluck the beam out of their own eye before they undertake to remove the mote out of their subordinate's eye."[101]

This chapter, in describing the policy and system that drove training in divisions and corps, Imperial and Dominion, has laid the foundation for further examination of the training problem. While the danger of overtraining did not go unrecognized (it could seriously affect morale), few, if any, commanders risked having troops less ready than it was possible to make them; Louis Lipsett, for example, considered rest "merely as a change of work from trench warfare to training, for there can be no real repose . . . until . . . the defeat of the enemy . . . To effect this . . . the fighting efficiency of all arms [must] be raised to as high a standard as possible."[102] A recruiting poster said it even better:

What in the end will settle this war?
TRAINED MEN
It is *Your Duty* to become ONE.[103]

This being so, the subject turns to what had to be learned and how that was achieved.

Notes to Chapter Seven

1. Quoted in Ashworth, *Trench Warfare 1914–1918*, p. 178.
2. Both manuals were small (100 mm X 125 mm or 4 x 5 inches), maroon cloth-covered books that could be carried conveniently in a pocket.
3. Corelli Barnett, *Britain and Her Army, 1509–1970: A Military, Political and Social Survey* (London: Penguin, 1970), p. 379.
4. *Notes for Commanding Officers* was issued to students by name, instead of on the usual basis of "Oh, just grab a copy." This shows its importance.
5. A.G.S. Enser, *A Subject Bibliography of the First World War Books in English 1914–1978* (London: Andre Deutsch, 1979), p. 284.
6. John Baynes, *Far from a Donkey: The Life of General Sir Ivor Maxse* (London: Brassey's, 1995), p. 136; Critchley, *Critch!*, p. 70, quotes Byng; LAC, RG9IIIC1, Vol. 4854, Folder 71, File 7, Corps to Second Army, 20 November 1917; MG 30E100 (Currie Papers), Vol. 1, Currie to H.C. Brewster, Premier of B.C., 31 May 1917; RG9IIIC3, Vol. 4037, Folder 2, File 5, Allan to company commanders, 27 November 1915.
7. LAC, MG 30E100 (Currie Papers), Vol. 15, Folder 43, letter to Charles Vining, 2 April 1927.
8. *Infantry Training (4-Company Organization), 1914*, pp. 1–2.
9. Baynes, *Far from a Donkey*, p. 150.
10. Samuels, *Command or Control?*, p. 120; *Army Council Instruction. No. 1968* (London: War Office, 6 August 1916), p. 2. After the Somme the course for infantry recruits over

the age of 18 years and eight months was reduced from six months to 14 weeks.

11. Pitt, "Writers and the Great War," p. 247; LAC, RG 41, CBC interview, Colonel D.H.C. Mason.

12. LAC, RG9IIIC1, Vol. 3859, Folder 85, File 2, Lipsett to Corps, 30 November 1917.

13. LAC, RG9IIIC3, Vol. 4032, Folder 28, File 1, 30 October 1918; Brig.-Gen. R.C.B. Haking, *Company Training* (London: Hugh Rees Limited, 1915), p. 1. Haking's book has an originality and freshness that make it a worthwhile read even today.

14. Charles Douie, *The Weary Road: Recollections of a Subaltern of Infantry* (Stevenage, Herts.: Strong Oak Press Ltd., 1988), p. 74.

15. Hamilton, *The Commander*, p. 2.

16. Curry, *From the St. Lawrence to the Yser*, p. 155, is referring to the CDS series *Notes from the Front* and probably *Notes on Field Defences* issued throughout 1915.

17. Imperial War Museum, IWM 86/53/1, Memoirs of W. Kerr, 5th Battalion, pp. 73–74.

18. Morton, *When Your Number's Up*, p. 91; LAC, Brigade War Diary, February 1917.

19. LAC, RG41, CBC interview.

20. LAC, RG9IIIC1, Vol. 3879, Folder 113, File 3; MG30E46 (Turner Papers), Vol. 8, Folder 49.

21. Tuxford, "The Great War as I Saw It," p. 149. Tuxford returned to France in March as GOC 3rd Brigade, which command he held until the Armistice.

22. Griesbach was not referring to Royal Engineers (RE) or Canadian Engineers(CE). *FSR* in 1914 had not precisely said which arm was to do what when it came to preparation of field defences but the tenor was that sappers did all field engineering except simple digging. By the time of his visit, and in fact long before that, it had become apparent that sapper resources were so limited that the infantry had to do most of the wiring. Consequently, infanteers had to be trained in that task, and the standard expected of them is outlined in Chapter Eight of this book.

23. LAC, RG9IIIC3, Vol. 4031, Folder 26, File 7, Griesbach to Macdonell, 15 July 1917; 2 October 1917.

24. LAC, RG9IIIC1, Vol. 3842, Folder 43, File 9, 23 August 1916; RG9IIIC3, Vol. 4026, Folder 11, File 3, Findings of Board of Inquiry, October 1916.

25. LAC, RG9IIID3, 3rd Brigade War Diary, 12 June 1918; MG 30E100 (Currie Papers), Vol. 2, General Correspondence (S–Z), 27 June 1918.

26. *Infantry Training (4-Company Organization), 1914*, pp. 3–4.

27. LAC, RG9IIIC1, Vol. 3827, Folder 6, File 1, Record of C-in-C Conferences, Corps G Staff conference record, 19 February 1916. Haig's remarks may be the basis of the post-war notion that the division had replaced the battalion as the basic "unit." (See John Terraine, "The Texture of the Somme, 1916," *History Today* (October 1976): p. 561).

28. Dominick Graham, "*Sans* Doctrine: British Army Tactics in the First World War," in Timothy Travers and Christon Archer, eds., *Men at War: Politics, Technology and Innovation in the Twentieth Century* (Chicago: Precedent, 1982), p. 82.

29. *SS 152*, p. 4.

30. LAC, RG9IIIC3, Vol. 4037, Folder 2, File 5, Major W.D. Allan to OCs, 27 November 1915; Gillon, *The Story of the 29th Division*, pp. 99–100. The GOC the 29th estimated that officer wastage averaged 100 percent every six months. This statistic made the old system whereby the CO was totally responsible for training of officers obsolete. The figure for 1st Division may have been higher or lower (accurate figures are not possible) but officer casualties were certainly high and probably comparable.

31. LAC, RG9IIIC3, Vol. 4007, Folder 4, File 4, Record of GOC Conference, 3 November

1915; Vol. 4010, Folder 14, File 14, 1st Division memorandum, 11 August 1917. 2ICs were responsible for unit administration: transport, rations, quarters, sanitation, Officers' Mess, postal services, band, ordnance, salvage and claims. Vol. 4032, Folder 28, File 1, Macdonell to units, 26 October 1918.

32. Fraser, *In Good Company*, pp. 213–15.
33. Travers, "Learning and Decision-Making on the Western Front," p. 95. Kentish, GOC 76th (Imperial) Brigade, became the Commandant of the Senior Officers School at Aldershot early in 1918.
34. Miles, *2nd July 1916 to the End of the Battles of the Somme*, p. 571.
35. Travers, "Learning and Decision-Making on the Western Front," p. 96.
36. Some Imperial corps commanders, Maxse, for example, had a deep interest in training. His interest and strong personality made him active in anything in which his corps was involved. Divisions joining his corps rapidly became aware of his firm commitment to training.
37. LAC, RG9IIIC1, Vol. 3827, records of Army, corps and divisional conferences, 1915–1917; RG9IIIC3, Vols. 4007 and 4046, "Conferences of Corps Commander, Divisional Commanders and Senior Officers, November 1915–February 1918."
38. Baldwin, *Holding the Line*, pp. 128–29.
39. LAC, RG41, H. Campbell, CBC radio program *Flanders' Fields*, No. 4, "Baptism of Fire," p. 12; G.W. Twigg, *Flanders' Fields*, No. 5, "The Second Battle of Ypres," p. 14; H.C. Brewer, *Flanders Fields*, No. 6, "A World of Stealth," p. 3; Birchall is quoted in Critchley, *Critch*, p. 54. Birchall wrote *Rapid Training of a Company for War* (Gale and Polden Ltd), a manual reprinted three times in early 1915.
40. Wallace, *From Montreal to Vimy Ridge and Beyond*, p. 214.
41. LAC, MG30E75 (Urquhart Papers), Vol. 2, File 3, 9 December. We can only guess as to what extent Currie realized that little or nothing could be expected from Carson.
42. Feilding, *War Letters to a Wife*, pp. 63, 66, 114; Lieut.-Col. J. Shakespear, *The Thirty-Fourth Division, 1915–1919* (London: H.F. & G. Witherby, 1921), p. 20.
43. Dancocks, *Gallant Canadians*, p. 44.
44. Ibid., p. 59.
45. LAC, 3rd Brigade War Diary, 5 December. 2nd Brigade's War Diary for December 1916 and January 1917 is full of complaints about the poor state of training of drafts.
46. Fraser, *In Good Company*, pp. viii–ix.
47. Greenhous and Harris, *Canada and the Battle of Vimy Ridge*, p. 36.
48. Fraser, *In Good Company*, p. 127.
49. *Training in Canadian Reserve Battalions*, January and October 1917. *ACI No. 1968* is included in full in the January edition. *ACI No. 1230* is included (extracts on recruit training only) in the October edition. The full text was published at the War Office in August 1917. Having set up the testing, *ACI No. 1230* then did some backsliding: failures would not be retained for remedial training but would proceed overseas as "special" drafts, presumably on the theory that training establishments in France would cure their shortcomings. Inevitably, some ended up being trained at units, which would not have pleased COs. Still, *ACI No. 1230* was a step in the right direction.
50. *SS 143 Instructions for Training Platoons for Offensive Action* (February 1917). *Notes for Commanding Officers* (1917) was also based on the new platoon organization.
51. *Training in Canadian Reserve Battalions*, January and October 1917 editions, Appendix 1.
52. Maj.-Gen. Sir Ernest Swinton, "The Bull Ring at Etaples," *Twenty Years After*, Supple-

mentary Volume, Part 16, Chapter XXXIII, p. 555. Graves, *Goodbye to All That*, p. 161.

53. Pedley, *Only This: A War Retrospect*, p. 19.

54. LAC, RG9IIIC1, Vol. 3870, Folder 112, Files 13 and 14, "Notes on the Training of Reinforcements at the Basic Training Camps," 18 October; Reid to BGGS, 16 June 1917 and to COs, 27 June. No. 1 Canadian Infantry Base Depot was established in 1915. LAC, MG30E100 (Currie Papers), Vol. 43, "Canadian War Establishments," p. 20.

55. Murray, *History of the 2nd Canadian Battalion*, p. 146.

56. LAC, RG9IIIC3, Vol. 4008, Folder 7, Files 4 and 5; Vol. 4031, Folder 27, File 2.

57. LAC, RG9IIIC1, Vol. 3870, Folder 112, File 14; *SS 152*, p. 7; *SS 135*, p. 58.

58. LAC, RG 41, CBC interview with Colonel H.S. Cooper.

59. LAC, MG30E100 (Currie Papers), Vol. 43, "Canadian War Establishments," p. 9. By August 1916 each Canadian division had an entrenching battalion (26 officers and 1,203 ORs). Of these, only four officers and 19 ORs were permanently on strength. While these battalions dug trenches and performed other manual labour, they functioned primarily as holding units for reinforcements going to line battalions. Private Wallace Carroll, 15th Battalion, who served in 1st Division's entrenching battalion before Hill 70 (August 1917), called it a "Navvy [or] pick and shovel battalion" that also provided reinforcements when necessary. During his time there the battalion had men on its rolls from all 16 battalions of the division, which makes sense since the battalion supplied men to all 16 (RG 41, Vol. 9). Fielding, *War Letters to a Wife*, p. 11, called an entrenching battalion "a kind of advanced depot—a stepping stone to the trenches" where new officers and soldiers could get accustomed to the sounds of war before joining fighting battalions.

60. LAC, RG9IIIC3, Vol. 4008, Folder 7, Files 4 and 5; Vol. 4031, Folder 27, File 2, HQ Canadian Corps to 1st Division, 5 September and 23 November 1917; GHQ to First Army 15 July 1918 and subsequently to Canadian Corps, 19 July. The figure of 100 men per infantry and pioneer battalion (5,200 infantry reinforcements all told) was based on calculations showing the 1917 "wastage % per month" at 10 percent for the infantry. Such calculations are a sad but necessary aspect of ensuring a timely sufficiency of reinforcements. The figures are from LAC, MG30E100 (Currie Papers), Vol. 43, "Canadian Corps Reinforcement Camp." Most of the documents pertaining to reinforcements were issued over the signature block of Major Wilfred Bovey, Deputy Assistant Adjutant General of the Canadian Corps. They provide a clear and concise statement of the reinforcement problem and a thorough and comprehensive description of how the new system was to work. The detailed document (22 foolscap pages) entitled "Canadian Corps Reinforcement Camp" epitomizes good SD. Bovey assesses the attributes of an efficient reinforcement system (speed of replacement, training, control of personnel, accuracy of records and realistic calculation of losses) and then traces the flow of reinforcements from England to France, through base depots to the camp and on to units. One comes away from these documents knowing how the system worked and feeling comfortable with it. In March 1916 1st Canadian Pioneer Battalion (30 officers and 980 ORs) joined 1st Division. The purpose of pioneer battalions was "to strengthen the Engineering Branch," and their tasks were digging or deepening trenches, burying signals cable, maintaining narrow gauge railways and constructing deep dugouts (Major W. Tait White, *1st Canadian Pioneers, C.E.F.: Brief History of the Battalion, France and Flanders, 1916–1918* [Calgary: 1st Pioneer's Association, 1938], pp. 1, 12). Because they were not trained engineers, pioneers required engineer supervision. Division commanders tended to consider them as

infantry first, pioneers second. In December 1916 the 1st Pioneer Battalion was replaced by the 107th Pioneer Battalion. All pioneer units were absorbed by the new engineer brigades in May 1918 (LAC, MG30E100 [Currie Papers], Vol. 43, "Canadian War Establishments," p. 9; Cave, "The Canadian Corps Order of Battle, pp. 9–12).

61. Nicholson, *Behind the Lines*, p. 198; Edmonds [Carrington], *A Subaltern's War*, p. 128.

62. Edmonds and Wynne, *Battle of Neuve Chapelle: Battles of Ypres*, pp 11–12. Bombing schools also existed at divisional level (see Nicholson, *Behind the Lines*, p. 198) and at brigade level (see LAC, 1st Division A & Q War Diary, entry for 30 April 1916). Ashworth, *Trench Warfare 1914–1918*, p. 69, says they also existed at Army level in some Armies. Nicholson, *Behind the Lines*, p. 196. Those who ate Army cooking must have wondered why a cookery school was necessary, for all they ever got was stew.

63. Adams, *Nothing of Importance*, pp. 73–84.

64. *SS 152*, p. 4. Canadian documents generally refer to divisional "training centres" rather than "classes of instruction." See LAC, RG9IIIC1, Vol. 3868, Folder 109, File 10, Canadian Corps to division 2 July 1917.

65. Edmund Blunden, *Undertones of War* (Harmondsworth, Middlesex: Penguin Books, 1982), p. 232; Sheldon-Williams, *The Canadian Front in France and Flanders*, p. 62; Military Advisory Board, *Canada in the Great World War: An Authentic Account of the Military History of Canada from the Earliest Days to the Close of the War of the Nations,*. Vol. IV, *The Turn of the Tide* (Toronto: United Publishers of Canada Limited, 1920), p. 104; Carrington, *Soldier from the Wars Returning*, p. 126.

66. Military Advisory Board, *Guarding the Channel Ports*, p. 211; Sheldon-Williams, *The Canadian Front in France and Flanders*, pp. 62–64.

67. Critchley, *Critch!*, pp. 74–75.

68. Griffith, *Battle Tactics of the Western Front*, p. 191.

69. Shakespear, *The Thirty-Fourth Division 1915–1919*, p. 75.

70. *SS 152* (Appendix XV) estimated annual output of instructors per battalion from schools in France as follows: Army Schools, 29; and Corps schools, 129.

71. LAC, MG 30E100 (Currie Papers),Vol. 43, "Canadian War Establishments," p. 21. Italics by author.

72. LAC, RG9IIIC1, Vol. 3870, Folder 112, File 6, Corps to First Army, 26 February 1917.

73. Ibid., 1st Division response, 25 February. *SS 143 The Training and Employment of Platoons* was published in February, and was just one of the indications that the platoon and the platoon commander were becoming *the* focus.

74. LAC, RG9IIIC3, Vol. 4046, Folder 4, File 2, "Summary of Subjects Discussed," March 1917; Vol. 4064, Folder 15, File 3, First Army "Schools of Instruction," March 1917; Vol. 4058, Folder 37, File 5, GHQ to First Army, 7 September 1917. GHQ senior and junior staff courses were held at Hesdin, France. *SS 152*, p. 5, lists GHQ schools.

75. LAC, RG9IIIC3, Vol. 4058, Folder 37, File 5, July 1917; *SS 152*, Appendix I.

76. *SS 152*, pp. 5–7. Training syllabi for each Army and Corps school are in Appendices I–XII.

77. LAC, RG9IIIC3, Vol. 4031, Folder 26, File 8, corps to 1st Division, 17 January 1918.

78. LAC, RG9IIIC1, Vol. 3870, Folder 113, File 3, Corps to Second Army, 11 July, 22 and 31 October 1916; Corps General Staff War Diary, July 1916, Appendix 1/4; Critchley, *Critch!*, pp. 68, 72.

79. MG30E100 (Currie Papers), Vol. 43, 1–31 January 1917.

80. LAC, RG9IIIC3, Vol. 4024, Folder 4, File 9, Currie to brigades and units, 16 July 1916; Vol. 4079, Folder 8, File 6, 21 July. For the background to Harington's remarks see

Chapter Four herein.
81. LAC, RG9IIIC1, Vol. 3868, Folder 109, File 10, corps to divisions and corps school, 2 July 1917; RG9IIIC3, Vol. 4047, Folder 6, File 1, 1st Division to 2nd Brigade, 21 July.
82. LAC, MG30E100 (Currie Papers), Vol. 43 "Canadian War Establishments"; RG9IIIC3, Vol. 4031, Folder 26, File 8, Canadian Corps to 1st Division, list of available courses, 17 January 1918.
83. LAC, RG9IIIC1, Vol. 3870, Folder 113, File 3, First Army to Canadian Corps, 22 October 1916; 3rd Brigade War Diary, entries for 19 and 26 November 1916; 1st Division A & Q War Diary, entry for 30 April 1916; MG30E100 (Currie Papers), Vol. 43. The importance of the school for junior Officers is evident in the fact that its commandant was a lieutenant-colonel.
84. LAC, RG9IIIC1, Vol. 3870, Folder 113, File 3, First Army to Canadian Corps 22 October 1916; Corps to divisions 31 October; Vol. 3868, Folder 109, File 10, Canadian Corps to divisions and Corps School, 2 July 1917; 3rd Brigade War Diary, June 1917, Appendix 30, "Policy Regarding The Divisional School."
85. LAC, RG9IIIC1, Vol. 3860, Folder 87, File 1, "Weekly Summaries of Operations." weekly summaries were started in September 1915. From March 1916 they included training, simply as "Battalions Training" or "Brigades Training." By late 1916 the summaries were specific, showing schools and numbers training by brigade (and sometimes by battalion). The statistics are based on 35 weekly reports for the year.
86. LAC, 1st Division General Staff War Diary for October 1917, "Infantry Brigade Training Schools"; RG9IIIC1, Vol. 3860, Folder 89, File 1. Such difficulties obtaining facilities resulted in requests that schools be assigned permanent homes and that corps ensure availability of suitable training areas before divisions went into reserve. This became a responsibility of the GSO2 (Training) at corps HQ.
87. LAC RG9IIIC1, Vol. 3860, Folder 89, File 2; 1st Division General Staff War Diary for 1917.
88. Tuxford, "The Great War as I Saw It," pp. 331–32. 1st Brigade War Diary, 16 June 1918; 3rd Brigade War Diary, Appendix 16, June 1918. Loomis had replaced Louis Lipsett at 2nd Brigade in June 1916 when Lipsett was promoted to command 3rd Division. Dan Ormond (10th Battalion) was similar in style to Tuxford, Griesbach and Dyer but he was not commanding a brigade in 1917.
89. LAC, 3rd Brigade War Diary, June 1917, Appendix 30; Murray, *History of the 2nd Canadian Battalion*, pp. 152–53; Goodspeed, *Battle Royal*, p. 171.
90. *SS 135*, p. 58; Imperial War Museum, 76/70/1, memoirs of Private E.W. Russell, 5th Battalion, p. 20; LAC, RG9IIIC3, Vol. 4064, Folder 15, File 3, Macdonell to brigades, "General Instructions Regarding Training While at Rest," 21 August 1917; RG9IIIC1, Folder 109, File 3, 1st Division to brigades, 12 December 1916.
91. LAC, 3rd Brigade War Diary, Appendix 31, June 1917, Report of Visit of BM.
92. LAC, 1st Division A & Q War Diary, entry for 2 July 1917.
93. LAC, 2nd Brigade War Diary, July 1917; 3rd Brigade War Diary, October 1917.
94. LAC, 1st Division A & Q War Diary, 11 December 1917. Lieutenant-Colonel A.C. Critchley assumed command of the school at Bexhill (near Hastings in Surrey) when it opened in early 1917. The Machine-Gun School at Seaford and the schools for artillery officers at Witley and Bordon also opened in 1917. For Critchley's time at Bexhill see *Critch!*, pp. 60–79. LAC, RG9IIIC3, Vol. 4079, Folder 8, File 6, Canadian Corps Officers' School, "Training for Battalions When Resting Out of the Line."; *Notes for Commanding Officers*, 1917 and 1918 editions, pp. 373 and 399 respectively,

"Some of the Things That Please an Infantry Brigadier."
95. Hamilton, *The War Diary of the Master of Belhaven*, p. 458.
96. Ernest Junger, *Copse 125*, trans. Basil Creighton (London: Chatto and Windus, 1930; reprint, n.p. Zimmermann and Zimmermann, 1985), p. 78.
97. Tuxford, "The Great War as I Saw It," pp. 69, 331.
98. Fraser, *In Good Company*, p. 111; Edmonds, *A Subaltern's War*, p. 26; Sheldon-Williams, *The Canadian Front in France and Flanders*, p. 59.
99. IWM 76/170/1, Russell memoirs, p. 15; Edward Fraser and John Gibbons, *Soldier and Sailor Words and Phrases* (London: George Routledge and Sons, Ltd., 1925), p. 92.
100. LAC, RG9IIIC1, Vol. 3868, Folder 109, File 3.
101. LAC, RG9IIIC3, Vol. 4031, Folder 26, File 7, "General Instructions Regarding Training Whilst at Rest"; Matthew 7:3, "And why beholdest thou the mote that is in thy brother's eye but considerest not the beam that is in thine own eye?"
102. LAC, RG9IIIC1, Vol. 3868, Folder 109, File 3, 24 June 1916.
103. Philip Orr, *The Road to the Somme: Men of the Ulster Division Tell Their Story* (Belfast: The Blackstaff Press, 1987), p. 40.

CHAPTER EIGHT

Training: Content and Conduct

An officer's first duty is, and always has been so to train the private soldiers under his command that they may, without question, beat any force opposed to them in the field.
—ARTHUR WELLESLEY, DUKE OF WELLINGTON

A commander's personality and qualities decisively shape the performance of his command. When it comes to training, he aims to produce a unit or formation fit in every respect to fight. *Notes for Commanding Officers*, 1918 edition, said nothing new in declaring that fighting efficiency depended almost entirely upon the quality of training. This had been a fact long before then and long before a senior staff officer said, "We have to win this war and we must win it by training."[1] For senior commanders and staffs, training included handling masses of men and material as well as preparing and conducting operations. For them and for all officers and men, training gave the knowledge and confidence that enabled them to become professional, rather than remaining amateur, in the exercise of their responsibilities. This also applied to their commands, be they unit, brigade or division.

This chapter makes several important observations on training, which set the scene for discussion of the content and conduct of divisional, individual and collective training. It aims to show that training, like staff work and command and control, reflected consistent professionalization and improvement, and enhanced divisional performance. Training in the 1st Division became increasingly realistic, progressive and dynamic; it was also deliberately made hard. Many commanders, while they did not express it in such terms, had a personal philosophy that training hard made actual operations easier and enabled the troops to stand up to anything. The chapter concludes with a wrap-up of both chapters on training.

An officer of any rank who is a bad trainer is a disgrace. On the other hand, men ignorant of their duties cannot be effective, even if led by the best of officers. Anyone, officer or other rank, who is to train others and is indifferent to training is suicidal. Clearly, each should know how to teach. During the first half of the war almost no guidance existed on teaching. *Field Service Regulations* focussed on leading troops, not training them. Despite its title, *SS 135 Instructions for the Training of Divisions for Offensive Action* taught only fighting. *Training in Canadian Reserve Battalions* detailed *what* to teach rather than *how*, as did *SS 152 Instructions for the Training of the British Armies in France*. Not until 1917 did publications devoted to training appear: *Notes for Commanding Officers* and *SS 143 Instructions for the Training of Platoons for Offensive Action, 1917*.

It would be difficult to refute Field-Marshal Montgomery's conviction that "training is a great art," and equally insensible to refuse Robert Browning's idea that "art's long, though time is short." Currie agreed: "Training in earnest . . . We need it very badly and training time is all too short."[2] A lecture in early 1915 recommended that officers and NCOs conducting a lesson or exercise should

> take it step by step. Do not leave any exercise until you have got the whole Company to carry it out correctly and *intelligently*. The successful Company trainer is the one who brings his whole section, half-Company and Company up to a certain mark of proficiency— not the one who has twenty very sharp men and eighty dull half-trained men.[3]

This ideal came up hard against the usual reality: "It is probable that the Canadian Corps will only be out of the line for a short period."[4] Commanding Officers yearned for four to six weeks for training, which would make for a splendid battalion, "but otherwise one must just rub along."[5] A myriad of things interfered: active operations, moving, preparing for moving and work parties. Even when there was time, circumstances often inhibited training. Commenting on "Battle Practise" in July 1917, Paul Villiers, BM of 3rd Brigade, observed, "Owing to the fact that the Training Course is under Hostile Observation, not more than one battalion at a time can practise." On the final day Tuxford took the risk, and his entire brigade did the course.[6] Despite this and other difficulties, more training was done that month than in several previous months. During one 30-day period the previous autumn 3rd Brigade had had only five training days and during three of them it had had to provide 2,750 men, more than half its strength, for working parties.[7] Admittedly, this was a "worst case." At times formations got three or four solid training weeks, usually when in corps reserve but, nevertheless, Currie's point about too little time remains valid.

Many work parties involved assisting sappers, a task so despised that Sergeant William Curtis of 2nd Battalion said he "would rather be in the front line all the time . . . You work all of the time when in reserve and that gets on the nerves." As 8th Battalion's second commandment expressed it, "remember that thou workest on the Sabbath . . . Six days shalt thou labour and do more than thou oughtest . . . but the seventh day is the day of the C.R.E., on it thou shalt do all manner of work." Infantry work parties began to refer to the sapper as "Boss" and to themselves as "goats." The debilitating effect of work parties and hard training when out of the line at "rest" became the subject of a popular marching song:

> *Nobody knows how tired we are,*
> *Tired we are,*
> *Tired we are,*
> *Nobody knows how tired we are,*
> *And nobody seems to care.*

As much as possible, commanders and staff tried to minimize work party demands but when this was unavoidable they tried to ensure a fair division of the labour; they had mixed success, as the song indicates. No doubt, labour negatively affected 1st Division but this was true of every division. Fighting and work were the infantry's lot. In 1st Division, officers were asked to lead in fighting and in work, too: "Young officers need not be afraid or ashamed of taking off their coats and setting an example to their men." Sometimes, when major ventures loomed, such as Vimy, training received priority over work. In January 1917 1st Division excused battalions in reserve from all working parties. 2nd Brigade, taking Currie at his word, scheduled comprehensive training for not only its reserve battalion but for brigade HQ, its machine-gun company and its trench mortar battery. Each battalion, upon going into reserve, trained for five and one-half days at bombing, range work, anti-gas drills, first aid and tactical exercises. Nothing was allowed to interfere. A battalion exercise filled the last half of day six, after which the troops prepared to return to the line.[8]

The teaching of tactics was particularly difficult and contentious. Before 1914 they were considered far less important than basic infantry skills. Cohesion and discipline, the keys to success, did not come from tactics. Field-Marshal Wavell, a BM in the Great War, thought that men who had not held command attributed too much importance to tactics.[9] Considerable truth abides in this. Tactical *sense* is the hardest of all things to impart to young officers and NCOs. The teaching of tactics often came down to teaching tactical drills on a blackboard or as set-piece demonstrations. These alone do not ensure comprehension. Tactics was best learned in genuine situations where someone in a different uniform was shooting ball, not blank at you. Another officer thought, "Active service at a quiescent period . . . the best training ground for battle." In some things, even actual battle could not ensure the best tactics. No matter how much "Don't bunch up!" was stressed in training, green troops in action did exactly that. Sergeant Raymond Chandler of the 7th Battalion recalled, "If you had to go over the top . . . all you seemed to think of was trying to keep the men spaced, in order to reduce casualties . . . It's only human to want to bunch . . . in face of heavy fire."[10] Death loves a crowd!

Training was also eternal: "Military education never ended and the troops who went over the top on 1 July [1916] were very different from the greenhorns [of] a year earlier."[11] All ranks learned and trained in response to actual or perceived shortcomings, to what the enemy did, and how he did it. His weapons, tactics and organization drove training to considerable extent and only he could teach certain skills, such as taking cover. Officers and men had also to be trained to perform the duties of a higher rank. Casualties and too little time for training meant that units usually soldiered on only half (or less) trained. After 2nd Battalion was "virtually destroyed" at Second Ypres it received many reinforcements "untrained in every way."[12] It had then to revert to individual training, putting collective training in abeyance. Every rebuilding entailed loss of expertise, every "hand-over" saw some wisdom disappear. Consequently, even the finest of formations reached a point where efficiency began to decline. If you keep squeezing an orange soon all the juice is gone. Had "The Hundred Days" in 1918 lasted beyond that, 1st Division, as good as it was, would have felt the sting of diminishing capability, just as Imperial Regular divisions became "flogged out" in 1916.[13]

Finally, no matter how well planned it was, training narrowed and became repetitive. The system—explain, demonstrate, exercise—gave it a fearful symmetry. A second part of the tiger was Army insistence on having all things *pukka*: "smartening-up drill," "spit and polish," and some degree, in modern terminology, of "chicken shit." "New drafts pretend an ignorance," said Macdonell, "that in many instances is merely 'Swinging the Lead' . . . We cannot afford to let them smirch the 'Old Red Patch.' They . . . glory in slouching around with dirty buttons, coats open, caps on the back of their head."[14] Down at the "smartening-up" end one subaltern described his part: "You have to play the game . . . Spit and polish is the word . . . for the good of the service." He observed, as the days went by, platoons becoming smarter and cleaner.[15] Perhaps they realized that while a particular practise might well be "bull," each practise built toward a common will and cohesion.

SS 152 proclaimed individual training "the keynote of efficiency" because it prepared each man to do his duties in war.[16] It began with recruit training which was reduced to 14 weeks, making a gradual decline in the standard inevitable. Two weeks of preliminaries "to accustom the recruit to military training" consisted of 12 hours each of drill, marching and physical training and 36 hours of anti-gas training, care of arms and equipment, and miscellaneous lectures. The remaining 12 weeks provided 553 hours of training, the big six subjects being musketry (155 hours), drill (96 hours), entrenching, wire, field work and route marching (87 hours), physical training and marching (75 hours), bayonet fighting (54 hours) and bombing (35 hours).[17] Each subject, plus anti-gas drills, occupied a chapter in *Training in Canadian Reserve Battalions* (January 1917 edition), wherein instructors learned the object and stages of the training, the standard to be achieved and the references to consult. Most chapters included a detailed syllabus of courses for instructors before they commenced instructing. *Notes to Assist Company Officers in Preparing Lectures for the Training of Category "A" Infantry Recruits* also provided useful guidance, although more on content than on conduct of training.[18]

The October edition of *Training in Canadian Reserve Battalions* included *Army Council Instruction (ACI) No. 1230*, which set the total hours of instruction for recruits at 608, down 17 hours from the superseded *ACI No. 1968*. The top five subjects were as above and bombing fell to a three-way tie for seventh place (12 hours), its spot taken by rifle bombing or Lewis gunnery at 24 hours (half the recruits were trained on one and half on the other). These changes reflected the experience of the front and the new platoon doctrine of early 1917. Sections on rifle handling and Lewis gunnery had been added so that training would conform to *SS 143 Instructions for the Training of Platoons for Offensive Action, 1917*. Testing in basic skills also became mandatory.[19] Despite the number of hours spent on musketry, musketry skills declined due to shortened recruit training, trench warfare and specialization. Colonel Ronnie Campbell's bayonet fighting "Circus," which toured the BEF before the Somme and staged dramatic exercises emphasizing the "Spirit of the Bayonet," had not done the rifle any good either. Many officers were aghast at training that treated the rifle as nothing more than a handle for a bayonet. To A.A. Hanbury-Sparrow, any officer who had his men sticking bayonets into training dummies was either lazy or incompetent. He went round urging subalterns to leave off:

'The enemy are shooting at you from that hill with a machine gun. Do something about it.' A pause. Then, 'You've already lost half your platoon whilst you've been making up your mind.' 'Now you've lost the whole of it and you're dead too, simply because you will waste your time with this nonsense instead of practising tactics.'[20]

After the Somme the rifle reasserted its dominance. Commanders began telling their men of the superb musketry skills of the "old Regular Army," but they knew better than to expect that standard since men of the new Army, seeing a German 300 yards away, would be wanting to throw a bomb at him! Practical advice on musketry training urged simplifying it as much as possible by shortening the pre- and early-war firing practises of grouping, application, snap-shooting and rapid fire: "Don't try to do 15 rounds per minute . . . The average man will never be good enough . . . It takes time to make a really good rapid shot." Of the four practises, the most valuable was grouping since it permitted instructors to see most readily where the shooter had gone wrong, if he had. Grouping was also the simplest practise to run and was done at 50 or 100 yards distance, which was half the length of the range required for application—a prime consideration in view of the difficulty in France of finding suitable ranges.[21]

Range work improved greatly after the publication of *SS 143*, the "best guide," according to *SS 152*. In fact, *SS 143* was the first really practical infantry guide. In September 1917 the General Staff also issued *SS 185 Assault Training*, parts of which had been in use since March. At that time 1st Division had strongly recommended one particular "Individual Assault Practise" because it made every man realize that "he must be trained to use his three weapons equally well, i.e., rifle, bomb and bayonet."[22] *SS 185* included several similar exercises, plus a collective exercise designed for platoons, all far superior to exercises in *SS 152* (January 1917) and in *Training in Canadian Reserve Battalions* (October 1917). By any yardstick, they were imaginative, interesting and challenging for platoons. "Notes on Carrying Out This Exercise" (the collective one) aimed to prevent this "practical fighting" exercise degenerating into simple range firing practise. No doubt, *SS 143* and *SS 185* pleased the GOsC 1st and 2nd Divisions. The latter commander had wanted two days out of every week in reserve spent on musketry. The former had urged that less time be spent on rifle mechanism and more on rapid loading and firing.[23] *SS 185*, in particular, shows how far training had come since 1915 when "2nd Lts . . . dug no trenches, handled no bombs, thought of the company, not of the platoon, still less of the section, as the smallest independent tactical unit."[24]

Specialists were another category of individual to be trained. Chapter Three examined their impact on fighting strength. Over-specialization revealed itself in over-organization and complicated doctrine and training, one of the best examples of this being the "trench storming party," March 1915 style, as laid out in "Memorandum on the Training and Employment of Grenadiers." One officer categorized its tactics as having "the stately solemnity of trooping the colour and the unhastening precision of a minuet." The whole of the memorandum bristled with conditionals ("if" and others), which soldiers of any nationality view askance.[25] Once the specialists were returned to their platoons, the minuet gave way to the sense and simplicity of "Rapid Trench Clearing," involving "fighting with rifle and bayonet over the top, not with bomb and bayonet along the trench." The key, said *SS 143*, was all-arms attack above ground, a method also incorporated in the October 1917 edition of *Training in Canadian Reserve Battalions*.[26]

Specialization posed another danger to training, which the C-in-C himself reiterated in May 1918:

> It is fully realized that the short period available for training generally, more especially for the training of officers, has necessitated the employment of specialists to a far greater degree than was the case before the war. It is feared that this is having an adverse effect in so far that Battalion Commanders, company commanders and platoon commanders are failing to realize that responsibility for the instruction and training of their command, in all military subjects, rests with them and that it is their duty to qualify themselves as thoroughly as possible to carry these out.
>
> Although expert instructors in musketry, Lewis gun, gas services ... are necessary for training instructors and supervision generally, this must not be allowed to relieve the regimental commander of his responsibility for the instruction of his officers and men.[27]

That this had long been a Canadian problem, too, shows on the first page of the second edition of *Training in Canadian Reserve Battalions*.[28] The message, paraphrased, is: "Commanders, build your own house. Do not rely on contractors or agents to do it."

Individual training also included training on enemy weapons. At Regina Trench on the Somme one bomber related how he and his mates held their positions thanks to their training on German bombs, which they hurled at their former owners. Corps schools in early 1917 also trained large numbers of men on enemy machine-guns. The 1st Division Wing of the CCRC had one German heavy machine-gun for training purposes.[29]

As for officer and NCO training, the former has always been largely centralized, usually with the CO in attendance and the training bearing his personal imprint, while NCO training falls largely to company commanders under the CO's general supervision. The exception is tactics training, where officers and NCOs learn together. *Infantry Training (4-Company*

Organization), 1914 provided for training NCOs and potential NCOs in minor tactics during unit classes. At corps reinforcement camps and later at corps schools they also received "special instruction to fit them for the duties of an N.C.O." as soon as possible after they had joined their units.[30] NCOs also attended GHQ and Army schools and learned by "doing" at their units. Lieutenant-Colonel A.W. Sparling, like most COs, reminded company commanders of their responsibility to make senior NCOs "more efficient [to] assist . . . in training your junior NCOs."[31] In mid-1917 one battalion implemented a system of training and selecting men for appointment as lance-corporals that was so good that HQ 1st Division wanted all battalions to copy it. Companies sent their three best soldiers to Battalion HQ where they became runners: "To be a good runner a soldier must be intelligent, reliable, fearless, and have initiative. It therefore follows, that he will make a good N.C.O." When a vacancy arose, the runner who had shown the most promise received the single stripe of a "Lance-Jack" and off he went to his new duties. His parent company replaced him with another promising soldier. OCs liked the system because they got their men back and gained the benefit. Battalion HQ got a chance to get to know the men who would soon be senior NCOs.[32]

SS 152 lists no schools for junior NCOs. Archival records reveal much about senior NCO training but very little about school instruction of potential and actual juniors. Given the level of their responsibility, almost all of their training was done at units. In late 1917, however, junior NCO training began assuming more importance. In October, recognizing that open warfare would demand "great initiative and power of command" from junior NCOs and privates, Corps sought divisional opinions as to whether or not they should receive more training in open warfare and, if so, how best to carry it out. All four divisions responded "Yes," but only 1st Division offered ideas on how: participation by junior ranks in small exercises and more opportunity for junior NCOs to command a platoon—an excellent idea but one that was far easier said than done because divisions out of the line had so much other training to do that such opportunity was rare. Moreover, platoon officers needed all the experience they could possibly get. Only the CO of 1st Battalion recommended "classes of instruction" for junior NCOs.[33]

Overall, NCOs remained a weak link in the chain of command. First of all, many were killed, and many others were commissioned. Commissioning from the ranks aimed not just to replace casualties but to maintain quality to the extent that was possible. GOC 1st Brigade (Griesbach), expressing his concern and that of his superiors that only the best men be commissioned, issued careful guidance to his COs on what he expected in any recommendations they made for commissioning. He cautioned that a man not likely to make a good NCO might make a good officer but "the fact that a man is a good NCO does not necessarily qualify him for commissioned rank." He also warned that he had rejected recommendations because he had thought some of them "would have had the result of losing a good NCO to gain a poor officer." In every case, the performance and character of a man had to be reviewed carefully before a recommendation went forward. An example of what he cautioned against appears in a letter by a former NCO, who was commendably forthright regarding his confusion and anxiety about his new status:

> The difference between being an officer . . . and an NCO is quite some difference. My job is to see that my NCOs and men are on their job, keep my distance and dignity and growl and snap. I'm afraid I'm a poor snapper. You see my inclination is to sit down and make friends like I used to do, and let someone else worry about 'discipline' and 'smartness.' Only you see, there isn't anyone else— it's *my* job. I'm a much better NCO than loot [Lieutenant]. You know some guys just naturally love to walk on people, and I like to treat other people's feelings with respect, which doesn't make for efficiency. Training in the ranks isn't necessarily the best way to make an officer. Maybe it'll help when it comes to fighting but it raises difficulties when you know just how your men think.

The contradictions are readily apparent. This new officer had things backward: it is the officer who demands discipline and the NCO who enforces it. If his attitudes were more or less common, and keeping in mind that about half of all Canadian officers who served in the infantry overseas were former ORs, then another major training requirement had surfaced. It was a fact that perfection was unlikely: as one officer remarked, while "you can't make a silk purse out of a sow's ear . . . you can make a good leather one." A good many leather ones were required. The system had to cure the leather, that is, indoctrinate the new officer, resolve any ambiguity about roles and make the transition as easy as possible. Imperial divisions were required to send 10 NCOs per month for officer training. No figure for Canadian divisions was found but it is not unreasonable to suggest a figure of at least that.[34] So much commissioning from the ranks resulted in serious bleeding of NCO talent. Secondly, being second-string quarterbacks, NCOs had much less prestige. So long as his platoon commander was healthy an NCO got little chance to call the play. When he did, it was for only a few days pending the arrival of a new subaltern. In the normal course of events NCOs were left to do more mundane chores.

Training NCOs, junior or senior, also meant training instructors. All leaders, in theory, had to be capable of instructing but few actually received training in it until mid-1917 when the system began to produce large numbers of instructors. The annual output per battalion from schools in France alone totalled 41 officers and 117 NCOs, giving a very large potential total in just one division, four times that in the Corps, and many times that for the BEF.[35] These figures show the concerted effort made to enlarge the cadre. An equally determined effort to maintain quality is apparent in both editions of *Training in Canadian Reserve Battalions*. Normally an instructor served a maximum of six months on staff of a school in Britain, after which he returned to the front and was replaced by another experienced officer or NCO. This time limit also appeared in *SS 152*, which advised that the best way to maintain high standards was to protect instructor "interests as to advancement" (promotion), to provide opportunity for "refreshing their minds" (courses) and to keep them in touch with fighting troops.[36]

In their training, officers first had to be made aware of their responsibilities. Many new officers did not initially comprehend that their command had to be their first thought. This came only with experience, as did such fundamentals as how much a subordinate should tell his superior about his worries and difficulties and how much account the superior should take of these. While it took "many months to make a *good* platoon commander" it took even longer to make a good CO. In wartime such time could not be had. Urgency exacerbated the difficulties facing the officer who had to learn not only his own art but the art of his subordinates. "Regimental soldiering is not the simple, common-sense affair that some think it. It becomes a matter of plain common sense only when you know how; and when by constant training it has developed into a second nature."[37] Private Russell, 2nd Battalion, put this in more homely fashion: "Your officer is your officer and he is human same as anybody else . . . By and large a green officer he is in trouble till he finds . . . his feet."[38] This explains why Alderson saw officers as the weak point, why some British Regulars said officers were not initially a strength of the CEF and why "The problem was not so much in the training of the men as in that of their officers and NCOs."[39] But how could it have been otherwise? Similar comments were made about Territorial and New Army officers and even about the Guards. Kipling puts his finger on it: "the men made their Officers and the Officers their men."[40] Neither initially possessed soldierly skills. The best way to apply these skills to ground (and the ground itself) also went largely unappreciated.

Clearly, officer training had to be a priority. Louis Lipsett knew this. In early 1916 he told his COs to train their officers continuously: "Avoid allowing officers to consider that all they are required to know or think about is their daily routine work. They must realise [they] are expected to supply the thinking part of the Army." Having listed what officers had to know about their own troops, the enemy, the terrain and "how [to] train their men . . .

even in the trenches," he urged COs to take every opportunity to set small tactical problems for them to solve. Lipsett did this constantly. His "Notes on Tactical Work for Officers" emphasize his desire to teach. One exercise taught the sequence and content of an appreciation, then set an actual requirement at company level. Every officer in his division received a copy of his "Notes" which were sent to other divisions as well. Annotations on archival copies show that it was used extensively in every division.[41]

In the training of senior officers, including COs, appreciations featured prominently. So did the conduct of training, one of the three primary responsibilities of a CO (the others were discipline and fighting efficiency). "We all agreed," said the C-in-C at a Conference of Army Commanders, "on the need for the training of battalion commanders, who . . . must train their company and platoon commanders." Battalion 2ICs instructed the "younger officers in their duties," while Adjutants were responsible for the "drill and instruction of drafts, both of Officers and other ranks."[42]

Finding trained and experienced officers to command battalions was always of great concern. As early as July 1916 Army schools offered short courses to a few officers selected for, or having just assumed command of battalions but vacancies and facilities did not suffice. In October GHQ established formal courses for such officers.[43] That same month the first "COs' Course" commenced at Aldershot. It, like the Army school courses in 1916, was designed to guide officers "suddenly finding themselves . . . in command of battalions without knowledge as to how to train them."[44] Over 10 weeks its 120 students, including two from 1st Division, studied organization, tactics, all-arms cooperation, lessons from recent fighting, battalion training during rest, discipline and morale. Thereafter COs' courses ran regularly. The Canadian Corps' first in-house course for COs and 2ICs commenced in the fall of 1916 as authorized by *SS 152*.[45] The necessity for such a course for COs was beyond doubt: "Many officers who proved themselves capable commanders in action were not as successful out of the line when the reconstitution and training of their battalions, companies, or platoons became the vital need."[46] Also, any course that provided opportunities to discuss tactics with other officers was pure gold since it enabled students to better plan and execute operations. The former BGGS, C.H. Harington, neatly summed up the value of officers' schools and the COs' course in particular:

> These Schools are the very greatest value to the Army . . . It is these Schools which have got to set the standard of thought and training. *This is the premier School, the one for COs*, and then we have the Army Schools for Company Commanders . . . Whatever is evolved from lessons of recent fighting and training must be started at these

schools . . . and when you go from these Schools you are in a position to act as agents to disseminate that information.[47]

One student on the January 1917 course at Aldershot (he returned to 1st Division in time for Vimy) described his course as 200 to 250 officers, nearly all majors, usually 2ICs of battalions, and from every division in the BEF. He thought the Commandant, Brigadier-General R.J. Kentish, "a first-class Officer . . . who put on marvelous demonstrations" that made students laugh but drove home lessons "that none of us forgot."[48] The whole course, he enthused, featured realistic problems of the sort that would face men returning to the front as COs. The numerous problem solving exercises, suitably modified, would have greatly helped COs train their officers in reconnaissance and in the preparation and writing of Operation Orders and other SD, including appreciations. Candidates also studied how to prepare exercises for the training of NCOs.[49]

Senior officer training was not limited to COs. Upon being ordered in June 1916 to regain certain positions at Hooge, Currie planned to attack with two brigades, each with a different Zero. Byng commented:

> When an attack does not start together, generally it will not assault together and so fail. I would prefer to see the two brigades start together but I realize you have made the reconnaissance and if you still think your plan the better, then it becomes my plan and I authorize and approve it. Think it over and let me know the result of your decision later.

This shows his "marvelous strength of character." No wonder men trusted and admired "Inspiring, tough, competent and sympathetic" Byng. Had Currie stuck to his original plan and had it gone wrong Byng would have been responsible.[50]

In 1914 companies were the principal training "unit" but by late 1916 the platoon had become the focus. In 1915 and early 1916 the prevailing view considered subalterns "ignorant of the small things of leadership" and their general standard of training very low, so low that battalion commanders and training staff preferred them to remain with their units under close supervision for at least three months before being considered for courses.[51] As casualties mounted, this became policy because ever less experienced subalterns simply had to receive some basics before attending formal training. One of these basics, *SS 143 Instructions for the Training of Platoons for Offensive Action, 1917*, aimed to assist subalterns in "training and fighting" their commands. Regimental officers considered this manual "the most important War Office Publication issued during the war."[52] Its 26 pages, which must have helped platoon commanders immensely, listed the requirements to be attained by training as:

(a) *The Offensive Spirit* [close with and destroy the enemy].
(b) *Initiative* [act without waiting for orders].
(c) *Confidence* [attain skill at arms].
(d) *Cooperation of Weapons* [employ the all-arms concept].
(e) *Discipline* [practise battle discipline].
(f) *Morale* [build and maintain].
(g) *Esprit de corps* [build and maintain].[53]

SS 143 expounded seven steps that platoon commanders had to take to attain the seven requirements. First, conduct progressive training—individual, section, platoon—and run evening refresher training of section commanders to confirm each day's training and prepare for the next. Second, attain proficiency in all platoon weapons and be capable of instructing in every one. Third, train every man in drill, bayonet fighting, bombing, mopping-up, musketry, physical fitness, fire discipline, wiring, field works, gas drills, and tactics. Fourth, make sections proficient in their weapons: the Bombing Section in bombing, the Rifle Grenadier Section in rifle bombing, the Lewis Gun Section in gunnery and the Rifle Section in marksmanship, bayonet, and bombing (as either rifle grenadier or Lewis gunner). Fifth, train section commanders in fire control, target indication, map reading, message writing and tactics. Sixth, make all training competitive. Finally, train "on the actual ground and situation . . . [and] turn out . . . always in fighting order . . . with the full complement of arms and ammunition [as for] battle." *SS 143* emphasized that the platoon held all infantry weapons and that specialist commanders for infantry sub-units and units were undesirable: "over to you, mister platoon commander" was its unmistakable message.[54]

As useful as it proved, *SS 143* could not resolve everything. Platoon commanders had still to decide how best to use men, weapons and ground—*tactics*. Still, *SS 143* was unique in how it extolled that valuable and scarce quality known as initiative. Schools also highlighted it. One lecture at the Canadian Corps Officers' School offered some lessons about initiative in a memorable way:

Here are some bad types of initiative:

(i) For the cowardly initiative consists in refusing information so as to shirk responsibility.
(ii) For the ambitious initiative consists in seizing every opportunity of increasing notoriety.

(iii) For lazy people initiative is the right to pass all irksome duty on to their subordinates.

(iv) For [the] easy going initiative consists in modifying to their liking any order they may receive.

Initiative, like obedience, must be cultivated. The only way to cultivate it is to distribute responsibilities. The only way to foster it is to acknowledge it openly.[55]

Another lecture, this one by William Rae just before he took command of 4th Battalion, concerned "The Command and Training of a Platoon." He offered sound advice: keep your men healthy so as to bring into action the maximum possible number; know your men and ensure orders are properly carried out; know your work and every weapon; immediately replace section commanders not up to the mark; plan training and work carefully; teach the primacy of rifle and bayonet over bomb and rifle grenade and stress constantly one word, "fight." This, after all, was the sole object of training. A platoon, he said, was nothing more than a reflection of its commander, and its actions indicated its standard of training. An officer who did not make himself the best that he could be failed in his duty.[56]

As vital as a CO was, new organization and doctrine in early 1917 made the platoon commander his rival for training. *SS 143* and *SS 135*, which called the platoon the "unit" of assault, also turned the war into a "platoon commander's war." GOC 1st Brigade (Griesbach) directed that the "instruction and the general conduct of these Officers should receive . . . careful attention [so they] will . . . have a greater sense of their responsibilities. I desire particular attention to be paid to [their] training." Platoon commanders had to be held responsible for their platoons in all respects.[57] This awakening to platoons and their training featured in the BEF as a whole; for example, the GOC XIII Corps (Lord Cavan) had remarked early in January 1917 that "victory depended more on the leadership of platoon commanders than on anything else." Nicholson believed that "every general in every army in Europe might have said the same thing with equal truth. The platoon commanders were the axis on which the whole fighting machine turned."[58]

This focus on the platoon and its commander wrought significant improvement. While content differed for officers and sergeants attending the two week Platoon Commander and Platoon Sergeant Course run by the Canadian Corps Officers' School, both officers and sergeants received concentrated instruction in their responsibilities. By the fourth course (February 1916), one third of total course hours concerned practical tactics. In fact, most of the course consisted of practical exercises, only 20 of the 127 hours of instruction being given over to lectures. These were not frippery, either. Topics included trench mortars, machine-guns, training of bombers, supply, intelligence, and infantry/artillery cooperation, all useful to the all-arms commander. Course content had been determined from experience—the lessons of operations—and from what senior officers and training staff believed to be the shortcomings of junior commanders. This led to increasing emphasis on practical tactics. As a whole, the course provided what was required to lead a platoon effectively.[59] In July the course was extended by 10 days. The material to be covered is indicative of the challenge facing platoon commanders:

Leadership	Principles of Attack	Map Reading
Discipline	Fire Discipline	Messages and Reports
Moral(e)	Defence	Arrest
Command	Trench Warfare	Intelligence
Organization	Defensive Works	GHQ Routine Orders
Care of Arms	Trench Orders	Supply
Sanitation	Machine-guns	Drill
Billets	Grenades	PT
Duties	Personal Weapons	All-Arms cooperation
Protection	Patrols.[60]	

Similar developments were underway in Imperial formations. By the spring of 1917, 29th (Imperial) Division confidently said, "Much had been done . . . to effect an improvement, and good results were seen."[61] While this was true in many divisions, and certainly in 1st Division, it should not be supposed that platoon commanders considered all subjects of equal importance, or that they shone at them all. Necessarily, they focussed on those they believed directly relevant to combat: leadership and tactics. Map reading remained the exception in that little improvement was evident. The standard, Canadian and Imperial, remained very low as was seen in the constant errors during 1917 by officers reporting their locations. Reading a map and reading the ground can be two very different skills. The CO of 10th Battalion found that "many Officers on arrival from England knew nothing about map reading or [had] a smattering that . . . in many cases proved worse than useless."[62] Mistakes invariably meant tardiness and that, in turn, frequently meant failure. Moreover, as one platoon commander said, "To lead men wrong is always bad; but when they are tired out it is unpardonable and not quickly forgotten." Obliteration of most natural landmarks made accurate location of positions more difficult. Consequently, schools began to teach such methods as resection. That map reading remained a problem for COs, too is evident in *Notes for Commanding Officers* (1918), which contained a new section on resections, finding true bearings, and other compass work.[63]

Leadership featured strongly in courses for platoon commanders. One lecture listed the qualities of a leader as knowledge, skill, determination, endurance, courage and cunning. Mutual confidence between officer and man was critical. Another lecture suggested that while a platoon commander could not always know what the enemy was going to do, he could usually know what his men were going to do by examining himself: "As you are, so will your men be. As you have done, so will your men do." The lecturer then asked: "Are you a good leader? Are you worthy to lead men? Have you confidence in your men? Have your men faith in you?"[64] Such questions were fleshed out in a series of pamphlets ("flyers" might be a better word as they were usually one page long) each having a title that began "Some Questions a Platoon Commander Might [or Should] Ask Himself . . . " and then ended with a specific subject. One of the first (which had added the words "in the Line.") was signed personally by Byng. Another ended "Before an Attack," and yet another, "on Taking Over a Trench." The last was notable for the question, three times in block capitals, "AM I AS OFFENSIVE AS I MIGHT BE?"[65] This question featured in many of the pamphlets, a constant refrain that greatly annoyed those who did the fighting:

> "Am I offensive enough?" is one of the questions laid down in a pamphlet that reaches us from an Army School some 30 miles behind the line. It is for the subaltern to ask himself each morning as he rises from his bed. Most laudable! But, as the Lewis Gun Officer remarked today, it is one of the paradoxes of war that the further you get from the battle-line the more "offensive" are the people you meet![66]

The best individual training in the world does not make a division effective. It becomes that only when its arms, services and staff can work together. *Infantry Training (4-Company Organization), 1914* said that the objective of collective training was "to render sections, platoons, companies, and the larger units and formations capable of manoeuvre and cooperation in battle." Collective training could be as simple as a few men on a night patrolling exercise, or learning a better way of erecting or cutting through wire, or a platoon doing extended order drill, or it could involve a full-scale brigade or divisional exercise. Units customarily referred to "routine" training, which, according to 14th Battalion, was bayonet fighting, gas drills, musketry and platoon and company formations, and to "special" training such as tactical schemes, demonstrations and practise attacks at all levels.[67]

SS 143, SS 135 and *SS 144* manuals were considered the best guides for collective training.[68] *Notes for Commanding Officers* (1917) was also extremely useful. In January 1917, a month after the issue of *SS 135*, 2nd Brigade directed that "training is to be carried out in the spirit as well as in the exact words of this manual." The BM, Captain W.H.S. Alston, hoped for discussion of its content, adding that company commanders had to ensure platoon commanders thoroughly understood that the platoon was a self-contained all-arms organization and success would largely depend upon its commander. Those who received instruction had themselves to transmit it to all ranks; in other words, platoon commanders, not outsiders, trained their platoons.[69] Formation commanders kept close watch, insisting on approving all training programs. Lipsett not only set content and methodology (he liked demonstrations, thinking them very instructive) but he also stressed what he saw as the purposes of training: to strengthen discipline and offensive spirit, maintain physical fitness, and increase self-confidence.[70] When divisions went into corps reserve, they could expect, barring a crisis, to remain in that role for four weeks and to train long hours daily. At such times GOsC became especially interested in training because of the relative stability offered by the time and the ready availability of better training facilities than usual. The wise CO kept himself much in evidence at all unit training.

One widely used appendix in *SS 152* offered step-by-step guidance on "Training a Battalion" over four weeks, including how to prepare and run programs for training the new battle platoon.[71] A central principle said that training had to be progressive: first week, platoon; second week, company; third week, battalion; and the final week, brigade. Alternatively, four weeks out of the line for a battalion could have been: Week One—four days sub-unit, one day unit and one day brigade training; Week Two—three days sub-unit, two days unit and one day brigade training; Week Three—two days sub-unit, two days unit, and two days brigade training; and Week Four—the same as Week Three. As important as the manuals were, the guidelines set by commanders had the most direct impact, for they decided emphasis, specific direction and training methods, these being based on the expectation of what might come on return to the line. Griesbach (1st Brigade) insisted on night training during the first week, and at least one afternoon had to be devoted to exercises such as the platoon attacking a pill box. Company week had to feature more night training and dealing with strongpoints. Battalion week had to include a major exercise, stressing lessons he thought especially salient. In December 1917, for example, he wanted exercises on consolidation and forming defensive flanks. That same month Loomis of 2nd Brigade demanded tactical exercises and more tactical exercises. In both brigades individual training also continued for specialists, NCOs and officers, the latter concentrating on map reading and message writing. As always, perceived shortcomings drove the training.[72]

The routine and intensity of training depended largely upon location. Brigades in corps reserve could train daily, and work parties did not usually deter, most requirements being minor. Units in divisional and brigade reserve could still do considerable collective training despite more limited facilities in the forward area and the requirement to provide more men for work parties. The better trainers let nothing deter. Griesbach listed 36 items on which men could be usefully trained in as little as 15 minutes: duties of NCOs, use of ground, judging distance, enemy grenades and equipment, enemy ruses, offensive spirit and communications. He urged officers to take every opportunity to stimulate interest, improve training, clear up obscure points and secure valuable suggestions, and he added tactics, cooperation with aircraft, means to surprise the enemy, sanitation and trench discipline. Ivor Maxse, too, insisted that training opportunities were always there, "on any bit of odd ground near any billet in any odd quarter of an hour every day . . . without any facilities . . . if you only make up your mind to do something . . . and to do it quick."[73] In bad winter weather some outdoor training suffered but demonstrations and company level training went ahead most days, and officer training continued, including lectures on all-arms cooperation, heavy artillery support and other operational matters, and many administrative topics, such as courts-martial.[74]

Daily routine also depended on anticipated operations and on the brigadier's wishes, meaning that training hours varied widely. Most brigadiers preferred that mornings be spent on training, and afternoons on sports, or rest perhaps one afternoon out of every three or so. Training generally commenced at 9:00 A.M., or at 7:00 A.M. in some brigades. Usually the training day ended at 3:00 or 4:00 P.M. Sundays featured church parade, sports and rest. Shorter periods out of the line—a week was the norm—were left to unit training. *Notes for Commanding Officers* recommended the following program:

> *Day One:* Baths, clean arms and equipment, pay, CO's meeting to discuss the week's training, concert in the evening.
> *Day Two:* Drill, including ceremonial march past, ranges, sports.
> *Day Three:* Drill, including ceremonial march past, ranges, sports.
> *Day Four:* Company in the attack, ranges.
> *Day Five:* Battalion in the attack, ranges.
> *Day Six:* CO's Meeting to discuss training done.

According to this manual, a battalion so occupied when out of the line would return that evening to the trenches "in good heart, the men ready for any effort their Officers may call upon them to make."[75]

One type of special training was rehearsals on replicas of the actual ground over which an attack would be made, or on ground taped and marked to portray enemy deployment. Rehearsal after rehearsal preceded the Somme, with platoons, companies, battalions and brigades training incessantly on "miles of fields . . . laid out to represent enemy positions." Canadian and Imperial battalions conducted practise attacks over and over, the objectives being to get assault formations right, to ensure understanding of leap-frogging, reinforcement and consolidation and to confirm that "every man from a battalion's Colonel downwards knew precisely what to do and when to do it."[76] Such preparations were even more thorough before Vimy. Training consisted of "entirely one thing: . . . attack . . . Something . . . was in the air."[77] Every feature of the German defence was laid out on the ground and units went over it: first just walk-throughs to get the feel of it, then walk-throughs in formation, then practise assaults in slow time, then practise assaults in actual speed—over and over until every officer and man was as ready as it was humanly possible to be. 2nd Battalion, for example, began practising attacks daily in February, including firing at targets while advancing, as Byng had wanted. In fact, he had 10 "wants." His first ordered all ranks to carry during training exactly what they would carry in the actual assault. Two, he directed that every leader practise leading an assault. Numbers three to nine concerned weapons (handling and fire discipline) and formations, in which platoon commanders were allowed to move sections within waves. Ten stressed dealing with enemy strongpoints. These preparations were a "triumph."[78] So was Vimy.

Before Hill 70 in August every battalion in 1st Division trained on a taped course. In addition, 2nd Brigade School made a 1:40 scale model available for study. For Passchendaele much the same applied: training on replicas of enemy positions and scale models, and endless rehearsals. 2nd Battalion, for example, practised battalion attacks every second day, in all cases using the leapfrog method against two objectives, as they would in the actual assault. Platoon practises ran 40 minutes, company attacks one hour and battalion practises a half-day or more depending on what observers thought of them.[79] With GOsC around almost constantly, units were on their toes.

The second category of special training was tactical schemes, in which GOsC were deeply interested since schemes not only taught but tested.

> The tactical knowledge and power of command of Platoon, Company and Battalion Commanders should be developed by simple tactical schemes carried out without troops, either on the ground or on a map, or rough large-scale model. These schemes might be based on actual incidents . . . during recent operations, and might subsequently be carried out as exercises with troops on the ground. The important thing is to produce a situation that requires quick decision and the issue of definite orders on the spot.[80]

Other benefits included attaining better appreciation of ground, confidence in writing and issuing orders and improved map reading, a skill that had continued to decline. Loomis, GOC 2nd Brigade, liked the way in which schemes encouraged "individuality of thought and action, resourcefulness, judgement, doing the right thing at the right time."[81]

One type of scheme involved no troops and was carried out either on the ground or on models for the benefit of officers and, depending on the tactical level, for NCOs, too. When Byng became GOC he instituted such training for COs. A few at a time gathered at his HQ where over five or six days they worked out solutions to exercises, which were presented by individual COs and discussed each evening by the GOC, various staff officers and other COs.[82] Later, these tactical exercises without troops (or TEWTs, their modern acronym) were run at all sub-unit and unit levels. GOC 1st Division (Macdonell) directed that TEWTs

> resemble reality as much as possible, and that the Officers . . . receive the Scheme in the same form they would . . . in reality. Hence it is better for the purpose of instruction, instead of handing an Officer a general and specific idea, to hand him a Brigade Order which contains his task, and allow him to make any reasonable assumption . . . Only straight forward schemes should be set: unnatural situations call for unnatural solutions.

Macdonell outlined a sample exercise and how to stage it. To exercise officers in outpost operations each syndicate received sufficient information to set the problem in context, an order to hold certain ground and the line that the outposts had to cover. Each syndicate member had to prepare and give his orders. Similar exercises tested companies and platoons, some situations demanding verbal orders and some written orders.[83]

When groups of officers could not be gathered, "correspondence" lessons were conducted; Griesbach, for example, set company level TEWTs, giving company commanders, via COs, four days to come up with solutions, which he vetted. One TEWT demanded written plans, orders and situation reports and detailed attack battle procedure. Another required written solutions to the tactical problems of a platoon sized patrol tasked to locate the enemy. Platoon commanders had to decide how to organize and deploy, select bounds for movement, determine the actions of scouts, and establish liaison with flanking forces. In Part Two, which began with the enemy in his new line, they had to report upon and recommend further operations.

Tactical training conducted on cloth models that were painted with terrain, or on sand-table models, did not need to be especially sophisticated, particularly at lower levels, since principles were the focus. Virtually any situation could be studied on such models. Loomis held numerous exercises, "illustrating the principles of attack . . . employment of artillery and machine-guns, communications, use of the ground . . . fire control . . . and flanking fire." The writing and issue of appreciations, orders and reports quickly and clearly was a primary requirement. Other training stressed close all-arms cooperation and reconnaissance and warned of the dangers of stereotyped practises and of overtasking sub-units. Each TEWT concluded with a wrap-up to ensure that the training had been understood and that no false lessons had been learned. In 1st Division the GOC and G Staff attended as appropriate to the level of training.[84] Brigadiers strongly encouraged COs to conduct minor tactical exercises for their officers. To help them, the COs' Course at Aldershot provided take-away sample exercises for issue of orders, fire control, deployment, sentry duties and defensive preparations. While at Aldershot COs participated in several lengthy series of problem-solving exercises. One series, Problems *A* to *Z*, required them to write numerous sets of orders and to solve a wide range of tactical problems. Another long series posed problems (and solutions) relating to conduct of training.[85] The whole point was practical problem solving.

Whenever possible, TEWTs were followed by the same exercise, this time with troops participating. Obviously, this was easier to do at sub-unit level. Here, too, the keynote was simplicity. When it became apparent that the lessons had been driven home, the exercise ceased and was criticized, the unit then moving to the next position where it faced another situation for solution and learned another lesson, thus making maximum use of the time available. Macdonell also suggested that practise attacks could flow easily into tactical exercises: "Attacks should be first practised as a drill slowly, each situation discussed . . . if necessary, done over again in a better way; lastly, you may with profit be able to have schemes worked out by two opposing sides with criticism when finished."[86]

A salient feature of exercises with troops at every level from platoon to brigade was "live" play with an "enemy." This heightened the competitive spirit but it had to be watched to ensure it did not get out of hand. During a stay in corps reserve in August 1916, 2nd Brigade conducted, in addition to routine training, sub-unit exercises over a four day period, followed by major exercises:

21 August: Battalion level exercise, one-half battalion friendly forces, the other half as "enemy."

22 August: Brigade exercises: two battalions acting as assault battalions, one battalion in support, providing moppers-up and dug-out clearing parties, and one battalion in reserve. At the close, GOC and observers from 1st Division critiqued the exercise.

23 August: Unit training.

24 August: Attack and Defence brigade exercise, two battalions as attack force and two as "enemy" in defence. Activities centred around the aims of opposing advance and rear guards. Both sides had artillery and mortar support, fire being indicated by coloured flags; 'A very satisfactory practise.'

25 August: Conference of all brigade officers to review the exercise and critique by GOC.

Other examples of brigade training during periods in corps and divisional reserve in 1916 and 1917 could be offered but the above suffices to show the progressive nature of training, always culminating with major exercises. Three such exercises may not seem particularly intensive but given the other demands on a brigade the three days were a major investment. 2nd Brigade was fortunate to have been spared work parties.[87]

Beginning in the summer of 1917 the emphasis shifted to training for the "open warfare" senior commanders anticipated. Training schemes increasingly featured scenarios associated with offensive operations. 16th Battalion's training for the last two weeks of June mostly consisted of platoon schemes involving reconnaissance and platoon in the attack and company schemes covering patrols, advanced guards and night advances. Such training highlights the syllabi of many of the battalions of 1st Division, which is not surprising since the GOC set priorities and the brigadiers amplified them. In the fall of 1917 exercises working up to battalion level featured in most training plans.[88] 1st Brigade's training directive for December emphasized open warfare: advance guards and pursuit. Unit training included deployment and operations of advance guards and the provision of their own flank protection. Since rapid advances could result in open flanks, they had to guard against ambush but avoid "stickiness and stiffness." If the enemy were retiring in a disorganized manner the advance could be less cautious. As usual, Griesbach told COs exactly what he wanted: mutual support, fire and movement; maintenance of contact with the enemy; and rapid passage of information.[89]

By late 1917 divisions spent as much time as possible training for open warfare, paying special attention to "obtaining superiority of fire, mutual support, fire and movement, advancing in artillery formation and skirmishing." At unit level this translated into training in the use of machine-guns and Lewis guns for offensive action, renewed emphasis on musketry (accuracy became more important in the longer distances), and, as Herbert Mowat of the 8th Battalion recalled, brigade exercises that stressed mobility, flexible assault formations and initiative. Officers avidly studied *SS 197 The*

Brig Gen D.M. Ormond, GOC 9th Brigade, January 1919. As a Lt Col Ormond was CO 10th Battalion from September 1916 to May 1918. Note the badge of rank, at the time only a crossed sword and baton. (LAC PA-003900)

Col M.A. Colquhoun (right) CO 4th Battalion from June 1915 to June 1916. (LAC PA-007038)

Lt Col L.J. Lipsett, CO 8th Battalion and later Brig Gen, GOC 2nd Brigade and then Maj Gen, GOC 3rd Division. (LAC PA-007442)

Lt Col W. Rae, CO 4th Battalion, July 1916. (LAC PA-000376)

Lt Col A.E. Swift, CO 2nd
Battalion, July 1916.
(LAC PA-000422)

Brig Gen V.W. Odlum, formerly
CO 7th Battalion from April
1915 to July 1916.
(LAC PA-002117)

Lt Col W.F. Gilson, CO 7th Battalion (right) and Maj D. Philpott, 2IC 7th Battalion, December 1917. (LAC PA-002243)

Officers of the 5th Battalion, July 1918. Front row, l–r:William (mascot); Lts G.W. Young; T.F. Carter; W.W. Code; T.W. Cogland; W.T. Bebbington; T.B. Chapman; E.C. Foot; D. Gibson; J.H.S. Laidlaw. Centre, l–r: Hon Capt G.J. Gray; Capt A.A.E. Batchelor; Capt P.J.A. Andrews; Maj K.A. Mahaffy; Maj E. Day; Maj I.L. Crawford; Lt Col L.P.O. Tudor; Capt G.E. Hocking; Maj C.K.L. Pyman; Capt H. George; Capt W.E. Lloyd; Lt H. Robertson. Back row, l–r: Capt R. Lingford; Capt J.S. McGlashan; Lt J.W. Slaughter; Lt A.S. Pither; Capt J.L. Evans; Capt E.P. Osler; Lt J. Rowe; Lt H. Maguire; Capt T. Whitmore. (LAC PA-002848)

8th Battalion Grenade Section at rest; a card game in progress, May 1916.
(LAC PA-000151)

Canadian Highlanders cleaning "cooties" from kilts, June 1916. (LAC PA-000159)

A private of 15th Battalion (48th Highlanders) cleaning his Lee Enfield rifle, June 1916. (LAC PA-000163)

This photo has been identified variously as Canadians in actual attack on the Somme and as a staged "photo op" in reserve trenches. Archival records state that it shows training at a trench mortar school at St Pol, France, in October 1916. (W.I. Castle/LAC PA-000648)

Canadians returning from forward trenches, Battle of the Somme, November 1916.
(William Ivor Castle, LAC PA-000832)

Canadian platoon commander briefing his platoon during training, October 1916.
(LAC PA-000877)

Canadians jubilant after Courcelette, September 1916. (LAC PA-000809)

Jolly 10th Battalion private, November 1917. (LAC PA-003678)

Tactical Employment of Lewis Guns and carefully reviewed *Infantry Training (4-Company Organization), 1914*, which had been written for open warfare and put aside for trench warfare.[90] Corps also stressed "Training in Marching," just to make sure the ability to make long, rapid marches was retained.[91] Infantry-artillery cooperation became a training priority because of the numerous complaints about "shorts" at Passchendaele: "There is nothing so disconcerting as our guns landing short," said 8th Battalion. All told, six battalions had suffered casualties from friendly artillery fire, field and heavy. In January 1918 the heavy artillery attached an LO to each infantry brigade HQ. Prior to this, field artillery LOs had also been responsible for obtaining heavy support on the highly optimistic premise that they had "complete knowledge" of heavy artillery methods and deployment. In April, 1st Division ordered brigades to resume attaching one officer per infantry battalion to divisional artillery for five-day periods "in order to obtain . . . practical knowledge of the . . . artillery in all its phases."[92] Canadian formations and units also trained with tanks, participating in tactical exercises.[93]

Another aspect of operations that received increasing training attention in 1917 was cooperation with tactical aircraft which had, in fact, been of interest as early as September 1915 when First Army published "Preparatory Measures to be Taken by Armies and Corps Before Undertaking Offensive Operations on a Large Scale." One of its "Principal Points to be Attended To" described aircraft employment on reconnaissance, artillery observation, bombing, and contact patrols. Fourth Army "Tactical Notes," issued in May 1916 in preparation for the Somme offensive, concentrated on contact patrols, ordering each corps to designate such patrols. It also detailed aircraft markings and patrol procedure, including liaison and communications, with signalling devices such as flares, lamps and ground markings. GHQ disseminated these instructions to all Armies.[94]

In early August 1st Division practised establishing contact with aircraft under the supervision of the GOC, which indicated Currie's high interest in the matter. Staff officers also attended to monitor the progress of the participants from several of the battalions. 1st Division Training School had previously conducted classes in contact procedures for platoon commanders and platoon sergeants.[95] When 1st Division went into Army reserve in mid-August for a 10-day period, its brigades conducted brigade exercises involving patrol contact procedures. 3rd Brigade, in particular, paid very close attention to contact training. Notes prepared by the BM, Major M.O. Clarke, stressed that troops must not disclose their positions until the aircraft had signalled for them to do so, and they must continue to display their ground signals for as long as the aircraft remained in their area, thereby increasing the chance that the signals would be seen and understood. Loomis of 2nd Brigade warned his COs that "great care" had to be taken in instructing all ranks in contact procedure.[96]

SS 135, published in December 1916, contained an entire section on "Cooperation With Contact Aeroplanes" and a very detailed appendix specifying procedures for infantry and artillery, including the use of flares and klaxon horns; pre-arranged codes for establishing contact and for indicating what support the ground units required; marking of HQs; and aircraft recognition. The appendix further refined and improved the procedures first in effect in mid-1916.[97] Brigade War Diaries for 1917 show that officers and men routinely attended courses of instruction in contact work held by various air squadrons. *SS 135* directed that whenever possible aircraft tasked to support a division during operations would also support it during training. In 1st Division training in contact work became a common feature of tactical exercises from mid-1917 in preparation for the more open warfare that was anticipated.[98] *SS 152* (June 1917) indicates that ground-air cooperation training had also become part of the training at Army infantry, artillery and scouting, observation and sniping schools, at corps infantry schools and at cavalry schools.[99]

One of the most valuable training vehicles was competitions, which received great emphasis. Participants ranged in number from 6 or fewer men to whole sections, platoons and sometimes companies. Arrangements for the competitions and their results were considered significant enough to be included routinely in unit and formation war diaries. Competitions included officer revolver matches and sports (team and individual), bayonet fighting, bombing, scouting, sniping, marksmanship (rifle), forced marching, physical training, Lewis gunnery, wiring, patrolling, and even cooking; "Military Efficiency" competitions featured several events that in the aggregate tested sub-unit skills. Senior officers often put up a trophy for award to the winner, as did Major Hugh Urquhart, BM of 1st Brigade, when he donated one in mid-1917 for marksmanship. A platoon from 2nd Battalion took top honours.[100]

A platoon competition that eventually became *the* competition to win was based on *Army Rifle Association: Platoon Competition*, published in February 1917 just after *SS 135* and *SS 143*. It reinforced the importance of the platoon and the platoon commander.[101] During 1917, 10 such competitions took place. GOC 29th (Imperial) Division (Major-General de Lisle) aptly summed up their training value: "Target practise is for duffers and snipers. Field firing competitions are the real battle practise."[102] 1st Division saw their value as a demonstration of the power of surprise and of the great volume of fire under the control of the platoon commander.

Each team consisted of a platoon commander and 28 ORs in three sections:

one Lewis gun section and two rifle sections. The general idea had the platoon moving as the reserve of an advance guard. Upon entering a village the OC received warning of a small enemy force on one flank. He then had to reconnoitre, locate the enemy, plan and issue orders and then attack. The competition had five parts: first, an inspection to check that the men were dressed and equipped in accordance with the rules (30 points maximum with deductions for any deficiencies); second, deployment by the platoon commander, and his orders and fire orders (60 points maximum); third, the advance and covering fire (120 points); fourth, handling of the Lewis gun section (60 points maximum); and, finally, each hit on the various targets (a quarter point, five points being deducted for each miss; maximum possible, 715 points). Each man had 120 rounds, except for commanders and the two-man Lewis gun crew. The total possible score was 985 points.

For the platoon commander, the competition proved very demanding: he had only 10 minutes to make his plan and targets remained exposed for a limited time from the first shot. Slow fire orders or movement meant some targets would go down before anyone could fire at them. Moreover, he had to take care that his Lewis gunners did not fire on rifle targets, for that meant immediate disqualification. The targets themselves in their configuration and deployment offered a considerable challenge to shooters. Overall, the competition tested the platoon commander's ability to execute his fundamental tasks: find the enemy, issue orders to deal with him and direct his resources to achieve that end. To succeed, he had to understand the weapons available to him and grasp clearly the task. In short, it provided an opportunity for him to display his tactical *sense* (or not).

Many senior officers, including GOC 1st Division, attended the brigade eliminations on 11, 12 and 13 January 1918. The next day, 14 January was a day of intense preparation by the three winning platoons, one each from 2nd, 8th and 15th Battalions. At 10:00 A.M. on 15 January, with Macdonell again in attendance, the competition began, and the rain fortunately held off until the afternoon. A distant third, at 135½ points, was the platoon from 15th Battalion. The platoon representing 8th Battalion, cursed by a jammed Lewis gun, compiled 230¼ points. Number 2 Platoon (Lieutenant P.J. Browne) of 2nd Battalion rang up 254 points, walking off with the Challenge Cup and the grand prize of two weeks' leave in Paris for the whole platoon. The loss must have been particularly galling to the 8th, which had won its brigade heat by 150 points, while 2nd and 15th Battalions had won theirs by a scant 9 and 5 points respectively. In fact, 2nd Battalion's nearest rival in its brigade heat also had Lewis gun failure, causing it to lose the chance to represent 1st Brigade.

The post-competition report of the Chief Judge, Lieutenant-Colonel J.H.

MacKenzie, GSO1 (Training), First Army, was quite complimentary to the three platoons. His major criticisms concerned marksmanship and fire control, both of which needed considerable improvement: none of the platoons managed better than 100 points for marksmanship. His comments must have been taken to heart. In the next competition, held in May 1918, the scores improved considerably, 16th Battalion winning with almost 400 points and 2nd Battalion losing by only 19 points.[103]

It remains to wrap up this chapter in much the same way that a TEWT is concluded. Usually, the officer running a TEWT concludes by stressing its training value, with reference to the lessons taught. While training had its flaws—most criticisms focus on particular content—it was far more dynamic than was usually acknowledged. Despite GHQ's failure to assert itself until late 1916, the enormous commitment to training cannot be doubted. The proliferation of schools, the inclusion of training staff officers at senior formation HQs, the many *SS* publications (the series exceeded 500), and the mountain of lesson documents are indicative of dedication to training. Many of the lessons were featured in the revised editions of SS publications; *SS 135*, for example, was revised five times. Lessons also featured in a long series of publications under the overall title *The Experiences of Recent Fighting*. New publications appeared frequently, especially after major actions. The constant quest for lessons and the continuous analysis of them reflect a strong desire to learn and improve.

Canadian training as a whole took place in units and formations, schools, bases and facilities in France and training centres in Britain, all set within the larger Imperial system. Training policy, standards, directives and publications were virtually identical. Content and methods of instruction, while they reflected national identity, were similar. Instructors at schools, bases and formations met the Imperial requirement that they have combat experience. Canadians trained at Imperial facilities such as the senior officer, CO and staff schools in Britain, where they improved themselves and their divisions. In France, Imperial corps schools were restricted to training junior officers, but Dominion corps schools also trained senior officers, it having been recognized that Dominions should be directly influential in the training of their senior commanders.[104] Instruction of Canadian reserve battalions that supplied reinforcements to the front was always a Canadian responsibility.

The Canadian Corps had a GSO2 (Training), just as Imperial Corps did but Canadian Corps HQ exercised an influence on training far beyond that of most Imperial corps. During his time as GOC 18th (Imperial) Division, Ivor Maxse was touted as one of the best trainers in the BEF. Currie and Macdonell must surely be considered his equal. 1st Division was also fortunate in its brigadiers, especially Lipsett, Tuxford and Griesbach, who consistently trained their brigades intelligently. It is regrettable that Griesbach's better snippets on training from his "Book of Wisdom" did not become better known outside 1st Division for many were as pithy and valuable as Maxse's "Training Leaflets," if not more so. It must be said, though, that Canadians improved upon training concepts and content more than they conceived them. While they made an art and a science of rehearsals for attacks, the idea originated with others even before the Somme.

Both Currie and Macdonell saw the key to success as fresh troops that were specially and thoroughly trained for the task at hand. One particular strength of Canadian training was its consistent response to the lessons, complaints and requirements stated by field commanders, who were quick to express their concern about too much (or too little) of this or that. Content and conduct were always contentious. Few commanders, if any, were satisfied with the standard of marksmanship and weapons handling. As repetitive as such training was, the only way to achieve the skill at arms that marked the good soldier was constant practise. The whole purpose of weapons training was to confer the ability to kill.[105]

The modern reader is entirely at liberty to decry training content in one aspect or another. The usual complaint is drill, upon which too much time was spent, although also doing the same attack exercise over and over again *ad nauseum* became just as tedious and artificial. The reasonable and the best way to look at 1st Division's training is to consider the aggregate and the result. In the final analysis, training in 1st Division met the requirement and stood it in good stead. Training produced a division fit to fight, which was the aim. As Private E.H. Russenholt said, "We had mastered our job . . . Training, training, training!"[106] In fact, Old Red Patch became not only a well-trained division but a supremely confident one, ready in all aspects for the decisive struggle of 1918.

Notes to Chapter Eight

1. *Notes for Commanding Officers* (1918), p. 16; LAC, RG9IIIC3, Vol. 4032, Folder 28, File 1, IGT, GHQ, October 1918.

2. Field-Marshal Montgomery, "Some General Notes on What to Look for When Visiting a Unit," Appendix A in English, *The Canadian Army and the Normandy Campaign*, p. 317; LAC, MG30E100 (Currie Papers), Vol. 52, Diary entry 15 August 1916.

3. Lyn Macdonald, *1914–1918 Voices and Images of the Great War* (London: Michael Joseph, 1988), p. 57. Italics in original.

4. LAC, MG30E18 (3rd Battalion), Vol. 20, Folder 143, 1st Division to brigades, 1 May, 1917.

5. Fraser, *In Good Company*, p. 109.

6. LAC, 3rd Brigade War Diary, June 1917, Appendices 29 and 30.

7.   Ibid., September 1916.

8.   LAC, MG30E505 (Curtis Papers), diary entry, 3 August 1915. Curtis was killed in action on 8 October 1916. MG30E60 (Matthews Papers), Vol. 3, Folder 12, "The Ten Commandments"; Urquhart, *History of the 16th Battalion*, p. 113; John Brophy and Eric Partridge, *The Long Trail What the British Soldier Sang and Said in the Great War of 1914–18* (London: Andre Deutsch, 1965), p. 37; LAC, 2nd Battalion War Diary, July 1917, Appendix 11/2 and 3rd Brigade War Diary, September 1916, Appendix 16A, "Instructions for the Coordination of Work in the Area of the 1st Canadian Division"; 2nd Brigade War Diary, January 1917. Canadian privates, gunners and sappers received $1.00 per day plus $0.10 field allowance. Specialists such as tunnellers received extra, a bonus few infanteers begrudged because they realized the extreme risks inherent in the troglodyte existence of the tunneller (Love, "*A Call to Arms*," p. 237). In the British Army the fact that ordinary sappers were paid more than the infantry (*Field Service Pocket Book*, p. 179) created much resentment: "the bees do the work and the bees make the honey, but the [insert unit] do the work and the REs draw the money." Clarrie Jarman, "My Experiences in the Great War," *Stand To!* 8 (Summer 1983): 5.

9.   Field Marshal Earl Wavell, *Soldiers and Soldiering, or Epithets of War* (London: Jonathan Cape, 1953), pp. 14–15.

10. C.E. Carrington, "Kitchener's Army: The Somme and After," *Journal of the Royal United Services Institute* (March 1978): p. 17. Quoted in Frank MacShane, *The Life of Raymond Chandler* (Harmondsworth, Middlesex: Penguin Books, 1978), p. 29. Chandler, who later became a famous mystery novel writer, enlisted in Victoria, B.C. in August 1917. A brief sketch entitled "Trench Raid" was his only writing about his war service.

11. Carrington, "Kitchener's Army," p. 18.

12. Murray, *History of the 2nd Canadian Battalion*, p. 69; LAC, MG30E432 (Sinclair Papers), Vol. I, Diary, 9 February 1915.

13. Carrington, "Kitchener's Army," p. 18.

14. LAC, RG9IIIC3, Vol. 4077, Folder 3, File 13, 14 September 1918.

15. Pedley, *Only This: A War Retrospect*, pp. 294–95.

16. *SS 152*, p. 12.

17. *Infantry Training (4-Company Organization), 1914*, pp. 6–10 and Appendix II. Drill included close order drill (parade-square) and extended order drill (tactical). The latter was rudimentary, formal and still parade-square oriented. Field work included field engineering, advancing under fire, patrolling, night firing and operations.

18. *Notes to Assist Company Officers in Preparing Lectures for the Training of Category "A" Infantry Recruits* (London: HMSO, January 1917). Pages 1–8 provided helpful hints on teaching drill, musketry, discipline, crimes and punishment, interior economy, pay and messing, trench warfare, hygiene and anti-gas measures.

19. *Training in Canadian Reserve Battalions*, October 1917, pp. 66–67. Tests included the standard rifle handling test (now called "Tests on Elementary Training"), firing the annual fire practise and field firing, including moving and firing at surprise targets and rapid firing at short range. To pass the wiring test the recruit had to have been one of a party of one NCO and nine men who erected a 50-yard length of wire within 15 minutes.

20. Campbell, who served with the Canadian contingent during the Boer War, died in 1963. Lieutenant-Colonel A.A. Hanbury-Sparrow, *The Land-Locked Lake* (Canberra: Broderick Pty. Ltd., 1977), p. 156. While Hanbury-Sparrow quite rightly condemned

the overemphasis on the bayonet, it had (and still has) a place. At Tumbledown Ridge during the Falklands War one company commander of the Scots Guards led his company, bayonets fixed, into the attack. He personally killed one Argentine with his bayonet. Others died on other bayonets.

21. *Notes for Commanding Officers* (1917), pp. 36–37, 41, 49. Prior to the war, in accordance with *Musketry Regulations Part I, 1909, Reprinted 1914* (HMSO, 1914), p. 152, the range qualification entailed firing 250 rounds at ranges of 100 to 600 yards, sometimes firing kneeling or lying prone, sometimes firing with a fixed bayonet. More dramatically, qualification included the famous "mad minute," when the soldier had to fire 15 rounds at a target 300 yards distant. At this rate of fire, to expect accuracy as well would have been somewhat "mad." The more usual rapid fire rate was eight rounds per minute. During Part III of the pre-war annual classification the soldier fired 50 rounds at various ranges. The maximum possible score was 200 points. The qualifications and scores required were: marksman, 130 points; first-class, 105 points; and second-class, 70 points. The excellence of British pre-war shooting at ranges under 600 yards was well known on the continent.

22. *SS 152*, p. 12; *SS 185 Assault Training* (London: Harrison and Sons, September 1917), pp. 11–12; LAC, RG9IIIC3, Vol. 4031, Folder 26, File 7, 1st Division to brigades and Divisional School, 28 March 1917. This particular practise was done over a 100 yard course. Having left the start line the soldier walked at a steady pace for the first 40 yards, practising firing from the hip as he went. At the 40-yard point a sniper target suddenly popped up from a hole. He was required to bayonet the target and cross the obstacle, whereupon he had to bayonet another dummy and deal with a second pop-up target, this time with rapid fire. He then doubled forward 20 yards or so to a trench occupied by three more dummies. Having dealt with these, he threw two bombs at a target, built a fire step in the trench and fired five rounds rapid at a target about 20 yards farther on. Each man did a "dry" run, no firing or bomb-throwing, followed by a "live" practise.

23. NAC, RG9IIIC1, Vol. 3859, Folder 85, File 2, November 1917.

24. Graves, *Goodbye to All That*, p. 78.

25. LAC, 1st Division General Staff War Diary, March 1915, Appendix 16; Military Advisory Board, *Guarding the Channel Ports*, pp. 166–67. Junger, *Copse 125*, p. 23, severely criticized similar German tactical instructions.

26. Carrington, *Soldier from the Wars Returning*, p. 174; *SS 143*, p. 8; *Training in Canadian Reserve Battalions* (October 1917): pp. 39–40.

27. LAC, RG9IIIC3, Vol. 4022, Folder 51, File 9. First Army repeated Haig's direction to its corps, which then included the Canadian Corps.

28. *Training in Canadian Reserve Battalions*, October 1917, p. 4.

29. McClintock, *Best O' Luck*, p. 93; LAC, RG9IIIC1, Vol. 3868, Folder 109, File 3, Canadian Corps to First Army, 10 May 1917; RG9IIIC3, Vol. 4031, Folder 26, File 8. The best grenades of the war, still in use during the Second World War, were the German made "stick grenade" and an improved British Mills No. 36 grenade.

30. *Infantry Training (4-Company Organization), 1914*, pp. 11–12; LAC, RG9IIIC3, Vol. 4031, Folder 27, File 2, GHQ to First Army, 15 July 1918 and First Army to Canadian Corps, 19 July.

31. LAC, RG9IIIC3, Vol. 4031, Folder 26, File 8, 15 January 1918, CO 1st Battalion to company commanders.

32. LAC, RG9IIIC3, Vol. 4031, Folder 26, File 7, 1st Division to brigades, 22 May 1917.

The battalion was only identified as being from 1st Brigade.

33. LAC, RG9IIIC1, Vol. 3859, Folder 85, File 1, Corps to divisions, 26 October 1917, and division responses 30 November, 3 and 16 December (1st Division); RG9IIIC3, Vol. 4028, Folder 17, File 20, 1st Division query 16 November and response 28 November.

34. LAC, MG30E15 (Griesbach Papers), Vol. 3, File 16A, letter to COs, March 14 1917; Hanbury-Sparrow, *The Land-Locked Lake*, p. 214; Lieutenant Armine Norris, *Mainly for Mother* (Toronto: The Ryerson Press, 1917), p. 208. Norris was killed in action in September 1918; Samuels, *Command or Control?*, p. 226; John Terraine, ed., *General Jack's Diary: War on the Western Front, 1914–1918* (London: Cassell, 2000), p. 195. Jack's diary entry for 18 February 1917 (he was then CO of a Yorkshire battalion) says that each month battalions had to submit the names of five NCOs or privates for commissioning.W.F. Stewart, "Attack Doctrine in the Canadian Corps 1916–1918." Master's thesis, University of New Brunswick, 1978, p. 253. Of 10,063 officers who served in the infantry overseas, 4,265 were commissioned from the ranks. Love, "A Call to Arms," p. 83, says that each Canadian reserve unit in Britain maintained a small reinforcement pool of officers, most of them officers from disbanded battalions who had chosen to remain with a reduction in rank rather than return to Canada. Some trained officer reinforcements were also available at the CCRC. Officer casualties were replaced from the CCRC pool, which then filled its gaps from the pools in Britain.

35. *SS 152*, Appendix XV.

36. *Training in Canadian Reserve Battalions*, January 1917 (pp. 5 and 21) and October 1917 (pp. 5–6, 21); *SS 152*, p. 14.

37. Nicholson, *Behind the Lines*, p. 137. Keeping firmly in mind the enormous difference between soldiering in peace and in war, and the time that had elapsed since 1914–18, it is still useful, considering how much had to be learned, to reflect on the fact that most Canadian infantry subalterns during the 1950s and 1960s commanded a rifle platoon for three years or so before moving on to a junior staff position or another command, such as a support weapons platoon.

38. LAC, RG41, Vol. 7, CBC interview.

39. Morton, *When Your Number's Up*, p. 108; Williams, *Byng of Vimy*, p. 147.

40. Rudyard Kipling, *The Irish Guards in the Great War: The First Battalion* (New York: Sarpedon, 1997), p. 62.

41. LAC, MG30E60 (Matthews Papers), Vol. 6, Folders 16 and 21; MG30E100 (Currie Papers), Vol. 37, File 165.

42. Haig quoted in Dancocks, *Spearhead to Victory*, p. 7; *Notes for Commanding Officers* (1917), pp. 319, 321.

43. Miles, *2nd July 1916 to the End of the Battles of the Somme*, p. 571.

44. *Notes for Commanding Officers* (1918), p. 35.

45. *SS 152*, p. 6; LAC, RGIIIC3, Vol. 4023, Folder 1, File 10, Canadian Corps to 1 Division, 19 December 1916 and 3rd Brigade War Diary, 15 and 20 November 1916. The first two students to attend Aldershot from 1st Division were Major Cy Peck, 16th Battalion, and Lieutenant-Colonel G.E. McCuaig, 13th Battalion.

46. Miles, *2nd July 1916 to the End of the Battles of the Somme*, pp. 571–72.

47. *Notes for Commanding Officers* (1917), pp. 355–56 and *Notes for Commanding Officers* (1918), pp. 393–94, 397, italics added.

48. LAC, RG41, CBC interview transcript, Colonel D.H.C. Mason.

49. The exercises are in Chapter X, *Notes for Commanding Officers* (1917) and Chapter XII, *Notes for Commanding Officers* (1918).

50. Williams, *Byng of Vimy*, pp. xiii, 125. Senior officers were not always so amenable. Victor Odlum, at Vimy GOC 11th Brigade (4th Division), would not allow his COs to rotate as battalions; rather they had to rotate by companies, meaning that battalions were half in and half out of the line all the time. The negative impact on training is obvious. (See Pierre Berton, *Vimy* [Toronto: McClelland & Stewart, 1986], pp. 261–62).

51. *SS 152*, p. 5, LAC, RG9IIIC3, Vol. 4007, Folder 4, File 4, Corps Conference minutes 3 November 1915. See Lieutenant Adams's account in Chapter Seven.

52. Graves, *Goodbye to All That*, p. 215.

53. *SS 143*, pp. 3, 11–13. In concept and guidance *SS 143* compares more or less to *Infantry Section Leading and Platoon Tactics*, the infantry officer's bible in the 1950s and 60s.

54. *SS 143*, p. 3.

55. LAC, RG9IIIC3, Vol. 4079, Folder 8, File 6, Canadian Corps Officers' School, November 1916, "Notes on Marches and March Discipline."

56. LAC, RG9IIIC1, Vol. 3873, Folder 120, File 11, 11 June 1916. Rae commanded 4th Battalion from June 1916 to June 1917. For an assessment of Rae and other COs of the 4th see Pedley's account in Chapter Three. Rae was awarded the DSO in 1916.

57. *SS 135*, p. 17; *SS 143*, pp. 3, 14; LAC, MG30E15 (Griesbach Papers), Vol. 3, File 16A, Griesbach to COs, 18 February 1917.

58. Quoted in Nicholson, *Behind the Lines*, p. 136. During his tenure of command (September 1916–March 1918) Cavan emphasized the importance of the leadership of platoon commanders and their training. The latter included attaining proficiency in the employment of all weapons in the platoon. He made the comments at about the time *SS 143* was issued.

59. The syllabi of the January and the February/March 1916 courses are in LAC, 1st Division General Staff War Diary, January 1916, Appendix 5 and RG9IIIC1, Vol. 3868, Folder 109. The January course, in contrast, had only 19 hours of tactics (practical), more time having been spent on lectures on musketry, topography, tactics and other subjects.

60. LAC, RG9IIIC3, Vol. 4042, Folder 20, File 5, Syllabus, 28 July 1916. All-arms cooperation included cooperation with aircraft.

61. Gillon, *The Story of the 29th Division*, p. 99.

62. LAC, RG9IIIC3, Vol. 4032, Folder 28, File 1, Canadian Corps "Notes on Training," November 1917; Vol. 4051, Folder 19, File 8, Ormond to brigade, 15 November 1916. Adams, *Nothing of Importance*, p. 55. One can only speculate to what extent *The Complete Guide to Military Map Reading* (Aldershot: Gale & Polden, Ltd., 1911 and subsequent editions) was issued and studied. It is in many respects a remarkable manual, notable especially for its clarity and for its numerous exercises, filling 42 of its 151 pages.

63. *Notes for Commanding Officers* (1918), pp. 324–33. Resections are possible providing you can locate two places (three is better) on the ground and on the map. If so, take a compass bearing on each and work out the back bearings (the back bearing is always 180 degrees different: if the bearing is under 180 degrees, add 180 degrees to get the back bearing; if the bearing exceeds 180 degrees, subtract 180 degrees). Where the back bearings intersect is your location.

64. The leadership lecture is in LAC, RG9IIIC3, Vol. 4079, Folder 8, File 6.

65. LAC, RG9IIIC1, Vol. 3866, Folder 102, File 19; Vol. 3868, Folder 109, File 10; RG9IIIC3, Vol. 4079, Folder 8, File 6.

66. Feilding, *War Letters to a Wife*, pp. 248–49.

67. *Infantry Training (4-Company Organization), 1914*, p. 6; Fetherstonhaugh, *The Royal Montreal Regiment*, pp. 161, 211.

68. *SS 152*, p. 13.

69. LAC, 2nd Brigade War Diary, January 1917.

70. LAC, RG9IIIC1, Vol. 3859, Folder 85, File 2; Vol. 3868, Folder 109, File 3. In 1917 Lipsett proposed the establishment of demonstration platoons (one per division). These would tour brigades demonstrating all-arms cooperation.

71. *SS 152*, Appendix XIII.

72. The training plans of Griesbach and Loomis, 9 and 11 December respectively, are in LAC, RG9IIIC3, Vol. 4031, Folder 26, File 7 and Vol. 4064, Folder 15, File 4.

73. LAC, RG9IIIC3, Vol. 4031, Folder 26, File 7, Griesbach to units, 3 March 1917; MG30E15 (Griesbach Papers), Vol. 3, File 16B; Baynes, *Far from a Donkey*, p. 170.

74. LAC, 3rd Brigade War Diary, January 1917.

75. *Notes for Commanding Officers* (1917), Chapter One; (1918), pp. 49–57.

76. Beattie, *48th Highlanders of Canada*, p. 157; Fetherstonhaugh, *The 13th Battalion*, pp. 119–20, 137; Macdonald, *Somme*, p. 27.

77. Beattie, *48th Highlanders of Canada*, p. 20.

78. Ibid., p. 213; MG30E318 (3rd Battalion), Vol. 9, File 63, War Diary, March–April 1917; 2nd Battalion War Diary, February 1917, Appendices 2–4; RG 9IIIC3, Vol. 4011, Folder 81, File 1, Byng to divisions, 22 March 1917.

79. LAC, RG9IIIC3, Vol. 4064, Folder 15, File 3; Prior and Wilson, *Passchendaele*, p. 116; LAC, 2nd Battalion War Diary, October 1917, Appendices 11/14 and 11/16.

80. LAC, RG9IIIC3, Vol. 4032, Folder 28, File 1, Notes on Training, 27 November 1917.

81. LAC, RG9IIIC3, Vol. 4046, Folder 4, File 2, Minutes of COs' Conference, Chairman, GOC 2nd Brigade, 22 March 1918.

82. Urquhart, *History of the 16th Battalion*, p. 191.

83. LAC, RG9IIIC3, Vol. 4022, Folder 51, File 9, Macdonell to brigades, 27 April 1918. Syndicates consist of eight or ten officers, a group large enough to ensure several opinions and hence discussion but small enough to ensure that everyone gets a chance to participate and in fact, has no choice but to participate. Syndicates are the system in use in Commonwealth Staff Colleges and in TEWTs.

84. LAC, MG30E15 (Griesbach Papers), Vol. 3, File 16A, 1st Brigade to battalions, 25 June 1917; RG9IIIC3, Vol. 4024, Folder 3, File 4, 1st Brigade, "A Scheme for Solution by Subalterns," 10 February 1918; Vol. 4046, Folder 4, File 2, 22 March 1918; Vol. 4022, Folder 51, File 9. 1st Division to brigades, 23 April 1918.

85. *Notes for Commanding Officers* (1917), Chapters IX and X; *Notes for Commanding Officers* (1918), Chapters XI and XII.

86. LAC, RG9IIIC3, Vol. 4031, Folder 26, File 7, 1st Division "General Instructions Regarding Training Whilst at Rest," 21 August 1917.

87. LAC, 2nd Brigade War Diary, August 1917.

88. LAC, War Diaries of 2nd, 5th, 10th, 13th, 14th, 15th and 16th Battalions for June, August and September 1917.

89. LAC, MG30E15 (Griesbach Papers), Vol. 3, File 16A, 21 December 1917.

90. LAC, MG30E318 (3rd Battalion), Vol. 20, Folder 143, order of 1 May 1918; RG 41, CBC interview, Herbert Mowat; *SS 197 The Tactical Employment of Lewis Guns* (HMSO, January 1918), pp. 14–17, 22–23; *Infantry Training (4-Company Organization), 1914*, Sections 116, 118–19, 121–24.

91. LAC, MG30E318 (3rd Battalion), Vol. 20, Folder 143.
92. LAC, RG9IIIC3, Vol. 4052, Folder 21, File 2; Vol. 4023, Folder 1, File 10.
93. LAC, 2nd and 3rd Brigade War Diaries, March 1918. A series of one day exercises paired two infantry battalions with one tank battalion. (At the time a tank battalion consisted of three companies each of 12 tanks [later four companies].) The aim of the training was to practise infantry-tank cooperation. RG9IIIC1, Vol. 3867, Folder 107, File 8, contains copies of various lectures on infantry-tank cooperation.
94. Edmonds, *Haig's Command to the 1st July: Appendices* (London: Macmillan, 1932), Appendices 16 and 18.
95. LAC, RG9IIIC1, Vol. 3868, Folder 109, 1st Division Training School; MG30E100 (Currie Papers), Vol. 35, File 176.
96. MG30E100 (Currie Papers), Vol. 35, File 176; RG9IIIC3, Vol. 4051, Folder 19, File 9, 2nd Brigade Exercise Operation Order, 10 August; 3rd Brigade War Diary, August 1916, Appendix 28.
97. The appendix was also published later in *Notes for Commanding Officers* (1917). *SS 135* was designed to convert the lessons of the Somme into practise.
98. *SS 135*, pp. 33–34 and Appendix B (pp. 68–72). Courses and exercises are in brigade War Diaries, January–March and July–August 1917.
99. *SS 152*, Appendices I–IV, VII, IX.
100. Murray, *History of the 2nd Canadian Battalion*, p. 188.
101. *Army Rifle Association, Platoon Competition* (France: Army Printing and Stationary Services, December 1917). This four-page leaflet, folded in half, fit a tunic pocket nicely. The rules of the competition could be amended to suit local conditions.
102. Gillon, *The Story of the 29th Division*, p. 101.
103. LAC, MG30E318 (3rd Battalion), Vols. 20 and 63; RG9IIIC3, Vol. 4031, Folder 26, Files 7 and 8, and Vol. 4064, Folder 15, File 4; War Diaries for January and May/June 1918 of 1st, 2nd and 3rd Brigades and 1st, 2nd, 3rd and 13th Battalions. 2nd Battalion's War Diary for March 1918 describes an enemy raid on 21 March during which three Lewis guns jammed, failings that allowed the raiders to get into the battalion's trenches. Despite this the CO stressed the usefulness of the Lewis guns. In the end, they broke up the enemy raid. He also emphasized that it was of the "utmost" importance to keep the Lewis gun in the best possible condition.
104. *SS 152*, p. 6.
105. *Notes for Commanding Officers* (1918), p. 87.
106. LAC, RG 41, *Flanders Fields*, No. 9, "The Battle of Vimy Ridge," p. 6.

CHAPTER NINE

And It All Came Together

*The progress of the Canadians was well known to all Australians
and I know that (to use his own expressive vernacular) it was
Currie's invariable habit to deliver the goods.*

—SIR JOHN MONASH, 1918

The superlative performance of the Canadian Corps during the "Hundred
Days" commencing in August 1918 resulted from three years of fearful hard
times. The many lessons learned during those years made operations go very
well. So, too, did the first half of 1918 during which the Corps reached its
maximum fighting efficiency when "it" all came together: command and control, staff work, and training. As the title suggests, this chapter examines
their contribution to 1st Division's performance in the last half of 1918,
specifically during the Amiens offensive (August), the breaking of the
Drocourt-Queant Line (August–September) and the Canal du Nord-Bourlon
Wood operation (September). For 1st Division these were the most significant
operations in 1918 and the ones that demonstrated its full development as a
good division.

First, though, a brief word on organization is necessary since certain
changes in establishments in the first half of 1918 enhanced Canadian effectiveness. In May Currie gave each division a sapper brigade (three battalions
each of 30 officers and 969 other ranks) and a pontoon bridging unit (66
all ranks) capable of bridging 225 feet. This organization would admirably
meet the needs of the "Hundred Days."[1] The other major change gave each
division 96 Vickers machine-guns, 30 more than in an Imperial division.
Canadian divisions retained the four-battalion infantry brigade. By August
the Corps could punch considerably above any other. The four Canadian divisions stood at 84,000. With the addition of over 35,000 Corps troops, this

made the Canadian Corps the strongest in the BEF and the equal in assault and firepower of a small Army.[2] Knowing this and the Corps' reputation, Haig made it the vanguard of the summer offensive.

Training was critical. The Deputy Chief of Staff at GHQ, Major-General Guy Dawnay, quite rightly believed that "the training of infantry [was] probably the greatest factor of all" behind the victory that came in 1918.[3] Soon after his appointment in January, he began to issue "Notes on Recent Fighting," a series on the lessons of the fighting in progress, including translations of enemy documents and a covering page or two of comment—the idea being to get such doctrinal information out quickly.[4] These notes, Currie said, "were carefully studied and, to a large extent, inspired our training." Notes and Canadian experience were also featured in instructions "precising the methods of Employment of Artillery, Engineers, and Machine Guns in combination with the tactics of the Infantry." When the Corps went into GHQ reserve on 7 May, Currie assigned top priority to "combined training by brigades . . . to familiarise the Commanders and Staffs with the handling of troops in open warfare, and so give the different Arms and Services an opportunity of practising cooperation and mutual support." Because of the Corps' permanent order of battle and the knowledge that it would likely remain in GHQ reserve for some time, he could impose coherence and continuity in training.[5] Training had, in fact, been intensifying since the New Year. During the first quarter Currie held his front with three divisions, leaving one to rest and to train. Each division had about a month out of the line. Of the three in the line, two deployed two brigades up and the other one brigade up, meaning that some brigade level training could continue.[6]

Individual training, especially in musketry, remained a priority and subunit training was not neglected. Before the New Year Currie had warned that while divisional and corps schools would help all they could, COs remained responsible for training their officers. To him, the efficiency of company officers was "the criterion of a Battalion Commander's capacity for commanding and further advancement." That platoon commanding and platoon commanders remained the greatest concern is evident in the responses of division commanders to specific questions about how best to achieve a high standard of all-arms cooperation. The consensus was sub-unit tactical exercises (platoon and company) run by battalions whenever they were out of the line. Training in 1st Division also emphasized the best use of weapons: rifle grenades were effective against emplacements but rifles and machineguns were better against personnel.[7]

In February, Currie expressed his regret that the inexperience of platoon commanders and the necessity for close supervision of platoon training distracted formation commanders. GOC 1st Division (Macdonell) saw the competence of platoon commanders as his most challenging training problem.[8] This should not surprise since platoon commanders, generally young men, had much to learn and be concerned about. He reminded COs of their duty to ensure they came up to the mark: "INSTRUCTION TO BE GINGERED UP all along the line." To him the major shortcoming was

> too much complacency. Officers are inclined to say 'I have been three years on the Western Front; you can't teach me anything.' Possibly not but are you imparting this wonderful experience and knowledge . . . to those you . . . command? Teach, teach, teach . . . make sure the Junior has learnt the lesson correctly, then make him stand on his feet, teach others and play the game.[9]

Brigade commanders echoed his concern. In mid-February Griesbach ordered all company officers in 1st Brigade to attend a series of lectures by various COs, his BM, Staff Captain (Int) and himself on such subjects as

> —What I Expect of Platoon Commanders in the Line
> —What I Expect of Company Commanders in the Line
> —What I Expect of Platoon Commanders While Battalions Are at Rest
> —What I Expect of Company Commanders While Battalions Are at Rest
> —What the Brigade Expects of the Battalions in the Line
> —What the Brigade Expects of the Battalions in the Line in the Way of Reports and Intelligence.

Such lectures seem very basic but he thought them necessary because if nothing were done the standard of company officers would decline to the point where "they will fail us in a great emergency. Officers attending these lectures should be required by Battalion commanders to hand in a written précis of the lecture which they have listened to." Griesbach's conviction that rank had no monopoly on brains shows in his insistence that anyone with "a good idea or suggestion upon any subject connected with the war could count on having it actively considered."[10] Brigadiers also received useful guidance from the COs' course at Aldershot. When Hugh Urquhart, a student on the course in mid-1918 and the former BM of 1st Brigade, forwarded a copy of the school's "Attack in the Open" précis, which took a battalion through the deployment, assault and consolidation stages of an attack, Griesbach sent copies to units, having added notes stressing that the précis was only a guide; ground must dictate and officers had to think out situations for themselves. Nevertheless, his brigade used it extensively, which says much for its quality and for the excellence and reputation of the COs' course itself.[11]

By May, with individual skills at their peak and the units having conducted many sub-unit and unit exercises, brigades commenced a series of sophisticated exercises, each emphasizing a specific lesson. Participants also came from divisional artillery, trench mortars and machine-guns, and contact patrol aircraft from several squadrons. Before the first exercise (2nd Brigade), Macdonell, his GSO1 (Lieutenant-Colonel Parsons), the brigade commander (Loomis) and his BM, Major Lionel Heron, walked the exercise area, paying close attention to the "enemy" strong points and machine-gun emplacements that the two exercising battalions would have to take out. On 15 May the exercise kicked off, the whole affair "quite successfully" carried out. Afterward, Currie conducted the critique, which included comments by the judges, who had observed the events at each strongpoint, and explanations by the COs of their attack methods. Loomis, Macdonell and Currie then offered their criticisms, the two main ones relating to inadequate liaison between the battalions and insufficient use of rifle grenades.[12]

The next day 1st Brigade's exercise had similar participants, results and aftermath, the critique being conducted by the BGGS, Brigadier-General Webber. Griesbach, as usual, bluntly criticized the Operation Orders that the COs had written. 1st Battalion's order, for example, was unclear and far too long. He cautioned COs against overdirection: tell the mortars their task but not how to deploy or operate; find the right balance between "interfering too much or not interfering at all." Well-trained units, he said, made concise orders possible. After many months of trench warfare the need for special instructions in an Operation Order had almost disappeared, experience having made them virtually unnecessary; commanders now had the training and the experience to recognize the problems and how to solve them. But "now open fighting is the novelty and we are getting back to the training in the manuals. If every officer knew his manuals [*Infantry Training* and *Field Service Regulations*] and could . . . apply the principles there laid down, no special instructions would be required." Re-education was necessary.[13]

3rd Brigade conducted exercises on 22 May and again on 28 May, three battalions attacking one: "Keen rivalry was displayed between the opposing forces and many strategies and tricks were resorted to." The first exercise also included sappers, who built bridges and practised demolition of strongpoints. Currie and Macdonell attended, their critique stressing shortcomings in the control of support weapons. Unfortunately, an interdivisional exercise set for 24 May had to be cancelled due to projected operational movements but additional brigade exercises went ahead on 29 and 31 May. The units of 3rd Brigade, as had those of the other brigades, carried out contact work with the Royal Air Force, during which contact procedures were further refined; red flares, for example, proved more visible than white, and smoke grenades were found to be another good way to mark locations. Generally, battalions reported the exercises and procedures as very successful. 1st Division personnel continued to attend RAF courses in contact work.[14]

There was no let-up in June. Commencing on the 8th, brigades conducted several major exercises, ending with a 2nd Brigade exercise on the 27th. 1st Brigade's exercise on 8 June was the most interesting, perhaps because it was apparently the least successful, thereby giving all concerned more to say. Less controlled exercise play created certain artificialities that reduced its effectiveness. The main problem with free play was that participants' reactions could not be known and, as it turned out, neither the "friendly" nor the "enemy" force commander produced sound appreciations or plans, in Griesbach's opinion. "Commanders," he said, "must learn to appreciate situations. They must learn to deliver a real punch based upon a sound conception." Movement and mutual support and fire did not please him either, sub-unit leaders not having exercised proper control. Six weeks of strenuous field work probably had something to do with this; perhaps the series had gone on too long. However, the transition that would have to be made from static to open warfare worried commanders. Griesbach assured his COs "in the most earnest manner that this training is most essential and is the one respect in which the Canadian Corps may fail if put to the test." However, he went on to say that as a result of the training he had confidence in them and he believed they had confidence in him. For once, he may have felt he had pushed too hard for he concluded by describing the relationship as that of a "happy family." Nevertheless, he thought the training had achieved its aim: " to draw attention . . . to the vital differences between trench . . . and open warfare . . . with, it is hoped, a general turning to the manuals for light and guidance upon those principles . . . which have to some extent been lost sight of during the past three years."[15]

In late July while unit training continued, brigades sent several officers to 6 Squadron, Royal Air Force for training in aircraft contact procedure. Currie sent large numbers of Regimental officers to a series of demonstrations of tank and infantry cooperation. These continued into early August. On 5 August officers from 2nd Brigade watched a demonstration and heard about the methods of infantry-tank cooperation learned at Hamel. Overall, training with the tanks seems to have consisted mostly of demonstrations and lectures rather than "hands-on," at least in the case of 1st Division, which found the time too short "to permit of training with tanks, except . . . 13th Cdn. Bn. did carry out company exercises on Aug. 4th." This training fell considerably short of the "brigade-sized scheme" reported by 3rd Brigade. Fortunately, 1st Division battalions had had some training with tanks in March when a series of one-day exercises had paired two infantry battalions with one tank battalion, the aim being to practise formations and tactics.[16]

Loomis provided the best wrap-up of the six weeks of intensive training. He listed the lessons learnt thus:

(1) That an advance, to be successful, must be continuous.

(2) That an attack with unlimited objectives must be organized to go through, before it is launched.

(3) Impossibility of bringing into action in open warfare, unaided by personnel outside its establishment, the Light and Medium Trench Mortars.

(4) Impossibility of a Battalion Commander controlling the action of Tanks and Artillery from Battalion Hdqrs.

(5) Impossibility of Company Commanders handling both of those weapons at the same time, and the extreme difficulty of him handling either of them effectively.

(6) Machine Guns must work in close cooperation with the Infantry.

(7) The danger of stereotyped practises, and of attempting to lay down detailed rules applicable to any two operations.

(8) An attack, to be successful, must be carried out by all arms, properly controlled, and organized for cooperation.

(9) The danger of giving Battalion and Company Commanders too much to do.[17]

Currie believed that the climax of training was Operation Delta, a projected but never delivered Army level attack in the Lys Salient. The intense work that went into its planning tested staff proficiency at all levels. As he said, the preparations "exercised a most vivifying influence on the training; . . . it familiarised all Arms and Services with the difficulties . . . inherent to a surprise attack intended to penetrate suddenly to a great depth." Much of the Delta concept came to pass at Amiens: large numbers of tanks, the key factor of surprise, rapid infantry advance, and special fire planning.[18]

Summing up pre-Amiens training, battalions did considerable work in infantry skills at individual, sub-unit and unit levels; they sent significant numbers of officers and ORs away on courses of every description; they did some training with tanks and aircraft and participated in divisional competitions, despite the influenza that caused the brief illness of many men (260 still sick in 3rd Brigade alone at the end of June). The numerous battalion and brigade exercises during the spring and the comprehensive critiques of them by Currie, Webber, Macdonell and his brigadiers show that 1st Division's training philosophy during the earlier part of the war still applied in 1918: train hard in order to fight easy and push commanders to the limit.

Not much had changed, it seems, since Thucydides had exclaimed that he is best who is trained in the severest school. As ever, formation commanders exhibited their dedication to training. According to George Tuxford, "open warfare was the whole trend," including cooperation with artillery, machine-guns, tanks and aircraft.[19] 1st Division had determined to master the principles of open warfare, just as it had mastered those of trench warfare. By August, Currie thought his divisions as ready as they could possibly be, although the enemy had not yet had his say. While actual operations would vindicate much of the training, a great deal remained to be learned once the offensive began. As well, commanders would soon see their command and control skills tested. For the staff the test came earlier.

When the Canadian Corps returned to the line, relieving XVII Corps on 15 July, Currie held his front with two divisions, and the two in reserve continued training as much as possible. The receipt on Saturday 20 June of a verbal warning order for the impending offensive marked the start of battle procedure and the beginning of intense and prolonged staff work. GOC Fourth Army (Rawlinson) outlined his plan the next day: a limited operation in early August to relieve the pressure on Amiens and to free the Amiens-Paris railway. His concept visualized a one-day assault by the Canadian and Australian Corps supported by over 500 tanks, the objective being the old (1916) Amiens line that was 6 to 10 miles behind the German line. The flanks would be covered by III (Imperial) Corps on the left and XXXI Corps of the French First Army on the right. Once the heavy tanks had broken through, cavalry and light tanks (Whippets) would exploit.

The Canadian Corps had first to move 50 miles south from First Army (Horne) to Fourth Army and have concentrated the following in assembly areas in the Amiens sector by the night before Zero:

> four divisions of infantry, one cavalry corps, two motor machine-gun brigades, four battalions of large tanks, two battalions of whippit tanks, seventeen brigades of field and ten of heavy artillery, and a brigade of horse artillery—representing an actual fighting strength of 30,000 rifles, 2,500 machine-guns . . . 10,000 sabres, 450 field guns, 160 heavy guns . . . and 300 tanks . . . on a frontage of 7,000 yards without the enemy becoming aware that anything untoward was happening.[20]

Movement by road and rail marked the start of worry for the Administration and Quartermaster branches. On arrival in the new area, which had just passed from French to Australian control, the Corps found "none of the organisations necessary for British troops," nothing having been changed for fear of arousing enemy suspicions. No dumps for artillery and "trench ammunition" (small arms and bombs) existed, and advance refilling points had not even been selected, meaning that forward dumping would be delayed and difficult. Army dumps were so distant that trucks could manage only one trip per day, a situation worsened by shortages of trucks and gas. Where to put the thousands of horses that would arrive posed another tough question. Routes, too, barely sufficed since they had to be shared with the Australians and for security reasons, traffic control could not be in place early.[21]

Scant time for preparation exacerbated these formidable challenges. Time was short because of the central operational requirement for: "absolute secrecy" in order "to effect a surprise." Rawlinson's orders on 21 July had a very small audience: his MGGS, GOCRA and GSO1 Operations; the GOC and BGGS of the Australian, Canadian, III (Imperial) and Cavalry Corps; a representative of the RAF; and the GSO1 of the Tank Corps, Lieutenant-Colonel J.F.C. Fuller, who would later call Amiens "the most decisive battle" of the Great War. On 29 July Currie's division commanders and their GSO1s received preliminary orders, one division at a time, and a warning not to advise brigadiers until 1 August. Orders to anyone below this were prohibited until after the move. The A and Q branches learned nothing of the real destination until the 29th, one day before redeployment began, despite the fact that the operation was "essentially an administrative operation until the troops reached the assembly area on 6 and 7 August."[22]

During the week of 21 to 28 July those commanders and staff officers who were not in the know prepared for what they thought would be the capture of Orange Hill, an operation Currie had considered earlier. Those officers selected to attend the Australian tank-infantry demonstrations did so thinking that the tanks had a part in the operation. G Branch arranged more deception, or *maskirovka* (the Russian word for camouflage), which is rather appropriate here since 1st Division several times referred to the arrangements as "camouflage." Convincing the enemy that the Canadian Corps was going north to Second Army demanded careful planning and imagination. First Army widely broadcast its phoney order that the Corps move to Second Army. The order contained no destination since that would have been too good to be true, in the enemy's mind. To add veracity, two battalions actually went into the line near Kemmel (Ypres Salient), together with wireless and power buzzer sections and two casualty clearing stations. Another nice touch saw the establishment in Second Army area of several Canadian railheads.[23]

For A and Q staffs, the 24 hours preceding the move on 30 July were sleepless and frantic. Troops had to be relieved, moved to departure points, put aboard buses and trains, or set on the march, moved nearly 50 miles to concentration areas and then marched or moved forward to assembly areas.

The rail move proved more complicated than anticipated, Army having allocated trains on the basis of the smaller Imperial division: "Owing to the strength of a Canadian division . . . it took nearly three hours to work out a scheme whereby the Division could be moved with the number of trains allotted." Post-Amiens A and Q reports reveal some understandable resentment about the lack of warning but secrecy rightly took precedence.[24] Currie himself set the tone for the move and for the march discipline that would achieve it.

March discipline is:

1. The ceremonial of war
2. A battalion . . . slack in march discipline is slack in war
3. Make section commanders feel that when a man falls out . . . his unit is disgraced. A fit man can march 50 min. [per hour]
4. The more tired the men are, the stricter must be the march discipline
5. Inspect feet immediately after every march
6. Officers must march in rear of platoons, companies, battalions, etc
7. Once more . . . [march] discipline is the discipline of the battle.[25]

On 1 August Macdonell told all ranks wearing the Red Patch what he expected:

The Corps Commander directs that discipline is to be tightened up all along the lines; especially is this to be the case with 'March Discipline.'

He had recently had an occasion to summarily remove a Battalion Commander for bad march discipline, and been forced to withdraw his recommendation reconfirming the Acting Brigadier of the Brigade. Let it be thoroughly understood . . . that the strictest and most rigid discipline on the line of march and in billets is required.

Wise precautionary measures are to be taken on the line of march to ensure that no straggling, etc.—reposting police and sentries to prevent any breaches of discipline such as wandering about in daylight, tampering with abandoned houses, etc. etc.

The standard has been raised throughout the Canadian Corps during the last six months but I am satisfied they can't raise it too high for the Old First Division.

We lead, others follow. The best is none too good for this Division, and nothing but the best will do.[26]

The move went off in splendid fashion, "without serious hitch," said

Currie, and good solutions were found to all the problems encountered on arrival, "thanks to the energy, discipline, training and untiring efforts of all concerned." Virtually every unit ended up in place on time as ordered, ready for Zero Hour, 4:20 A.M., Thursday, 8 August 1918.[27] Major-General W.H.S. Macklin was undoubtedly right in saying that "surprise can be achieved through good staff work."[28] The MGGS of the receiving Fourth Army thought Canadian security and the move as a whole were excellent:

> August 8th is an example of what degree of secrecy can be obtained
> if proper steps are taken and every detail is worked out, and of the
> thorough staff work which is required to collect such a large num-
> ber of men, horses and material on a front of about 22,000 yards
> without the Germans discovering or having the slightest idea that
> such a force had been collected there. It was done solely by paying
> due attention to secrecy and by really efficient administrative staff
> work. It was the administrative arrangements on August 8th that
> made that victory possible probably more than anything else.[29]

Macdonell considered himself "especially fortunate" in staff officers, the relationship between G Branch and A and Q Branches being so excellent that he could boast they were really interchangeable if the need arose. He jokingly referred to "Q," Lieutenant-Colonel James ("Buster") Sutherland Brown, as "the best supply officer since Moses." He was equally appreciative of his GSO1, Lieutenant-Colonel John Rowlett ("Rowly") Parsons, with his "fine analytical brain."[30] Preparations by G Branch, underway since 21 July, became the focus once the Corps began moving. In fact, the focus had widened even before the move. On 28 July Foch redefined the operation, which had been, in Currie's words, "of a purely local character," into an attempt at reducing the entire salient created by the German spring offensive. Now to be "pushed as far as possible" on a front of 22,000 yards, the attack would be mounted north to south by III (Imperial) Corps, the Australian Corps, the Canadian Corps and XXXI Corps of First French Army. The first and the last would no longer just cover the flanks but would mount serious attacks. All would aim at deep and rapid penetration.[31]

The divisional G Staff package for Amiens, Drocourt-Queant and Canal du Nord-Bourlon Wood stacks almost five inches high. The only documents in that accumulation not of 1st Division origin are the two initial corps instructions (19 pages in all) for Amiens. Corps ordered a surprise attack on an 8,500-yard front by 3rd Division (right), 1st Division (centre) and 2nd Division (left), with 4th Division in reserve. Each received one tank battalion (42 tanks) under command. The artillery available came to 17 field artillery, nine heavy brigades and four long-range siege batteries—in all 646

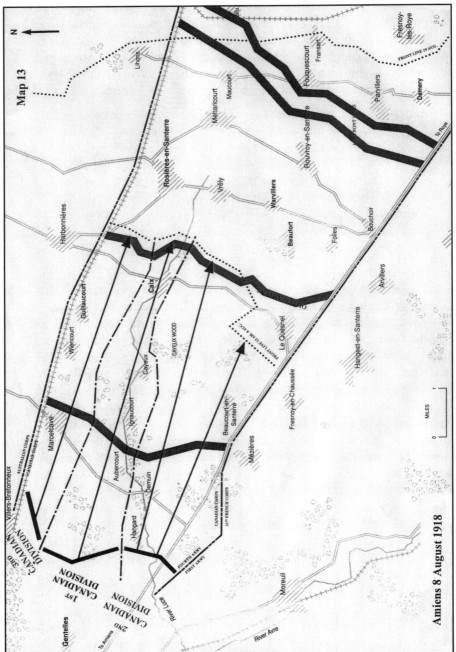

Map 13

Amiens 8 August 1918

Courtesy of the Calgary Highlanders and The Calgary Highlanders Regimental Funds Foundation (map prepared by 2Lt I.R. Spratley)

guns. Of these, 14 field artillery brigades would provide the rolling barrage (200 yards per minute); the other three, which would move forward at Zero, would be on call to engage targets specified by divisions. No preliminary bombardment was planned. For the first day three objectives were set: the first two (the Green and Red Lines) corresponded more or less to the depth of the enemy forward zone (about 5,000 yards) and the final was the Blue Line some 14,000 yards, or eight miles, distant. Currie emphasized surprise and infantry-tank cooperation. Instructions for the former included several restrictions: no movement except at night; troops to remain under cover during daylight; no move by troops in the line except in trenches; no wireless stations to open; very limited reconnaissance and no artillery registration. To ensure good infantry-tank cooperation, Corps ordered:

> The commander of every Infantry detachment to which a detachment of tanks is allotted, will detail one infantryman to ride in each tank. This man will be responsible for watching the Infantry advance and the Infantry signals and keeping the tank commander informed as to the Infantry progress and requirements. He will also operate the signals from the tank to the Infantry.[32]

Currie's plan stemmed in part from the labour of intelligence staffs who had sorted out the enemy order of battle, made terrain assessments, provided maps and interpreted air photographs, which were so valuable in determining the enemy's defensive footprint and capabilities and less so in estimating his intentions,. The enemy was thought to have 24 battalions (less than three divisions) forward, with six more battalions in support and four understrength divisions in reserve. His forward battalions held wide frontages, mostly without significant wire obstacles, and his field defences consisted chiefly of unconnected stretches of trenches with a "vast number of machine gun posts . . . here and there, forming a fairly loose but very deep pattern."[33]

The large stack of G documents mentioned above breaks down into three roughly equal bundles, one each for Amiens, Drocourt-Queant and Canal du Nord. Each contains 1st Division's report, plus warning orders, preliminary instructions, Operation Orders for reliefs, moves and attacks and any subsequent instructions; brigade reports with similar accessories; and those battalion reports and orders that contain interesting aspects of command and control, staff work and training. For Amiens, 1st Division issued the customary warning order, followed by preliminary instructions and then five Operation Orders (30 July–5 August) pertaining to reliefs, moves and approach marches to assembly areas prior to the attack. On 7 August (Zero minus 24 hours) the division issued its executive Operation Order for the attack, followed on 8 August by a similar order for the continuation on the next day. Brigades and battalions issued fewer orders since warning orders and preliminary instructions could be combined at these levels. The operational paper trail for Drocourt-Queant is similar—relief and movement orders were required for the return to First Army—but longer because two preliminary operations had to establish suitable jumping-off lines for the actual assault on 2 September. Canal du Nord-Bourlon Wood presents a similar profile.[34] In each operation, staff and commanders faced unique problems, which will be discussed later as part of command and control.

Several features of the entire staff package are remarkable. The first is the brevity of most documents: battalion orders seldom exceed three pages, brigade orders the same (often only two pages) and divisional operation orders mostly three pages (in three cases, four pages). There is no sign here of the detailed reiterations of higher formation tasks that had so complicated and lengthened operation orders earlier in the war. Each order includes only the relevant detail required by the commander executing it. Such a marked improvement would have pleased former G staff officers who had worked so hard to end the propensity for encyclopedic and ever-longer orders. Time, training and experience had worked their magic. Second, clarity is evident, especially in the mission statement, which almost invariably begins with the identity of the unit or formation, followed by the imperative "will" and ending with exactly what is to be achieved; for example, "3rd Canadian Infantry Brigade will relieve the Centre battalion of the 13th Australian Brigade in the line on the night of 7th/8th August 1918."[35] In this simple, direct sentence we see four of Kipling's six honest serving men: who, what, where and when. How and why followed in the execution paragraphs. The point about clarity may seem obvious (and surely it is just common sense) until one remembers the style of orders and instructions in 1915 and 1916, and even in early 1917 (although infrequently), where one has to dig well down to be sure who is issuing the order, what the mission is and who is going to execute it.

Third, orders and instructions are free of vague terms such as "dawn" and conditionals such as "should" appear only where additional discretion was permitted or when it was simply not possible to be more definitive. The fourth observation concerns the test of a good order: "could I take it and execute it?" In every case in the package the answer is "Yes," although the comfort factor would be higher with some cases and higher still providing some questions could be asked. Nevertheless, the answer remains "Yes." This had not always been so in earlier days when several or many additions and other amendments complicated matters, not always because the situation had changed but because there were ambiguities in the first effort. A fifth point is the format. The documents for the three operations are standardized:

one always finds grouping, say, in the same place and in the same style. Sequencing throughout is also the same. Minor SD is impeccable, a quality that always adds to the confidence of the recipients of an order. Finally, in examining the ladders formed by division Operation Orders, the brigade orders written from them and the 12 battalion orders written from brigade orders, one sees continuity, relevance to the originating level of command, and above all, presence of the essentials. The sense of the whole, whether individual order, ladder or package, is easy to understand, which is commendable and critical because it is tired, even exhausted, distracted, or anxious men who must read and execute orders, usually under severe pressure of time and circumstance.

A blanket assessment of staff work for the three operations remains to be rendered. While it is entirely possible to find fault with this or that order, the whole is of a very high standard, far superior to the staff work of earlier days in the life of 1st Division. A good order is clear, concise, timely and accurate. In 1918 orders in 1st Division met these criteria, and the staff work has the mark of the professional. The GSO1, Lieutenant-Colonel John Parsons, wrote fine, clear orders that invariably contained all the essentials. The BMs, Majors Foster and Wilson (1st and 3rd Brigade respectively) and Captain Herridge (2nd Brigade) took Parson's orders and translated them into fine, clear orders for their brigades. The harried and battle-worn adjutants and other Regimental officers produced good battalion orders from brigade orders, often under appalling conditions. All of these officers owed much to their predecessors who had set Old Red Patch on the road to staff excellence. That 1st Division had come to be a solid and effective formation stemmed in no small part from the sturdy performance of its staff, G and A & Q. The latter did an outstanding job before Amiens. Perhaps the best way to emphasize this, and the enormous improvement over three years of war is to quote a front-line battalion: "it can be placed on record that the troops had hot meals, hot tea, never missed a meal and were only 24 hours without receiving mail—surely a great record." This is a far cry from June 1916 when one Imperial officer at Hooge considered 1st Division careless, disorganized, hungry and undisciplined.[36]

By 1918 staffs at HQ 1st Division and at brigades had reached the point where they routinely met the two tests of staff work: they got the right troops to the right place at the right time with all they needed to achieve their mission and the staffs' written work had reached such high calibre that virtually any officer could take a written order and execute it. 1st Division staffs demonstrated quick thinking in abundance in 1918. They had learned that the art of good staff work was the art of saving time. In short, 1st Division's staff work spelled "excellent" as a result of senior staff officers, especially GSO1s and BMs, employing the lessons of three years of war: delegate responsibility sensibly and work subordinates hard, thereby remaining free to handle the really thorny problems; train and supervise subordinates carefully; be able to write very well; have a sense of humour and share it; be courteous, especially to subordinates, which costs nothing and provides a great deal; and appreciate how vital teamwork is at every level. Above all, 1st Division staffs practised loyalty to superior and subordinate staffs, to units and lower formations and to principles. Most accounts praise the soundness of divisional staff and line relationships. Old Red Patch seems to have been a happy division: its commanders were admired, G and A and Q staffs were on good terms, GSO2s and GSO3s were conscientious and sensible, and the HQ as a whole seemed helpful and open to all. It is always easy for the staff to be wise—afterwards. In 1918 1st Division staff was *wise—during*. That, perhaps, says it all.

Watching the troops marching toward their assembly areas on 7 August, the day before Zero, and listening to them sing "Hail, hail, the gang's all here; what the hell do we care now!" Currie remarked to his staff, "God help the Boche tomorrow."[37] Three days earlier, as Canadians prepared for Zero, Ludendorff, "uneasy about . . . the German Armies . . . no longer *'jauchzend'* (shouting hurrah!) but [at] the other extreme . . . *'zur Holle betrübt'* (depression down to Hell)," issued an order of the day: "We occupy everywhere positions which have been strongly fortified . . . we can await every . . . attack with the greater confidence . . . we should wish for nothing better than to see the enemy launch an offensive."[38] At Zero on the day these words would become mockery, the whole of the BEF attack making "satisfactory progress from the outset."[39]

At 4:20 A.M. on Thursday, 8 August, the offensive opened on a 12 mile front supported by over 2,000 guns and covered by a mist so thick that in some places direction keeping was by compass. 1st Division, which had the farthest to go of the Canadian divisions, attacked on a one brigade front, the lead brigade (Tuxford's 3rd) to take the first objective, the Green Line, and secure it so 1st Brigade (Griesbach) could pass through to its objective, the Red line, at which point 2nd Brigade (Loomis) would pass through to the Blue Line, the final objective. Tuxford attacked three battalions up and two in support, the extra one from 2nd Brigade to be used only in dire need. Six Stokes mortars, 12 Vickers machine-guns and 22 tanks accompanied the infantry. The brigade of field artillery that followed closely to provide fire had little to do since, as Tuxford later said, little serious fighting took place until the enemy main line was reached, where it was fierce but brief. According to Andrew McNaughton, enemy artillery was not a factor for any of the Canadian divisions: "little hostile retaliation. It appears . . . we swamped his batteries."

Nevertheless, casualties were fairly heavy (62 officers and 1,062 ORs).[40]

1st Brigade began advancing at 5:10 and by 8:20 had passed through 3rd Brigade and the Green Line, three battalions up, with 18 tanks (six of its own and 12 of the 22 allotted to 3rd Brigade), six mortars and 12 Vickers. The latter weapons and the artillery remained mostly inactive, enemy resistance not being "very serious" and the infantry "everywhere successful;" the whole of the Red Line was secure before noon.[41] 2nd Brigade, which had left its assembly areas at 6:20 A.M., rapidly traversed the Red Line and continued to the Blue Line, having met little resistance, the advance being "extremely rapid . . . without striking incident and with hardly a casualty." 7th Battalion, which encountered only isolated machine-gun posts, had not a single casualty! None of 2nd Brigade's battalions paid much attention to the flanks: when 10th Battalion could not locate 6th Brigade of 2nd Division it pushed on regardless in "very dashing manner."[42] This, in itself, is indicative of how well 1st Division had adapted to open warfare.

By early afternoon the Canadian Corps "had gained all of its objectives with the exception of a few hundred yards on the right near Le Quesnel [4th Division area] . . . the day's operations . . . representing a maximum penetration of . . . over eight miles." Surprise had been complete and overwhelming.[43]

The next day (9 August) did not go as smoothly. Currie did not get his orders from GOC Fourth Army (Rawlinson) until late the day before, which had adverse impact on divisional battle procedure. The order must have surprised Currie in that it left him and GOC III Imperial Corps (Butler) to set their own Zero hours, in each case advising GOC Australian Corps of the time. This departure from normal battle procedure virtually guaranteed uncoordinated attacks, during which the Australians suffered "losses which need not have been incurred" due to "lack of coordination [and] uncertainty about Zero hour." The requirement for 4th Division to tidy up at Le Quesnel created a redeployment problem for Currie, one greatly complicated by the sudden holding back of 32nd (Imperial) Division, which had been promised to him and which he had incorporated in his plan for 9 August. It was "an unfortunate change [that] was to cause considerable disruption . . . bringing back into action a tired division [the 3rd] . . . and, what was more serious, delaying the attack on 9 August for more than five hours, thereby giving the enemy . . . additional time to bolster his resistance." The requirement for a major redeployment and the issue of new orders proved very difficult since the previous day's rapid advance had so outpaced and disrupted communications that some divisions did not receive the new orders until 5:00 A.M., by which time Zero had been postponed to 10:00 A.M. "instead of 5:00 A.M. as at first settled." III Corps had already determined to start at 5 o'clock. The British official history neatly summarizes the unravelling:

It may be fairly assumed that had not a counter-order been given as regards the employment of the 32nd Division, the general advance of the Canadian Corps could have begun at 5 A.M. as originally fixed by Lieut.-General Currie, or at any rate very soon after that hour. Even with the same delays as occurred in the execution of the 10 A.M. (postponed to 11 A.M.) advance, the divisions of the Canadian Corps would have been under way by 9 A.M., with a whole day instead of only an afternoon before them.[44]

Poor communications also greatly hindered the cooperation between infantry and supporting arms. 2nd Brigade complained of "serious" casualties caused by the artillery "constantly" firing short. 10th Battalion estimated that nearly half of its casualties were due to friendly fire after the unit reached the Blue Line: "our own 4.5 howitzers shelled Battalion Headquarters . . . for about 30 minutes." Throughout the night some units of 1st Division also suffered severely from enemy aircraft that bombed and machine-gunned the newly won positions on the Blue Line.[45]

Almost from the start on 9 August resistance had "stiffened considerably, whatever gains there were resulting from heavy Infantry fighting against fresh troops, with only a few Tanks available for support."[46] Seven fresh enemy divisions had reached the forward area, three opposite the Canadian Corps. Nevertheless, and despite heavy enemy machine-gun fire, 1st and 2nd Brigades, each supported by six tanks and Vickers machine-guns, achieved gains of up to four miles but could do no more. Momentum had gone. With Haig's approval, Rawlinson suspended operations on 11 August.[47] When on 13 August Currie suggested moving his Corps north to the Arras front to launch a surprise attack toward Bapaume, Haig seized on this idea, ordering First Army to prepare an offensive against the Monchy-le-Preux and Orange Hill areas, the latter having been the focus of the proposed attack in July. Commencing on the night of 19/20 August the Canadian Corps began moving to rejoin First Army.

Total Canadian casualties from 8 to 20 August were almost 12,000, 1st Division's casualties being a quarter of that. The Corps had taken 9,000 prisoners (1st Division took over 4,000), 200 guns (the 1st took 80) and over 1,000 mortars and machine-guns. Overall, the Corps "met and defeated elements of 15 German divisions, completely routing four . . . penetrated up to 14 miles on a frontage which had risen from 7500 to 10,000 yards—an area of 67 square miles—and had liberated 27 villages."[48] The former GOC Canadian Corps extended his congratulations. "Gen. Byng was good enough to say that he considered the operations of the Canadian Corps in the Battle of Amiens to be the finest operation of the war."[49]

The other gains, as always, were lessons and improvements to command and control. Many arose from the fact that Amiens had been "almost entirely a battle of tanks and infantry against a machine-gun defence." Griesbach, amongst others, considered the tank "the answer to the machine-gun." 3rd Battalion reported that tanks had sometimes been decisive: "at one point it is very doubtful if we would have been able to get forward . . . had it not been for . . . a tank, which exterminated a series of machine gun nests which held up the whole Battalion." 3rd Brigade, too, found the tanks "invaluable."[50] Adverse comments on tank tactics also surfaced. Griesbach bluntly stated, "I am of the opinion that the handling of the tanks . . . mechanically and tactically leaves much to be desired." 3rd Brigade blamed the heavy tank losses on "insufficient use . . . of dead ground" and a predilection for the sky line that made the tanks easy marks.[51] 1st Division agreed with this and with Loomis' strong preference for keeping tanks under the tactical control of brigade commanders. Obviously, tanks had to avoid wooded areas since therein lurked anti-tank weapons. Most senior commanders concluded that once the tanks had taken out wire and machine-gun nests, they should drop back behind the infantry for protection. The operation also "conclusively proved" the necessity of smoke protection for tanks. Clearly, doctrinal refinement and more training were required.[52]

The air arm does not feature strongly in Canadian documents relating to preparation for the Amiens offensive. Canadian Corps Instruction No. 2 (4 August) advised that contact patrols would be provided by 5 (Corps Reconnaissance) Squadron, RAF, while bombing and machine-gun work on Fourth Army's front would be provided by five day-bombing squadrons, four night-bombing squadrons and eight scout squadrons. 1st Division's preliminary instructions say only that contact aircraft would fly after Zero at times to be notified. Divisional operation orders on 7 and 8 August, immediately before Zero, do not mention air units or operations at all.[53] Colonel Nicholson notes that on 8 August a heavy morning mist covered the Canadian sector and interfered with all forms of air support. 1st Division made no mention of air operations on 8 and 9 August other than to say, "Heavy mist render[ed] observation impossible."[54] None of the 12 battalion reports refer to air support. Brigade reports only mention contact aircraft.[55]

As for support weapons, 1st Division found that the weight of the Stokes mortar and the difficulties of ammunition resupply negated the Stokes' usefulness. 1st Brigade reported negatively on the Stokes: "too immobile to be of much use," said 1st Battalion; "rarely in operation . . . principal difficulty immobility," said 2nd Battalion, whose CO went so far as to call mortars "useless"; 3rd Battalion considered the Stokes not "adaptable to open warfare"; and 4th Battalion thought it "too immobile and vulnerable" but added that mortars had helped break up counterattacks.[56] The two other brigades and most of the battalions echoed these complaints. What was needed was a better means of carriage.[57] The mortarmen who made a real contribution were those assigned to accompany the infantry, their role being to man any captured weapons against the enemy: "In some instances on our arrival the pieces were too hot to touch, showing that the Germans had fired until the last moment."[58]

For the Amiens attack, Corps stipulated that no coordinated machine-gun barrage would be fired along the whole of the 8,500-yard Corps front, a distance approximating about one third of the entire attack frontage. Divisions were free to arrange machine-gun barrages as they wished within their frontages, about 3,000 yards in 1st Division's case.[59] Macdonell put one machine-gun battery under the tactical command of each of his brigadiers, tasked three more to move at Zero and help provide a barrage at the first objective (the Green Line), and allocated another to the consolidation phase, leaving three batteries (a total of 12 Vickers) to thicken the barrage at Zero along the divisional front.[60]

Reports of 1st Division's constituent brigades and battalions show that machine-guns in the direct and indirect roles played a lesser part in the operations on 8 and 9 August. Nine of the 12 infantry battalions made no mention at all of the Vickers in their reports. Another battalion said only that "very little" was seen of them. 2nd Battalion reported that machine-guns "came under notice" on only one occasion. 10th Battalion praised the battery that had been attached to it for its "excellent work" and "splendid cooperation," but gave no specifics. Griesbach of 1st Brigade summarized machine-gun support thus: "They did very little offensive firing and did not materially assist the attack." One reason for this is evident in 2nd Battalion's report: "They [machine-gunners] were unable to get forward their guns and ammunition quickly; . . . their range of action was decidedly limited." Men carrying the Vickers simply could not keep up and were as short of ammunition as were the mortarmen. GOC 2nd Brigade (Loomis) reiterated his strong desire to see Vickers and Stokes integrated into infantry battalions. He did not comment on machine-gun effectiveness in either the direct or indirect role. Finally, Tuxford (GOC 3rd Brigade) merely noted that machine-guns had engaged "targets of opportunity" and had had a "certain amount" of fighting. The vagueness and brevity of his comments suggest that machine-guns were of marginal use, at least in his brigade.[61] 1st Division's report mentioned machine-guns only briefly. Regarding direct fire, it echoed 3rd Brigade's comments that the rapidity of the advance on 8 August made it very difficult for machine-guns to assist in winning the fire fight. Apparently, some machine-guns engaged "distant" targets (that is, overhead fire) but no details were offered and barrage fire was not reported.[62]

The artillery in the case of 1st Division supplied an effective barrage for the initial advance, and counterbattery fire was such that enemy artillery fire was noticeable only by its absence; thereafter 1st Division's artillery came into action "on only a few occasions," the advance being so fast that "Brigade commanders could not get information down to Batteries in time to have it acted upon. Result was that Batteries were advancing at all times more or less out of range." 2nd Brigade categorized the advance as so rapid that the "artillery could give very little assistance to the assaulting troops until they had reached their final objective."[63] Griesbach thought the gunners had not adapted as well as they might have. The three brigades that had moved forward at Zero to engage targets indicated by the infantry had not been bold enough: "our artillery also require to be ginned up in . . . offensive fighting. Trench warfare ideas . . . still prevail."[64] He wanted the guns to move quickly in bounds, always one leg on the ground (that is, always with some guns in fire position). As required, they had to halt, unlimber, get the trails down and rapidly engage (what today is called a crash action). The gunners, no doubt, tried to oblige but they were not mobile enough to get forward quickly. Recognizing this, 1st Division thought the immediate remedy was to attach two field artillery guns to each battalion, the section commander to move with the CO so the guns could go quickly into action. 10th Battalion liked the idea. 8th Battalion thought a "light field gun which could be man-handled (say a horse artillery gun) would be of inestimable value to break up machine gun nests by direct fire." Loomis urged the taking into service of a light infantry gun, which leads one to suppose that as well as being imaginative, he had also read *SS 356 Handbook of the German Army*, which described the 76mm gun found in German assault battalions (six per battalion), and that he knew from intelligence of at least 50 enemy infantry-gun (77mm) batteries.[65] Overall, more training and experience would help but technology was the real problem.

Most of the other lessons concerned tactics during the advance, especially with regard to the role of the Lewis gun, described by Griesbach in his initial report on Amiens as "the weapon par excellence and we may attribute our success to it and to the men who handle it." He devoted another report entirely to the Lewis gun, concluding that intensive training had produced gunners superior in every way to their enemy counterparts: they used ground better, practised mutual support better and exercised more initiative.[66] More vindication of the training in minor tactics that was held during the spring and summer appears in Loomis' reports. Having observed all his units press the advance without worrying unduly about their flanks, he praised the training for having freed "the minds of all Regimental officers of the old ideas and obsessions of trench warfare." 7th Battalion considered the effectiveness of the training "fully demonstrated by the rapidity of the advance," which had placed greater responsibility on junior officers, who had proven they could handle the challenge. Tuxford thought the excellence of the training revealed itself in the fighting that went on simultaneously in several sectors of the attack frontage, "that is to say that the advance wave continued . . . by outflanking tactics, and pushed vigorously forward." 15th Battalion saw the value of the training as the imprint of open warfare basics "with special attention to Lewis gun tactics and overcoming defensive localities."[67] 1st and 2nd Battalions also appreciated the training, which had stood them in good stead, section commanders displaying "splendid initiative" in out-flanking manoeuvres. The training had been of "inestimable value," and the principles of open warfare and the methods of eliminating deeply sited enemy machine-guns had been so thoroughly rehearsed "that they were automatic."[68]

Division had two comments. First, "the methods of infiltration taught . . . were sound [the] combination of fire and movement . . . with scouts and Lewis guns . . . proved effective." The second stressed the tactical sense in pushing on boldly and quickly regardless of flanks.[69] At unit level, infiltration meant working around strongpoints and machine-gun nests, finding the easiest line, pushing on and isolating any enemy still fighting; infiltration that demanded abundant initiative, battle discipline, cooperation with flanking units, flanking attacks and avoidance of the mindset of two years that had found gaps unacceptable. How this worked in practise is evident in the guidance of Lieutenant-Colonel A.L. Saunders, CO 8th Battalion, on "normal" platoon formations and the platoon in the attack. "Normal" had the two Lewis gun sections in the first line on a frontage of 100 yards with the two rifle sections as a second line about 100 yards behind the first, all four sections in either file or diamond formation. Two scouts from each Lewis gun section moved slightly ahead, looking always for good fire positions. Behind them the Lewis guns leap-frogged, one always firm on the ground in a good fire position, followed by the rifle sections. In this way the platoon advanced rapidly with minimum exposure and less risk of surprise, and with the rifle sections, which must make any assault, least fatigued. On coming under fire, the riflemen quickly "dribbled" forward to become the first line. Meanwhile, the Lewis guns took up the best positions to support the assault by the riflemen, the platoon's shock troops. They maintained covering fire until their fire was masked and then followed the riflemen in the assault. Saunders stressed two things: ground and circumstance might recommend variations from "normal," and the Lewis gun was the best provider of covering fire.[70] Such ideas were not peculiar to 8th

Battalion or 2nd Brigade. 16th Battalion (3rd Brigade) operated in similar fashion, all its platoons often in file or diamond formation, the depth of the attack making rapid manoeuvre possible and necessary.[71]

In 1st Division tactical commanders decided on the assault formation, the choice depending upon ground, mission and the commander's judgement and preference. Diamond formation, although slower for movement, was preferred by most. In June Macdonell had ordered thorough practise in diamond, it being so "handy and convenient, especially in dealing with surprise attacks in open warfare." Platoon commanders preferred it because of its flexibility (a platoon could quickly change front in any direction). On the other hand, it was vulnerable to frontal fire and was not very good for producing fire to the front. Another option was arrowhead, which was harder to control but did not have the disadvantages of diamond.[72]

Based on his experience Griesbach, realistic as usual, injected a note of caution and a reminder after Amiens that while sub-unit tactics had improved, officers still had much to learn:

> All officers, and particularly young officers, must be required to forget many of the rules of trench warfare and rapidly master the principles of open warfare . . . In trenches, everything is cut and dried. In open warfare, everything is wide open. Officers not trained in open warfare are often at sea. They ask for a barrage, worry unduly about their flanks and think in terms of the continuous line. Officers . . . must think, read and talk about open warfare. The men are all right, it is the officers who need the training.[73]

5th Battalion identified part of the problem: "on too many occasions officers *fought* instead of *directing*." Situations in which an officer had to fight as a private were so absolutely extreme that direction no longer mattered, just survival, but in the normal course of events and even when "the crisis could not now be long deferred, . . . to meet it [he] would have to be fighting as an officer and not as a private."[74] The parallels between Griesbach's caution and the following, written some 29 years later, are obvious:

> The years of trench warfare, the necessary issue of lengthy orders entering into meticulous detail, and the rehearsal of attacks over a marked-out practise course with fairly well-defined objectives, had produced an army . . . [whose] only tactical principle which was thoroughly ingrained, . . . was that of safeguarding the flanks. . . . A young divisional commander said at the time that there was "still too much blue, red and green line"—that is, fixed objectives—about the battles . . . In view of the imperfect tactical training of the regimental

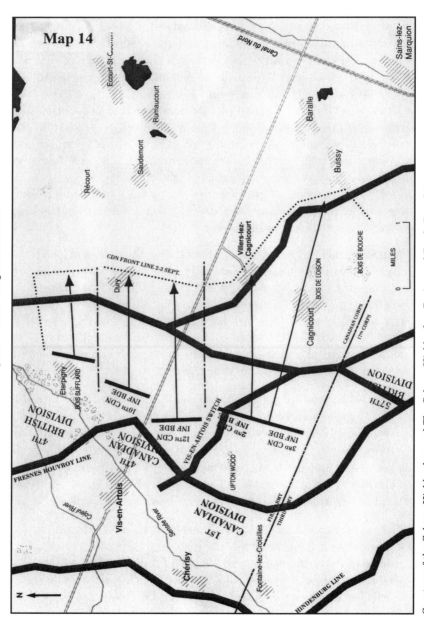

Map 14

Drocourt-Queant Line 2 September 1918

Courtesy of the Calgary Highlanders and The Calgary Highlanders Regimental Funds Foundation (map prepared by 2Lt I.R. Spratley)

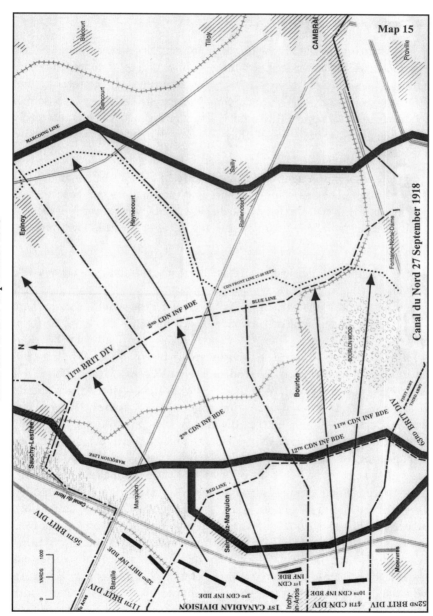

Canal du Nord 27 September 1918

Map 15

Courtesy of the Calgary Highlanders and The Calgary Highlanders Regimental Funds Foundation (map prepared by 2Lt I.R. Spratley)

officers . . . the system of limited advance was inevitable . . . On the
other hand, the patrol work of small parties, . . . was magnificent;
the use of ground, the value of the indirect approach and envelop-
ment were well understood.[75]

Nevertheless, in the aggregate, battalion and brigade commanders had
responded well to new ideas, exhibiting a high degree of adaptability and
skill in the methods of open warfare. They had generally appreciated that
"the tenets of trench warfare, hung fondly about our necks, [were] a burden
too heavy to be carried swiftly or far."[76] Perhaps Loomis, who had repeatedly
proven himself one of the most innovative Canadian brigadiers, should have
the last word:

The prospect of a fight, after long months of trench warfare and of
still more irksome training, had brought the troops to that cheerful
humour in which the British soldier fights his best. Never was the
2nd Brigade in better shape; never was it better trained; never was
its morale higher.[77]

This applies in full measure to 1st Division, whose infantry as a whole had
demonstrated a sound grasp of all-arms tactics.

On 23 August Canadian Corps HQ opened in First Army's sector where
Currie assumed command of the front formerly held by XVII Corps. The divisions arrived separately from the Fourth Army area between 20 and 28
August. Currie's new orders, received verbally from the C-in-C in the presence of GOC First Army on the 22nd, ordered the Corps, on the right of First
Army, to attack eastwards, the axis of advance being the Arras-Cambrai
road; break the Drocourt-Queant Line south of the Scarpe and reach Canal
du Nord, thereby unhinging the Hindenburg Line; and prevent the enemy
rallying behind his formidable defences. This entailed penetrating four
strong defensive lines, thick in places with wire obstacles, innumerable
machine-gun posts and deep dugouts: the old German line east of Monchy-
le-Preux (including Orange Hill), the Fresnes-Rouvroy Line, the Drocourt-
Queant Line and the Canal du Nord Line. Surprise would not be possible,
except perhaps as to time. Because of heavy tank losses at Amiens each
attacking division would have only nine tanks and these would follow rather
than precede the infantry, a principle laid down "as a result of lessons
learned" during that operation. Zero was set for 3:00 A.M., Monday, 26 August.
What enabled the Corps to undertake "the hardest battle in its history" with
only three days' notice was excellent trench railways, good communications
and administrative facilities, and the fact that much of the planning had
already been done for the proposed and never executed Orange Hill attack in

July. Currie ordered a night attack by 2nd and 3rd Divisions, each on a one-brigade front, the idea being that both divisions could then fight for three consecutive days.[78] That Currie could opt for a night attack, one of war's most difficult operations, by two divisions is indicative of his complete confidence in the command and control abilities of his formations. The advantages of having a well-experienced and efficiently organized staff were also obvious. He would not have been so sure of such an operation in 1916 or 1917.

By nightfall on 26 August, the Corps had secured Orange Hill and the whole of the Monchy Heights. The next day's advance slowed in the face of stiffer opposition and slowed even more the following day, the enemy having brought reinforcements forward. While the Fresnes-Rouvroy Line had been pierced in several places, it had not been compromised. 2nd and 3rd Divisions gradually became exhausted. On 28 August, Zero for the attack on the Drocourt-Queant Line by the Canadian and XVII Corps was set for 1 September, the intention being to cross Canal du Nord in the same operation. First, 1st Division and 4th (Imperial) Division relieved 2nd and 3rd Divisions on the night of 28/29 August. On 30 and 31 August the Imperials and 2nd and 3rd Brigades accomplished the initial task of establishing a good jumping-off line for the assault.

1st Brigade's attack is the most interesting of these preliminaries. Griesbach planned a bold night march by two battalions into the enemy's open southern flank, a similar approach by another battalion in the northern part of the brigade sector, then a convergence of attacks launched from flanks and rear along southerly and northerly axes—the whole supported by an ingenious rolling barrage moving not west to east but south to north. Such innovation was typical of Griesbach who was, in Macdonell's words, "the quickest officer that I have ever had anything to do with to grasp the tactical advantage or disadvantage of a given situation . . . The way . . . it was done was his own idea." The plan was a "masterpiece," brilliantly supported by the CRA, H.C. Thacker, who in a very few hours prepared a complicated fire plan, described by Griesbach as an "ingenious barrage [that] boxed in the whole area of attack and moved in front of the attack of each battalion." It proved to be "perfect." 1st Division later described the barrage as L-shaped as it crept forward, thereby serving both for the eastward attack by the 3rd Battalion and the northward attack of 1st and 2nd Battalions.

As it turned out, the most difficult part of the attack was the "curious psychological" disorientation suffered by the three units. Having attacked north and south, they oriented their consolidation toward those directions rather than toward the east, a fact the enemy exploited in counterattacks that had some success until 4th Battalion entered the fray from the west, the conventional direction. Even after consolidation the three units persisted in moving north or south with prisoners and wounded rather than take the short route west. "This matter of attacking in one direction and then facing another," said Griesbach, "calls for more than passing attention as a study of tactics." 1st Division agreed, noting that training was required in such tactics as forming front to a flank.[79] That battalions could execute such a complicated operation and 1st Brigade and 1st Division could contemplate improving upon it is indicative of the calibre of command and control in the division by 1918. It is unlikely that such an operation could have been mounted in 1917; certainly it could not have been executed then on such short notice and with the equanimity that is so evident in the reports on the operation.

For the actual Drocourt-Queant attack, Currie deployed 1st Division right and 4th Division left, with over 700 guns in support. Zero was postponed until 5:00 A.M. on 2 September, thereby allowing time for minor operations to improve the jumping-off line, for additional wire-cutting and for 4th Division's redeployment to replace 4th (Imperial) Division, which had suffered crippling losses in helping tidy up the jumping-off line. Currie had also to defeat elements of two fresh enemy divisions that launched strong counter-attacks astride the boundary between 1st and 4th Divisions on 1 September; they broke in twice but were expelled each time.[80] Hand-to-hand fighting continued until Zero and even beyond it, the troops moving forward to attack the Drocourt-Queant Line becoming involved in the ongoing fight along the jumping-off line.[81] That the attack could still go forward testifies to the superb battle discipline, the elan and the physical and mental toughness of those wearing Old Red Patch. Such characteristics had not appeared out of the blue; they had been absorbed as a result of over three years' hard experience. The action says a great deal about the confidence and competence of 1st Division. The main Canadian attack, launched by two brigades, with 1st Brigade close behind to pass through to the final objective, gained the Drocourt-Queant Line and its supporting line but could not cross the Canal du Nord, behind which the enemy had retired. Nevertheless, Currie thought the results "gratifying":

> a battle fought . . . with six divisions for nine days, on a front of 10,000 yards, that resulted in an advance of nearly twelve miles straight down the Arras-Cambrai Road, that outflanked the enemy's defences west of Douai and caused a retirement from Arras to Armentieres, that protected the left flank of the great attack of the Third and Fourth British Armies . . . That the enemy put forth every effort to stop our advance is shown by the fact that . . . the Canadian Corps alone met and defeated thirteen German divisions.[82]

The Corps took over 10,000 prisoners, 100 guns and over 1,000 machine-guns, 1st Division's haul being 4,000, 60 and 250 respectively. Currie especially praised Old Red Patch, assessing its achievements in taking the Fresnes-Rouvroy and the Drocourt-Queant lines as "one of the finest performances in all the war." Of the whole attack he said, "It is a question whether our victory of yesterday or of August 8th is the greatest but I am inclined to think yesterday's was."[83]

Since the main participants were infantry and artillery, tanks being little involved, most of the lessons learned concerned the two older arms. For the attack each battalion had one 18-pounder under command, the gun being under the immediate direction of an artillery officer. These guns generally gave good service in the direct fire role. At brigade level, artillery and infantry commanders worked and moved together, such an excellent arrangement according to Tuxford (3rd Brigade), that he was "surrounded by artillery officers clamouring for targets." 2nd Brigade thought its HQ was "embarrassed with a multitude" of artillery liaison officers. Loomis, not surprisingly, again repeated his demands for a lighter field gun to accompany the infantry.[84]

HQ 1st Division thought that while artillery and machine-guns had been generally effective, their owners had been hesitant "to risk their too highly prized guns." Showing more initiative and pushing batteries forward rapidly would be "a long step in the required direction. The idea is to eliminate stickiness."[85] Lieutenant-Colonel J.P. Girvan of 15th Battalion complained that the Vickers had no ammunition when he needed them, another instance of the inability to get sufficient ammunition forward quickly. Only Tuxford commented on indirect fire by machine-guns; he, too, complained that when called upon for such fire they could not respond due to insufficient ammunition. Griesbach thought machine-gun tactics left much to be desired: "I would like to treat machine guns as other arms . . . ought to be treated by the Infantry but I am now of opinion that . . . [they] must be attached to the Infantry and specific orders given by the Infantry Commander."[86] As for the battalions, five did not mention machine-guns in their reports. Those that did praised the machine-gunners for their prompt and effective direct fire and for their contributions to consolidation and to flank protection. Most COs were effusive about their Lewis guns, being delighted with how "the men advanced in section rushes, with covering fire from Lewis guns, exactly as they had done during our manoeuvres in the back areas." This effective integration of the Lewis gun presents a very different picture from *SS 143 Instructions for the Training of Platoons for Offensive Action, 1917* (February), which had considered the Lewis gun only as a "weapon of opportunity."[87]

1st Division had very limited air support during the Drocourt-Queant attack. Its report on operations from 26 August to 4 September refers only briefly to contact aircraft. 1st and 2nd Brigade reports make no reference to air at all. 10th Battalion complained that the enemy's complete mastery of the air allowed him to seriously damage the battalion with machine-gun fire. Other units (and 3rd Brigade) remarked that friendly aircraft did not seem to know where the objective was, this being evident in their repeated requests for flares at 3,000 yards and more behind the leading assault troops.[88]

No complaints arose about platoon commanders. 1st Battalion thought success was entirely due to their initiative and their "outstanding" application of the lessons of training and of recent operations. 14th Battalion, despite having only two officers per company and very few senior NCOs, had been able to push on, lance-corporals leading platoons and privates leading sections. Tuxford praised his COs, who moved their battalions quickly eastward without regard to their flanks. Lieutenant-Colonel Girvan, explaining why things had gone so well and why 1st Division had become such a formidable and effective fighting formation, said, "It was a Platoon Commander's battle and they all delivered the goods."[89] The contrast between this and 1916, when subalterns were thought ignorant of their duties, including leadership, is striking. Clearly, the time and effort spent on their training had paid off.

From the perspective of the GOC (Macdonell) the operation had proven the value of enveloping tactics and the necessity of rapid movement (eliminate "stickiness," be bold, "Always Bold") and of offensive thinking. How far 1st Division had come in three years is evident in the conclusion of his report:

> These operations . . . were only possible in the limited time (4 days) by reason of . . . sound training and splendid elan . . . These operations had to be decided upon quickly, frequently the tasks had to be set with insufficient time for full explanation, relying upon the training, initiative and thrust of Juniors to instantly grasp them and push them through . . . The truism was amply demonstrated that if the training of Junior ranks has been sound it can be relied upon and instructions need not be clogged with items which have been a matter of training. Training must be continued along these lines; all officers must be able to switch rapidly to any new plan. Facility in map reading and the use of ground are essential. In short, in the operations under review, there was not sufficient time for the minute instructions which were thought necessary during the Trench Warfare phase. The D–Q operations, with the necessary preliminary fighting for the J.O.L. [jumping-off line] were all carried out

in a much shorter time than would have been considered necessary for the preparation of a trench raid last winter.[90]

A "bounce" crossing of the Canal du Nord, one of the objectives assigned for the Drocourt-Queant operation, had proven optimistic. In fact, it was beyond the capabilities of the Canadian Corps alone. Once on the western bank, First Army ceased active operations for about three weeks and commenced preparations for a larger scale attack. On 22 September the C-in-C issued orders: First Army on the left will capture the heights of Bourlon Wood, push forward to anchor the left flank on the Sensee River and protect the left flank of Third Army; Third Army will cooperate with First Army, press forward to secure the passages of the Canal de l'Escaut and cooperate fully with Fourth Army; Fourth Army will advance in the direction of Bohain commencing on Zero plus two days. Horne, GOC First Army, having been warned, issued his formal orders on 18 September, confirming the verbal orders that three days earlier had assigned Canadians the leading role: "The operations of the First Army will be carried out by the Canadian Corps with the cooperation of XXII and VIII Corps."[91] He visualized a narrow crossing on a front of 2,500 yards where the canal was dry or nearly so and then a fan-out to a frontage of nearly 15,000 yards along the Sensee and Schelde Canals. For the Canadian Corps this entailed a canal crossing, penetrating the Canal du Nord Line some 500 yards east of the canal, the Marquion Line another 1,500 yards to the east and, finally, the Marcoing Line farther east still. Once over the canal, the Corps in advancing northward would roll up the enemy.

The depth of the attack necessitated phasing. In Phase One 1st Division on the left on a front of 800 yards where the canal was dry, and 4th Division on the right would cross on a front of 2,500 yards and capture Bourlon Wood, the high ground north of the wood and the entire valley of the Canal du Nord as far north as the village of Sauchee Lestree, about 1,000 yards north of the Arras-Cambrai road. 3rd Canadian and 11th (Imperial) Divisions would then come into line right and left respectively in preparation for Phase Two, during which all four divisions would advance north to the Sensee Canal, seize the bridges over the Schelde Canal northeast of Cambrai and establish bridgeheads on the far bank. When this last task was added on 22 September, Currie received 11th (Imperial) Division under command. Artillery available included 22 field artillery and nine heavy brigades, with over 800 guns in all. Zero was set for 5:20 A.M., Friday, 27 September.

Well might Currie say "This attack was fraught with difficulties." Such a narrow crossing front, which could mean extreme congestion and presentation of lucrative targets, worried him; he thought a concentrated enemy bombardment, or gas attack, a "dreaded possibility." Also, the "intricate manoeuvre" of expanding rapidly to a wide front from a narrow bridgehead "called for most skillful leadership . . . and the highest state of discipline." In such an operation many "ifs" could not be avoided, but there must have seemed to be too many "ifs." The perilous nature of the operation shows in Griesbach's reassurance of subordinates that the attack (he called it a "knock-out blow") had been well planned and would be well supported.[92] Fortunately, only two command changes had occurred. Neither unduly worried Currie. He knew these would present a learning curve but he had confidence in the abilities of the two new commanders: on 13 September Loomis (2nd Brigade) replaced Lipsett as GOC 3rd Division and Lieutenant-Colonel W.F. Gilson (CO 7th Battalion) replaced Loomis.

Sappers and gunners would play key roles. The very able GOCRA (Morrison) again exercised his usual thoroughness and imagination. To ensure fire support would always be available, field artillery had to cross behind the first infantry just as soon as space for gun positions became available. He decided to leapfrog the guns forward, with some of them firing and others moving to new positions where they in turn would fire, the whole process rather like going hand-over-hand up a rope. The fire plan also featured back barrages, which would start at the limits of range and then walk backward to meet the usual creeping barrage, thereby causing the enemy to think his own guns were dealing death. The key to maintaining continuous fire support was getting over the canal fast. This was where the sappers came in. They had, in fact, been preparing for exactly this since the issue on 28 August of the amendments to the Drocourt-Queant plan. Light railways had been constructed and the men and material required to bridge the canal had been concentrated and readied to do their part. On Zero Day (27 September), just 90 minutes into the attack, 4th Division's guns were clattering across the first bridge to the east bank. An hour later eastbound traffic crowded two more bridges. In 1st Division's area heavy and persistent fire on the sappers delayed completion of bridges until early afternoon, at which time the artillery crossed. Fire support did not slacken, however, since Morrison had wisely kept all guns under Corps control, thereby guaranteeing fire wherever required. To compensate for his not allowing divisional fire control, machine-guns thickened the artillery barrage in addition to providing direct fire.[93]

1st Division had the most difficult operational task, which in itself was recognition of its high reputation. The operation required commanders and staff "to prepare minutely" as far before Zero as possible. Even before receiving their orders on 16 September, they had several times reconnoitered assembly and crossing areas: "The value of time spent on . . . this . . . is unquestionable." When not so engaged, they studied air photographs of the canal and the eastern bank.[94] Starting from a front only 1,100 yards wide, the division would fan out to cover 6,000 yards at its final objective, some 6,000 yards distant. Macdonell ordered a two-up attack, 1st Brigade right and 3rd Brigade left. Once they were secure on the Marquion Line, 2nd Brigade would come into line between them, whereupon the advance would continue to the high ground along the Marcoing Line. After crossing the canal 1st Brigade had to take three trench lines, all frontally, ending up some 6,000 yards to the east, where it became responsible for 1,500 yards of front. 2nd Brigade had a similar mission, a frontal advance of about 3,500 yards and a final responsibility for 2,000 yards of front. 3rd Brigade had a more complicated part involving crossing the canal and then wheeling north and even west, "thus presenting the unique spectacle of . . . attacking directly toward our own lines." It would continue rolling up the Marquion Line, crossing the Arras-Cambrai road and pushing on right up to the Canal de la Sensee. Tuxford's men had 6,000 yards to go and on arrival at the Sensee would have to defend a front of 2,500 yards. Such an operation necessitated a fire plan out of the ordinary. H.C. Thacker, CRA 1st Division, came up with what he called a "monkey puzzle barrage": fire would move forward as usual and then drop back toward our guns, meaning fire would be between our troops and the guns. At some point Old Red Patch would be fighting east, north and west in the "most intricate large-scale operation ever contemplated for the division."[95] Again, such an operation would have been highly problematic earlier in the war.

The very narrow brigade frontage at the canal (500 yards) forced Griesbach to attack with only one battalion. In a "whirlwind" assault, led by the young (aged 28) and tactically shrewd Harry Nelles, the 4th Battalion crossed in 12 minutes and quickly secured the first trench line, whereupon another battalion passed through and took the second objective. By 1:00 P.M., not quite eight hours after Zero, 1st Brigade was firm on its final objective, the whole attack having gone "exactly as planned."[96] 3rd Brigade took somewhat longer due to thick enemy wire and heavy machine-gun fire but by 2:30 P.M. 1st Division had everywhere accomplished its Phase One tasks.

In Phase Two (the continued advance from right to left of 3rd, 4th and 1st Divisions and 11th (Imperial) Division) 2nd Brigade led for 1st Division. The initial rapid advance ceased when leading troops encountered very thick wire and extremely heavy defensive fire just east of the Douai-Cambrai road. Attempts to regain momentum continued until 1 October but the attack could not be sustained, communications being chaotic and coordination faltering. On 1 October, 3rd Brigade achieved but quickly lost some significant gains, a clear sign that it was time to pause for reorganization. That night 2nd Division began relieving the 1st, which went into reserve, thus ending 12 straight days of fighting.

During Canal du Nord-Bourlon Wood, the third panel of the triptych of this chapter, and of Canadian participation in three major offensives by two Armies within two months, the Canadian Corps advanced 23 miles, defeated 31 German divisions and took 18,585 prisoners, 371 guns and 1,023 machine-guns. More important than the numbers was the net result of the three operations in which Canadians had been the vanguard: two enemy Army groups had been forced out of Germany's last prepared defensive line. Pursuit followed. A high value is always placed on leadership but a high price is always exacted. Corps casualties for the period 27 September–7 October exceeded 13,000 all ranks. In comparison, XXII Corps lost less than 2,000. The three offensives together during August, September and the first week of October cost 30,000 Canadian casualties.[97]

Before looking at 1st Division reports on Canal du Nord-Bourlon Wood and its GOC's view of this operation, reflection upon the division's capabilities in August 1918, as opposed to earlier days, is useful. It is inconceivable that 1st Division as it was in the beginning, or even at the mid-point of its career could have executed the Drocourt-Queant or the Canal du Nord operations. The first, a highly sophisticated operation, demanded precise execution founded in sure exercise of assault power, as well as fire power. The second operation was even more challenging, involving not only coordination of assault and fire power but management of great risk in negotiating a defile at a canal, followed by a rapid fan-out on a wide frontage, with rather tenuous flank protection during that manoeuvre, and then the capture of ground vital to the German defence.

It is equally inconceivable that gunners earlier in the war could have planned or executed the complex fire plans that supported the two operations. First of all, until mid-1917 the command structure to conduct such "shoots" did not exist, CRA being at that time an advisor, not a commander, and without the staff, communications and authority to contribute to operations in such decisive fashion. Even when he became commander in fact as well as in name, competence and confidence in the new system did not instantly exist. Only time and experience could achieve that as well as the liaison and other control measures that ensured good fire support, such as Forward Observation Officers (FOOs) at all levels down to brigade (and sometimes even down to battalion) for both field and heavy artillery; short-term officer exchanges between infantry and artillery to permit each arm to see what the other had to do and how; and dedicated artillery communications to permit rapid execution of fire orders. Technology, too, improved over time, such as the 106 fuze that made wire cutting easier and the sound-ranging and flash-spotting techniques that made Canadian counterbattery fire so effective. It took a great deal of experience, time and hard work before mutual confidence grew to the point where gunners and infanteers alike knew that fire would usually come down upon the desired target. In the same way, only when CRE became a proper commander did engineer resources get put to best use. These changes allowed the infantry and the two support arms to develop the superb teamwork displayed throughout the Hundred Days.

It took almost as long to achieve the best integration of machine-guns and mortars, this process extending even into the Hundred Days when it became evident that these weapons should be *in* the battalions, not merely *with* them. Canadian commanders continued to grow in competence during the last half of 1918, yet another example of the command excellence that had been developing since 1915. The brigadiers of 1st Division, the COs and the GOsC the division had consistently displayed their adaptability and their ability to anticipate during three years of war. Throughout, they had demonstrated their strong willingness to learn; for example, everyone learned from the Regina Trench "disaster" of October 1916. Moreover, 1st Division came to see that the critical elements were the platoon, its OC, and the soldier with his rifle, the number one weapon. It took time to recognize this, cast aside the extravagant enthusiasm for specialists such as bombers, achieve the most efficient mix of platoon weapons, provide the platoon with sound doctrine, and motivate and train its OC to make himself and his command the best they could possibly be.

In sum, 1st Division effectively integrated man and machine in its operations. Henry Lloyd's wisdom about principles and their effective practise, which was hard to achieve, applies to 1st Division: "If the perfection we aim at is not attainable, to approach it is a great merit, and will in some measure answer the end proposed."[98] It can fairly be said, in view of its record, that Old Red Patch shared in and often stood in the forefront of the general Canadian and BEF recognition of what the anonymous author of *Kritik des Weltkrieges* referred to as the "fundamentally important value of . . . technical invention." In his view, a major cause of German defeat was an underestimation of the effect of firepower and a failure to perceive the need to effectively assimilate man (morale and tactics) and firepower.[99]

Throughout the whole of the learning process, and even before, commanders and staff worked hard to inculcate battle discipline, the attribute that kept men in the trenches, kept them organized and alert, and helped them to develop and adhere to routines, which had to become as automatic as possible so that commanders could focus on planning and conducting active operations. Battle discipline and all of the command and staff functions described in this book resulted from another lengthy process: the identification, implementation and validation of control measures in grouping, movement, fire; HQ locations; communications; assembly areas and jumping-off lines;

intelligence resources and products; and consolidation procedures. Training was critical in all of this. 1st Division commanders and staff learned how to train so successfully that the training as described earlier in this chapter and in this book prepared Old Red Patch for any eventuality.

Good battle procedure, too, did not just appear. Commanders spent months discovering the meaning of "appreciating the situation" and applying that skill to planning. Another fundamental aspect of improved command, the development of initiative, made possible the open warfare success of the second half of 1918. Open warfare, being less structured and less predictable than trench warfare, demanded habitual initiative, ability to improvise and rapidity of thinking and manoeuvring. Senior commanders demonstrated how very successfully they had adjusted from the limited set-piece attacks of 1917 to the rapid succession of set-piece attacks in 1918, which in essence formed a continuous coordinated advance during the Hundred Days. Moreover, the three operations showed that by mid-1918, as opposed to former days, Canadian battle procedure provided the "hustle to be ready on time," no matter how difficult and complex the mission.[100]

In short, three years and the best efforts of every officer and man took the division from raw militia to a good, professional formation. By mid-1918, well-equipped, well-trained and well-motivated men, their material wants ensured by good staff work, were led by commanders who had become professional, capable of operating at a level far superior to that of the war's earlier days. 1st Division had become, in Robert Graves' word, "top-notch."[101]

Griesbach's report on Canal du Nord, where 1st Brigade had the leading role, offers few lessons of interest. Our artillery was effective; theirs was not. He did not comment on mortars and machine-guns, other than to say that the latter provided a heavy barrage at Zero. As was usually the case with indirect fire, he could not say what damage had actually been done to the enemy. Nor could the machine-gunners say. The tenor of all 1st Division reports during the Hundred Days shows that machine-gun barrages, from the division's perspective, were most effective at Canal du Nord. Griesbach also commented on enemy machine-gunners, who continued to fire and cause casualties until the attacking troops were on top of them and then tried to surrender, "our men [being] disinclined to admit that the enemy could have it both ways." Battalion reports are very brief, even cryptic, very little being offered by way of lessons, except in minor tactics. 2nd Brigade offered only one lesson: the necessity for a light field gun for battalions. 3rd Brigade's only significant observation complimented the artillery for its excellent support. One battalion reported shortages of machine-gun ammunition, another instance of the inability to get it forward quickly continuing to inhibit effectiveness.[102] As for air support, while the divisional report on

Canal du Nord, Bourlon Wood and Cambrai operations (27 September–2 October) covers engineers, artillery, tanks, signals, machine-guns and the services in considerable detail (the report exceeds 60 pages), it scarcely mentions air. Brigade and battalion reports for the same period refer only to contact aircraft. The only comment in any length came from 2nd Battalion, angry about the scarcity of friendly aircraft during the Canal du Nord crossing and the following day (28 September):

> Enemy aircraft were very active and harassed us continuously . . . It did not enhance the morale of our men to see the enemy's aircraft disporting themselves at our expense, and to see numerous German balloons in the air . . . directing his artillery against the attacking troops.[103]

For 1st Division, for the Canadian Corps, for the BEF and, indeed, for all the Armies, air photography, contact patrols, reconnaissance and bombing in enemy rear areas, although useful, could not be decisive. The RFC/RAF was an auxiliary arm during the Great War and again during the Second World War. Even if the air arm in 1914–1918 had been given everything by way of resources, it is difficult to see, *given the technology of the time*, how it could have been of more value to the Army than it was.

1st Division's report does not contain the usual section on "Observations and Lessons." One appendix, written by the CO of 1st Battalion, Canadian Machine Gun Corps, is interesting for its comments on the relationship between a machine-gun commander and the GOC/CO of the formation or the unit to which he was attached. Not surprisingly, the writer stuck to his corps doctrine, concluding that machine-gun commanders should not be tied down to specific tasks but must have a free hand and direct and control their machine-guns "in the same manner as any other commander of a formation [obviously meaning 'arm']." None of the brigade commanders agreed.[104]

Reports after Canal du Nord and Bourlon Wood are far less comprehensive than they were after Amiens and Drocourt-Queant, first because "tremendous exertions and considerable casualties had made heavy inroads."[105] Also, as the three operations followed one another in close succession, the lessons of the last operation had mostly been already highlighted and learned or studied in the first two. As Captain Herridge, BM of 2nd Brigade, said, "the principles enunciated in earlier narratives were instinctively followed . . . there occurred . . . no concrete illustration . . . that had not before been mentioned."[106] Third, there was less to say since the Canal du Nord and Bourlon Wood operation had been executed in very fine fashion, which revealed how professional the division had become:

From a 1st Division point of view I have always felt that the smooth accurate working of the old Division when we broke the Canal du Nord . . . was our high water mark.

I firmly believe no Division on the Western Front could have done better than the Old Red Patch that day and few could have done so well. My faith in the Brigades was so strong that I felt . . . it was a perfectly feasible scheme . . . I wrote the appreciation myself . . . and felt absolutely confident.[107]

Finally, as one of the first post-war histories said,

By the autumn of 1918 the Canadian Corps had learned all there was to know about war . . . We had learned many things in a hard school . . . We had been educated largely by our mistakes. And, while profiting by these, we had also taught ourselves greater adaptability . . . We had learned what to go out and look for, what to take infinite pains over, and what to bother about not at all. The victory of Cambrai was the achievement of an army which knew its business from butt-plate to fore-sight.[108]

The first sentence of this extract is an impossibility but the rest is accurate.[109] Another early account saw the learning thus: "Canada's first contingent has been described as a mob of amateur[s] . . . Discipline was lax, officers unproved, and though the stuff was there, it took time to transmute it into the perfect fighting machine it became."[110] Perfection is not attainable but by late 1918 perhaps 1st Division was advancing upon that.

The officers and men of Old Red Patch had good reason to be proud of their record. Outsiders, too, admired the division. The use that the C-in-C made of the Canadian Corps is testament to his high regard for Currie and the Corps. A stream of congratulations reached the Corps from senior officers. GOC Fourth Army (Rawlinson) was especially impressed with the Canadian performance. The former BGGS of the Canadian Corps, Percy Radcliffe, wrote that "the old Corps has beaten its own brilliant record. How I wish I was still with you."[111]

The British official historian, writing after the war, considered the leadership of Dominion officers and NCOs to be superior to that of their British counterparts because "they had been selected for their practical experience and power over men and not for theoretical proficiency and general education."[112] Lieutenant-Colonel A.A. Hanbury-Sparrow, an officer of strong will and courage (his tunic featured DSO and Bar, and the purple and white of the MC), spoke of the "indomitable resolution" of the Canadians, those "invincible Overseas Storm Troops."[113] Another Imperial, echoing this sentiment, said Dominion troops scarcely bothered "to break it to us gently that they were the 'storm troops' . . . that, out of all us sorry home troops, only the Guards Division, two kilted divisions and three English ones could be said to know how to fight."[114] Charles Carrington, describing the start of the Amiens offensive in August 1918, called the 10 divisions of the Dominions "the best fighting troops in any army."[115] The opinions of Hanbury-Sparrow and Carrington must count heavily. Some men enjoy combat. These two certainly did; their verve and talent for it is obvious in their writing. They knew good fighting men when they saw them.

This chapter has defined 1st Division's effectiveness in the last half of 1918. The splendid performance of the division during the three operations that occupied about 60 of the Hundred Days is striking evidence of its superb state of training, the competence of its staff and the effectiveness of the firm command and control it practised. Its commanders demonstrated mastery of the all-arms battle using weapons and equipment that had been totally new, or had not existed in 1914. They fought Canada's first modern war, employing sophisticated fire support, tanks, tactical air support, chemical warfare, intelligence, reconnaissance and *maskirovka*. 1st Division stood in late 1918 at the highest state it would ever achieve. Unfortunately for the generation of soldiers to come, the usual focus after the war was on the set-piece aspects of Canadian operations and the hurricane artillery fire that supported them. The ability of officers like Lipsett, Tuxford, Loomis and Griesbach to imagine, innovate and impress their will upon the enemy through fire *and manoeuvre*, and the combination of the two as the essence of war, were largely forgotten. Forgotten, too, was Currie's tenet, expressed as early as 1916:

> Too often, when our infantry are checked, they pause and ask for additional preparation before carrying on. This artillery preparation cannot be quickly and easily arranged and is often not necessary. Our troops must be taught the power of manoeuvre and that before giving up they must employ to the utmost all the weapons with which they are armed and have available.[116]

1st Division had come a long way since Second Ypres. By September 1918 "the finest spear in the British Army" was the Canadian Corps, and "the polished point of that spear [was the] grand old 1st Division."[117] As it turned out, it still had a very long way to go. Upon hearing of the Armistice, Andrew McNaughton was disgusted: "Bloody fools! We have them on the run. That means we shall have to do it all over again in another twenty-five years."[118] Macdonell, in saying farewell to his division, the "Old Guard," wished officers and men well and that "you will all live to see the day when your son wears the 'Old Red Patch' the same as 'Dad' wore, and just as proudly."[119]

Notes to Chapter Nine

1. Hertzberg, "The Reorganization of the Engineering Troops of a Canadian Division, Great War, 1914–1918," p. 42. The new battalions never quite attained full establishment but each in August 1918 stood at almost 800 men.

2. LAC, MG30E100 (Currie Papers), Vol. 37, File 166; RG9IIIC1, Vol. 3757.

3. Andrew Whitmarsh, "The Development of Infantry Tactics in the British 12th (Eastern) Division, 1915–1918," *Stand To!* 48 (January 1997): 32.

4. Dawnay's "Notes" were published by the Army Printing and Stationary Services, which also issued the CDS/SS series of manuals and instructions. LAC, RG9IIIC3, Vol. 4061, Folder 9, File 13, provides an idea of the range of topics of these "Notes." As an example, German 18th Army's "Notes on the Creeping Barrage" dated 29 March 1918, was issued under cover of "Notes on Recent Fighting: No. 10 The Creeping Barrage" on 6 May. It usefully compares creeping barrages, German and BEF.

5. Currie, *Interim Report*, pp. 23–24. After Ivor Maxse became Inspector-General of Training (IGT) in July 1918, it was soon evident that he was not to have much authority over training because of Haig's policy that it was the responsibility of commanders to train the men they had to lead into action. Dawnay summed up the continuing incoherence thus: "Our training system is neither perfectly coordinated nor evenly distributed through the Armies. I am constantly being told by divisions . . . that they are being taught different doctrines as they move from one command to another." (Quoted in Samuels, *Command or Control?*, pp. 122–23). Canadian divisions were spared this.

6. Currie, *Interim Report*, p. 1.

7. LAC, RG9IIIC1, Vol. 3859, Folder 85, File 2, November 1917.

8. LAC, RG9IIIC3, Vol. 4007, Folder 4, File 4, Notes on Conference of Divisional Commanders at Canadian Corps HQ, 5 February 1918; Vol. 4024, Folder 4, File 8, Macdonell to brigades, 27 July 1918.

9. LAC, RG9IIIC3, Vol. 4032, Folder 28, File 1, Canadian Corps "Notes on Training"; Vol. 4077, Folder 3, File 6, 1st Division to brigades, 24 February 1918.

10. LAC, MG30E15, (Griesbach Papers), Vol. 3, File 16B, 19 February 1918.

11. LAC, RG9IIIC3, Vol. 4113, Folder 45, File 6; MG30E15 (Griesbach Papers), Vol. 3, File 16B, Griesbach to battalions, 20 May and 14 June 1918; *Notes for Commanding Officers* (1918), Chapter VII. The précis broke an attack into a preliminary phase (including reconnaissance, administration, passage of orders and battle procedure) and six stages ranging from the unit first coming under artillery fire to their consolidating the captured position. For each stage a checklist of likely developments and decisions to take was offered. The guide also made recommendations on such matters as the location of unit commanders (too far forward was as bad as being too far back).

12. LAC, 2nd Brigade War Diary, May 1918.

13. LAC, RG9IIIC3, Vol. 4024, Folder 3, File 4, Griesbach to battalions, 17 May 1918.

14. LAC, brigade and 1st Division General Staff War Diaries, May 1918; Fetherstonhaugh, *The 13th Battalion*, p. 240; 5th and 15th Battalion War Diaries, May 1918.

15. LAC, RG9IIIC3, Vol. 4022, Folder 51, File 6, 1st Brigade "Narrative," 7 June 1918; Vol. 4028, Folder 17, File 20, "Critique," 17 June; Vol. 4113, Folder 44, File 2; 1st Division War Diary, June; Vol. 4031, Folder 27, File 2, Griesbach to COs, 2 July.

16. LAC, 1st Division General Staff War Diary, June 1918; 2nd and 3rd Brigade War Diaries, March and July 1918.

17. LAC, 2nd Brigade War Diary, July 1918, Appendix 2.

18. Currie, *Interim Report*, p. 24; LAC, RG9IIIC1, Vol. 3854, Folder 72, File 1, First Army to Canadian Corps, 4 May; File 4, Outline Scheme for Delta, 19 June. Of the battalion histories Urquhart's *History of the 16th Battalion* is the only one to mention Operation Delta (p. 263). Swettenham, *McNaughton*, and Nicholson, *Official History of the Canadian Army*, contain a paragraph each on Delta (pp. 133 and 382 respectively).

19. LAC, 3rd Brigade War Diary, June 1918; Tuxford, "The Great War as I Saw It," p. 331. In its work with contact aircraft 1st Division had concluded, based upon its experience in 1917, that flares were the best means of contact. Training stressed the importance of answering calls made by aircraft without delay. The other Canadian divisions agreed that flares were the best means, despite the continuing belief of forward troops that flares gave their positions away. These opinions were forwarded to Canadian Corps HQ in response to a demand for "Lessons Learnt During the Year's [1917] Fighting" (LAC, RG9IIIC3, Vol. 4028, Folder 17, File 20). 1st Division's response is dated 16 December 1917.

20. Captain John Dixon Craig, *The 1st Canadian Division in the Battles of 1918* (London: Barrs & Co., 1919), p. 11.

21. Currie, *Interim Report*, pp. 31–32.

22. Ibid., pp. 27–28; Major-General J.F.C. Fuller, *The Decisive Battles of the Western World and Their Influence Upon History*, Volume Three, *From the American Civil War to the End of the Second World War* (London: Eyre & Spottiswoode, 1956), p. 276; LAC, RG9IIIC3, Vol. 4081, Folder 5, File 1, 1st Division report on Amiens.

23. Currie, *Interim Report*, p. 29; LAC, RG9IIIC3, Vol. 4081, Folder 5, File 1, 1st Division report; Craig, *The 1st Canadian Division*, pp. 10–11; Nicholson, *Official History of the Canadian Army*, p. 389, points out what an uncertain business deception is: German intelligence noted the signs of a Canadian presence with Second Army but did not draw the conclusions desired by the deceivers.

24. LAC, RG9IIIC3, Vol. 4081, Folder 5, File 1, 1st Division report.

25. At its simplest, march discipline relates to getting from Point A to point B not only the marching men and horses but the supply and ammunition columns, and the horse and motor vehicles. Bad march discipline could be more destructive than enemy fire. Good march discipline, according to *Infantry Training (4-Company Organization), 1914*, conferred "The power of undertaking long and rapid marches without loss in numbers and energy [which] is one of the chief factors of success in war." In 1914 march discipline had to be taught, it not being a feature of civilian life. Learning it did not necessarily mean adherence to it. Proficiency did not come overnight. March discipline required constant monitoring if the ability to march rapidly over long distances was to be retained. Currie in 1918 was reiterating what he and all officers had been saying since 1915. From Second Ypres on formation commanders prodded units constantly (and punished inefficiency as necessary) to ensure a high standard of marching. Their efforts paid off in the summer of 1918. Currie is quoted in Dancocks, *Spearhead to Victory*, p. 32.

26. LAC, RG9IIIC3, Vol. 4043, Folder 1, File 15.

27. Currie, *Interim Report*, pp. 31–32; LAC, RG9IIIC3, Vol. 4081, Folder 5, File 1, "1st Canadian Division Report on Amiens Operations." Section V of this inch-thick document contains 17 pages on the actual march, detailing the planning and execution of the relief on the Arras front, secrecy, entrainment and detrainment, move of divisional HQ, the approach march, traffic control, transport and roads. Remarkably

few problems are noted. Billetting in some cases had been "difficult" because certain units (not identified) had not moved according to plan, a problem exacerbated by the Corps operation order, which had sent "several" battalions to wrong areas, thus causing congestion. The move had involved extensive use of light railways and trains. No problems were noted with the former but there were some with the trains. The divisional ammunition column (DAC) had marched to a location that was 10 miles from where the column was supposed to go, causing several trains to be four hours late. Disciplinary action was taken against those responsible. Every other unit arrived at its assigned entraining point on time. Administrative staffs thought that detraining points should have been closer to assembly areas in the forward area to spare troops "long" marches, in some cases 10 miles but G Staff vetoed this, not wanting trains too far forward lest they give the show away.

28. Maj.-Gen. W.H.S. Macklin, *An Introduction to the Study of the Principles of War* (Ottawa: King's Printer, 1952), p. 17. Macklin, who served in the infantry in the Great War, was Adjutant-General of the Canadian Army in 1949.

29. Lieut.-Gen. Sir Archibald Montgomery-Massingberd, "8th August 1918," *Journal of the Royal Artillery* 55 (January 1929): 16.

30. Lieut.-Gen. Sir Archibald Macdonell, "The Old Red Patch at the Breaking of the Drocourt-Queant Line, the Crossing of the Canal du Nord and the Advance on Cambrai, 30th Aug.–2nd Oct. 1918, I, The Preliminary Operations of August 30th, 31st and September 1st, Comprising the Attack and Capture of the Fresnes-Rouvroy Line, Upton Wood, the Vis-en-Artois Switch, Ocean Work and the Crow's Nest," *Canadian Defence Quarterly* 4 (July 1927): 389–90.

31. Currie, *Interim Report*, p. 33; Nicholson, *Official History of the Canadian Army*, p. 388.

32. LAC, RG9IIIC3, Vol. 4015, Folder 30, File 4, Instructions No. 1 and 2 (3 and 4 August). Right flank security was the responsibility of a mobile "Canadian Independent Force" consisting of 1st and 2nd Canadian Motor Machine Gun Brigades, the Corps Cyclist Battalion and a section of truck-mounted 6-inch mortars, all under Brigadier-General R. Brutinel. This force, with 3rd Cavalry Division and the Whippet tanks of 3rd Tank Brigade, was to exploit success and act as a link between cavalry and infantry.

33. Useful with regard to air photography and the air aspects of the operations as a whole is S.F. Wise, *Canadian Airmen and the First World War: The Official History of the RCAF*, Vol. 1 (Toronto: University of Toronto Press, 1980). A.J. Peacock, *Gun Fire No. 36: Illustrations to Accompany Notes on the Interpretation of Aeroplane Photos* (Easingwold, York: G.H. Smith & Son, n.d.) and Nicholas C. Watkis, *The Western Front from the Air* (London: Imperial War Museum, 1997) consist almost entirely of interpreted and annotated air photos. Watkis also provides the corresponding trench maps for his examples of aerial photography. These together provide an idea of the difficult work of the photographic interpreter.

34. The Amiens reports are in LAC, RG9IIIC3, Vols. 4081 (division), 4015, 4077 and 4052 (brigades and battalions). For Drocourt-Queant see Vols. 4016 and 4033. Canal du Nord is the subject of Vols. 4081, 4028 and 4074.

35. LAC, RG9IIIC3, Vol. 4015, Folder 30, File 7.

36. LAC, 1st Battalion War Diary, 12 August 1918. See also Hooge in Chapter Five.

37. Daniel G. Dancocks, *Sir Arthur Currie: A Biography* (Toronto: McClelland & Stewart, 1985), p. 152. Currie is quoted in Military Advisory Board, *The Triumph of the Allies*, p. 132.

38. Quoted in Brigadier-General Sir James E. Edmonds, *Military Operations, France and*

Belgium, 1918, Volume IV, *8th August–26 September, The Franco-British Offensive* (London: Macmillan, 1947), pp. 37–38.

39. Currie, *Interim Report*, p. 37.

40. LAC, RG9IIIC3, Vol. 4015, Folder 30, File 7, 3rd Brigade report, 20 August; McNaughton quoted in Swettenham, *McNaughton*, p. 144; Craig, *The 1st Canadian Division*, p. 12.

41. LAC, RG9IIIC3, Vol. 4081, Folder 5, File 1, 1st Division report; Vol. 4015, Folder 30, File 5, 1st Brigade and battalion reports; File 6, 2nd Brigade and battalion reports; File 7, 3rd Brigade and battalion reports; Craig, *The 1st Canadian Division*, p. 13. Overall, Vickers machine-guns did not "materially assist the attack" (Griesbach's assessment) because of heavy ground mist and the rapidity of the advance.

42. LAC, RG9IIIC3, Vol. 4015, Folder 30, File 6, 2nd Brigade report; Vol. 4052, Folder 22, File 4, 7th Battalion report; Vol. 4081, Folder 5, File 1, 1st Division report.

43. Currie, *Interim Report*, p. 38.

44. Rawlinson's initial order is in Edmonds, *The Franco-British Offensive*, pp. 95–96 and Appendix XI (pp. 576–77). It was untimed and the Canadian Corps General Staff War Diary does not note when it was received. Edmonds, pp. 21–22, says that the 32nd "whilst remaining at the special disposal of G.H.Q. [had been] allotted to the Canadian Corps" on 31 July. The Fourth Army order of 6 August (Appendix IX) allotted the 32nd, with two other Imperial divisions, to "General Reserve." Nicholson, *Official History of the Canadian Army*, pp. 408–409, speaks of the "unfortunate change" and goes on to say that when Rawlinson visited Canadian Corps HQ on 9 August (he meant the 8th), he told the BGGS (Webber) that the 32nd would join the Corps for the 9th. Two hours later MGGS Fourth Army countermanded this. The success of the 8th apparently caught Fourth Army short, little or no thought having been given to exploitation: the result was order, counter-order, disorder. The impact of Fourth Army's decision to let its corps set Zero and the confusion surrounding the 32nd are in Edmonds, pp. 102–103, 106.

45. LAC, RG9IIIC3, Vol. 4052, Folder 22, File 4, 2nd Brigade report dated 14 August on operations 7–9 August; Vol. 4081, Folder 5, File 1, 1st Division "Log of Events (Battle of Amiens)," pp. 4, 6. 2nd Brigade stated that the enemy air attacks continued all through the night of 8 August, a performance repeated the next night, his aircraft "dominating and attacking our troops with M.G. fire and bombs." 1st Brigade reported "Hun planes all over the place." Urquhart, *History of the 16th Battalion*, p. 279, graphically described the enemy air attacks on 9 August, the low flying aircraft causing "widespread" injuries. Shane B. Schreiber, *Shock Army of the British Empire: The Canadian Corps in the Last 100 Days of the Great War* (Westport, Conn.: Praeger, 1997), p. 53, states that 2nd Brigade reported that friendly aircraft did the bombing and machine-gunning. However, the aircraft were at low altitude and clearly recognizable by 2nd Brigade as enemy in the light of parachute flares on both nights.

46. Currie, *Interim Report*, p. 39; Nicholson, *Official History of the Canadian Army*, p. 408.

47. Edmonds, *The Franco-British Offensive*, Appendix XVI, Fourth Army order, 11 August, p. 582.

48. Ibid., p. 419; Craig, *The 1st Canadian Division*, p. 18; Currie, *Interim Report*, p. 41.

49. LAC, MG30E100 (Currie Papers), Vol. 43, diary, 22 August.

50. LAC, MG30E15 (Griesbach Papers), File 4, 24 August; RG9IIIC3, Vol. 4015, Folder 30, Files 5 and 7, 3rd Battalion and 3rd Brigade reports.

51. Currie, *Interim Report*, p. 28; LAC, RG9IIIC3, Vol. 4015, Folder 30, Files 5 and 7, 1st and 3rd Brigade reports; Vol. 4081, Folder 5, File 1, 1st Division report.
52. LAC, RG9IIIC3, Vol. 4081, Folder 5, File 1, 1st Division report; Vol. 4015, Folder 30, Files 5 and 6, 1st and 2nd Brigade reports; Vol. 4028, Folder 17, File 20, 2nd and 3rd Battalion reports. 1st Division's expedient of having one infanteer ride on each tank seems to have kept tanks and infantry together. If gaps did develop, these were uncommon or insignificant since none of the divisional reports mention any difficulty with infantry-tank cooperation. Vol. 4033, Folder 4, File 4. Concerned after Amiens about the "tendency on the part of the tanks to act as an arm independent of the other arms, and to forget that their action must be auxiliary to that of the infantry," First Army directed that tanks would be under command of the formation to which they were attached and that their CO must be at the HQ of the formation they were supporting. 1st Division's Preliminary Instructions for Amiens (LAC, RG9IIIC3, Vol. 4027, Folder 13, File 3) had specifically warned that tanks must not get too far ahead of the infantry to which they are allocated. As the tanks were under tactical command of the infantry, by definition they were required to conform to the movement of the infantry.
53. LAC, RG9IIIC3, Vol. 4015, Folder 30, File 4; Vol. 4081, Folder 5, File 1.
54. Nicholson, *Official History of the Canadian Army*, p. 397; LAC, RG9IIIC3, Vol. 4081, Folder 5, File 1, Appendix C, Log of Events. In "Lessons Learned From Recent Fighting" dated 11 September (Vol. 4016, Folder 33, File 13) air support is not mentioned. Artillery and tank support are commented upon at length. Either Macdonell saw no lessons in regard to the air arm, or air support to 1st Division was so limited that no comment was possible or necessary.
55. LAC, RG9IIIC3, Vol. 4015, Folder 30, Files 5–6; Vol. 4052, Folder 22, File 4; and Vol. 4077, Folder 3, File 13 contain brigade and battalion reports on 8–9 August. All the reports are dated between 12 and 14 August.
56. LAC, RG9IIIC3, Vol. 4016, Folder 33, File 13; Vol. 4053, Folder 24, File 16; Vol. 4028, Folder 17, File 20.
57. LAC, RG9IIIC3, Vol. 4052, Folder 22, File 8 and Vol. 4053, Folder 24, File 16. One development addressing the complaints was the "GHQ Equipment," a lightweight version of the Stokes. See Chapter Three, note 93 for details. 1st Division was not allocated any heavy mortars. All of the heavy mortars (one section) that had been mounted on trucks were grouped with the two Canadian Motor Machine Gun brigades working with 4th Division on the right of the Canadian Corps (Currie, *Interim Report*, p. 36).
58. LAC, RG9IIIC3, Vol. 4081, Folder 5, File 1, 1st Division report.
59. Currie, *Interim Report*, p. 34; Craig, *The 1st Canadian Division*, p. 8, gives the Corps frontage as approximately 7,000 yards. Currie's figure is the more accurate.
60. LAC, RG9IIIC3, Vol. 4015, Folder 30, File 4, Canadian Corps Instruction No. 2, 4 August 1918; Vol. 4081, Folder 5, File 1, 1st Division report on Amiens and Operation Order 272, 7 August; Vol. 4077, Folder 3, File 6; Vol. 4043, Folder 2, File 1, "Notes for the Information and Guidance of All Officers Regarding the Organization of Machine Gun Battalions and Their Employment." This document, signed by N.W. Webber, BGGS, on 30 April 1918 describes machine-gun organization, tactics, command, liaison, training and communications. It also lists the duties of the DMGO and contains charts showing battalion organization in detail (three companies of four 4-gun batteries) and battery organization. In strength—63 officers and 1,497 ORs—a

machine-gun battalion was half again the size of an infantry battalion. It is significant that sub-units of companies were called batteries rather than platoons. Their fire was to be controlled much as artillery fire was. Macdonell's allocations in this case clearly stress direct, as opposed to indirect, machine-gun fire.

61. Brigade and battalion reports are in LAC, RG9IIIC3, Vol. 4015, Folder 30, Files 5–7. See also Chapter Three of this present study for a fuller account of Loomis' views on machine-guns.

62. LAC, RG9IIIC3, Vol. 4081, Folder 5, File 1, Section IV, Narrative of Operations.

63. Ibid.; Vol. 4015, Folder 30, File 6, 2nd Brigade report; Craig, *The 1st Canadian Division*, p. 17.

64. LAC, RG9IIIC3, Vol. 4016, Folder 31, File 5, 1st Brigade report, 31 August.

65. LAC, RG9IIIC3, Vol. 4081, Folder 5, File 1; Vol. 4052, Folder 22, File 4; Vol. 4053, Folder 24, File 16, reports of 2nd Brigade and 8th and 10th Battalions. The Lessons sections of the reports of 1st Division and 2nd and 3rd Brigades indicate that the 18-pounder attachments to infantry were not implemented at Amiens. *SS 356*, p. 91, describes the 76mm *Infanterie Geschutz*, which had a shortened barrel, no long-range sight and a lighter carriage. These guns accompanied attacking infantry to provide direct fire on hardened targets. The 77mm gun, which was found unsuitable for the purpose, was replaced at the end of 1917 by 37mm and 50mm light guns.

66. LAC, RG9IIIC3, Vol. 4015, Folder 30, File 5, 1st Brigade reports 8, 9 and 17 August.

67. LAC, RG9IIIC3, Vol. 4015, Folder 30, Files 6 and 7, 2nd and 3rd Brigade reports; Vol. 4077, Folder 3, File 13, 15th Battalion report.

68. LAC, RG9IIIC3, Vol. 4015, Folder 30, File 5, battalion reports 11 and 12 August.

69. LAC, RG9IIIC3, Vol. 4081, Folder 30, File 1.

70. LAC, RG9IIIC3, Vol. 4069, Folder 12, File 3, Lieutenant-Colonel A.L. Saunders, DSO, MC and Bar, "The Normal Formation of a Platoon and a Platoon in Attack," undated. Saunders assumed command of the 8th Battalion on 13 September 1918. A graduate of the fifth COs' Course(1917) at the Senior Officers' School, Aldershot, he was one of 18 Canadians (six from 1st Division) on that serial of the course (*Notes for Commanding Officers* [1917], List of Students). His course report described him as having "any amount of common sense and imagination in appreciating situations quickly, with undoubted powers of leadership and strong personality . . . should do well in command." (LAC, RG9IIIC3, Vol. 4058, Folder 37, File 5). He did. 1st Division had gone to this platoon organization in May. Chapter Three discusses the variants in platoon organization within the four Canadian divisions. Tactical formations also varied within the divisions, which was acceptable to Corps HQ. Experimentation in platoon organization and tactical formations was an evolutionary process.

71. LAC, RG24, Vol. 1828, GAQ 7–16, "Details of Battles and Raids Engaged In By the 16th Cdn. Bn. Including Particulars of Battalion Tactical Organizations."

72. LAC, RG9IIIC3, Vol. 4022, Folder 51, File 9, Macdonell to brigades, 10 June 1918; Captain B.H. Liddell Hart, "The 'Ten Commandments' of the Combat Unit," *Journal of the Royal United Services Institute* (May 1919): p. 292.

73. LAC, MG30E15 (Griesbach Papers), Vol. 2, File 4, letter to 1st Division, 24 August.

74. LAC, RG9IIIC3, Vol. 4053, Folder 24, File 16; Hanbury-Sparrow, *The Land-Locked Lake*, p. 201. Hanbury-Sparrow, DSO and Bar, MC, commanded an Imperial battalion in 1918.

75. Edmonds and Maxwell-Hyslop, *The Advance to Victory*, pp. 575–76. Captain G.C. Wynne, who co-authored (with Edmonds) one volume of the British official history,

said that arbitrary objectives drawn in "continuous blue, green and brown lines . . . across the map . . . regardless of reverse slopes and death-traps" had in the past (he referred specifically to the failure to exploit Canadian success at Vimy) "dissipated . . . strength." He pointed out that the exceptions after Vimy were the capture of Arleux and Fresnoy by Canadian battalions (See Wynne, *If Germany Attacks*, pp. 245, 248, 252). In addition to ignoring the ground, such artificial lines also inhibited exploitation or, conversely, created expectation that could not always be satisfied.

76. LAC, RG9IIIC3, Vol. 4052, Folder 22, File 2, Lieutenant-Colonel R.P. Clark, CO 14th Battalion, to 1st Division, 28 October 1918.

77. LAC, RG9IIIC3, Vol. 4015, Folder 30, File 6, 2nd Brigade report.

78. Currie, *Interim Report*, pp. 44, 46–47; LAC, Canadian Corps General Staff War Diary, August 1918.

79. LAC, MG30E15 (Griesbach Papers), Vol. 5, File 34B. This file also contains several wartime newspaper accounts of the attack, which for security reasons, did not identify the brigade or its commander. The attack is also described in 1st Brigade's War Diary for August and in 1st Division's report, Section VI, Lessons and Observations (RG9IIIC3, Vol. 4016, Folder 31, File 1). The reports of 1st Brigade and its battalions are in File 5.

80. Locating formation and unit boundaries is enormously helpful in determining order of battle. Once located, boundaries become a prime axis of attack because they are considered the weakest part of the defence, or, at the very least, the point where inter-formation or inter-unit coordination is less definitive.

81. Currie, *Interim Report*, p. 52; Craig, *The 1st Canadian Division*, p. 27. One of the battalions involved was 5th Battalion. See Chapter Three, note 24, for an account of the fine leadership of its CO, Lieutenant-Colonel Lorn Tudor, DSO and Bar.

82. Craig, *The 1st Canadian Division*, p. 31.

83. Ibid., Nicholson, *Official History of the Canadian Army*, p. 440.

84. LAC, RG9IIIC3, Vol. 4016, Files 2 and 7, reports of 2nd and 3rd Brigades and 14th Battalion.

85. LAC, RG9IIIC3, Vol. 4016, File 1, 1st Division report, Section VI, Lessons and Observations.

86. LAC, RG9IIIC3, Vol. 4016, Folder 31, Files 5 and 7, reports of 1st and 3rd Brigades and 13th and 15th Battalions. Griesbach had thought exactly the opposite during his visit to the Machine Gun School at Grantham in July 1917. At that time he was convinced that infantry commanders should not assign specific targets to machine-gun officers and that they should be treated in the same way as artillery commanders (Vol. 4031, Folder 26, File 7, report on visit to Grantham).

87. LAC, RG9IIIC3, Vol. 4016, Folder 31, File 7, report of 13th Battalion; *SS 143*, p. 7. The other battalion reports are in Files 5–6, Folder 31, Vol. 4016.

88. LAC, RG9IIIC3, Vol. 4016, Folder 31, Files 1, 5–7.

89. Since mid-1917 junior leaders had been trained in taking command. See Chapter Four, note 121. LAC, RG9IIIC3, Vol. 4016, Folder 31, Files 5 and 7, reports of 1st Battalion (8 August), 14th and 15th Battalions and 3rd Brigade; Vol. 4033, Folder 4, File 1, report of 1st Battalion, 9 August; Vol. 4007, Folder 4, File 4.

90. LAC, RG9IIIC3, Vol. 4016, Folder 31, File 1, 1st Division report, Section VI, Lessons and Observations; Vol. 4033, Folder 4, File 4, Lessons Learnt From Recent Fighting.

91. Edmonds and Maxwell-Hyslop, *The Advance to Victory*, pp. 14–17.

92. Currie, *Interim Report*, p. 57; LAC, RG9IIIC3, Vol. 4033, Folder 3, File 6, 26

September. Bourlon Wood was also a formidable obstacle. Taken and lost by Third Army in November 1917, the wood, which covered a commanding spur north of the Bapaume-Cambrai road, was the key to the capture of Cambrai.

93. Edmonds and Maxwell-Hyslop, *The Advance to Victory*, pp. 24–25; LAC, RG9IIIC3, Vol. 4081, Folder 5, File 1; Currie, *Interim Report*, p. 58.

94. Currie, *Interim Report*, p. 54; LAC, RG9IIIC3, Vol. 4028, Folder 15, File 5, 1st Brigade report.

95. Murray, *History of the 2nd Canadian Infantry Battalion*, p. 296.

96. LAC, RG9IIIC3, Vol. 4028, Folder 15, File 5, 1st Brigade report; Edmonds and Maxwell-Hyslop, *The Advance to Victory*, p. 23.

97. Currie, *Interim Report*, p. 68; Edmonds and Maxwell-Hyslop, *The Advance to Victory*, p. 155; Craig, *The 1st Canadian Division*, p. 47. Although comparisons are odorous (so Shakespeare said), sometimes one is forced into them, as Griesbach was when after the war he felt compelled to respond to an American brigadier (one Henry Reilly) who had publicly disparaged the Empire's war effort and claimed that the American Army had won the war. Griesbach's irrefutable answer to the slander showed the vainglorious Yank that the First American Army in the Meuse-Argonne had not done nearly as well as the Canadian Corps during the Hundred Days (LAC, MG30E15 [Griesbach Papers], Vol. 1, File 2). See John Swettenham, *To Seize the Victory The Canadian Corps in World War I* (Toronto: The Ryerson Press, 1965), p. 238: "A comparison of the American performance . . . with that of the Canadians . . . is not without interest. This is done . . . to show what can be accomplished by a country with a small but well-trained force as opposed to another able to furnish larger numbers of troops but not so well prepared. The favourable results obtained were made possible only by the fact that the Canadians had benefitted by the experience of training and hard fighting during the previous years." Swettenham provides the following statistics:

Category	Meuse-Argonne	Hundred Days
Number of troops engaged	650,000	105,000
Duration of operation (days)	47	100
Maximum advance (miles)	34	86
German divisions defeated	46	47
Casualties suffered for every German division	2,170	975
Total battle casualties	100,000	47,830
Prisoners captured	16,000	31,537
Guns captured	468	623
Machine-guns captured	2,864	2,842
Trench mortars captured	117	336

In September 1918 the Americans faced roughly 19 German divisions. The BEF had to contend with about four times that, First Army's share alone being most of the 17 divisions of the German Eighteenth Army and some of the divisions of the German Seventh Army. German and Allied deployments at the time are shown on the map facing page 248 in R.C. Fetherstonhaugh (ed), *The 24th Battalion, C.E.F., Victoria Rifles of Canada, 1914–1919* (Montreal: Gazette Publishing Co., 1930). Cyril Falls, *The Great War, 1914–1918* (Toronto: Longmans, 1959), p. 17, called the extreme American view that France and the British Empire muddled eleven-twelfths of the war, leaving it to the Americans to put it right in the last twelfth, "moonshine." Reilly served in the American "Rainbow" Division, so named, according to another American General, because it "came out after the storm." (LAC, MG30E20, Vol. 1, unpublished biography of Macdonell by J.A. Kennedy-Carefoot, p. 215). Many think the comment applicable to all Americans in the Great War.

98. Quoted in Brigadier-General Vincent J. Esposito and Colonel John Robert Elting, *A Military History and Atlas of the Napoleonic Wars* (New York: Praeger, 1964). The quoted sentence appears under the heading "Recommended Reading." Lloyd, a Scot who served as an Austrian General during the Seven Years War, was an influential military writer until his death in 1783.

99. Wynne, *If Germany Attacks*, pp. 320–21.

100. Currie quoted in Terraine, *Douglas Haig: The Educated Soldier*, p. 454.

101. Graves, *Goodbye to All That*, p. 161.

102. LAC, RG9IIIC3, Vol. 4016, Folder 32, Files 2 and 4; Vol. 4028, Folder 15, File 5; Vol. 4052, Folder 22, File 7; 14th Battalion War Diary, Appendix 5, September 1918. 1st Division's Instruction No. 2 (Vol. 4081, Folder 5, File 4) provided for an initial barrage by 20 machine-gun batteries (160 machine-guns in all). Tuxford said the machine-guns were "confined to barrage work" (Vol. 3016, Folder 32, File 2).

103. LAC, RG9IIIC3, Vol. 4081, Folder 5, File 4; Vol. 4028 Folder 16, File 3; Vol. 4052, Folder 22, File 7; 3rd Brigade War Diary, May 1918, Appendix 4.

104. LAC, RG9IIIC3, Vol. 4081, Folder 5, File 4, 1st Division report. For Griesbach's opinion, which was the consensus, see earlier in this chapter. See also Chapter Three for Loomis' views. Few, if any, infantry officers of today, would argue against their views. Machine-guns are an integrated support weapon whose fire must not be separated from assault power.

105. Currie, *Interim Report*, p. 61.

106. LAC, RG9IIIC3, Vol. 4016, Folder 32, File 4, 2nd Brigade report.

107. LAC, MG30E100 (Currie Papers), Vol. 12, File 36, letter, Macdonell to Currie, 21 April 1922.

108. Sheldon-Williams, *The Canadian Front in France and Flanders*, p. 143.

109. Everard Wyrall, "On the Writing of 'Unit' War Histories," *Army Quarterly* (July 1923): p. 388, applies this to historians: "It is no use your saying to yourself 'I know all about the war!' That honour is reserved for some learned historian yet unborn."

110. Livesay, *Canada's Hundred Days*, p. 10.

111. LAC, RG9IIIC3, Vol. 4062, Folder 11, File 6.

112. Edmonds, *The Franco-British Offensive*, p. 515.

113. Hanbury-Sparrow, *The Land-Locked Lake*, pp. 210, 223.

114. Montague, *Disenchantment*, p. 131.

115. Carrington, *Soldier from the Wars Returning*, p. 233.

116. LAC, RG9IIIC3, Vol. 4053, Folder 24, File 16, "Notes on French Attacks, North-East of Verdun in October and December 1916," p. VI.

117. LAC, RG9IIIC3, Vol. 4077, Folder 3, File 13, Macdonell to units 14 September.

118. Quoted in Swettenham, *McNaughton*, p. 168.

119. Final Order of the Day by Major-General Sir Archibald Cameron Macdonell Commanding 1st Canadian Division, 17 November 1918.

CHAPTER TEN

Finis

Life is short, the art long, timing is exact, experience treacherous,
judgement difficult.

—HIPPOCRATES

This applies equally well to war and divisions. Old Red Patch achieved a
reputation and a distinction during the Great War that largely eluded it in
the rematch. 1st Division in 1939–1945, unlike 1st Division in 1914–1918,
was almost entirely Canadian born; however, what really differentiates them
is their respective experiences. In early 1915 1st Division engaged the main
body of the main enemy, the struggle ending over three years later. In the
rematch 1st Division did not see action until Sicily, July 1943, almost four
years after it had left Canada. It was 10 times longer at training. How it
would have done in the Western Desert with other Dominion and the Imperial
divisions that made up the Eighth Army is a very interesting "might have
been." It might have become as famous as 7th Armoured Division (the Desert
Rats); on the other hand, it might have ended up defending Tobruk in 1942
in place of, or with, 2nd South African Division, which the Germans "put in
the bag." For the 1st, it could have been "The lyf so short, the craft so long
to lerne."[1]

Both vintages of 1st Division were initially unready to fight. After 1918
the politicians left the Canadian Army to "moulder away," which it did, becoming encrusted over the years of neglect with cobwebs, its organization and
training degenerate and its whole persona "hopelessly bureaucratic."[2] The
militia, as in 1914, was a social club and the regulars, having been deprived
for too long of the means to train, forgot almost everything. As for equipment, in the late 1930s the Army had 29 Bren guns (the replacement of the
Lewis gun), 23 anti-tank rifles, four 2-pounder anti-tank guns and five 3-inch

mortars.[3] Tragically, the military legacy of the Great War—the competence and professionalism purchased at very high cost—was squandered by the politicians, partly because of the legend of the Canadian Corps, which contributed to

> an unbounded popular faith in the citizen-soldier which parsimonious post-war governments would utilize with devastating effect to forestall the development of a regular army . . . That the country's enviable war record . . . would contribute as well, under the oppressive weight of the militia myth, to the speedy undoing of the professional military system ultimately responsible for such victories must rank as one of the Canadian Corps' most confounding and unfortunate legacies.[4]

Before 1914 there had been nothing for them to squander. The Army then had little training or experience, either in commanders or staff; it had no reputation of worth or credibility; and it was inadequately equipped and armed. Fortunately, 1st Division did not proceed directly to France. If it had, it would have become involved, in all likelihood, in the great retreat from Mons and might not have survived. But, to keep this in perspective, Imperial Territorial divisions were mostly as unready.

What 1st Division experienced was remarkably similar and mutually understandable to many Imperial divisions. All divisions shared the neophyte stage of competence, which entailed awaiting and conducting training and undergoing baptism of fire. After a time, they became trained and engaged in attaining additional experience more or less throughout 1915. By late 1916 the consistent performers had been identified, among them Old Red Patch. At Vimy and afterwards, 1st Division burnished its reputation, demonstrating its ability to achieve virtually any mission, given sufficient support and preparation time. As Kipling said, Canadians and Australians were "always inquisitive and seldom idle . . . and between [them] the enemy suffered."[5]

A superb class of leaders—command and staff—at division, brigade and battalion enabled 1st Division to integrate and effectively use new weapons, doctrine and organization, which taken together represented change. 1st Division coped well with that change. Speaking of leaders, men like Louis Lipsett, William Griesbach, George Tuxford and Frederick Loomis come immediately to mind. Lipsett, in particular, catches the eye. His operational writing is striking; one comes away impressed with the superior quality of anything he wrote, especially appreciations, which are well reasoned and thorough textbook examples of first class SD. Griesbach, with his "Book of Wisdom," which provided homely but useful advice and instructions, approaches Lipsett's standard. All four officers were tough, resourceful commanders, no nonsense and hard-fighting, but careful of the lives of their soldiers. Lipsett went on to another division, as did many other leaders, where they set the newer formations on the path trod earlier by 1st Division.

1st Division recognized early on that organization and tactics hung together and that the key to success was the infantry platoon and its commander, a young officer who had to become skilled in the best use of a blend of weapons while on the job. Platoon commanding was a difficult and complex task that was still evolving by war's end. Along the way Old Red Patch used its experience and that of others to improve the effectiveness of its platoons. As the men of 1st Division became regimental, they became cognizant that, like the rivets in Kipling's "The Ship That Found Herself," they were fundamental to the ship. They took on some of the characteristics of the regular soldier, quite spontaneously since they had very few Canadian Regulars to imitate, but at the same time they retained overall a less structured approach that worked for Canadians.

Canadian Corps' claims to have established its "own tactical doctrine"[6] seem somewhat ingenuous. Every corps and every division worth its salt did that—or more accurately, each established a tactical method. Corps and divisions implemented the doctrine set by higher formation, mostly Army rather than GHQ, and they used training manuals that drove the conduct of operations rather more than was acknowledged. This is especially true of *SS 143 Instructions for the Training of Platoons for Offensive Action, 1917*, the bible for subalterns, those young men who became the key in operations. The Canadian Corps did not establish a reputation for doctrinal innovation, except where 1st Division seems to have been the first to engage in large-scale raids, but its methods became greatly admired and imitated. Canadians made errors, too, which is not surprising. Attaching artillery to infantry units, for example, did not work well, although this concept did not get the trial that it should have. And 1st Division had, perforce, to accept the separation of close support weapons (machine-guns and mortars) from the infantry. Of the brigade commanders, Loomis protested loudest (and at length) against this. In the end, he was proven right; the battalion, like the platoon, had to be an all-arms team and the process of returning these weapons to the battalions began.

While the training system could be said to be incomplete because of the absence at GHQ of a central focus until late in the war, the other components were in place: schools at every level, depots and reinforcement camps, and unit training, collective and individual. Commanders like Currie, Macdonell, Lipsett, Griesbach and Tuxford demanded and ensured a high level and standard of training. Earnest training, such a prime factor in combat effectiveness, had one purpose: to prepare men for combat. All efforts were bent to that purpose.

Training had other flaws: inadequate liaison between front and rear, for one. Despite improvement it could never satisfy, simply because they were two worlds. Also, for many months, teaching officers how to train, as opposed to training them how to lead, received insufficient attention. Shortages of qualified instructors also presented significant problems. Because officers had to know not only their own jobs, but those of every man under them, it took a long time to make a good officer. Platoon commanders, in particular, were always in short supply. The need to replace casualties bled off the better NCOs through commissioning from the ranks, a course of action that created yet another problem: a less capable senior NCO corps. Their authority suffered consequently.

Training of necessity was hard, constant and usually a priority over rest. 1st Division's training system, which was a sub-set of the larger system, enabled it to absorb the lessons of war and to implement in a timely fashion the changes suggested by those lessons. This book has discussed some of the many lessons that had to be learnt, ranging from the most mundane trench routines to the highly complicated attack options. At its most basic, 1st Division, along with every other division had to learn open warfare and then trench warfare, and then had to relearn open warfare.

Battle was the culmination and the proof of training. The evidence shows nothing seriously wrong with command and control in Old Red Patch. While one should try to avoid that human failing of judging the general by the particular, there is a strong case for extending that judgement to the Canadian Corps. Competent command and control gave 1st Division a confidence that could be tested and stretched but not broken. Even after the worst of times, like Festubert and Regina Trench, given rest and reinforcement the division showed amazing resilience. Had the war continued this might not have endured, for divisions, like men, become used up.

It remains to sum up what took 1st Division to effectiveness. First, its excellent staff officers, G, Q and A Branches, set a high standard. Second, it had throughout strong and competent command and control. Third (and finally), it was highly trained, master of its equipment and weapons, which became good and sufficient, and it effectively incorporated doctrinal innovation based on knowledge of the enemy and experience. From this came a fighting division with a strong personality: aggressive in offence and defence, especially tenacious in the latter, and innovative within its limits in both phases of war. 1st Division eventually demonstrated what Ian Hamilton saw as the military essence: system, education, soul and fire.[7] The self-belief at the centre of the 1st Division soldier's mind was reinforced constantly. Each man became convinced of unit and formation superiority, and each man knew that when the time came, each man would demonstrate its worth to friend and foe. Men and divisions that are modest about their talents will be taken at face value. 1st Division was never modest. If 1st Division had not believed it was the best, it would have been no good at all!

While this book has separated the three components in order to deal with them better on the printed page, it recognizes, as did the commanders of Old Red Patch, their inseparability. No single component could be the way ahead or the explanation for 1st Division's effectiveness. As it travelled along the very hard road from early 1915 to the Armistice the division established a reputation that Canadians were soldiers larger than life. At Second Ypres, on the Somme, at Vimy, Hill 70, Passchendaele and Amiens, and across Canal du Nord it showed its stalwart strength and the noble virtues of the warrior.

Grossly unfair to the men of the BEF, including 1st Division, and damaging to the national spirit of Canada was the misconception described by Charles Carrington: "A legend has grown up, propagated not by soldiers but by journalists, that these men who went gaily to fight . . . lost their faith . . . and returned in anger and despair."[8] The contention of a comparative few, usually those who had not fought, of utter futility, hopelessness and incompetence does not square with the record. While it would be naive to think that disillusionment with the conduct of the war did not exist in 1st Division (and in the Canadian Corps), anger and despair hardly feature in any of the Canadian regimental histories, or in any of the recollections and memoirs penned by veterans of 1st Division. The historians of the 10th and 15th Battalions, for example, said cheeriness was a quality that never left those units.[9]

Also damaging for a long time was the fashion to condemn everything, *totus porcus*, about command and control and staff work in the Great War. Denis Winter, Leon Wolfe, John Laffin and Alan Clark wrote the most unbalanced books, doing their very best to denigrate the endurance, efficiency, leadership and achievements of the BEF. One example of their negative effect was the student who in writing about the morale and discipline of the BEF suggested that British officers in 1918 did not radiate confidence, "and, here again, the Army failed in 1918." This is devoid of even a pretension of reality. The student, while he accepted the bilge pumped out by Winter et al, must have had some doubts, for greatly to his credit he had the honesty to place himself amongst those "who have never experienced battle or lived in a close-knit group like a platoon."[10] Charles Carrington reminds them (and us) that it was the BEF that knocked the enemy out, and he challenges:

> Now tell me, you historians, how it is that three million volunteered, subdued themselves to discipline, fought four arduous campaigns, came back to the battlefield again and again after every kind of setback and painful surprise, won the war at last by traditional

methods under their old commanders and, after the war, formed Old Soldiers loyal associations, over which Lord Haig, the one man whom all trusted, was President. They held happy, laughing, joking reunions for 20, 40, even 60 years.[11]

In their thousands Canadian veterans formed regimental associations and joined the Royal Canadian Legion, a branch of the British Empire Service League. They, too, held reunions for many years after the Great War.

The tendency to badmouth British generals and generalship, training, doctrine, equipment and, indeed, virtually anything under the sun, and the failure to make proper comparisons, or any comparisons at all, have resulted in much of the unbalanced criticism. Jeffery Williams provides a salutary and necessary antidote in his biography of Byng:

> As a Canadian who has known the British Army well for forty years, I find it difficult to believe that all its senior officers could have been so incompetent, unfeeling and unimaginative as they have been portrayed. Hundreds of thousands of Canadian veterans would attest that one at least could not be cramped into that dismal mould . . . [Byng] made them into a superb fighting force and set them on the road to victory.[12]

It was said of Currie that it was his "invariable habit to deliver the goods."[13] This was 1st Division's habit, too. The battles of Vimy, Hill 70, Passchendaele, and Amiens and the thousands of 1st Division casualties are the signposts of the division's skill at arms. This being so, the national amnesia about the achievements of our men in the Great War is sad—and ironic, too, in an era in which people are desperately seeking heroes. People are ever eager to apply the word—most often on the flimsiest of grounds—to participants in just about anything—be it business, sport, party or other politics—and including every "ism" that captures some interest's fancy. The very word "hero" is fast becoming meaningless, if it is not already. Away from the battlefield it should apply only in the most exceptional circumstances; even in reference to the battlefield it should be used sparingly. It can be applied unhesitatingly to 1st Division's 24 VC winners; it can be applied to the winners of other decorations for valour. Perhaps it can even be applied to every man who remained true and did his duty: "dearer yet the brotherhood that binds the brave of all the earth."[14] "It was from this spirit," said John Masters, "that no man was alone, neither on the field of battle, which is a lonely place, nor in the chasm of death, nor in the dark places of life."[15]

First Canadian Division, Old Red Patch, "You stand for more than your own name."[16]

Notes to Chapter Ten

1. Geoffrey Chaucer, quoted in Emily Morison Beck, ed., *John Bartlett, Familiar Quotations*, Fourteenth Edition (Boston: Little, Brown and Company, 1968), p. 163.

2. G.R. Stevens, *The Royal Canadian Regiment, 1933–1966* (London, Ont.: London Printing, 1967), p. 2.

3. Colonel C.P. Stacey, *Official History of the Canadian Army in the Second World War*, Volume I, *Six Years of War: The Army in Canada, Britain and the Pacific* (Ottawa: Queen's Printer, 1955), pp. 11, 20. In 1936 the Mackenzie King government reduced the sum allocated for armament acquisition to almost nil. King, aged 40 in 1914, and in apparent good health, judging by contemporary photographs, did not serve in the armed forces. Like the country he so admired, he opted for neutrality, acting during the war as a labour consultant, working for the Rockefeller Foundation and writing a ponderous thesis on labour relations.

4. Dean Oliver, "The Canadians at Passchendaele," in Peter H. Liddle, ed., *Passchendaele in Perspective The Third Battle of Ypres* (London: Leo Cooper, 1997), p. 268.

5. Kipling, *The Irish Guards in the Great War: The First Battalion*, p. 252.

6. Desmond Morton, "'Junior But Sovereign Allies': The Transformation of the Canadian Expeditionary Force, 1914–1918," in Norman Hillmer and Philip Wigley, eds., *The First British Commonwealth Essays in Honour of Nicholas Mansergh* (London: Frank Cass, 1980), p. 57.

7. General Sir Ian Hamilton, *The Soul and Body of an Army* (London: Edward Arnold & Co., 1921), p. 23.

8. Edmonds [Carrington], *A Subaltern's War*, p. 192. How easily journalistic imagination runs to self-deception!

9. Dancocks, *Gallant Canadians*, pp. 69, 196–97; Beattie, *48th Highlanders of Canada*, p. 96.

10. James Brent Wilson, "Morale and Discipline in the British Expeditionary Force, 1914–1918," Master's Thesis, University of New Brunswick, 1978, pp. viii, 7.

11. Carrington, "Kitchener's Army," p. 20.

12. Williams, *Byng of Vimy*, p. xiii. The present author, who was stationed in the United Kingdom for three years and has worked closely with the British Army for over 20 years, shares Williams' assessment.

13. Lieutenant-General Sir John Monash's comment on Currie's statement that the Canadian Corps would deliver the goods. See Urquhart, *Arthur Currie*, p. 227.

14. Sir Henry Newbolt, "Clifton Chapel," in *The New Oxford Book of English Verse*, ed. Sir Arthur Quiller-Couch (New York: Oxford University Press, 1955), pp. 1066–67.

15. John Masters, *Bugles and a Tiger* (New York: The Viking Press, 1956), p. 123.

16. From a poem that hangs in the regimental chapel of The Green Howards, Alexandra Princess of Wales' Own Yorkshire Regiment, at Richmond, North Yorkshire, England.

Abbreviations

2IC	Second in Command
A	Administration/Administrative
A & Q	Administration and Quartermaster
AA & QMG	Assistant Adjutant and Quartermaster General
ACI	Army Council Instruction
ADC	Aide-de-Camp
ADMI	Assistant Director of Military Intelligence
ANZAC	Australia New Zealand Army Corps
APM	Assistant Provost Marshal
ASC	Army Service Corps
BEF	British Expeditionary Force
BGGS	Brigadier-General General Staff
BM	Brigade Major
BMGO	Brigade Machine-Gun Officer
C-in-C	Commander-in-Chief
CB	Commander of the Bath
CCRC	Canadian Corps Reinforcement Camp
CE	Canadian Engineers
CEF	Canadian Expeditionary Force
CFA	Canadian Field Artillery
CGS	Chief of the General Staff
CIGS	Chief of the Imperial General Staff
CMG	Commander of the Order of St. Michael and St. George
CO	Commanding Officer
CRA	Commander Royal Artillery
CRE	Commander Royal Engineers
DA & QMG	Deputy Adjutant and Quartermaster General
DAA & QMG	Deputy Assistant Adjutant and Quartermaster General
DAAG	Deputy Assistant Adjutant General
DAC	Divisional Ammunition Column
DMGO	Divisional Machine-Gun Officer
DSO	Distinguished Service Order
FOO	Forward Observation Officer
FSR	*Field Service Regulations*
G/GS	General Staff
GHQ	General Headquarters
GOC (GOsC)	General Officer(s) Commanding
GOCRA	General Officer Commanding Royal Artillery
GSO1	General Staff Officer (1st Grade)
GSO2	General Staff Officer (2nd Grade)

GSO3	General Staff Officer (3rd Grade)
HE	High Explosive
HQ	Headquarters
IGT	Inspector-General Training
IO	Intelligence Officer
LO	Liaison Officer
LOB	Left Out of Battle
MC	Military Cross
MGGS	Major-General General Staff
MO	Medical Officer
NCO	Non-commissioned Officer
NDHQ	National Defence Headquarters
OC	Officer Commanding
OP	Observation Post
OR(s)	Other Rank(s)
p.s.c.	passed staff college
Q/QM	Quartermaster
RAF	Royal Air Force
RCD	Royal Canadian Dragoons
RCHA	Royal Canadian Horse Artillery
RCR	Royal Canadian Regiment
RE	Royal Engineers
RFA	Royal Field Artillery
RFC	Royal Flying Corps
RMC	Royal Military College
RUSI	Royal United Services Institute
SAA	Small Arms Ammunition
SD	Staff Duties
TEWT(s)	Tactical Exercise(s) Without Troops
TO	Transport Officer
VC	Victoria Cross

APPENDIX II

Formations, Battles and Engagements

In August and September 1914, 1st Division assembled at Valcartier preparatory to sailing for Plymouth on 3 October. Upon arrival the division moved to Salisbury Plain where it conducted training until departure for France in February 1915. Thereafter 1st Division served on the Western Front until the Armistice.

Its commanders were Lieutenant-General E.A.H. Alderson (29 September

1914), Major-General A.W. Currie (13 September 1915) and Major-General A.C. Macdonell (9 June 1917).

1915
Battle of Ypres

22–23 April	Battle of Gravenstafel
24 April–4 May	Battle of St. Julien
15–25 May	Battle of Festubert
15–16 June	Second Action of Givenchy

1916

2–3 June	Battle of Mount Sorrel

Battles of the Somme

15–22 September	Battle of Flers–Courcelette
26–28 September	Battle of Thiepval
1–18 October	Battle of Le Transloy
1 October–11 November	Battle of the Ancre Heights

1917
Battles of Arras

9–14 April	Battle of Vimy
28–29 April	Battle of Arleux
3–4 May	Third Battle of the Scarpe
3 June – 26 August	Operations near Lens (Hill 70)

Battle of Ypres

26 October–10 November	Second Battle of Passchendaele

1918
The Advance to Victory

8–11 August	Battle of Amiens
15–17 August	Damery

Second Battle of Arras

26–30 August	Battle of the Scarpe
2–3 September	Battle of Drocourt–Queant

Battle of the Hindenburg Line

27 September–1 October	Battle of Canal du Nord
8–9 October	Battle of Cambrai

Order of Battle

FORMATIONS	CONSISTING OF	COMMANDED BY	APPROXIMATE SIZE
Army	Two or more corps	General	200,000 +
Corps	Two or more divisions	Lieutenant-General	60,000–100,000
Division	Three brigades	Major-General	15,000–20,000
Brigade	Four battalions	Brigadier-General	5,000

UNITS	CONSISTING OF	COMMANDED BY	APPROXIMATE SIZE
Battalion	Four companies	Lieutenant-Colonel	1,000

SUB-UNITS	CONSISTING OF	COMMANDED BY	APPROXIMATE SIZE
Company	Four platoons	Major	200
Platoon	Four sections	Lieutenant or 2nd Lieutenant	40
Section		Corporal	12

Division

Headquarters
> Infantry Brigade(s) (3)
> Artillery Brigades ....Gun Brigades (3)
> ....Howitzer Brigade
> ....Heavy Battery
> Ammunition Column
> Engineer Companies (2, later 3)
> Medium Trench Mortar Batteries (3)
> Field Ambulances (3)
> Sanitary Section
> Veterinary Section
> Divisional Train
> Signals Company
> Cavalry Squadron
> Employment Company
> Machine-Gun Company (later a Battalion)

Note: An Entrenching Battalion and a Pioneer Battalion joined 1st Division for varying periods.

Victoria Cross Roll of Honour

Corporal Colin Fraser Barron	3rd Battalion	
Captain Edward Donald Bellew	7th Battalion	
Corporal Alexander Brereton	8th Battalion	
Private Harry Brown	10th Battalion	Posthumous
Lieutenant Frederick William Campbell	1st Battalion	Posthumous
Corporal Leonard Beaumaurice Clarke	2nd Battalion	
Corporal Frederick George Coppins	8th Battalion	
Private John Bernard Croak	13th Battalion	Posthumous
Lance-Corporal Frederick Fisher	13th Battalion	Posthumous
Corporal Herman James Good	13th Battalion	
Company Sergeant Major Frederick William Hall	8th Battalion	Posthumous
Lieutenant George Fraser Kerr	3rd Battalion	
Sergeant Arthur George Knight	10th Battalion	Posthumous
Captain O'Kill Massey Learmouth	2nd Battalion	Posthumous
Lieutenant George Burton McKean	14th Battalion	
Sergeant William Merrifield	4th Battalion	
Lance-Corporal William Henry Metcalfe	16th Battalion	
Private William Johnstone Milne	16th Battalion	Posthumous
Private Michael James O'Rourke	7th Battalion	
Lieutenant-Colonel Cyrus Wesley Peck	16th Battalion	
Private Walter Leigh Rayfield	7th Battalion	
Piper James Cleland Richardson	16th Battalion	Posthumous
Captain Francis Alex Scrimger	14th Battalion	
Sergeant Raphael Lewis Zengel	5th Battalion	

Commanders

Canadian Corps

GOC

13 September 1915	Lieutenant-General E.A.H. Alderson
28 May 1916	Lieutenant-General J.H.G. Byng
9 June 1917	Lieutenant-General A.W. Currie

1st Division   GOC

29 September 1914	Lieutenant-General E.A.H. Alderson
13 September 1915	Major-General A.W. Currie
9 June 1917	Major-General A.C. Macdonell

1st Brigade   GOC

22 September 1914	Brigadier-General M.S. Mercer	later Major-General, Killed in action 1916
25 November 1915	Brigadier-General G.B. Hughes	
14 February 1917	Brigadier-General W.A. Griesbach	
27 February 1919	Brigadier-General G.E. McCuaig	

2nd Brigade   GOC

22 September 1914	Brigadier-General A.W. Currie	later Major-General
13 September 1915	Brigadier-General L.J. Lipsett	Killed in action, 1918
2 July 1916	Brigadier-General F.O.W. Loomis	
1 January 1918	Brigadier-General J.F.L. Embury	
18 March 1918	Brigadier-General F.O.W. Loomis	
13 September 1918	Lieutenant-Colonel W.F. Gilson	
6 October 1918	Brigadier-General R.P. Clark	

3rd Brigade   GOC

22 September 1914	Brigadier-General R.E.W. Turner
12 August 1915	Brigadier-General R.G.E. Leckie
12 March 1916	Brigadier-General G.S. Tuxford

Commanding Officers

1st Battalion

22 September 1914	Lieutenant-Colonel F.W. Hill	
24 January 1916	Lieutenant-Colonel F.A. Creighton	Died of wounds
27 June 1916	Lieutenant-Colonel G.C. Hodson	
17 August 1917	Lieutenant-Colonel A.W. Sparling	

2nd Battalion

22 September 1914	Lieutenant-Colonel D. Watson
26 August 1915	Lieutenant-Colonel A.E. Swift
26 October 1916	Major W.M. Yates
10 January 1917	Lieutenant-Colonel R.P. Clark
12 May 1917	Lieutenant-Colonel L.T. McLaughlin
30 August 1918	Major R. Vanderwater
10 October 1918	Lieutenant-Colonel L.T. McLaughlin

3rd Battalion

22 September 1914	Lieutenant-Colonel R. Rennie
10 November 1915	Lieutenant-Colonel W.D. Allan
1 October 1916	Lieutenant-Colonel J.B. Rogers

4th Battalion

22 September 1914	Lieutenant-Colonel R.H. Labatt	
26 February 1915	Lieutenant-Colonel A.B. Birchall	Killed in action
29 April 1915	Lieutenant-Colonel J.B. Rogers	
14 May 1915	Lieutenant-Colonel R.H. Labatt	
7 June 1915	Lieutenant-Colonel M.A. Colquhoun	
25 June 1916	Lieutenant-Colonel W. Rae	
2 June 1917	Lieutenant-Colonel A.T. Thomson	Killed in action
20 November 1917	Lieutenant-Colonel L.H. Nelles	
10 August 1918	Major G.G. Blackstock	
4 September 1918	Lieutenant-Colonel L.H. Nelles	

5th Battalion

22 September 1914	Lieutenant-Colonel G.S. Tuxford
11 January 1916	Lieutenant-Colonel H.M. Dyer
29 June 1917	Lieutenant-Colonel L.P.O. Tudor
8 March 1918	Lieutenant-Colonel L.L. Crawford
4 April 1918	Lieutenant-Colonel L.P.O. Tudor

7th Battalion

22 September 1914	Lieutenant-Colonel W. Hart McHarg	Killed in action
29 April 1915	Lieutenant-Colonel V.W. Odlum	
20 July 1916	Lieutenant-Colonel S.D. Gardner	Died of wounds
9 October 1916	Lieutenant-Colonel W.F. Gilson	

8th Battalion

22 September 1914	Lieutenant-Colonel L.J. Lipsett	Killed in action 1918
28 September 1915	Lieutenant-Colonel H.H. Matthews	
14 July 1916	Lieutenant-Colonel K.C. Bedson	
3 September 1916	Lieutenant-Colonel J.M. Prower	
20 April 1918	Lieutenant-Colonel T.H. Raddall	Killed in action
13 August 1918	Lieutenant-Colonel A.L. Saunders	

10th Battalion

22 September 1914	Lieutenant-Colonel R.L. Boyle	Killed in action
1 June 1915	Lieutenant-Colonel J.G. Rattray	
25 September 1916	Lieutenant-Colonel D.M. Ormond	
24 May 1918	Lieutenant-Colonel E.W. Mcdonald	

13th Battalion

22 September 1914	Lieutenant-Colonel F.O.W. Loomis	
5 January 1916	Lieutenant-Colonel V.C. Buchanan	Killed in action
27 September 1916	Lieutenant-Colonel G.E. McCuaig	
20 December 1917	Lieutenant-Colonel K.M. Perry	
1 April 1918	Lieutenant-Colonel G.E. McCuaig	
14 September 1918	Major J.M.R. Sinclair	
14 October 1918	Lieutenant-Colonel K.M. Perry	
28 February 1919	Major J.M.R. Sinclair	

14th Battalion

22 September 1914	Lieutenant-Colonel F.S. Meighen
19 June 1915	Lieutenant-Colonel W.W. Burland
29 July 1915	Lieutenant-Colonel F.W. Fisher
19 March 1916	Lieutenant-Colonel R.P. Clark
15 January 1917	Lieutenant-Colonel G. McCombe
19 April 1918	Lieutenant-Colonel D. Worrall

15th Battalion

22 September 1914	Lieutenant-Colonel J.A. Currie	
28 June 1915	Lieutenant-Colonel W.A. Marshall	Killed in action
20 May 1916	Lieutenant-Colonel C.E. Bent	
29 December 1917	Lieutenant-Colonel J.W. Forbes	
15 April 1918	Lieutenant-Colonel C.E. Bent	
10 August 1918	Lieutenant-Colonel J.P. Girvan	
3 October 1918	Lieutenant-Colonel C.E. Bent	

16th Battalion

22 September 1914	Lieutenant-Colonel R.G.E. Leckie
12 August 1915	Lieutenant-Colonel J.E. Leckie
13 December 1916	Lieutenant-Colonel C.W.Peck
3 January 1919	Major J. Hope
28 March 1919	Lieutenant-Colonel J.A. Scroggie

Senior Staff Appointments

Canadian Corps

Brigadier-General General Staff

Brigadier-General C.H. Harington*
Sep 1915–Aug 1916   To Second Army as MGGS

Brigadier-General P. deB. Radcliffe*
Aug 1916–Apr 1918   To War Office as DMO

Brigadier-General N.W. Webber*
 Apr 1918–Oct 1918   Ex GSO1, 2nd Div(1917)

Brigadier-General R.J.T. Hayter*
 Oct 1918–Armistice   Ex GOC 10th Bde

Deputy Adjutant and Quartermaster General

Brigadier-General T.B. Wood*   Sep 1915–Jun 1916

Brigadier-General G. Farmar*   Jun 1916–Armistice

1st Division

General Staff Officer (1st Grade) (Lieutenant-Colonel unless otherwise shown)

INCUMBENT	PREVIOUS APPOINTMENT	SUBSEQUENT APPOINTMENT(S)
E.S. Heard* (Oct 1914–Feb 1915)	Imperial Army	
Col C.F. Romer, psc* (Feb–Jul 1915)	GSO1 5th (Imperial) Div	BGGS (Imperial) III Corps and later Major-General
R.H. Kearsley, psc* (Jul 1915–Aug 1917)	GSO2 Indian Cav Corps	BGGS VI (Imperial) Corps
R.J. Hayter, psc* (Aug–Dec 1917)	BM 1st Bde (Sep 1914–Sep 1915)	GOC 10th Bde to Oct 1918, then BGGS Cdn Corps
J.L.R. Parsons (Dec 1917–Jan 1919)	GSO1 5th Div	SSO Cdn Section GHQ

*British Army Officers

Assistant Adjutant and Quartermaster General

Col T.B. Wood* Oct 1914–Jul 1915	DA & QMG Cdn Corps
G. Frith* Jul 1915–Mar 1917	
J.S. Brown Mar 1917–May 1918	AQMG Cdn Corps

Brigade Major 1st Brigade (Major unless otherwise shown)

INCUMBENT	PREVIOUS APPOINTMENT	SUBSEQUENT APPOINTMENT(S)
R.J.T. Hayter, psc* (Oct 1914–Sep 1915)	Imperial Army	GSO2 1st Div (Sep 1915) GSO1 3rd Div (Jun 1916) GOC 10th Bde (Jan 1918)
A.B. Incledon-Webber* (Sep 1915–May 1916)	Imperial Army	GSO2 1st Div (May 1916)
H.F. McDonald (May–Sep 1916)	GSO3 2nd Div (Sep 1915)	Wounded, hospital, UK (Sep 1916)
P.S. Villiers (Acting) (Sep 1916)	GSO3 1st Div	BM 3rd Bde (Oct 1916)
W.A. Adams (Sep 1916–Feb 1917)		UK
H.M. Urquhart (Feb–Dec 1917)	Staff Captain 3rd Bde (Jan 1916–Jan 1917)	CO 43rd Bn
J.D. Simpson (Acting) (Nov 1917–Jan 1918)		
L.D. Heron (Feb–Jun 1918)	GSO3, 1st Div	GSO2, GHQ
H.W.A. Foster (Jun–Nov 1918)		

Brigade Major 2nd Brigade (Major unless otherwise shown)

INCUMBENT	PREVIOUS APPOINTMENT	SUBSEQUENT APPOINTMENT(S)
LtCol H. Kemmis-Betty, psc (Oct 1914–May 1915)		GSO2 1st Div

G. Meynell (Acting) (May 1915)		
LtCol J.H. Elmsley (May–Sep 1915)	Cdn Cav Bde	GOC 8th Bde(June 1916)
J. Prower (Sep 1915–Aug 1916)	8th Bn	CO 8th Bn
Captain W.H.S. Alston* (Aug 1916–Jul 1917)	GSO3 63rd Div	BM, 172nd Bde, 57th Div
J.P. MacKenzie (Jul 1917–May 1918)	2IC 8th Bn	Lieutenant-Colonel & BM, Engr Bde
Captain W.D. Herridge (Jun–Nov 1918)	Staff Captain 2nd Bde (Jun 1917–Jan 1918) GS03, 4th Div (Jan–Jun 1918)	

Brigade Major 3rd Brigade (Major unless otherwise shown)

INCUMBENT	PREVIOUS APPOINTMENT	SUBSEQUENT APPOINTMENT(S)
LtCol G.B. Hughes (Oct 1914–May 1915)		GSO2, 2nd Div (May 1915) GOC 1st Bde (Nov 1915)
P.F. Villiers (Jul 1915–Jan 1916)	Staff Captain 3rd Bde (May–Jul 1915)	GSO3 1st Div (Jan 1916)
M.O. Clarke	GSO2 Second Army (Jan–Oct 1916)	
P.F. Villiers* (Oct 1916–Jan 1918)	GSO3 1st Div Staff Captain, 3rd Bde	GSO2 29th Div (Jan 1918)
Gordon Aikins (Apr–May 1918)	Staff Captain 2nd Bde (Feb–Apr 1918)	Wounded and evacuated
A.D. Wilson (May–Nov 1918)	Staff Captain 12th Bde	

BIBLIOGRAPHY

Government Records

Library and Archives Canada. Record Groups 9, 24 and 41.

———. Service Records.

———. Personal Papers and Unit Records: 3rd Battalion (MG 30E 318); 10th Battalion (MG 30E 349); Ackland, Peregrine (MG 30E 222); Alldritt, William Alexander (MG 30E 1); Baxter, Frank (MG 30E 417); Creelman, John Jennings (MG 30E 8); Currie, Arthur W. (MG 30E 100); Curtis, William Howard (MG 30E 505); Griesbach, William Antrobus (MG 30E 15); Griffith, Aubrey (MG 30E 442); Leckie, John Edward (MG 30E 83); Leckie, Robert Gilmour (MG 30E 84); Macdonell, Archibald Cameron (MG 30E 20); Matthews, Harold Halford (MG 30E 60); Morrison, Edward Whipple (MG 30E 81); Odlum, Victor Wentworth (MG 30E 300); Parsons, Johnson Lindsay (MG 30E 117); Phelan, Frederick (MG 30E 54); Russell, E.W. (MG 30E 220); Sinclair, Alexander Gibson (MG 30E 237); Sinclair, Ian MacIntosh Rae (MG 30E 432); Turner, Richard E.W. (MG 30E 46); Urquhart, Hugh MacIntyre (MG 30E 75); Villiers, Paul Frederick (MG 30E 236); Watson, David (MG 30E 69); Woods, William B. (MG 31 G29-31).

Saskatchewan Provincial Archives. R.2.247. "The Great War as I Saw It." Memoirs of Brigadier-General George Tuxford.

Imperial War Museum—Personal and Other Papers: Stanley Brittain, William Kerr and E.W. Russell.

Manuals and Instructions

Army Council Instruction No. 1968. Training of Infantry Recruits. London: War Office, 1916.

Army Council Instruction No. 1230. Training of Infantry Recruits. London: War Office, 1917.

Army Rifle Association, Platoon Competition. France: Army Printing and Stationery Services, December,1917.

Canadian Army Manual of Training, CAMT 1-36 Staff Procedures, Volume 3, *Staff Duties in the Field.* Ottawa: Queen's Printer, 1963.

Canadian Corps Trench Orders. London: HMSO, 21 October 1915.

Canadian Corps Trench Orders. Army Printing and Stationery Services, July 1916.

Canadian Corps Trench Standing Orders. Army Printing and Stationery Services, 1917.

Field Service Pocket Book. London: General Staff, War Office, 1914.

Field Service Regulations, Part I: Operations. London: HMSO, 1909; reprint 1912.

Infantry Platoon Commander's Aide Memoire. Camp Borden, Ontario: The Royal Canadian School of Infantry, 1959.

Infantry Section Leading and Platoon Tactics, 1954. Ottawa: Queen's Printer, 1955.

Infantry Training (4-Company Organization), 1914. London: HMSO, 1914.

Instructions Governing Organization and Administration. Ottawa: Government Printing Bureau, 1916.

Musketry Regulations, Part I, 1909, Reprinted 1914. London: HMSO, 1914.

Notes for Commanding Officers. Aldershot: Gale and Polden, 1917 and 1918 editions.

Notes to Assist Company Officers in Preparing Lectures for the Training of Category "A" Infantry Recruits. London: HMSO, January 1917.

Organization of an Infantry Battalion and the Normal Formation for the Attack. London: HMSO, April 1917.

Platoon Organization. London: War Office, January 1917.

SS 109 Training of Divisions for Offensive Action. GHQ: May 1916.

SS 119 Preliminary Notes on the Tactical Lessons of the Recent Operations. Army Printing and Stationery Services, July 1916.

SS 135 Instructions for the Training of Divisions for Offensive Action. London: HMSO, December 1916.

SS 143 Instructions for the Training of Platoons for Offensive Action. London: HMSO, February 1917 and September 1917.

SS 143 The Training and Employment of Platoons. Army Printing and Stationery Services, February 1918.

SS 144 The Normal Formation for the Attack. London: HMSO, February 1917.

SS 152 Instructions for the Training of the British Armies in France (Provisional). London: HMSO, June 1917.

SS 185 Assault Training. Harrison and Sons. September 1917.

SS 192 The Employment of Machine Guns. London: HMSO, January 1918.

SS 197 The Tactical Employment of Lewis Guns. London: HMSO, January 1918.

SS 356 Handbook of the German Army in War. April 1918. London: HMSO, 1918.

SS 415 The Duties of an Officer: Knowledge and Character. London: HMSO, 1917.

Training in Canadian Reserve Battalions. London: HMSO, January and October 1917.

Training Leaflet No. 1 Sample of a Day's Training for a Company. B.E.F. France: Army Printing and Stationery Services, August 1918.

Training Leaflet No. 2 Programme of Training for a Battalion Out of the Line for Ten Days. B.E.F. France: Army Printing and Stationery Services, August 1918.

Training Leaflet No. 3 Battalion Commander's Conference. B.E.F. France: Army Printing and Stationery Services, August 1918.

Training Leaflet No. 4 Attack Formations for Small Units. B.E.F. France: Army Printing and Stationery Services, September 1918.

Books

Abbott, P.E. and J.M.A. Tamplin. *British Gallantry Awards*. Guinness Superlatives Ltd and B.A. Selby Ltd., 1971.

Adams, Bernard. *Nothing of Importance: A Record of Eight Months at the Front with a Welsh Battalion, October 1915 to June 1916*. 1917. Reprint, Uckfield, East Sussex: The Naval and Military Press, n.d.

Allen, Capt. E.P.S. *The 116th Battalion in France*. Toronto: privately printed, 1921.

Annals of Valour: Empire Day, Friday, May 23rd, 1919. Toronto: King's Printer, 1919.

Ashworth, Tony. *Trench Warfare, 1914–1918: The Live and Let Live System*. New York: Holmes & Meier Publishers, Inc., 1980.

Atkinson, C.T. *The Seventh Division, 1914–1918*. London: John Murray, 1927.

Bailey, J.B. *Cinquante-Quatre Being a Short History of the 54th Canadian Infantry Battalion*. Belgium: privately printed, 1919.

Baldwin, Sergeant Harold. *"Holding the Line."* Chicago: A.C. McClurg & Co., 1918.

Banks, Arthur. *A Military Atlas of the First World War.* 2nd ed. London: Leo Cooper, 1989.

Barker, A.J. *British and American Infantry Weapons of World War II.* London: Arms and Armour Press, 1969.

Barnard, Lieutenant Colonel W.T. *The Queen's Own Rifles of Canada 1860–1960: One Hundred Years of Canada.* Don Mills: Ontario Publishing Company, 1960.

Barnett, Corelli. *Britain and Her Army, 1509–1970: A Military, Political and Social Survey* London: Penguin, 1970.

Baynes, John. *Morale, A Study of Men and Courage: The Second Scottish Rifles at the Battle of Neuve Chapelle, 1915.* London: Cassell, 1967.

———. *Far From a Donkey: The Life of General Sir Ivor Maxse.* London: Brasseys, 1995.

Bean, C.E.W. *The Official History of Australia in the War of 1914–1918.* Vol. VI. *The A.I.F. in France: May 1918—The Armistice.* Sydney: Angus and Robertson Ltd., 1942.

Beattie, Kim. *48th Highlanders of Canada, 1891–1928.* Toronto: 48th Highlanders of Canada, 1932.

Beck, Emily Morison., ed. Bartlett, John. *Familiar Quotations.* 14th ed. Boston: Little, Brown and Company, 1968.

Becke, Major A.F. *History of the Great War Order of Battle of Divisions, Part 1: The Regular British Divisions.* London: HMSO, 1935.

———.*Part 4: The Army Council, G.H.Q.'s, Armies, and Corps, 1914–1918.* London: HMSO, 1945.

Bennett, Captain S.G. *The 4th Canadian Mounted Rifles, 1914–1919.* Toronto: Murray Printing Company Limited, 1926.

Berton, Pierre. *Vimy.* Toronto: McClelland & Stewart, 1986.

Bidwell, Shelford and Dominick Graham. *Fire-Power: British Army Weapons and Theories of War 1904–1945.* London: George Allen & Unwin, 1982.

Bird, Will R. *Ghosts Have Warm Hands.* Nepean, Ontario: CEF Books, 1997.

Bishop, Arthur. *Our Bravest and Our Best: The Stories of Canada's Victoria Cross Winners.* Toronto: McGraw-Hill Ryerson, 1995.

Blackburn, George G. *The Guns of Normandy: A Soldier's Eye View, France 1944.* Toronto: McClelland & Stewart Inc., 1995.

Blunden, Edmund. *Undertones of War.* Harmondsworth, Middlesex: Penguin Books, 1982.

Bond, Brian. *British Military Policy Between the Two World Wars.* Oxford: Clarendon Press, 1980.

Bond, Brian, ed. *The First World War and British Military History.* Oxford: Clarendon Press, 1991.

Borthwick, Alastair. *Battalion: A British Infantry Unit's Actions from El Alamein to the Elbe, 1942–1945.* London: Baton Wicks Publishing, 1994.

A Brief History of the 3rd Battalion, C.E.F. (Toronto Regiment). N.p., 1934.

A Brief Outline of the Story of the Canadian Grenadier Guards and the first months of the Royal Montreal Regiment in the Great War. N.p., 1926.

Brophy, John and Eric Partridge. *The Long Trail: What the British Soldier Sang and Said in the Great War of 1914–18.* London: Andre Deutsch, 1965.

Brown, Malcolm. *Tommy Goes to War.* London: J.M. Dent & Sons Ltd., 1978.

Burns, Lieut.-Gen. E.L.M. *General Mud: Memoirs of Two World Wars.* Toronto: Clarke, Irwin and Company Limited, 1970.

Bush, Captain Eric Wheeler, ed. *Salute the Soldier: An Anthology of Quotations, Poems and Prose.* London: Allen & Unwin, 1961.

Calder, Major D.G. Scott. *The History of the 28th (Northwest) Battalion, C.E.F. (October 1914–June 1919).* Regina: privately printed, 1961.

Canada in Khaki: A Tribute to the Officers and Men Now Serving in the Overseas Military Forces of Canada. London: Pictorial Newspaper Co., 1917–19.

Carrington, Charles. *Soldier from the Wars Returning.* London: Hutchinson, 1965.

Chappell, Mike. *The Canadian Army at War.* Osprey Men-at-Arms Series, no. 164. London: Osprey Publishing, 1985.

Clark, Alan. *The Donkeys.* London: Hutchinson, 1961.

Clausewitz, Carl von. *On War.* Edited and translated by Michael Howard and Peter Paret. Princeton, N.J.: Princeton University Press, 1976.

Clyne, H.R.N. *Vancouver's 29th.* Vancouver: Tobin's Tigers Association, 1964.

Cobb, Humphrey. *Paths of Glory.* New York: Avon Books, 1973.

Collyer, Brigadier-General J.J. *The Campaign in German South West Africa, 1914–1915.* Pretoria: Government Printer, 1937.

Commonwealth War Cemeteries and Memorials: France & Belgium. Maidenhead, Berkshire: Commonwealth War Graves Commission, 1974.

Cooke, O.A. *The Canadian Military Experience, 1867–1983: A Bibliography,* 2nd ed. Ottawa: Department of National Defence, 1984.

Cooper, Major Bryan. *The Tenth (Irish) Division in Gallipoli.* London: Herbert Jenkins, 1918.

Corrigall, Major D.J. *The History of the Twentieth Canadian Battalion (Central Ontario Regiment), Canadian Expeditionary Force, in the Great War, 1914–1918.* Toronto: Stone & Cox Limited, 1935.

Craig, Captain John Dixon. *The 1st Canadian Division in the Battles of 1918.* London: Barrs & Co., 1919.

Craig, W.J. *The Complete Works of William Shakespeare.* London: Magpie Books, 1993.

Critchley, Brig.-General A.C. *Critch! The Memoirs of Brigadier-General A.C. Critchley.* London: Hutchinson, 1961.

Currie, Lieut.-General Sir A.W. *Canadian Corps Operations During the Year 1918.* Ottawa: Department of Militia and Defence, 1919.

Curry, Frederic C. *From the St. Lawrence to the Yser with the First Canadian Brigade.* London: Smith, Elder & Co., 1916.

Dancocks, Daniel G. *Sir Arthur Currie: A Biography.* Toronto: McClelland & Stewart, 1985.

———. *Legacy of Valour: The Canadians at Passchendaele.* Edmonton: Hurtig, 1986.

———. *Spearhead to Victory: Canada and the Great War.* Edmonton: Hurtig, 1987.

———. *Welcome to Flanders Fields: The First Canadian Battle of the Great War: Ypres, 1915.* Toronto: McClelland & Stewart, 1988.

———. *Gallant Canadians: The Story of the Tenth Canadian Infantry Battalion 1914–1919*. Calgary: The Calgary Highlanders Regimental Funds Foundation, 1990.

Davies, F., and G. Maddocks. *Bloody Red Tabs*. London: Leo Cooper, 1996.

Douie, Charles. *The Weary Road: Recollections of a Subaltern of Infantry*. Stevenage, Herts: Strong Oak Press Ltd., 1988.

Duff, Maj.-General A.C. *Sword and Pen: Some Problems of a Battledress Army*. Aldershot: Gale and Polden Limited, 1950.

Duguid, Col. A. Fortescue. *Official History of the Canadian Forces in the Great War, 1914–1919* General Series, vol. I, *From the Outbreak of War to the Formation of the Canadian Corps, August 1914–September 1915.*

———. *Official History of the Canadian Forces in the Great War, 1914–1919*. General Series, vol. I, *Chronology, Appendices and Maps*. Ottawa: King's Printer, 1938.

Dunn, Captain J.C. *The War the Infantry Knew, 1914–1919*. London: Jane's Publishing Company Limited, 1987.

Eden, Anthony. *Another World, 1897–1917*. London: Allen Lane, 1976.

Edmonds, Charles [Charles Carrington]. *A Subaltern's War*. London: Peter Davies Ltd, 1929.

Edmonds, Brig.-General J.E. *Military Operations, France and Belgium, 1915: Battles of Aubers Ridge, Festubert, and Loos*. London: Macmillan, 1928.

———. *Military Operations France and Belgium, 1916: Sir Douglas Haig's Command to the 1st July: Battle of the Somme*. London: Macmillan, 1932.

———. *Military Operations France and Belgium, 1916: Sir Douglas Haig's Command to the 1st July: Battle of the Somme. Appendices*. London: Macmillan, 1932.

———. *Military Operations France and Belgium, 1916: 2nd July 1916 to the End of the Battles of the Somme*. London: Macmillan, 1938.

———. *Military Operations France and Belgium 1917: The German Retreat to the Hindenburg Line and the Battles of Arras. Appendices*. London: Macmillan, 1940.

———. *Military Operations France and Belgium 1917*. Volume II. *7th June–10th November Messines and Third Ypres (Passchendaele)*. London: Macmillan, 1948.

———. *Military Operations France and Belgium, 1918: March–April, Continuation of the German Offensives*. London: Macmillan, 1937.

———. *Military Operations France and Belgium 1918*. Volume IV. *8th August–26 September, The Franco-British Offensive*. London: Macmillan, 1947.

Edmonds, Brig.-General J.E., and Lieut.-Colonel R. Maxwell-Hyslop. *Military Operations France and Belgium 1918* Volume V *26th September–11th November The Advance to Victory*. London: Macmillan, 1947.

Edmonds, Brig.-General J.E., and Captain G.C. Wynne. *Military Operations, France and Belgium, 1915: Winter 1914–15, Battle of Neuve Chapelle, Battles of Ypres*. London: Macmillan, 1927.

Elliot, Major S.R. *Scarlet to Green: A History of Intelligence in the Canadian Army, 1903–1963*. Toronto: Canadian Intelligence and Security Association, 1981.

Ellis, John. *Eye-Deep in Hell: The Western Front, 1914–1918*. London: Croom Helm, 1975.

English, John A. *The Canadian Army and the Normandy Campaign: A Study of Failure in High Command*. Westport, Conn.: Praeger, 1991.

Enser, A.G.S. *A Subject Bibliography of the First World War Books in English, 1914–1978*. London: Andre Deutsch, 1979.

Falls, Captain Cyril. *Military Operations, France and Belgium, 1917: The German Retreat to the Hindenburg Line and the Battles of Arras*. London: Macmillan, 1940.

———. *The Great War, 1914–1918*. Toronto: Longman's, 1959.

———. *War Books: An Annotated Bibliography of Books About the Great War*. London: Greenhill Books, 1989.

———. *The History of the 36th (Ulster) Division*. London: M'Caw, Stevenson & Orr, Ltd: 1922.

Feilding, Rowland. *War Letters to a Wife: France and Flanders, 1915–1919*. London: The Medici Company, 1929.

Fetherstonhaugh, R.C. *The 13th Battalion Royal Highlanders of Canada, 1914–1919*. Montreal: The 13th Battalion Royal Highlanders of Canada, 1925.

———. *The Royal Montreal Regiment, 14th Battalion, C.E.F., 1914–1925*. Montreal: The Gazette Publishing Co. Limited, 1927.

———. *The 24th Battalion, C.E.F., Victoria Rifles of Canada, 1914–1919*. Montreal: Gazette Printing Company, 1930.

———. *The Royal Canadian Regiment, 1883–1933*. Montreal: Gazette Printing Company, 1936.

Fifth Battalion Year Book. Saskatoon: Fifth Battalion Association, n.d.

Fortescue, Sir John. *The Vicissitudes of Organized Power: The Romanes Lecture*. Oxford: At the Clarendon Press, 1929.

Fosten, D.S.V. and R.J. Marrion. *The British Army, 1914–18*. Osprey Men-at-Arms Series, no. 81. London: Osprey Publishing, 1978.

Fraser, David, ed. *In Good Company: The First World War Letters and Diaries of The Hon. William Fraser Gordon Highlanders*. Salisbury, Wilts.: Michael Russell, 1990.

Fraser, Edward, and John Gibbons. *Soldier and Sailor Words and Phrases*. London: George Routledge and Sons Ltd., 1925.

Fuller, Major-General J.F.C. *Memoirs of an Unconventional Soldier*. London: Ivor Nicholson and Watson Limited, 1936.

———. *The Decisive Battles of the Western World and Their Influence upon History*. Volume Three. *From the American Civil War to the End of the Second World War*. London: Eyre & Spottiswoode, 1956.

Fuller, J.G. *Troop Morale and Popular Culture in the British and Dominion Armies 1914–1918*. Oxford: Clarendon Press, 1990.

Gibbs, Philip. *Realities of War*. London: Heineman, 1920.

Gibson, Capt. W.L., ed. *Records of the Fourth Canadian Infantry Battalion in the Great War, 1914–1918*. Toronto: MacLean Publishing Company Limited, 1924.

Gilbert, Martin. *The Challenge of War: Winston S. Churchill 1914–1916*. London: William Heinemann Ltd., reprint, London: Mandarin, 1990.

Gillon, Captain Stair. *The Story of the 29th Division: A Record of Gallant Deeds*. London: Thomas Nelson & Sons Ltd., 1925.

Glover, Michael. *A New Guide to the Battlefields of Northern France and the Low Countries*. London: Michael Joseph Limited, 1987.

Goodspeed, Major D.J. *Battle Royal: A History of the Royal Regiment of Canada, 1862–1962*. Toronto: The Royal Regiment of Canada Association, 1962.

———. *The Road Past Vimy: The Canadian Corps, 1914–1918*. Toronto: Macmillan, 1969.

Gould, L. McLeod. *From B.C. to Baisieux, Being the Narrative History of the 102nd Canadian Infantry Battalion*. Victoria, B.C.: Thos. R. Cusack Presses, 1919.

Graham, Stephen. *A Private in the Guards*. London: Macmillan, 1919.

Graves, Robert. *Goodbye to All That*. London: Cassell, 1957.

Greenhous, Brereton, and Stephen J. Harris. *Canada and the Battle of Vimy Ridge 9–12 April, 1917*. Ottawa: Canada Communication Group, 1992.

Griffith, Paddy. *Battle Tactics of the Western Front: The British Army's Art of Attack, 1916–18*. New Haven, Conn.: Yale University Press, 1994.

Griffith, Paddy, ed. *British Fighting Methods in the Great War*. London: Frank Cass, 1996.

Gudmundsson, Bruce I. *Stormtroop Tactics: Innovation in the German Army, 1914–1918*. New York: Praeger, 1988.

Hahn, Maj. J.F. *The Intelligence Service Within the Canadian Corps*. Toronto: Macmillan, 1930.

Haking, Brig.-General R.C.B. *Company Training*. London: Hugh Rees Limited, 1915.

Hamilton, General Sir Ian. *A Staff Officer's Scrapbook During the Russo-Japanese War*. London: Edward Arnold, 1906.

———. *The Soul and Body of an Army*. London: Edward Arnold & Co., 1921.

———. *The Commander*. London: Hollis and Carter, 1957.

Hamilton, Nigel. *Monty: The Making of a General, 1887–1942*. London: Hamish Hamilton, 1981.

Hamilton, Master of Belhaven, Lieut.-Colonel The Hon. Ralph. *The War Diary of the Master of Belhaven*. London: John Murray, 1924; reprint, Barnsley, South Yorkshire: Wharncliffe Publishing Limited, 1990.

Hanbury-Sparrow, Lt.-Col. A.A. *The Land-Locked Lake*. Canberra: Broderick Pty. Ltd., 1977.

Harington, General Sir Charles. *Tim Harington Looks Back*. London: John Murray, 1940.

Harris, Stephen J. *Canadian Brass: The Making of a Professional Army, 1860–1939*. Toronto: University of Toronto Press, 1988.

Hay, Ian [Major-General John Hay Beith]. *The First Hundred Thousand, Being the Unofficial Chronicle of a Unit of "K(I)"*. Toronto: William Briggs, 1916.

Haycock, Ronald. *Sam Hughes: The Public Career of a Controversial Canadian, 1885–1916*. Waterloo, Ont.: Wilfred Laurier University Press, 1986.

Haycock, Ronald, and Keith Neilson, eds. *Men, Machines and War*. Waterloo, Ont.: Wilfred Laurier University Press, 1988.

Hayes, Lieut.-Col. Joseph. *The Eighty-Fifth In France and Flanders*. Halifax: Royal Print & Litho Limited, 1920.

Headlam, Lieut.-Col. Cuthbert. *History of the Guards Division in the Great War, 1915–1918*. 2 vols. London: John Murray, 1924.

Heinl, Robert D. *Dictionary of Military and Naval Quotations*. Annapolis, Md.: U.S. Naval Institute, 1966.

Hill, R.J.T. *Something About a Soldier.* London: Lovat Dickson Limited, 1934.

Hitchcock, Captain F.C. *Stand To: A Diary of the Trenches, 1915–1918.* Norwich, Norfolk: Gliddon Books, 1988.

Hogg, Ian V. *Grenades and Mortars.* New York: Ballantine, 1974.

———. *The Guns.* Ballantine, 1971.

Holland, J.A. *The Story of the Tenth Canadian Battalion, 1914–1917.* London: Charles and Son, 1918.

Holmes, Richard. *Firing Line.* Harmondsworth, Middlesex: Penguin Books, 1987.

Holt, Tonie and Valmai, eds. *The Best of Fragments from France by Capt. Bruce Bairnsfather.* Cheltenham, Gloucestershire: Phin Publishing Limited, 1978.

Horner, D.M. *Crisis in Command: Australian Generalship and the Japanese Threat, 1941–43.* Canberra: Australian National University Press, 1978.

Huntford, Roland. *The Last Place on Earth.* London: Pan Books, 1985.

Hyatt, A.M.J. *General Sir Arthur Currie: A Military Biography.* Toronto: University of Toronto Press, 1987.

James, Robert Rhodes. *Gallipoli.* London: B.T. Batsford Limited, 1965.

Jessel, Major R.G. *G, A, and Q: An Introduction to the Staff.* Aldershot: Gale and Polden, 1947.

Junger, Ernst. *The Storm of Steel.* London: Chatto and Windus, 1929; reprint, London: Constable, 1994.

———. *Copse 125.* Translated by Basil Creighton. London: Chatto and Windus, 1930; reprint, Zimmermann and Zimmermann, 1985.

Kearsey, Lieutenant-Colonel A. *The Battle of Amiens 1918 and Operations 8th August–3rd September, 1918.* Aldershot: Gale & Polden, 1950.

Kerr, Wilfred Brenton. *Arms and the Maple Leaf Memories of Canada's Corps, 1918.* Seaforth, Ontario: Huron Expositor Press, 1943.

———. *Shrieks and Crashes.* Toronto: Hunter-Rose Company, 1929.

Kipling, Rudyard. *Barrack-Room Ballads and Other Verses.* Reprint, London: Methuen and Co. Ltd., 1929.

———. *The Irish Guards in the Great War: The First Battalion.* New York: Sarpedon, 1997.

Leader, Major W.K.M., MC, p.s.c. *An Elementary Study of Appreciations Orders and Messages.* London: Sifton, Praed & Co. Ltd., 1936.

Lewis, Lieut. R. *Over the Top with the 25th.* Halifax: H.H. Marshall, Limited, 1918.

Liddle, Peter H., ed., *Passchendaele in Perspective: The Third Battle of Ypres.* London: Leo Cooper, 1997.

Lipscomb, Capt. W.P. *Staff Tales.* London: Constable & Company Ltd., 1920.

Livesay, J.F.B. *Canada's Hundred Days. With the Canadian Corps from Amiens to Mons, Aug. 8–Nov. 11, 1918.* Toronto: Thomas Allen, 1919.

Long, A.L. *Memories of Robert E. Lee.* New York: J.M. Stoddart & Company, 1887.

Love, David W. *"A Call to Arms": The Organization and Administration of Canada's Military in World War One.* Calgary: Bunker to Bunker Books, 1999.

Lucas, Sir Charles, gen. ed. *The Empire at War.* 5 vols. Oxford: Oxford University Press, 1921–26. Vol. 2, *Canada*, by F.H. Underhill. London: Clarendon Press, 1923.

Lukacs, John. *The Hitler of History.* New York: Knopf, 1997.

Lupfer, Timothy T. *The Dynamics of Doctrine: The Changes in German Tactical Doctrine During the First World War*. Leavenworth Papers, No. 4. Fort Leavenworth, Kansas: Combat Studies Institute, 1981.

MacDonald, F.B. and John J. Gardiner. *The Twenty-Fifth Battalion, Canadian Expeditionary Force*. Sydney, N.S.: City Printers Limited, 1983.

Macdonald, Lyn. *They Called it Passchendaele: The Story of the Third Battle of Ypres and the Men Who Fought In It*. London: Michael Joseph, 1978.

———. *Somme*. London: Michael Joseph, 1981.

———. *1914–1918, Voices and Images of the Great War*. London: Michael Joseph, 1988.

———. ed., *Anthem for Doomed Youth: Poets of the Great War*. London: Folio Society, 2000.

MacGowan, S. Douglas, Harry (Mac) Heckbert, M.M. and Byron E. O'Leary. *New Brunswick's "Fighting 26th": A History of the 26th New Brunswick Battalion, C.E.F., 1914–1919*. Saint John, N.B.: Neptune Publishing Company Limited, 1995.

Macklin, Maj.-General W.H.S. *An Introduction to the Study of the Principles of War*. Ottawa: King's Printer, 1952.

MacShane, Frank. *The Life of Raymond Chandler*. Harmondsworth, Middlesex: Penguin, 1978.

Manning, Frederick. *The Middle Parts of Fortune*. London: Peter Davies, 1929.

Masters, John. *Bugles and a Tiger*. New York: The Viking Press, 1956.

———. *The Road to Mandalay*. New York: Harper & Brothers, 1961.

Mathieson, William B. *My Grandfather's War: Canadians Remember the First World War*. Toronto: Macmillan, 1981.

McClintock, Alexander. *Best O'Luck*. Toronto: McClelland, Goodchild & Stewart, 1917.

McEvoy, Bernard and Capt. A.H. Finlay, M.C. *History of the 72nd Canadian Infantry Battalion Seaforth Highlanders of Canada*. Vancouver: Cowan & Brookhouse, 1920.

McHarg, W. Hart. *From Quebec to Pretoria with the Royal Canadian Regiment*. Toronto: W. Briggs, 1902.

McWilliams, J.L. and J.R. Steel. *Gas! The Battle for Ypres, 1915*. St. Catharines: Vanwell Publishing, 1985

———. *The Suicide Battalion*. St. Catharines: Vanwell Publishing, 1990.

Meek, John F. *Over the Top! The Canadian Infantry in the First World War*. Orangeville, Ontario: n.p., 1971.

Meinertzhagen, Colonel R. *Army Diary, 1899–1926*. Edinburgh: Oliver and Boyd, 1960.

Middlebrook, Martin and Mary. *The Somme Battlefields: A Comprehensive Guide from Crecy to the Two World Wars*. London: Viking, 1991.

Miles, Captain Wilfrid. *Military Operations, France and Belgium, 1916: 2nd July 1916 to the End of the Battles of the Somme*. London: Macmillan, 1938.

———. *Military Operations, France and Belgium, 1917: The Battle of Cambrai*. London: Macmillan, 1948.

Military Advisory Board. *Canada in the Great World War: An Authentic Account of the Military History of Canada from the Earliest Days to the Close of the War of the Nations*. Vol. III, *Guarding the Channel Ports*. Toronto: United Publishers of Canada Limited, 1919.

———. Vol. IV, *The Turn of the Tide*. Toronto: United Publishers of Canada Limited, 1920.

————. Vol. V, *The Triumph of the Allies*. Toronto: United Publishers of Canada Limited, 1920.

————. Vol. VI, *Special Services, Heroic Deeds, etc.* United Publishers of Canada Limited, 1921.

Miller, Carman. *Painting the Map Red: Canada and the South African War, 1899–1902*. Montreal: McGill-Queen's University, 1993.

Monash, Lieut.-General Sir John. *The Australian Victories in 1918*. New York: E.P. Dutton and Co., n.d.

Montague, C.E. *Disenchantment*. London: Chatto and Windus, 1922.

Montgomery, Major-General Sir Archibald. *The Story of the Fourth Army in the Battles of the Hundred Days, August 8 to November 11, 1918*. London: Hodder & Stoughton, 1920.

Moran, Lord. *The Anatomy of Courage*. London: Constable, 1945.

Morton, Desmond. *A Peculiar Kind of Politics: Canada's Overseas Ministry in the First World War*. Toronto: University of Toronto Press, 1982.

————. *When Your Number's Up: The Canadian Soldier in the First World War*. Toronto: Random House, 1993.

————. *Ministers and Generals: Politics and the Canadian Militia, 1868–1904*. Toronto: University of Toronto Press, 1970.

————. *Canada and War: A Military and Political History*. Toronto: Butterworths, 1981.

Morton, Desmond, and J.L. Granatstein. *Marching to Armageddon: Canadians and the Great War, 1914–1919*. Toronto: Lester & Orpen Dennys, 1989.

Murray, Colonel W.W. *The History of the 2nd Canadian Battalion (East Ontario Regiment) Canadian Expeditionary Force*. Ottawa: Mortimer Ltd., 1947.

Nabokov, Vladimir. *The Real Life of Sebastian Knight*. Norfolk, Conn: New Directions, 1968.

Nichols, Captain G.H.F. *The 18th Division in the Great War*. London: William Blackwood and Sons, 1922.

Nicholson, Colonel G.W.L. *Official History of the Canadian Army in the First World War: Canadian Expeditionary Force, 1914–1919*. Ottawa: Queen's Printer, 1962.

Nicholson, Col. W.N. *Behind the Lines: An Account of Administrative Staffwork in the British Army, 1914–1918*. London: Jonathan Cape, 1939.

Norris, Lieutenant Armine. *"Mainly for Mother."* Toronto: The Ryerson Press, 1917.

Orr, Philip. *The Road to the Somme: Men of the Ulster Division Tell Their Story*. Belfast: The Blackstaff Press, 1987.

Peacock, A.J. *Gun Fire No. 36: Illustrations to Accompany Notes on the Interpretation of Aeroplane Photos*. Easingwold, York: G.H. Smith & Son, n.d.

Peat, Harold R. *Private Peat*. Indianapolis: Bobbs-Merrill Co., 1917.

Pedley, James H. *Only This: A War Retrospect*. Ottawa: Graphic Publishers, 1927.

Perry, F.W. *History of the Great War, Order of Battle of Divisions*. Part 5A, *The Divisions of Australia, Canada and New Zealand and Those in East Africa*. Newport, Gwent: Ray Westlake, 1992.

Powell, Geoffrey. *Plumer, the Soldier's General*. London: Leo Cooper, 1990.

Prior, Robin, and Trevor Wilson. *Command on the Western Front: The Military Career of Sir Henry Rawlinson, 1914–18.* Oxford: Blackwell, 1992.

———. *Passchendaele: The Untold Story.* London: Yale University Press, 1996.

Radley, Kenneth. *Rebel Watchdog: The Confederate States Army Provost Guard.* Baton Rouge, La.: Louisiana State University Press, 1989.

Rae, Herbert. *Maple Leaves in Flanders Fields.* Toronto: William Briggs, 1916.

Rawling, Bill. *Surviving Trench Warfare: Technology and the Canadian Corps.* Toronto: University of Toronto Press, 1992.

Riddle, David K., and Donald G. Mitchell, eds. *The Distinguished Service Order to the Canadian Expeditionary Force and Canadians in the Royal Naval Air Service, the Royal Flying Corps and Royal Air Force, 1915–1920.* Winnipeg: Kirkby-Marlton Press, 1991.

———. *The Military Cross to the Canadian Expeditionary Force.* Winnipeg: Kirkby-Marlton Press, 1991.

Roy, Reginald H. *For Most Conspicuous Bravery: A Biography of Major-General George R. Pearkes, V.C., Through Two World Wars.* Vancouver: University of British Columbia Press, 1977.

Roy, Reginald H., ed. *The Journal of Private Fraser, 1914–1918 Canadian Expeditionary Force.* Victoria: Sono Nis Press, 1985.

Royle, Trevor. *A Dictionary of Military Quotations.* London: Routledge, 1990.

Russenholt, E.S. *Six Thousand Canadian Men, Being the History of the 44th Battalion Canadian Infantry, 1914–1919.* Winnipeg: The Forty-Fourth Battalion Association, 1932.

Samuels, Martin. *Command or Control? Command, Training and Tactics in the British and German Armies, 1888–1918.* London: Frank Cass, 1995.

Schreiber, Shane B. *Shock Army of the British Empire: The Canadian Corps in the Last 100 Days of the Great War.* Reprint, St. Catharines, Ont: Vanwell Publishing, 2005.

Seely, Maj.-General the Rt. Hon. J.E.B. *Adventure.* London: William Heinemann Limited, 1930.

Serle, Geoffrey. *John Monash: A Biography.* Melbourne: Melbourne University Press, 1982.

Shakespear, Lieut.-Colonel J. *The Thirty-Fourth Division, 1915–1919.* London: H.F. & G. Witherby, 1921.

Sheldon-Williams, Inglis and Ralf Frederic Lardy Sheldon-Williams. *The Canadian Front in France and Flanders.* London: A & C Black Ltd., 1920.

Simpson, Andy. *The Evolution of Victory: British Battles on the Western Front, 1914–1918.* London: Tom Donovan, 1995.

———. *Hot Blood & Cold Steel: Life and Death in the Trenches of the First World War.* Staplehurst, Kent: Spellmount Limited, 2002.

Singer, Major H.C. *History of the 31st Canadian Infantry Battalion, C.E.F.* Calgary: privately printed, [1939].

Smyth, Brigadier the Rt Hon Sir John. *Leadership in Battle, 1914–1918: Commanders in Action.* London: David & Charles, 1975.

Spaight, Robin. *British Army Divisions in the Great War, 1914–1918: A Checklist.* Richmond, Surrey: Robin Spaight, 1978.

Sprung MC, CD, Colonel G.M.C. *The Soldier in Our Times: An Essay.* Philadelphia: Dorrance, 1960.

Stacey, C.P. *Canada and the Age of Conflict: A History of Canadian External Policies.* Vol. 1:, 1867–1921. Toronto: Macmillan, 1977.

———. *A Date with History.* Ottawa: Deneau, 1983.

———. *Official History of the Canadian Army in the Second World War.* Volume I, *Six Years of War: The Army in Canada, Britain and the Pacific.* Ottawa: Queen's Printer, 1955.

Stanley, George F.G. *Canada's Soldiers, 1604–1954: The Military History of an Unmilitary People.* Toronto: Macmillan, 1954.

Statistics of the Military Effort of the British Empire During the Great War, 1914–1920. London: The War Office, March 1922.

Stevens, G.R. *A City Goes to War.* Brampton, Ont.: Charters Publishing Company Limited, 1964.

———. *The Royal Canadian Regiment, 1933–1966.* London, Ont.: London Printing, 1967.

Swettenham, John. *To Seize the Victory: The Canadian Corps in World War I.* Toronto: The Ryerson Press, 1965.

———. *McNaughton.* Vol. 1, *1887–1939.* Toronto: The Ryerson Press, 1968.

Swinton, R.E., Major-General Sir Ernest [Ole Luk-Oie]. *The Green Curve and Other Stories.* London: William Blackwood & Sons, 1916.

Tascona, Bruce, and Eric Wells. *Little Black Devils: A History of the Royal Winnipeg Rifles.* Winnipeg: Frye Publishing, 1983.

Terraine, John. *The Smoke and the Fire: Myths and Anti-Myths of War, 1861–1945.* Sidgwick & Jackson, 1980.

———. *White Heat: The New Warfare, 1914–18.* London: Guild Publishing, 1982.

———. *Douglas Haig: The Educated Soldier.* London: Hutchinson and Co. Ltd., 1963; reprint, London, Leo Cooper, 1990.

———, ed. *General Jack's Diary: War on the Western Front, 1914–1918.* London: Cassell, 2000.

The Times History of the War Vol. XVI. London: *The Times*, 1918.

Topp, Lieut.-Colonel C. Beresford. *The 42nd Battalion, C.E.F. Royal Highlanders of Canada.* Montreal: Gazette Printing Co. Limited, 1931.

Travers, Tim. *The Killing Ground: The British Army, the Western Front and the Emergence of Modern Warfare, 1900–1918.* London: Unwin Hyman, 1987.

Urquhart, Hugh M. *The History of the 16th Battalion (The Canadian Scottish Regiment) Canadian Expeditionary Force in the Great War, 1914–1919.* Toronto: Macmillan, 1932.

———. *Arthur Currie: The Biography of a Great Canadian.* Toronto: Macmillan, 1950.

Vokes, Maj.-General Chris. *Vokes: My Story.* Ottawa: Gallery Books, 1985.

Wallace, O.C.S., ed. *From Montreal to Vimy Ridge and Beyond: The Correspondence of Lieut. Clifford Almon Wallace, B.A. of the 8th Battalion, Canadians, B.E.F., November 1915–April 1917.* Toronto: McClelland, Goodchild & Stewart, 1917.

Watkis, Nicholas C. *The Western Front from the Air.* London: Imperial War Museum, 1997.

Wavell, Field Marshal Earl. *Soldiers and Soldiering, or Epithets of War.* London: Jonathan Cape, 1953.

White, Major W. Tait. *1st Canadian Pioneers C.E.F.: Brief History of the Battalion France and Flanders, 1916–18.* Calgary: 1st Pioneer's Association, 1938.

Who Was Who, 1916–1928: A Companion to Who's Who Containing the Biographies of Those Who Died During the Period 1916–1928. London: Adam & Charles Black, 1947.

Who Was Who, 1941–1950: A Companion to Who's Who Containing the Biographies of Those Who Died During the Decade 1941–1950. London: Adam & Charles Black, 1952.

Williams, Jeffery. *Byng of Vimy, General and Governor General.* London: Leo Cooper, 1983.

Winter, Denis. *Haig's Command: A Reassessment.* London: Viking, 1991.

Wise, S.F. *Canadian Airmen and the First World War: The Official History of the RCAF.* Vol. 1. Toronto: University of Toronto Press, 1980.

Wood, Herbert Fairlie. *Vimy.* Toronto: Macmillan, 1967.

Wynne, Captain G.C. *If Germany Attacks: The Battle in Depth in the West.* London: Faber and Faber Ltd., 1940.

Wyrall, Everard. *The History of the Second Division, 1914–1918.* 2 vols. London: Thomas Nelson & Sons Ltd., 1921.

Articles

Anderson, Lieut.-General Sir Hastings. "Lord Horne as an Army Commander." *Journal of the Royal Artillery* 56 (September 1930): 407–18.

Anderson, Maj.-General Sir W.H. "The Crossing of the Canal du Nord by the First Army, 27th September, 1918." *Canadian Defence Quarterly* 1 (October 1924): 63–77.

———. "The Breaking of the Queant-Drocourt Line by the Canadian Corps, First Army, 2nd–4th September, 1918." *Canadian Defence Quarterly* 3 (January 1926): 120–27.

"Army Notes Staff College Casualties." *Journal of the Royal United Services Institute* (November, 1938): 876–90.

Bailey, Jonathan. "British Artillery in the Great War." In *Britsh Fighting Methods in the Great War,* edited by Paddy Griffith. London: Frank Cass, 1996.

Beattie, Kim. "The Song of Death." In *"And You!"* Toronto: Macmillan, 1929.

Becke, Major A.F. "The Coming of the Creeping Barrage." *Journal of the Royal Artillery* 58 (January 1932): 19–40.

Bovey, Lieutenant-Colonel Wilfrid. "General Sir Arthur Currie: An Appreciation." *Canadian Defence Quarterly* 3 (July 1926): 371–79.

Brennan, Patrick H. "From Amateur to Professional: The Experience of Brigadier General William Antrobus Griesbach." In *Canada and the Great War: Western Front Association Papers,* edited by Briton C. Busch. Montreal: McGill-Queen's University Press, 2003.

"The British Army and Modern Conceptions of War." *Journal of the Royal United Services Institute* (September 1911): 1181–1204.

Broad, Lieut.-Colonel C.N.F. "The Development of Artillery Tactics 1914–1918." *Journal of the Royal Artillery* 49 (1922–23): 371–79.

Brooke, Lieut.-Col. A.F. "The Evolution of Artillery in the Great War: III, The Evolution of Artillery Equipment." *Journal of the Royal Artillery* 51 (April 1924): 37–51.

———. "The Evolution of Artillery in the Great War: IV, The Evolution of Artillery Organization and Command." *Journal of the Royal Artillery* 52 (April 1926): 369–87.

Brown, R. Craig, and Desmond Morton. "The Embarrassing Apotheosis of a 'Great Canadian': Sir Arthur Currie's Personal Crises in 1917." *Canadian Historical Review* 60 (January 1979): 43–44.

Butcher, Bob and Terry Cave. "Some Further Notes on Army Organisation." *Stand To!* 41 (Summer 1994): 15–17; 42 (January 1995): 18–19.

Butcher, R.W. "The Infantry Division, 1914." *Stand To!* 19 (Spring 1987): 13.

———. "Changes in BEF Divisions." *Stand To!* 20 (Summer 1987): 4.

Carrington, C.E. "Kitchener's Army: The Somme and After." *Journal of the Royal United Services Institute* (March, 1978): 15–20.

Cave, Colonel Terry. "The Canadian Corps Order of Battle." *Stand To!* 24 (Winter 1988): 6–12.

Clifton, Ronald. "What is an Artillery Brigade?" *Stand To!* 31 (Spring 1991): 31–34.

———. "What Is a Divisional Train?" *Stand To!* 33 (Winter 1991): 24–27.

———. "What Is a Heavy Battery?" *Stand To!* 35 (Summer 1992): 29–30.

———. "What Is a Signal Company?" *Stand To!* 36 (Winter 1992): 6–8.

Duguid, Colonel A. Fortescue. "Canadians in Battle, 1915–1918." *Canadian Defence Quarterly* 13 (October 1935): 12–27.

"Editorial." *Canadian Defence Quarterly* 2 (July 1925): 320–22.

Edmonds, Brigadier-General Sir James. "The Staff College Fifty-Four Years Ago." *Owl Pie*. Staff College, Camberley, 1949.

Goodspeed, D.J. "Prelude to the Somme: Mount Sorrel, June 1916." In *Policy by Other Means: Essays in Honour of C.P. Stacey,* edited by Michael Cross and Robert Bothwell. Toronto: Clarke, Irwin and Company Limited, 1972.

Graham, Dominick. "*Sans* Doctrine: British Army Tactics in the First World War." In *Men at War: Politics, Technology and Innovation in the Twentieth Century,* edited by Tim Travers and Christon Archer. Chicago: Precedent, 1982.

Grasset, Colonel. "How to Write a Description of a Battle." Translated by Brig.-General W. Evans. *Journal of the Royal Artillery* 56 (January 1930): 91–9.

Griffith, Paddy. "The Lewis Gun Made Easy The Development of Automatic Rifles in the Great War." *The Great War 1914–1918* 3 (September 1991): 108–15.

———. "The Extent of Tactical Reform in the British Army." In Paddy Griffith, ed., *British Fighting Methods in the Great War.* London: Frank Cass, 1996.

Hart, Captain B.H.L. "The 'Ten Commandments' of the Combat Unit." *Journal of the Royal United Services Institute,* May, 1919, pp. 288–93.

———. "The Soldier's Pillar of Fire by Night: The Need for a Framework of Tactics." *Journal of the Royal United Services Institute* (November 1921): 618–25.

Harvey, Colonel R.N. "The Effect of the War on Field Engineering." *Journal of the Royal United Services Institute* (May 1922): 193–218.

Herbert, A.P. "The Cookers." In *Anthem for Doomed Youth: Poets of the Great War,* edited by Lyn Macdonald. London: The Folio Society, 2000.

Hertzberg, Colonel H.F.H. "The Reorganization of the Engineering Troops of a Canadian Division, Great War, 1914–18." *Canadian Defence Quarterly* I (July 1924): 39–47.

Holmes, Dr. Richard. "Indirect Fire: Its Consequences and Countermeasures: An Historical Reflection." *Journal of the Royal Artillery* 122 (March 1995): 2–24; (September 1995): 8–12.

Hudson, Major N. "Trench Mortars in the Great War." *Journal of the Royal Artillery* 47 (April 1920): 17–29.

Hyatt, A.M.J. "Official History in Canada." *Military Affairs* (Summer 1966): 91–99.

Ironside, Major-General Sir W.E. "The Modern Staff Officer." *Journal of the Royal United Services Institute* (August 1928): 435–47.

James, Robert Rhodes. "Thoughts on Writing Military History." *Journal of the Royal United Services Institute* (February 1966): 99–108.

———. "Britain: Soldiers and Biographers." *Journal of Contemporary History* 3 (1968): 89–101.

Jarman, Clarrie. "My Experiences in the Great War." *Stand To!* 8 (Summer 1983): 5.

Kerr, W.B. "Historical Literature on Canada's Participation in the Great War." *Canadian Historical Review* 14 (December 1933): 412–36.

———. "Supplementary List of Historical Literature Relating to Canada's Part in the Great War." *Canadian Historical Review* 15 (March 1934): 181–90.

"Letters from France." *Stand To!* 31 (Spring 1991): 34,36.

Lewendon, Brigadier R.J. "The Cutting of Barbed Wire Entanglements by Artillery Fire in World War One." *Journal of the Royal Artillery* 112 (September 1985): 115–16.

Liddle, Peter A. "Battle of the Somme: Image and Reality." *Stand To!* 39 (Winter 1993): 11–17.

Macdonell, Lieut.-General Sir Archibald. "The Old Red Patch at the Breaking of the Drocourt-Queant Line, the Crossing of the Canal du Nord and the Advance on Cambrai, 30th Aug.–2nd Oct. 1918." *Canadian Defence Quarterly* 4 (July 1927): 388–96; 6 (October 1928): 7–19.

———. "'The Old Red Patch.' The 1st Canadian Division at the Breaking of the Canal du Nord Line." *Canadian Defence Quarterly* 9 (October 1931): 10–26.

"Major-General Louis James Lipsett, C.B., C.M.G." *Canadian Defence Quarterly* 6 (April 1929): 293–300.

Maxse, Brigadier-General F.I. "Battalion Organisation." *Journal of the Royal United Services Institute*, January, 1912, pp. 53–86.

McNaughton, Brigadier General A.G.L. "The Development of Artillery in the Great War." *Canadian Defence Quarterly* 6 (January 1929): 160–71.

Montgomery-Massingberd, Lieut.-General Sir Archibald. "8th August, 1918." *Journal of the Royal Artillery* 55 (January 1929): 13–37.

Morison, Lt.-Colonel Frank. "The 16th and 10th Canadians at St. Julien." *Hamilton Association Journal and Proceedings* (1920): 132–49.

Morton, Desmond. "The Short, Unhappy Life of the 41st Battalion, CEF." *Queen's Quarterly* 81 (Spring 1974): 70–80.

———. "The Limits of Loyalty: French Canadian Officers and the First World War." In *Limits of Loyalty,* edited by Edgar Denton. Waterloo: Wilfred Laurier University Press, 1979.

———. "French Canada and War, 1868–1917: The Military Background to the Conscription Crisis of 1917." *In War and Society in North America*, edited by J.L. Granatstein and R.D. Cuff. Toronto: Thomas Nelson and Sons, 1971.

———. "'Junior but Sovereign Allies': The Transformation of the Canadian Expeditionary Force, 1914–1918." In *The First British Commonwealth Essays in Honour of Nicholas Mansergh*, edited by Norman Hillmer and Philip Wigley. London: Frank Cass, 1980.

Newbolt, Sir Henry. "Clifton Chapel." In *The New Oxford Book of English Verse*, edited by Sir Arthur Quiller-Couch. New York: Oxford University Press, 1955.

"An Officer's Code." *Canadian Defence Quarterly* 3 (July 1926): 479.

Oliver, Dean. "The Canadians at Passchendaele." In *Passchendaele in Perspective: The Third Battle of Ypres*, edited by Peter H. Liddle. London: Leo Cooper, 1997.

Phelan, Major F.R. "Army Supplies in the Forward Area and the Tumpline System." *Canadian Defence Quarterly* 6 (October 1928): 20–35.

Pitt, Barrie. "Writers and the Great War." *Journal of the Royal United Services Institute* (August 1964): 246–48.

Robbins, Simon. "The Right Way to Play the Game: The Ethos of the British High Command in the First World War." *Imperial War Museum Review* 6 (1991): 39–50.

Scott, Peter T. "The CDS/SS Series of Manuals and Instructions: A Numerical Checklist." *The Great War, 1914–1918,* 1 (February 1989): 50–54; (May 1989): 115–16; (August 1989): 155–57; 2 (February 1990): 70–71; (May 1990): 106–107; (August 1990): 153–54; 3 (November 1990): 33–35; (February 1991): 68–70; (May 1991): 100–101; (September 1991): 134–36.

———. "Mr. Stokes and His Educated Drainpipe." *The Great War, 1914–1918* 2 (May 1990): 80–95.

———. "Trench Weaponry: 3 The West Spring Gun." *Stand To!* 5 (Summer 1982): 16.

Scott, Peter T., ed. "With France The 'W.F.' Plan and the Genesis of the Western Front: A Previously Unpublished Account by General Sir Percy Radcliffe, KCB, KCMG, CB, DSO." *Stand To!* 10 (Spring 1984): 6–13.

Sharpe, C.A. "Enlistment in the Canadian Expeditionary Force, 1914–1918: A Regional Analysis." *Journal of Canadian Studies* (Winter 1983–84): 15–29.

Simkins, Peter T., ed. "Co-Stars or Supporting Cast? British Divisions in the 'Hundred Days,' 1918." In *British Fighting Methods in the Great War,* edited by Paddy Griffith. London: Frank Cass, 1996.

Simpson, Keith R. "Capper and the Offensive Spirit." *Journal of the Royal United Services Institute* (June 1973): 51–56.

Slim, Field-Marshal Sir William. "Higher Command in War." *Military Review* (May 1990): 10–21.

"The Staff? The Myth? The Reality?" *Stand To!* 15 (Winter 1985): 44–51.

Stanley, George F.G. Review of *Welcome to Flanders Fields: The First Canadian Battle of the Great War, Ypres, 1915,* by Daniel G. Dancocks. *Queen's Quarterly* 97 (Spring 1990): 186–89.

Sweetman, John. "A Territorial Subaltern at War, 1917–18." *Journal of the Society for Army Historical Research* 77 (1999): 210–17.

Swinton, Maj.-General Sir Ernest. "Intelligence and Spies." *Twenty Years After.* Supplementary Volume, Part 16, Chapter XXXIII, 552–56.

Sykes, Julian. "Lt. Henry Webber." *Gun Fire* No. 7: 162–67.

Terraine, J.A. "Passchendaele and Amiens." *Journal of the Royal United Services Institute* (May 1959): 173–83; (August 1959): 331–40.

———. "The Texture of the Somme, 1916." *History Today* (October 1976): 559–68.

———. "'Wully' Field Marshal Sir William Robertson, Bart, GCB, KCVO, DSO." In *1914–1918, Essays on Leadership and War.* Poole, Dorset: The Western Front Association, 1998, 55–89.

Travers, Tim. "Learning and Decision-Making on the Western Front, 1915–1916: The British Example." *Canadian Journal of History* (April 1983): 87–97.

———. "Currie and 1st Canadian Division at Second Ypres, April 1915: Controversy, Criticism and Official History." *Canadian Military History* (Autumn 1996): 7–15.

Travers, Timothy H.E. "Allies in Conflict: The British and Canadian Official Histories and the Real Story of Second Ypres (1915)." *Journal of Contemporary History* 24 (1989): 301–25.

Whitmarsh, Andrew. "The Development of Infantry Tactics in the British 12th (Eastern) Division, 1915–1918." *Stand To!* 48 (January 1997): 28–32.

Winterbotham, Lieutenant Cyril. "O.C. Platoon Enquiries." In *Anthem for Doomed Youth: Poets of the Great War,* edited by Lyn Macdonald. London: The Folio Society, 2000.

Woodward, Lieutenant-Colonel Walden. "The British Army Staff." *Military Review* (April 1952): 3–13.

Wright, Major R.M. "Machine-Gun Tactics and Organization." *Army Quarterly* (January 1921): 290–313.

Wyrall, Everard. "On the Writing of 'Unit' War Histories." *Army Quarterly* (July 1923): 386– 90.

Young, Alan R. "The Great War and National Mythology." *Acadiensis* 23 (Spring 1994): 155–66.

Unpublished Materials

Bezeau, Captain M.V. "The Role and Organization of Canadian Military Staffs, 1904–1945." Master's Thesis, Royal Military College, Kingston, 1978.

Eyre, Kenneth Charles. "Staff and Command in the Canadian Corps: The Canadian Militia, 1896–1914, as a Source of Senior Officers." Master's Thesis, Duke University, 1967.

Stewart, W.F. "Attack Doctrine in the Canadian Corps, 1916–1918."Master's Thesis, University of New Brunswick, 1978.

Tuxford, George. "The Great War as I Saw it." Memoirs.

Wilson, James Brent. "Morale and Discipline in the British Expeditionary Force, 1914–1918." Master's Thesis, University of New Brunswick, 1978.

INDEX

Note: Ranks shown are the highest attained during or after the war

MEMBER OF SCABRINI GROUP

Québec, Canada
2006